AWAKENING A CURATE'S LIBRARY

AWAKENING A CURATE'S LIBRARY

*The Rev. William Arderne Shoults (1839–1887):
His life, his book collection, and his legacy to
New Zealand*

DONALD JACKSON KERR

THE BIBLIOGRAPHICAL SOCIETY OF AUSTRALIA AND NEW ZEALAND

2022

Donald Kerr is the former Special Collections Librarian at the University of Otago. His particular research area is book collecting and the formation of private libraries in New Zealand. His publications include *Amassing Treasures for All Times. Sir George Grey, Colonial Bookman and Collector (Oak Knoll; Otago University Press*, 2006), and *Hocken. Prince of Collectors* (Otago University, 2015).

First published in 2022 by The Bibliographical Society of Australia and New Zealand

This publication is copyright. Apart from any fair dealing for the purpose of private study, research, criticism or review, as permitted under the Copyright Act 1968, no part may be reproduced by any process without written permission. Enquiries should be made to the publisher.

© Donald Jackson Kerr

ISBN: 9780645666205 (hardback)

Design and Layout: Caren Florance, Ampersand Duck.
Typeset in Garamond.

Cover: detail from *Formularium procuratorum et advocatorum Curiae Romanae* (1493). Shoults Collection, University of Otago. Swb 1493 F

CONTENTS

Foreword	vi
Acknowledgements	ix
Selected Timeline	xii
List of Illustrations	xiii
List of Abbreviations	xv

Chapters

1.	Introduction	1
2.	Southwark, Ramsgate, and Educational Beginnings	9
3.	St. John's College, Cambridge, and Sizar Shoults	23
4.	Certainties at College, 1856–59	45
5.	Book Collecting Contextualised	54
6.	First Step: Assistant Curate, St. Peter's, Walworth, 1863–65	71
7.	St. Paul's, Hoxton, 1866–69	103
8.	Father Ignatius and 'Father Cyril'	112
9.	St. Michael's, Shoreditch, 1873–75	130
10.	Hymns at St. Edmund the King and Martyr, Lombard Street, 1875–79	143
11.	A Loving Marriage and Travel	159
12.	The Collection I: Church Fathers and the Scriptures	169
13.	The Collection II: The Middle East	200
14.	The Collection III: European Manuscripts, Incunables, and Tools of the Trade	219
15.	The Collection IV: Last Readings and Contemporary Magazines	239
16.	Provenance and the Traffic of Books	256
17.	Lists and Jottings: Evidence of Use	276
18.	Treasures to New Zealand, and Shoults's Legacy	291

Bibliography	311
Index	336

FOREWORD

Dunedin is fortunate in the historic collections kept in its libraries. Some of these are internationally renowned, such as the medieval manuscripts and early printed books gathered by Sir Alfred Reed (1875–1975), and now housed in the Dunedin Public Library.[1] Thomas Morland Hocken (1836–1910), a local doctor, was one of the first to make a systematic collection of books and manuscripts relating to New Zealand: it is now in the Hocken Library, University of Otago.[2] In the University Library itself are key parts of the collections assembled by Esmond de Beer (1895–1990), including an invaluable assemblage of European guide books and the eighteenth-century English poetry gathered by Iolo Williams (1890–1962). Born in Dunedin, de Beer spent most of his life in England, and is now widely remembered as the editor of two magnificent editions: the diary of John Evelyn, and the correspondence of John Locke. The New Zealand modern poetry and prose collection of Charles Brasch (1909–73), de Beer's cousin and editor of the New Zealand literary journal *Landfall*, adds a further dimension. Such collections augment others prominent in New Zealand, such as the books and manuscripts of Sir George Grey (1812–98), now in Auckland City Library,[3] or that of Alexander Horsburgh Turnbull (1868–1918), now in Wellington.[4]

William Arderne Shoults is a much less well-known name; unlike those just mentioned he was neither born in, nor ever visited, New Zealand. Yet his collection is of exceptional interest. Its contents, including many rare books, add materially to the bibliographical resources of the country. It is also of considerable international interest as a collection in its own right. There have been many instances of whole libraries being brought by settlers, and some have found their way into public collections. There have been rather fewer nineteenth-century examples of libraries bought or otherwise acquired from an overseas source in their entirety.

Quite apart from its contents, explored in the following pages, the interest of the collection is at least twofold. First, it provides a portrait of a man who was neither wealthy nor socially well-connected. There have been plenty of studies of what we may call the high end of British collecting: of people, generally wealthy or at least reasonably so, who have concentrated on fifteenth-century printing, classical authors, English literature (especially Shakespeare), antiquarianism, and other specialisms. Second, while

---

[1] Reed (1968); Manion (1989).
[2] Kerr (2015).
[3] Kerr (2006).
[4] McCormick (1974).

Shoults had several interests, there is little sign that he was able to collect systematically to any great extent. Not for him first editions or author collections. Whether he was pursuing an interest or he was prompted simply by curiosity, he seems to have mostly bought books for the moment. The result is a collection that is at once notably eclectic, and yet also where we can see some of his long-term overall commitments: in a selection of the Church fathers, in some antiquarian subjects, in some aspects of linguistics, in bibliographical history, in some classical authors. Contemporaries attested to his knowledge of languages of the Middle East, and he was a respected scholar of early hymns.

We cannot tell how far the books now in Dunedin represent the whole of his interests. Dr Kerr has provided details of what is known of dispersals since the arrival of the books in New Zealand. But when Shoults died in 1887 his books were left in the care of his widow. She did not die until 1914. The books now in Dunedin were his working library, those that he needed or wanted as a clergyman of scholarly leanings. It must at least be possible, and even probable, that there were many other books in the house, whether for recreational reading or for different kinds of interests. Did she retain a few of the books he had acquired? Certainly, to judge by the books she gave him, she seems to have appreciated and shared his interests. Simply put: there is little sign of what most people would regard as light reading or, for example, of everyday interests in travel that took him and his wife to the continent and Rome in the early 1880s. Detailed though it is, the portrait of him that emerges on the basis of his surviving books may be only a partial one.

Shoults was never a wealthy man, though his marriage brought some change. His family background was modest, and his stipends as curate in successive parishes were not large. His personal exploration of some of the multifarious by-ways of Victorian religious practices and beliefs brought support, but not much spare cash. Scholarly by instinct, and with interests honed by his years as an undergraduate at Cambridge, he continued to buy books until this tailed off in the face of the gradual progression of tuberculosis in his final years. Like other parish priests, he almost certainly caught the disease through his work. By the time that he died, aged just 48, he had accumulated a significant library. We may guess that most of his books were bought either in minor second-hand bookshops, or from book barrows in some of the markets that then were so much a feature of the London street scene. Some of the best-known stalls were in Faringdon Road, just north of the City, in Whitechapel and in Shoreditch to the east, or New Cut in Lambeth, south of the Thames. Here books could be found for a few pence, or a few shillings. These were not affluent neighbourhoods, yet stories abounded of lucky finds in such places, and good profits to be made from selling books on to the more fashionable shops of the West End. While Shoults certainly possessed some rarities, we do not know that he ever went in for this kind of trading. Some of his books were rare, but there was little cash value in his incomplete set of John Chrystostom (Eton, 1610–13). In any case, many of the books that he chose were distinctly recondite, of interest to only a few people and hence with limited appeal.

Certainly he paid little attention to binding. Although some books were repaired after his death, this was never a collection remarkable for its fine bindings. That is one of its very great attractions, and part of its very great value today. To anyone working on nineteenth-century reading, its physical condition is in its own way as instructive as its literary content. Here, on the shelves now in the University Library, we can recover something of the realities of buying second-hand books in Victorian London: books that had been little read since they were published several generations previously, books whose neglected condition speaks of use, and sometimes care, but not of lavish expense. In keeping with his resources, Shoults seems to have bought new books only sparingly. There are few collections, anywhere, that provide such a graphic portrait of what, for hundreds if not thousands of people, it meant to gather a private library.

Dr Kerr relates the circumstances in which Shoults's books came to New Zealand: how his wife was persuaded by an energetic and far-seeing bishop that they would be particularly welcome for the new theological college being established in Dunedin. This was a sensible decision, providing the historical context for training Anglican clergy that was considered so central to the curriculum. If many of his books were often more of antiquarian interest than doctrinal, the historical dimension was important, and the fact that his books included much on other subjects was a bonus for a diocese that had only been established for a few years. Today they stand not only as witnesses to a personal intellectual and religious voyage in an influential part of the late nineteenth-century church, but also as a resource of unique and more general value to historians of books, their making, their circulation and their use since the fifteenth century.

David McKitterick
Cambridge

ACKNOWLEDGEMENTS

It is a pleasure to acknowledge the many debts incurred during the years in which this work on the Rev. William Arderne Shoults has been written. As Special Collections Librarian at the University of Otago, I have had valuable access to the Shoults Collection. I have received support and encouragement from the Central University staff, but, importantly, also from colleagues at the Hocken Library when accessing the Selwyn College Archive and the small cache of Shoults Papers. I offer special thanks to my Hocken colleagues Anna Blackman, Katherine Milburn, David Murray, and Mark Quarrie. For permission to view the Selwyn College files particular thanks go to Ashley Day (former Warden, Selwyn College), Graeme Sykes, and Bishop Stephen Benford of the Anglican Diocese of Dunedin. Thanks also to Romilly Smith, former assistant at Special Collections, and Dr Tony Fitchett.

In 2017, I received an inaugural award from the Ian Willison Book History Trust which helped facilitate my research in the United Kingdom. This award enabled me to visit institutions in England, including St. John's College Library and Archives, Cambridge University, the British Library, the British Museum Library and Archive, Lambeth Palace Library, and the London Metropolitan Archive. The institutions are nothing without the people working within them. Thanks must go to those who assisted me in my work. They include Fiona Colbert, Adam Crother, Tracey Deakin, and Kathryn McKee (St. John's College Library and Archives), Jacky Cox, Frank Bowles, Louise Clarke, Nicola Hudson, and Johanna Ward (Cambridge University Library), Steven Archer and Nicolas Bell (Trinity College Library), Clemens Gesser (Divinity Library, University of Cambridge), Mary Burgess (the Cambridgeshire Collection, Cambridge Public Library), Ken Gibb, Jessica Hudson, Anna James, John Lancaster, Becky Loughead, and Giles Mandelbrote (Lambeth Palace Library) Francesca Hillier (Archives, British Museum), and Mark Arnold (London Metropolitan Archive).

In the search for relevant material on Shoults I have been helped by many people, and their responses (in person, by letter, or by email) have greatly refined my research. My thanks go to: Eleni Angelomati, Karen Attar, Mark Ballard, Alan Bell (current owner of 37 Camberwell Grove, London), Sebastian Brock, Kellie Clinton, Anne Coldiron, Dennis Duncan, Jack Eckert, Christopher Edwards, Falk Eisermann, Roland Folter, Mitch Fraas, Stephen Gamble, Gordon Giles, Gregory Girolami, John Goldfinch, Wendy Hawke, Rosemary Hill, Boyd Hilton, Oliver House, Edmund King, Deborah Leslie, Jessica Murphy, Gillian Neale, Peter Nockles, Glenda Norquay, John Orens, Robyn Orr, Becky Payne, Piergiorgio Parodi, David Pearson, Jeremy Potter, Stephen Potter, Michael Reading, Emma Roberts, Alexandra Saunders, Chris Scales, David J.

Shaw, Jon Shepherd, Christopher Stray, Timothy Stunt, Tom Townsend, Jenny Uglow, Emily Walhout, and Jane Wells.

New Zealand libraries and institutions and their personnel also deserve thanks for their support and encouragement. Thanks to Damian Cairns (University of Canterbury, Christchurch), Lorraine Johnstone and Julian Smith (Heritage Collection and Rare Books, Dunedin Public Library), and Anthony Tedeschi (Alexander Turnbull Library, Wellington). Special thanks are to Keith Giles (Sir George Grey Special Collections, Auckland City Libraries), whose magical work with census materials has been enormously helpful, and Rowan Gibbs (Wellington), who responded positively and promptly to my requests for translations from Greek and Latin.

Individuals associated with Otago University also deserve thanks: Alan Edwards (former Law Librarian), John Hughes (Reprographics, Library), Don Jamieson (former Reference and Medical Librarian), Keith Maslen (former lecturer in English), Mark Seymour, John Stenhouse, and Pamela Treanor (former rare books cataloguer). I would also like to thank Emeritus Professor Erik Olssen, and Shef Rogers, my colleague at the Centre for the Book at the University of Otago.

Quite by chance, I made contact with the Father Ignatius Memorial Trust, and I have to thank Caroline Woollard for putting me in touch with Hugh Allen, Father Ignatius's most recent biographer. I spent a wonderful day with Hugh and Peter Davies driving from Abergavenny to Llanthony, visiting the area of Capel-y-ffin, which Ignatius and Shoults knew well. Peter's driving skills were a match for the winding roads, and their knowledge of the area was invaluable. Another serendipitous link was with Sisters Clare and Paula at Curzon Park Abbey, Chester, who provided valuable insight into Shoults's involvement with the 'rebel' followers of Ignatius. A special thanks to them all.

As I started this project, I came across four books that were not only extremely informative, but also pushed my personal learning to another level. They are: Hubertus R. Drobner's *The Fathers of the Church* (2007), Robert Irwin's *For Lust of Knowing. The Orientalists and their Enemies* (2007), John Shelton Reed's *Glorious Battle. The Cultural Politics of Victorian Anglo-Catholicism* (2017), and David McKitterick's *The Invention of Rare Books. Private Interest and Public Memory, 1600–1840* (2018). To these authors I offer a special thanks.

Another personal thanks is given to Dr Majid Danesghar, formerly lecturer at the University of Otago and now at the Oriental Studies section at the University of Freiburg, Germany. Dr Danesghar's knowledge of and expertise in Middle Eastern languages helped identify books and manuscripts in the Shoults Collection. His teasing out the nuances of Arabic and Persian languages (see chapter 13) has been invaluable.

A number of individuals in England deserve special thanks. The first is Christopher de Hamel, who has always encouraged my work on Shoults. He has helped me greatly on providing provenance details, and improving my shaky Latin. The second are Nicolas and Joanna Barker, who have also given encouragement. Their Clarendon Road home is always a great refuge for a visiting New Zealander. The third are David and Rosamond McKitterick, who were extremely welcoming while I was at Cambridge. I have to thank Rosamond for not only arranging accommodation at Sidney Sussex College, but also for giving me advice and reminders on the use of the University of Cambridge Library catalogue system. And finally, Rick Watson, who opened his home to me while I was in London. I appreciated not only the book-talk, but also the company after a heavy day devoted to research.

A book like this is not completed alone. At various stages, a number of people have read the typescript and provided invaluable suggestions for its improvement. I am very grateful for their time and energy spent on the drafts. Thanks to Jeanette Wikaira (Dunedin), Peter Skegg (Dunedin), John Pickles (Cambridge), David McKitterick (Cambridge), and George Woodman (Belfast), who have each taken the red pen to passages, phrases, and grammatical errors. George Woodman's efforts deserve special note, as he has painstakingly worked through the text, adding comments based on his expertise in Anglo-Catholicism and other ecclesiastical matters. I have taken on board all the suggestions and comments. Nevertheless, all mistakes and misconceptions are mine alone.

A very special thanks is also offered to Brian McMullin, editor in charge of the Occasional Publications of the Bibliographical Society of Australia and New Zealand, who has laboured hard on refining the text for publication. And it is to the BSANZ and the Executive, especially Amanda Laugesen, that I offer a huge thank-you for their commitment to publish this book. I will be forever grateful.

And finally, warm and sincere thanks to Jude for her patience and tolerance while I have been working away on the Rev. William Arderne Shoults. Without her support, the completion of this book would not have been possible.

Donald Kerr
Dunedin

SELECTED TIMELINE

29 March 1839	Born Southwark
1847	Moved to Ramsgate
1851	First book purchase in Glasgow, *The Poetical Works of Shelley*
1 July 1856	Admitted to St John's College, Cambridge
November 1858	First appearance in print, the *Eagle*
1859	First significant book purchases
January 1860	Qualified B.A.
April 1863	Proceeded to M.A.
December 1863	Ordained deacon
December 1863	Curate at St Peter's, Walworth
December 1864	Ordained priest
December 1865	Curate at St Paul's, Hoxton
1867	First meeting with Father Ignatius
June 1868	Contact with the convent at Feltham
December 1870	First recorded visit to Capel-y-ffin
September 1873	First book gift from Eliza Katharine Ogle
December 1873	Curate at St Michael's, Shoreditch
March 1874	Admitted to Bachelor of Divinity studies
1875	Curate at St. Edmund the King and Martyr, Lombard Street
1 August 1878	Married Eliza Katharine Ogle
1883	Visited the Vatican Library, Rome
14 June 1887	Died at family home, 37 Camberwell Grove, Camberwell
September 1888	Bishop Nevill mets Eliza Shoults
1892	Publication of John Julian's *Dictionary of Hymnology*
1893	Shoults Collection arrived at Selwyn College, Dunedin
1965	Shoults Collection transferred to the University of Otago Library on permanent loan

LIST OF ILLUSTRATIONS

Plate 1. William Arderne Shoults (1839–1887)
Plate 2. Old Chapel, St John's College, Cambridge, c.1847. From John Le Keux, *Memorials of Cambridge*, vol. 1 (Cambridge, 1847)
Plate 3. *The Cambridge University Calendar for the Year 1860* (1860)
Plate 4. Charles Wisbey's 'Cottage Ornéé with Garden & Land' auction promotion sheet, *Cambridge University Library Maps PSQ.bb.18.210*
Plate 5. St. Peter's Church, Walworth, 2018
Plate 6. St. Paul's Church, Bunhill, Hoxton, from St. John Adcock, ed., *Wonderful London* (1926)
Plate 7. Joseph Leycester Lyne, (1837–1908)
Plate 8. The monastery at Capel-y-ffin, 2018
Plate 9. Rev. Henry Anstey's *Munimenta academica: Or, Documents Illustrative of Academical Life and Studies at Oxford* (1868)
Plate 10. Rev. Henry Anstey's *Munimenta academica: Or, Documents Illustrative of Academical Life and Studies at Oxford* (1868)
Plate 11. St Michael's Church, Shoreditch, 2018
Plate 12. St. Edmund the King and Martyr, Lombard Street, London City. From William Maitland, *History of London* (1753)
Plate 13. Harvest Festival at St Edmund the Martyr, *Graphic*, 30 October 1875
Plate 14. John Julian, *Dictionary of Hymnology* (1892)
Plate 15. *Nonarum inquisitiones in curia scaccarii* and *Placitorum abbreviatio* (1807–1811)
Plate 16. No. 37 Camberwell Grove, Camberwell, 2018
Plate 17. Livy's *Historiarum ab urbe condita libri* (1738–1746), Vol. II
Plate 18. Ruard Tapper, *Opera* (1582)
Plate 19. Vulgate Bible (1481)
Plate 20. Astesanus de Ast's *Summa de casibus conscientiae* (c.1473)
Plate 21. Petronius's *Satyricon* (1693)
Plate 22. John Fisher, *Assertionis Lutheranae confutatio* (1545)
Plate 23. Erpenius, *Rudimenta linguae Arabicae* (1628)
Plate 24. Qurʾān (Koran), c.1846
Plate 25. Samuel Tarratt Nevill (1837–1921), Bishop of Dunedin
Plate 26. The Shoults Collection, Selwyn College, c.1900
Plate 27. Printed notice of the Shoults Collection, c.1893.

Plates 1, 9-10, 12, 14-15, 17-24, and 27 are reproduced by permission of the Shoults Collection, University of Otago Library, Dunedin. Plate 2 is reproduced by permission of the Masters and Fellows, Trinity College, Cambridge. Plate 4 is reproduced by kind permission of the Syndics of Cambridge University Library, Cambridge: *Maps PSQ. bb.18.210*. Plate 6 is reproduced by kind permission from Special Collections, University of Canterbury, Christchurch. Others are from a private collection.

ABBREVIATIONS

AC *Alumni Cantabrigiensis*, Part II, 1752–1900. Compiled by John Venn and J. A. Venn. Cambridge: University Press, 1940–1954
Vol. I. Abbey – Challis (1940)
Vol. II. Chalmers – Fytche (1944)
Vol. III. Gabb – Justamond (1947)
Vol. IV. Kahlenberg – Oyler (1947)
Vol. V. Pace – Spyers (1953)
Vol. VI. Square – Zupitza (1954)

EB *Encyclopaedia Britannica*, Eleventh edition. New York: Encyclopaedia Britannica Co., 1910–1911

ISTC *Incunabula Short-title Catalogue,* www.bl.uk/catalogues/istc/

OCD Oxford Classical Dictionary. Second edition. Oxford: Clarendon Press, 1970

ODCC Oxford Dictionary of the Christian Church. Third edition. Oxford: Oxford University Press, 1998

ODNB Oxford Dictionary of National Biography. Oxford University Press, www.oxforddnb.com

STC A. W. Pollard and G. R. Redgrave, *A Short-title Catalogue of Books printed in England, Scotland, & Ireland, and of English Books printed abroad, 1475–1640*. Second edition, revised by W. A. Jackson, F. S. Ferguson, and Katharine F. Pantzer, with a chronological index by Philip R. Rider. 3 vols. London: Bibliographical Society, 1975–91

Wing Donald G. Wing, *Short-title Catalogue of Books printed in England, Scotland, Wales, and British America, and of English books printed in other countries, 1641-1700*. Second edition, rev. by John J. Morrison and Carolyn W. Nelson, and Matthew Seccombe. New York: Modern Language Association of America, 1972–1998

Plate 1. William Arderne Shoults (1839–1887)

The only image of William Arderne Shoults (1839–1887), curate and book collector, probably taken around the time of his wedding on 1 August 1878, aged 39.

1   INTRODUCTION

Throughout history, pages and pages have been written on lost libraries, those book and manuscript treasures that, through human or natural mishap, have completely disappeared. Sadly, all that are left now are the records and reports on what was in a certain library, and the vague titles or summations of what existed. This bio-bibliographical study of the Rev. William Arderne Shoults and his book collecting presents the reverse: not what is lost, but what has survived. It is not only the first study to provide an account of Shoults's life and his book collecting, but it is also the first detailed examination of a true survivor, his book collection.

William Arderne Shoults was born in 1839 and died in 1887, age 48. In his short life he amassed some 5600 books and manuscripts that formed a working library. He surrounded himself with his books, many at easy reach. He was educated at St. John's College, Cambridge University, and, like most of his contemporaries, entered the Anglican Church, spending most of his professional life as a curate in some of the toughest parishes located in London in the mid-nineteenth century. Shoults married late, and from all accounts Eliza, his wife, loved him dearly and supported his endeavours. In fact, she wanted to keep his library intact, initially earmarking it for St. John's College at her death. Their relationship began when he was about 34 but was cut short after nine years of marriage. He travelled beyond Britain, but such travel was not extensive. He never became the vicar or the rector of a parish, much less canon of a cathedral, a position to which New Zealand commentators elevated him long after his death. Above all, Shoults seems to have been a caring man, dedicated to his mission of spreading the Gospel of Jesus Christ.

There are no biographies of Shoults, or articles on this relatively obscure curate, who glided through life unnoticed as an unremarkable parish clergyman. From the one account available (see chapter 7), he was conscientious in his parish work, although not deemed a great preacher. He remained at the level of a curate and was said to be a good backup man. He was a bookish intellectual, an assessment borne out by the books that he collected and by the small number of published articles that he wrote. As an intellectual, however, he does not seem to have grappled with the big issues of the day, as reflected in the works—with their big questions and conclusions—of Hume, Gibbon, Bentham, Mill, Kant, Comte, and Froude. There are no works by any of these men in his collection.

Shoults was actively involved in parishes that were known to be ritualistic: St. Peter's, Walworth; St. Paul's, Hoxton; St. Michael's, Shoreditch; and St. Edmund the King and Martyr, Lombard Street. Fortunately, there are records of his taking part in such ritualistic practices. A longer tradition of wanting to restore the Anglican Church to its primitive form, back to its roots of a single Christian Church, was promoted by seventeenth-century divines such as Lancelot Andrewes, Archbishop William Laud, and Jeremy Taylor. In the 1830s, advocacy of this tradition was represented in England by the Oxford Movement, the Catholic revival in the Church of England, led by John Henry Newman (1801–90), Edward Bouverie Pusey (1800–92), John Keble (1792–1866), and supporters such as Henry Edward Manning (1808–92). In the 1860s, there was a wave of revival and renewal, manifest in the ritualistic accoutrements such as colourful vestments, incense, candles, and the like, in the efforts of John Mason Neale and his contemporaries in the Cambridge Camden Society, and the Society of the Holy Cross, an organisation of Anglo-Catholic priests that included founders Charles Fuge Lowder, Charles Maurice Davies, and Alfred Poole.

Throughout this period, there were controversies surrounding ritualism and the Anglo-Catholic movement, which generally subscribed to doctrines such as the Real Presence and baptismal regeneration. The influence surrounding the Anglo-Catholic movement was strong, particularly at institutions such as Oxford and Cambridge, and, through various iterations, it spread throughout English society. Shoults was not immune from it, and his involvement with the Rev. Joseph Leycester Lyne (1837–1908), the controversial, enthusiastic revivalist known as 'Father Ignatius', founder of his own Benedictine Order in the Anglican Church, certainly confirms this particular religious slant, although the approach by Ignatius was somewhat eccentric.[1] However, Shoults escaped controversy, unlike some of the men he knew or mixed with.

Although swayed by Father Ignatius, Shoults retained a sense of personal identity, maintaining, by what seems a quiet determinism, something of his own individuality. Seemingly quiet by nature, private, and scholarly, he evinced, as is evident in the contrary works held in his collection, some tolerance of various religious controversies. These publications offer a balance to issues that he had to work through as a curate and in his private life. The world he embraced was bookish and locked into the past. It was a private world that he obviously enjoyed.

Apart from a small number of books and medieval manuscripts sold in 1938 and 1962, Shoults's library is complete. It stands as a fine example of what a nineteenth-century curate could collect on a small stipend (his first curacy paid £80 per annum), a small inheritance, and judicious choosing. It is not a deluxe collection, filled with

---

[1] The cult of personalities is noted by J. S. Reynolds: 'The history of the evangelical revival is in a considerable measure a history of personalities. It is perhaps hardly necessary to add that spiritual leadership and devotion are not essentially associated with special prominence in the visible church. As with other schools of thought, many of the greatest names in the evangelical movement [...] are of men who lived out all their days as plain parish clergymen.' Reynolds (1967), 2.

high-spot items such as those in libraries amassed by the wealthy. He did, however, collect medieval manuscripts, incunables (books printed before 1501), works by classical authors, and those publications on and by the Church Fathers. These areas of collecting place him in the 'Dibdinian' tradition, representing good old-fashioned fields of collecting that reflected the tastes of many nineteenth-century gentlemen.² Collecting, however, is a highly individualistic activity, defined by one modern commentator, Werner Muensterberger, as 'the selecting, gathering, and keeping of objects of subjective value'.³ Shoults followed his own collecting path, driven by purely personal interests in ecclesiastical history, primitive church rites and rituals, philology, a general antiquarianism, and an enjoyment of books and manuscripts on or about the Middle East. He was also interested in bibliography and records of institutional collections and private sales. Works by individuals such as Robert Bellarmine, Edward Bernard, Jacques-Charles Brunet, Guillaume-François de Bure, Friedrich Benedict Carpzov, Louis Ellies du Pin, Johann Albert Fabricius, Conrad Gessner, Daniel Georg Morhof, and Joseph Justus Scaliger feature. They reflect his scholarly interests. He also seemed to have a working knowledge of German, but the publications he owned in that language are very few.⁴ He did own works by Friedrich Schlegel, August Schlegel, Goethe, Bunsen, and Schiller, yet these are all in English translation.

As is evident from an examination of his collection, the titles that he collected are solid, serious works. There are no novels or light reading in this library, which is filled with Latin, Greek, Arabic, Persian, Hebrew, and, naturally, English texts. The Shoults family surely had some light reading in the house. However, it can only be presumed that Eliza omitted these publications from the donation, deeming them as not suitable for educational purposes, especially for young theology students. A few English poets are represented: Alexander Pope, Matthew Prior, Thomas Gray, Lord Byron, and Percy Bysshe Shelley.

Shoults's collection is a true working library. There are books with cheap bindings, there are volumes that stand alone, divorced from others in a set, and the condition of some is poor: covers detached, ripped and torn leaves, water-damage, foxing, and

---

² Seymour de Ricci wrote that 'nearly every library built up in England during the first half of the nineteenth century conformed to the Dibdinian type of Bibliotheca Spenceriana.' See de Ricci (1969), 85.
³ Muensterberger (1994), 4.
⁴ It took some time for German language instruction to be formalised as a foreign language in Britain, for example, German was first included as a subject at the University of Cambridge in 1858. See McLelland (2014). Note Will Ladislaw's remark to Dorothea in George Eliot's *Middlemarch*: 'If Mr Casaubon read German he would have saved himself a great deal of trouble'. Cited in Eliot (1998), II, xxi, 194. And A. P. Stanley to Mark Pattison: 'How different the fortunes of the Church of England might have been if Newman had known German.' Pattison, *Memoirs* (1885), cited in Wilson (2000), 144.

many bindings wormed. It was formed by piecemeal accumulation in a relatively short period of time, with content seemingly more important than condition. And it is without doubt that his collecting efforts saved many of the printed books and manuscripts from loss. Of this role it is pertinent to remember A. W. Pollard's remark: 'It is mainly by the zeal of private collectors that books which would otherwise have perished from neglect are discovered, preserved and made to yield up their secrets, with the result that almost every great library owes more on its historical side to their generosity than to the purchases from its own resources.'[5] Given that judicious choosing and perhaps a little serendipity dictated much of Shoults's collecting, his achievement was remarkable.

The books that he collected range from unprepossessing medieval manuscripts on paper, incunables, Arabic-Latin texts, and Elzevirs, to sermons, works by the Church Fathers, philological dictionaries, and accounts of travel to Italy and France. Those books printed in Britain dominate, numbering just over 3100 volumes (55%). Books from presses in the Low Countries follow, with some 800 volumes (14%); his holdings of Elzevirs (105) raise the percentage. German publications follow closely, with some 710 volumes (12%). Then there are French (415; 7.4%), Italian (319; 5.7%), and Swiss (163; 2.7%) publications, with minors such as Swedish and Spanish publications making up the rest.

Imprints from the nineteenth century dominate, with some 2200 falling into that period. The eighteenth century follows, represented by some 1500 volumes, then the seventeenth century with 1350, and the sixteenth century, with just over 500. Incunables number 28, while there are three medieval manuscripts. Overall, it is an impressive array.

The classification by which the Shoults Collection is arranged at Special Collections, University of Otago, is a novel one. It consists of four elements, for example, Eb 1700 A. The 'E' represents the country of publication, in this case, England. The others are A (America), D (Denmark), F (France), G (Germany), I (Italy), L (Low Countries; Holland and Belgium), O (China and Turkey), Sn (Sweden), Sp (Spain), and Sw (Switzerland). In the past E represented the wider British Isles, which included Ireland, Scotland, and Wales. These countries now have their own classification, being Ir, Sc, and W.

The lower case 'b' in the classification Eb 1700 A represents the height of the book. The sizes are 'a', less than 13 cm; 'b', from 13 to 27 cm; 'c', from 27 to 40 cm; 'd', from 40 to 50 cm; and 'e', greater than 50 cm (horizontal shelving). These letters roughly equate to bibliographical formats such as octavo, quarto, folio, and elephant

---

[5] Pollard, cited in Thomas (1975), 271. See also Pollard, 'Book collecting', in *EB*, IV, 221-5.

folio. The date of '1700' is the year of publication. And finally, the letter A, which is based on the main entry in the catalogue and is usually the first letter of the author's surname, or the title.

The books are shelved chronologically within the designated place of publication and size, that is, all the 'a' formats for each country, A, D, E, F, G and so on. Then the 'b' format follows, with all its countries. These are followed by the larger 'c' format and then the 'd's and 'e's. Although this arrangement creates various size sequences, it does allow the book historian an opportunity to isolate particular periods of printing and view what publications of a particular country are held between, say, 1660 and 1680, 1760 and 1770, and so on.

The remarkable thing about this library is where it is now located: not in Cambridge, where it was destined to go, nor in London. In 1893 it was shipped halfway around the world to Dunedin, New Zealand, where, through the initiatives of Bishop Samuel Tarrett Nevill (1837–1921), first Bishop of Dunedin, it was to form the library of the new Selwyn College. The story of how this migration happened through the generosity of Shoults's wife, Eliza, is told in chapter 18.

Little is known about Shoults's collecting. He left no invoices, no copies of letters to book dealers, and no account of his book collecting. As he was primarily London-based, one can assume that his chief method of purchase was over the counter, from the many book barrows and bookshops. He also bought from the occasional auction. There are a small number of book-dealer catalogues in his collection, and it can be presumed that he also bought from them.

With such a paucity of information about his book-collecting, it is necessary to create a narrative from what actually survives. In essence, this study of Shoults is one of reconstruction. The prime resource is his library, which is substantially intact. A physical examination has revealed the types of books that he collected, the condition of them, the presence of annotations, some provenance details, and a variety of interesting bibliographical information. When acquisition details are present, such as in the years 1859, 1874, and 1875, they usually consist of an inscription and a date, almost always in black ink. Because there are so few details for the other years, establishing an overall pattern of buying is just not possible.

The first ten chapters of this narrative are chronological, beginning at Shoults's birth and early life in Southwark from 1839 to the end of his curacies and travel with his wife Eliza, about 1880. While a number of new facts of his life are revealed, especially those centring on his years at St. John's College, on his activities as a curate, and on his involvement with Father Ignatius, they do not impact much on his development and activities as a book collector. They do, however, offer context. A chapter on book collecting (5) is embedded within these first chapters. This chapter not only provides a brief history of the collecting tradition that he was part of, but also, from the evidence of his library, his more precise positioning within that tradition.

The reconstruction approach adopted centres on his library. Four thematic chapters deal with specific areas: Church Fathers and the Scriptures (12), the Middle East (13), Manuscripts and Incunables (14), and Contemporary Magazines (15). Although an artificially constructed approach, this forensic exercise enables a teasing out of the sorts of books that he collected, either for his professional requirements as a Church of England curate or for his own intellectual needs. It is a necessary approach in the light of the fact that there is no information available about him as a book collector.

Nevertheless, it is a difficult, near impossible, task. It is pertinent to quote from *Still Dead* (1934), a detective novel by Ronald Knox, a classical scholar who was at one time one of England's most prominent and articulate Anglo-Catholics. He converted to Catholicism in 1917. In chapter 9, Knox's detective hero looks into the room of a dead man and, by perusing the shelves of his library, tries to ascertain something of his character:

> He turned to the books first, as we all do; tried to conjure up, as we all do, some picture of the man who had inhabited the room from the silent friends with which he had surrounded himself. But the test is a precarious one, especially when you are dealing with the young; for the most part they accumulate books at haphazard, as the need or the whim of the moment suggests; there is no policy, and therefore no self-revelation, about their choice. Here were school-books, Oxford textbooks, illustrated Christmas-present books, one or two very modern novels, and even collections of poetry; there was the usual congeries of odd volumes which knit the brows of the searcher with the question 'What on earth did he buy that for?' You could hardly expect to get the atmosphere of the young man who had died so tragically from a library like this – Hall and Knight's *Algebra*, *Statuta et Decreta Universitatis Oxoniensis*, Pliny's *Letters* (selected), *Clubfoot the Avenger*, Dulac's *Arabian Nights*, *Angel Pavement*, *Wheels*, *Three Men in a Boat*, *How to Breed Rabbits*, Walsham How on *Confirmation*, *The Mysterious Universe*.[6]

T.A. Birrell is more positive: 'A private library is part of its owner's biography. The known facts of his life may help in the understanding of his choice of books. Conversely, his choice of books may add to the understanding of the known facts of his life, and perhaps reveal unknown facts. A private statistical analysis of contents is

---

[6] Taylor (1987), 146.

inadequate.'[7] And for enthusiastic sage advice there is always Holbrook Jackson: 'A man in the last resort must choose his own books. His library must be the expression of himself, rather than he of it, for a book, or any number of books, can do no more than bring out what is in him.'[8] Books do record the tastes and interests of their owners, and for the attempt to flesh out this aspect of Shoults it is fortunate that his library is largely intact.

After the chapters on provenance and his use of the collection, there is a return to the chronological, a chapter centring on what is surely one of the most important, certainly to those in New Zealand who are interested in book history: the arrival of the collection, Shoults's legacy, and its current state and use.

Shoults must have had some notion of how he expected to see himself remembered. It is also without doubt that he and his wife talked about the life of the library after his death. In fact, as already mentioned, Eliza was proud of his achievements and was prepared to keep the library intact as a monument to him, intending to bequeath it on her death to St. John's College. This intention was fixed in place until Bishop Nevill raised the notion of the library going to Selwyn College. It is interesting to speculate on the library's standing — and the Shoults association — if it had gone to St. John's College or perhaps the University Library at Cambridge, almost certainly to be integrated into and subsumed by their much larger collections.

The Shoults Collection has remained relatively unknown outside Dunedin for many years, used by only a few. It has suffered the fate of being a 'sleeping-beauty' library, much like Briar Rose in the Brothers Grimm fairy tale, sitting quietly at Selwyn College and then at the University of Otago Library. The composition of the materials has played a part in this invisibility. It is a library full of serious, complex texts, many printed in languages that are no longer part of the linguistic toolkit of the modern student and scholar, especially in a predominantly monolinguistic country such as New Zealand. In truth, because of its specific nature, the Shoults Collection's contribution to the literary and cultural heritage of New Zealand has been small thus far. On the other hand, there have been periods of recognition, with publications by scholars such as David Taylor (1955) and Christopher de Hamel (See Manion, 1989) especially on the medieval manuscripts. The manuscripts and other printed works such as the incunables certainly add to the general storehouse of book resources in New Zealand, especially for those interested in early printing, ecclesiastical history (especially ritualism and Anglo-Catholicism), philology, and the history of the book.

---

[7] Birrell (1991), 116–18.
[8] Jackson (1981), 349.

One goal of this study is to raise the profile of William Arderne Shoults and his book collection, to date a little-known contributor to New Zealand's intellectual and cultural tradition. It is hoped that a greater awareness of the riches in this collection will spur others to carry out contrasts and comparisons with other libraries both in New Zealand and overseas. An adjunct to this aspect is the hope that further work will be carried out by scholars on other book collectors in New Zealand such as Robert McNab, A.H. Reed, and Esmond de Beer, thereby offering contrast and comparison to Shoults, and of course greater awareness of the formation of their own particular collections. In considering the notions of contextualisation and connectivity, the thoughts of Étienne Geoffroy Saint-Hilaire are relevant:

> Such is the character of our epoch that it becomes impossible today to enclose oneself strictly within the framework of a simple monograph. Study an object in isolation and you will only be able to bring it back to itself; consequently you can never have perfect knowledge of it. But see it in the midst of beings who are connected with each other in many different ways, and which are isolated from each other in different ways, and you will discover for this object a wider scope of relationships. First of all, you will know it better, even in its specificity: but more important, by considering it in the very center of its own sphere of activity, you will know precisely how it behaves in its own exterior world, and you will also know how its own features are constituted in reaction to its surrounding milieu.[9]

This book represents a metaphorical kiss that I hope will awaken William Arderne Shoults's book collection from its current repose. Prospects are bright. Through shining a light on the story that follows, this rich resource will become better known, thereby generating greater use by scholars, students, and the wider community.

---

9   Saint-Hilaire, in Said (2003), 144.

2 SOUTHWARK, RAMSGATE, AND EDUCATIONAL BEGINNINGS

SOUTHWARK

Southwark is bound north by the River Thames, east by Bermondsey, south-east by Camberwell, and west by Lambeth. The area is connected to the City of London by bridges such as London, Southwark, and Blackfriars. It has Bankside, an area where, in the late sixteenth century, entertainment (bull and bear-baiting) and theatre dominated, with William Shakespeare and his contemporaries actively involved in the *Rose* and *Globe* theatres. It has Guy's Hospital, founded in 1721 by Thomas Guy, a Bible-selling speculator who made his fortune from the South Sea Bubble initiative. John Keats studied medicine there between 1814 and 1816. It had Bethlehem (Bedlam) Hospital, one of Europe's oldest psychiatric institutions for the care and treatment of the insane. This house for unfortunates was moved to St. George's Fields in 1815. It had the Marshalsea Prison, faithfully described by Dickens in *Little Dorrit*, which was based on his visits to see his father, who was imprisoned for debt there. The prison closed around 1860. And there was the Elephant and Castle, a major road, and eventual rail and tube junction, and an important entrance to and exit from the City. One controversial religious institution that developed in the area was the Metropolitan Tabernacle, which had worshipping congregations as early as the 1650s, but found greater popularity in Victorian times with Particular Baptist Charles Haddon Spurgeon, who was known as the 'Prince of Preachers'.[1] Spurgeon initiated the move of the church to the Elephant and Castle area; it was completed in 1861.

The population of Southwark was 99,562 in 1821, 116,006 in 1831, 134,225 in 1841, 152,371 in 1851, and 173,900 in 1861.[2] Among the constant smells from factories, streets, and houses, the area pulsated: river traffic, road traffic, dock workers, shopkeepers, builders, artisans, and children, young and old. There was a certain vibrancy. It was, however, a tough place, and poverty was rife.[3] In the nineteenth century, Southwark was 'a maze of streets and courts crowded in many parts' famed for its 'low life, criminality, and heathenism'.[4] Two later commentators (Hollingshead and Greenwood) described it thus:

---

[1] See Drummond (1992); see also *ODCC* (1998), 1534.
[2] Cited in Williams (1999), 25.
[3] Booth (1902–1903), especially 4: Inner South London.
[4] Williams (1999), 24.

A very vast and melancholy property, lighted up at intervals with special markets of industry, or budding into short patches of honest trade, sinking every now and then into dark areas of crime, and covered everywhere with the vilest sores of prostitution. It has scores of streets that are rank and steaming with vice; streets where unwashed, drunken, fishy-eyed women hang by dozens out of the windows, beckoning to the passerby.

A more general observation of the area suggests it a place of: 'the very nests and nurseries of crime. Here are to be found the lowest of the low class of beershops in London, and probably in the world, the acknowledged haunts of "smashers", burglars, thieves and forgers.'[5]

Eighteen thirty-nine might be called the year of the 'Big Storms'. It started in January with a huge storm off the Irish and English coasts called the 'Big Wind' and ended in late November and December with a huge cyclone that slammed south-eastern India with high winds and a 40-foot storm surge, destroying the city of Coringa (now Korangi). An estimated 300,000 people were killed. Selected events tucked between these two included the announcement at the French Academy of Science of the Daguerreotype photo process; the assassination of the Earl of Norbury near his house Kilbeggan, County Meath in Ireland; a request to the British government to formally take ownership of New Zealand, leading to the signing of the Treaty of Waitangi in 1840; the issuing of an Edict by King Kamehameha III of Hawaii that established some toleration towards Roman Catholics and freedom to worship; Chartist riots in Birmingham; and various anti-Corn Law meetings in northern towns such as Leeds and Manchester.[6]

In this year, on 29 March, William Arderne Shoults was born in Southwark to William and Elizabeth Shoults.[7] The family lived at 8 Weston Street, which had Guy Street, Manning Street and the Bermondsey Market running off it, and ran south, dog-legging from Thomas Street to Old Dover Road. Today, the house has long gone, but the street remains snug against the modern-day expansions of Guy's Hospital. Almost a month later, on 24 April 1839, young William was baptised at St. Olave's Church on Tooley Street, a short walk from Weston Street and situated on the east-side of the entrance into High Street from London Bridge. The baptismal record was signed by the Rev. Arthur Kenney, a University of Dublin graduate, who began his Rectorship at St. Olave's in 1817.[8] In 1839,

---

[5] Hollingshead (1986), 85; see also Greenwood (1981), 111.
[6] Irving (1880).
[7] 1841: England and Wales census, St. Olave, William Arderne Shoults.
[8] 1839: Bermondsey, St. Olave, Southwark baptisms.

2 SOUTHWARK, RAMSGATE & EDUCATIONAL BEGINNINGS

Kenney's *The Dangerous Nature of Popish Power in these Countries* was published.

There were other churches nearby, including St. Saviour, the principal Church of England building in Southwark, an ancient parish with registers starting in 1538.[9] Roman Catholic worship in the area centred around a chapel dedicated to St. George on London Road, which became St. George Cathedral on land in St. George's Fields, opening on 4 July 1848.[10] The designer of the Cathedral was Augustus Welby Northmore Pugin (1812–52), the first person to be married in it.

The fact that William was baptised at St. Olave's points to this church being the preferred family one for worship. The church was an ancient one, mentioned in the Domesday Book. It was called after Olav (or Olaf, 995–1030), King of Norway, and Saint of the Roman Catholic Church, who was canonised in 1030. He earned his association with Southwark by supposedly raiding London and pulling down the old London Bridge. The parish of St. Olave stretched to the east and south, limited by nearby Bermondsey parish. In 1740, architect Henry Flitcroft (1697–1769) was tasked with designing a new church, replacing the eleventh-century one. By 1759, the parish area included a free school, two charity schools, an alms house, a workhouse, and a bridge house, which stored materials for the repair of London Bridge.[11] There were adjudged some 2012 houses within the parish.[12] In 1831, the free Queen Elizabeth's Grammar School attached to the parish was demolished to make way for the approach to the new London Bridge.[13]

Fire in such close built-up neighbourhoods was always a hazard. On 21 June 1841, when William was two, there was a disastrous fire that affected the family residence.[14] Starting in Maze Street about 3 a.m., it spread to Weston Street. The Shoults family home suffered only 'slight damage' to furniture and stock, and, fortunately, they were insured. Two years later, on the night of 19 August 1843, another fire took hold in Tooley Street that severely damaged St. Olave's Church, leaving only the bare walls standing. The fire took six hours to subdue, and the total loss was estimated at £50,000.[15] William was four at the time. If in the crowd viewing the conflagration, he may have had vague recollections of all the commotion. Under the direction of George Allen, the church was restored, re-opening on 17 November 1844 at a cost of

---

[9] Stevens (1930), 11.
[10] Hill (2007), 375, 401.
[11] Lambert (1806), III, 155–6.
[12] *Universal Magazine*, 25 (1759), 59.
[13] *History of the County of Surrey* (1967), 125–162, with specific reference to St. Olave's Church, 151–2.
[14] *Morning Chronicle*, 22 June 1841, 7.
[15] *Gentleman's Magazine*, XX. N.S. (July–December 1843), 309. See also 'Interior of the Church of St. Olave before the late fire', *Illustrated London News* (23 September 1843), 203.

£8000.[16] In 1845, the Rev. William Corbet Le Breton (1815–88), later dean of Jersey, began his curacy there. St. Olave's was demolished in 1928, a victim of increased industrialization and a declining parish population. A building on the old Church plot is now called St. Olaf's House, a private hospital. It has a Norseman image on one corner of the building, a fitting reminder of the association with St. Olav.

Attracting individuals to church services was not an easy task in the nineteenth century. Indeed, the 'Census of Religious Worship of 1851' reveals disturbing trends in attendance for the established Church. Although deeply flawed, the survey reveals that 7.3 million individuals in England and Wales went to church, which, in 1851, was 41% of the total population of 17.9 million. This was about 58% of the calculated 'eligible day' population. It was disconcerting to the church authorities that some 7.5 million did not attend Church at all. What was particularly alarming was that numbers present at Dissenting and Roman Catholic Services exceeded numbers of those attending Anglican services.[17]

The use of music and hymn-singing was often used as a way in which to attract new folk to church services and a strategy to hold on to seasoned parishioners. St. Olave's was fortunate to have Henry John Gauntlett (1805–76) as the church organist between 1827 and 1846. He not only built and designed a new organ for the church, but also composed songs and hymns.[18] Although speculation, Gauntlett's undoubted enthusiasm for this aspect of church service may have rubbed off on young William. He enjoyed singing and, while there is no evidence that he played an instrument, he obviously had some musicality. As will be shown in chapter 10, he later developed an intellectual interest in hymns, writing about them.

THE FAMILY

Shoults's paternal grandfather, also named William (1777–1846), was a carpenter and builder. In 1825, aged 48, he fell from an attic to the cellar of a house in the Maze, Southwark, suffering some injury. In 1831, he was a partner with one Richard Henry Vinson rebuilding the St. Olave Parish Workhouse on Fair and Parish streets. By April 1832, grandfather Shoults was adjudged bankrupt. Despite insolvency notices, there was some financial recovery.[19] When he died, in December 1846, his will of 31 October 1846 distributed his worldly goods amongst his five children: Ann, married to John Kingstone; Cecila, married to James Davis; Frances; Edward; and William (1812–78),

---

[16] *Gentleman's Magazine*, XXIII. N.S. (January–June, 1845), 86.
[17] Williams (1999), 14; see also Pickering (1967).
[18] Crolley (2004).
[19] *Times*, 10 February 1838, 7.

the younger William's father. Edward, as the older son, inherited the majority of the estate, including a plot of land in Maze Place. William, as the younger son, got very little: £5 and a mourning ring. Ann, the oldest daughter, received the household furniture, plate and china, and an unspecified number of 'books'.[20]

Carpentry was in the blood. In 1841, William's father was registered as a carpenter.[21] It seems, however, that William Senior had aspirations. As evidenced by property ownership recounted below, and what his wife Elizabeth brought to the marriage, he slowly moved up the English social scale. He became a gentleman, a man of money and leisure. He moved past being a mere tradesman. Part of his aspirations were bookish: he was a reader and displayed the beginnings of being a book collector. Some of the books in his son's library in Special Collections, University of Otago, had obviously been his. They include three volumes of *The Builder. An Illustrated Weekly Magazine for the Architect, Engineer, Archaeologist, Constructor, & Artist* (1858–60), and a large run of Charles Knight's *Penny Magazine*, a popular Victorian magazine that provided a growing number of readers information on all manner of scientific and technical knowledge, travel, art, and cultural subjects. Twelve issues of this magazine, those from 1834 to 1841, are of special interest. They each contain a simple printed book label bearing the name 'SHOULTS' pasted over another label, belonging to an unidentified owner who resided at 'George Street, Hanover Sq., 13A.' The production of any sort of printed label or bookplate is a considerable step for any book owner. The decision to create a permanent provenance record—even the design and printing of a simple name label—shows a strong regard for what has been collected. In the eyes of the owner, the books amassed are worthy of such an action, seen and designated as a collection rather than simply a gathering of books. It is a serious move, and something that Shoults's father carried out. There are no other books in the Shoults Collection that contain the 'SHOULTS' label; thus any other books possibly owned by his father remain unidentified.

One book came directly from Shoults's father. In March 1870, Shoults Senior gave his son a birthday present, a first edition of William Nanson Lettsom's translation of *The Fall of the Nibelungers: Otherwise the Book of Kriemhild*, published by Williams and Norgate in 1850. This medieval German epic poem is a very specific gift, and unless he got it quite wrong, he must have had good knowledge of the sort of book that appealed to his son. A warm filial relationship is certainly reflected in the

---

[20] 1846: will for William Shoults (1777–1846), 30 December 1846, PROB 11/2047/19/901–950 (1846)/254.
[21] 1841: England and Wales census, St. Olave, William Arderne Shoults.

retrospective inscription by Shoults: 'William Arderne Shoults The Gift of his dear Father March 29th 1870. April 22 1870 W. Shoults.'

On 24 April 1836, Shoults Senior married Elizabeth Arderne Dodds, at St Mary's, Whitechapel, on Whitechapel Road. She was born in Stockwell, south of the Thames, about 1811. Her occupation, according to the 1841 Census, was 'School Mistress'.[22] She died in Cambridge in July 1859, and the family estate passed to her husband and the two children: William and his sister Maria Susannah, born 7 April 1842. She was also baptised at St. Olave's Church, on 4 May 1842.[23]

Elizabeth's mother was another Elizabeth, second daughter to John Dodds, a successful retailer of corn, who, at his death in 1819, was living at Phoenix Place, East Street, Walworth parish of St. Mary's Newington, Surrey. Dodds's estate was valued at some £4000 and divided among his three children: John (b.1789), Mary Ann (b.1787), who married William Woodthorpe Faulkner of Saddlers Hill, Cheapside,[24] and Elizabeth (b.1792), Shoults's maternal grandmother, who married Henry Arderne. Elizabeth inherited considerable property from her father: a freehold house at No 71 Tooley Street, some leasehold premises on lease to the Tooley house; a leasehold house at Rose Buildings Camberwell Green, and part ownership of Vine Yard, Southwark.[25] Important to this study of Shoults as a book collector is that John Dodds's will records books, perhaps a substantial library: 'My books be sold by public auction in manner my Executors shall deem best or allotted out for my children to share out amongst themselves or by private contract as my children and my executors, the major part of them, agree to do after all my just debts and funeral expenses are paid share and share alike.'[26] One title filtered through to young William: Benjamin Martin's *The Natural History of England, Or, A Description of Each Particular County: Illustrated by a Map of Each County* (London, 1759–63). Volume 1 of this two-volume work is in Shoults's library. It contains the inscriptions 'Dodds' and a later-added 'W. A. Shoults B. D'. If there are others, they are not identifiable.

One other important factor must be noted. In view of the various properties owned, and the success of Shoults's father's business, the family were not poor. They

---

[22] 1841: England and Wales census, St. Olave, William Arderne Shoults.

[23] Maria Susannah was born 7 April 1842. She did not marry. She moved from the family home (No. 37 Camberwell Grove, Camberwell) to 235 Shakespeare Road, Brixton. She died on 15 February 1907, aged 64. She was buried in the Shoults family plot at Norwood cemetery.

[24] Faulkner (c.1990).

[25] Southwark Local Studies Library, Deed Reference SLS 4638. One deed refers to the compulsory purchase of a piece of land in Vine Yard, Southwark, 22 March 1834. Much later, in Cambridge, 1858, William Arderne Shoults was a witness to a document concerning this Vine Yard property.

[26] Faulkner (c.1990).

no doubt enjoyed a standard of living well above that of the average Southwark folk. Young William certainly benefited from the result of this status.

RAMSGATE

By 1847, the Shoults family were living in Ramsgate, a coastal resort in East Kent, some 78 miles from London. The area around Ramsgate was enjoying a boom, with tourists attracted to the area to enjoy sea-water bathing, steamer trips to Dover, Boulogne, and Calais, and summer resort and holiday activities. The population in 1851 was 11,838; rising ever so slightly in 1861 to 11,865. Houses numbered 2209.[27] About the time that the family moved, the town had three notable churches: St. George, built in 1827; St. Lawrence (Laurence) in Thanet, built in 1844; and St. Augustine's Catholic church on the West Cliff. This last was designed by Augustus Pugin in 1847 in the Gothic Revival style and was part of the Roman Catholic Archdiocese of Southwark. Pugin resided in Ramsgate and over time designed The Grange, West Cliff, and other buildings, such as the Granville Hotel. He died at Ramsgate in 1852, aged 40.

There is no evidence of how and why the Shoults family moved to Ramsgate. At that time, Pugin was employing various men and women in the area as carvers, painters, and carpenters for his various projects. The prospect of building and carpentry work may have been a factor, especially considering the economic downturn in other parts of the country.[28] If anything, it provided a pleasant change of scenery from the Tooley and Weston Street environment.

In 1847, the family were living at 5 Trafalgar Place, Ramsgate.[29] It was a sizeable home, described in an auction notice of the 9 March 1847 issue of the *Kentish Gazette* as containing 'two parlours, drawing room, four bed rooms, and back and front kitchen, with garden at rear'.[30] There is no reason why they sold the 'freehold tenement', but the fact is that they did not move far. In 1851, the family were registered as living at 33 South Wood (now Southwood), St. Lawrence. And it was here that William, now 12, was recorded as a 'Scholar', a term allocated by Census officials to children who were above the age of five and were being schooled at home or receiving regular tuition under a master or governess.[31] Unfortunately, there is no record whatever of his educational progress in these early, formative years. As his mother was a school mistress, she may have given him regular 'home-school' lessons. Coincidentally, the

---

[27] Young (2011).
[28] Hill (2007), 375, 378.
[29] Bagshaw (1847), II, 202.
[30] *Kentish Gazette*, Canterbury, 9 March 1847, 1.
[31] 1851: England census, Thanet St. Lawrence.

family's South Wood address had Pugin connections. The designer's daughter, Anne, and her husband John Hardman Powell, a pupil of Pugin's and himself a stained-glass designer, lived at 3 Southwood Terrace. It was also a house that Pugin helped decorate and furnish.[32] It was possible that the two families rubbed shoulders on occasion.

FIRST BOOKS

In 1851, young William, aged 12, secured what may have been his first book purchase. During that summer, and for some unknown reason, he was in Glasgow and acquired there a copy of *The Poetical Works of Percy Bysshe Shelley* (1845). This dumpy, faded-cloth 580-page work, with no statement of publisher, is the only Shelley title in his collection. Whatever the reason for its purchase, he thought enough of it to inscribe within brief acquisition details.

Four years later, in 1855, another book arrived through family links. In that year his great-aunt Mary Ann Faulkner died. William's father was co-executor of her will, along with Mary Ann's husband, William Woodthorpe Faulkner.[33] In her will, she bequeathed to her sister Elizabeth the sum of £50, silver goods, linen, and jewellery. She must have had some awareness of her grand-nephew's interests, as she bequeathed young William a copy of 'Wilson's Bible in 3 Volumes bound in Red'. This set, published in Bath by R. Cruttwell in 1785, is titled *The Holy Bible Containing the Books of the Old and New Testaments and the Apocrypha: with Notes by the Right Reverend Father in God Thomas Wilson*. These impressive volumes are still in the collection, and represent another 'first'. His collection had begun.

EDUCATIONAL BEGINNINGS

Young William was obviously a bright lad, and, at some point, the family decided that he was 'University material'. This decision meant not following his father's line of business, but rather a career in Holy Orders. He may have already expressed a desire to enter the Church, and certainly the gift of the Bible indicates some leaning towards this career choice.

In the middle of the nineteenth century, an education at Oxford or Cambridge was seen as a socially elite achievement. It was still a place of the privileged, and the progression from school to university was not a given. Indeed, only a third of the boys who left the seven major public schools, including Eton, Harrow, and Rugby, went on

---

[32] Hill (2007), 443.
[33] Faulkner (c.1990).

2 SOUTHWARK, RAMSGATE & EDUCATIONAL BEGINNINGS

to university.[34] More generally, the mass of children left school without proceeding to higher education, and few boys remained at school over 16.[35]

There were no formal requirements for admission into a Cambridge College other than a headmaster's letter. In the 1860s, Robert Potts wrote, adding one small proviso: 'There is no College or University examination to be passed before admission to residence, except at Trinity College; but a certificate, signed by a Master of Arts, is required for every candidate for admission, that he [the student] possesses a competent knowledge of the elements of the Latin and Greek languages, and of the principles of Arithmetic, Geometry, and Algebra. Some colleges require, in addition to the certificate of competent knowledge, a certificate of good moral character; and others also a certificate of baptism.'[36]

It was still hard to gain admission, especially when faced with economic and conservative social-class advantages that existed in nineteenth-century England. And this difficulty persisted, despite the fact that after the 1830s there was a general opening-up of admission to universities. Getting in remained hard; completing the degree course was another issue. However, on completion the degree offered the student undoubted self-satisfaction, increased standing within his family, greater respect in the community, and the general perception that he was now an educated 'gentleman'.[37] In 1853, one ebullient commentator offered his opinion that classics and mathematics were of great value, since they instilled principles which made it easy to acquire any branch of knowledge and taught 'mental habits of analysis and discrimination'.[38] In a sermon, Thomas Gaisford, Dean of Christ Church, was more forthright: 'Nor can I do better, in conclusion, than impress upon you the study of Greek literature which not only elevates above the vulgar herd, but leads not infrequently to positions of considerable emolument.'[39] The Shoults family obviously recognised young William's potential and for him to succeed would provide another opportunity for the family to improve their general station in life. Possession of an Oxford or Cambridge degree was an important social marker worth acquiring. After all, he was William and Elizabeth's only son.

---

[34] Bamford (1967), 47. The top seven public schools were: Eton, Harrow, Winchester, Rugby, Westminster, Shrewsbury, and Charterhouse.
[35] Roach (1986), 5.
[36] Potts (1863), II, 61.
[37] Stray (1998).
[38] Roach (1986), 11, from an examiner's report in Trustees' Minute Book 1840–1889, Warrington Grammar School, 23 January 1854.
[39] Tuckwell (1901), 129.

So, at one point it was decided. One certainty on choosing a career in Holy Orders was that there were requirements that young Shoults had to fulfil, and these were followed without question. It involved an education in Latin and Greek—simply put, lessons construed, parsed, construed, parsed, repeated, and repeated *ad nauseam*. As T.W. Bamford wrote of the stark reality: 'At least three-quarters and in some cases four-fifths, of the time was spent in class on Latin and Greek.'[40] And any thought of the University scholarship—in part or whole—meant classical scholarship.[41] Latin was, after all, still the language of international scholarship.

One example of classical curricula delivered was in Louth in Lincolnshire. The teaching in this school was based on the Eton Latin and Greek grammars. Boys used Valpy's Latin *Delectus* and spent two hours a day in spelling and reading English, writing and arithmetic. The classical texts used included the Fables of Phaedrus, Caesar, Virgil, Horace, Cicero, Livy, and Tacitus. When the rules of prosody were learnt, the students moved on to Latin verses, working through nonsense verse and imitations of English poets to original composition. When about 11, they began Greek and followed similar exercises with authors Xenophon, Homer, the tragedians, Demosthenes, Pindar, Herodotus, and Thucydides. Each day began with Bible reading in Greek, Latin, and English. There were also morning and evening prayers. Rote learning of Greek and Latin texts was favoured, with writing out texts and translating them into English and then back into Greek and Latin.[42] Another less strict classical programme cited by John Roach was at Bury in Lancashire. In December 1835, the eight boys in the first class faced Latin verses and prosody; Greek Testament; Scripture questions; Virgil Book 9; Questions in Geography and History; Livy Book 22; Euclid and Natural Philosophy; Arithmetic; and Maps of France, Italy, Greece, and Palestine. The theme was *Scientiâ nulla res est praestantior* [No matter is superior to science]. The eight in the second class faced Latin Grammar, Watt's *Scripture History*, History, Ellis's *Exercises*, Caesar, Geography, and Arithmetic.

It was this sort of curriculum and its grinding routine that Shoults would have faced within a formalised school setting. If the desire to secure a place at university was strong enough, it meant passing, or at least showing some competence in, the subjects covered.

'Would have' is the key here. There is no evidence that Shoults attended any of the local Ramsgate schools, any of the older public schools, or the newer ones such as Cheltenham and Marlborough. No school is mentioned at all. As a consequence,

---

[40] Bamford (1967), 62; see also Shrosbree (1988), 33.
[41] Shrosbree (1988), 25.
[42] Roach (1986), 70–1.

2 SOUTHWARK, RAMSGATE & EDUCATIONAL BEGINNINGS

there are no anecdotes or tales about school life, be it as a boarder or a day pupil. There are no remarks extant about classmates, games played, punishments faced, fees paid, good or 'rotten' masters, or examination results after the Latin and Greek grind inevitably faced. In addition, there is no evidence that the Shoults family had any social connections that could ease the path to educational advancement. In the 1841 Census, Shoults's mother is classified as a 'school mistress'.[43] She may have taught him rudimentary school lessons, and while she had some Latin, as evidenced from inscriptions in her son's books, she may not have had enough to deliver the full gamut of Latin and Greek required for University entrance. Wherever he went, or whether he had a private tutor or not, it was a fact that Shoults had first to acquire a fair knowledge of Latin and Greek. Somewhat bleakly, Colin Shrosbee writes: 'The requirement for a classical qualification made it virtually impossible for a poor but able man to achieve entry into this elite by natural ability and through private study.'[44] Even when considering his family's rising middle-class background, their undoubted enthusiasm for advancement through their son, and the statistical evidence of boys not attending university, Shoults's achievement was a very good one.

In the same issue of the *Kentish Gazette* that advertised the auction of the family home in Trafalgar Place, there is an advertisement for an election to Corpus Christi College, Oxford.[45] This notice gives details that on a given day candidates must present themselves to Electors of the College. They must be under 19 years of age, have with them a certificate of marriage of their parents and of their own baptism, 'competent evidence' of the day and place of birth, testimonials from their college or school, and a Latin epistle to each of the Electors.

With the opening-up of admissions to universities, a fitness of study certificate was a relatively common requirement in the university admissions register. Some certificates were issued by independent masters rather than from established colleges or schools. Ecclesiastical reformer Canon Samuel Augustus Barnett (1844–1913) was one recipient of such a certificate. He was home-schooled, and in 1859, aged 15, passed the Cambridge Junior Local examination. Two years later, he took the Senior Papers. His preparation – that is 'cramming' – for entrance to Oxford University was monitored by the Rev. T. Hulme.[46] Perhaps St. John's College, Cambridge, published a similar advertisement. If so, it indicates one possible way in which the young William

---

[43] 1841: England and Wales census, St. Olave.
[44] Shrosbee (1988), 59.
[45] *Kentish Gazette,* Canterbury, 9 March 1847, 1.
[46] Barnett (1921), 7–8.

Arderne Shoults made his way to the College. And it was to St. John's College, in essence a seminary for the Anglican Church, that he would go.

An index card in the archives at St. John's College gives brief biographical details for him.[47] There is mention of a certificate of fitness to study signed by the Rev. William Dixon, who was, at the time that Shoults entered St. John's College, vicar of Shepreth, a village some 120 miles from Ramsgate, some 50 miles from London, and eight miles south east of Cambridge.[48] Born in 1819 at Cowes, the seaside resort on the Isle of Wight, Dixon attended Cowes School, under the tutelage of a Mr Matthews. On 20 October 1839, Dixon entered Trinity College, Cambridge as a sizar.[49] He secured a B.A. in 1845 and proceeded to an M.A. in 1848. In 1845, he was ordained a deacon in the diocese of Bath and Wells and, in that same year, a priest at Hereford. Between 1845 and 1847, he was Perpetual Curate of Pensax in Worcestershire. In 1847, he was appointed curate of Haslingfield, Cambridgeshire, staying there until 1853. In that year he became vicar of Shepreth, staying until 1872. He later became vicar of Over and died there on 1 August 1891.

In 1858, the parish area of Shepreth was 1300 acres, and the annual value of the vicarage was £92.[50] In 1851, just before Dixon's arrival, the parish congregation for morning service averaged 30; in the afternoon some 100 were attracted.[51] In that year, the village's population was 321. In 1856, during Dixon's tenure, a new Independent Chapel was registered, listed as an out-station of the Independent Church at Melbourn. In 1859, the Church was sufficiently fenced, was in tolerable condition, and the poor were being looked after, with certain monies allocated to them within the parish.[52]

Little is known about Dixon and his wife Mary Ann. Mystery surrounds how the Shoults family and Dixon connected, and what the nature of their relationship was, if any. However, somehow the family decided to search out Dixon, who must have had some reputation as a tutor. Shoults died young at 48, and he may have been a sickly boy, susceptible to illnesses and not made for the rigours and stresses of

---

[47] St. John's College Biography Card Index, St. John's College Archives, St. John's College, Cambridge; see also Hilton (2011), 242.
[48] Dixon, *AC* (1944), II, 307.
[49] Originally a sizar was an undergraduate who financed his studies by undertaking menial chores and tasks within a college. It later extended to those undergraduates who received small grants from the College. At St John's and Trinity, there was further demarcation: a Proper Sizar, who obtained specific endowments; and subsizars, those maintained by Fellow-commoners and Fellows.
[50] Kelly & Co (1858), 70.
[51] Bolton (1973), 251–63; see also *British History Online* http://www.british-history.ac.uk/vch/cambs/vol5/pp251-263 [accessed 8 April 2020], particularly footnote 305 and reference H.O. 129/140/3/6/5.
[52] Presentment of the Churchwardens of Shepreth, 7 May 1859. Ely Diocesan Records, Visitation Packets, Archives, GBR/0012/MS EDR, Cambridge University Library.

attending school, whether boarding or as a day pupil. Mystery also surrounds how long Dixon tutored young Shoults. Did he board with Dixon at Shepreth? Or were there daily visits? The coaching fee, as there would certainly have been, is also unknown. Whatever the arrangement, and for how long, it obviously suited both parties. There is one certainty: for Dixon to sign the certificate and assure proficiency, he would have had personal contact with Shoults.

In the end, Dixon must have been pleased with the progress of his charge. On 1 July 1856, Shoults was admitted to St. John's College. The family, obviously proud of their son's achievements, were committed to offer William financial and filial support. At some point, certainly prior to his acceptance into St. John's College, they moved from Ramsgate to Cambridge. They lived in a substantial house on Madingley Road, near the Observatory, near Toft's Farm, and a ten-minute walk to the University colleges. In an auction notice issued by Cambridge auctioneer Charles Wisbey in November 1859, the house was described thus: a brick and slate 'Cottage Ornée' with an entrance hall, study, dining room, drawing room, and kitchen, on the ground floor, four 'remarkably cheerful' bed-rooms, and a large basement cellar. There were outhouses suitable for a chaise-house and stable, and a conservatory with a large garden, 'abundantly stocked with the most choice young fruit trees and prolific asparagus beds'.[53] (See pl. 4.) According to Wisbey, Shoults's father had spent large sums fixing the place up, his building skills obviously coming into play.

A few records also situate the family there. The poll list for Madingley Road for 30 March 1857 records Shoults's father, albeit called Edward.[54] And his father is listed in *Kelly's Directory* for 1858 and the *Cambridge Independent Press* of 14 May 1859 as 'William Shoults, gent'.[55] Young William is also firmly placed there. On 23 January 1858, he was at Madingley Road, a witness for his father and mother to a Covenant to produce Deeds to the Board of Works for St. Olave's District Southwark.[56]

Shoults's mother died on 19 July 1859, during term time at College.[57] Her death was the catalyst for the sale of their 'comfortable' and 'most perfect' Madingley home. Nothing is known of when Shoults Senior moved back to Camberwell, but he still felt sufficiently connected to the University town to donate £1 to support the

---

[53] Charles Wisbey Auction sheet, November 1859. Cambridge University Library: Map Room: Maps. PSQ.bb.18.210. Ornéé can be translated as adorned or ornamental.
[54] *Cambridge Independent Press*, 25 April 1857, 6.
[55] Kelly & Co (1858); *Cambridge Independent Press*, 14 May 1859, 2.
[56] See Southwark Local Studies Library: Vine Yard, Southwark Indenture, 23 January 1858, MS 40638.
[57] See 'Deaths', *Morning Chronicle*, 22 July 1859, 8.

building of the new All Saints' Church in February 1860.⁵⁸ All of these events were timely. William had completed the gruelling Mathematical Tripos and was listed under the heading of 'Examined & Approved' Honours men for the Bachelor of Arts on 28 January 1860.⁵⁹ He was at the beginning of his own career, and he no doubt accompanied his father and sister south.

---

⁵⁸ *Cambridge Chronicle and Journal*, 11 February 1860, 4.
⁵⁹ 'University Intelligence, Cambridge, 27 January 1860, Bachelor of Arts Announcements', in *Morning Chronicle*, 28 January 1860, 4.

3 ST. JOHN'S COLLEGE, CAMBRIDGE, AND SIZAR SHOULTS

On 1 July 1856, Shoults was admitted to St. John's College, Cambridge. However, before his matriculation and first residency began, he and twenty-seven other students sat an examination, which not only gave the Fellows an idea of the abilities and standards of their new charges, but also settled sizarships, awards given to freshmen and tenable for three years.[1] The results of the 'Sizar Elected Examination' on 26 June 1856 are extant, and they offer a first glimpse of how Shoults compared with his contemporaries. The subjects tested included Euclid, Arithmetic-Algebra, Latin, Greek, Latin Composition, and Greek prose translation, with marks assigned to each. The top mark was obtained by one Thomas Hoare, whose total was 116. The lowest mark was for George Chell, later Vicar of Kneesall, whose total was 23. Shoults was ranked 17 out of 28, just below the middle. His total was 67, scoring 25 in Euclid (18th), 18 in Arithmetic-Algebra (4th), 10 in Latin (12th equal), 7 in Greek (19th equal), 4 in Latin Composition (25th), and 3 in Greek translation (19th equal). From this first glimpse, he was a bright but middling student, and with his 67 he was below the average of 71.9. Indeed, on the results sheet there is a line drawn under his name and his equal, Andrew John Yarranton.[2]

The Hare Exhibition had been created in 1623 by Sir Ralph Hare, who, by deed of 30 April of that year, allocated £64 per annum 'to and for the only relief, maintenance, &c of *thirty of the poorest, and best disposed poor Scholars* of and within the foundation or College of St. John'.[3] The Exhibition money was accrued through the rectoral tithe of Cherry Marham in Norfolk, and, in 1854, the scholarship was worth about £14 per annum, which went towards college fees and charges. The Shoults family were certainly in the category of the rising middle class, with some affluence (and perceptions of such), as indicated by a substantial house, some land, and Shoults's father's gentlemanly status. They were by no means poor. However, the line mentioned above was a demarcation, indicating a cut-off point. It meant that Shoults's position secured him a Hare Exhibition. He was thus regarded as one of the 'best disposed poor Scholars'. The Hare was not a prestigious scholarship, but it helped.[4]

At the time Shoults entered Cambridge as an undergraduate, there were some 2000 resident students and some seventeen Colleges, overseen by a Chancellor, a

---

[1] Mayor (1910), 189–209 (190).
[2] Hoare, *AC* (1947), III, 390; Chell, *AC* (1944), II, 22; Yarranton, *AC* (1954), VI, 610.
[3] Potts (1855), I, 315. Italics in the original.
[4] Bonney (1921), 15.

Vice-Chancellor, assessors, proctors, and innumerable other office-holders, such as Assessors and Moderators.[5] Matriculation numbers rose and fell for St. John's College. In 1856 there were 421; in 1857, 451; in 1858, 382; in 1859, 399; and in 1860, Shoults's last year, 443.[6] These could be considered bumper years, if one considers Thomas George Bonney's calculation of 270 undergraduates in 1852, the year he matriculated at St. John's.[7]

The men holding Professorships included William Sterndale Bennett, Professor of Music; Edward Harold Browne, Norrisian Professor of Divinity; Charles Hardwick, Hulsean Professor of Divinity; Thomas Jarrett, Regius Professor of Hebrew; James Amiraux Jeremie, Regius Professor of Divinity; Theodore Preston, Lord Almoner's Professor of Arabic; William Selwyn, Lady Margaret's Professor of Divinity; William Hepworth Thompson, Regius Professor of Greek; and Henry Griffin Williams, Sir Thomas Adams's Professor of Arabic.[8] These men gave occasional lectures, which Shoults may have attended. It was extremely unlikely that he ever came into personal contact with any of them.

There were four categories of undergraduate: fellow-commoners (generally sons of the nobility), scholars, pensioners, and sizars.[9] They paid different fees, enjoyed particular rights and privileges, and, in some instances, even the academic dress worn was visibly different. For example, the sons of noblemen wore top hats and were known as hat-fellow-commoners.[10] There were strict observances about academic dress: students had to wear them at all times on Sundays, even outside Cambridge, as well as after dark on week days, and in the earlier part of the morning. Carrying the gown was not permissible, nor letting it or a cap fall into 'a collapsed condition'.[11]

Shoults was a Proper Sizar, one funded by a scholarship.[12] The others were just sizars, funded somehow by the College. Nevertheless, like all sizars, he paid 15 shillings per quarter for tuition and faced the same examinations and exercises as all the other students. In previous years, sizars—students with limited funds—often waited on tables or were assigned valet duties to a master or a fellow in return for board and

---

[5] Gardner (1851). Further references in this chapter on Cambridge are from Roach (1959), 235–65; Searby (2004); Brooke (2004); and Hilton (2011).
[6] *Historical Register* (1917), 990.
[7] Bonney, (1909), 294–310 (295); see also Raby (1991), 45.
[8] *Historical Register* (1917).
[9] Gardner (1851).
[10] Bonney (1921), 19.
[11] Bonney (1909), 308.
[12] Shoults is listed with eight others under the title Proper Sizar. See *Cambridge University Calendar* (1859), 317.

lodgings.¹³ By 1856, the year that Shoults entered College, these 'servant-like duties' had largely diminished. His gown, like those of other Bachelor of Arts candidates, was made of bombazine or poplin, with large sleeves terminating in a point. He later embarked on a Bachelor of Divinity degree; his gown then was made of the same material but had the sleeves extended to the feet, with the sleeve points square.¹⁴

From the 1850s onwards, there was an increased mix of students, each bringing with them a wide range of educational backgrounds, abilities, misconceptions, and boyhood naiveties. Sons of noblemen, doctors, merchants, tradesmen, and clergymen came from schools such as Rugby, Shrewsbury, and Eton, or from backgrounds and situations similar to Shoults's.¹⁵ Although this influx caused a general change in the make-up of the Colleges, most of the men were like-minded individuals, inculcated with strong, conservative, deeply entrenched social, economic, and class traditions. Despite their individual differences, they all came together in a rather strange classroom intimacy towards learning, whether it be Euclid, Latin composition, or Greek. Many formed sets based on common areas of interest or shared experiences that helped them get through the rigours of College life. There was the athletic set, the musical set, the loafing set, the reading set, the fast set, and many other iterations.¹⁶ The fast set—or man—was aptly described by John Delaware Lewis:

> The fast man usually rises at a late hour [...] The fast man hurries off to chapel with curses both loud and deep [...] his surplice unbuttoned, and holds his prayer book upside down. In the evening, there are his billiards, his whist, his soirees at the 'Emperor's Head' with oysters, and horse-dealers and blacklegs. Hating solitude, he cannot study, and he hates the University, as a matter of course, longing for the time, as he tells you, when he is to get out into the world.¹⁷

By contrast, there were the 'reading men', those undergraduates consumed by study and amusingly described by John Smith: 'He [the reading man] seldom reads an English work, and of the history of his native country is strangely, almost supernaturally, ignorant. Passing occurrences do not affect him.' Smith continued:

> The fields with which he is best acquainted are not battle fields, but rectangular

---

¹³ Searby (2004), 70; see also Venn (1913), 131.
¹⁴ Gardner (1851), 70.
¹⁵ Some of the schools that provided students to Cambridge included Charterhouse, Cheltenham, Eton, Harrow, Manchester Grammar, Marlborough College, Rugby, Sedbergh, Shrewsbury, and Uppingham. See Hilton (2011), 299–300.
¹⁶ Besant (1902), 80.
¹⁷ Lewis (1849), 10–22, cited in Searby (2004), 67.

ones with mathematical properties, through which he fights his way to a solution over the carcases of x's and y's. Beautiful landscapes fail to delight him. He looks upon hills, and valleys, and rivers, as interesting or otherwise, according to their capabilities of furnishing a sum.[18]

Samuel Butler, author of *Erewhon* and *The Way of All Flesh*, entered St. John's College as a pensioner on 2 May 1854, two years earlier than Shoults. Butler secured a First Class in the Classical Tripos (12th equal) in 1858.[19] In *The Way of All Flesh* (1903), he offers a description of the 'labyrinth', tumbledown rooms behind the then chapel of St. John's, and the 'poor fellows'—that is, sizars—who inhabited the area:

> In the labyrinth there dwelt men of all ages, from mere lads to grey-haired old men who had entered late in life. They were rarely seen except in hall or chapel or at lecture, where their manners of feeding, praying and studying, were considered alike objectionable; no one knew whence they came, whither they went, nor what they did, for they never showed at cricket or the boats; they were a gloomy, seedy-looking *conferie*, who had as little to glory in clothes and manners as in the flesh itself [. . .] Unprepossessing then, in feature, gait and manners, unkempt and ill-dressed beyond what can be easily described, these poor fellows formed a class apart [. . .] To most of them the fact of becoming clergymen would be the *entrée* into a social position from which they were at present kept out by barriers they well knew to be impassable; ordination, therefore, opened fields for ambition which made it the central point in their thoughts.[20]

Parts of Butler's 'class apart' description could well apply to Shoults. However, there is no evidence that Shoults belonged to any one group or set. Significantly, he lived at home on Madingley Road, a ten-minute stroll to and from College. This last fact may have had some influence on his chance to connect with contemporaries, if this is what was desired. By not being around after hours, he certainly missed the conviviality and camaraderie, the banter and skylarks and conversations. It could be grim, as Walter Besant (1836–1901), a student at Christ's College and another near contemporary of Shoults, wrote:

> But nobody cared about any of the students; during the whole time I was there I never remember a single word of personal interest or encouragement. The men went to lectures; if they failed to attend, a letter was sent to their people

---

[18] Searby (2004), 600.
[19] Raby (1991), especially Chapter four: St. John's.
[20] Butler (1970), chapter 47, 216–18.

at home; of individual interest or encouragement there was absolutely none. I believe it was much the same thing at most of the colleges of Oxford and Cambridge at this time. The men were left severely alone.[21]

Shoults may have opted for this option: an individual comfortable in his own skin as the bookish loner, getting on with his own thing, whatever that was. It certainly seems that way, although he must have appreciated the collegiality found with like-minded souls at the College.

REFORM

In the years before 1850, reform was in the air.[22] In 1828, there was the removal of civil religious tests (the Test and Corporation Acts); in 1829, there was Catholic emancipation; in 1832, the Reform Act was passed; and in 1833 there was the Irish Church reform. Albeit glacial, reforms were also seeping into College life. In 1849 and 1860, there were important Statute changes that, according to Edward Miller, 'represented a substantial breach in the old order'.[23] One reform was that official recognition was given for the first time to ten College Lecturers, whose classes could now be attended by all students, and not just by a select few. Importantly, in 1856, the Cambridge University Reform Act was passed, abolishing religious tests for B.A. degrees, except for those taking Divinity studies. Although religious restrictions were maintained for those who proceeded to the M.A. degree, and celibacy requirements for Fellows were not yet abolished, there was a general loosening up of statutes and procedures that opened Cambridge up to students of dissenting religious factions. In fact, the dissenting factions could enrol and attend classes, although graduating with a degree was still not possible. Unlike Oxford, which as an institution demanded that students should know and be tested on the Thirty-nine Articles of the Anglican faith, Cambridge was lenient, requiring only that a student declare that he was a *bona fide* member of the Church of England. Peter Searby has termed the reforms 'remarkably gentle and moderate'.[24]

---

[21] Besant (1902), 74.
[22] Roby (1909–10), 189–209; see also Mayor (1910). William Hamilton cited in Searby (2004), 434, says: 'This is the age of reform. Next in importance to our religious and political establishments, are the foundations for public education; and having now seriously engaged in a reform of "the constitution, the envy of surrounding nations", the time cannot be distant for a reform in the schools and universities which have hardly avoided their contempt.' See also earlier work by Hamilton (1852), 386–434 (386–7).
[23] Miller (1961), 86 cited in Hilton (2011), 274.
[24] Searby (2004), 433.

THE CURRICULUM

Although small changes had occurred, the curriculum followed very much the traditional and somewhat narrow degree that was confined to mathematics and classics. It was designed to offer the men a shared common experience, all 'well calculated to inform the mind, and strengthen judgment'.[25] Instruction was given under the four headings of:

> Theology: the Historical Books of the Old Testament, the Greek Testament, William Paley's *Evidences of Christianity*, and Church History
>
> Natural Philosophy: Euclid's *Elements* (the first three books, and six propositions of Book VI), Algebra, Trigonometry, Conic Sections, Mechanics, Hydrostatics, Optics, Astronomy, Differential and Integral Calculus, Isaac Newton's *Principia*, etc.
>
> Moral Philosophy: Bishop Butler's *Analogy of Religion*, and William Paley and Dugald Stewart's *Moral Philosophy*
>
> Belles Lettres: the most celebrated Greek and Latin Classics.[26]

Mathematics, rather than classics, dominated at Cambridge. The regime in place was tough, and those with any literary pretensions were disadvantaged by the heavy bias towards mathematics. Examinations dominated student life. The Previous Examination, known as 'Little-Go' or 'smalls', was perceived as less strict and important than the final one. It was established in 1822 and first held in 1824. The 'Little-Go' examination was obligatory for all undergraduates in the Lent term of the second year, and they were expected to pass a written examination, demonstrating knowledge of one of the Gospels in Greek, a Greek or Latin classic, William Paley's *Evidences of Christianity*, and the first three books of Euclid.[27] The Mathematical examination followed at the end of the first May term.[28] All students were judged on results, and some scholarships were awarded to deserving candidates. Shoults passed his 'Little-Go' but did not qualify for any scholarships.

The endgame for most students was to pass the Mathematical Tripos, a number of written examinations which were faced after attendance of ten terms (reduced to nine in February 1853). The Tripos (established in 1747) was fiercely competitive, with almost everyone aiming for the highest score and the much-desired position of

---

[25] Gardner (1851), 56.
[26] Gardner (1851), 56. See also Potts (1863), II, 255–56.
[27] Chadwick, (1987), II, 30.
[28] Venn (1913), 260.

Wrangler.[29] By way of example, in 1854 the Tripos consisted of sixteen papers spread over eight days, totalling 44.5 hours. The total number of questions was 211.[30] William Everett, an American pensioner and scholar at Trinity about the same time as Shoults was at St. John's, recalled what was involved. On the first day the paper contained questions on the elements of mathematics, Euclid, and other geometrical subjects. After three hours:

> Art one, another three hours' paper. The next day, the same, and the next. Then a pause of ten days, while the work of the previous three, all on the easier departments of mathematics, is looked over. All those who have passed the minimum asked by the examiners, are now announced as 'having acquitted themselves so as to deserve mathematical honours'. The rest are [...] plucked. The degree of Bachelor of Arts is not for them as far as mathematics goes. With these three days, the ambition of most stops.[31]

What followed was another five days' examination on areas such as 'tough' mathematics, especially differential calculus, and then to the highest calculation of astronomy and optics. The results were then processed and posted, with individuals ranked from high to low. As mentioned, the prize of Senior Wrangler was uppermost in the minds of many. Then followed Second Wrangler, and so on down through second-class honours (Senior Optimes), and third-class honours (Junior Optimes). Noel Annan succinctly wrote: 'the Tripos was a trial of memory and nerves', adding:

> Much of the preparatory work consisted of practising manipulations which would increase the rate of solving and writing out the solutions of propositions. Part of the test lay in the speed at which a candidate could work, and this in turn depended on how fast he could make his pen skim over the sheets of paper. Hence it paid to learn endless propositions by heart so that not a moment would be wasted in the examination room in thinking them out.[32]

For those less mathematically inclined, there was Classical studies. In 1824, the Classical Tripos was introduced, effectively broadening existing study. The twelve papers consisted of four for composition (translating verse or prose into Latin or Greek)

---

[29] A Wrangler is a student who gains first-class honours in the third year of the University's undergraduate degree in mathematics. The highest-scoring student is the Senior Wrangler, the second highest is the Second Wrangler, and so on. Students who achieve second-class and third-class mathematics degrees are known as Senior Optimes (second-class) and Junior Optimes (third-class).
[30] Stray (2001), 33–50.
[31] William Everett cited in Searby (2011), 179.
[32] Annan (1984), 'The Early Years' chapter.

and the remaining eight for the translation of classical prose or verse into English.[33] In 1857, a year after Shoults entered, the requirement that any student (noblemen excepted) must pass the Mathematical Tripos before entering this programme was dropped. One person, so named 'Y.Z', tabulated the passages set from Classical authors between 1824 and 1860. Too numerous to detail, a small sample included Thucydides and Demosthenes (Greek prose); Homer's *Iliad* and Sophocles (Greek verse); Livy and Cicero (Latin prose); and Lucretius and Virgil (Latin verse).[34] The exercises often focused on pertinent literary passages that illustrated points of syntax or grammar. And, in matters of verse composition, the range was from Iambics and Trochaics to Hexameters and Lyrics. As in classes in early school, there was much rote repetition and much translation.

The Tripos was by then a multi-day written examination ordeal, answered in English rather than in Latin. One staunch classical studies advocate was Richard Shilleto (1809–76), who tutored Shoults at St. John's. He defended the use of Latin and disliked the encroachment of English in texts. John Venn (1834–1923), a student at Gonville and Caius College, and a near contemporary of Shoults's, wrote: 'There was probably not a single College [except Trinity and St. John's] which provided what would now be considered the minimum of necessary instruction, even in classics and mathematics.'[35] J.W. Headlam similarly wrote in about 1885:

> It is often said among Cambridge men, and I daresay by many others too, that Cambridge is now the only place in England where pure classics retain their old importance as an educational subject. Pure classics is of course the technical expression used among scholars to denote the critical study of the language of the ancient authors as distinguished from that of the matter: the study of Literature in its simplest and primary aspect, abstracted as far as possible from all Historical, Philosophical or even Philological questions.[36]

Shoults was extremely fortunate that he attended St. John's.

In 1848, with pressure from Trinity College, two new Triposes were introduced: Moral Sciences and Natural Sciences, which required a knowledge of history, law, political economy, botany, geology, mechanics, and engineering. About 1853, Joseph Bickersteth Mayor (1837–1921) and George Downing Liveing (1827–1924) were appointed as Lecturers to teach Moral and Natural Sciences respectively. And in that same year, 1853, a chemistry laboratory was opened, the 'haunt' of Liveing. In

---

[33] Searby (2004), 171.
[34] 'Z, Y.' (1860), 207–11.
[35] Venn (1913), 256.
[36] J.W. Headlam, c.1885 cited in Stray (1998), 123.

3 ST. JOHN'S COLLEGE, CAMBRIDGE & SIZAR SHOULTS

1857, William Henry Bateson (1812–81) was the Master; the eccentric stickler George 'Betsy' Fearns Reyner (1817–92) was Senior Bursar.[37] The Junior Bursar during Shoults's tenure was Simeon Hiley (1854–60).

And what of theological instruction? What was offered to students as intending clergy?[38] In 1841, George Peacock, the Dean of Ely, wrote: 'At least one-half the students in the university are designed for the church, and no provision (the lectures of the Norrisian professor alone excepted) is made for their professional education; this is a deficiency in our academical system.'[39] Perhaps Peacock had forgotten that in 1837 divinity, along with hydrostatics and mechanics, had been added as a topic of study, albeit somewhat rudimentary: candidates were tested on the Acts of the Apostles and one or two of the Epistles.[40] It was a small advance. In 1843, the Voluntary Theological Examination was introduced. In 1850, it became a requirement that candidates for the examination should, by means of a certificate, show that they had 'attended the lectures delivered during one Term at least by two of the three Theological Professors'.[41]

The bias towards mathematics and classics remained, and it seemed that any theological instruction was a 'hit or miss' affair, largely dependent on the enthusiasm and initiative of the student and the availability of willing lecturers. Walter Besant later wrote, reflecting on his own university experience:

> Those of the undergraduates who were religiously disposed indulged in a sort of gluttonous banquet of services. One man, I remember, would take Sunday school at eight a.m., go to chapel at half-past nine; to a morning service at eleven; to the university sermon at two; to King's College Chapel at three; to the college chapel at six; to evening service in some church of the town at seven, and end with a prayer meeting and hymn singing in someone's rooms. But such men were rare.[42]

He continued:

> For my own part, though still proposing to take orders, I was so little moved by the responsibilities before me that though it was necessary, in order to obtain the proper college testimonials, to attend three celebrations of Holy Communion in the three years of residence, I forgot this requirement, and,

---

[37] See Hilton (2011), chapter four, 'The Nineteenth Century'.
[38] Searby (2004), 262, 266–7.
[39] George Peacock, the Dean of Ely cited in Searby (2004), 265.
[40] Searby (2004), 267.
[41] Searby (2004), 268.
[42] Besant (1902), 91.

on discovering this omission, attended all three in the last two terms. This was thought somewhat scandalous and I nearly lost my college certificate in consequence.[43]

John Venn commented on a 'good natured mathematician' he knew who grappled with theology—his 'grotesque attempts at comment and interpretation' were the joke of the College.[44] Venn did mention Alford's *Greek Testament* as a popular handbook of the day; perhaps Shoults used this work as well.

COLLEGE ROUTINE

Each student faced routine, cramming, and Chapel and Hall. Chapel started at 7.00 a.m. Charles Astor Bristed, an American student at Trinity College in 1840, had his personal servant (known as a 'gyp'[45]) call him at 6.30 a.m. for Chapel. He then went to breakfast, which for him was rolls, butter, and tea. John Venn dined on bacon and eggs.[46] As he recorded, lunch was bread and cheese. A common meal—usually a simple affair—was eaten in the Hall, usually at about 4.00 or 5.00 p.m. This consisted of meat joints, potatoes, and cabbage; sweets, cheese, and ale were regarded as 'sizings' and had to be specially ordered, and were charged separately. To Venn, soup, fish, and game were 'absolutely unknown', while of the 1860s Thomas George Bonney (1833–1923), a St. John's College student who graduated as 12th Wrangler in 1856, wrote of a more appetising fare: dinner of a meat course with pies, puddings, and cheese and, at supper time, cold turkey, boar's head, ham, and game pie, with home-brewed punch.[47] And everyone drank beer, 'Bitter and Swipes' being the most common.[48]

In theory, Chapel was compulsory. Although the requirement for undergraduates was to 'keep' seven chapels per week, many slid out of the habit. To be seen at morning and evening prayers was obviously the key, as W. E. Heitland wrote somewhat cunningly: 'If you kept two Chapels on Sunday, you could get off with three in the rest of the week.'[49] Evening Chapel began at 6.00 p.m. It was all a matter of keeping your nose clean, as Bristed wrote: 'I believe if a Pensioner keeps six chapels, or a Fellow-Commoner four, *and is quite regular in all other respects*, he will never be troubled

---

[43] Besant cited in Searby (2004), 274.
[44] Venn (1913), 257.
[45] A 'gyp'—from the Greek word for vulture—was a personal servant who worked for about 20 or so undergraduates. He called them in the morning, brushed their clothes, carried parcels and notes, etc. See Brooke (2004), 597.
[46] Venn (1913), *270*.
[47] Venn (1913), *270*; see also Bonney (1921), 33–4; and Roach (1959), 235–65.
[48] Besant (1902).
[49] Bristed (1852), 5–6, 19–29; see also Searby (2004), 272, 593; and Stray (2008).

by the Dean.'⁵⁰ Neglect of rules bought trouble from the Junior Dean, a monitor of all activities, who recorded transgressions in the Junior Dean's Books. Some students broke up the monotony by frequenting pubs, gambling, womanising, and general skylarking. This behaviour was also monitored, sometimes with dire consequences. There is no evidence of Shoults ever transgressing the rules. Some of his contemporaries did, however: Spurrier—'Found in a house of ill-fame by the Proctors reported by them to the College. The Master, without consulting the Seniors, arranged that the case should be settled by the Proctors & his Tutor. The Proctors insisted upon his being sent down for a Term. Told, through his tutor, that College testimonials for Holy Orders will be objected to.' Salmon—'Out of College all night. Traced to London. Seems to have gone off from fear of his father, who had just come down to enquire into his progress & conduct.' And Stone—who was 'in residence after putting on an "exeat". Took lodgings under the name of Leicester. Explanations very unsatisfactory'.⁵¹ For most, the evening's work began after Chapel, with reading before bed.⁵² Rooms varied in size, with sizars usually getting the inferior ones.⁵³ Most were spartanly furnished. Bedmakers—perhaps the only females that students came into contact with apart from the wives of Masters or members of their own family—undertook daily rounds. College gates were closed at 10.00 p.m., with transgressors often fined. Then, as now, everyone looked towards the Long Vacation, which was the middle of June to the middle of October.

PRIVATE COACHING

William E. Heitland—one of the best annalists of the College, who himself entered as a pensioner in 1867—commented that 'college lectures and examinations were futile'.⁵⁴ There was all too much rote learning, with the eye forever fixed on the position of Wrangler, the main academic prize. Of course, some men were just ill-equipped intellectually to face what was involved. The path to the prize demanded speed and accuracy; these attributes were paramount.

Classics instruction had good and competent students mixing with those who could not decipher the Greek alphabet. And it was often construe, construe, construe, with a follow-up commentary on a particular passage. Often mathematics lecturers merely dictated various questions and walked around the class answering questions,

---

⁵⁰ Stray (2008), 18.
⁵¹ Additional entries in the Junior Dean's Register, Week 17 October 1856–1857, and Week 16 October 1857–1858. DS3.2-6. St John's College Archives, Cambridge.
⁵² Bonney (1909), 308.
⁵³ Romilly (2000), 316, fn 13.
⁵⁴ William E. Heitland cited in Hilton (2011), 285.

if they were forthcoming. Of his experience Bonney wrote: 'The lectures at St. John's, at any rate for the Freshmen, then left much to be desired. The system, in fact, was a survival of one which had become obsolete, and which apparently assumed that little or no mathematics had been learnt at school. So men likely to be Wranglers were obliged to attend lectures on Euclid of a very elementary kind; those on algebra being rather better, but the lecturer unattractive.' He was critical: 'the great fault of our system was that at first it wasted the time of the better men.'[55] John Venn painted a vivid picture:

> The brilliant scholar from the best public schools, and the young man who had given up business and was beginning his Greek letters with a view to taking Orders; the destined high wrangler, who had read his conic sections as a school boy, and the youth to whom Euclid and his mysterious pictures were a daily puzzle, sat side by side on the benches of our lecture room, and tried to make the most of the lecture, or at any rate of the time during which the lecture was delivered.

He made further comment: 'This arrangement, prevalent I believe in most if not all the Colleges, was probably one of the worst features in the system of the day.' And it seemed that not much was forthcoming about what one studied. Venn wrote: 'As to Honour-men: we had few or no 'tips' or notes of lectures, or suggestions as to what books or parts of books we should read. There was but little of this, I think, from private tutors, and nothing, I should say from the lecturer.'[56]

Underlying Heitland, Venn, and the recollections of Bonney was the need for a private coach. Lectures were just not enough. And it was recognised that to obtain a reasonably high place in a Tripos 'coaching' was vital. Indeed, 'getting men through' was the aim in areas such as composition, unseen translation, and advanced mathematics.[57] William Henry Bateson's dictum was that 'The greatest part of a man's education here consists of what he does by himself and with his private tutor [. . .] The College Tutors I can assure you are of very little assistance, especially to a classical man'.[58]

During his first years at St. John's, Shoults's primary tutors were Francis France (1816–64) and Dr Stephen Parkinson (1823–89).[59] France had been a sizar, admitted to St. John's on 12 May 1835. He secured his B.A. in 1837 and his M.A. in 1843. While

---

[55] Bonney (1909), 15–6, 300–1.
[56] Venn (1913), 258, 265.
[57] Heitland (1921–1922), 284; see also Hilton (2011), 286.
[58] William Henry Bateson cited in Hilton (2011), 281.
[59] France, *AC* (1944), II, 561–62; Parkinson, *AC* (1953), V, 30–1.

a Fellow, he completed a Bachelor of Divinity degree in 1850. In 1859 he became Archdeacon of Ely and Chaplain to the Bishop of Gloucester and Bristol. He was a lecturer in Greek and the author of *The Example of Christ* (1861).

Parkinson was admitted as sizar at St. John's on 25 February 1841. He graduated as Senior Wrangler in 1845, famously beating William Thomson (later 1st Baron Kelvin) into second place. He was elected to a Fellowship at St. John's in the same year. He served his College as lecturer in mathematics, tutor (1864–82), and President (1865–89). Parkinson also served on the committee of the University Senate (1866–78) and became a Fellow of the Royal Society in 1870. He was ordained in 1851 and received his Bachelor of Divinity in 1855 and his D.D. in 1869. He married Elizabeth Lucy Welchman Whateley on 15 August 1871. Parkinson was the author of two mathematical textbooks, *Elementary Treatise on Mechanics* (1855) and *A Treatise on Optics* (1859), both of which went through several editions and remained in use at Cambridge for 25 years. Samuel Butler passed comment on these two: 'Parkenson [sic] and [...] France are awfully jolly dons far the nicest in the college.' He was less complimentary about others: 'Reyner and Mayor are brutes.'[60] France was 40 and Parkinson 33 when Shoults came under their tutelage.

Samuel Butler mentioned his schedule with Parkinson: 'I go to Parkenson [sic] in Euclid on Tuesday Thursday and Saturday mornings from 8 to 9.'[61] Bonney also left a description of Parkinson's teaching methods:

> [He] was at that time in great repute as a mathematical coach. He took his pupils, as a rule, singly. On reaching the inner room, where he sat, you received a manuscript paper, with about half a dozen questions, and went to work at it in the outer room. Presently he called one back to a chair by his side, when he looked over one's last lot of papers, indicating mistakes, sketching out a solution of a posing problem, and dealing with any other difficulty. His explanations were terse, but lucid, and he never 'snubbed' a pupil. His great merit as a teacher for Cambridge examinations was, as I thought, that, when you received a paper of questions at one of these, you felt as if you had already seen something rather like it. In short, he was a first-rate trainer for the Senate House races.[62]

Shoults's experience with this 'jolly' don was no doubt similar.

While Parkinson, France, and Shilleto were experts in their respective fields,

---

[60] Raby (1991), 44–5.
[61] Raby (1991), 44.
[62] Bonney (1921), 16.

it was not enough.[63] It was customary for undergraduates to engage a private coach, a necessary boost to increase chances of passing.[64] While there is no evidence that Shoults engaged a coach, he surely conformed, like the others, paying whatever was the going rate. He did have other expense—charges for groceries, the tailor, the hosier, the shoemaker, and the bookseller—but, as already noted, he lived at Madingley Road and did not have a room at College.[65] Living at home, his costs were certainly much less than the average student's. There was the 'tolerably prudent' sizar who could manage on a yearly sum of £73, and there was the more extravagant student, spending upwards of £250.[66] Whatever his costs per year were—presumably not exceeding £100—it was customary that his tutors were involved in any financial transactions.

ATTENDANCE & EXAMINATIONS

Two of the most important markers that reveal firm evidence of Shoults at St. John's College are the attendance registers and the examinations he sat. Attendance registers at St. John's College record his passage in and out of College during Lent, Easter, and October Terms, with dates given for returning or 'exeat' (a formal leave of absence).[67] They also included absences over Long Vacation. Throughout his tenure he 'kept' the statutory nine terms—including regular Chapel attendance, with morning chapel beginning at seven. His 'first residence' was on 13 October 1856, and he quickly adopted the practice of going home. His last appearance in the Register was just before finals in October 1859, when only his name is recorded.

There are also registers for the years 1856 to 1859 that reveal Shoults's attendance under the guidance of Francis France. In one register he is designated 'S' (perhaps

---

[63] Venn (1913), 262–3: writes: 'In all respects we were left very much to ourselves in the matter of our studies. The tutor Mr Clayton, never lectured. We saw him for a few minutes at the beginning and end of term; that is, to report our arrival and to secure our exeats.'

[64] Bristed, cited in Stray (2008), 138, gives £7 per term and states that noblemen and fellow commoners paid more, with sizars about one half. Bonney (1921, 16) confirms the coaching fee of £7 per term and £15 for the vacation, and in a later reflection, gives his coach costs at £36 a year. See also Hilton (2011), 281.

[65] See St. John's College (1895) and (1984) for lists of occupants in college rooms. By 1860 there was a high percentage of non-residents at College. See also Brooke (2004), 112.

[66] H. W. Cookson, a tutor at Peterhouse, cited by Searby (2004), 125, cites a 'tolerably prudent' sizar, whose first year's costs were £72 11s 7d after securing various prizes and scholarships. W. H. Thompson, cited in Roach (1959), 235-65, maintained the average expenses of a pensioner were between £150 and £250. William Collings Mathison, Fellow of Trinity 1840–68, was a little more specific: 'he thinks the *necessary* expenses of a sizar are £53—and the *actual* expense of a careful Sizar ought not to exceed £100 a year.' See Romilly (2000), entry: Thursday, 7 April 1859, 316.

[67] SJAR/6/1/5/4. Residence Book (Archives) and St. John's College Admission and Register, SJAR /6/1/6/2. St. John's College Archives.

'sizar'), with entries confirming his attending nine terms.[68] The registers also reveal the names of classmates, including Henry Frederic Codd, Samuel Farman, William Grist, John Hodgson, John Read Marrack, Joseph Merriman, and Charles Sellwood.[69] Another register covers October 1856 and has Shoults bracketed with three other students: George Green, William Lucas, and Stephen Condon Adam. They each have a small note 'Rd13' beside their names, which is surely 'Rediit' (the record of a student's date of return to Cambridge after an exeat), for 13 October.[70] Green was a sizar, who matriculated at St. John's on 5 July 1855 and died age 40 in March 1870; Lucas was the son of a wire-worker, who was admitted as a sizar on 3 July 1854 and, as 12th Wrangler (1858), went on to become Vicar of Ottringham, and then of Burstwick, Yorkshire; and Adam, son of an excise officer, who was admitted as a sizar on 3 July 1854 and eventually became Vicar of St. Jude, Wolverhampton.[71] Another register, of January 1857, has Shoults by himself, with 'Rd26' by his name.[72] In June 1857, he is again bracketed with Lucas, along with George Jackson and John Bullivant Slight.[73] Another 'Rediit' note is beside their names.[74] That same month, Shoults is registered with the note 'Ex11' (exeat) beside his name.[75]

EXAMINATIONS

The Archives at St. John's College also have examination records that provide information on Shoults's placement and progress while at College. They are not complete, and there are mysteries surrounding some of the markings in the records— for example, the meaning of '15+ 15-', and '3+ 27-'. Nevertheless, they offer a further snapshot of him and his contemporaries. In December 1856, Shoults and seventy-nine others sat the Christmas 'Freshman' examinations. Of the thirty-four men listed and ranked in the First Class section, he was placed twenty-second, another middling result. Sizar Hoare is positioned five below Shoults; Chell is still under-performing, listed in the Third Class section, placed eighth.

In June 1857, Shoults and thirty others sat the Midsummer 'Freshman' Examinations. If the results reflect ranking, he improved his position, being placed

---

[68] SJAR 6/1/13/8. Rediit Register, St. John's College Archives.
[69] SJAR 6/1/6/2. College Admission and Register, St. John's College Archives. See *AC* volumes: Codd, *AC* (1944), II, 83; Farman, *AC* (1944), II, 460; Grist, *AC* (1947), III, 161; Hodgson, *AC* (1947), III, 400; Marrack, *AC* (1951), IV, 321; Merriman, *AC* (1951), IV, 395; and Sellwood, *AC* (1953), V, 461.
[70] SJAR 6/1/13/8. Rediit Register, St. John's College Archives.
[71] Green, *AC* (1947), III, 127; Lucas, *AC* (1951), IV, 229; Adam, *AC* (1940), I, 7.
[72] SJAR 6/1/13/8. Rediit Register, St. John's College Archives.
[73] Jackson, *AC* (1947), III, 536; Slight, *AC* (1953), V, 533.
[74] SJAR 6/1/13/8. Rediit Register, St. John's College Archives.
[75] SJAR 6/1/13/8. Rediit Register, St. John's College Archives.

seventh in the First Class section. Like others in this section, he was listed as a 'St. John's College Prizeman'.[76] In December 1857, he and sixty-five others sat the '2nd Year' Examinations. Of the fifteen students listed in the First Class section, he was placed tenth, securing a mark of 15-, just below Hoare, who obtained 15+.[77] The highest mark in the First Class section was registered to Walter Baily, scoring 29-.[78]

Just before Easter 1858, Shoults faced the rigorous Lent Term 'Little-Go' examination. Although no specific results for him have been found, he continued his good form, ranking in the First Class section and in the 'Additional Subjects and Approved' list.[79] Thanks to Parkinson's collecting efforts, examination papers for that year survive. They reveal subjects Shoults faced, including arithmetic, algebra, Euclid, mechanics, the Gospels (especially St. Luke), Herodotus, Virgil, and William Paley's *Principles of Moral and Political Philosophy* (1785) and *Evidences of Christianity* (1794). The two entries below carry samples of what Shoults had to answer. In relation to William Paley's *Evidences*, he had to answer numerous questions, of which three are shown here:

> 1. Explain the abuse of words which consists in defining a miracle to be *contrary to experience*, and answer the argument hereupon founded that all testimony in favour of miracles is inadmissable.
>
> 2. Shew that the *actual existence* of Christianity is strongly in favour of the truth of the proposition 'that the original teachers voluntarily passed their lives in labours, dangers, and sufferings'.
>
> 7. What is meant by *momentary miracles, tentative miracles*? Shew that the miracles of our Lord were not of this character.[80]

In relation to Virgil's *Aeneid*, he had to translate into English the text beginning 'Murranum hic, atavos et avorum antiqua sonantem' and ending at 'olli per galeam fixo stetit hasta cerebro'. (Book XII, 529–37)

Shoults also had to complete the following example tasks:

> 1. Derive *atavus, praeceps, excutio, jugum, scopulus, proculco*.
>
> 2. Parse *incita, actum, provolvere*

---

[76] *Cambridge Chronicle and Journal*, 13 June 1857, 4; see also *Cambridge University Calendar* (1858), 317.
[77] *Cambridge Chronicle and Journal*, 19 December 1857, 4.
[78] Baily, *AC* (1940), I, 121.
[79] *Cambridge Chronicle and Journal*, 3 April 1858, 7.
[80] 'Previous Examination March 1858', in *Cambridge Examination Papers* (1858), 8.

3. Derive *crimen, funditus, demens, luctus*. What are the perfects and supines of *prospicio, sono, discindo, credo, necto*.

4. Describe the position of Latium with the names both ancient and modern of the surrounding countries.[81]

In June 1858, Shoults faced another examination, the final of his second year. Out of twenty-one students, he secured twelfth place in the First Class section. He got 19+ 37–, while C. J. E. Smith was first, scoring 37– 60, and Henry Clements Barstow last, number twenty-one, scoring 3+ 27–.[82] In the local newspapers and the University calendar, Shoults was listed under 'Junior Sophs' (a second-year undergraduate at Cambridge) and the more general heading of 'Prizemen, June 1858'.[83] In his collection in Special Collections, University of Otago, there is a beautifully-bound three-volume edition of Virgil's *Opera* (1852). Volume one has a brief inscription: 'A prize secured by W. A. S. at Cambridge.' Perhaps this edition was awarded to him for his achievement in the above Examination.

In the December '3rd year' Examination of 1858, something went awry. He did not make the First Class list. In fact, the abbreviation 'Susp' (Suspended?) is written above his name and that of eighteen others, including contemporaries Codd, Grist and Sellwood. The score beside his name is a mysterious '10, 21'. There is no certainty of why this hiccup occurred. One explanation, however, is plausible in that his home life was proving tough. His mother died in July the following year, and she may have been exhibiting the first signs of an illness.[84] One can well understand his shifting priorities if this was the case.

Shoults's performance was still below par in the Third year Midsummer 1859 Examinations. He missed out on the First Class section, making it into the Second Class list, ranking number three of eleven students. His mark was 16+. It was perhaps because of his poor showing that he was not listed as one of the 'Scholars Elected Nov. 7 1859', along with contemporaries such as Hoare, Marrack, and Merriman.

---

[81] 'Previous Examination March 1858', in *Cambridge Examination Papers* (1858), 188, and from Stephen Parkinson's large run of Examination Papers, CA Exam.L.9 1824-83, and Exam.L.68. St. John's College Library, Cambridge.
[82] SJAR/1/2/Parkinson/2/1/1. Examination Book. St. John's College Archives. For Smith, see *AC* (1953), V, 544; Barstow, *AC* (1940), I, 172.
[83] Listed under 'Prizemen, June 1858' under 'Junior Sophs', in *Cambridge University Calendar for 1859* (1859), 313; see also *Cambridge Chronicle and Journal*, 12 June 1858, 4.
[84] Published death notice on 19 July 1859 of Elizabeth, wife of William Shoults, Esq., of Madingley Road (See 'Deaths', *Morning Chronicle*, 22 July 1859, 8). She was taken back to London and buried on 29 July 1859 at Norwood cemetery, otherwise, South Metropolitan Cemetery. South Metropolitan Cemetery Company (West Norwood Cemetery). See 1914: Surrey Church of England Burial Registers, EKS no. 2391, reference: P33/1/42.

In early January 1860, Shoults sat the Mathematical Tripos (Senate House) examinations along with 121 others. Throwing off personal anxieties in what must have been a very trying time, and buckling down to what was deemed a very important examination, he improved his performance. He made the top of Senior Optimes, just missing out on the much-desired Wrangler category.[85] (See pl. 3.) That year there were thirty-eight Wranglers, with Stirling, a Trinity man, securing first place. Shoults headed fifty Senior Optimes. There then followed thirty-three Junior Optimes. Fourteen St. John's men were placed ahead of him. They included Walter Baily, George Richardson, John Vavasor Durell, Joseph Merriman, Charles James Eliseo Smith, William Shrubsole Foster, Thomas Hoare, Robert West Taylor, John Read Marrack, William Addy Proctor, Richard Saul Ferguson, William Previte, Charles [Isabel] Scott, and Jason Smith.[86] Like Shoults, all of the above men had matriculated in 1856. Only six of the fourteen entered the Church; the remaining eight became legal men, educationalists, or civil servants. According to records in *Alumni Cantabrigienses*, four, like Shoults, would marry.

On 21 January 1860, Shoults's name appeared along with twenty-six others under the heading 'Questionists Deserving Mathematical Honors' in the *Cambridge Independent Press*.[87] He also was mentioned in the B.A. 'Honours' list under 'University Intelligence' in the *Morning Chronicle* of 27 January 1860.[88] It was an excellent achievement, and even though his mother missed the occasion, his father must have been very proud.

EXTRA-CURRICULAR ACTIVITIES

Shoults was a bright young intellectual. He probably enjoyed the tussle over language passages and mathematical formulae, the grind (e. g. Greek, 'the gerund grind'), and the eventual examination cram. He was certainly bookish, and, from the small amount of evidence available, it seems that he enjoyed his time at Cambridge.

Although there is no evidence that Shoults played a musical instrument, he did sing, and, in one instance, led a parish congregation in singing hymns. As will be shown in chapter 10, he displayed some intellectual interest in the history and origins

---

[85] *Cambridge University Calendar* (1860), 114.
[86] For details on these students see *AC* entries: Baily, *AC* (1940), I, 121; Richardson, *AC* (1953), V, 292; Durell, *AC* (1944), II, 361; Merriman, *AC* (1951), IV, 395; Smith, *AC* (1953), V, 544; Foster, *AC* (1944), II, 549; Hoare, *AC* (1947), III, 390; Taylor, *AC* (1954), VI, 129; Marrack, *AC* (1951), IV, 321; Proctor, *AC* (1953), V, 208; Ferguson, *AC* (1944), II, 483; Previte, *AC* (1953), V, 191; Scott, *AC* (1953), V, 441; and Jason Smith, *AC* (1953), V, 559.
[87] *Cambridge Independent Press*, 21 January 1860, 5.
[88] See also CA Exam.L.68, Special Collections, St. John's College Library.

of hymns, especially Latin ones. Given this presumed musicality, he may have attended choir and music sessions organised through the Cambridge University Musical Society, which was formed at Peterhouse in 1843 for the study and performance of choral, orchestral, and chamber music. Shoults is not listed as a member in any of the existing Society registers, yet he came to know the Rev. John Robert Lunn (1831–99), a Fellow of St. John's College, composer of ecclesiastical music, strong advocate of the works of J. S. Bach, and one time President of the Musical Society.[89] The extent of their relationship is unknown, but there was familiarity. In fact, in 1863, Shoults felt comfortable enough to ask Lunn to add his name to a testimonial on his character and moral conduct for entrance into Holy Orders.

There was another Cambridge musical connection that Shoults would have certainly acknowledged. John Mason Neale (1818–66) was a Trinity College undergraduate who established in 1839 the Cambridge Camden Society, which later became the Ecclesiological Society in London (1845) and then, with a division, the Cambridge Architectural Society (1846).[90] Importantly, Neale was a hymnologist, who recognised that good melodic hymns were of immense importance in teaching the orthodox faith of the Church. He wrote hymns for children and the sick, gathered hymns from monasteries and libraries while travelling overseas, and translated hymns from the Latin and Greek into English, hoping that they would inspire congregations within the Church of England.[91] He also worked on carols, his most famous being *Good King Wenceslas*. Shoults not only referenced some of Neale's publications in his own work on hymns, but also owned a number of them, including his hymnbook *Sequentiæ ex missalibus Germanicis, Anglicis, Gallicis aliisque Medii Aevi, collectæ* (1852); *The Ancient Liturgies of the Gallican Church* (1855), co-authored by G. H. Forbes; a tract entitled *A Few Hints on the Practical Study of Ecclesiastical Antiquities* (1840); two copies of *A Few Words to Churchwardens on Churches and Church Ornaments. Part I: Suited to Country Parishes* (1842; 1846); a third edition of *History of Pues* (1843); and *Church Enlargement and Church Arrangement* (1843).

There were other commonalities with Neale that Shoults may have warmed to. Through the Society Neale promoted 'the study of Ecclesiastical Architecture and Antiquities, and the restoration of mutilated Architectural remains'.[92] Neale was convinced that the revival of church architecture would bring about a revival of Catholic ceremony in the Church of England. He was attracted to Tractarianism

---

[89] Lunn, *AC* (1947), IV, 236.
[90] Lough (1962); see also Brooke (2004), 109; Drain (2004); and 'John Mason Neale' in *ODCC*, 1134.
[91] Some of Neale's hymn works included *Hymns for Children* (1842), *Hymns for the Sick* (1843), *Mediaeval Hymns and Sequences* (1851), and *Hymns of the Eastern Church* (1862).
[92] Lough (1962), 8, 156.

(otherwise the Oxford Movement), initiated by John Henry Newman, John Keble, and Edward Bouverie Pusey.[93] He loved the celebration of the Catholic tradition in Anglicanism, and it was his desire to have the Church return to the purity of the Middle Ages, to be locked into festival times, to go back to fasting on Fridays, and to rise at 4.15 a.m. to say lauds. Neale was also an advocate for the reunion of the three churches: the Church of Rome, the Eastern Church, and the Church of England.[94] Finally, in 1854, he formed an order for women, St. Margaret's Sisterhood, basing this enterprise in East Grinstead, Sussex.[95] Shoults certainly had some knowledge of the building industry through his father's business, and he collected books that had a focus on antiquities and antiquarianism. Importantly, Shoults was a ritualist, although perhaps not classified as such then. All of the London parishes he subsequently worked in were ritualistic. In addition, he became associated with the Anglican Benedictine monk Joseph Leycester Lyne (1837–1908), otherwise known as Father Ignatius, who, in his own eccentric style, promoted both ritualistic and revivalist services. It was through Shoults's association with Father Ignatius that he became deeply involved in monastery and convent life.

Shoults was not a member of the Cambridge Camden Society, the Ecclesiastical Society, or the Cambridge Architectural Society. Although there is no evidence that he and Neale met, it is hard to dismiss such an influence on him. Indeed, the influence of Neale and the Society was long-lasting, permeating through the close-knit Anglo-Catholic community by word of mouth or through publications. As A. G. Lough writes: 'During the latter half of the nineteenth century churches all over England were restored and new churches built. It would be true to say that there was hardly a church in the country which was not affected in some way by the Cambridge Camden Society.'[96]

---

[93] The beginnings of the Oxford Movement started on 14 July 1833, when John Keble, a Fellow of Oriel College, gave the annual assize sermon in Oxford, choosing the theme 'National Apostasy'. The sermon discussed the interference of the state in the affairs of the Church of Ireland—that is, the Irish Church Temporalities Act that suppressed some bishoprics to provide augmentation for poor livings in Ireland. It offended some High Churchmen as an effort to make the church the state's creature. Keble, Newman, and Pusey all saw the church's authority as derived from the Protestant Reformation. In *Tracts for the Times* (1833–41), a work consisting of 90 essays, they emphasised the church's Catholicity, and, hoped to revitalise the Anglican Church of England. Shoults owned a copy; his holdings of the *Tracts* are the first double issue of April and July 1844, June 1845, October 1845, March 1846, and June 1848.
[94] Works by Neale relating to Eastern Churches include *A History of the Holy Eastern Church – The Patriarchate of Alexandria* (1847) and *History of the Holy Eastern Church – General Introduction* (1850).
[95] Lough (1962), chapter 5; see also Anson (1964), 337–50.
[96] Lough (1962), 36.

And what was on offer outside College studies for a student like Shoults? Golf and lawn tennis were unknown. There were no bicycles, although some enterprising soul owned a velocipede, sometimes seen (and ridden) on the streets of Cambridge. Football and cricket were played by some, but there were no designated grounds, and no uniforms. Any rough and tumble team sport activity more than likely did not attract him, especially if he had underlying health issues. The only image extant of him reveals that he wore glasses. (See pl.1.) Short- or long-sighted, his vision may have limited his activities. Rowing was a favourite extracurricular activity at St. John's. T. G. Bonney's doctor said to him: 'You may read hard or row hard, but you cannot do both.'[97] There is no evidence that Shoults belonged to the rowing fraternity, and, again, his health may have precluded such vigorous activity. It seems that he opted for reading hard.

John Venn remarked on his formative educational influences: 'I had learnt something from my lecturers, more from my coach, but most of all from conversations with friends; and the main opportunity for such conversation was the daily walk.'[98] Walking was the way in which most students got about, and Shoults would have certainly enjoyed walking the lanes and roads around the countryside of Cambridge. The most popular was 'The Grind', out through Grantchester, then to Trumpington, and then back to town along the main road.[99] There is no certainty in this, but perhaps one or two of his fellow students accompanied him, giving him an ideal opportunity to discuss meaty theological or philological issues, or discuss Tennyson's *Maud* or perhaps the works of Carlyle, Dickens, or Kingsley.[100]

National sentiments on contemporary events such as the Crimean War and the Indian Mutiny spread through the College. There were also more localised events that may have attracted Shoults. Visiting speakers came and went, and he may have attended the talk on 'Faith' by the popular Charles Spurgeon on Good Friday, 10 April 1857, or listened to the explorer David Livingstone at Senate House and then at the Town Hall on 4 December 1857, or heard the naturalist Richard Owen delivering a paper called 'On the classification and geographical distribution of Mammalia' at the Senate House on 10 May 1859, or that Victorian draw-card Charles Dickens, who spoke at the Town Hall on 17 October 1859.[101] While there are no certainties about his involvement in the above events, there are a few while he was at College, aside from the registered examination marks and general attendance. As will be revealed in

[97] Bonney (1909), 305.
[98] Venn (1913), 280–1.
[99] Bonney (1909), 307.
[100] See Besant (1902).
[101] Romilly (2000), 277–8, 299–300, 319–20, and 331.

the next chapter, he started amassing books for his personal use, books that became part of his growing book collection. Obtaining them was one small pleasure for this budding bookman.

4 CERTAINTIES AT COLLEGE, 1856–59

THE EAGLE

The *Eagle* was a College magazine started by poet Thomas Ashe and Joseph Bickersteth Mayor in 1858, towards the end of Shoults's second year.[1] In its early days, it had five editors: J.B. Mayor, Frederic Charles Wace, Edward Delanoy Little, William Edward Mulling, and Edward Woodley Bowling.[2] Its stated aims were to encourage the study of English literature, to offer an opportunity for the practice of English composition, and to afford a necessary stimulus for more serious reflection upon subjects which did not feature prominently in College courses.[3] The editors hoped that the magazine would become 'a rallying point and a watchword among us; something to fasten College spirit upon when here'.[4]

Shoults was an early subscriber, and there is a record of his annual payment of 7s 6d noted in issue no. 3, November 1858.[5] His subscription lasted until 1869; on his death in 1887 he was given a one-line notice in the obituary section of the *Eagle* (1888).[6] Importantly, he was also a contributor. In the November issue of 1858, there is his first appearance in print. Under 'Answers to Queries' is his three-plus-page article entitled 'On Cupid's Blindness'.[7] The article begins:

> The notion that the representation of Cupid as blind is not to be found in the Greek and Latin writers, is of old standing. Caelius Rhodiginus (tutor of Julius Caesar Scaliger, who calls him the Varro of his age), in his *Lectiones antiquae* (lib. XVI. Cap. 25, col. 760, in the edition of 1599) after quoting from Theocritus (*Idyll*. X.; given below), says that some denied that it could be found in the writings of the ancients.

Shoults continues his argument with quotations from authors such as Proclus, Lilius Gyraldus (1479–1552), Virgil, Servius, Julius Pomponius Sabinus (a commentator on Virgil), Plato, Plutarch, and the above-mentioned Lodovicus Caelius Rhodiginus

---

[1] The eagle is the symbol of St. John the Apostle.
[2] For biographical details on these men see *AC* entries: Mayor, *AC* (1951), IV, 379; Wace, *AC* (1954), VI, 299; Little, *AC* (1951), IV, 180; Mulling, *AC* (1951), IV, 495; Bowling, *AC* (1940), I, 344.
[3] From a sheet headed '*The Eagle. A Johnian Magazine*', dated 16 October 1858, tipped in Shoults's copy of the first volume of the *Eagle*.
[4] *Eagle*, I (1859), 4.
[5] Shoults's name is underlined in ink in the Michaelmas Term issue (November, 1858).
[6] Shoults's brief obituary, *Eagle*, XV (1888), 103.
[7] 'On Cupid's Blindness', *Eagle*, III (November 1858), 168–71.

(1469–1525). He ends by quoting a few verses from a fragment of the *Phaedrus* of Alexis, preserved by Athenaeus; these ten lines are in Greek. The article is signed 'G. de A. Decurio', a nom de plume that can be expanded to Gulielmus de Arderna Decurio, that is, William Arderne Shoults, with the variants Schultz or Schultheiß in German being the head of a municipality, that is, decurio.[8]

In the article he also quotes from the historian Dionysius of Halicarnassus (c.60– after 7 BC). Shoults owned four copies of his works: *Scripta qvae exstant, omnia, et historica*, published in Frankfurt in 1586, *Antiqvitatvm Rom. libri XI*, published in Lausanne in 1588, a Greek edition of *Dionysiou tou Halikarnasseōs tés Rhomaikēs archaiologias ta sózomena*, published in Oxford in 1704, and *Opera omnia*, published in Leipzig in 1829. Three of these titles he may have had at hand as he penned the article; the Oxford edition was obtained later.

He presumably felt that there was a need for clarification. In the April issue he added a small 'Note' to his article, similarly signed, and again ending in a flourish of Greek.[9] Interestingly, in this piece, Shoults mentions the eleventh-century London-born monk Albricus and specifically Thomas Muncker's *Mythographi Latini*, published in Amsterdam in 1681. Shoults owned an extremely battered copy of *Mythographi*, and it may well have been used as a resource for the article. There is no indication of when he purchased it, or from whom.

Shoults also owned a copy of Caelius Rhodiginus's *Lectionum antiquarum libri triginta*, published in Frankfurt in 1599. This work, a collection of notes on the classics and general topics such as oracles, contains a bookmark resting between the pages that correspond to his specific reference in the first article of 'col. 760'. The marker (with some inky notes on it) was likely placed there as he extracted the information from it. And the contents of this book were perused relatively quickly. It had been given to him by this mother on his birthday in 1858, when he turned nineteen. The Latin inscription reads: 'Gulielmo Arderne Shoults muneri natalicio hunc librum dedit, carissima ejius [sic] Mater MDCCCLVIII'.

The two articles are impressively erudite, especially coming from a twenty-year-old. They are important on various levels. They confirm not only Shoults's knowledge of Latin and Greek, but also the range of materials that he was reading in order to construct what are densely-packed pieces. Importantly, they mark out for the first time the scholarship and rigour associated with work that he undertook. They display close, accurate work, and he was obviously at home dabbling in such detail. The pieces

---

[8] Thanks to Drs David J. Shaw and Anne Coldiron for information on 'Schultheiß' and 'decurio'. Email correspondence: 10 June 2020.

[9] 'Note', *Eagle* (April 1859), 240.

are strongly bibliographical and, at a glance, are markedly different from the more general contributions by others found in the first three volumes. Any prospective reader would need a high level of Greek under their belt and familiarity with those writers mentioned. Perhaps the editors were conscious of what their readers preferred because there are no more contributions from 'G. de A. Decurio'.

The Shoults Collection contains 36 issues of the *Eagle*, covering Lent Term, March 1858 to December 1869. Bound in six volumes, they were once owned by Wace, one of the editors. Fortunately, Shoults's authorship of the two pieces is revealed by a hand-written inscription in black ink of his name under his nom de plume. Black ink was Shoults's favourite medium, and these scribal revelations were done by him. Wace was an editor, Shoults a contributor, albeit fleetingly. They must have rubbed shoulders, if only over editorial matters. They may also have had a more personal relationship, perhaps close enough for Wace to give his copies of the *Eagle* to Shoults, sometime after 1869.

COLLECTION BEGINNINGS

Despite a 'paper-tax' on books and newspapers, printed matter—old and new— was readily available in Cambridge from shops and stationers, at the Union library (the Debating Society), and through circulating libraries.[10] There was also a raft of periodicals and journals available, a growing selection that provided for all tastes. These ranged from the *Edinburgh Review* (1802) and the *Examiner* (1808), to the *Illustrated London News* (1842) and the *London Quarterly Review* (1853). Although periodicals offered a wider content range, and in the main offered a currency in news and reviews, bound books were still king.

As mentioned, there are occasional dated inscriptions made by Shoults in his books. In 1859, three years into his study, he acquired ten books, perhaps from a local bookseller such as Deighton, Bell & Co, or a London-based book dealer. The titles that follow are significant in that they not only give a good indication of what he acquired for personal use, and, specifically, where his interests lay, but also proof that he was frequenting bookshops (and auctions) to purchase books. They are serious titles and certainly not frivolous.

On or about 1 January 1859, he acquired a second-hand copy of William Palmer's *Treatise on the Church of Christ: Designed Chiefly for the Use of Students in Theology*. Published in 1842, this two-volume set is the third edition, revised and enlarged. It

---

[10] See Hewitt (2013).

carries the previous owner's name: 'G. Bainbridge, 1845'.[11] In both volumes Shoults inscribed his name and the date of purchase: 'W. A. Shoults. The Feast of the Circumcision, 1859'—that is, 1 January. William Palmer (1803–85) was a graduate of Trinity College, Dublin, before transferring his association to Worcester College, Oxford. He was a supporter, for a time at least, of the Oxford Movement. Although there are no marginalia or other marks, both volumes have cracked spines, indicating that they may have been well read. Shoults may have dipped into this densely-packed 'magisterial' work on 'Branch Theory'.[12]

Some twenty-three days later, Shoults acquired two more books. The first was the third French edition of the works of Salvian (or Salvianus), a Christian writer of the fifth century in Gaul. This copy, published in 1684, was edited by the French scholar Étienne Baluze (1630–1718) and contains Salvian's best work, *De gubernatione Dei*. This copy, with its outer lower corners of the calf board covers eaten away, once belonged to the English College in Rome (Perigle Coll. Inglese Roma) and to Juan Francisco Marco y Catalán (1771–1841), a Spanish Roman Catholic cardinal, whose collection was sold in Rome in 1841. It was then passed to an unknown buyer at the sale, who made a pencil note within about the cardinal. The book finally ended up in Shoults's hands, who dated its acquisition to a particular Feast day: 'W. A. Shoults. St. John Evangelist's College, Cambridge. The Feast of the Conversion of St Paul, 1859'—that is, 25 January.

The second book acquired was a folio edition of *The Historical and Miscellaneous Tracts of the Reverend and Learned Peter Heylyn, D.D.*, published in London in 1681. Heylyn (1600–1662) was a theologian and historian, who seems to have been a natural curmudgeon. According to Anthony Milton, Heylyn had 'a taste for combat'.[13] Some of his 'tracts' in this volume include 'Ecclesia Vindicata, or the Church of England Justified', 'Of Liturgies, or Set Forms of Worship', and 'The Undeceiving of the Peoples in the point of Tithes', preceded by a biography of a man who did not like a quiet life. The first preliminary leaf and the title page of Shoults's copy are torn, and the imprint details—M. Clark, for Charles Harper, 1681—have been lost. Shoults may have bought the book in this state, not worrying too much about its condition. Obviously, the content—all 700 pages plus—was enough. This fact will be repeated: his books constitute a working library, which he read and from which he extracted

---

[11] Perhaps George Bainbridge, a St. John's College man, who died on 3 August 1858 aged 49. See *AC* (1940), I, 121.

[12] 'Branch Theory' provided that both the apostolic succession and the Faith of the Apostles are kept intact and that there the Church exists, albeit in one of its branches. Nockles (2004) calls Palmer's work 'magisterial'.

[13] See Milton (2015), *ODNB* entry on Heylyn.

content when needed. Condition was secondary. The Heylyn contains no ink marks or notations except for the inscription on the title page: 'W. A. Shoults. St. John Evangelist's College, Cambridge. The Feast of the Conversion of St Paul, 1859.'

Ten days later, Shoults purchased a third edition copy of John Keble's sermon *Primitive Tradition Recognised in Holy Scripture*, published in London in 1837. It is inscribed 'W. A. Shoults. St. John the Evangelist College, Cambridge. The Feast of the Purification of the Blessed Virgin Mary, 1859', which equates to Candlemass, 2 February.

Twenty-three days later—on 25 March—he acquired two more books, inscribing them: 'W. A. Shoults, St. John the Evangelist's College, Cambridge. The Feast of the Annunciation of the Blessed Virgin Mary, 1859.' The first was a copy of the second edition of Robert Isaac Wilberforce's *The Doctrine of the Holy Eucharist*, published by Mozley in London in 1853. Wilberforce (1802–57) was the second son of William Wilberforce, the abolitionist, who, like his Oriel College counterparts John Henry Newman and Henry Edward Manning, joined the Roman Catholic Church. Wilberforce's work was an important and scholarly contemporary treatment of the Eucharist, where he argued that the body and blood of Christ are sacramentally present in the Eucharist (in the form of bread and wine) and that the Eucharist itself was a sacrifice. Alf Härdelin has described the work as 'the crowning effort of Tractarian thinking on this subject'.[14] It is a very clean copy.

The second was a Parisian edition of Roberto Francesco Romolo Bellarmino's *De scriptoribus ecclesiasticis liber unus*, published in 1630. Bellarmine (1542–1621) was an Italian Jesuit and Cardinal famous for his involvement in the Giordano Bruno and Galileo trials. He was an erudite scholar, who among other things produced in 1613 his *De scriptoribus ecclesiasticis*, a work on Church Fathers and Church theologians. Shoults read this small-format book enough to make one annotation. In black ink, he added in the index at the front: 'S. Gregorius Nyssenus, 134', which relates to the entry on Gregory in the text.

The Feast of Saint Mark the Evangelist is celebrated on 25 April. On this day, Shoults acquired a copy of the second edition of Edward Welchman's Latin explanation of the Thirty-nine Articles (*XXXIX articuli Ecclesiæ Anglicanæ*), published in Oxford, 1718. He marked his acquisition thus: 'W. A. Shoults. St. John the Evangelist's College, Cambridge, The Feast of St. Mark. 1859.' This particular copy is interleaved, full of numerous manuscript notes on each Article. The notes are not by Shoults, and it is

---

[14] Härdelin (1965), 21; see also Newsome (2006). The *Holy Eucharist* by Wilberforce was the last of a trilogy. The first two were *The Doctrine of the Incarnation* (1848), and *The Doctrine of Holy Baptism* (1849).

a pity that there is no indication whatsoever in the book of what he thought of the unknown reader's notes on Welchman (1665–1739), an English Calvinist churchman, or of the Articles. By this time Shoults was surely fixed on entering Holy Orders; these defining principles on doctrines and practices of the Church of England were an integral part of his obligations towards that chosen career path.

On 26 May, Shoults acquired a copy of the first edition of John Henry Newman's *An Essay on the Development of Christian Doctrine*, published in 1845, the year that Newman was received into the Roman Catholic Church. This work was Newman's articulation of Catholic ways that were historically present but unnamed in the 'one and one only great doctrinal Council in Ante-nicene times'—that is the time in Christian history up to the First Council of Nicaea, AD 325.[15] Much of this work is based on studies of the early Church Fathers. Somewhat fittingly with the book's Romanist slant, Shoults's dated inscription reads: W. A. Shoults In Fest. S. Philippi Nerii, 1859', which is celebrated on 26 May. Philip Neri (1515–1595) was known as the 'Apostle of Rome' and was famed, among other achievements, for founding the Congregation of Oratory, a type of monastery that allowed certain freedoms of action and religious practice which were mostly approved by Pope Paul V.[16] In the late 1860s, when Shoults was involved in the monastery established by Father Ignatius (see chapter 8), he may have reflected on Neri's work in this area.

A few days later, on 11 June, on the Festival of St. Barnabas, Shoults obtained a copy of the fourth edition of Christopher Bethell's *A General View of the Doctrine of Regeneration in Baptism*, a doctrine that had direct relevance to Roman Catholics, Lutherans, and High Church and Anglo-Catholic adherents. Published in 1845, Shoults's copy is a repackaged one, containing an eight-page prospectus of 'New Books' that was printed later and dated February 1849. The publishers were Francis and John Rivington, who had High Church connections. They had published the Oxford Movement's *Tracts for the Times* in 1833, which Shoults also owned, and did much publishing for the Society for Promoting Christian Knowledge (SPCK). Bethell (1773–1859) also had High Church connections, and this work, which first appeared in 1821, is regarded as his best book. The inscription within reads: 'W. A. Shoults In Fest. S. Barnabae, 1859.' It is a clean copy.

Four months later, on 14 September 1859, Shoults moved away from nineteenth-century publications and chose a large folio Latin edition of Stanislaus Hosius's *Opera quae hactenus extiterunt omnia*, published in Antwerp in 1566. Hosius (1504–79), a Roman Catholic Cardinal, was at one time the Prince-Bishop of Warmia in Poland

---

[15] Newman (1845), 12.
[16] See 'St. Philip Neri', in *ODCC*, 1276.

and papal legate to the Holy Roman Emperor's Imperial Court in Vienna. He was an ardent anti-Protestant and a man of extremes. He not only desired a repetition of the St. Bartholomew Day massacre, but also claimed that the Bible was the property of the Roman Church, regarding it as having no more worth than the fables of Aesop.[17] This edition of his 'Works' contains various theological doctrines and information on the Council of Trent (1545–63). Beautifully bound in brown calf, it has blind-stamped rectangular frames on the covers that depict crucifixion scenes, doves, skulls, and medallion busts of Cicero, Ovid and Virgil. Blind-stamped on the front cover is the name: Hosii. In addition to the dated inscription: 'W. A. Shoults, The Feast of the Invention of the Holy Cross, 1859', there is slight evidence of use: underlining of text and marginal notes in red and black ink.

All of the above books not only reconfirm Shoults's serious intellectual interests, but they also represent some of the theological issues that he was grappling with, or at least had to come to terms with in regard his own beliefs. Some of these included the unity of the Christian Church, the place of rituals in services, the Eucharist, and regeneration through baptism. The other marked feature is that on purchase he wrote in every book a particular Feast-Festival day. He obviously had a high regard for Christian feast days, those celebratory days dedicated to a saint or martyr throughout the liturgical year. He was twenty, and these are very personal responses. Indeed, what better way to commemorate a book purchase than to add in by hand significant, and to him meaningful, Feast days. Incidentally, and somewhat serendipitously, the chronological arrangement of books in his collection at the University of Otago Library means that a copy of Edward Vansittart Neale's *Feasts and Fasts: An Essay on the Rise, Progress, and Present State of the Laws Relating to Sundays and Other Holidays, and Days of Fasting* (1845) sits snugly beside the Newman mentioned above.

By 1859, Shoults owned a copy of Shelley's *Works*, a Wilson Bible, a copy of Muncker's *Mythographi Latini* (1681), a copy of Caelius Rhodiginus's *Lectionum antiquarum libri triginta* (1599), and the above titles. There were no doubt others, but, if so, they cannot be identified. Non-identification aside, there are three books that he may have acquired during his time in Cambridge. While acquiring them at this time is not definite, they do, as a disparate group of books, add to the mix greatly and point further to the subject areas that he was interested in.

Francis Procter (1812–1905) was a pensioner admitted to St. Catharine's College,

---

[17] 'Hosius', in *EB*, XIII, 790; see also 'Stanislaus Hosius', in *ODCC*, 793.

Cambridge, in 1831 who later became Vicar of Witton, Cheshire.[18] He wrote *A History of the Book of Common Prayer: with a Rationale of its Offices*, first published in 1855. Shoults owned a first edition, which has the inscription 'With the author's respects'. The imprint date makes it possible that it could have been a presentation copy to Shoults, although there is nothing definite about this claim. The topic was certainly an area of interest to him. With mention of Feast days above, it is noted that Procter's preface to this work carries a festive sign-off: 'Witton Vicarage, The Feast of the Circumcision, 1855.'

During this time, Shoults may also have acquired a copy of *De arcanis Catholicae veritatis* by Pietro Colonna Galatino (1460–1540), an Italian friar, philosopher, theologian, and orientalist, who wrote the work at the request of Pope Leo X and Emperor Charles V. The work is decidedly Catholic and anti-Jewish and was first published by Gerson Soncino in Ortona in 1518. Shoults's copy is the second edition, published in Basel in 1550. Although the title page states the presence of 'De Arte Cabalistica', Johannes Reuchlin's controversial treatise on the authority of the Jewish writings, it is actually missing from Shoults's copy.[19] Once belonging to the 'Bibliotheca Regia Monacensis' (Bayerische Staatsbibliothek; the Bavarian State Library), it passed somehow to the Rev. Richard Wilson of Carlton Hill, Leeds, who has written '1856' inside it. This copy was obviously disposed of from his library before his death in 1890.[20] There is a pencil note of 'Rare' on the front pastedown and a number of fragments of manuscript writings, probably sixteenth century, sewn into the binding of the volume. Perhaps these two aspects caught Shoults's eye and induced him to buy the book.

Adrian and Peter Walenburch (1609–69; 1610–75 respectively) were Dutch Roman Catholic theologians. In the years 1669 and 1670, a two-volume folio edition of their collected works was published in Cologne: *Tractatus generales de controversiis fidei*. This work covered fundamental principles of the Catholic Church and various treatises, such as on the Eucharist, Purgatory, and transubstantiation. Shoults's copy is badly battered and badly foxed. Volume II contains an inserted sheet listing in ink each treatise and a small hand-written note in ink pasted at the bottom of the endpaper reading: 'A Valuable & scarce work, priced in Nutts Catalogue (1857) at £3 10. It is the best book of controversy with which I am acquainted, both as regards its candor & learning.' Both notes may have been written by Shoults, perhaps when it was acquired about 1858 or 1859. However, there is a caveat, especially in regards the last

---

[18] Procter, *AC* (1953), V, 207.
[19] For Reuchlin and his Cabbalistic interests see 'Johannes Reuchlin', in *ODCC*, 1389–90.
[20] See the Rev. Richard Wilson in *AC*, VI (1954), 527.

4 CERTAINTIES AT COLLEGE

sentence. At this time, he was about nineteen or twenty, and it is hard to credit him with such wisdom and experience to make such a pronouncement. But it is possible.

In November 1859, after writing his articles for the *Eagle*, the works of Dionysius of Halicarnassus were still fresh in his mind. On Friday, 11 November 1859, the Cambridge auctioneer Charles Wisbey sold off duplicates from Trinity College Library in a catalogue entitled *Valuable Collection of Books, Being Duplicate Volumes from Trinity College Library, Cambridge*. Within it, there are four entries describing works by Dionysius, including *Opera omnia graece & latine*, published in Oxford in 1704.[21] Shoults obtained this particular edition, edited by John Hudson. It contains the Trinity College Library bookplate, an oval stamp with the date of 1859, and a shelf number: W.11.9. There is no indication of what he paid for it.

Again, these books hammer home two important, and constant, features. They represent the type of books that Shoults was interested in: solid, serious tomes. They also reflect his high level of language skills, his erudition (for a twenty-year-old), and his particular interest in a number of issues faced by the established Church of England.

---

[21] Wisbey (1859). The four works by Dionysius are listed briefly at lot numbers 137, 144, 154, and 163.

5   BOOK COLLECTING CONTEXTUALISED

A few months before she died, Elizabeth Shoults gave her son on his twentieth birthday a copy of Part II – *Acts of the Apostles,* one volume of the five-volume *The New Testament of our Lord and Saviour Jesus Christ: in the Original Greek,* with notes and introductions by Christopher Wordsworth. This work, the last birthday present he would receive from her, is inscribed in her hand: 'William Arderne Shoults the Gift of his Mother as a Birthday Present, March 29th 1859.' It was published in 1857 and was no doubt readily available in bookshops in Cambridge and London. Was this the only volume she bought for him? Did she acquire the companion volumes, now since disappeared? It is a publisher's trade book and not an expensive one. It was surely purchased locally, in Cambridge.

So, how common was the buying of such items in the early nineteenth century and into the Victorian period? Who were the prominent bookdealers and auctioneers? What did they offer to high-spot well-heeled book collectors and to those bookish students like Shoults? What were the dominant trends within the book collecting scene in England? And lastly, who were the prime book collectors in this burgeoning activity? There were book collectors—not well-heeled ones—that assembled similar book collections to Shoults's. How did he stand in contrast to these individuals? Here three collectors offer some useful comparison: Joseph Mendham (1769–1856), William Maskell (1814–90), and John Mitford (1781–1859).

From the early nineteenth century, there was a rise of booksellers, all vying for custom as each new generation of book collectors took on the search for items. They became prominent in the field, especially in London, which was the centre of book collecting. They included the firm of Payne and Foss (1813–50), who handled the Heber sales; Thomas Rodd (1796–1849), who included in his client-base the British Museum; Thomas Thorpe (1791–1851), who focused on historical, genealogical, and topographical materials, as well as on manuscripts and autographs; William Pickering (1796–1854), who became the British Museum agent after Rodd's death; Henry George Bohn (1796–1884), who produced the famous 'Guinea' catalogue of 1841, the largest single catalogue ever issued by a British bookseller; Thomas (d.1873) and William (1794–1869) Boone, who as publishers and bookdealers became the agent for the British Museum after Pickering retired; and Joseph Lilly (1804–70), who was involved in a large number of sales, most notably of the libraries of Warren Hastings (1853), William Conybeare (1858), Sir Henry and Sir John Savile (1860), Archbishop Tenison (1861), and Sir Edward Dering (1862). Lilly also had a large share in the formation of Henry Huth's library (said to be over £40,000-worth of business).[1]

As the years progressed into the 1850s and 1860s, the book trade grew. Later book dealers (in some cases publishers) established themselves and sold to a growing clientele. Some of the dealers included W.H. Smith (1848), Francis Edwards (1855), Maggs (1855), Bell and Daldy (1856), Sotheran & Willis (1856), Elliot Stock (1859), and F. S. Ellis (1860). By 1860, 812 booksellers were situated in London; 211 of these were also publishers. Indeed, the role of publisher and bookseller was blurred.

There were other factors to the growth: educational and juvenile trade increased; the popular press began with Routledge's Railway Library series (1849); lending and subscription libraries such as Mudie's (1852) developed; scientific publishing increased; and the important 1870 Forster Education Act was passed, introducing free compulsory secular education for all children. As a result, there was a print explosion.

The 1840s also saw changes among book-auctioneers. The Roxburghe auctioneer R.H. Evans of Pall Mall retired from business in 1846. He had handled many celebrated sales, including Hibbert's, Valpy's, the Duke of Sussex's, and part of Heber's extensive collection. Samuel Sotheby (1771–1842) retired and left the business in the hands of his son Samuel Leigh Sotheby (1805–61) and his new partner John Wilkinson (1803–94). In 1846, the partnership of Thomas Puttick and William Simpson was formed, taking over from James Fletcher and William Stewart.

It is a truism that there has to be a flow of objects to collect. Both during and after the Napoleonic Wars there was a large dispersal and destruction of libraries. There was thus an influx of books from abroad, specifically from Europe. Booksellers snapped these books and manuscripts up and organised book auction and sales to a growing number of book collectors.

One important book sale in the early nineteenth century was the Duke of Roxburghe's Library, sold by Evans in May 1812. It was on this occasion that a book— the Valdarfer Boccaccio—realised a four-figure sum, an unprecedented first: £2260. On 22 May 1813, Evans auctioned off the first portion of the library of Stanesby Alchorne, one-time Master of the Mint. Although small in comparison with the aristocratic libraries of Spencer and Grenville, there were some choice volumes in it for sale, including a copy of Fabyan's *Chronicle* (1533), Edmund Spenser's *Complaints* (1591), and nine Caxtons. Buyers at this auction included William Cavendish, the Sixth Duke of Devonshire (1790–1858), the Marquess of Blandford (1766–1840), Sir Francis Freeling (d.1836), Sir Mark Masterman Sykes (1771–1823), Richard Heber (1773–1833), the Earl of Powis (1754–1839), and Thomas Grenville (1755–1846). Changes during the 1830s and 1840s were dramatic. There were two major reasons.

---

[1] Munby (1956), IV, 4.

The first was the death of many principal book collectors; the second was—as noted—the huge glut of books and manuscripts on the market. In 1834, George John, second Earl Spencer, died. Seymour de Ricci called him 'one of the greatest book-collectors, not only in English history, but even in the history of the world'.[2] His library at Althorp, with a focus on English and Latin Bibles, incunables (many rare William Caxton imprints), and first editions (*editiones principes*) of all the great Italian authors, was called 'the most beautiful and richest private library in Europe'.[3] In 1834, the first sale of Richard Heber's extensive book collection began. Before he died in 1833, he amassed over 200,000 volumes that were found strewn throughout eight houses in England and Europe.[4] The sales—sixteen of them—resulted in the market being glutted. In 1839 Richard Grenville, first Duke of Buckingham and Chandos, died. His library was passed on to his son Richard Plantagenet, second Duke, but as a result of straitened circumstances the entire collection, comprising 6212 lots, was sold at auction by Sotheby and Wilkinson, beginning on 8 January 1849. Books in the first Duke's collection included the *Apocalypse* blockbook, a *Nuremberg Chronicle* (1492), various editions of Dante's *Divina Commedia*, the First, Second and Third Shakespeare Folios, and some 900-plus medieval manuscripts. In 1843, the Duke of Sussex, Prince Augustus Frederick, sixth son of George III, died. His library of more than 50,000 volumes included theological books, numerous early Hebrew manuscripts, and 1000 editions of the Bible. His collection was sold by Evans, beginning on 1 July 1844. In 1844, William 'Vathek' Beckford died. His library was rich in incunables and early books printed on vellum, Aldines, English, French and Spanish literature, and rare voyages and travels. It was passed to his son-in-law, the tenth Duke of Hamilton (1767–1852), and was eventually sold in 1882. The last and truest representative of this period was Thomas Frognall Dibdin, who died on 18 November 1847. He was not only a great collector, but also a commentator par excellence, producing his now classic *Bibliomania; or Book Madness* (1808), *The Bibliographical Decameron* (1817), *Bibliotheca Spenceriana* (1814–1815), *Aedes Althorpianae* (1822), and *The Library Companion* (1824). Zealous enthusiasm reigns in each work, as do inaccuracies and error.

Other book collectors included Sir Thomas Phillipps (1792–1872), who amassed a collection of over 100,000 manuscripts and 50,000 printed books, acquiring them from sales such as that of Page Turner (1824), Celotti (1825), Drury (1827), Frederick North, fifth Earl of Guilford (1830), and George Harbin (1831). There was also Robert

---

[2] De Ricci (1969), 73.
[3] Renouard, cited in Fletcher (1902), 311.
[4] Simmons, 184 (1997), 219–26.

Stayner Holford (1808–92), who, according to de Ricci, built a library as an exact replica of the Bibliotheca Grenvilliana, including incunabula, first editions of the classics, Aldines, Shakespeare Folios, and medieval manuscripts.[5] Phillipps's only rival was Bertram, fourth Earl of Ashburnham (1797–1878), who at 17 began his collecting by buying a copy of *Secretes* of Albertus Magnus and who continued to purchase in most of the major sales until the Perkins sale of 1872–3, when prices were high and when competition was keen, especially between the Earl of Crawford, Henry Huth (1815–78), and the American James Lenox (1800–80).[6] The sale of Lenox's collection occurred in 1897 and 1898 (4075 lots) and featured works by Petrarch and Dante, over 200 incunabula, 189 Bibles and New Testaments, 54 Books of Common Prayer, 46 Books of Hours, and 27 works by Chaucer. There was also Frances Mary Richardson Currer (1785–1861), one of the few nineteenth-century female bibliophiles, the Rev. Thomas Corser (1793–1876), Sir William Tite (1798–1873), the Earl of Gosford (1806–64), the Duke of Buccleuch (1806–84), W. E. Gladstone (1809–98), John Ruskin (1819–1900), and the American John Carter Brown (1797–1874).

From 1860 onwards, Shoults lived in the Camberwell and Hoxton areas of London. It is tempting to speculate whether he visited some of the local antiquarian book dealers in London mentioned above. These men offered a whole range of old and new books, along with advice, especially enticing for a neophyte book collector. It must be stressed that all of the above book collectors represent a league of collecting that was well beyond his level. Shoults was entering a career in Holy Orders and would work as a curate in some of the poor parishes of London. His first stipend was £80 *per annum* and it may have gone up to £100. Even though he gained some money from his father's estate in 1878 and had a few leisure pounds to spend, it was probably not much. In reality, he did not have the monetary resources of Blandford, who secured the Valdarfer. He did not have the inclination to demand fine bindings (like Currer), nor did he exhibit that obsessional bibliomanic drive of Phillipps or Dibdin. He was a much lesser player in the English book collecting scene, buying in a field that did not generally command great prices and buying books that were not necessarily in pristine condition. The library he amassed by slow acquisition was a very personal one, primarily for his own reading and scholarly use.

BOOK DEALER CATALOGUES

There are only two nineteenth-century book dealer catalogues in the Shoults Collection. The first is a copy of *The Museum*, a catalogue of bound together issues from January

---

[5] De Ricci (1969), 116.
[6] De Ricci (1969), 11.

and December 1855 (the September issue is missing). This catalogue was issued by Bernard Quaritch, that Napoleon of booksellers who bought aggressively from various libraries when they came onto the market.[7] The libraries included that of Thomas Jolley (1843 and 1845), the Rev. David Thomas Powell (1848), Neville Holt (1848), the Stowe library of the Duke of Buckingham (1849), John Dunn Gardner (1854), Dr Edward Hawtrey (1853 and 1862), Edward Vernon Utterson (1857), and Dawson Turner (1853 and 1859). The books and manuscripts described in each issue of *The Museum* no doubt constituted only a small portion of the great bookseller's stock.

Shoults's volume was once in the library of the Royal Institute of British Architects; ownership stamps appear on the first page. The only evidence of use in this volume is that there are six entries excised from the March, April and November issues.[8] As these are all listed under 'Fine Arts', 'Books of Prints', and 'Architecture and Engineering', it is more than likely that the cuts were done in-house at the RIBA Library, or perhaps by a previous unknown owner. It is very doubtful that they were done by Shoults, because the subject areas fall (in the main) outside his collecting interests. Apart from these cuts, each issue is remarkably clean, with no markings.

The second catalogue is one issued by Charles J. Stewart, who operated from 11 King William Street, West Strand, London. One area that Stewart concentrated on was theological books. Indeed, the volume Shoults owned is titled: *Catalogue of Works in Patristic and Mediaeval Literature* (1862).[9] It contains 1638 entries, plus glowing reports and extracts from Stewart's own *Catalogue of the Fathers of the Church and Ecclesiastical Writers to the Fifteenth Century*. Stewart was also a publisher, producing the revised catalogue of the Eshton Hall Library, amassed by Frances Mary Richardson Currer, and a facsimile of an early block-book, *Speculum humanae salvationis*.[10]

The catalogue Shoults owned is clean, except for a small, loosely tipped-in, unidentifiable paper fragment of inked text between pages xii-xiii, a deletion in ink of an unknown fifth-century writer listed between Caedmon (670) and Adamnanus (679) in a 'Chronological Table of Writers' (xvii), and a pencil mark at the entry on Severus, No. 1338 (102). This last item is described as a limited edition of 100 copies of *De mortibus boum carmen* (1838), edited by John Allen Giles, published by Bohn in London, and priced at 9s. No such copy of this bucolic poem on the death of cattle is in Shoults's library. Indeed, even Stewart got it wrong, attributing this work to

---

[7] De Ricci (1969), 158.
[8] Quaritch (1856): March 15: Lot 815, 23–4; April 15: Lot 717, 22; Lots 735–6, and 745, 23; November 15: Lots 2724–5, 79, Lot 2792, 82; Lots 2939, 2942–3, and 2946, 89. Shoults Eb 1856 Q.
[9] Stewart (1862). Shoults Eb 1862 S.
[10] Obituary for C. J. Stewart, *Athenaeum*, 29 September 1883, 402. Elkin Mathews called Stewart 'the last of the learned old booksellers', cited in Nelson (1989), 5.

Sulpicius Severus rather than Severus Sanctus Endelechius, a Christian writer of the fourth century. However, it is this 'other' Severus, a writer of a chronicle of sacred history and the miracle work of St. Martin of Tours, that was of interest to Shoults. He owned four works, all titled *Opera*: an edition published by Christopher Plantin in 1574, two Elzevir publications of 1656 and 1665, and an early-eighteenth-century Leipzig publication of 1709. Shoults hardly ever left a trail of where he got his books from, yet three of these books offer tantalising provenance clues.

The 1656 Elzevir contains two inscriptions on the front free endpaper: 'John Heynes' and 'Richard Price'. These two individuals remain unknown, although the latter may be Richard Price (1723–91), philosopher, mathematician, and non-conformist preacher. The Leipzig edition of 1709 is a little more promising. This contains the inscription of 'Christopher Benson' and the date 1835. This could well be the Cambridge-educated theologian Benson (1788–1868), who was first Hulsean lecturer and later, in 1825, canon of Worcester Cathedral. As an evangelical engaged in ecclesiastical controversies, especially in his opposition to the 'Tractarian' movement, Benson would certainly be versed in Severus. His library may have been dispersed after his death. If so, it was after that time that Shoults obtained it.

The last, the Plantin edition of Severus's works, contains the bookplate of the Rev. Charles James Blomfield (1786–1857), former Trinity College pensioner who became Bishop of London, a post that he held for twenty-eight years. As an ecclesiastical reformer, Blomfield was particularly interested in patristics, and over a long career published on the Jewish tradition and the understanding of scripture. While his papers are at Lambeth Palace Library, most of his books were sold at auction by S. Leigh Sotheby and John Wilkinson on 30 November 1857 (and over four following days), being listed in the *Catalogue of the Principal Portion of the Classical & Theological Library of the Right Honourable and Right Reverend C. J. Blomfield, D.D. late Lord Bishop of London*.

Shoults may have attended the auction in London or, more than likely, later purchased the book as it drifted into the marketplace, bought from a Cambridge or London dealer. He actually obtained six other books that contain Blomfield's bookplate: a Greek edition of Hesiod (1603), Leone Allacci's *Excerpta varia Graecorum sophistarum* (1641), a copy of the two-volume edition of Isaac Casaubon's *Museum philologicum et historicum* (1699–1700), a Latin edition of Robert Huntington's letters (1704) edited by Thomas Smith, a copy of Artemidorus Daldianus's *Oneirokritikon* (1805), and a copy of Homer's *Hymni et Batrachomyomachia* (1805).

Shoults does not offer anywhere a comment on or a regard for provenance, and thus the Blomfield ownership may have just been a pleasant surprise to him. It was obviously the content that appealed. The letters by Huntington may have resonated a little more with him. Huntington, an Oxford graduate, was devoted to the study of theology and Eastern languages. His travels to the Levant enabled him to acquire numerous books and manuscripts, mainly Arabic and Hebrew, but also Coptic, Syriac, Samaritan, Persian, and Turkish.[11] As will be revealed, Shoults also had a penchant for such materials, collecting Middle Eastern manuscripts and rare books and displaying a working knowledge of Arabic, Hebrew, and perhaps Syriac.[12] In addition, he obtained a copy of an eighth edition of Blomfield's *Prometheus of Aeschylus* (1846), which was once owned by the Rev. Daniel Nihill (1791–1867), Chaplain and Governor of Millbank Penitentiary, Lambeth, and Perpetual Curate of Forden, Montgomeryshire, 1826–44. Daniel Nihill's son was the Rev. Henry David Nihill (1834–1913), vicar at St Michael's Church, Shoreditch, who, in 1873, engaged Shoults as a curate. Passed from father to son, the book was either borrowed by Shoults (and not given back) or was a gift.

THREE CONTENDERS

Joseph Mendham

And what of book collectors who, like Shoults, gathered together theological materials? Three candidates offer something of a contrast to him. Joseph Mendham (1769–1856) who, although collecting a little earlier than Shoults, is the first.[13] Mendham was Oxford-educated (St. Edmund Hall) and became a priest in 1794. The county of Warwickshire was his home, and he died at Sutton Coldfield on 1 November 1856, aged 87. He involved himself in Catholic versus Protestant controversies and wrote numerous tracts and other publications, often under nom de plumes such as 'Catholicus', 'Emancipatus', or 'A Plain Man'. Some of his sermons included *Exposition of the Lord's Prayer* (1803), *Episcopal Oath of Allegiance to the Pope* (1822), *Account of Indexes, Prohibitory and Expurgatory, of the Church of Rome* (1826), *Some Account of Discussion on Infallibility at Cherry Street Chapel, Birmingham, 30 Sept. and 1 Oct. 1830* (1830), *Life and Pontificate of Saint Pius the Fifth* (1832), and *Index Librorum Prohibitorum a Sixto V Papa* (1835). He also contributed to *Notes and Queries,* the *Protestant Journal,* and the *Christian Observer.* In the process of writing the above works, he amassed a supporting library of controversial theology. This collection eventually went to his nephew, the Rev. John Mendham, on whose death his widow, Sophia, placed the books at the disposal of Charles Hastings Collette, a solicitor in Lincoln's Inn Fields, by

---

[11] See Hamilton (2008). Items not donated to the Bodleian or Merton College were later bought by Oxford University. Huntington's library of 1700 books were sold at auction in January 1702.

[12] See Daneshgar (2017).

[13] Ditchfield (2006).

whom a selection was presented to the Incorporated Law Society in Chancery Lane, London. A printed catalogue was issued in 1871: *Catalogue of the Mendham Collection Being a Selection of Books and Pamphlets from the Library of the Late Rev. Joseph Mendham*, with a supplement appearing in 1874.[14] The alphabetically arranged entries, occupying over 334 pages, were compiled by John Nicholson, the librarian at Lincoln's Inn. Mendham's collection number about 6000-plus items.

The Mendham collection has a definite focus, with books and pamphlets relating to the controversies between the churches of England and Rome, especially during the year 1688. Shoults's collection does not have this particular focus. The Mendham collection includes rare editions and versions of the Old and New Testaments, liturgies, expurgatory indexes, catalogues of prohibited books, proceedings of councils, writings of the fathers, early printed books of great rarity, and some manuscripts. While the Shoults Collection certainly contains books within these fields, it is far more catholic, covering other topics such as science, travel, philology, and the Middle East.

William Maskell

The second collector is William Maskell (1814–90), another Oxford-educated (University College) student, who entered Holy Orders in 1837, after graduating B.A. in 1836.[15] He proceeded to M.A. in 1838. In 1842 Maskell was given the rectory of Corscombe, Dorset, and while there devoted himself to learned researches into the history of Anglican ritualism and Catholic doctrine. His publications include *Ancient Liturgy of the Church of England according to the Uses of Sarum, Bangor, York, and Hereford, and the Modern Roman Liturgy* (1844), *A History of the Martin Marprelate Controversy in the Time of Queen Elizabeth* (1845), *Monumenta ritualia Ecclesiæ Anglicanae, or Occasional Offices of the Church of England according to the Ancient Use of Salisbury, the Prymer in English, and other Prayers and Forms, with Dissertations and Notes* (1846), and *Holy Baptism: a Dissertation* (1848). It was through these works that Maskell gained a solid reputation amongst English ecclesiastical antiquaries. Eventually resigning from the rectory at Corscombe in 1847, this 'learned theologian'—so termed by de Ricci—moved to the vicarage of St. Mary the Virgin, Marychurch, near Torquay, and became domestic chaplain to the Bishop of Exeter,

---

[14] Law Society (1871). Since 1985, the Mendham Collection has been on loan to Canterbury Cathedral Library and the University of Kent. In July 2012 the Law Society removed some of the most valuable books with the intention of selling them to raise funds. An auction sale took place at Sotheby's, London on 5 June 2013, when 106 out of the total of 142 lots were sold at a total price of £1,180,875. Some manuscripts concerning the Council of Trent were bequeathed to the Bodleian Library, Oxford. See Law Society (1994).

[15] See Rigg (2004).

Henry Phillpotts.[16] Controversies surrounding the Gorham case led Maskell to resign his living.[17] He eventually became a Roman Catholic. He never took orders and spent his later life in retirement in the west of England.

Over the years Maskell amassed a large library of patristic literature. He was also an enthusiastic collector of medieval service books, enamels and carvings in ivory. Indeed, he produced a catalogue of the last: *Ivories Ancient and Mediaeval in the South Kensington Museum* in 1875.[18] Obviously proud of what he collected, he printed two catalogues of his library. Privately printed, the first was *Selected Centuries of Books from the Library of a Priest in the Diocese of Salisbury* (1843); the second, of English liturgies, a *Catalogue of Books Used in and Relating to the Public Services of the Church of England during the Sixteenth and Seventeenth Centuries* (1845). The first, with a focus on early English theology, consisted of some 300 items arranged under the headings: 'First Century', 'Second Century', and 'Third Century'. Numerous printed Bibles, Missals, Books of Hours, and Books of Common Prayer feature alongside many anti-Papist publications. English imprints predominate. While his collection was no doubt useful to the research Maskell undertook, de Ricci claims that he was in the habit of building up collections of books (and art) to sell to public institutions such as the British Museum. After his death, the remaining portions of his library were disposed of at auction, with a final sale occurring on 26 February 1891.[19]

The Shoults Collection contains a few Bibles and missals, but again the strength of the collection is not in such works. Indeed, it lacks the sheer number of copies of these works in Maskell's collection, and there are no examples of Books of Hours such as those by Vérard. The anti-Pope/Papist field was one that Shoults did not venture into, nor industrial arts. A good number of the books in Shoults's collection are European imprints, from Swiss and Venetian incunables onwards. There are of course numerous nineteenth-century titles, ranging from travel and history through to philology and science. And, for all of his bookishness, there is no existing list or printed catalogue of his library. Perhaps if he had lived longer, he might have got around to producing one.

---

[16] De Ricci (1969), 143. William Maskell features in Hazlitt (1968), XII, 21.

[17] In 1847 the Rev. G.C. Gorham was presented to the vicarage of Brampford Speke. The Bishop of Exeter, H. Phillpotts, found him unsound on the doctrine of baptismal regeneration and refused to institute him. Gorham appealed to the Judicial Committee of the Privy Council, which, attributing to him a view which he did not hold, declared it to be not contrary to the doctrine of the Church of England. The decision caused controversy and many defections to the Roman Catholic Church. See entry on Gorham in *ODCC* (1998), 692.

[18] Other Maskell-related catalogues include a later published *A Description of the Ivories Ancient & Medieval in the South Kensington Museum* (1872) and *The Industrial Arts* (1876).

[19] De Ricci (1969), 143.

John Mitford

The last collector is John Mitford (1781–1859), who was an English clergyman and man of letters. Educated at Richmond and Tonbridge Grammar School (under Vicesimus Knox), and then Oriel College, he graduated B.A. on 17 December 1804. Ordained as a priest on 22 December 1808, he secured a curacy at Kelsale in Suffolk. He later moved to the vicarage of Benhall, near Saxmundham, and then later (August 1815) became domestic chaplain to his relative John Freeman-Mitford, 1st Baron Redesdale (1748–1830). Mitford was also appointed to the rectory of Weston St. Mary, and nominated to the rectory of Stratford St. Andrew, both in Suffolk. He retained these livings until his death.

At Benhall, Mitford began forming an extensive library, mainly of English poetry, which Bernard Barton claimed, in a letter of 1823 to Letitia Landon, was 'the most valuable library to which I ever had access'.[20] His library was also well stocked with Latin and Greek Classics and many books by French, German, and Italian authors. The English poet Thomas Gray was of particular interest to him: in 1814, Mitford edited the first accurate edition of Gray's *Poems*, with critical notes. He later, in 1853, edited the *Correspondence of Gray and Mason*. In 1834, he became editor of the new Aldine British Poets series, initiated by William Pickering, the then part-owner of the *Gentleman's Magazine*. His own literary output was prolific, including *Agnes, the Indian Captive*, a poem (1811), *Lines Suggested by a Fatal Shipwreck near Aldborough, 3 Nov. 1855* (1855), *Miscellaneous Poems* (1858), and edited works such as *Sacred Specimens Selected from the Early English Poets, with Prefatory Remarks* (1827) and the *Correspondence of Horace Walpole and Rev. W. Mason* (1851). His friendships included Samuel Rogers, Alexander Dyce, William Beattie, and Henry Luttrell.

Even though Mitford married Augusta Boodle on 21 October 1814, and had children, his collections were dispersed after his death by Sotheby and Wilkinson.[21] His Latin and Greek books were sold off on 17 December 1859 and 6 days following, realising £1029 19s. The library of English history, plays, and poetry was sold on 24 April 1860 and the eleven days following, producing £2999 2s, many of them going to the libraries of Alexander Dyce, John Forster, or the British Museum. Mitford's manuscripts sold on 9 July 1860, producing £817 3s.

The Shoults Collection contains very few books of English poetry and no play books. These were just not areas of collecting that attracted him. He did, however,

---

[20] See Courtney (2004); see also 'The Rev. John Mitford of Benhall, Suffolk (1860)' in Hazlitt (1968), XII, 21.

[21] An annotated copy of the *Catalogue of the Collection of Greek and Latin Classics Forming the First Portion of the Library of John Mitford* is in the British Library. See Leigh, Sotheby (1859).

own a number of Latin and Greek works that would certainly match Mitford's, although without doubt not as many, to judge from the number of sale days it took to disperse the Mitford books.

THE MITFORD CACHE

Shoults actually owned twenty-seven titles that were once in Mitford's library. Each contains Mitford's bookplate, bibliographical references written in his hand, and further provenance details. It is not known whether Shoults purchased this cache in one go or by gradual accumulation over some years. The content obviously appealed, and the fact that the books were from Mitford's library may have held some attraction. The books are significant on two levels: they reflect something of the make-up of Mitford's own collection and they offer an excellent glimpse of what sort of books Shoults was particularly interested in.

The Mitford books Shoults obtained are mainly older imprints: six sixteenth-century; fifteen seventeenth-century; four eighteenth-century; and two early nineteenth-century. They are scholarly tomes, and all but one in Latin.

The oldest now in the Shoults Collection is a copy of Guillaume Budé's *De asse et partibus eius*, published in Paris by Josse Badius in 1527. With the inscribed date of 1804, it was likely obtained by Mitford while at Oriel College, Oxford. Deemed a masterpiece on coins and measures, this work, with the iconic image of a printing press on the title page, was the one that gained Budé (1468–1540), friend of Erasmus and Thomas More, his high reputation. Budé also wrote *Commentarii linguae Graecae* (1529), a lexicographical work that encouraged Greek learning in France. Shoults also owned a copy of this work, a later edition of 1548, but it is not a Mitford book. The 'youngest' book in the Mitford cache is a copy of the German philologist Karl August Ludovic Feder's *Observationum criticarum in auctores veteres Graecos atque Latinos specimen quadruplex*, published in London in 1818. This work is bound in with philologist John Hill's 60-page *De C. Corn. Taciti stilo observationes criticae* (1817).

Between these two titles fall the others, which are treated here in a chronological order. Shoults obtained a copy of Eustathius's commentaries on Homer's *Iliad* and *Odyssey*. This large-folio Greek-language edition not only contains Homer's works, but also deals with issues in the text of grammar, mythology, history, and geography. It was published in Basel by Froben in 1558. On the front endpaper is Mitford's name and the date of 1815, as well as a pencil notation by a later owner, one 'J. W. B.' The note reads: 'Bt at Westall's Oxf. St. Sat Feb 16' and the date '1861'. And someone, perhaps Westall, got it wrong: there is an additional note that reads: 'autograph of Mitford, author of History of Greece overleaf', thus confusing the Rev. John Mitford with his cousin, William Mitford (1744–1827), best known for that work.

The English humanist Thomas Linacre (1460–1524) was a physician and teacher of Erasmus. Shoults obtained a copy of his *De emendata structura Latini sermonis libri VI*, a book about Latin sermon construction that was published in Leipzig in 1569. It contains Mitford's name and the date 'September 1850'. At the back there is a small list in ink with the names 'Laur. Valla' and 'Prodigiosa' with their corresponding page numbers.[22] Reference to the text reveals very discrete pencil ticks beside each that may have been added by Shoults.

The next is a simple calf-bound copy of Lucas Fruterius's *Librorvm qui recuperari potuerunt reliqviae* published by Christopher Plantin in Antwerp in 1584. An early Leiden-based owner added his name on the title page—'Job Henr. Cociejus, Lugd. Bat., 1666'—most likely Johann Heinrich Cocceius, son of the Dutch theologian, Johannes Cocceius (1603–69). Mitford has dated the book 1827 and added bibliographical notes, including 'See account of L. Fruterius Irving's Life of Buchanan, p. 208'.

Fabius Planciades Fulgentius's *Expositio Virgilianae continentiae secundum philosophos moralis* follows. Published in Heidelberg in 1589, the book offers a hint of when Shoults bought it—and perhaps some of the other Mitford books. With the inscriptions of previous owners 'Hieronymus Cornelius Gruteros' and 'J. Mitford, 1823' present, there is also the additional name of 'J. A. Jeremie, 1862'. The Rev. James Amiraux Jeremie, D.D. (1802–72), Regius Professor of Divinity in University of Cambridge, amassed a large library of classical authors. His inaction and dithering on what to do with his collection meant that it was dispersed after his death.[23] In 1872, Shoults was between curacies, and perhaps he had a little more leisure-time to read a work like this. Although not Mitford books, Shoults also owned Fulgentius's chief work, *Mythographi Latini* (1681), *Liber de expositione Virgilianae* (1589), and an early compendium featuring Virgil's *Aeneid* and *Georgics*, published in Geneva in 1636.

Shoults also acquired a first edition of an anthology of epigrams, a small octavo titled *Epigrammata et poematia vetera*. It was edited by Pierre Pithou and published in Lyon in 1596. It contains Serenus Sammonicus's didactic medical poem *Liber medicinalis*, which details a number of popular remedies and magic formulae, including the famous abracadabra spell. Again, this book has Mitford's signature in his neat hand, his usual bibliographical notes, and the date 1806. Shoults owned another version of Serenus Sammonicus's *De medicina*, contained in another compilation, *Poetae Latini minores*, published in Leiden in 1731.

---

[22] The 'Valla' reference may be Lorenzo Valla (c.1407–57), the Italian priest who proved that the Donation of Constantine was a forgery.

[23] See Matthew (2004).

Another Mitford book that Shoults obtained was an edition of Vincenzio Contarini's *Variarum lectionum liber*, published in Venice in 1606. The content of this tidy, vellum-bound book is on the development and improvement of Greek and Latin classics. Shoults also picked up a copy of Antonio Cerri's *Satyrarvm scholiasticarvm centuriae duae*, published in Rimini in 1607. This book is dated 1804 and was more than likely purchased by Mitford while at Oxford.

The French Protestant scholar Joseph Justus Scaliger (1540–1609) stands tall in classical historical scholarship, and his contextual approach, which included not only Greek and Roman history, but also Persian, Babylonian, Jewish, and ancient Egyptian, was ground-breaking.[24] His publications include editions of the *Catalecta* (1575), of *Festus* (1575), *Catullus, Tibullus and Propertius* (1577), *Manilius* (1579), and *De emendatione temporum* (1583), all of which were produced by the application of rigorous textual criticism and emendation. Shoults acquired a copy of Scaliger's *Opuscula*, a posthumously-edited work published in Frankfurt in 1612. Mitford dated this copy 1804. It contains a fragmentary English manuscript tipped in at the back, which may have caught Shoults's eye.

Shoults had a penchant for works of grammar and language. He acquired a first edition of Claude Dausque's two-volume *Antiqui novique Latii orthographica*, published in Tournai, Belgium, in 1632. On purchase, he may have read the note by Mitford on the forged date of the book ('See La Libreria de' Volpi, p. 57') and on the fact that the bibliographer Daniel Georg Morhof (1639–91) gave the work high praise ('Morhof Polyh. Liter. Tom I, p. 812; Index: I, 4, 9, I').[25] Shoults also owned another work by the Jesuit Dausque (1566–1644), a compilation titled *Orationes XLIV* by St. Basil. This edition was published in Heidelberg in 1604, but it is not a Mitford book.

Another language work Shoults obtained was a copy of *Observationes singulares in linguam Latinam* by the German philologist and lawyer Hubert van Giffen (1534–1604). Shoults's copy is a vellum-bound first edition published in Frankfurt in 1624. Mitford has again inscribed his name and date ('J. Mitford, 1816') and a few bibliographical references. A '7' is present, which may represent seven shillings or pence, the price Shoults paid for this rather foxed copy.

At some point, Shoults obtained a vellum-bound duodecimo edition of Piero Valeriano's *De literatorvm infelicitate libri duo*, published in Amsterdam in 1647.

---

[24] Grafton (2001), particularly chapter 15, 'Jacob Bernays, Joseph Scaliger, and Others', 279–98 (286).
[25] According to Taylor (1987), 265, the Volpi catalogue: *La Libreria de' Volpi, e la stamperia Cominiana* (1756) was more on the history of the press than of the Volpi family library. For reference to Morhof's encyclopedic *Polyhistor* (Lübeck, 1688–1707) and his earlier *Unterricht von der Deutschen Sprache und Poesie* (1682), the first attempt in Germany at a systematic survey of European literature, see 'Morhof', in *EB*, XVIII, 836; see also Taylor (1987), 117–18, 179–80.

This was Valeriano's most famous work, and Mitford dated his copy 1806, with a bibliographical note: 'See an account of J. Pierius Valerianus in Burman's Pref: to Virgil. See a list of the editions of this work in Brydges Res Literature No. 1 212 ii. 54.'[26] This reference was a retrospective one, because Samuel Egerton Brydges's very limited *Res literariæ* appeared first in Naples in 1820 and then in later editions: Rome in 1821 and Geneva in 1822. Shoults also owned another work by Valeriano (1477–1558), his *Hieroglyphica*, a study on hieroglyphics and their use in allegory. His copy, not a Mitford book, is a later edition, published in Lyon in 1621.

The next work is a copy of *De rebus gestis imperat. Constantinop. Ioannis & Manuelis, Comnenorum, historiar. libri IV* (1652) by the twelfth-century Greek historian Joannes Kinnamos or John Cinnamus. This, his major work, is a history that covered the reigns of John II Comnenus (1087–1143) and Emperor Manuel I (1143–80) and the latter's unsuccessful campaign against the Turks. Inscribed and dated 1806 by Mitford, this particular copy was a presentation copy to the German historian Antonius Aemilius (1589–1660) from Cornelius Tollius (c.1628–54), the Dutch scholar. It also has manuscript notations in Greek at the back, which may have been made by Shoults.

Shoults's copy of Latino Latini's *Epistolae*, published in Rome in 1659, has a firm provenance. This work by the Italian humanist was in Mitford's hands in February 1835, as evidenced by the inscription: 'With E. H. Barker's best wishes to the Rev. John Mitford, Febr. 21, 1835.' Edmund Henry Barker (1788–1839) was an English classical scholar educated at Trinity College, Cambridge, earning in 1809 the Browne medal for Greek and Latin epigrams. Barker worked closely with the Rev. Samuel Parr (1747–1825), schoolmaster, vicar of Hatton, Warwickshire, and literary bon vivant. Parr, whom we will meet again in chapter 16, had an excellent library at Hatton, and this book was once part of it.[27] Thus the Latini has a pedigree: Parr-Barker-Mitford-Shoults. Shoults owned another work by Latini (1513–93), his Tertullian, published in Paris in 1616.

The next Mitford book is a copy of Josephus Laurentius's *Polymathia*, published by Anisson in Lyon in 1666. This folio edition contains Mitford's signature and a bibliographical note referencing Morhof's *Polyhistor*, which Shoults also owned, in a dumpy one-volume edition published in 1714 and a two-volume edition published in 1747.

---

[26] The Dutch scholar Pieter Burman the Elder (1668–1741) started the Virgil edition, but it was his nephew, philologist Pieter Burman the Younger (1713–78), who actually finished the work.

[27] Latini's *Epistolae* (1659) is listed on page 310. See *Bibliotheca Parriana* (1827).

Matthias Bernegger (1582–1640) was a friend of Johannes Kepler, Elia Diodati, and Galileo Galilei. Shoults did not own any of Bernegger's translations of Galileo's works, but he did own a copy of his *Observationes miscellae*, published in Strasbourg in 1669. This volume contains some bibliographical notes by Mitford and mention again of Morhof: 'See Job: Magisi Thonal Lib. 1, 121; Morhof Poly ii c.b. p.381.' Shoults's *Observationes* has a pencil price of '2s 6d', a sum that he could have paid for it.

Another dumpy vellum-bound book owned by Mitford is a copy of *Manuductio ad excerpendum* by Johann Peter Tietz, a professor of pronunciation and poetry. Mitford's copy of this work on note-taking and on Latin sermons and prosody, published in Gdańsk in 1676, is dated 1836.

The next Mitford book is a copy of *De libris varioque eorum usu et abusu libri duo* by the Utrecht-based William Salden (1627–94). This vellum-bound octavo edition was published by Henry and Theodore Bloom in Amsterdam in 1688 and was judged by some 'a curious book with which every collector would wish to enrich his library'.[28] Mitford has inscribed his name, 'Oriel Coll, Oxon', and the date 'July 1819' on the frontispiece. He has added a bibliographical note: 'See an account and analysis of this work in Anecdotes of Eminent Persons, Vol. II, p. 201.'[29] The work also shows use by Shoults. On the rear free endpaper there is a list of thirteen references in his hand that refer to passages within the text—for example: 'p. 16 Cornelius Vossius; p. 52 Thomas Gataker [actually p. 113]; p. 75 de Origene; p. 169 Alphons. Ciccarles'. The relevant text passages have small pencil ticks beside them.

A work by the French Protestant scholar Claude Saumaise (1588–1653), friend of Isaac Casaubon (1559–1614) and Joseph Scaliger, follows. Shoults owned a copy of Saumaise's *magnum opus*, a commentary on Solinus's *Polyhistor*, which had the author learning Arabic for the botanical component of the book. Shoults's copy is a large-folio two-volume edition published in 1689, which Mitford acquired in 1803. It passed through Sotheby's auction house (sale codes are present) to an early owner, 'W. Heath', who was no doubt the bookseller William Heath, 497 Oxford Street.[30] Noting condition and completeness, Heath inscribed on a front preliminary leaf: 'preserve this leaf, WH'. Shoults owned four other works by Saumaise: two Elzevir editions of *De annis climactericis et antiqua astrologia diatribae* (1648) and *Specimen confutationis animadversionum Desiderii Heraldi* (1648); an edition of Florus, published in London in 1683; and another edition of *Polyhistor*, published in Paris in 1629.

---

[28] *European Magazine* (1812), 110.

[29] The author of *Anecdotes of Eminent Persons* was Charles Henry Wilson (c.1756–1808). The work was first published in 1804 under the title, *The Polyanthea: Or A Collection of Interesting Fragments*.

[30] See Roberts (1895).

One book heavily marked up by Mitford is a copy of *Julius Celsus de vita et rebus gestis C. Julii Caesaris*, published in London in 1697. The Celsus attribution is erroneous. The work was extracted from Petrarch's *De viris illustribus*.

One Greek text that Shoults acquired was *Kata alphabeton Onomatón Attikón Eklogai*, published in Franeker, Netherlands, in 1698. This work, by the Byzantine grammarian Thomas Magister (1282–1328), is an alphabetically-arranged lexicon of Attic words and phrases based on the works of Ancients such as Ammonius, Herodian, and Moeris. It was edited by the classical scholar Nicolaus Brancard (1625–1703), Professor of Greek and Antiquities at Franeker. Mitford obtained it in 1810, following the dispersal of books previously owned by 'William Windham, October 1792'—surely the British Whig statesman William Windham (1750–1810).

Thomas Reinesius (1587–1667) was a busy German physician who was also interested in philology.[31] He corresponded with many like-minded scholars such as Johann Andreas Bose (1626–74), the German historian and philologist. Shoults obtained a badly-foxed copy of Reinesius's *Epistolae mutuae* (1700), which featured work by Bose. Mitford acquired it in 1806.

The next publication is a copy of *Presbyteri Ecclesiae Anglicanae, & Bibl. Lambethanae curatoris opera*, a compilation of scriptural histories and curatorial matters by Paul Colomiès (1638–92), a French librarian who visited England and spent time at Lambeth Palace Library. Published in Hamburg in 1709, it was edited by the German classical scholar Johann Albert Fabricius (1668–1736). Mitford acquired this calf-bound copy in 1804. It contains a short biographical reference inscribed in his minuscule hand.

Shoults acquired a two-volume folio edition of the ancient sceptic Sextus Empiricus's *Opera* in Greek and Latin, published in Leipzig in 1718. Sextus's works had a great influence on philosophers such as Montaigne, David Hume, and Hegel, and this particular copy was once in the library of Richard Porson (1759–1808), the English classical scholar, who, in 1792, became the Regius Professor of Greek at Cambridge. At Porson's death, his library was divided into two: the first portion was purchased by Trinity College, Cambridge, for 1000 guineas; the second was sold off at auction by Leigh and S. Sotheby on Friday 16 June 1809, and the following six days. Mitford attended the sale, securing 11 items at a cost of £15 4s 6d.[32] The Sextus—dated by Mitford 1809—was part of the booty.

The French Huguenot Michel or Michael Maittaire (1667–1747) was a classical scholar and bibliographer who lived much of his life in England, eventually becoming

---

[31] Bayle (1737), IV, 859; see also Thomas (1887), IV, 1879–80; and Hoche (1889).
[32] Naiditch (2011), xlvi, 136.

tutor to the young Philip Dormer Stanhope, fourth Earl of Chesterfield (1694–1773). Maittaire focused not only on facets of the Greek language, but also on the history of printing. His works included *Graecae lingvae dialecti* (1706), *The English Grammar* (1712), a New Testament (Greek) (1714), and the two-volume *Historia typographorum aliquot Parisiensium* (1717). Shoults owned Mitford's copy of Maittaire's *Graecae lingvae dialecti*, a much-improved early nineteenth-century edition (1807) edited by Friedrich Wilhelm Sturtz. Shoults also owned Maittaire's *Terence* (1713), and his *Annales typographici*, published by Vaillant in the Hague in 1719. These last two are not Mitford books.

The one English-language Mitford book that Shoults acquired was a decidedly unattractive cloth-bound volume of eleven tracts, which, according to a written note, may have cost Shoults 1s 6d. Among the tracts are a copy of a second edition of Richard Tickell's *Anticipation* (1778), *The Speech (at length) of the Hon. C.J. Fox, against the Address to His Majesty, Approving of the Refusal to Enter into a Negotiation for Peace with the French Republic* (1800), R.B. Sheridan's 'second edition faithfully reported' of *The Genuine Speech against Warren Hastings* [1787], and *Dr. Friend's Epistle to Dr. Mead* (1719). On the surface, most of them fall outside Shoults's collecting interests. Yet perhaps it was the copy (a second edition) of William Vincent's *Considerations on Parochial Music* (1790) that caught his eye. Vincent (1739–1815) was Dean of Westminster, who, as a classical scholar, had a strong interest in ancient geography. This small tract was written when Vincent was rector of All-Hallows-the-Great, in the City of London. Shoults's interest in hymns would certainly have justified purchase. The tract is heavily marked up, but the annotations are severely cropped, which suggests that the inked notes were added before it was bound up in this volume. Further details on this volume of Tracts will be covered in chapter 17.

While the above books do not reveal any discernible pattern within the Shoults Collection, they do reveal the sort of books that he wanted—and used. They are solid, serious books that not every nineteenth-century reader would tackle. With his interest in hymnology, philology, ecclesiastical history, and antiquarianism, they suited him exactly.

6 FIRST STEP: ASSISTANT CURATE, ST. PETER'S, WALWORTH, 1863–65

William Arderne Shoults's career was in the Anglican Church, centred on four parishes in Southwark and Shoreditch. In the nineteenth century these were tough areas, with mass and chronic pauperism, and with begging and crime prevalent. Misfortune and suffering were rife. Lord Shaftesbury, speaking in 1884, but of the 1860s, about a district in Bermondsey, stated: 'It was a large swamp where a number of people lived, as they do in Holland, in houses built upon piles [. . .] So bad was the supply of water there that I have positively seen the women drop their buckets into the water over which they were living, and in which was deposited all the filth of the place, that being the only water they had for every purpose of washing and drinking.'[1] It was also a period when a number of societies and agencies were established to try and ameliorate the suffering —for example, the Society for the Relief of Distress (1860) and the Parochial Mission Women Fund (1860).

Canon Samuel A. Barnett, a near contemporary of Shoults working at St. Jude's in Whitechapel about 1869, was a social reformer who saw parish work as much a civic as a spiritual responsibility. He was also something of a pragmatist, aiming to decrease sin, but not necessarily suffering. Barnett's congregation sometimes numbered 30 in the morning and 50 to 100 at evenings.[2] His duties were comparatively light: one sermon a fortnight, with ample time to prepare. He taught school, which included scripture lessons, history, and preparation for Confirmation.

In the Census of 1861, Shoults is recorded as visiting 2 Grove Place, St Giles, Camberwell, where his father (48), his sister Maria Susannah (19), and servant Martha Baker were living.[3] He is registered as 'B.A. Cantab. Visiting Tutor', a designation that suggests that he may have schooled a few students on a private basis. It was certainly a way in which he could supplement any other income. Two years later, on 15 April 1863, he fulfilled College requirements and qualified for the award of M.A, along with a number of his College contemporaries, including Durell, Hoare, Merriman, Previte, Proctor, Richardson, C. J. E. Smith, and Taylor.[4] They had all matriculated in 1856, the same year as Shoults.

---

[1] Helen Bosanquet, *Social Work in London, 1869 to 1912: A History of the Charity Organisation Society* cited in Barnett (1921), 18.
[2] See Barnett (1921).
[3] 1861: England and Wales census, Camberwell, under William Arderne Shoults.
[4] 'University Intelligence', *The Times*, 17 April 1863, 10; see also *Morning Post*, 17 April 1863, 6.

TOWARDS HOLY ORDERS

Shoults obviously still desired to proceed to Holy Orders. However, he had much to do before he could climb onto the first rung, which was that of deacon. There were numerous protocols to carry out. First, he had to compose a letter to the bishop of the diocese in which the curacy was situated and notify his candidacy for the position. He had also to be in contact with the incumbent rector or vicar, who was obliged to acknowledge the application, to state categorically an annual stipend, and to confirm that the candidate – in this case Shoults – lived on the premises of the Parish house, or nearby. What was also to be confirmed was that the candidate was not committed to any other ecclesiastical preferment. On receiving all these documents, and no doubt scrutinising credentials, the bishop set in train a number of events. First and foremost, 'necessary papers' were passed to the secretary of the diocese. These included the nomination to a curacy, a certificate of baptism, a certificate from the Divinity Professor verifying attendance at lectures, a certificate attesting to having passed the Voluntary Theological Examination, testimonials from St. John's College, three testimonials from beneficed clergymen (especially if the candidate had long left College), and finally the 'Si Quis' ('if anyone'), which not only indicated the candidate's intention to enter Holy Orders, but provided an opportunity for anyone to provide evidence of the candidate's suitability.[5] At this point, an examination date was set by an Examining Chaplain, who was required to certify that the candidate 'be well acquainted with':

1. The Greek Testament to the end of the Acts of the Apostles
2. Bishop Beveridge on the XXXIX Articles
3. The History of the Church of England, especially of the Reformation (e. g. Short's Sketch of the History of the Church of England)
4. The History of the Prayer Book, e. g. *The Narrative* portion of Dr Cardwell's History of the Conferences, &c respecting the Revision of the Book of Common Prayer
5. The Old and New Testament History

In addition, some acquaintance was required with Latin composition and with the composition of a sermon in English.[6] The examinations in some instances were often perfunctory. Tindal Hart cites two cases that could only be classified as superficial: the

---

[5] Pinnock (1855), 'Ordination', 23–36. If a certificate of baptism was not possible, a signed affidavit from a JP was suitable. Often a non-resident position would receive free use of the glebe house, garden, and offices (if relevant), surplice fees paid, and a freedom from rates and taxes. (87).

[6] Pinnock (1855), 25.

chaplain and son-in-law of Bishop North (1741–1820) once examined two candidates for Holy Orders at a cricket match while waiting to go in to bat, while the chaplain of Bishop Douglas did the same while shaving.[7] Above all, candidates had to be over 23.

The examination lasted three or four days, and at the conclusion — a happy one in this instance — the time and place for ordination would be set. On Sunday 20 December 1863, Shoults was ordained, along with 21 others, as deacon at a service at Her Majesty's Chapel Royal, Whitehall.[8] In the presence of the others, he had to subscribe to the Thirty-nine Articles and the Liturgy and to take the Oaths of Allegiance and Supremacy. Three of the Articles included:

1. That the *Queen's Majesty*, under God, is the only Supreme Governor of this realm, and of all other her Highness's Dominions and Countries, as well in all Spiritual or Ecclesiastical things or causes, as Temporal: and that no foreign prince, person, prelate, state, or potentate, hath, or ought to have, any jurisdiction, power, superiority, pre-eminence, or authority, Ecclesiastical or Spiritual, within her Majesty's said Realms, Dominions, and Countries.

2. That the *Book of Common Prayer*, and of Ordering of Bishops, Priests, and Deacons, containeth in it nothing contrary to the Word of God, and that it may lawfully so be used; and that he himself will use the form in the said Book prescribed in Public Prayer, and Administration of the Sacraments, and none other.

3. That he alloweth the Book of *Articles of Religion* agreed upon by the Archbishops and Bishops of both provinces, and the whole Clergy in the Convocation holden at London in the year of our Lord God, 1562; and that he acknowledgeth all and every the Articles therein contained, being in number IX and XXX, besides the Ratification, to be agreeable to the Word of God.[9]

Like the other candidates, Shoults had to kiss the book after the Oaths had been taken, and he received a parchment copy of 'Letters of Orders' and Licence after paying a fee of 60 shillings. On this day, Archibald Campbell Tait (1811–82), Bishop of London, was in attendance to ordain him, the prayers were organised by the Rev. J.H. Howlett, the choral service by a Mr Massey, and the sermon by the Rev. William Gilson Humphry. The sermon was entitled *Our Sufficiency is of God*, based on 2 Corinthians III. 5. The sermon was printed, and Shoults saved a copy, having it bound up in a volume of other

---

[7] Hart (1970), 169.
[8] 'Ordinations', *The Times*, 21 December 1863, 5.
[9] Pinnock (1855), 40–1.

Church tracts. It began: 'We are now about to celebrate one of the most solemn and certainly one of the most affecting ordinances of our Church, the setting apart and dedication of a number of young men for the work of the ministry. From henceforth these young men will bear a new character in the sight of God and man.' It ended: 'We believe that if you are faithful to Him, He will never leave you nor forsake you; for He sends you forth with this gracious promise, "Lo, I am with you always, even unto the end of the world."'[10]

Shoults and his fellow ordinands were presented by the Rev. Joseph Barber Lightfoot (1828–89), Fellow of Trinity College, Cambridge, and Hulsean Professor of Divinity. Two other contemporaries from St. John's College were present: William Greenaway Bullock and Edmund George Peckover.[11] On this occasion, and as part of the procedure, Shoults was licensed to his first curacy: St. Peter's Church, at nearby Walworth, in the Woolwich Episcopal Area of the Anglican Diocese of Southwark.[12] Bullock was assigned to St. Philip's, Earl's Court, Kensington, Peckover to Christ Church, Lee, Kent.

DIOCESAN ORDINATION RECORDS

The Ordination Records for Shoults's candidacy towards his diaconate exist, and more or less follow the details laid down by W. H. Pinnock in *The Laws and Usages of the Church and Clergy* (1855), a work that Shoults owned.[13] In the London Metropolitan Archive there is a thin pocket tied with aging pink ribbon that contains the ordination papers for Shoults and a document that not only verifies his date of birth (29 March 1839) but also of his baptism, 24 April 1839. The latter is signed by the Rev. A.H. Kenney, rector of St. Olave's. A blue-paper certificate acknowledges the fact that he had passed a theological examination, which he sat in 1863, and signed by H. R. Seward, 2 May 1863.[14] There is a testimonial from St. John's College verifying his moral conduct. In its rather formulaic wording, it reads in full:

> Testimonial: Whereas our well-beloved in Christ William Arderne Shoults, Master of Arts, hath declared unto us his intention of offering himself in

---

[10] Humphrey (1864). Shoults Eb 1839 T.

[11] 'Ecclesiastical Intelligence', *Morning Post*, 21 December 1863, 3.

[12] 'London Ordination', *Daily News*, 19 December 1864, 2; *Crockford's* (1865), 571.

[13] London Diocese Ordination Papers, St Peter's Walworth, 1863–1865, Deacon and Priest Folder, 9651–10390 no.12: DL/A/B/004/MS10326/269 – 2751863. December 1863–November 1864. London Metropolitan Archives, London (LMA).

[14] H.R. Seward remains unidentified. He does not appear in *Crockford's Clerical Directory*, nor in the alumni lists for Cambridge and Oxford. He was obviously sufficiently well-respected to oversee examinations.

candidate for the sacred office of a Deacon, and for that end, hath requested of us Letters Testimonial of his good life & conversation, we the Master and Senior Fellows resident of the College of Saint John the Evangelist in the University of Cambridge, according to the ancient and approved custom of this University do hereby testify that the said William Arderne Shoults conducted himself soberly and regularly during the time of his residence amongst us, which began in October one thousand eight hundred and fifty six and ended in June one thousand eight hundred and fifty nine. And that in moral conduct, we think him a proper person to be admitted into Holy Orders. Nor do we know that he hath believed or maintained any opinion contrary to the doctrines and disciplines of the Church of England. In witness whereof we have here unto set our hands and seal, this seventeenth day of June in the year of our Lord one thousand eight hundred and sixty three.

This document is signed in order by W. H. Bateson, Master; F. France B.D. President; the Rev. George F. Reyner B.D.; Churchill Babington; A. Calvert; Joseph B. Mayor; John Robert Lunn; J.E.B. Mayor; and T. G. Bonney.

There is also a testimonial addressed to Tait from three clergy vouching for Shoults's character, they having known him for at least three years. It reads:

To the Right Honourable and Right Reverend Archibald Campbell Tait, Lord Bishop of London. Whereas our well-beloved in Christ, William Arderne Shoults of St. John's College, Cambridge, M.A., hath declared to us his intention of offering himself a candidate for the sacred office of Deacon, and for that end hath required of us letters testimonial of his good life and conversation. We therefore, whose names are hereunto subscribed, do certify that the said William Arderne Shoults hath been personally known to us for the space of three years last past; that we have had opportunities of observing his conduct; that during the whole of that time we verily believe him to have lived, in all respects, piously, soberly, and honestly; nor have we at any time heard anything to the contrary thereof; nor hath he at any time, so far as we know, or have heard, maintained, said, or written anything contrary to the doctrine or discipline of the United Church of England and Ireland: and, moreover, we do believe him in our consciences to be, as to his moral conduct, a fit person to be admitted into the sacred Ministry.

This document is dated 7 August 1863 and signed by: William Dixon, Vicar of Shepreth, Cambridgeshire; the Rev. Henry Algernon Baumgartner (1821–1909), incumbent of Emmanuel, Camberwell, and later that year moving to the vicarage of St. Paul's, Worcester; and Samuel Smith (1803–97), incumbent of St. George's, Camberwell.

Dixon, whom we have already met in chapter 2, was 44; Baumgartner was 42; and Smith, the oldest signatory, was 60.[15]

An additional note clarifies the credentials of these men: 'William Dixon, a subscriber to this testimonial, is a benefited clergyman in the diocese of Ely, and is worthy of credit. T [Thomas Turton]. Ely. 16 Oct. 1863' and 'The Rev. Samuel Smith is beneficent in my diocese. The Rev. H. Baumgartner was incumbent of Emmanuel, Camberwell, until the latter end of the month of August, when he resigned. Both are worthy of credit.' This addendum is dated 20 October 1863.

Another testimonial is from the Rev. Thomas Joseph Gaster, of St. Giles, Camberwell, who was prepared to announce publicly Shoults's candidacy. It reads:

> Notice is given that William Arderne Shoults, Master of Arts, of St. John's College, Cambridge, now resident in this parish, intends to offer himself as a candidate for the holy office of Deacon, at the ensuing ordination of the Lord Bishop of London; and if any person knows any cause or just impediment, why the said William Arderne Shoults ought not to be admitted into Holy Orders, he is now to declare the same, or to signify the same forthwith to the Lord Bishop of London. We certify, that, on Sunday, the fifteenth day of November instant, the foregoing notice will be publicly and audibly read by the undersigned Thomas Joseph Gaster, in the church of St. Giles, Camberwell, in the time of Divine Service, and that no impediment was alleged. T. J. Gaster, curate of St. Giles, Camberwell.

It was witnessed on 15 November 1863 by two churchwardens, one of whom was James Pew, the Camberwell representative on the Metropolitan Board of Works.

Importantly, there is a notice by the Rev. Francis Freeman Statham, who was prepared to employ Shoults at St. Peter's. It gives Shoults's stipend, his position, and the fact that he was to be a non-resident assistant curate. It reads:

> To the Right Honourable and Right Reverend Archibald Campbell Tait, Lord Bishop of London. I, Francis Freeman Statham, B.A., Incumbent of St. Peter's, Walworth, in the county of Surrey, and your Lordship's diocese of London, do hereby nominate William Arderne Shoults, Master of Arts, to perform the office of assistant curate in my church of St. Peter's, Walworth, aforesaid, in the place of the Rev. Samuel B. Webb, B.A., late licensed curate; and do promise to allow him the yearly stipend of eighty pounds, to be paid by equal quarterly payments: and I do hereby state to your Lordship that the said William Arderne Shoults intends to reside in the said parish, distant from my

---

[15] Baumgartner, *AC* (1940), I, 191; Smith, *AC* (1953), V, 568.

church under one mile, and that the said William Arderne Shoults does not serve any other parish or incumbent or benefice, and does not officiate in any other church or chapel.

This is dated 20 November 1863. A codicil of sorts is attached, whereby each—Shoults and Statham—signed what was a binding agreement regarding money given and received. It reads:

> We the undersigned Francis Freeman Statham and William Arderne Shoults, do declare to the said Archibald Campbell Tait, Lord Bishop of London, as follows, namely, I, the said Francis Freeman Statham, do declare that I bona fide intend to pay, and I, the said, William Arderne Shoults, do declare that I bona fide intend to receive, the whole actual stipend mentioned in the foregoing nomination and statement, without any deductions or reservation whatsoever.

This paper is signed by both men, 20 November 1863.

Who were these men that Shoults felt comfortable in asking for testimonials? Obviously they were men he knew and respected. Of the Cambridge contingent, France is understandable, not only because he was President, but because he was tutor to Shoults. Bateson was Master, and his signature was undoubtedly a formality. The eccentric George Fearns Reyner also signed; this horse-riding, whip-flaying Senior Bursar, who was both loved and hated at College, had come up through the ranks and, like Shoults, had been a sizar, admitted in July 1835.[16] Churchill Babington (1821–89) was a classical scholar, Fellow of St. John's, and Disney Professor of Archaeology at Cambridge; author of various works on numismatics, botany, and ornithology, he was, when he signed, between curacy appointments.[17] Arthur Calvert (1830–91) had orientalist interests, and was a great promoter of Edward Henry Palmer (1840–82), the English orientalist and explorer. At the time of signing, Calvert was Perpetual Curate of Horningsea, Cambridgeshire, taking over from Babington. As already mentioned, J.B. Mayor was an editor of the St. John's College magazine *Eagle*, and, in the year that he signed Shoults's testimonial, he had just begun his stint as headmaster of Kensington School (1862–68), before becoming Professor of Classical Literature (1870–79) and, later, Professor of Moral Philosophy (1879–83) at King's College, London. J. B's brother, John Eyton Bickersteth Mayor (1825–1910), was an English classical scholar, and, from 1863 to 1867, the University of Cambridge Librarian. At various points in his career, he was President of the Cambridge Antiquarian Society,

---

[16] Reyner, *AC* (1953), V, 278; see also Hilton (2011), 262–3.
[17] See Seccombe (2004).

the Philological Society, and the Vegetarian Society. As mentioned in chapter 2, the Rev. John Robert Lunn was President of the University Musical Society and, in 1863, vicar of Marton-cum-Grafton, Yorkshire.[18] The last of the College signatories was the Rev. Thomas George Bonney, who was Junior Dean at St. John's College, taking up the post in 1861.[19]

Perhaps the most interesting person to sign the testimonial was the Rev. Thomas Joseph Gaster (1832–1909), of St. Giles, Camberwell.[20] Gaster was ordained a priest in Calcutta by Bishop George Cotton in 1858 and served as a Church Mission Society missionary in Agra until 1860. In 1861, he moved to the hill station of Simla, all the while undergoing language study and doing missionary work among expatriates and the indigenous population. He arrived in London in May 1863 and was almost immediately made a curate at St. Giles, Camberwell, working for the priest in charge, the Rev. Robert Tapson. Gaster's appointment was slightly unconventional, differing markedly from Shoults's experience. Gaster wrote to the Rev. Stephen Bridge, an old friend and incumbent of St. Matthew's, Denmark Hill, asking for a curacy. Bridge enticed him to his area of London to start 'a second church', but in recognising that this would take time, recommended that Gaster work with the Clapham-connected Tapson, who needed a curate. Gaster 'accepted at once' and was licensed by the Bishop of Winchester, Dr Sumner. Gaster was an enthusiastic evangelist. He signed the testimonial in November 1863, meaning that it was a mere six months that Shoults and he had had to become familiar. Although the announcement procedure was no doubt formulaic, Gaster obviously felt comfortable in agreeing to support Shoults's candidacy. There was then the Rev. Francis Freeman Statham, of whom more below.

ST. PETER'S, WALWORTH

St. Peter's, the first church designed by Sir John Soane, was built between 1823 and 1825. With four large columns at front, it sits tucked between Trafalgar and Liverpool Streets, and is bordered by Walworth Road and parts of East Street and Albany Road, a quiet fenced oasis with a small shrub garden at back. The church was consecrated on 28 February 1825 by Charles Manners-Sutton (1755–1828), the Archbishop of Canterbury.[21] It remains an impressive building. (See pl. 5.)

It was at St. Peter's that Shoults started as an assistant curate, beginning in December 1863 and staying there until December 1865. He lived at 24 New Olney Street,

---

[18] Mayor, J.B, *AC* (1947), IV, 379; Mayor, J.E.B, *AC* (1947), IV, 379; Lunn, *AC* (1947), IV, 236.
[19] See Oldroyd (2004); see also Bonney, *AC* (1940), I, 318.
[20] Orr-Ewing (2018).
[21] Darlington (1955), 95–8.

a 35-minute stroll north to old familiar haunts in Tooley Street and a 30-minute walk south to his family, who, by 1863, had moved to 37 Camberwell Grove.

As already mentioned, the rector at St. Peter's was the Rev. Francis Freeman Statham (1814–84), a Magdalen Hall, Oxford man who was ordained a deacon in 1843 and priest in 1844. Between 1843 and 1845 he was curate of Verulam Episcopal Chapel, Lambeth, near the asylum. He began his tenure at St. Peter's in 1848 and remained there until his death.[22] About the time that he started, the population of the parish was 13,963, and the living attached amounted to some £500 plus a house. The rectory must have been a full one: Statham married Jane Lee, second daughter of William Kington, Gloucester, in 1836, and they had seven children. He was a Fellow of the Royal Geographical Society, was known as a good preacher, and had scientific interests that might have interested Shoults. In July 1848, Statham published a sermon: *Loyalty—a Christian Duty*, preached at St. Peter's on 2 July after the insurrection in Paris. In 1850, he produced a small pamphlet titled *Our Protestant Faith, as Distinguished from the Corruptions and Superstitions of Popery, Being a Course of Lectures upon the Distinctive Errors of Romanism*. The publication proving sufficiently popular, Statham produced a second edition in 1851. He was 49 when Shoults began at St. Peter's.

In 1861, the population of Walworth was 44,463, and poverty was rife.[23] The clergy worked hard to combat these conditions. Parish work was not easy, and Statham had his own crosses to bear. Prior to Shoults's arrival, some unpleasantness had occurred between one E. N. Willson and Statham, even though the latter had extolled the former's good character in a previous testimonial, dated 5 June 1861.[24] By March 1862, Statham was proclaiming: 'he [Willson] has caused me first and last so much trouble and annoyance that I might justly decline having anything more to do with him.'[25] Defamation proceedings were initiated by Willson, which carried on to just before Shoults's arrival at St. Peter's.[26] To compound matters, in early January 1862, Statham lost a good, reliable man—Mr Helden—who had been at St. Peter's for three years. Statham wrote: 'I shall be extremely sorry to lose his services and scarcely know where to look for one who will fill up the gap occasioned by his contemplated removal.'[27] As part-time counsellor, Statham also had to deal with the personal

---

[22] *Alumni Oxoniensis* (1888), 4, 1346; see also *Crockford's* (1884), 1147.
[23] Booth (1902–1903), 4, opp. 58.
[24] Tait Papers, 127, f. 24, Statham, testimonial for E. N. Willson, 5 June 1861. Lambeth Palace Library (LPL).
[25] Tait Papers, 127, ff. 26–29, Statham to Lord Bishop of London, 27 March 1862. LPL.
[26] See Tait Papers, 131, ff. 47–8, Jan–April 1863. LPL.
[27] Tait Papers, 127, ff. 89–90, Statham to Lord Bishop of London, 20 January 1862. LPL.

problems of the Rev. George Alcock Macdonnell, who had incurred debts through his wife's extravagances.[28] All this was percolating when Shoults began his term there.

As an assistant curate, Shoults's duties included assisting Statham in Divine Service (officiating at Morning and Evening Services), assisting him in the Ministration of the Holy Communion, aiding in the collection of Alms (the Offertory), reading the Holy Scriptures and Homilies in the Church, instructing children in the catechism, baptising infants in the absence of Statham, preaching, performing the Churching of Women, and officiating at ceremonies to bury the dead. One chief duty was to search out the sick and the poor and report the details to Statham.[29] This function of parish work was particularly important. Indeed, in 1898, an unknown missionary wrote: 'I am more than ever convinced that [. . .] the backbone of mission work is visit, visit; and then begin again and visit consecutively [. . .] the only real, vital way to reach them is to visit them single-handed.'[30] Shoults would surely have recognised this obligation.

Occasionally deacons could solemnise matrimony.[31] On 8 February 1864, Shoults officiated at the marriage service between George Green and Ellen Ewing.[32] Perhaps this was his first such undertaking. What he could not do was to pronounce the Absolution, consecrate the Elements of the Lord's Supper, pronounce the Blessing, or hold any Benefice or Ecclesiastical preferment.[33] In short, he was an assistant and learnt the church procedures through the leadership offered by Statham, who may have been a good role model. It must be remembered that Shoults's yearly stipend was £80, which was the minimum established by law in 1817 (57 George III c.99) and confirmed through the Pluralities Act of 1838, 1 & 2 Victoria c.106.[34]

A deacon was obliged to stay in the role for at least one year. This requirement made sense, as a period such as this gave time for the novice to gain experience in all ecclesiastical and administrative matters. It was a serious undertaking, and not to be rushed. Pinnock (1855) detailed the importance of being in Holy Orders: 'I would now strongly impress upon you, that when you are once in HOLY ORDERS, those ORDERS are *indelible*.' This sentiment was reiterated in Canon 76: 'No man being admitted to a Deacon or Minister shall from henceforth voluntarily relinquish the

---

[28] Tait Papers, 136, ff. 129, Statham to Lord Bishop of London, January 1864. LPL. Aside from clerical duties, MacDonnell (1830–99) was also a chess master and writer.
[29] See Pinnock (1855), 69.
[30] Nichols (2003), 91, citing an unknown missionary in 1898.
[31] Pinnock (1855), 25.
[32] *The Essex Standard*, 12 February 1864, 3.
[33] Pinnock (1855), 71.
[34] Hart (1970), 128.

same, nor afterward use himself in the course of his life *as a layman*, upon pain of excommunication.'³⁵ Pinnock also offered advice on the next rung, that of Priest.

> Established in your Curacy, it will perhaps be well for you, as early as possible, to obtain from the Bishop's Examining Chaplain a list of subjects in which you will be examined for *Priest's Orders*, so that you may employ what leisure hours you may have in preparing them. You must not expect to have much time at your disposal: the Occasional Duties of your Parish. The Pastoral Visiting, the Overlooking of the Schools, the Composition of your Sermons for the Sunday; and possibly, Daily Service, and an additional Lecture or Discourse on some day of the week, will deny you the luxury of deep reading, and leave but few opportunities for connected study.³⁶

On 21 May 1863, Shoults visited the British Museum, where he applied for a reader's ticket. He was given ticket no. 2109, as recorded in the 'Directions Respecting the Reading Room'. He used his father's address at 37 Camberwell Grove as a point of contact. Access to the books and manuscripts in the British Museum required character references and a statement that the Museum was the only place in which such information could be obtained. The Principal Librarian had the final say on gaining access. Unfortunately, the records of applications up to 1880 no longer exist, and so it is now impossible to ascertain who Shoults's referees were, or what books he consulted.³⁷ He may have been there to consult items as part of his forthcoming examination, or perhaps it afforded an ideal opportunity to grab a few minutes of that much-desired 'luxury of deep reading'.

Just before Christmas 1864, Shoults was back at the Chapel Royal for another ordination service, this time towards full priesthood. Again, the Bishop of London officiated, with Howlett organising the prayers for the service. The sermons were arranged by the Rev. E.H. Parowns, with the Rev. J.B. Lightfoot present as Examining Chaplain. Shoults joined his two familiars from St. John's: Bullock, now attached to the curacy of All Saints' Church, Notting Hill, after a year at St. Philip's, and Peckover, who would remain at Christ Church, Lee, Kent. Shoults was reconfirmed in his position at St. Peter's.³⁸

Of course, prior to acceptance into the priesthood, he had to carry out the same procedures as he had had with his diaconate, although in reality much less was

---

³⁵ Pinnock (1855), 93.
³⁶ Pinnock (1855), 81.
³⁷ Thanks to Francesca Hillier, Archivist, Central Archive, British Museum, for supplying the BM Index archive records on Shoults.
³⁸ 'London Ordination', *Daily News*, 19 December 1864, 2.

required. Papers again were forwarded, with an emphasis on testimonials confirming his sound doctrine, his good behaviour, and his living a pious, sober and honest life.[39] Apart from gleaning useful hints, Shoults may have noted in his copy of Pinnock the pronouncement: 'What is said to you in these pages is grounded on the assumption that you have entered into Holy Orders with single and pure motives, and with a steadfast determination of heart to submit yourself to the guidance of that Holy Spirit by whom you at first professed yourself to be inwardly moved. Since, then, you have declared the work of the ministry to be the business of your life, make it so in reality.'[40] And again, an examination time was set, where 'competent knowledge' was expected in:

1. Greek Testament, especially the Epistles.
2. Pearson on the Creed, the notes as well as the text.
3. Church History, more particularly the periods embracing the first five centuries, and the Reformation.
4. The Scripture History and an acquaintance of the Hebrew text of the Book of Genesis.[41]

Shoults then attended the service of ordination, where the Bishop and, usually, three others invested him by the laying on of hands and by giving him the 'authority to preach the Word of God', to consecrate, and to 'administer the Holy Sacraments in the congregation'. He received another parchment, which not only reiterated his obligations to the Thirty-nine Articles and to the three Articles contained in the 36 Canons. The cost of this ordination was 60 shillings.[42]

The above requirements are confirmed by the Ordination for Priesthood records relating to Shoults held at the London Metropolitan Archives.[43] As expected, there is less documentation than in those items required for his diaconate. His residency at 24 New Olney Street, Camberwell was confirmed; his intention to become a priest was duly noted; and it was written that Statham was prepared to read publicly and audibly Shoults's intention of this in St. Peter's on a given day: Sunday, 13 November 1864. The last document was signed by Statham, churchwarden F.J. Prewett, and J.E. Sach, clerk. One other document was signed by fellow clergy, who testified to Shoults's good character. It reads (in part):

---

[39] Pinnock (1855), 85.
[40] Pinnock (1855), 116.
[41] Pinnock (1855), 81–2.
[42] Pinnock (1855), 91–2, 94–104.
[43] London Diocese Ordination Papers, St Peter's Walworth, 1863–1865, Deacon and Priest Folder, 9651–10390 no.12: DL/A/B/004/MS10326/269 – 2751863. December 1863–November 1864. LMA.

6 FIRST STEP: ASSISTANT CURATE, ST. PETER'S, WALWORTH

We therefore, whose names are hereunto subscribed, do certify that the said William Arderne Shoults hath been personally known to us for the time which has elapsed since his ordination as Deacon; that we have had opportunities of observing his conduct; that during the whole of that time we verily believe him to have lived, in all respects, piously, soberly, and honestly; nor have we at any time heard anything to the contrary thereof; nor hath he at any time as far as we know, or have heard, maintained, said, or written anything contrary to the doctrine or discipline of the United Church of England and Ireland; and moreover, we do believe him in our consciences to be, as to his moral conduct, a fit person to be admitted into the sacred order of priest.

This testimonial was witnessed by the Rev. John Going, perpetual curate, St. Paul's, Walworth, the Rev. George Toulson Cotham, perpetual curate, St. John's, Walworth, and the Rev. Daniel Alfred Moullin, incumbent at Holy Trinity, Newington. It was dated 12 November 1864.

Going was well-known for his ritualistic ceremonies at St. Paul's. His services were known to be festooned with brass crucifixes, tall wax candles, bannerets of the Virgin and Child and the Cross, richly embroidered crimson and gold vestments, Gregorian music, and incense.[44] His ceremonies closely resembled High Mass in the Roman Catholic Church. In fact, in 1870, Going was one of five ritualistic clergy called to the Bishop of London's house to clarify issues surrounding the introduction of various prohibitions—for example, mixing water with wine at the Holy Communion, wearing stoles at the communion service, and the ceremonial use of candles at particular times.[45] Not only was there disgruntlement over 'Romanism' in the newspapers, but concerned individuals voiced their opinions, often quite vehemently. A Mr Smith wrote to Bishop Tait on 7 February 1866 complaining of 'the gee-gaw practices organised by J. Going', even though the writer termed Going 'an esteemed gentleman, kind, [and] benevolent'.[46]

Cotham was a graduate of Trinity College Dublin, who became a deacon in 1847 and priest in 1848.[47] Prior to his perpetual curacy at St. John's, he was minister at Collingham All Saints, Newark. He was a member of the Kent Archaeology Society. Moullin was another graduate who attended Trinity College Dublin, ordained in

---

[44] As noted in 'St Paul's Walworth', *The Times*, 4 January 1869, 3.
[45] 'The Bishop of London and the Ritualists', *The Times*, 4 April 1870, 12. The other four were the Rev. C. F. Lowder, St. Peter's London Docks; the Rev. H. D. Nihill, St Michael's, Shoreditch; the Rev. C. J. Le Geyt, St. Mathias, Stoke Newington; and the Rev. A. H. Mackonochie, St. Alban's, Holborn.
[46] Tait Papers, 143, ff. 400–1, November 1865 to February 1866. LPL. The *South London Chronicle*, 17 February 1866, recorded Going heading a semi-popish procession. f.415.
[47] *Crockfield's* (1868), 153.

1843.⁴⁸ Before being appointed to Holy Trinity, Walworth, he was curate of Carleton Rode, Norfolk (1843–4) and then of St. Stephen's, Norwich (1844–88).⁴⁹

Shoults knew the above men and was obviously comfortable in asking them for their backing—evidential proof of his good character. A month after the testimonial was signed, Shoults assisted Going in the marriage service of Clare Newbold, daughter of Francis Newbold, to Robert Bendle Moore on 12 December 1864.⁵⁰ On another occasion, in August 1865, Shoults attended the consecration of All Saints Church, Newington, a church that was under the spiritual charge of Statham at St. Peter's, Walworth. Fellow attendees with Statham included the Revs. Going, Cotham, Moullin, J. W. Erskine Knollys, permanent curate at Aldborough Hatch, Essex, and later at Holy Trinity, Twickenham, and Alfred Cay, briefly curate in charge at St. George's-in-the-East, the church to which the Rev. Bryan King (1811–94), an early advocate of the Catholic Revival in England, was appointed.⁵¹ It is quite possible that Shoults mixed with these men socially.

The Clerical Registers for St. Peter's, at the London Metropolitan Archive, offer a small glimpse of what Shoults's duties and activities were for the two years he spent in the parish.⁵² They do not offer evidence of his visiting duties or of the pastoral care he carried out, but they do give details of his preaching and sermon activities. Statham worked his new curate hard, right from the start. On 27 December 1863, which may have been his first day, Shoults delivered his first prayer and sermon to his new congregation. The outgoing curate, the Rev. Samuel B. Webb, was there too, giving his last. Understandably, Statham was the most frequent preacher.⁵³

The first month of the new year, 1864, offers a glimpse of Shoults's workload and schedule. On 3 January, he gave a reading in the afternoon and then preached in the evening to the congregation. Four days later, on 7 January, he gave a reading, preached, and was involved in a Thursday-night lecture. On 10 January, he gave a reading and preached. On 14 January, he shared duties with the Rev. Oliver Mitchell, curate, in an evening service.⁵⁴ Three days later, on 17 January, he gave a reading and preached. On 21 January, he gave an evening prayer, with Statham preaching, on Isaiah III. 5: 'And the people shall be oppressed, every one by another.' That night Shoults also

---

⁴⁸ See *Alumni Dublinenses* (1924).
⁴⁹ *The Guardian*, 6 March 1889, 349.
⁵⁰ Cited in *Cheshire Observer & Chester, Birkenhead, Crewe and North Wales Times*, 17 December 1864, 6.
⁵¹ 'Consecration of All Saints Church, Newington', *The Standard*, 8 August 1865, 3.
⁵² St Peter's, Walworth, Clerical Registers, P92/PET1/97: January 1850–January 1864, and P92/PET1/98: January 1864–1870. LMA.
⁵³ St Peter's Clerical Register, P92/PET1/97. LMA.
⁵⁴ Mitchell, *AC* (1947), IV, 430.

gave an evening lecture. On 24 January, he gave a prayer reading and preached in the afternoon. In the evening he shared duties with Statham on another reading. The next morning, 25 January, Shoults gave a morning prayer and preached, basing his sermon on the conversion of St. Paul. On 28 January, he gave an evening reading and shared preaching duties with Statham. In the month of March 1864, leading up to Easter, Shoults presided fifteen times, sometimes doing double duties as reader and preacher.

This pattern of reading, preaching, and giving lectures became the norm, and, from the records kept, he was busy almost every other day. Sometimes the records provide a text reference to the sermons—for example, on 24 February, the Feast for St Mathias, Luke XX. 17–19: 'And the seventy returned again with joy, saying Lord, even the devils are subject unto us through thy name. / And he said unto them, I beheld Satan as lightning fall from heaven. / Behold I give unto you power to tread on serpents and scorpions, and over all the power of the enemy: and nothing shall by means hurt you' and Luke XII. 42–43: 'And the Lord said, Who then is that faithful and wise steward, whom his lord shall make ruler over his household, to give them their portion of eat in due season? / Blessed is that servant, whom his lord when he cometh shall find so doing.' Communion services also took up much time.

The Register occasionally contains congregation numbers, and, perhaps understandably, the largest are for when Statham was presiding. Figures such as 25, 27, and 36 were usual, with the highest over the two-year period being 52 on Easter Day, 27 March 1864. A pencil note beside this figure reads: 'Celebration!' In 1864, there were 234 times when the clergy and parishioners came together. In 1865, it was 232. Of the 234 for 1864, Shoults appeared 110 times, Statham 65. For 1865, Shoults appeared 86 times, Statham 57.[55] On 31 December 1865, Shoults carried out his last duties: he gave an afternoon reading and preached.

In his role as curate, Shoults was expected to be involved in the community, visiting the sick, elderly, and poor. While there is no account of his outreach activities, there is again a glimpse of his involvement in the National Parochial Charity and Sunday Schools programme attached to St. Peter's.[56] At one point, on 2 February 1863, there were 123 boys in the Shaftesbury Street school, 105 girls in the Girls' School, and 94 infants at Church Gates School. In January 1864, Shoults was secretary of the parish committee, most certainly a position that came with the duties of a new curate. Statham was the chairman.

Over the 1864–65 period, the content of the minutes—recorded in Shoults's slanting hand—detail troubles over recruiting good teachers and sorting out their

---

[55] St Peter's Clerical Register, P92/PET1/98. LMA.
[56] St. Peter's, Walworth Schools, 1846–1870, P92/PET1/137. LMA.

salaries and general working conditions. Eventually a Miss Ellen Weldon was hired as school mistress at £20 *per annum*, while a Mr Crampon was appointed not only as schoolmaster, but also the Church organist; his salary was fixed at £80 *per annum*. In June 1864, some boys stole the tap off the water butt and Shoults was instructed to write a letter to the Superintendent of Police about this matter, detailing the damage done. Other matters covered included offertory totals for morning and evening services, the piggery (which was a health nuisance), the blocked sewer drains, and the fact that the toilets at the school needed repair. Often there was no quorum at the meetings, a fact that Shoults dutifully recorded in the minutes. On 4 December 1865, he noted his own resignation as secretary, because he had accepted a curacy at St. Paul's, Bunhill Row.

Legally, Shoults was able to move to another post after twelve months. However, he chose to stay another full year under Statham's tutelage. It was, after all, his first appointment, and he had much to learn and put into practice. He may have read his Pinnock, taking to heart the words:

> Wandering about from Curacy to Curacy, merely for the sake of change, is wrong in principle, and injurious in fact. It not only retards the full development of your aptitude for the Ministerial work, but also interferes materially with the practical efficiency of your pulpit teaching, and your pastoral labours: and, I may add, in no small degree interrupts your future advancement. Above all, let not fastidiousness or caprice impel you to such a step; much less allow yourself in so great a matter to be swayed by a captious irritability.[57]

Shoults was bookish, and he surely browsed in some of the London bookshops. To the trade, he was probably regarded as another nameless young man walking around the shelves, picking up a volume, putting it back, and deliberating over making a purchase. He was not a high-spot buyer flush with funds. He did, however, manage during his busy schedule to get back to the British Museum. On 22 September 1865, he applied for and received another Reader's ticket, no. 3975: 'William Arderne Shoults (Rev'd), 24 New Olney St., Walworth.' There is no inkling of what he consulted, nor his referees, but, as he had passed his examinations for the diaconate and full priesthood, one can only assume that it was for personal study, perhaps a bibliographic point over an ancient church text or a particular over a certain hymn.

About 1865, his personal library could well have been termed a 'collection', and not just a disparate gathering of volumes. Although there is no evidence on how many books he actually had at this time, the number was certainly growing. Certainly he

---

[57] Pinnock (1855), 92–3.

had accumulated some large thick folios, and to house them required space and a degree of stability. As he was on the move again, he stored most at his father's house in Camberwell Grove, a three-storey building which could accommodate the growing collection. Importantly for him, it was the family home, a place to which he could return at will.

Plate 2: Old Chapel, St John's College, Cambridge, c.1847. From John Le Keux, *Memorials of Cambridge*, vol. 1 (Cambridge, 1847).

Shoults was enrolled at St John's College, Cambridge, between 1856 and 1860. The interior of the old chapel at St John's College was certainly a place that he was familiar with. This smaller mediaeval chapel, which dated back to the thirteenth century, was demolished about 1865 and replaced by the current chapel.

MATHEMATICAL TRIPOSES.

1860.—MODERATORS { Henry William Watson, M.A. *Trin.*
{ Edward John Routh, M.A. *St Peter's.*

EXAMINERS { Percival Frost, M.A. *St John's.*
{ Norman Macleod Ferrers, M.A. *Caius.*

Wranglers.		Senior Optimes.		Junior Optimes.	
Ds Stirling (1)	*Trin.*	Ds Shoults	*Joh.*	Ds Beddome }	*Trin.*
Baily (2)	*Joh.*	Moodie	*Trin.*	Brownlow } Æq.	*Emman.*
Richardson	*Joh.*	Clarke } Æq.	*Pemb.*	Howard }	*Clare.*
Durell	*Joh.*	Smith }	*Christ's.*	Cowell β } Æq.	*Trin.*
Merriman	*Joh.*	Raban	*Trin.*	Peach }	*Emman.*
Snooke γ	*Trin.*	Graham	*Trin.*	Imrie	*Christ's.*
Smith, C. J. E.	*Joh.*	Langdon } Æq.	*Trin.*	Brooks	*Trin.*
Crosthwaite } Æq.	*Trin.*	Young, Sir G. β }	*Trin.*	Shattock	*Pemb.*
Stephenson }	*Trin.*	Cachemaille	*Caius.*	Binyon } Æq.	*Trin.*
Foster	*Joh.*	Farman	*Joh.*	Bower }	*Joh.*
Eve β	*Trin.*	Harvey	*Christ's.*	Barwell	*Trin.*
Fisher	*Trin.*	Buszard γ } Æq.	*Trin.*	Dunning	*Christ's.*
Brown	*Caius.*	Howell }	*Cath.*	Bullock }	*Caius.*
Macfarlan	*Trin.*	Pennethorne	*Jesus.*	Cripps } Æq.	*Christ's.*
Churton	*King's.*	Codd	*Joh.*	Clayton γ }	*Trin.*
Candler	*Trin.*	Jackson β	*Joh.*	Attwood	*Emman.*
Hoare }	*Joh.*	Wyer	*Emman.*	Coode	*Trin.*
Taylor α } Æq.	*Joh.*	Mortimer	*Trin. H.*	D'Almaine	*Queens'.*
Watkins }	*Caius.*	Adams } Æq.	*Caius.*	Hart	*Corpus.*
Lee	*Emman.*	Weekes }	*Sidney.*	Bigg	*Caius.*
Braithwaite	*Clare.*	Fisher	*Jesus.*	Collier }	*Caius.*
Marrack	*Joh.*	Festing	*Trin.*	Everett }	*Clare.*
Proctor	*Joh.*	Metcalfe	*Joh.*	Lawson }	*Corp.*
Williams	*Trin.*	Nunn } Æq.	*Emman.*	MacCalmont }	*Tr. H.*
Brent	*Queens'.*	Watkins }	*Christ's*	Whittington }	*Pet.*
Blissard	*Emman.*	Bunbury } Æq.	*Joh.*	Smith	*Trin. H.*
Ferguson } Æq.	*Joh.*	Love }	*Sidney.*	Vines	*Corpus.*
MacCarthy }	*Emman.*	Blyth	*Joh.*	Fox	*Trin.*
Bates	*Magd.*	Boulby } Æq.	*Queens'.*	Davenport } Æq.	*Trin.*
Evans	*Corpus.*	Crombie }	*Trin.*	Frere }	*Emman.*
Booth } Æq.	*Trin.*	Johnston }	*Trin.*	Scargill β } Æq.	*Trin.*
Makgill }	*Trin.*	Hodgson α	*King's.*	Waddell }	*Trin.*
Previté	*Joh.*	Nisbet	*Jesus.*	Wedgewood	*Trin.*
Mason	*Christ's.*	Cooper } Æq.	*Christ's.*		
Scott	*Joh.*	Grist }	*Joh.*		
Bayford } Æq.	*Tr. H.*	Andras	*Joh.*		
Smith, Jason }	*Joh.*	Ewen	*Trin.*		
Walsh }	*Emm.*	Mules } Æq	*Trin.*		
		Sellwood }	*Joh.*		
		Ward	*Trin.*		
		Farrant	*Trin.*		
		Peile α	*Christ's.*		
		Bosanquet α } Æq.	*King's.*		
		Graham }	*Emman.*		
		Methold	*Trin. H.*		
		Storrs	*Cath.*		
		Jessop	*Trin.*		
		Nixon	*Corpus.*		
		Paley } Æq.	*Joh.*		
		Westcott }	*Pemb.*		

Plate 3. The Cambridge University Calendar for the Year 1860 (1860).

In January 1860, Shoults sat the Mathematical Tripos examinations and secured first place in Senior Optimes, as recorded in the University of Cambridge Calendar for 1860. Although he missed out on the much-desired Wrangler status, it was a significant achievement.

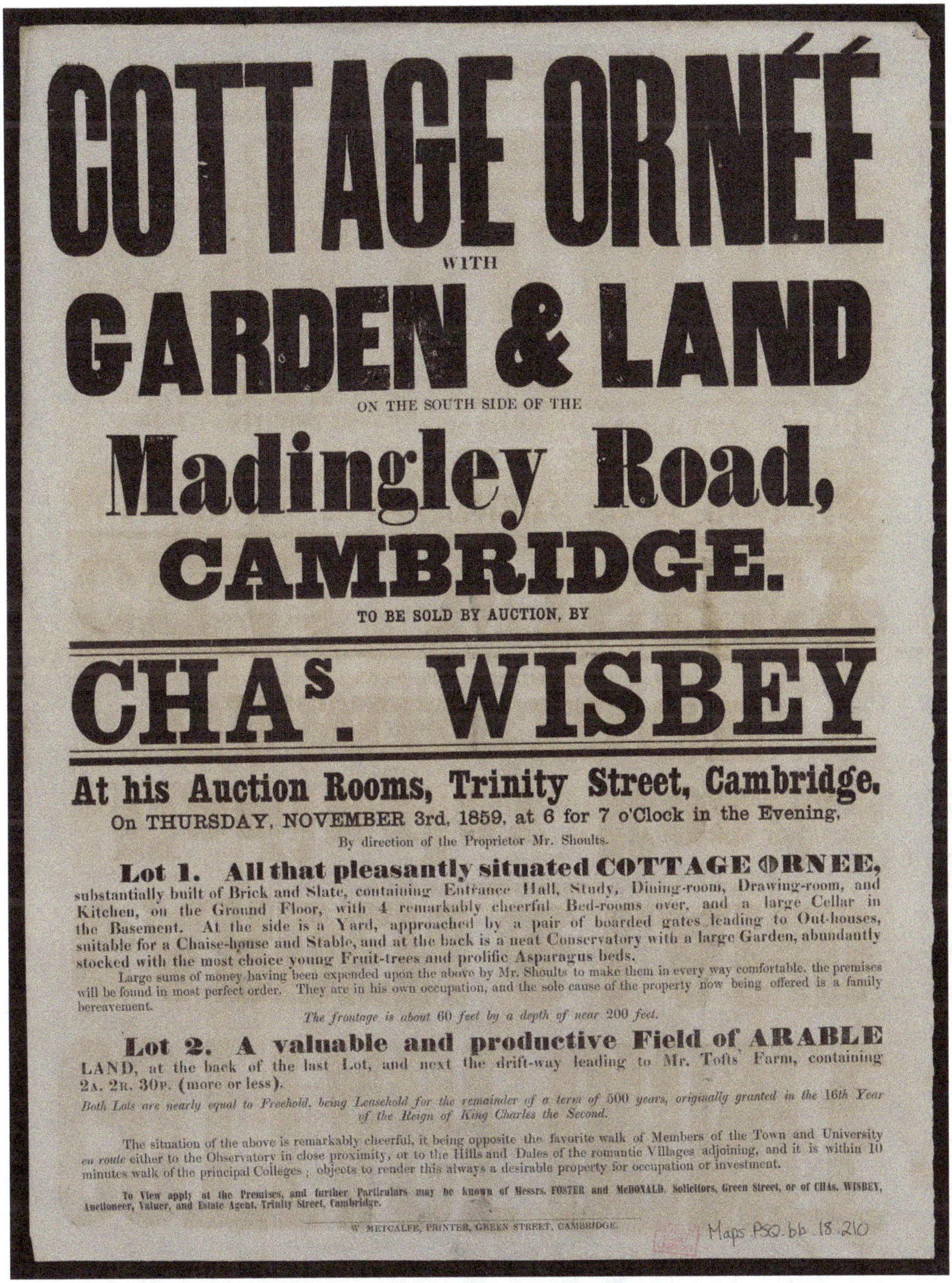

COTTAGE ORNÉÉ

WITH

GARDEN & LAND

ON THE SOUTH SIDE OF THE

Madingley Road,

CAMBRIDGE.

TO BE SOLD BY AUCTION, BY

CHA^{S}. WISBEY

At his Auction Rooms, Trinity Street, Cambridge.

On THURSDAY, NOVEMBER 3rd, 1859, at 6 for 7 o'Clock in the Evening,

By direction of the Proprietor Mr. Shoults.

Lot 1. All that pleasantly situated COTTAGE ORNEE, substantially built of Brick and Slate, containing Entrance Hall, Study, Dining-room, Drawing-room, and Kitchen, on the Ground Floor, with 4 remarkably cheerful Bed-rooms over, and a large Cellar in the Basement. At the side is a Yard, approached by a pair of boarded gates leading to Out-houses, suitable for a Chaise-house and Stable, and at the back is a neat Conservatory with a large Garden, abundantly stocked with the most choice young Fruit-trees and prolific Asparagus beds.

Large sums of money having been expended upon the above by Mr. Shoults to make them in every way comfortable, the premises will be found in most perfect order. They are in his own occupation, and the sole cause of the property now being offered is a family bereavement.

The frontage is about 60 feet by a depth of near 200 feet.

Lot 2. A valuable and productive Field of ARABLE LAND, at the back of the last Lot, and next the drift-way leading to Mr. Tofts' Farm, containing 2A. 2R. 30P. (more or less).

Both Lots are nearly equal to Freehold, being Leasehold for the remainder of a term of 500 years, originally granted in the 16th Year of the Reign of King Charles the Second.

The situation of the above is remarkably cheerful, it being opposite the favorite walk of Members of the Town and University *en route* either to the Observatory in close proximity, or to the Hills and Dales of the romantic Villages adjoining, and it is within 10 minutes walk of the principal Colleges; objects to render this always a desirable property for occupation or investment.

To View apply at the Premises, and further Particulars may be known of Messrs. FOSTER and McDONALD, Solicitors, Green Street, or of CHAS. WISBEY, Auctioneer, Valuer, and Estate Agent, Trinity Street, Cambridge.

W. METCALFE, PRINTER, GREEN STREET, CAMBRIDGE.

Plate 4. Charles Wisbey's 'Cottage Ornéé with Garden & Land' auction promotion sheet, Cambridge University Library Maps PSQ.bb.18.210.

Charles Wisbey's 'Cottage Ornéé with Garden & Land' auction promotion sheet for the Shoults family home, Madingley Road, Cambridge, 3 November 1859. It was from this substantial house that he walked back and forth to classes at St. John's College.

Plate 5.   St. Peter's Church, Walworth, 2018.

St. Peter's Church, Walworth. This church, which was designed by Sir John Sloane, was where Shoults spent his first two years as assistant curate, 1863 to 1865.

Plate 6. St. Paul's Church, Bunhill, Hoxton, from St. John Adcock, ed., *Wonderful London* (1926).

A photograph of St. Paul's Church, Bunhill, Hoxton, before it was demolished in 1933. Shoults was curate at this church, which was nestled beside the famed Bunhill Fields, a graveyard for Protestant dissenters.

Plate 7. Joseph Leycester Lyne, (1837–1908).

Joseph Leycester Lyne, (1837–1908), the controversial, enthusiastic, revivalist known as 'Father Ignatius', founder of his own particular Benedictine Order in the Anglican Church in nineteenth-century England. Shoults, a near-contemporary, was about 27 when he met Ignatius.

Plate 8. The monastery at Capel-y-ffin, 2018.

The monastery at Capel-y-ffin, four miles from Llanthony Priory, South Wales, established by Father Ignatius in September 1869. Shoults's first recorded visit to this desolate site was Christmas 1870, when he was asked to assist in the celebrations of midnight Mass in the newly built chapel.

The Revd W. A. Shoults, M.A.
With the respectful love
Of his grateful and affectionate spiritual children
The Mother & Sisters of Convent, Feltham.
Christmass
1874.

The Revd Father Cyril M.A.
With the respectful love
Of his grateful and affectionate spiritual children
The Mother & Sisters of Benedictine Convent, Feltham
Christmass. 1874.

SELWYN
COLLEGE
LIBRARY

Plates 9 & 10. Rev. Henry Anstey's *Munimenta academica: Or, Documents Illustrative of Academical Life and Studies at Oxford* (1868).

The inscriptions by the Mother and Sisters of the Feltham Convent to Shoults in his copy of the Rev. Henry Anstey's *Munimenta academica: Or, Documents Illustrative of Academical Life and Studies at Oxford (1868).* Volume one is inscribed to Shoults; volume two to 'Father Cyril'.

Plate 11.   St Michael's Church, Shoreditch, 2018.

St Michael's Church, Shoreditch, where Shoults was curate between 1873 and 1875. The vicar at the time was the Rev. Henry David Nihill (1834–1913), an uncompromising Anglo-Catholic, who was a member of the Society of the Holy Cross, an organisation that supported Catholic revival in the Church of England.

Plate 12. St. Edmund the King and Martyr, Lombard Street, London City. From William Maitland, *History of London* (1753).

St. Edmund the King and Martyr on Lombard Street, London City (middle) from William Maitland's History of London (1753). Shoults was curate between 1875 and 1879, his longest stint in any one parish. The rector was the ritualist Pascoe Grenfell Hill (1804–1882), who enlivened his church by employing charismatic preachers such as Father Ignatius, and using music as a way to attract parishioners.

Plate 13.
Harvest Festival at St Edmund the Martyr, *Graphic*, 30 October 1875.

The accompanying text to this image of a Harvest Festival at St Edmund the Martyr in the Graphic, 30 October 1875, cites Shoults as a prime organiser and lead hymn singer, depicted standing at right. Harvest Festival events were an Anglo-Catholic innovation that is now deemed almost universal in the Church of England.

292   DEUS PATER PIISSIME

ed., 1856, p. 251, it is altered, and begins: "Now hush your cries, and shed no tear," and repeated thus in her *C. B. for England*, 1863, No. 97. Also in *Ps. & Hys.*, Bedford, 1859, No. 269, and the Rugby *School H. B.*, 1866, No. 208.

ii. **Nun lasst uns den Leib begraben.** This version has so little from the Latin that it is noted under its own first line (q. v.). [J. M.]

Deus Pater piissime. [*Saturday Evening.*] This hymn occurs as a vesper hymn for the Saturday before the 3rd Sunday in Lent to Passion Sunday, in a MS. Breviary, written about the 14th century, formerly belonging to the Monastery of Evesham (*MS. Barlow*, No. 41, in the Bodleian Library at Oxford). It is also in a 12th cent. MS. in the *British Museum* (Harl. 2928, f. 115 b.), and in a Bodleian MS. of the 13th cent. (Ashmole 1285, f. 38). In 1851 it was given in the *Hymnarium Sarisburiense*, p. 73. *Tr.* as :—

O God, O Father kind and best. By J. D. Chambers, in his *Companion to the Holy Communion*, 1855, and his *Lauda Syon*, 1857, p. 139, in 6 st. of 4 l. It is repeated in the *Appendix* to the *Hymnal N.*, 1863, and in Skinner's *Daily Service Hymnal*, 1864. [W. A. S.]

Plate 14.   John Julian, *Dictionary of Hymnology* (1892).

'This hymn occurs as a vesper hymn for the Saturday before the 3rd Sunday in Lent to Passion Sunday'. So begins the entry for the hymn 'Deus Pater piissime', which was written by Shoults [W.A.S.]. It and 59 others written by Shoults were published in John Julian's Dictionary of Hymnology, published in 1892. Shoults did not see his entries in print.

Plate 15.   *Nonarum inquisitiones in curia scaccarii* and *Placitorum abbreviatio* (1807–1811).

This rather ornate inscription was written by Shoults's wife Eliza, whom he married on 1 August 1878. It is found in two Record Commission publications: Nonarum inquisitiones in curia scaccarii *and* Placitorum abbreviatio *(1807–1811), books that she gave him on 28 March 1877. As an 'S' is used rather than an 'O' (her maiden name was Ogle), it is certainly a retrospective inscription.*

Plate 16. No. 37 Camberwell Grove, Camberwell, 2018.

On 14 June 1887, William Arderne Shoults died at the family home at 37 Camberwell Grove, Camberwell. The imposing brick four-storey Georgian house still stands, and one can imagine his book and manuscript collection (some 5600 volumes, including large, fat folios) sitting on book shelves in the house.

7 ST. PAUL'S, HOXTON, 1866–69

In about October 1865, Shoults handed to Statham a notice of his intention to leave St. Peter's. As with his entrance into Holy Orders, there was a process to be followed, which included permission from the Bishop and a suitable lead of three months' notice before his departure.[1] The move, however, was not a big one. His new curacy was just some three miles over the river (an hour's stroll) to St. Paul's, Bunhill Row, 11 Buckland Street, New North Road, Hoxton.[2] This 'ordinary little church with a spire' stood within the borough and civil parish of St. Luke, Old Street, Finsbury.[3] (See pl. 6.) It was built in 1839, 'when little or no attention was paid to Ritual arrangement'.[4] With overhanging galleries obstructing light and air, the church was deemed dark and cheerless. Repairs to it began just before Shoults's arrival and continued during his tenure. The parish population in 1868 was 5896.[5]

The surrounds of the church had a rich history, especially Bunhill Fields, which over time became a dumping ground for human bodies and bones, especially when the plague ravaged the city in the seventeenth century. It was about 1665 that Bunhill Fields ('Bone Hill' to 'Bunhill') became established as a burial ground. It was never consecrated, and it became popular as a non-conformist burial ground, especially as a result of the Corporation and Test Acts of 1661 and 1673, which excluded from burial those who had not been prepared to take the sacrament according to the rites of the Church of England. Those excluded included Roman Catholics and those following the Jewish faith. And, by chance, Bunhill became the resting place of many famous dissenters and non-conformists. The graves of writers John Bunyan and Daniel Defoe, of artist-poet William Blake, and of Isaac Watts, the 'Father of English Hymnody', are there. The poet Robert Southey claimed that dissenters regarded Bunhill Fields as their 'Campo Santo' (Holy Ground).[6] At one time there were about 1600 burials per year, and because of the large numbers, a crisis point was reached. In January 1854, the cemetery was classified as full, and it was closed to further interments.[7] Bunhill

---

[1] Pinnock (1855), 146–9.
[2] St. Paul's, Bunhill Row, Islington, Records: P76/PAU1/008. LMA.
[3] *Scenery of London* (1905).
[4] 'S. Paul's, Bunhill Row', *Church News*, 28 August 1867, 386–7.
[5] See Crockford's (1868), 438. In 1883, the church was further restored. It closed in 1932, and the parish united with Saint Mary, Charterhouse. The building was demolished in 1933.
[6] Cited in 'Review of Books' (1830).
[7] After the Burials Act of 1852, on 29 December 1853, Bunhill Cemetery was closed for burials, with the final burial of a 15-year-old girl taking place in January 1854. See *Official Guide* (1991).

Fields was obviously held in strong regard by the local community, because in 1867, when Shoults was working nearby, an Act of Parliament was passed that preserved the Fields 'as an open space' for the public's use. It was also 'enclosed', gaining iron railings and gates. In October 1869, more improvements were made to the cemetery, actions that Shoults may have been involved with. Despite massive bomb damage during the Blitz in the Second World War, the area has survived and retains that very useful public function: a quiet oasis surrounded by modern smart glass office buildings.

It is unknown why Shoults swapped Walworth for Hoxton. While the former was considered tough and had its full share of the poor, Hoxton was somewhat worse. At least that was the general claim. At the end of the century, Charles Booth began his overview of the area with 'Hoxton is the leading criminal quarter of London, and indeed of all England', and followed with a cry of 'Wall Off Hoxton!' Booth described mass poverty, low life, building demolitions, crowded quarters and conditions, drunkenness, and a degraded population. To him, the conditions in Hoxton made 'religious work exceptionally difficult'. He added: 'we find everywhere small congregations – sometimes hardly any congregation at all,' and '[a]s to the mass of the residents in Hoxton we hear without contradiction that not one grown-up person in thirty, or some say not one in fifty, and some again not one in eighty, attends any religious service.'[8]

Perhaps Shoults liked a challenge. After all, it was the Ministry's way: to throw yourself into the people – the poor and the slums – and do your best by your congregation, no matter how little, nor how difficult it might appear. With youthful patience and untiring zeal, Shoults was obviously prepared to discharge his duties, perhaps remembering the strictures from Ecclesiastes IX. 10: 'whatsoever thy hand findeth to do, do *it* with thy might.' Booth wrote somewhat positively: 'The people come to the clergy when in trouble'.[9]

Shoults was employed as curate at St. Paul's between late December 1865 and November 1869, carrying out parish duties under the incumbent, the Rev. Lewis Marcus (c.1801–79). Admitted as a sizar to Queens' College, Cambridge, on 13 December 1823, Marcus was ordained deacon in 1827 and priest in 1828. Between 1827 and 1841, he was curate of Biggleswade, Bedfordshire, and then headmaster of Holbeach Grammar School, Lincolnshire.[10] He was appointed as permanent curate to St. Paul's in May 1846, the value attached to the position £200, with the Patron being the Rector

---

[8] Booth (1902–1903), 2, 111, 117–18.
[9] Booth (1902–1903), 2, 132.
[10] Marcus, *AC* (1951), IV, 317.

of St. Luke's, Hoxton.[11] Marcus was to remain at St. Paul's until his death. During his tenure he found time to be appointed Professor of Latin at the City of London College for Ladies, compile a *Comparative Vocabulary of the German and English Languages* (1852), and write a text book: *A Latin Grammar; Elementary Latin, A Delectus of Exercises* (1861), which had various iterations, such as *Elementary Latin: A Delectus of Progressive Exercises in Construing and Composition Adapted to the Rules of Syntax* (1862–4). Some years earlier, Marcus had composed a *Jubilate Deo, for the Episcopal Jews Chapel, Bethnal Green* (1819; reprinted 1823) and a *Village Psalmody, A Collection of Plain Psalm Tunes for Use of Country Churches* (1825).

Music was a successful method of attracting people to church. In the New Year of 1866, the Rev. L. Marena, who was based at the Parsonage at St. Paul's, advertised in the *Musical Times and Singing Class Circular* for members of a voluntary surpliced choir.[12] Booth agreed: 'good music will always draw a congregation in the evening.'[13] Yet attracting and keeping parishioners was no doubt patient ongoing work, and as a new curate, who had some musical talent, if even just for singing, Shoults was surely involved in playing his part in these strategies. St. Paul's seemed a good match, and the musical offerings and encouragement by Marcus may have attracted him to the church. At this time, Marcus was about 64; Shoults 27.

As a small parish, St. Paul's faced hard times, even before Shoults arrived. In 1861, Marcus drew attention to the plight of his church by writing to Tait, Bishop of London, stating that St. Paul's had 'at length fallen into such a state of dilapidation as to render it, I fear, almost impossible for me to perform divine service within its walls'.[14] He backed his claim by quoting legal obligations: 'By the Act of Parliament under which the chapel of St. Paul Finsbury was built, it is enacted that "chapels built under the provisions of such Act whether with or without a district for ecclesiastical purposes, shall be repaired by the parishes to which such chapels respectively belong."' He not only pressed those involved to be 'kind enough to make arrangements for stopping any further injury to the fabric and for the putting the church of St. Paul Bunhill Row in a proper state of repair', but also issued an ultimatum: 'May I also beg your early attention to this request for in the event of my discontinuing to perform divine service in the church I shall have to give notice thereof to the ordinary forthwith.'[15] To judge by private responses, Marcus did not have a good reputation.

---

[11] *The Times*, 21 May 1846, 7; see also Crockford's (1879), 641, which gives 'Gross Inc. 420 pounds. Net 300 pounds plus house.'

[12] In *Musical Times and Singing Class Circular*, 12, 275 (1 January 1866), 1.

[13] Booth (1902–1903), 2, 130.

[14] Tait Papers, 121, ff. 39–40, Lewis Marcus to Tait, 4 January 1861. LPL.

[15] Lewis Marcus to Tait, 4 January 1861.

A note in Tait's papers reads: 'Rev. L. Marcus, incumbent of St. Paul's Bunhill Row. Horrible fellow, neglected his parish shamefully. To this hour the parish is suffering from his ill doings. There are heaps of letters complaining of him.'[16] And, perhaps in response to Marcus's begging letter, one James Richardson wrote of the plight of St. Paul's:

> one instance of a church being all but deserted, in the midst of a large district, is proved in the case of St. Paul's Bunhill Row. I think I shall rather exceed, than go beyond the truth, if I state that the last time I was in that church, there were less than 18 people present. Since that time it has been, I believe, closed. The disgraceful state the building was in, broken windows, etc. It had all the look of a deserted place.[17]

Complaints continued to roll in: in November 1863, the Rev. Frederic George Blomfield, rector of St. Andrew Undershaft, London and chaplain to the Bishop of London, wrote of Marcus to the Lord Bishop:

> he does not visit his people but spends his time in writing and editing Latin exercise books. He has difficulties about money and has continually borrowed from his neighbours. His influence in parish is nil. Would it be possible to obtain from any source the stipend for a curate? Perhaps if the inhabitants know that an efficient man was to be curate & virtually incumbent they might contribute his stipend.[18]

Marcus's reputation lingered. In a note dated 19 July 1889, his delinquency is mentioned with the rather cutting: 'To this day the parish is suffering from the memory of Rev. Marcus. The people loathe his memory'.[19]

In December 1863, Tait informed Marcus that 'to justify the enforcement of the Act of Parliament, which requires that, where the duties of a parish are inadequately performed, the Bishop shall appoint a curate. It would seem to me to be your only right course to appoint a curate, who would assist you in bringing the parish into a more hopeful state'.[20] Marcus had problems securing a second curate, and the Rev. Mr Stenner eventually took up the challenge, lasting the normal two years.[21]

---

[16] 'Note' in Tait Papers, 132, ff. 369. LPL.
[17] Tait Papers, 132, ff. 370, James Richardson to Tait, June 1863. LPL.
[18] Tait Papers, 134, ff. 394–7, F. G. Blomfield to Tait, 16 November 1863. LPL.
[19] 'Note' in Tait Papers, 134, ff. 393. LPL.
[20] Tait Papers, 135, ff. 105–6, Tait to Lewis Marcus, 31 December 1863. LPL.
[21] Tait Papers, 135, ff. 107–8, Lewis Marcus to Tait, 30 January 1864; Tait Papers, 136, ff. 241–2, Lewis Marcus to Tait, 1862; 'Note' in Tait Papers, 138, ff. 108. LPL. Stenner may be John Flavell Stenner, a King's College graduate.

Enter Shoults, whose services as a curate must have been appreciated. He stayed at St. Paul's for almost four years, and one can only presume that he saw another side to this 'horrible fellow'. And to give Marcus his due, he stuck with his duties and fought for the church and parish. Architects were called in, quotes for repairs were sought, and a general parish survey was carried out.[22] Marcus received £50 for repairs from the Ecclesiastical Commission, which included making alterations to the pulpit and pews and the removal, cleaning and repair of the organ and pipes. In 6 April 1866, when Shoults was there, Marcus replenished his stock of Bibles and New Testaments, ordering 500 copies from a local stockist J. Palette on Beech Street. Marcus also subscribed to the *Church Times* and the *Church News*, as well as to numerous City newspapers.[23]

In August 1867, during Shoults's curacy, the Church underwent further alterations, much of them under the direction of Robert Jewell Withers (1824–94), a well-known Church architect.[24] The desire of Marcus, and Churchwardens Rawlins and Fry, was to put 'the Church into more Ritual order and making such repairs and improvements as should render the interior, especially the chancel, more suitable for its sacred object'.[25] The huge galleries positioned on three sides, and the lofty pulpit and reading tower were removed. Stalls were placed on the sides of the sanctuary, and gas-standards were installed.[26] The organ was moved down into the choir, and seats were removed to provide space for a chancel. Further funds were required to raise floors, to erect a footpace (predella) for the altar, to place above the altar a five-light window, to clean the church throughout, and to colour the walls. A general appeal for funds was called for.[27]

The services at St. Paul's were ritualistic, and this seemed to suit Shoults. In fact, all the City parishes he was later associated with—St. Michael's, and St. Edmund the King and Martyr—were identified with the Anglo-Catholic revival movement. Although there were often vocal denunciations of ritualism and its associated services and of the Anglo-Catholic revival, there was a tangible groundswell of support. In July 1864, just before Shoults joined St. Paul's, well over ten thousand Anglican clergymen—just under half of the total in England and Ireland—signed the Oxford Declaration (as it was known), declaring that the Church of England was Catholic in maintaining 'without reserve or qualification' the inspiration and divine authority

---

[22] Tait Papers, 135, ff. 101–2, Rev. W. Fry to Tait, 2 December 1863. LPL.
[23] St. Paul's, Bunhill Row, Islington, Records: P76/PAU1/008. LMA.
[24] 'The Catholic Revival', *Church News*, 3 April 1867, 54.
[25] 'S. Paul's, Bunhill Row', *Church News*, 28 August 1867, 386–7.
[26] *Church News*, 8 April 1867, 54.
[27] 'S. Paul's, Bunhill Row', *Church News*, 28 August 1867, 386–7.

of the Bible and in teaching that the punishment of the 'cursed' and the 'life' of the righteous were everlasting.[28]

Shoults began his curacy just in time to be included in the long-awaited survey, carried out in the summer of 1866. It painted an already-recognised gloomy picture, as the Rev. F. G. Blomfield reported to the Lord Bishop: 'My dear Lord, The Church is still not of repair and it's unsatisfactory. Its condition in this respect is given as one reason why the attendance is so small. I am told £200 would put it in decent order.' He then gave attendance figures for Sunday morning, 15 July 1866: 'the Clergyman, Pew Opener, organist, 4 cloisterers, 3 children, 3 adults, and an informant.'[29] Blomfield then reported on Marcus, confirming once more the inherent problems within the parish: 'The incumbent has never recovered from the prejudice created by his former pecuniary embarrassments. He is now free from debt, but the old prejudices have in no way diminished, and he has absolutely no influence in the District. Those who are most friendly to him are of opinion that nothing can be done to place matters on a satisfactory footing so long as he remains. He does not visit at all in the District.'

The survey is significant because it names Shoults (albeit misspelt) as curate and offers the only extant record of his character, abilities, and performance: 'The Curate: Rev. Schultz was appointed last Christmas. He is well spoken of as a conscientious painstaking man desirous of doing his duty, and as visiting the sick & others; but he is not a good Preacher and has not sufficient ability to take the lead. But it is thought he would make a good second. He is paid by the Eccl. Commissioners.' Shoults's effort in keeping a school open is also mentioned, even though it did not meet with success. Aware of the dire situation of the parish, and no doubt conscious of Shoults's strengths and weaknesses, Blomfield suggested that the Ecclesiastical Commissioners hire a second 'senior curate', even as a temporary measure, to assist Marcus.[30]

PROSPECTIVE READING?

While Shoults was at St. Paul's, there is no indication at all of what books he read or acquired. And yet, as a reader, he must have been attracted by contemporary publications and have extracted information from them, if not for personal interests, then certainly for his professional duties and development. A glance at the books from his library published during this period is instructive in that those within the four-year span (1866-9) reveal a diversity and confirm a general pattern that reflects his scholarly interests. Again, they are solid, serious works; there is nothing light or frivolous,

---

[28] Cited in Chadwick (1987), II, 85.
[29] 'St Paul's Survey', Tait Papers, 145, ff. 175–6, Rev. F. G. Blomfield to Tait, 28 July 1866. LPL.
[30] 'St. Paul's Survey', Tait Papers, 145, ff. 175–6, Rev. F. G. Blomfield to Tait, 28 July 1866. LPL.

certainly no novels or short stories. After rejecting titles that carry evidence of being acquired later, such as presentation copies and those that have dates written within, there are eight volumes. While these books—all published between 1866 and 1869—could well have been acquired after this time, their brief description offers another glimpse of the sort of materials that attracted Shoults.

One item he owned was a single bound volume of the *Church News*, a short-lived London-based Anglo-Catholic magazine, with issues from 13 March to 24 December 1867. This volume contains chatty notes, queries, articles on ecclesiastical matters, wide-ranging correspondence, and book reviews. It complemented the *Church Times*, the much longer-living Anglo-Catholic periodical founded in February 1863 by George Josiah Palmer. Headings in the *Church News* include 'The Bishops on Ritualism', 'Anglican Charges and Roman Pastorals', 'The City Churches', and 'The Church and Political Parties'. There are no marks or annotations in it.

The second title is a volume of nine tracts consisting of items such as Thomas Carlyle's *Inaugural Address at Edinburgh, April 2nd, 1866* (1866), *Addresses at the Inauguration of Thomas Hill, D.D., as President of Harvard College, Wednesday, March 4, 1863* (1863), A. J. Scott's *On the Academical Study of a Vernacular Literature: An Inaugural Lecture delivered in University College, London, November 25, 1848* (1849) and B. Waterhouse Hawkins's *The Science of Drawing Simplified; Or, The Elements of Form Demonstrated by Models* (1843). Most of the tracts are clean, with no markings. There are two, however, that carry some provenance details. The first is a copy of George Granville Bradley's *Oratio cancellarii præmio donata*, delivered at the Sheldonian Theatre, Oxford, on 6 June 1845. Bradley (1821–1903) was a schoolteacher who in 1881 became Dean of Westminster and wrote a biography of Dean Stanley, his predecessor. This thin Latin-language item has the name of a previous owner on the flyleaf: John Langford Capper, who was admitted to Merton College, Oxford, in June 1843 and later graduated from Wadham College, Oxford, in 1865. The other tract is John Frederic Daniell's *A Letter on the Study of Natural Philosophy: As a Part of Clerical Education* (1857), which was edited by Charles Anthony Swainson. Daniell (1790–1845) was an English chemist and physicist who, as a teacher and a writer, became known as a social philosopher. This tract is clean, except for an undated manuscript letter tipped-in, written by H. W. Ramsay, Gloucester Lodge, Somerset, to a Mr Beamish.

The third volume is a copy of *De rerum natura*, with a translation by H. A. J. Munro. This English language text of Lucretius's famed work was the second 'revised' edition, published in Cambridge in 1866. The fourth is Ahmad Fāris Shidyāq's *A Practical Grammar of the Arabic Language: With Interlineal Reading Lessons, Dialogues and Vocabulary*, first published in 1856. The Lebanon-born Shidyāq (1805-

87), also known as Fares Chidiac or Faris Al Chidiac, was Professor of Arabic at the University of Malta. He assisted the Cambridge University orientalist Samuel Lee in the Arabic translation of the Bible, published in 1857. Although a clean copy, it adds to the cache of Middle Eastern and Islamic materials that Shoults collected, and indicates, as will be discussed in chapter 13, the attraction that such materials had for him.

In 1833, Henry Edward Manning was a curate in the Church of England. In April 1851, he was received into the Roman Catholic Church and within two months was ordained as a Catholic priest. This move was after his High Church association with Tractarians such as Pusey, Keble, and Newman; the last had already crossed to the Roman Catholic Church. Shoults owned a copy of Manning's *England and Christendom* (1867). In the preface Manning wrote of his desire 'to bring England and Christendom once more a shade nearer in the unity of truth and peace', a sentiment that may have resonated with Shoults.[31] His copy is clean, but extremely battered, indicating heavy use, perhaps by Shoults. He also owned Manning's *The Temporal Mission of the Holy Ghost, or, Reason and Revelation*, published in 1865.

Three volumes of the *Gesta abbatum monasterii Sancti Albani* (The deeds of the abbots of the monastery of St. Alban) form the next possible acquisition in this period. The basis of this mammoth Latin text was Thomas Walsingham's work from the fourteenth-century text, found in the reference MS. Cotton Claudius E. iv. in the British Library. As part of the Rolls Series instigated by Sir John Romilly, it is truly an antiquarian work, one that is dipped into and not normally read from cover to cover. The content of these handsome volumes certainly suited Shoults's interest in antiquarianism, yet the publication beat him. The leaves of the latter half of the first volume and all of the remaining two volumes are unopened. Perhaps all he needed to extract was in the first part, with the rest of the text just not required.

The second edition of Georgina Molyneux's *The Curé d'Ars: a Memoir of Jean-Baptiste-Marie Vianney* (1869) must be considered the only lightweight tome of this cluster—an easy read. The facts of Vianney's life (1786–1859) are recorded: his humble beginnings; his very average intelligence; his luck, especially escaping prolonged army duties; his success in the orphanage for destitute girls that he started; his common-sense confessional advice to all comers; the miracles performed; and his role for some forty years as a quiet 'saintly' parish priest. Shoults's copy is extremely battered, which again suggests heavy use. Vianney's life was one of pious devotion to and love for a Christian God. He was canonised in 1925 by Pope Pius XI.[32]

---

[31] Manning (1867), x.
[32] See St. Jean-Baptiste-Marie Vianney under 'the Curé d'Ars' in *ODCC*, 439.

The last candidate possibly purchased in this period is the third revised edition of James Craigie Robertson's *How Shall We Confirm to the Liturgy of the Church of England?* (1869). Robertson was Canon of Canterbury and Professor of Ecclesiastical History in King's College London. As Shoults was a relatively new curate, and one who was actively involved in ritualistic practices within the Church of England, this book would have offered him an introduction to the history of liturgies. On page 311 there is a stroke down the margin that highlights the passage concerning the priest beginning his new office at the northern part of the west side of church. On page 312, there is a mark alongside the following passage: 'the priest, standing before the table [. . .] and in that position he is to break the bread "before the people" i. e. so that the act of breaking may be seen by the congregation.' These could well have been Shoults's 'note-taking'. In addition, this particular copy has three articles on ritualism pasted at the back. They are taken from newspapers—*The Times*, 25 February 1871 and *The Daily News*, 10 and 27 March 1871—and detail the Herbert v. Purchas case and the Judicial Committee's decision over the actions during service by the Rev. John Purchas. These actions included the administering of wine mixed with water, standing with his back to the people, using wafer bread instead of bread, and of wearing a chasuble during Communion.[33] Such were the issues (and more) that consumed many of the Church of England clergy of the day. In fact, the Rev. Lewis Marcus was a supporter of Purchas, signing a petition in 1871 entitled: 'An Alphabetical List of the Signatures to a Remonstrance Addressed to the Archbishops and Bishops of the Church of England on Occasion of the Report of the Judicial Committee of the Privy Council In Re Herbert *v*. Purchas' (1871).[34] So did Francis Statham, vicar at St. Peter's, and Henry D. Nihill, rector at St. Michael's and Shoult's future employer. As Shoults was intimately involved in ritualistic practices, it could well be that after he read the articles, he cut them out and pasted them into the book.

---

[33] 'Ritualism', *The Times*, 25 February 1871, 4.
[34] *Alphabetical List* (1871).

8 FATHER IGNATIUS AND 'FATHER CYRIL'

On 26 January 1867, the Rev. Lewis Marcus, incumbent at St. Paul's, Hoxton, wrote to Tait, Bishop of London:

> My Lord, For the last few months & upwards Mr Lyne has been in the habit of attending my daily evening service on Saturdays & at times taking a part of the duty. He has also preached one of my special Advent sermons. About a fortnight ago, he expressed a wish to preach once a week in my church for the benefit of his home for invalid & disabled men [. . .] I am an honorable man [. . .] May I beg an early reply from your Lordship in order that I may know how to deal with Mr Lyne after tomorrow. Mr Lyne is a person with whom I differ in toto on many points, but he appears so sincere & earnest that it is almost impossible to resist his entwining himself about one's best feelings.[1]

The Mr Lyne mentioned is Joseph Leycester Lyne (1837–1908), the controversial, enthusiastic revivalist known as 'Father Ignatius', founder of his own Benedictine Order in the Anglican Church in England.[2] (See pl. 7.) While Shoults was working at St. Paul's he met Lyne. Their association started when Shoults was working in the parishes of London and ended in isolated Capel-y-finn, four miles from Llanthony, South Wales. Because Father Ignatius was such an influence on Shoults—indeed a pivotal figure—this chapter focuses on him, his activities in Norfolk and London, some of his associates, and events surrounding the formation of his monastery and convent. Marcus's use of the word 'entwining' is an apt one. Ignatius certainly captivated Shoults—for a time. And for that period, from 1867 to 1874, Shoults was attracted to the charismatic Ignatius, to his particular religiosity, and to his dream of establishing a particular religious order, which was Ignatius's own unique creation. Shoults even followed him to Wales, albeit temporarily. His involvement with this eccentric monk confirms not only his stance towards revivalism in the Church of England, but also his preference for a church with a Catholic pattern to its services and worship.

JOSEPH LEYCESTER LYNE

Lyne was born in London in 1837. After first attending St. Paul's School, London, which he did not enjoy, he moved to Perth, Scotland, in 1856, where he attended

---

[1] Tait Papers, 149, ff. 166–7, Lewis Marcus to Tait, 26 January 1867. LPL.
[2] Canon Bateman cited in Calder-Marshall (1962), 143. Biographical details on Lyne are found in Ignatius (1896), De Bertouch (1904), Attwater (1931), Calder-Marshall (1962), Anson (1964) and (1973), and Allen (2016).

Trinity College, Glenalmond, an Anglican seminary and independent school founded in 1847. In 1860, he was ordained deacon at Wells Cathedral, and for two years he held an honorary curacy at St. Peter's, Plymouth, under the vicar George Rundle Prynne, a pioneer in the Catholic revival.[3] While in Plymouth, Lyne experienced a clear call from God to revive the medieval monastic system in the Church of England.[4] In this endeavour he was supported by Priscilla Lydia Sellon (1821–76), who founded the Church of England Sisterhood of Mercy and helped establish schools and an orphanage in Devonport.[5] Sellon was a disciple of Pusey; he called her 'the restorer after three centuries of the Religious Life in the English Church'.[6]

In January 1862, Lyne travelled to Belgium, where he gathered information on the rules of various religious orders, including the Benedictines. By June, he was back in London, meeting Bryan King (1811–95) and Charles Fuge Lowder (1820–80), respectively rector and priest-in-charge of St George's-in-the-East, Shadwell, London. There was a vacant curacy at St George's-in-the-East, and Lyne took it, under Lowder, founder of the Society of the Holy Cross, a society for Anglo-Catholic priests.[7] By this time, Lyne was 'Brother Joseph' and had adopted his distinctive habit, a rough serge cassock. Even though Lyne's enthusiastic preaching began to attract large crowds, there were rumbles. Lowder asked him to tone down the Benedictine dress, in order to be less provocative. Lyne was uncompromising, falling back on a personal defence: 'I felt called to come before the world as a Monk.'[8]

Lyne's dream of forming his own particular Order continued. By February 1863, he had adopted his patron saint's name: 'Ignatius'. He was helped in his cause by the Rev. George Drury, an Anglo-Catholic who was rector of Claydon, near Ipswich. Drury offered Ignatius the opportunity to install the Order in a large Suffolk rectory. As Peter Anson writes: 'Mr Lyne was thus enabled to found on Shrove Tuesday, 1863, the first Benedictine monastery in communion with Canterbury since the Reformation.'[9] The community lasted there until the end of January 1864.[10]

---

[3] Prynne was a so-called unsung 'hero' of the Catholic Revival, friend of Pusey, and advocate for the teaching and practice of penance in the English Church. See Reed (2017), 48, 263–4.

[4] See Anson (2015). In 1861, Lyne was visiting family (George Lynne) at 25 Wyndham Place, Plymouth in 1861. See 1861: England and Wales census, St. Andrew's, under Joseph Leycester Lyne.

[5] Allen (2016), 6–8.

[6] Dr Pusey cited in Allchin (1958), 127.

[7] The Society of the Holy Cross was formed on 28 February 1855 by Lowder, Charles Maurice Davis, David Nichols, Alfred Poole, Joseph Newton Smith, and Henry Augustus Rawes. See Lowder (1887).

[8] De Bertouch (1904), 133; see also Allen (2016), 19.

[9] Anson (1964), 54.

[10] Allen (2016), 23.

Some of the rituals and schedules carried out at Claydon are worth documenting, because they carry over to what was established by Ignatius later on in London and Wales and because, inevitably, Shoults was exposed to them.[11] The men rose for Matins (from 3 a.m. to dawn) and Lauds (dawn, about 5 a.m.). Ignatius was the only one who had Latin, and in the process of translating, he omitted portions of the text that were too 'Roman'. The Psalms were recited from *The Book of Common Prayer*, and Thomas Helmore and John Mason Neale's seminal *Hymnal Noted* (1851–54) provided translations of most of the hymns for the offices and plain-chant melodies. Ignatius also adopted the *Brevarium monasticum*. The services were all make-do: a hotch-potch of Latin, English, and later Welsh, when the Order was in Capel-y-ffin. After Lauds, the monks returned to bed until they rose for Prime (early morning, approximately 6 a.m.). At 8 a.m. George Drury, wearing vestments, celebrated the Holy Eucharist, using the Prayer Book rite. The midday meal was the main one, although on Sundays and feast days there was breakfast, at 9 a.m. A frugal supper was permitted after Vespers (sunset, approximately 6 p.m.). Nones was recited at 3 p.m. or 4 p.m. Compline was at the end of the day, before retiring, approximately 7 p.m.[12] Apart from worship, there were domestic duties such as housework, teaching in the church school mornings and afternoons, and supervising other activities without violating monastic rules—for example: never running. If there were breaches, penance followed. All the ritualistic accompaniments (gold cloths, black and gold crucifixes, scarlet cassocks, censers, and candles) set locals talking. Questions were asked: 'What are these monks doing?'; 'What monkery?'; and 'A "Catholic Faith" teetering towards the Papacy?'.

Ignatius continued to preach and attract crowds, a phenomenon which upset the established Church. In fact, from the 1860s onwards, it was not just locals that questioned the over-ornamented ritualistic services held: London papers—and some London clergy—raised questions about the idea of the religious life of men, exhibiting a general unease over certain peculiarities.[13] One of those clergy was John Thomas Pelham (1811–94), the Bishop of Norwich, who, with Ignatius in mind, declared that he did not want a monk preaching in a Church of England pulpit. He issued a directive that only the incumbent could preach in the churches of his diocese. Because of this ban, Ignatius preached his sermons (called 'lectures') in the Rectory barn.[14]

While sympathetic to Ignatius's overall cause, Drury ran out of patience, and an excuse was found to eject the community. As a result, Ignatius was forced to look

---

[11] Cited in Walker (1864), specifically, the Claydon experience; see also Allen (2016), 21–35.
[12] Anson (1964), 54–5.
[13] Allchin (1958), 193.
[14] Cited in Allen (2016), 32–3.

elsewhere for quarters. After a money-raising preaching tour, he had raised enough to buy a forty-room house in Norwich that was once part of the site of a pre-Reformation priory.[15] On 30 January 1864, the brothers moved into Elm Hill Priory. This move marked another significant beginning: Lyne became 'Father' Ignatius and started calling himself Abbot.

On being questioned on his authority for restoring Benedictine monasticism in the Church of England, Father Ignatius wrote: 'God put it in my heart to be the one after three hundred years to revive the glorious rule of St Benedict in the English Church.' He continued: 'In our convent the Benedictine rule is more strictly observed than in any Roman house of the order I have ever heard of, and I have heard of many [...] and wherever we go, crowds flock to the standard of the English Church, from dissent, and many from Rome.'[16] It is important to stress again that Ignatius's Benedictinism was a version of his own concoction. He came to Benedictine monasticism well after he had decided that he wished to restore the monastic life, and the rules of such communities differed from those that he established in his communities. For example, elaborate services were not part of Benedictine life, nor the elevation of priests to any point of privilege. And his habit bore no resemblance to anything worn by actual Benedictines.[17] Significantly, while Ignatius was positive about Roman monasticism, he had no sympathy with Popery.[18]

Ignatius was never ordained a priest, and so he could not celebrate the Eucharist, pronounce benedictions, or hear confessions. In 1865, he continued his persistence in obtaining this long-cherished, but unrealised goal.[19] He wrote to Dr Longley, Archbishop of Canterbury, asking to be ordained. Longley laid down conditions, which included the abandonment of both the monastic habit and the name of Benedictine Order. Ignatius disregarded these decrees and thereby lost the Archbishop's support. Ignatius even appealed to Samuel Wilberforce, Dean of Westminster and Bishop of Oxford, for advice and moral support. The Bishop's response was not positive, attacking his dress—'*never* suited to English habits'—and famously wrote: 'You are sacrificing everywhere the great reality for which you have sacrificed yourself to the puerile imitation of a past phase of service which it is just as impossible for you to

---

[15] Preaching up and down the country was the main income stream for Father Ignatius. As Allen states, this strategy was first suggested to Ignatius by Drury. See Allen (2016), 37.
[16] Ignatius from *Churchwork* (Magazine of the Guild of St Alban, 1863), 260, cited in Anson (1964), 57.
[17] *The Rule of Saint Benedict* (1997).
[18] Anson (1964), 53.
[19] In 1898 Ignatius did receive a rather dubious priestly ordination outside the established church from Joseph Rene Vilatte (Mar Timotheos), a French-North American prelate who would bestow orders in return for a fee. See Allen (2016), 323 ff.

revive in England as it would be for you to resuscitate an Egyptian mummy and set it upon the throne of the pharaohs.'[20] In short: *'Cucullus haud facit monachum'* ('The cowl hardly makes the monk').[21] Even Lyne's father, Francis Lyne, commented on his son's total disregard of the warnings from others: '[He] doesn't give up the Monk's dress [. . .] told to, says yes, but once out of sight, he resumes. He who deceives his friends deceives himself.'[22]

Ignatius's Norwich monastery lasted some two years, ending in late 1865. Its demise was due to public scandal, dissension, and loss of control. The last was caused by Ignatius spending much of his time away from Elm Hill, preaching and lecturing to raise the necessary funds for his primary mission: to revive the medieval monastic system in the Church of England. And, as so often happened with him in times of crisis, he suffered another nervous breakdown. Travel was one solution to this situation. He visited Llanthony, Bristol, and, further afield, Marseilles and Rome, where he had an audience with Pope Pius IX.

Back in England, Ignatius received in August 1866 a letter from Dr Pusey, inviting him to Southlands, Chale, on the Isle of Wight. While at Southlands, Ignatius experienced another Damascus-like epiphany that re-orientated his life's mission: a vision of Joseph and the Virgin Mary. With this 'born again' event, he found salvation, and from that point on he did not fear eternal damnation or hell-fire. In recognising the love of Jesus as his eternal Saviour, Ignatius developed the catch-phrase 'Jesus Only'. In that year, he travelled to London and 'preached' to raise much-needed funds. On 30 August, he preached at a crowded service at St. Michael's, Shoreditch, where the Rev. Henry Daniel Nihill was vicar. Nihill (of whom more later) was staunchly Anglo-Catholic, and, during the 1880s, Master of the Society of the Holy Cross. Ignatius's sermon that day, as reported in the *Bury & Norwich Post*, included the notion 'that all who loved Christ were members of the Church— Independents, Roman Catholics, Baptists—for, though he would not deny that differences existed, the unity of all who loved Christ should be the prayer of all Christians.'[23] Ignatius also preached at St. Bartholomew's, Moor Lane, Cripplegate, and his delivery was so impressive that the vicar, the Rev. William Denton, organised employment there as a curate at £120 *per annum*.[24]

With some stability in place, Ignatius set about re-establishing his Order. Indeed, as Arthur Calder-Marshall writes: 'During the week Ignatius was a conspicuous

---

[20] Cited in Anson (1964), 59.
[21] Calder-Marshall (1962), 129.
[22] Archbishop Sir Henry Longley Papers, 4, Francis Lyne to Longley, 22 September 1866. LPL.
[23] *Bury & Norwich Post*, 4 September 1866, cited in Allen (2016), 99–100.
[24] Calder-Marshall (1962), 153.

suburban monk; during the weekends he was a popular evangelical preacher, divested of his habit.'[25] He was a popular speaker, and crowds flocked to hear him at the church. This was all very appealing to Denton, certainly with the pews filling up. He did note, however, the beginnings of the 'cult of Ignatius'. And Ignatius secured more venues: St. Paul's, Bunhill Row (regular Friday evenings), St Ethelburga, Bishopsgate Street, and, after an invitation from the Rev. Pascoe Grenfell Hill, St. Edmund, King and Martyr, Lombard Street (Sunday evenings, and often Friday midday services). In November 1867, Ignatius resigned from St. Batholomew's and transferred to St. Edmund's, albeit temporarily.[26] All the while, he was gathering much-needed money towards financing the further establishment of his mission, and he continued to attract crowds:

> On Thursday in Holy Week, S. Ethelburga's, Bishopsgate-street, was densely crowded, it having been announced that 'Father Ignatius' (the Rev. J.L. Lyne) would preach, his subject being 'Crowned with Thorns'. So great was the rush for admission to the Church, and so many people blocked up the thoroughfare in Bishopsgate-street, opposite the sacred edifice, that a sergeant and three constables of the City police had to be procured to prevent accident and keep the pressure of those without from incommoding the congregation within. The Services were of very High Church order, and the Sermon was attentively listened to.[27]

The years 1867 and 1868 were the peak of Ignatius's preaching career, and it was claimed that 'the year 1867 brought many recruits'.[28] Shoults was one, susceptible at that point in time to what Ignatius offered. He was attracted to the charismatic Ignatius and the message that was promulgated. It was a powerful ensemble of sentiments and beliefs, including the mystical communion, especially the Eucharistic Presence, the observances, and the reverence, especially to the Veneration of the Virgin Mary. There were the austerities and fasting, often occurring in a monastic setting. There was also a perceived 'Romantic' simplicity of the Middle Ages, which was often accompanied by a rejection of the growing materialism that was becoming more evident in the nineteenth century.[29] Ignatius was enthusiastic towards his notion of the revival of the Church of England, and Shoults responded with a like enthusiasm.

---

[25] Calder-Marshall (1962), 151.
[26] De Bertouch (1904), 386.
[27] *Church News*, 24 April 1867, 103.
[28] De Bertouch (1904), 379; see also Calder-Marshall (1962), 156; and Allen (2016), 105.
[29] See Calder-Marshall (1962), 42.

LALEHAM, FELTHAM, AND HUNTER STREET, LONDON

As a measure of his growing popularity and increased finances, Ignatius secured a number of venues around London. In June 1867, he took out a lease of £35 *per annum* on a red brick house at Laleham-on-Thames, not far from Staines.[30] He converted the house into a monastery, where 'the first essential feature was a grille through which conversation between the monks and seculars of both sexes could be carried on without violating enclosure'.[31] Another house, with six small rooms, was leased at 51 Hunter Street, Brunswick Square, Bloomsbury. An outhouse was converted into a small chapel, where candles were burnt. Activities within attracted attention: 'Every Saturday evening at 6 is a special service held at the Benedictine home, 51 Hunter Street, Brunswick Square [. . .] the place was literally crammed with people, many of the men dressed in a hybrid, monkish attire, and not a few of the women as sisters of mercy.'[32] In June 1868, Ignatius realised another dream. Four miles north-east of Laleham was Feltham. It was in this village that he established an Anglican Benedictine convent, Feltham Priory, or Feltham Nunnery, which was dedicated to Saints Mary and Scholastica, the latter the twin sister of St Benedict. The convent was enclosed, and again red curtains and grilles were installed to secure the community within, as well as to facilitate some small communication with those outside. Sister Ella, who had come from the Plymouth Sisters of Mercy, became 'Mother Hilda, O.S.B.', first prioress of this female section of the Benedictine double community. Because Ignatius was not an ordained priest, the Sisters (including Mary Etheldreda, Cecilia, Werburgh, and Mary Agnes) were dependant on the occasional visits of other clergy to hear confession and celebrate Mass.

Both these communities—the monastery and the convent—were strict. By 1868, Feltham alone had 49 'Observances', which had to be read daily, each with its own special penance. Silence was the norm, as was blind obedience: 'Religious of both sexes had to genuflect before speaking to the Superior-General, and kiss the hem of his cowl. Because he firmly believed that he had held the place of Christ in his double-community, Ignatius of Jesus took for granted that he himself was dispensed from keeping any of the forty-nine "Observances", as well as the rigid rules of abstinence and fasting he imposed on his subjects.'[33] He even believed in self-flagellation as beneficial to spiritual life.

---

[30] De Bertouch (1904), 382–3.
[31] Anson (2015), 82.
[32] Excerpt from *Church Association Monthly Intelligence*, 1 November 1868, 195–8, in Tait Papers, 153, ff. 5–6. LPL.
[33] See a full description in Anson (2015), 88.

8 FATHER IGNATIUS & 'FATHER CYRIL'

In 1890, Sister Mary Agnes, formerly Jane Mercy Povey, published her *Nunnery Life in the Church of England,* which was about her life in the Feltham Convent. On one occasion, she wrote:

> I remember also that once he [Ignatius] ordered a young monk, who had come to Feltham with him, to put on a high hat, and then to hop up and down the centre path in the convent garden, so that all the nuns might see him. He did this to test the young monk's humility and obedience, and to see if he was willing to become a fool for Christ's sake. The nuns did see this extraordinary sight, and exclaimed: 'Dear Mother, do look at Brother. Is he not a perfect fool?' Nothing was too idiotic to impose in the name of holy obedience. I have seen, for instance, a brother, instead of kneeling to receive Holy Communion, standing afar off, holding up a black kettle, and at grace, in the refectory, with the muddy street door mat on his head.[34]

Shoults was a priest and not strictly part of the brotherhood. He no doubt escaped such embarrassments.

Among the three properties, Ignatius established a weekly programme. He divided himself between the two communities of monks and nuns and every Friday went to Hunter Street and fulfilled other mission engagements. However, controversy followed him. Crowds openly hostile to the content of his 'sermons' congregated around Laleham Chapel. They disrupted services, shouted out 'No Popery', and threatened violence. Police were often stationed at the Chapel to protect the premises. In September 1868, a riot occurred outside St. Edmund's as a consequence of one of a series of Friday-morning sermons he gave, in which he spoke disparagingly of the merchants and traders of Lombard Street.[35] His outspoken sentiments against the City bankers received wide popular support.[36] His early biographer, Baroness de Bertouch, quotes a crowd figure of 60,000—exaggerated no doubt. With scuffles and stampedes, 'Lombard Street was one swaying, heavy black body'.[37] And during this time, and in another desperate attempt to gain what he so long desired, Ignatius petitioned Bishop Tait for ordination as a priest. Tait refused, writing: 'Let me earnestly beg you to be contented that God has given you powers whereby you are able greatly to influence those whom you address in your pastoral character [. . .] Let me earnestly beg you to

---

[34] Sister Mary Agnes (1890), 59. See also Anson (1964), 423, fn.1, and Anson (1973), 82–93. Note, 'Ritualistic theatricals at Shoreditch', *Punch*, 21 September, 1867, 121.

[35] See Calder-Marshall (1962), especially chapter 14: Riots in Lombard Street: The Excommunication of Sister Gertrude, 164–71.

[36] Palmer (1993), 224.

[37] De Bertouch (1904), 415.

be contented with such means of influence, and to give up the attempt to engraft on the Church of England parts of the Roman system which are disapproved of by the whole of our Church governors.'[38] In fact, Ignatius was eventually suspended by the Bishop from officiating or preaching in the Diocese of London, owing in part to the action taken by Ignatius in respect to Sister Gertrude of the Third Order Sisterhood at the Mission House, Hunter Street. He had had her 'excommunicated'.[39] The lead up to this event was her general dissatisfaction with Ignatius's lack of understanding about her role and his mismanagement of the three communities. As an authoritarian, Ignatius called her in and asked her to resign. She refused to leave. He wrote a letter of excommunication and made her leave Hunter Street, which had been for so long her home. She imparted all this information to Bishop Tait, who denounced Ignatius in *The Times* and introduced the ban. Naively, and petulantly, Ignatius responded by telling Tait that from early youth he had vowed to be a monk. Tait replied: 'I will release you from your vows.' Ignatius fired back: 'My lord, what you ask of me is tantamount to asking me to go to Hell.' Tait's final remark was: 'Then really, Mr Lyne, I don't see what more I can say upon the subject.'[40] Ignatius was left with no priestly elevation and relegated to public halls to carry out his preaching.

HUNTER STREET AND SHOULTS

As mentioned, Shoults was attracted to Ignatius, the ecclesiastical outsider. Fortunately, there is a small piece of evidence that relates to Shoults's involvement with him in this London period. The Rev. Charles Maurice Davies (1828–1910) was a Church of England priest who briefly became a Roman Catholic only to return to the Anglican fold. He was a founding member of the Anglo-Catholic Society of the Holy Cross (along with the above-mentioned Lowder and Nihill), a journalist, an advocate of automatic writing (psychography), and a member of the British National Association of Spiritualists. In the 1860s and 70s, he spent time visiting 'unorthodox' congregations around London. He wrote his visits up in the *Daily Telegraph*, articles that became *Unorthodox London: Or, Phases of Religious Life in the Metropolis* (1875). One weekend Davies visited Ignatius's 'Monastery' at 51 Hunter Street.[41] It was a Saturday, and Davies recorded that the congregation at the Monastery 'scarcely exceed half a hundred'. The front row of the hall was full of some dozen females dressed in a 'quasi-religious costume of dark gown and white cap'. Since they ranged from teens to those

---

[38] Tait's letter, cited in Calder-Marshall (1962), 157.
[39] See Palmer (1993), 200–44 (226).
[40] Calder-Marshall (1962), 169–70.
[41] Davies (1875), particularly 'Father Ignatius "At Home"', 260–6.

aged forty, it is no wonder that Davies felt himself to be 'Jack among the maidens'. In a back drawing-room there was an altar, a large crucifix, and six candles. A procession began and 'the Rev. W.A. Shoults' (so named) is described as wearing a lace skirt and surplice. This is an important reference. It provides documentary evidence of Shoults's involvement with Ignatius and confirms his predilection for ritualistic practices. The procession continued, with Shoults followed by a 'scarlet acolyte with censer'. Ignatius then appeared, sandaled and head shaven. The service conducted by Ignatius included a number of psalms with 'curious interpolations of melody'. Davies then describes an amusing scene that suggests a nervousness or an over-enthusiasm in Shoults:

> Then the resplendent page came and put a blue cloak on Mr Shoults, handing him the censer at the same time. He was not *au fait* at swinging this at all, and once or twice I thought he would have thrown it into the congregation, and hurt some of us. As it was, he nearly poisoned us with the fumes; and there was an interval of coughing for several minutes, until someone reasoned with him, and he desisted.

After a final prayer, there was a light refreshment—a glass of sherry was served. And then followed Ignatius's sermon, which Davies was less impressed with, calling it 'an evident copy of Mr Spurgeon, equalling his eccentricities, but only faintly approaching his power'. On leaving, and on reflection, Davies remarked—in the words of Sam Slick—'*This is coming it rayther too strong*' and ended his piece on the note that Father Ignatius was '*playing at church*'.[42]

In August 1868, the Bishop of London wrote to J.B. Lee mentioning 'the clergyman who is Incumbent' at Laleham, who may have been Shoults.[43] There is firmer evidence of his involvement at the convent at Feltham in the reminiscences by Dame Paulina Bridges, one of the sisters.[44] The Feltham convent was opened on St. Peter's Day, 29 June 1868 and, according to Dame Paulina, Shoults was present the day before, giving help to the Prioress, Mother Hilda. On the day of the opening, a procession was planned by Ignatius, and Shoults was asked to carry the Blessed Sacrament, the consecrated sacramental bread and wine. According to Dame Paulina, 'Father Scholts' was 'the non-resident chaplain' from that day onward. He was, she maintained, 'a constant friend of the community'.[45] He made a lasting impression. In his library there is volume 1 of the Rev. Henry Anstey's *Munimenta academica; Or,*

---

[42] Davies (1875), 265–6. Italics in the original text.
[43] Tait Papers, 152, ff. 223–5, Tait to J. B. Lee, 19 August 1868. LPL.
[44] Cited in Bridges (1866–1936). Personal correspondence with Sister Clare, the Abbey, Curzon Park, Chester, August 2018.
[45] Cited in Bridges (1866–1936).

Documents Illustrative of Academical Life and Studies at Oxford (1868). An inscription in it reads: 'The Revd. W. A. Shoults. M.A. With the respectful love of his grateful and affectionate spiritual children. The Mother & sisters of Convent, Feltham. Christmass 1874.' (See pl. 9.)

CAPEL-Y-FFIN, SOUTH WALES

By the middle of 1869, Ignatius began looking for another venue, and, by September that year, he had secured one: Capel-y-ffin, four miles from Llanthony Priory, in the Valley of Ewyas, South Wales. (See pl. 8.) It was from there that he wanted 'to serve the Lord God apart from this most wicked age, in solitude, self-denial, labour and prayer'.[46] Part of his larger vision was that the Abbey Church be 'from floor to roof a monument of the living, energising belief of English Catholics in the great verity of the Real Presence'.[47] He continued:

> It seems to me that a church built as an act of reparation to the Blessed Sacrament in the Church of England should have tabernacle, altar—nay, floor, walls and roof, of purest gold, adequately to express what English Catholics owed to the outraged Majesty of God in this unhappy land. If we cannot thus lavishly show the intensity and reality of our faith and love, we can at least see that the first monastic church reared as a direct and perpetual act of reparation should be 'exceeding magnifical' in all its fittings; and that in it the worship of God should have restored to its tenfold those splendours and symbolical glories of which an unbelieving world would fain deprive it.[48]

As reported in the *York Herald* in 1878, Ignatius used the Sarum Missal in his services and not the Roman Catholic Missal.[49] He maintained that his establishment was 'the Benedictine Monastery of the Church of England', which he believed obtained the sanction of the Church of England before the time of Pope Gregory, from St. Augustine in 596, from St. Wilfrid in 660, and from Sts. Dunstan (c.946) and Oswald (c.975). He was adamant that he paid no allegiance to Pope or Bishop and that he belonged 'to the one Roman Church, which included Greek and Roman churches'. He did not believe in 'the dogma of the Papal Infallibility, the Immaculate Conception, nor that of Purgatory'.[50]

---

[46] Anson (1964), 61–2.
[47] 'Llanthony Abbey. Father Ignatius and his Benedictines', *York Herald*, 14 January 1871, 4.
[48] 'Llanthony Abbey. Father Ignatius and his Benedictines', *York Herald*, 14 January 1871, 4.
[49] The Use of Sarum, a variation of the Roman rite in use at the cathedral of Salisbury, England. See *ODCC* (1998), 1446.
[50] Cited in *York Herald*, 5 June 1878, 5.

FATHER CYRIL

Shoults ended his curacy at St. Paul's in late 1869 and did not begin his stint at St. Michael's, Mark Street, Shoreditch, until December 1873.[51] He simply disappeared, except for inclusion in the census of 1871. The main reason for this was that at this time he is known as 'Father Cyril', disappearing somewhat behind that honorific. According to Hugh Allen, Ignatius's most recent biographer, Ignatius loved to bestow honorary monastic status (with appropriate 'names in religion') on his outside followers: for example, John Spence, who became 'Brother Cuthbert', Douglas Boutflower ('Bernard'), William Henry Wicking ('Placidus'), and Albert Edward Giddy (another 'Cuthbert').[52] There is no ready answer as to why Shoults was named Cyril. Ignatius may have been thinking of Cyril of Jerusalem (c.313–86), the theologian who wrote on liturgy and who was venerated as a saint, not only by the Roman Catholic Church, but also by the Eastern and Oriental Orthodox Churches. Another candidate is the scholarly Cyril of Alexandria (c.376–444), who not only wrote on Christian controversies, but maintained Christ's union of divine and human nature, a 'God-man'.[53] One possible reason for 'Cyril of Alexandria' may be Ignatius's acknowledgement of Shoults's intellectual make-up and his penchant for the Middle East.[54] Whatever Ignatius's thinking was, Shoults's appellation of 'Cyril' is confirmed by records from the Benedictine nuns at Curzon Park, Chester, the lineal descendants of the Feltham 'rebels', as well as by an inscription in the second volume of Anstey's *Munimenta academica* (1868). The inscription has the exact wording of volume 1 except for the inclusion of 'Father Cyril'. It reads: 'The Revd. Father Cyril M.A. With the respectful love of his grateful and affectionate spiritual children. The Mother & Sisters of Benedictine Convent, Feltham. Christmass 1874.'[55] (See pl. 10.)

Shoults joined Father Ignatius in his effort to establish a monastery in Wales. He was designated 'Monastery Chaplain', thereby fulfilling an important role for Ignatius, who had to rely on a fully-ordained priest to preside over celebration of the

---

[51] 'The Church in the Metropolis', *Daily News*, 13 December 1873, 4.

[52] See Allen (2016), 108–13, and personal correspondence with Hugh Allen, 16 August 2018.

[53] See Cyril of Alexandria's Commentary on John 14. 20 and his *Unity of Christ* in McGuckin (1994) and Keating (2004).

[54] See entries on both Cyrils in *ODCC* (1998), 442–3. Another candidate, but a somewhat unlikely one, is Saint Cyril (826–69), who, along with his brother Methodius (815–85), was to become, through their joint missionary and linguistic work amongst the Slavic people, 'Apostles to the Slavs'. They were venerated as saints with the title 'equal-to-apostles'.

[55] Correspondence with Hugh Allen, 16 August 2018, reference to his book (2016), and correspondence with Sisters Clare and Paula, the Abbey, Curzon Park, Chester, 17 August 2018, in reference to memoirs by Dame Paulina Bridges [Elizabeth Mary Bridges], 25 January 1866 to 24 July 1936. See Bridges (1866–1936).

Eucharist on feast days, hear confessions, and pronounce benediction. This pattern of 'employing' visiting priests by Ignatius had already been established: the Rev. Gerard Moultrie, Vicar of South Leigh, Oxford, and the Rev. Edwin Augustus Hillyard, a pioneer of ritualistic observances in Norwich, had been two previous appointments.[56] It must be stressed that the move by Shoults was not complete. While prepared to take on the role, he decided not to reside at Capel-y-ffin, or Llanthony. He opted to be the non-resident Monastery Chaplain, travelling back and forth from London. This arrangement obviously suited both parties.

SHOULTS AT CAPEL-Y-FFIN

Shoults's first recorded visit to Capel-y-ffin was at Christmas 1870, when he was asked to assist in the celebrations of midnight Mass in the newly-built chapel. It was almost his last visit. According to Baroness de Bertouch, there was much preparation by the resident monks towards his arrival: decorating the chapel and making ready a warm welcome to 'Father Cyril', who faced an 11-mile walk from the railway station at Llanfihangel Crucorney, Monmouthshire, 5 miles north of Abergavenny and 18 miles from Hereford. The weather on the day was terrible. Snow lay upon the mountains, and it was very cold. As night fell, and with no appearance of 'Father Cyril', the notion of not having Mass at midnight became real. The doors were closed and locked; a Vigil was kept, and prayers were offered to the belated traveller. However, at about 11.30, Cyril (Shoults) appeared—cold and tired. He then related his own story, which to the Baroness was not only 'weird and wonderful', but verged on the miraculous.[57]

As Baroness de Bertouch related, Shoults had left London and had arrived at Hereford, where he visited the Cathedral, especially the shrine of St. Thomas Cantelupe [Cantilupe], 'Father of Modern Charity', for whom he felt a very special affection.[58] This delay caused the problem. After arriving at the station, and unaware of the worsening conditions, he pressed on, even though locals issued warnings not to continue. This so-called 'plucky Priest' walked on and, with more snow falling, lost his way, veering off the track onto open hills and past perilous cliffs. Acknowledging

---

[56] Calder-Marshall (1962), 96.
[57] De Bertouch (1904), 454–7.
[58] Perhaps it was Cantilupe's endless charitable works that appealed to Shoults. Thomas de Cantilupe (c. 1218–82), Lord Chancellor of England and Bishop of Hereford, was canonised in 1320 by Pope John XXII. He (St. Thomas De Cantilupe, or St. Thomas of Hereford) appears to have been an exemplary bishop in both spiritual and secular affairs. His charities were large and his private life blameless. He was constantly visiting his diocese, correcting offenders, and discharging other episcopal duties, and he compelled neighbouring landholders to restore estates which rightly belonged to the see of Hereford. Cantilupe has been lauded as the 'Father of Modern Charity'. See 'St. Thomas de Cantilupe', in *ODCC* (1998), 283.

his 'foolhardiness' he even considered retracing his steps. With on-coming tiredness and exposure to the elements, he not only gave himself up for lost, but prayed to God 'commending his spirit to the Merciful'. At that precise moment, a figure of a man stood behind him, surrounded by a bright light. Shoults believed that the man was St. Thomas, whose shrine he had visited that day. The figure then beckoned Shoults to follow him, retracing the steps taken until after a time, and guided by 'supernatural light', Shoults found himself at the door of the Abbey. Baroness de Bartouch claimed that the story was true, not fantastic, and she vouchsafed his word: 'it is the solemn testimony of a man whose reputation certainly lies above the level of an idle or malicious fable-monger.'[59]

Shoults's next recorded visit to Capel-y-ffin was on the Octave of the Assumption, 22 August 1872, when he took charge of the service to bless the foundation stone of the new monastery church. A solemn occasion, this first Llanthony 'Pilgrimage' established an important precedent for future years.[60]

One other account exists that proves that Shoults's association with Ignatius was still strong. On 4 August 1874, while he was the curate at St. Michael's, he went back to Capel-y-ffin. A service at the Monastery was described by a visiting journalist from the Cardiff-based periodical *The Weekly Mail* and reported in *Reynold's Newspaper*.[61] In this 'wilderness' spot, as he termed it, the reporter gave a good overview of the ritualistic practices that Father Ignatius had adopted and that Shoults—'Father Cyril', Monastery Chaplain—also accepted. He wrote:

> The service began with a chant and Latin prayers. The oratory is some eight or nine feet square, the altar blazing with candles, gold tinsel, and highly coloured images of saints and angels. The service was conducted by Father Ignatius and another personage, not a monk, but wearing long black hair, a full beard and moustache, and spectacles. Both were arranged [sic] in gorgeous vestments, which were from time to time changed for others. Now equally resplendent, now black and lowly.

After the ceremony of initiation of a young boy-monk (Dunstan), who was proclaimed by Ignatius a 'virgin bride of Christ', there were final hymns, prayers, and blessings. The service had lasted about two hours.

---

[59] De Bertouch (1904), 457. Losing one's way to New Llanthony Abbey at Capel-y-ffin was not unusual. Even in modern times, forgoing horse and dogcart in favour of a Morris Minor car, the trip along narrow roads to this desolate spot is treacherous. One needs all one's attention to keep on the road, and watch for turns.
[60] Anson (2015), 104.
[61] 'A Visit to Llanthony Monastery', *Reynold's Newspaper*, 16 August 1874, 2.

A shorter account appeared in the *Church Herald* of 21 September, which reported that Ignatius played the organ and that the service was delivered 'partly in Latin', although a portion of it was taken from the Book of Common Prayer, presumably in English. The procession was described thus:

> A monk with the processional crucifix of brass, attended by two others with lighted tapers in tall candlesticks; a novice with incense; the Brethren in order; a Monk with a red silk banner, on which was a rich jewelled gold crown, with palm leaves rising from it, the words 'Jesus Rex' were above and beneath the crown; after the banner followed the officiating Priest in surplice and a most gorgeous cope, the Superior closing the Procession.[62]

The 'officiating' bespectacled bearded priest was Shoults, immediately recognisable from the only extant image of him. (See pl. 1.) This is the last recorded mention of his visit to Capel-y-ffin.

THE SISTERHOOD

As already-mentioned, Shoults was the non-resident Monastery Chaplain, choosing not to reside at Capel-y-ffin full-time. In 1871, one place he was recorded as visiting while in London was 3 Hargrave Road, Islington, his designation: 'Clergyman, Church of England.'[63] This was the home of Frances Lack, a widow whose spinster sister Ann Easley (1822–1908) gave a large sum of money for the purchase of the Llanthony site.[64] Easley was known as 'Sister Winifred', and she had made contact with Ignatius when he was preaching at St. Bartholomew's in 1867.[65] Shoults obviously enjoyed these connections, and, from an account given, this 'college intellectual', as he was termed, introduced many other clergymen and useful friends to the Abbey.[66] One was Miss Charlotte Boyd (1837–1906), who would later be a keen financial supporter of the convent at Feltham. A friend of John Mason Neale, Boyd was involved not only in restoration projects such as that of Glastonbury Abbey through the trust of the Society of St. John the Evangelist, but also helped run an orphanage in Kilburn.[67]

---

[62] Cited in Allen (2016), 162.

[63] 1871: England census, Islington.

[64] Although the notes by Mrs Ann Winifred Caton on her great aunt Ann Easley (Winifred) mention £2000 given towards the purchase of the Capel-y-ffin site, Hugh Allen's thoughts are that it was only £1000. Apparently, the whole family at Hargrave Park were fascinated by Ignatius. Allen (2016), 116; see also Calder-Marshall (1962), 183. In reality some of the funds also came from Douglas 'Bernard' Boutflower, a naval chaplain. See Anson (2015), 91.

[65] Cited in Allen (2016), 210.

[66] Bridges (1866–1936).

[67] See Anson (2015), 124. In April 1793, Charlotte Boyd became the owner of Malling Abbey, which was

In 1874, Shoults was working at St. Michael's and no doubt busy undertaking parish duties. He did, as revealed by the inscriptions in Anstey's book quoted above, visit the convent at Feltham. The community of Sisters may have appealed to a softer side of Shoults, and the atmosphere at the convent was certainly more relaxed and less authoritarian than that at Capel-y-ffin. In her memoir, *Nunnery Life in the Church of England*, Sister Mary Agnes documented some of the chaos caused by Ignatius:

> Father Ignatius did not have very much to do with us there. The Mother, I think, used to let him know that she did not consider it a man's place to govern a number of women so entirely as he wished to do. Besides, he sometimes gave orders which she thought very indiscreet, from which great scandal might arise; and, being somewhat older than Father Ignatius, she took the liberty of representing to him, rather strongly, her views about his orders and doings. At times he would suddenly give orders from the so-called 'altar', where of course no one could well remonstrate, and which would put the household arrangements out for the whole day, though he seemed to be in a great state of consternation when matters did not go forward smoothly in consequence of his orders. Sometimes, before breakfast, he would order that no one, not even the reverend Mother, should speak for a whole day, thus causing the utmost confusion, especially amongst the servants in the kitchen, who were included in the eccentric command. And yet if his own dinner was not properly cooked and served in time, he would show great displeasure.[68]

Shoults obviously enjoyed the company of women, as witnessed by his association with Frances Lack, Ann Easley, and Charlotte Boyd. Archive records at the convent verify his presence and some of his activities there: 'Father Shoults was Chaplain to the Community soon after our beginning' and they, the Sisters, 'looked to him for their spiritual needs'. He was regarded 'far more stable than Bro. Ignatius', and in that capacity he 'guided the community spiritually', especially in delivering 'the sacraments'.[69] As an extension to his priestly duties, Shoults utilised his language skills and applied them to translations. As reported, he 'supervised and superintended the translation of the Latin Breviary' for use in the convent. He also gave advice on methods of worship, 'beginning with the Commons and going to the Propers afterwards'.[70] The Rev. Arthur

---

vested in the English Abbey Restoration Trust. The Abbey became the home for Mother Hilda after the split with Father Ignatius. Boyd eventually went over to the Roman Catholic Church. See also Anson (1964), 425.

[68] Sister Mary Agnes (1890), Chapter VII, Life at Feltham Convent, 57–8; see also Allen (2016), 203.
[69] Sister Clare, Curzon Park, Chester. Personal correspondence, 23 June 2019.
[70] Bridges (1866–1936). The Commons (or ordinary) are those elements of Christian worship that remain the same, for example: the Lord's Prayer, the offering. The Propers are those that change daily or weekly, for

Murray Dale was the son of the Rev. Thomas Pelham Dale, the ritualist who would be jailed in 1880 for wearing vestments and persisting in ceremonial services regarded as illegal by the Church of England. The younger Dale was Chaplain to the nuns at Feltham after Shoults. He gave lectures to the nuns on scripture, ecclesiastical history, and philosophy. Shoults also gave talks, and he must have initiated these programmes of instruction, a sure way of sharpening his preaching skills and his intellectual interests.[71] Father Ignatius did not bide a bookishness, maintaining that 'the only books a monk needed to study were the Bible and the Holy Rule, and that if he knew those well he required nothing else'.[72] Shoults was a book collector who read and used books frequently. Without doubt, he would have relished using his own books without restriction, especially when constructing the talks. Indeed, for that purpose such books were vital.

One other important thing that Shoults did was to introduce his friends to the convent community, many of whom offered further support.[73] Boyd was certainly one such supporter. Another was the Rev. G. Henry Worth, an Oxford Corpus Christi student who, in 1882, became the second curate at the ritualistic St. Agnes in Kennington Park.[74] In that year—further proof of Shoults's ongoing commitment to the convent—he introduced Worth to the Sisters. Worth became a strong advocate for the Sisterhood.[75]

In 1878, a split occurred within the Feltham community that Shoults was surely aware of. There is no record of his thoughts on this event except for the fact that he continued to support the 'Feltham' group. The schism was based on growing tensions between Ignatius and Mother Hilda concerning the former's demand for blind obedience. It ended bluntly with Ignatius stating to Hilda: 'You no longer belong to the order of the Monk Ignatius of Llanthony in the nineteenth century.'[76] Sister Mary Agnes was one of three that followed Ignatius, obviously not deterred by his unconditional demands.[77] These followers moved to Slapton, Devon, and later, in September 1881, to Llanthony. The 'rebel' faction under Mother Hilda remained at Feltham until the convent lease expired in 1889. With the assistance of the Revs.

---

example: reading different lessons, singing varied hymns, hearing a different sermon. See White (1990), 76.

[71] Sister Clare, Curzon Park, Chester. Personal correspondence, 23 June 2019.

[72] From a later 'Reminiscences of Llanthony' by Dom Cyprian Alston, cited in Anson (2015), 125.

[73] Sister Clare, Curzon Park, Chester. Personal correspondence, 23 June 2019.

[74] Cited in Anson (2015), 124, 132, 216. Worth was received into the Roman Catholic Church in 1895. He would later become a lay-oblate of Erdington Abbey and a member of the Vatican Commission on Plainchant, set up by Pius X.

[75] Sister Clare, Curzon Park, Chester. Personal correspondence, 3 September 2018.

[76] Cited in Allen (2016), 207.

[77] Sister Mary Agnes (1890), 59–60.

Arthur M. Dale, Reginald Camm, and Shoults's friend Henry Worth, they eventually moved to Twickenham and then to a pre-Reformation Abbey at West Malling, Kent.

While Shoults kept his association with the Sisters, his relationship with Ignatius diminished gradually. In 1873, he made a conscious decision to go back into a more formal position in the Church of England. He may also have been affected by events swirling around Ignatius, notably the Todd Case of 1873, the drawn-out Drury trial of 1876, and his personal preference for the Sisters at the Feltham convent.[78]

Father Ignatius died at Camberley on 16 October 1908, aged 71. Over his long career, he was called 'the Don Quixote of the Catholic Revival' and perceived as a madman.[79] Many were embarrassed by his eccentric activities, his persistent 'Monkery'.[80] Tait, Bishop of London, called him a 'wrong-headed donkey',[81] while Henry J.W. Shillingfleet (dubbed 'Clement' by Ignatius) was more damning in his criticism: 'the object Lyne aims at may be a good one, yet he is thoroughly unscrupulous as well as ill-judged in the means he employs. I have very strong doubts too as to the sincerity of his motives [...] Notoriety is what he has been aiming at & he has succeeded.'[82] He did, however, get some good press: 'Every monk, friar and clerk regular in England today owes gratitude to him for all he did to familiarise the people of England and Wales with the forgotten, misjudged or vilified idea of monasticism [...] He gave England the vision of a good, loving man who was nevertheless a monk. The path of all monks has been easier for the life and sacrifice of Ignatius.'[83] He was part of a general trend to improve the standing of the Anglican Church of England in England, a revitalisation which, in the eyes of Tractarians, Post-Tractarians (that is, Subtractarians), and other churchmen, was much needed. Although not living long enough to judge Ignatius's future reputation, Shoults may have looked kindly on the interlude when he was associated with him. He may also have acknowledged some of the achievements of his former mentor.

---

[78] Richard Todd. This was known as the Case of the Kidnapped Ward of Chancery. See Calder-Marshall (1962), 209–11; The Lyne v. Drury case concerned the Elm Hill monastery. See Calder-Marshall (1962), 172–182.
[79] Cited in Palmer (1993), 240.
[80] See Reed (2017), 13.
[81] Tait Papers, 14, ff. 156–7, Tait to Fisher, 14 December 1867. LPL.
[82] Tait Papers, 135, ff. 301–21, Henry J.W. Shillingfleet to an unknown correspondent, 14 December 1863. LPL.
[83] Donald Attwater, cited in Palmer (1993), 242.

9 ST. MICHAEL'S, SHOREDITCH, 1873–75

Father Ignatius was once recorded as saying: 'Our wish is to dwell apart from the world.'[1] Shoults was not of that disposition, having made the choice to be non-resident Monastery Chaplain at Capel-y-ffin and Feltham. Thus he not only fulfilled 'ecclesiastical' obligations to Ignatius, but was able to enjoy communal aspects of living in London. Although bookish, and perhaps by nature quiet, he was still a social creature. It was at this time that he made a conscious decision to again undertake ministry within formal church structures. He also faced changing ambitions and interests that were further catalysts for this decision. At this time too, his enthusiasm for Ignatius was obviously waning, no doubt disenchanted by the controversies that tended to follow the enthusiastic monk.[2]

Sometime before December 1873, Shoults approached the vicar of St. Michael's, Mark Street, Shoreditch, expressing interest in a parish vacancy. Around 13 December 1873, the Bishop of London installed him in the curacy of St. Michael's on the nomination of the vicar, the Rev. Henry David Nihill (1834–1913).[3]

HENRY DAVID NIHILL

As already noted, Nihill had been another of Ignatius's supporters for a number of years before the move to Capel-y-ffin, and, according to Francis Lyne, Ignatius's father, he had been dubbed 'Brother Basil'.[4] Nihill had been educated at Jesus College, Oxford, admitted there in 1852 aged 18. After obtaining a B.A. in 1857, he secured various curacies, including St. Alban's, Cheetwood, Manchester, between 1861 and 1867.[5] In August 1865, while assistant curate, he officiated in an Ignatius-driven procession in front of the Manchester Corn Office, verifying that at least by that date he not only knew Ignatius, but also had gravitated towards ritualistic practices. Indeed, it was on this occasion that Nihill was deemed one of the 'branch' leaders of Ignatius's Order.[6] While at St. Alban's, Nihill initiated an unauthorised ceremonial in one of his services (a sung Eucharist at which vestments were worn), which caused ructions

---

[1] 'A Visit to Llanthony Monastery', *Reynold's Newspaper*, 16 August 1874, 2. This statement by Ignatius is somewhat ironic, considering his frequent trips away from the monastery to raise money for his ventures, the travelling being a most un-Benedictine trait.
[2] 'Father Ignatius and the Llanthany. Contempt at Court', *Birmingham Daily Post*, 23 July 1873, 5.
[3] 'The Church in the Metropolis', *Daily News*, 13 December 1873, 4.
[4] Archbishop Sir Henry Longley Papers, 4, Francis Lyne to Longley, 22 September 1866. LPL.
[5] See *Crockford's* (1884) and (1888) for the Rev. Henry David Nihill.
[6] For full details on the procession, see Allen (2016), 64.

with his Bishop. This disagreement necessitated a move to London, where he secured the role of curate at St. Michael's under the Rev. Charles Lyford, who was a member of the Society of the Holy Cross. After Lyford's death, Nihill became the incumbent. When Nihill was installed on 30 August 1866, Father Ignatius was present, preaching to a large crowd during Evensong.[7]

Nihill promoted his own ritualistic practices. He was an ardent Anglo-Catholic, and, as a member of the Society of the Holy Cross, he managed to establish the parish rooms at St. Michael's as a base for the Society. On one occasion, on 26 October 1866, he officiated at 'Benedictine Vespers' in a gathering at Store Street Music Hall, Bloomsbury, and set up a 'gorgeously decorated' altar. The Hall was replete with ceremonial accoutrements: a high altar, white and red roses, some 60 to 70 wax candles, a crucifix, incense spilling out during the procession, a dozen altar boys in red and white, and embroidered vestments in white and gold.[8] He told the congregation that they would soon have a chapel of their own to worship in.[9] He also expressed the hope that he 'would soon find a way to live with his own monks all together in a monastery' and thereby 'encourage the religious life of the order'. Reality intervened, however, and he had to acknowledge the 'pressing necessities' of his own parish work.[10] Nihill published many sermons, of which Shoults owned one: *The Rights of English Churchmen. A Sermon Preached before the Church of England Working Men's Society, at their First Anniversary* (1870).[11]

Sometime after the October 1866 gathering, Nihill was summoned to an interview with the Bishop of London. It was suggested to him that all connections with Ignatius's Benedictine Order be discontinued. Sensibly, he responded positively: 'My Lord, Your very kind letter was more than I deserved, and I heartily thank you for it. I have at once withdrawn from the Order of S. Benedict altogether, and will try to confine myself entirely to parochial work.'[12] Nihill became a 'hard-working curate'.[13] Perhaps Shoults received the same episcopal advice.

Like the Cambridge Camden Society's John Mason Neale, Nihill wanted to establish a Sisterhood. In 1866, when at St. Michael's, he enlisted the 'sisters' from St. Alban's and formed his much-desired Community of St. Mary at the Cross, or

---

[7] See Allen (2016), 99.
[8] Tait Papers, 145, ff. 286–93, H.D. Nihill, 1866. LPL.
[9] Cited in Allen (2016), 101–2.
[10] Cited in Allen (2016), fn. 190, 102.
[11] Nihill (1870). Shoults Eb 1880 N.
[12] Tait Papers, 145, ff. 302–3, H. D. Nihill, to Lord Bishop, 6 November 1866. LPL.
[13] *Oswestry Advertiser*, 17 November 1866, 8.

the Sisters of the Poor, as it was known as.[14] The first Superior appointed was Miss Hannah Skinner, who became Sister Monica.[15] In 1873, the year that Shoults began work at St. Michael's, the community had secured land at Edgeware through the Ecclesiastical Commissioners, and the building, designed by James Brooks (1825–1901), the English Gothic Revival architect, was ready for occupation four years later, in 1877.[16] The services that Nihill's community adopted included the recitation of the Day Hours in Latin, with the *Breviarium monasticon* used for this purpose. Matins and Lauds were said in English, and the Lessons at Matins specifically translated and written out from a book that rested on a lectern. Nihill may have asked Shoults to undertake the translations needed, repeating what he had done at Feltham.

ST. MICHAEL'S CHURCH

St. Michael's Church was also designed by James Brooks.[17] (See pl. 11.) Completed in 1865, the church was designed for ritualistic ceremonial worship. A day before its consecration—on 25 August 1865—Tait, the Bishop of London, visited the church and took exception to 'four handsome bouquets on the altar' and the richly embroidered vestments worn by the clergy. As reported in *Punch* four months later, such was Tait's power and prestige that the flowers were removed and the clergy forced to take off their coloured stoles.[18] Tait also took exception to a rough sketch in charcoal of the Crucifixion, with figures of St. Mary and St. John, tucked behind the communion table. It was also removed. In response, the Rev. Charles Lyford published in the *Church Times* the very next day a request for a curate, with the accompanying note: 'St. Michael and All Angels, Shoreditch.—This Church was consecrated by the Bishop of London on Thursday last. We reserve our report until next week, merely mentioning that the Right Rev. Prelate displayed his iconoclastic propensities in reference to ornaments both of the Church and the Clergy, and altogether behaved both before

---

[14] Nihill (1887). In 1887, Nihill wrote about the Sisterhood: *The Sisters of the Poor and their Work* (1887).

[15] In January 1887, Nihill appeared before the Court of Chancery in a case which still has legal significance: Allcard v. Skinner. In 1871, three days after becoming a member of the Sisterhood Miss Allcard bequeathed all property, including railway stock, to Miss Skinner (Sister Monica). In 1879, after leaving the Sisterhood, she claimed the money back. Nihill, who was described as Vicar of Shoreditch and 'spiritual adviser of the Convent of St. Mary of the Cross', oversaw the community's finances, which included any donations and bequests. He claimed he received no stipend for his services. No judgement was pronounced on this case of undue influence, but it was unsettling for Nihill. See Burrows (2007). Incidentally, Miss Allcard greatly admired the preaching of the Rev. H.D. Nihill.

[16] Anson (1964), 400–2.

[17] Brooks also designed four churches in Haggerston: St. Saviour's, St. Mary's, St. Chad's, and St. Columba's. St. Michael's is now (2018) home of the London Architectural Salvage and Supply Company Limited ('Lassco').

[18] 'Flinching at St. Michael's, Shoreditch', *Punch*, 16 December 1865, 109; see also Anson (1964), 398–400.

and during the service with an amount of intolerance and irreverence which we were shocked to witness.'[19] On 21 September 1867, when Nihill was the incumbent, an item headed 'Ritualistic Theatricals in Shoreditch' appeared in *Punch*.[20] As reported, the 'Romanising' that day began with a procession and a processional hymn. The altar was festooned with fifty wax candles, two large candelabra, rows of lighted tapers, and flowers, their brilliance likened to 'the Horticultural Gardens'. The occasion was a sermon preached by Dr Gray, Bishop of Cape Town. There were cross bearers, choristers, clergymen—all dressed in red, gold, and other coloured vestments. The Bishop was in full episcopal robes; a deacon, shouldering a large white flag with a cross, ended the processional file. One attendant was overheard to say: 'Nothing couldn't be no finer than Nihill.' And after the sermon, everyone 'crossed themselves à la Romaine'. To top off the proceedings, Father Ignatius appeared with 'above two hundred members of his congregation'. His appearance, no doubt during one of his many fund-raising missions, was to offer thanks and gratitude to Gray. The whole congregation then begged the Bishop's blessing, going down upon their knees. As the unknown reporter for *Punch* wrote: 'Roman Catholics were never better acted.'

There was a general fear of 'Popery'. In fact, during Shoults's tenure at St. Michael's, Parliament passed the Public Worship Regulation Act (1874; in force 1875), which allowed any three parish residents to bring a clergyman before a judge on charges of unlawful ceremony. Those judged guilty could appeal to a Judicial Committee of the Privy Council, but, as this was a secular body, it was often ignored by hardened ritualists. It was to St. Michael's, this hotbed of ritualism, that Shoults went, his appointment lasting two years.[21]

The parish contained over 10,000 people, all housed within a square mile.[22] The area was vividly described about the 1860s and 1870s:

> Here lived the poor—not merely the respectable artisans, but the countless broken outcasts of the industrial system. These were pallid and gin-sodden; their ragged reeking clothes, which had passed through many phases of society in their long declining history, were so vile that they left a stain wherever they rested: they stank. They herded together in bug-ridden lodging houses and rotting tenements; they slept under railway arches. They were the 'submerged

---

[19] Cited in *Punch*, 16 December 1865, 109.
[20] 'Ritualistic Theatricals at Shoreditch', *Punch*, 21 September 1867, 121; see also Anson (1964), 398–9, fn 1.
[21] Other ritualistic hotspots included St. Alban's, Holborn, St. Saviour's, Hoxton, St. Peter's, London Docks, St. Alphege's, Southwark, and four churches in Haggleston. The Rev A.H. Mackonochie was at the first mentioned; the Rev. Charles Lowder at the third. See Anson (1964), 399–400.
[22] Nihill (1887), 8.

tenth', the skeleton at the rich Victorian feast, the squalid writings on the whitened wall.[23]

'Bug-ridden' was right. In 1866, there was an outbreak of cholera. In 1871, smallpox ravaged the area, which Nihill almost succumbed to.[24] St. Michael's was Shoults's Walworth and Bunhill Row experiences revisited, including the chaos surrounding the rebuilding of a church. It was a familiar scenario, back into the thick of a slum parish and all its problems. As a curate, he was back among parishioners offering assistance and help, and as was his mission, back trying to convert as many of the unchurched as possible.[25] It was tough, selfless work, and doomed to failure.[26] But at least he had support from Nihill, a sympathetic ritualist. There is no indication of his stipend, but presumably it was near £100 *per annum*.

BACHELOR OF DIVINITY

The move back into a more formal career path within the established Church was important for Shoults on an intellectual level. Part of the decision may have been the result of a growing aspiration to be more than just a curate. In April 1874, he enrolled for the degree of Bachelor of Divinity at Cambridge. One person he was in touch with at St. John's College was his old mathematics tutor, Dr Stephen Parkinson, who readmitted him.[27] Registered at a live-in curacy at 'S Michael's Vicarage, Mark Street, Finsbury', he no doubt had Nihill's support to undertake the necessary study.[28] He may also have received encouragement from Eliza Katharine Ogle, his future wife, with whom by this time he was certainly acquainted.

The degree was regarded as a high-status postgraduate one, requiring evidence of thorough scholarship. In 1841, George Peacock, the Dean of Ely, published his *Observations on the Statutes of the University of Cambridge*. In it, he complained that 'At least one-half the students in the university are designed for the church, and no provision (the lectures of the Norrisian professor alone excepted) is made for their professional education; this is a deficiency in our academical system'.[29] The B.D., like other higher degrees, negated this claim somewhat. It was certainly meant for those who were destined for the Church. A limited number took this degree: when Shoults received his, in June 1874, he was the only candidate listed.

---

[23] Taine (1872), 165; see also Anson (1964), 399.
[24] Cited in Nihill (1887), 45.
[25] See Orens (2003), 25.
[26] Reed (2017), especially chapter VIII 'Ritualism and the Urban Poor', 148–72.
[27] SJAR/1/3/1/2 Parkinson, 2/3, 4. St. John's College Archives.
[28] Parkinson/3/2/1 Address Book. St. John's College Archives.
[29] Searby (2004), 265.

Rules regarding the degree stipulated that there had to be a span of 14 years since matriculation before a candidate could enrol. Before changes were introduced in the mid-1850s, candidates were obliged to attend lectures in theology and Hebrew, to preach two sermons (one in English; the other in Latin) in the University church of Great St. Mary's, and to keep one divinity act and two opponencies (academic disputes). Before admission, the candidate had to acknowledge the Oath of Allegiance and subscribe to the Thirty-nine Articles. On admission, the 'sons', as they were called, were presented to the Vice Chancellor, who gave each of them a copy of the Greek Testament.[30] Another sermon had to be delivered at St. Paul's Cross within a year.[31] At this time, candidates had to be residents in the University.

By the mid-nineteenth century, modifications had begun to the curriculum, even though portions of the old degree were retained.[32] In 1850, J.A. Jeremie, the Regius Professor of Divinity, recognised the importance of these higher degrees. In his reply to the Graham Commissioners' enquiry about the exercises in Divinity, he wrote, 'I am inclined to think that, unless the period required for the degree of B.D. and D.D. be abridged, it is not desirable to change, to any considerable extent, the nature of the Exercises which being in conformity with long established usage, appear to be well adapted to the age and position of the candidates'.[33] The Commissioners accepted this stand. At that stage, the degrees still required good theological knowledge and a good command of Latin. In 1858, the Senate at Cambridge University made certain changes: the candidate was required to keep one Act, the Regius Professor of Divinity was charged with assigning times when exercises were to be carried out and to appoint supervisors, and, significantly, there was greater leniency towards the non-residency clause. The disputations remained, with the candidate reading a thesis, composed in Latin, on some approved subject. Arguments or objections to it followed in English, and there was mention of working the thesis into good copy for publication. Public notice of the defence was given well ahead of the time so as to allow any interested parties to attend.[34] Critical to this process was the judgement of the Regius Professor of Divinity, who acted as moderator. To some the intellectual test remained—as D.A. Winstanley wrote: 'a bachelor of divinity was not too easily won.'[35] There is no identifiable presentation copy of a Greek Testament in the Shoults Collection, and one suspects that, as with some of the lectures, this was one ritual that went by the way.

---

[30] Cited in Winstanley (1935), 78.
[31] Winstanley (1935), 64; see also Searby (2004), 262–3.
[32] Searby (2004), 262; see also Potts (1863), II, 96–7.
[33] Cited in Searby (2004), 263.
[34] *Cambridge University Calendar* (1860), 28–9.
[35] Winstanley (1935), 68.

The mention of publication above is particularly interesting.[36] The Trinity College-trained Fenton John Anthony Hort (1828–92) was a Hulsean Lecturer and Lady Margaret Professor of Divinity.[37] Called the 'greatest English theologian of the century', he lectured to theological students at Emmanuel College in subjects such as Origen, the Epistle of St. James, and the Apocalypse.[38] In his *Life and Letters*, edited by his son Arthur Fenton Hort, Hort mentions 'finishing for the press my dissertation for the B.D. degree which I took in the spring, …the essay is "on μονογενὴς θεός ['only-begotten God'] in Scripture and tradition" and has been greatly enlarged and laden with appended notes'.[39] The rules did not state that the B.D. thesis had to be published and so it must have been an action driven by the candidate, dependent on personal inclination and finances. While no physical copy of Hort's B.D. thesis, 'On the "Constantinople" Creed' exists, it is listed in a document entitled 'B.D. dissertations 1-22' in the Cambridge University Library, which spans the years 1873 to 1981.[40] It is second on the list, dated 16 December 1875, and has the format of '8°' (octavo) beside it. Hort also enrolled in a Doctor of Divinity degree, and his thesis topic was *On the "Constantinopolitan" Creed and other Eastern Creeds of the Fourth Century*, an expanded version of his B.D. thesis. It is present in the Cambridge University Library. Another published example is the Rev. J. Rawson Lumby's *The History of the Creeds. 1. Ante-Nicene, 2. Nicene and Constantinopolitan, 3. The Apostolic Creed*, which was submitted for his B.D. degree in 1873.[41] This 185-page work is listed as No.1 in the above list.

Shoults's topic of study for his B.D. is not known, and his name is missing from the above 'B.D. dissertations 1-22' list. There is also no public record of a *viva voce*. Dr Stephen Parkinson kept a register for 1874, and there are a several financial transactions attached to Shoults's name. He was charged a reading fee of 3s, and then on 11 April, the word 'caution' appears alongside a charge of £5, which must have been the initial deposit made. On 3 July, he was charged a further 16s for some unknown service. On 10 December 1874, he received a cheque for the sum of £4 1s, which was surely the balance of the original £5 paid.[42] By the time he received this small windfall, he had passed his 'Exercise'. Overall, the duration of his Bachelor of Divinity degree was

---

[36] See Thompson (2008).
[37] See entry on Hort in AC (1947), III, 448.
[38] According to Sanday (1897), 95–117 (97).
[39] Hort to the Rev. John Ellerton, 1 August 1875, in Hort (1896), II, 210. Thanks to Rowan Gibbs, Wellington, and Clemens Gresser, Librarian, Divinity Library, University of Cambridge, for the clarification of the Greek phrase 'Only-begotten God' (Gospel of John 1. 18) and the more common 'Only-begotten son'.
[40] 'Bachelor of Divinity Class Catalogue', Cambridge University Library.
[41] B.D. Dissertation No.1, in 'Bachelor of Divinity Class Catalogue', Cambridge University Library.
[42] SJAR/1/3/1/2 Parkinson, 2/3, 4. St. John's College Archives.

exceedingly short – just three months. On 4 June 1874, in front of a full congregation, which included the Vice Chancellor (Master of Peterhouse), Shoults had the degree conferred on him.[43]

1874

During the two years of 1874 and 1875, Shoults acquired 22 publications. Eighteen were purchases, and they are important on two levels. Firstly, they confirm his predilection for serious tomes. Secondly, some of them offer a possible hint of what the topic was for his B.D. degree—for example, centring on the antiquities of Greece through its ancient literature and histories. However, considering the nature of the degree, this area of research is improbable. As the topic of 'Creeds' dominates the Cambridge list, he may have undertaken research into something similar. The remaining four books were presentation copies, which are special in their own right.

On 3 March 1874, he picked up a copy of a second edition of *Clavis Homerica*, a dictionary that gives the names of things in Homer's *Iliad*. Published in London in 1638, it was compiled by Anthony Robert. On the title page of this closely-cropped duodecimo edition is the inscription of a previous owner: 'John Grant'. It is a clean copy. On the front endpaper is the inscription: 'W. A. Shoults M.A. March 3 1874.'

Four days later, he bought another three books: two duodecimos, and a sturdy octavo breviary. The first duodecimo is an edition of Thomas a Kempis's *De imitatione Christi libri quatuor*, published in Paris by B.P. Valleyre in 1762. This work is a classic, a much-reprinted Christian devotional text. The second is an Elzevir edition of Philipp Clüver's *Introductionis in universam geographiam*, published in Leiden in 1627. Clüver (1580–1622), a librarian and antiquary, is best known as a historical geographer. This was his most highly regarded work, the first comprehensive textbook on modern geography. The breviary that Shoults obtained is *Specimen breviarii monastici ad mentem regulae S. Patris Benedicti. pars prima*, published by Haener in Nancy, France, in 1771. Bound in red calf, it has the name 'Garnier' in gilt on the front and back covers. It was once in a Benedictine monastery: 'Des Benedictinis de Montangis', perhaps Montargis, South of Paris. All three books have Shoults's inscription: 'W. A. Shoults, M.A. March 7 1874.'

On 25 March he acquired a further four volumes. Three of them were part of John Potter's *Archaeologiae Graecae; or, The Antiquities of Greece*, published at Oxford between 1697 and 1699. These volumes (volume 2 of the 1697 printing and parts 5 and 6 of 1699) contain superb engravings of ships, fortifications, and formation marching; the text focuses on the military affairs of Greece and miscellaneous customs of that

---

[43] 'University Intelligence', *Daily News*, 5 June 1874, 6.

country. The volumes carry the ownership details of 'C. Chevallier, 1808', and 'Ric. Warren Coll. Jes. Cant.'. Chevalier may have been the Rev. Clement Chevallier (1765–1830), related to the Chevallier family of Aspen Hall, Suffolk. The latter was either Dr Richard Warren, archdeacon of Suffolk, rector of Cavendish, and editor of the Greek commentary of *Hierocles*, or his physician-son Dr. Richard Warren (1731–97), both of Jesus College. Parts 5 and 6 contain numerous pencil annotations, but they are not by Shoults. He has inscribed in all three volumes: 'W. A. Shoults, M.A. 25/3/74.' The last volume acquired was Robert Waring's *Amoris effigies: sive, Quid sit amor?* (1671), which is bound with Giovanni Baptista Ferrari's *Orationes* (1668). Waring (1614–58) was an English clergyman whose Latin love-verses were re-printed a number of times; an English version first appeared in 1680. The work certainly captured Shoults's attention, because there are ink crosses by him on various pages. Ferrari (1584–1655) was an Italian Jesuit who also produced illustrated botanical books and a Syriac-Latin dictionary. The title page of Waring has the inscription: 'W. A. Shoults. M.A. 25/3/74.'

Three days later, Shoults acquired a copy of Gratian's *Decretum aureum*, published by François Regnault in Rouen in 1519. It is a good example of French colour printing—black and red throughout—and has the imprint details and Regnault's device of an elephant in the colophon. This work on decretals contains the bookplate of Robert Chambers, who may be Robert Chambers (1802–71), the Scottish publisher and geologist and anonymous author of the popular *Vestiges of the Natural History of Creation* (1844). In addition, there is a note on the edge of the bookplate reading: 'Bought at Quaritch's Castle St. See Hook's Church Dictionary 1842 p. 117–118. Collated 24 July 1854. [1519. Printed in Rouen]', which may have been written by Chambers at the time of purchase. Shoults's inscription reads: 'W. A. Shoults M.A. March 28th 1874.'

On 10 April 1874, Shoults made another small purchase. He obtained a copy of Johannes Wolleb's *Compendium theologiæ Christianæ*, published in Cambridge, 1642. Wolleb (1589–1629) was a Swiss Protestant theologian, and this was his major work, first published in 1626. It was eventually translated into English by Alexander Ross in 1650. Shoults's copy is extremely battered, with both covers detached. It must be noted here that all of the above books contain Shoults's inscription denoting his M.A. status; the others that follow contain his soon-to-be-completed B.D.

In June, Shoults bought Robert Potts's *Liber Cantabrigiensis* (1855), an account of the aids and scholarships afforded to poor students, interwoven with common-sense maxims. His inscription reads 'William Arderne Shoults B. D. Corpus Christi 1874', giving his new status as well as a hint of when purchased, sometime early June but before the 24th.[44] It is not possible to explain why he acquired this particular book, given that he had just finished his studies. Perhaps he contemplated going further—an eye on a D.D.—and was thus interested to learn of possible scholarship funding.

In the month of August, Shoults acquired two books that harked back to his 'Greek' purchases before obtaining his B.D. The first is a Cambridge Latin and Greek edition of Henri Estienne's famous translation of Homer's *Iliad*, published in 1664 by John Field. An inscription by a previous owner—H. Ray—records beginning part 22 of Homer on 27 June 1814. Shoults used the book too: there is a folded sheet of handwritten notes loosely tipped in between pages 178 and 179 which are by him. His ink notes are extensive, including a select list of Greek words that appear in the book, with their Latin equivalents, and another of the actors in Homer's work. A few of the latter include: 'Hecuba daughter of Dymas a Phrygian second wife of Priam', 'Paris son of Priam and Hecuba also called Alexander', 'Menelaus King of Sparta son of Atreus', and 'Astyanax a son of Hector and Andromache.' The title page inscription registers his newly-acquired degree: 'W. A. Shoults B. D. August 2 1874.' The second book is another Cambridge publication, a copy of James Duport's *Thrēnothriambos* (1653), a bilingual translation of the book of Job, in Homeric Greek verse and Latin prose. This work is bound with Duport's *Proverbs of Solomon*. On the front endpaper, Shoults has inscribed it: 'Rev. W. A. Shoults B. D. 31/8/74.'

On 12 September Shoults purchased a copy of Alexandre de Rogissart's *Les Delices de l'Italie*, a popular travel book on Italy that describes Italian 'delights', enhanced by numerous fold-out engravings of (among others) Venice, boats on water, and papal processions. Shoults's Leiden edition, once owned by a J. Lawes, was published in French in 1706. He signed his name in all three volumes: 'Rev. W. A. Shoults B. D. Sept 12th 1874.' The acquisition of this travel book poses a question: perhaps he was contemplating travel overseas. This would have been a welcome break from work and just reward for completed studies.

A month later, on 17 October, he acquired a large Latin and French Catholic prayer book, *Le Paroissien, ou, l'Office Divine*, which contains the divine service for Sundays and holy days. This eucology was published by François Dolet in Boulogne in 1784, and, given Shoults's interest in feast and Saints' days, it seems an appropriate purchase. The title page has his inscription: 'Rev. W. A. Shoults, B.D. 17/10/74.'

---

[44] Corpus Christi is a moveable feast, celebrated on the Thursday after Trinity Sunday or, in countries where it is not a holy day of obligation, on the following Sunday. The earliest possible Thursday celebration falls on *May 21* (as in 1818 and 2285), the latest on 24 June.

1875

Eighteen seventy-five was a sparse year for Shoults as a book collector, with only four books identified as having been acquired. On 19 May, he obtained two books. The first is a copy of an Elzevir edition of Lucan's epic poem *Pharsalia*, published in 1651. Two previous owners have inscribed their names in the book: 'E. Libris H. Ingles, Coll: et Alumni, 1766'[45] and 'E. Balme Trin. Coll. Cant.', who may have been Edward Balme (1771–1822), barrister and Vicar of Finchingfield, Essex, whose valuable library was sold at auction at his death. The second was a copy of the anonymous *A Chronological Epitome of the Most Remarkable Events That Have Occurred During the French Revolution, from 1789 to 1796*, published in London in 1796. Both these books carry the familiar inscription: 'W. A. Shoults B.D. 19/5/75.'

The third title, acquired on 15 August 1875, is *A Brief Account of Durham Cathedral: with notices of the Castle, University, City Churches*, published by Blackwell in 1833. This clean copy has Shoults's inscription at front: 'W. A. Shoults. B.D. 15/8/75.' The last book is a puzzle. Captain Charles FitzGerald wrote a pamphlet titled *The Gambia and its Proposed Cession to France*, which was published by Unwin in 1875. The inscription 'With the Writer's Compliments Royal Colonial Institute, 15 Strand, WC, 2/12/75' is tantalising. The topic is an unlikely one for Shoults and is certainly outside his collecting interests. However, he may have met FitzGerald when the latter visited London, or through the below-mentioned the Rev. Pascoe Grenfell Hill (1804–82), whose own naval and slavery experiences match FitzGerald's. Captain Fitzgerald was Governor of Gambia from 1844 to 1847, and earlier, while in command of the *Buzzard* on the coast of Africa, had come into contact with slavers. His life was certainly not without incident: during his stint as Governor of Western Australia, from 1848 to 1855, he was speared by an Aboriginal man, Dga-bena, near Murchison.[46]

PRESENTATION COPIES

The remaining four books are presentation copies, all obtained in 1874. The first three are significant because they consolidate the growing relationship that was obviously developing between Shoults and Eliza Katharine Ogle, his future wife. The gift of a book on 16 September 1873 had already occurred, it being a copy of Joseph Marie Suarès's *Episcopi Vasionensis Praenestes antiqvae libri duo*, published in Rome in 1655.[47]

---

[45] Perhaps Henry Ingles, who added the name of Chamberlayne in 1874. See *Alumni Oxonienses* (1888), 234; for Balme see *AC* (1944), II, 137.

[46] See Shaw (2008).

[47] Joseph Marie Suarès, *Episcopi Vasionensis Praenestes antiqvae libri duo* (1655). Shoults Itb 1655 S. Suarès

The inscription in this volume reads: 'The Rev W. A. Shoults from E. K. Ogle Sept 16 1873.' This gift is important because it gives the earliest indication that the couple were acquainted at least five years before their marriage.

It is not known when and where William and Eliza first met, but it is quite possible that she was attached in some capacity to one of the Sisterhoods with which he was associated. The one significant fact is that she presented him with books that match his intellectual interests. Indeed, as mentioned, she may have had some input into encouraging him to undertake further studies, to go beyond being just a curate. She certainly seems to have adopted the seriousness that he displays, at least towards reading material. She seems to have learnt quickly, taking on board his reading preferences.

On 26 October 1874 Eliza gave him two books. The first is a Latin and Greek copy of Heliodorus, a paraphrase of Aristotle's 'Nicomachean ethics', published at Cambridge in 1679. This work is regarded as Aristotle's best-known work on ethics, and it was an important philosophical document in the Middle Ages. The second book was an Elzevir edition of Jacques Bongars's *Epistolae ad Joachimum Camerarium*, published in 1647. This duodecimo edition was once owned by 'Thomas S. Abercromby', whose name is inscribed within. The two books have inscriptions reading 'Rev W. A. Shoults B.D. from E. K. Oct 26, 1874' and 'Rev. W. A. Shoults, B.D. from E. K. S. Oct 26th 1874'. The last inscription is intriguing, because Eliza uses the capital 'S' rather than 'O' of her maiden name Ogle. Either she had some premonition of her future status or, more likely, the inscription was done later, sometime after their marriage.

The last book that Eliza gave to her future husband during this period was a copy of Anton van Dale's *Dissertatio super Aristea de LXX interpretibus*, published in Amsterdam by Wolters in 1705. Dale (1638–1708) was a Dutch Mennonite preacher, physician and writer on religious subjects. He was noted as an enemy of superstition and a strong critic of witch-hunting. His *Letter of Aristeas* is an epistolary concoction written in Greek by an unknown Jew to one Philocrates and contains the legend describing how the Septuagint came to be miraculously written. It was once in the library of Lord Elliock, who, as James Veitch (1712–93), was sometime Sheriff Deputy of Peebles and an elected MP for Dumfriesshire in 1755.[48] This and other Elliock books will be covered in chapter 16.

(1599–1677) was at one time custodian of the Barberini Library, now a core section of the Vatican's Biblioteca Apostolica.

[48] For Elliock or Eliock, see *Gentleman's Magazine* (1793), II, 675; Brunton (1832), 525–6; Scott (2004).

Sometime in 1874, Shoults was given a copy of the *Life of Napoleon III* (1869), by the Rev. Pascoe Grenfell Hill (1804–82), rector of St. Edmund the King and Martyr.[49] The inscription in the book reads: 'To the Rev. W. A. Shoults from his friend the author 1874.' Apart from the aforementioned books given to Shoults by the Sisters at Feltham, this presentation copy is the only one in his collection that reflects a close intimacy with anyone apart from family and Eliza. Shoults was 35, half the age of Hill. He and the elderly Hill obviously liked each other, certainly given the fact that the following year he would leave St. Michael's and transfer his allegiance to St. Edmund's.

Hill was certainly an interesting individual, especially considering his experience of the slave trade on the African coast. He had been educated at the nonconformist independent Mill Hill School, London, and Trinity College Dublin. In 1836, he graduated B.A. and was ordained and appointed chaplain in the Royal Navy. He served in this capacity until 1845, when he was placed on the retired list. It was during this time that he saw much of the slave trade, writing two accounts: *Fifty Days on Board a Slave Ship in the Mozambique Channel* (1843) and *A Voyage to the Slave Coasts of West and East Africa* (1849). He was also a budding poet, publishing *Poems on Several Occasions* (1845). From 1852 to 1857 he was chaplain of the Westminster Hospital and for some time morning reader at Westminster Abbey. In early January 1863, he was appointed rector of St. Edmund the King and Martyr with St. Nicholas Acons, Lombard Street, a role in which he continued in until his death. Despite the endearing inscription in the *Life of Napoleon III*, the leaves of the book remained unopened.

Shoults was not systematic in recording provenance or acquisition details in his books, signing some and others not. There were surely more books acquired during these years, but they remain unidentified. Given this paucity, it is fortunate that some, such as the above—a heterogeneous lot slowly accumulated—add to the picture of him as book collector and of the general make-up of his collection.

---

[49] See Boase (2018).

10 HYMNS AT ST. EDMUND THE KING AND MARTYR, LOMBARD STREET, 1875–79

In late 1874 or early 1875, Shoults left his curacy at St. Michael's and went to St. Edmund the King and Martyr on Lombard Street, City, some twenty-five minutes stroll south, back closer to the river.[1] Lombard Street was part of London's traditional financial district, including nearby Martin's Bank (No. 68 Lombard Street), with its distinctive Sign of the Grasshopper. With medieval beginnings, the church, sitting between George-yard and Birchin Lane, was styled as St. Edmund's, Grasschurch, from the adjoining market for hay and herbs in Grasschurch (or Gracechurch) Street.[2] The old St. Edmund's was destroyed in the Great Fire of 1666, and, as part of the greater reconstruction of London, the new one was built to the designs of chief surveyor Sir Christopher Wren between 1670 and 1679, with advice from his friends Robert Hooke, Edward Woodroffe, and John Oliver.[3] It was at this time that St. Edmund's was united with St. Nicholas Acons, another church that had been destroyed.[4]

The site of the new church was long and narrow, and, as a consequence, the tower, steeple and porch became the principal (south) front. The large tower, described by George Godwin as 'more Chinese than Italian', has ornamental flaming urns on it, a feature which, according to church historians, is an allusion to the Great Fire.[5] The church's spire was completed sometime after 1708. The interior was deemed elaborate, with oak carvings, a stained-glass window that contained the Arms of Queen Anne and commemorated the year of Union (1707), and two windows depicting St. Paul and St. Peter. Charles Booth had other ideas. To him, it was 'internally unattractive'.[6] The altar was situated on the west side of the church. Restored in 1864, the church

---

[1] St. Edmund is the patron saint of Kings, pandemics, the Roman Catholic diocese of East Anglia, Douai Abbey, wolves, torture victims, and protection from the plague. His name is given to the town of Bury St. Edmunds, Suffolk.
[2] In 1292, the church is first recorded as 'Saint Edmund towards Gracherche', and it reappears in 1348 as 'Saint Edmund in Lombardestrete'. John Stow, in his *Survey of London* (1598), refers to it also as St. Edmund Grass Church. St. Edmund's was damaged by bombing in 1917 and was designated a Grade I listed building on 4 January 1950. See Clarke (1966).
[3] For Wren, see Tinniswood (2001), especially chapter 11: Our Reformed Religion, and Beard (1982), 74. Clarke posits it was not a church that Wren designed. He merely approved the design. See Clarke (1966), 29.
[4] See Tinniswood (2001), 204–8, for a list of the churches and the complexity surrounding the rebuilds.
[5] Godwin (1839), 3.
[6] Booth (1902–1903), 3, 8; see also Clarke (1966), 151–2.

faced further alterations in 1880, just after Shoults left. St. Edmund's still exists, and its front entrance sits close to the road, some five feet away.[7] (See pl. 12.)

The rector when Shoults joined the church was Pascoe Grenfell Hill, whom we have met previously.[8] He was appointed on 26 January 1863 and continued at St. Edmund the King and Martyr (with St. Nicholas Acons) until his death in 1882. He was a ritualist who enlivened his church by providing a succession of preachers, many of whom proved attractive to worshippers. He also improved the choir, recognising that music was another method by which people were attracted to services. He was also the first to introduce a surpliced choir into a City church. Shoults was curate to 'his friend' Hill between 1875 and 1879.

One preacher that Hill engaged at St. Edmund's was the ubiquitous Father Ignatius, who was preaching there as early as 30 October 1867.[9] Hill was a strong supporter of the eccentric Ignatius, recognising his ability to attract a crowd.[10] As mentioned in chapter 8, Hill had invited Ignatius to preach on Sunday evenings and on some Fridays, when occasional midday services were held. The result was that, in November 1867, Ignatius resigned from St. Bartholomew's and transferred to St. Edmund's. It was a temporary move, and not without controversy, as Bishop Tait noted in March 1868: 'Superhuman case of stupidity on the part of a Rector of S. Edmunds, Lombard Street. O si sic omnes!'[11] Hill responded to Tait, not only offering an excuse over what was an embarrassment, but also, like the Rev. Lewis Marcus, revealing some naiveté towards Ignatius and his manipulativeness:

> My Lord, Mr Lyne wore my black silk gown, on the occasion to which the *Church News* refers. It is what is sometimes called the 'Geneva' or 'Preachers' gown; very large and round in the sleeves. On every other occasion he has worn a surplice, but on that day, we were three officiating clergymen and found that there were only two surplices between us. The rest having gone to the wash. I should never permit Mr Lyne to deviate from the customary mode of conducting Divine Service at St Edmund's: but the difference between a black and white gown I did not think of any consequence.[12]

---

[7] Although a consecrated Church, it no longer is used for regular worship. Since 2001, it has housed the London Centre for Spirituality and its associated bookshop.
[8] See Boase (2018); see also *Crockford's* (1879), 463.
[9] See Father Ignatius related-materials in Tait Papers, 148, ff. 340–53 (ff. 340). LPL.
[10] Tait Papers, 152, ff. 231–2, Pascoe Grenfell Hill to Father Ignatius, 12 October 1868. LPL.
[11] Father Ignatius-related materials in Tait Papers, 150, ff. 224–48. LPL; see also De Bertouch (1904), 386. In requesting permission to preach at St. Edmund's, Ignatius used the opportunity to secure his oft-held dream, priestly ordination. Tait held firm, not giving into him. See Tait Papers, 174, ff. 333–9. LPL.
[12] Tait Papers, 150, ff. 235–6, Pascoe Grenfell Hill to Tait, 10 March 1868. LPL.

10 HYMNS AT ST. EDMUND THE KING & MARTYR, LOMBARD STREET

The usual complaints rolled in, especially about Ignatius. J.C. Colquhoun, chairman of the Council of the Church Association, wrote to Tait on 15 May 1868: 'A small monkery in London [...] preaching Friday and Sunday evenings at St Edmunds.'[13] It got worse for Hill, because, as already mentioned, in September 1868 a riot occurred outside the church, a consequence of one of a series of Friday midday sermons given by Ignatius. He had made a general attack on the business traders of Lombard Street, and it did not go down well with local citizens and business folk. This was the ritualistic environment that had already been established at St. Edmund's by the time that Shoults arrived in 1875.

The registers for St. Edmund's—'the Preachers Book 1866–1883' and the 'Vestry Book 1871–1930'—are unlike the corresponding Walworth ones.[14] Shoults is mentioned once only, preaching on the morning of Good Friday, 19 April 1878.[15] In almost all cases, Hill dominates as the preacher, with a number of other ministers, such as the Revs. Rowland Beevor Hill (curate at Yorktown, Surrey), William Elisha Faulkner (curate at St. Agatha's, Shoreditch), and Freeman Crofts Wills (vicar of St Agatha's, Shoreditch), bought in to lead services.[16] There is no evidence of fraternisation, but it can be assumed that Shoults mixed with these men socially.

There is, however, one occasion on which Shoults is mentioned at St. Edmund's: the second of two significant printed records of his activity as a curate. An article in the *Graphic* of 30 October 1875 features a Harvest Festival, which was a truly Anglo-Catholic innovation that is now deemed almost universal in the Church of England.[17] On the occasion—16 October—St. Edmund's was tastefully decorated by Mr Athill, the verger, and, according to the report, it 'was crowded to excess'. There was a choir of seventy who began the service, which featured the processional hymn 'We March, We March, to Victory', written in 1867 by Gerard Moultrie (1829–85), the Anglican hymnographer and acquaintance of Father Ignatius. As reported, this hymn was intoned throughout by 'the Rev. W. Shoults, B.D. (curate)', who in this instance

---

[13] Tait Papers, 151, ff. 165–6, J. C. Colquhoun, chairman of the Council of the Church Association, to Tait, 15 May 1868. LPL.
[14] Preachers' Book for the United Parishes of St. Edmund the King and Martyr with St. Nicholas Acons, 1866-1883, P69/edk/a/015/Ms 18495/003, and Vestry Book for the United Parishes of St. Edmund the King and Martyr with St. Nicholas Acons, 1871–1930, P69/edk/b/004/Ms 11261/001. LMA.
[15] Preachers' Book for the United Parishes of St. Edmund the King.
[16] Preachers' Book for the United Parishes of St. Edmund the King. For Rowland B. Hill, son of Pascoe Grenfell Hill, see *Alumni Oxonienses*, 2, 662; for Faulkner, AC (1944), II, 466, and Wills, see Nicoll (1959), 5, 210.
[17] 'Harvest Festival Service in the Church of St. Edmund the King and Martyr, Lombard Street, City', *Graphic*, 30 October 1875, 16; see also Reed (2017), 73.

seemed to play a more significant role in the service than Hill. Part of the hymn that Shoults sang that day reads:

> We come in the might of the Lord of light,
> With armor bright to meet Him;
> And we put to flight the armies of night,
> That the sons of the day may greet Him,
> The sons of day may greet Him.
>
> Refrain:
>
> We march, we march to victory,
> With the cross of the Lord before us,
> With His loving eye looking down from the sky,
> And His holy arm spread o'er us,
> His holy arm spread o'er us.
>
> Our sword is the Spirit of God on high,
> Our helmet is His salvation;
> Our banner the cross of Calvary.
> Our watchword the Incarnation,
> Our watchword the Incarnation.[18]

An anthem followed, chosen from Psalm 145, A Song of Praise. Of David: 'I will extol you, my God and King, / and bless your name forever and ever.'

The ritualist the Rev. A. H. Mackonochie of St. Alban's, Holborn, was the preacher on the day, and the text he used was taken from Galatians II. 7: 'But contrariwise, when they saw that the gospel of the uncircumcision was committed unto me, as the gospel of the circumcision was unto Peter.' At this time, Mackonochie was at the height of his powers as a figure in the Anglo-Catholic movement, his presence confirming again the nature of the ecclesiastical circles that Shoults moved in.[19] The article is also significant in that it verifies once more Shoults's ritualistic tendencies and his preference for elaborate, ornamented church services. After Mackonochie's sermon, another hymn was sung: 'Come Ye Thankful People, Come'. Then followed Handel's 'Hallelujah Chorus'.[20] To close the service, another hymn was

---

[18] Julian (1892), 772.
[19] Mackonochie was constantly harassed by Church of England Protestant groups, especially concerning his ritualistic practices. The pressures led to his eventual breakdown and retirement in 1882.
[20] 'Come Ye Thankful People, Come' was written by Henry Alford (1810–71), an English churchman, theologian, and poet. It was deemed his most popular hymn. See 'Henry Alford' in Julian (1892), 39–40.

sung: 'Now Thank We All Our God', written by the German Martin Rinkart.[21] The musical arrangements were by Mr C. E. Tutill, and the 'Bishop' organ was played by Miss Kate Westrop. A large engraving accompanies the text in the *Graphic*, providing the reader with an opportunity to locate Shoults: Mackonochie is in the pulpit; Shoults, given his prominent role, is in the stall on the right. (See pl. 13.) The 'Harvest Festival' was an obvious success in increasing numbers, as on the following Sunday large congregations assembled at both the morning and evening services.

1877

There is no evidence of any books acquired in 1876. In 1877, however, there are three, all closely associated with monastic life, two specifically related to the Benedictines.

The first is a breviary, a composite volume that contains selections from various breviaries, mainly Benedictine, and a copy of *Supplementum novum ad breviarum monasticum*, published in 1832. This volume, certainly a working copy, contains printed and manuscript amendments to the various liturgical services. It is inscribed in red ink: 'W. A. Shoults, B.D. April 24 1877.' On the same day he bought a companion volume, a copy of *Breviaire monastique, disposé par le commandement du Pape Paul V. à l'usage des religieuses bénédictines*, published in Paris in 1690. This dark-calf-bound book, with its clasps still intact, contains prayer schedules for sisters of the Order. It is inscribed 'W. A. Shoults. B.D. April 24 1877', again in red ink.

On 11 August, he acquired a copy of the Rev. Joseph Oldknow's *The Validity of the Holy Orders in the Church of England Briefly Discussed and Proved* (1857). Oldknow was a good friend of John Mason Neale, the founder of the Cambridge Camden Society. The book contains the inscription: 'W. A. Shoults, B.D. 11/8/77.'

1878

On 3 April 1878, Shoults's father died at the family home, 37 Camberwell Grove, Camberwell. As written in the will, Shoults, aged 39, was the executor of the estate.[22] According to the terms of the will, which was dated 9 February 1878, he received from his father a part share in 'two freehold warehouses in Vine Street, St. John's, Southwark', and a 'freehold house at No.14 Sutherland Square, Walworth'. He shared the chattels of the family home with Maria Susannah, his sister, who was also the partner in the Vine Street warehouses. She received the family home as freehold. Shoults's father also owned a 'freehold house' at No. 37 Olney Street, Walworth,

---

[21] Julian (1892), 962–3.
[22] *Daily News*, 8 April 1878, 1. Will of William Shoults (1812–1878): Deed Reference SLS 4638, Southwark, England, 20 August 1878. no. 349 COW249612.

which went to Emma Smith, who may have been a home-caregiver. It was bequeathed to her 'in acknowledgements of the many acts of kindness shewn to [him]'.

Although the image conjured up of Shoults is that of an earnest, intellectual, bookish, and perhaps somewhat impractical churchman, there was obviously another side to him, one that reflected some business-like acumen. He had inherited property: warehouses in Vine Street, Southwark, and another house in Walworth. This injection of funds and accompanying property collateral were no doubt also welcome, certainly adding some financial security. While there is no evidence of his involvement in any business transactions, there is one financial aspect that he seemed to be interested in, although the extent of this remains sketchy and perhaps purely coincidental. This was the practice of tithing, an age-old tax system, usually found in rural areas, of allocating an agreed proportion (sometimes ten per cent) of the yearly profits from cultivation or farming in support of the parish church and its clergy. Often the local clergyman collected items 'in kind' from a farmer. In 1836, the government passed a law substituting money payments for payments in kind. Further legal changes were made in 1860, when Tithe Commissioners could determine the amount of rent-charge paid by a parish.

In late May 1878, Shoults bought a copy of *Tenants Law: Or, the Laws concerning Landlords, Tenants, and Farmers* (1777). His copy is of the seventeenth edition, its popularity attested by the sixteen editions published since 1718. Although the work carried some authority, it was well over 100 years old and did not have any of the new legislative changes pertinent to renting or tithing in 1878. Perhaps he just preferred a tried and trusted historical manual on the various ins and outs of the subject. He followed this purchase by acquiring in June 1878 a copy of a much older work: Richard Montagu's *Diatribae upon the First Part of the Late History of Tithes* (1621). The Rev. Richard Montagu (1577–1641), successively Bishop of Chichester and of Norwich, was a controversialist who entered into the debate over tithing.[23] Again, this work would not have been of any use to Shoults in his new role as landlord. If anything, it provided some intellectual musings on what was a contentious issue. As will be noted in chapter 15, the topic of tithes continued to be of interest to him.

JOHN JULIAN AND HIS *DICTIONARY OF HYMNOLOGY*

One particular field of interest that Shoults was intimately involved in, and one that engaged his intellectual ability, was the study of hymns. In 1892, John Julian produced his *Dictionary of Hymnology, Setting Forth the Origin and History of the Christian Hymns of All Ages and Nations*, a substantial publication that is widely recognised as

---

[23] See 'Richard Montagu' in *ODCC* (1998), 1106.

one of the most significant contributions to the study of hymnology (religious verse). The work survives as Julian's most significant contribution to ecclesiastical, poetical, and historical literature. A second, enlarged and revised, edition, with a supplement, was published in 1907.

The Rev. John Julian was born in 1839, the same year as Shoults. He was privately educated and in 1866 was ordained as deacon, serving as curate of Thornaby-on-Tees, Yorkshire. In that year he married, and he eventually had three children. In 1867, he was ordained priest and moved to St. Mark's, Liverpool. In 1871, he moved again, to St. Peter's, Preston, Lancashire. By 1874, he had begun hymn-writing, the first being: 'Father of all to thee'. Others followed, such as 'Hark, the voice eternal' and 'O God of God'. In 1876, Julian was the incumbent of Wincobank, Sheffield, Yorkshire, where he conducted most of his research for the *Dictionary*. Honours received included an honorary M.A. from Durham University in 1887; a Lambeth D.D. in 1894; and an honorary L.L.D from Howard University, Washington D.C. Julian later became vicar of St. Columba's, Topcliffe, near Thirsk, North Yorkshire. He died in 1913.

Manuscripts in the British Library point to Julian beginning the gathering in of hymns from his numerous correspondents about 1872–3.[24] It also seems that he started writing up articles on hymns about 1877. The *Dictionary* is particularly important for its research into early Latin, Greek, and German hymns, for which Julian had a particular penchant. It is an erudite work, and, in the preface to the first edition, he claimed:

> Where it could possibly be avoided, nothing has been taken at second-hand. Minute technical accuracy has been aimed at, and, after great labour and inevitable delay, has, it is hoped, in most instances, been attained. The pursuit of this aim has very frequently demanded, for the production of one page only, as much time and attention as is usually expended on one hundred pages of ordinary history or criticism.[25]

Ten thousand manuscripts were consulted, and over a thousand people wrote letters that assisted Julian's research. The result is truly a magisterial achievement. In the end, there were some forty-three contributors.

Shoults was one of them, but, unfortunately, he is not mentioned in any of the existing manuscripts or correspondence between Julian and the Rev. James Mearns, Vicar of Rushden, Buntingford, North Hertfordshire, who assisted Julian in editorial

---

[24] See John Julian, British Library Music Collections; see also Giles (2008).
[25] Julian (1892), Preface, ix.

work.²⁶ Embedded in the 1300 pages of the *Dictionary* are 60 pieces attributed to 'W.A.S.'—that is, as confirmed by the Contributors List: 'Rev. William Arderne Shoults, B.D. Late of St. John's College, Cambridge.'²⁷ All of Shoults's entries— of varying length—concern Latin hymns, such as *Adesto sancta Trinitas* (page 22), *Aeterna Christi munera, Et martyrum victorias* (page 24), *Auctor beate saeculi* (page 91), and *Beata nobis gaudia Anni reduxit orbita* (page 120).²⁸ He had no input into any of the biographies of writers such as Isaac Watts, John Wesley, Hermann Daniel or Franz Mone, or on any of the entries on the German or English hymns. The entries *A Patre Unigenitus*, *Aeterni Patris Unice*, and *Deus Pater piissime* (see pl. 14) are but three samples of his work:

> **A Patre Unigenitus.** *Anon. [Epiphany.]* Daniel, in vol. i., 1841, and later ed. No. 210, gives only the first four lines of this hymn as belonging to a hymn for the Feast of the Epiphany, of uncertain authorship, date between the 10th and 13th centuries. In the ancient mss. in the *British Museum*, however, this hymn is found in three of the 11th cent. (Harl. 2961, f. 230; Jul. A. vi. f. 36*b*; Vesp. D. xii. f. 43*b*). In the *Latin Hys of the Anglo-Saxon Church* (Surtees Society), 1851, p. 53, it is reprinted in full from a Durham MS. of the 11th cent.
>
> In 1853, *Mone* gave the full text in vol. i., No.59, in 6 st. of 4 l., heading it, 'In Epiphania ad nocturnum,' and added an extended note on the text, with

---

²⁶ James Mearns, British Library Music Collections.
²⁷ Thanks to Alan Edwards, Dunedin, for alerting me to Shoults's input into Julian's *Dictionary* (1892).
²⁸ The full list of hymn title entries by Shoults in Julian's *Dictionary*: *A Patre Unigenitus*, 3; *Adesto sancta Trinitas*, 22; *Aeterna Christi munera, Et martyrum victorias*, 24; *Aeterna coeli gloria*, 25; *Aeterna lux, Divinitas!*, 25; *Aeterne Rector siderum*, 26; *Aeterne rerum conditor*, 26; *Aeterne Rex altissime, Redemptor*, 26–27; *Aeterni Festi gaudia*, 27; *Aeterni Patris Unice*, 28; *Ales diei nuntius*, 38; *Alleluia, dulce carmen*, 48; *Alleluia piis edite laudibus*, 49; *Almum flamen, vita mundi*, 54; *Angelice Patrone, Beate Spiritus*, 68; *Aspice, infami Deus ipse ligno*, 87; *Aspice ut Verbum Patris a supernis*, 87–88; *Auctor beate saeculi*, 91; *Audi, benigne Conditor*, 91; *Aurora jam spargit polum*, 93; *Aurora lucis rutilat*, 94; *Ave Christi Corpus verum*, 98; *Ave maris stella*, 99; *Ave verum corpus natum*, 99–100; *Beata nobis gaudia Anni reduxit*, 120; *Chorus novae Hierusalem*, 224; *Christe, qui lux es et dies*, 227; *Christe, qui sedes Olympo*, 228; *Christe sanctorum decus angelorum, Gentis humanae Sator et Redemptor*, 229–230; *Christi perennes nuntii*, 231; *Christum ducem, Qui per crucem*, 232; *Coelestis aulae principes*, 240; *Coelestis O Jerusalem*, 240; *Coeli Deus sanctissime*, 241; *Crucis Christi mons Alvernae*, 271; *Crux benedicta nitet, Dominus qua carne pependit*, 272–273; *Da puer plectrum choreis ut canam fidelibus*, 276; *Deus Creator omnium Polique rector*, 291; *Deus Pater piissime*, 292; *Die dierum principe*, 293–294; *Dies absolutl praetereunt*, 294; *Dum, Christe, confixus cruci*, 315; *Dum morte victor obruta*, 315–316; *Ecce sedes hic Tonantis*, 320; *Eia recolamus laudibus piis digna*, 322; *Epiphaniam Domino canamus gloriosam*, 351; *Ex more docti mystico*, 359; *Ex quo, salus mortalium*, 359–360; *Forti tegente brachio*, 383; *Gloriosi Salvatoris*, 427; *Hujus diei gloria*, 541; *In domo Patris summae majestatis*, 563–564; *In passione Domini, qua datur salus homini*, 566; *Jerusalem luminosa*, 579; *Jubilemus pia mente*, 608; *Parvum quando cerno Deum*, 883; *Primo Deus coeli globum*, 912; *Quae gloriosum tanta coelis evocat*, 942; *Quando noctiis medium*, 943; *Tu qui velatus facia*, 1187.

references to a 15th cent. MS. at Stuttgart; and to *Thomasius*, &c. This text, with the notes and an addition or two including a reference to a MS. of the monastery of Rheinau, of the 11th cent. was repeated by *Daniel*, vol. iv. (1855), p. 151. It is also in the *Hymn. Sarisb.* Lond., 1851, p. 26, as a hymn at Lauds in the Epiphany, and through the octave; where are also given the variations of *York* (used at Matins during the same period); of *Evesham*; *Worcester*, &c. It is also in *Wackernagel*, i., No.173; in Card. Newman's *Hymni Eccl.*, 1838-65, and others. It may be noticed that the original is an acrostic from A to T inclusively. The *Gloria*, of course, does not follow this arrangement. [W.A.S.][29]

Aeterni Patris Unice. *Anon.* [*St. Mary Magdalene.*] This hymn has been ascribed to St. Odo of Cluny; and is found in a MS. of the 11th cent. in the *British Museum* (Vesp. D. xii. F. 153*b*) added to the 'Lauda Mater ecclesia' (q.v.). Both hymns are apparently in a later handwriting than the first part of the MS. *Daniel*, i, No. 348, reprinted in the text of Card. Newman, changing the opening word from 'Externe,' to *Aeterni*. *Mone* (iii, p. 424), reprinted the text of a MS. of the 14th cent. and added thereto numerous references to MSS. and various readings; and *Daniel*, iv. 244, the revised text of the *Roman Brev.* **Summi parentis Unice.** The text of the *York Brev.* is given in Card. Newman's *Hymni Ecclesiae*, 1838, and the *Rom. Brev.* form in Biggs's *Annotated H.A. & M.* with st. ii, 1. 2, 'Reconditur aerario,' for 'Reconditur est aerario,' in error. The older text sometimes reads, 'Patris Aeterne Unice'. [W.A.S.][30]

Deus Pater piissime. [*Saturday Evening*]. This hymn occurs as a vesper hymn for the Saturday before the 3rd Sunday in Lent to Passion Sunday, in a MS. Breviary, written about the 14th century, formerly belonging to the Monastery of Evesham (MS. Barlow, No. 41, in the Bodleian Library at Oxford). It is also in a 12th cent. MS in the *British Museum* (Harl. 2928, f. 115*b*), and in a Bodleian MS. of the 13th cent. (Ashmole 1285, f.38). In 1851 it was given in the *Hymnarium Sarisburiense*, p. 73. Tr. as:—O God, O Father kind and best. By J. D. Chambers, in his *Companion to the Holy Communion*, 1855, and his *Lauda Syon*, 1857, p.139, in 6 st. of 4 l. It is repeated in the *Appendix* to the *Hymnal N.*, 1863, and in Skinner's *Daily Service Hymnal*, 1864. [W.A.S.][31]

---

[29] Julian (1892), 3.
[30] Julian (1892), 28.
[31] Julian (1892), 292.

The pieces Shoults contributed are erudite, and show close, exacting textual and bibliographical scholarship. In the three entries, Shoults cites 12 printed sources such as J. M. Thomasius's *Hymnarium* in *Opera* II (1747), Hermann Adalbert Daniel's *Thesaurus hymnologicus* (1841–1856), Joseph Stevenson's *Latin Hymns of the Anglo-Saxon Church* (1851), *Hymnarium Sarisburiense* (1851 and 1855), Franz Joseph Mone's *Lateinische Hymnen des Mittelalters* (1853–1855), J.D. Chambers's *Companion to the Holy Communion* (1855) and *Lauda Syon* (1857), T. I. Ball's *Appendix to the Hymnal Noted* (1863), Carl Eduard Philipp Wackernagel's *Das Deutsche Kirchenlied* (1864), James Skinner's *Daily Service Hymnal* (1864), John Henry Newman's *Hymni ecclesiae* (1865), and Louis Coutier Biggs's *Hymns Ancient and Modern* (1867). Shoults notes two breviaries: the *Roman Breviary* and the *York Breviary*. He also records two English institutions: the British Museum and the Bodleian Library, Oxford. From the British Museum he cites Harleian MS 2961 and MS 2929. The first is known as the Leofric Collectar, which contains a collectar (a medieval liturgical book containing the collects used in the Divine offices), a hymnal, and series of sequences for a community of secular canons; the second is an eleventh-century French psalter, a breviary and other texts. Items from the Cotton Library included Vespasian D xi, Vespasian D xii, and Julius A vi. The first is the Lawrence of Durham manuscript (mid-twelfth-century), the second an eleventh-century Glossed Hymnal, and the last a late-eleventh-century manuscript comprising a calendar, computistical texts and tables, Expositio Hymnorum, and canticles and poems. The Bodleian Library item is Ashmole MS 1285, f. 38, part of a thirteenth-century miscellany of poetry and songs, once owned by Southwark Priory.

In the course of his 60 entries, Shoults cites a total of 50 books used to verify the origin, derivation, and first appearance of each hymn. Many are standard sources.[32] Apart from those already mentioned, they include Jacques-Paul Migne's *Patrologia latina* (1844–55), John Mason Neale's *Hymni ecclesiae* (1851) and *Mediaeval Hymns* (1851), Leon Gautier's *Oeuvres Poétiques d'Adam de St. Victor* (1859), St. Augustine's *De musica* (1871) and *Confessions* (1871), E. A. Dayman's *Hymnary* (1872), and references to the poems of John Keble, namely 'Annunciation of the Blessed Virgin Mary' in *The Christian Year* (9 March 1826) and *Miscellaneous Poems* (1869). There are also mentions of other breviaries and missals. Overall, it is an impressive array, revealing Shoults's familiarity with English, Latin, and French, a working knowledge of German, more than a passing knowledge of hymns and hymnology, an accuracy that befits bibliographical scholarship, and an obvious familiarity with primary materials.

---

[32] Julian (1892), 655–6; see 'Hymns', in *EB*, XIV, 181–98; see also 'Hymns', in *ODCC* (1998), 809–12.

The books and manuscripts that he cites are specialised ones. However, of the sources he used, he actually owned very few: some works on Aurelius Prudentius (348–c.405), a *Breviarium Romanum*, and two closely-related items to references made, namely the *Harleian Catalogue* (1743) and a work on the *Mozarabic Breviary*. He has no Daniel, Mone, or Wackernagel—writers of seminal bibliographies and works on hymns, whom he cites frequently.[33] He may have owned some of the books (say, Daniel or Mone) at one time, but, if so, they have since disappeared. If he did not own them (the manuscripts in particular), he would have had access to them through an institution such as the British Museum, with which he was familiar. Given the detail displayed in each entry, especially where he cites page or folio numbers, he must have consulted each book or manuscript closely.

The poet Prudentius follows St. Ambrose of Milan in importance in hymn-making. He composed highly poetic songs in his *Cathemerinon* ('Daily Devotions') and *Peristephanon* ('Crown-songs for Martyrs'), many of which have been described as 'full of fervour and sweeteness'.[34] The Spanish used many works by this Roman Christian in their liturgy, especially in the *Mozarabic Breviary*. Shoults owned a few works by Prudentius: an edition containing *Cathemerinon*, *Peristephanon*, *Psychomachia* ('Battle of Souls'), and *Hamartigenia* ('The Origin of Sin') published in Basel in 1527; a duodecimo 'Elzevir-like' copy of *Opera* published in Amsterdam in 1625; and an edition published by Plantin in 1564 that includes works by Prudentius and commentaries by Victor Giselinus, Erasmus, and Theodore Poelmann (1510–81), the house-editor of classics for Plantin. Given Shoults's strong interest in festivals and liturgy, and given that the twelve hymns in the *Cathemerinon* relate to use in the canonical hours and festivals, it is somewhat understandable that he acquired these books.

Given Shoults's ritualist leanings, it is equally understandable that he owned a copy of a *Breviarium Romanum*, a now-shabby spine-broken Parisian publication of 1828. This work contains the liturgical rites of the Roman Catholic Church: the public or canonical prayers, hymns, Psalms, readings, and notations for everyday use, especially by bishops, priests, and deacons in the Divine Office.

The two 'Hymnology'-related titles may well have proved handy in the formation of Shoults's entries. As mentioned, he owned a copy of the *Harleian Catalogue* (1743), a multi-volumed title that contains a list of 7000-plus manuscripts formed by Robert Harley, first Earl of Oxford, Edward Harley, the second Earl of Oxford, and their

---

[33] Entries on 'Daniel' and 'Mone' in Julian (1892), 279; 762.
[34] See 'Hymns', in *EB*, XIV, 185.

librarian, Humfrey Wanley, which are now housed in the British Library. This catalogue may have helped him identify manuscripts for consultation.

The second relates to the sixteenth-century Spanish *Mozarabic Breviary*, first published in Toledo in 1502 by Cardinal Ximenes, reprinted by Cardinal Lorenzana in 1775, and then published again by Migne in 1850. Although Shoults did not have any of these reprints on the 'Mozarabic Rite', he did own a copy of *The Ancient Liturgies of the Gallican Church: Now First Collected, with an Introductory Dissertation, Notes, and Various Readings, Together with Parallel Passages from the Roman, Ambrosian, and Mozarabic Rites,* published in 1855, and edited by John Mason Neale, co-founder of the Cambridge Camden Society.[35]

REFERENCE BOOKS CLOSE AT HAND

As already illustrated, Shoults mixed with clergy who were active ritualists. He was known as 'Father Cyril', a monastic appellation given to him by Father Ignatius. A number of his books are inscribed as being acquired on certain feast or saints' days, and he was obviously interested in the historical and antiquarian aspects of liturgical rites and hymns. There is reference to his undertaking some translation of breviaries and service books, but no samples survive. The breviary mentioned above was an important, seminal text, and Shoults owned other works that complemented it. To have such a cluster of books on hand cannot be considered out of the ordinary, especially given his interests. The ten books described briefly below form a useful collection that he no doubt enjoyed dipping into. In fact, some of them may have proved valuable as he formulated his entries on hymns.

The first is a copy of Bartolommeo Gavanto's *Thesaurus sacrorum rituum seu commentaria in rubricas missalis et breviarii Romani,* published in Venice in 1630. Gavanto (1569–1638) was an Italian Barnabite priest and liturgist, and this is his chief work, which traced the historical origin of the sacred rites and covers the mystical significance and rules relating to observance and obligation of the rubrics. With his strong interest in historical matters, especially pertaining to liturgy and hymns, Shoults could have used this book. Gavanto was known for his accuracy, something that must have pleased Shoults, who seems to have shared this concern.

The second is a copy of *Rituale romanum Pauli V. Pont Max,* published in 1635 by Balthasar Moretus (1574–1641), the head of the Officina Plantiniana in

---

[35] 'Mozarab' is a term used to describe Christians who lived under Muslim rule in Spain, although scholars believe it to be an anachronism coined in the eleventh century, as there is no evidence of its use through the first three centuries of Muslim rule. The ancient liturgy used by Christians of Toledo is called 'Mozarabic Rite', a synthesis of 'Visigothic' features and medieval Roman rite. See 'Mozarab', in *EB*, XVIII, 949.

Antwerp. This duodecimo sacerdotal handbook contains all of the services that may be performed by a priest or deacon and thus complements the *Brevarium romanum*. It contains prayers and texts for baptism, penance, burial, attendance at exorcisms, matrimony, extreme unction, the sick and infirmed, and processional songs with musical notations on four staves.

The third is an impressively-printed copy of *Ad rituale romanum commentaria*, published in Venice in 1752. This work contains commentaries on the different articles (blessings) of the Roman ritual by Girolamo Baruffaldi (1675–1755), a priest and poet of Ferrara. The fourth is an equally impressive publication, a first edition of *Opera omnia liturgia* by Giovanni Michele Cavalieri (1693–1757), the Augustinian hermit who was at one point Prior in Bergamo, Lombardy. This posthumous work on church rubrics and sacred rites was published in Venice in 1758. It contains a portrait of Cavalieri by Paolo Bonomini, engraved by the Italian Giovanni Volpato.

The fifth and sixth relate to the Benedictine Order: a copy of *Specimen breviarii monastici ad mentem regulae S. Patris Benedicti*, published at Nancy, France, in 1771, and a copy of *Benedictionale romanum sive sacrae benedictiones in rituali romano*, published in Regensburg in 1873. Although there was an effort to standardise liturgical practices across the whole Roman Catholic Church (instigated by Pope Pius V in 1568), there were exceptions. The Benedictines retained the use of their own breviaries, with differences such as a one-week psalter that includes prayers for terce (mid-morning), sext (mid-day), none (mid-afternoon), and compline (night); non-scriptural readings for Sunday and feast days; and special note and attention to monastic and Benedictine saints.[36]

The seventh is a copy of *Supplementum novum ad brevarium, et missale romanum*, published in 1795. The Roman Catholic James Peter Coghlan (c.1731–1800) published a large number of documents relating to Catholic emancipation, and, as a key figure in the dispersal of such material, he produced many supplements to the Breviary and Missal. This was one he published.

The eighth and ninth are two specific breviaries. One is a copy of *Brevarium cenomanense*, published in Paris in 1748: Shoults has the pars autumnalis (Autumn) volume only. This work was edited by Charles Louis Froulay de Tessé (1687–1767), Bishop of Le Mans. The 'Commune Sanctorum' and 'Intonationes, Mediationes' for the Psalms are bound at the back. The other is a copy of *Breviarium parisiense*, of which Shoults owned only two volumes: pars verna (Spring) and pars autumnalis.[37]

---

[36] See *The Rule of Saint Benedict* (1952) for a full account of the monastic code.

[37] The spring volume (pars verna) contains the Offices of Lent and Paschaltide to the Saturday of the Pentecost Ember Week, inclusive. In the main from 7 February to 19 June; the autumn volume (pars

Published in Paris in 1787, this work contains tables and calendar, dedications, music, and texts (psalms, lessons) relevant to the canonical hours and to a wider number of saints and martyrs (the 'Commune Sanctorum'). Some of the hymns that Shoults wrote about in Julian's *Dictionary* are mentioned in this breviary, notably: *Christe, qui sedes Olympo, Coelestis aulae principes, Coelestis O Jerusalem, Die Dierum principe, Ex quo, Salus mortalium,* and *Quae gloriosum tanta coelis evocat*.[38]

The tenth is *Marytrologium romanum ad novam kalendarii rationem*, of which Shoults owned two copies: the first of 1613, the second of 1630. Both works were created by Cardinal Caesare Baronio of Sora (1538–1607), who was responsible for updating the 'Roman Martyrology', the official catalogue of Catholic martyrs, into a chronological list. In essence, Baronio's work helped standardise liturgical rites and rituals. The 1613 edition is an impressive folio published in Paris, with striking red and black printing on the title page. The second was published in Venice in 1630, and, although dumpy in format, is still impressive. It was published under the authority of Pope Urban VIII (1568–1644), born Maffeo Barberini.

SHOULTS AND JULIAN

The circumstances in which Shoults and Julian met remain a mystery: by 1876 Shoults was at Lombard Street; Julian at Wincobank. There is no extant correspondence nor files documenting the creation of the *Dictionary*. In a majority of the entries on individual hymns, there are modern English translations and details on their common use. This component was almost exclusively done by Julian, who initialled each entry. Shoults did, however, have a hand in some, supplying translations to nine of his sixty entries. They are *Deus Pater piissime*; *Dies absoluti praetereunt*; *Dum, Christe, confixus cruci*; *Dum morte victor obruta*; *Jubilemus pia mente*; *Parvum quando cerno Deum*; *Quae gloriosum tanta coelis evocat*; and *Quando noctis medium*.[39] *Christe sanctorum decus angelorum, Gentis humanae Sator et Redemptor* is a joint effort, initialled by both Shoults and Julian.[40]

It is difficult to ascertain when Shoults began his work on his contributions to the *Dictionary*. It may have been about 1880, when he was settled as a married man, seemingly not employed, and, despite presumed ill-health, had a little more time on his hands to undertake research. It is more likely, however, that he had started his

---

autumnalis) covers the year from the eleventh Sunday after Pentecost till the day before Advent, 28 August to 2 December.

[38] Thanks to George Woodman, Belfast, for the identification of these hymns in the *Paris Breviary*.

[39] See Julian (1892), 292, 294, 315, 315–16, 608, 883, 942, and 948.

[40] Julian (1892), 230.

work on hymns in the 1870s. As revealed in chapter 6, Shoults was using materials in the British Museum as early as 1863 and 1865. This bookish habit surely continued, especially given the resources that the British Museum could provide, and especially given the number of manuscripts and books cited from its collections. It must be remembered that he enrolled in a Bachelor of Divinity degree in 1874; while no topic of research is known, it could well have been something related to hymns and hymnology.

Using the dates of books that Shoults cites, it is possible to establish the last point in time that he was working on his entries. One reference is of particular interest because it not only gives the latest date of his activity in constructing the entries, but also hints at his corresponding with Falconer Madan (1851–1935), the then Bodleian Librarian. Shoults definitely worked at the British Museum; why not a trip to the Bodleian to physically examine its resources? The date of 21 August 1884 is found in his entry on *Aeterna Christi Munera, et Martyrum Victorias*. It reads:

> Amongst the earliest MSS. in which it is found are two of the 11th century in the British Museum (Harl. 2961 f. 248; Jul. A vi. f.64*b*) and another, perhaps of the 8th or 9th cent., formerly belonging to that eminent scholar in the Anglo-Saxon and cognate languages, Franciscus Junius. The latter was No.110 among the MSS. bequeathed to the Bodleian by Fr. Junius at his death in 1677, but 'has been missing from the Library for more than 100 years.' [F. Madan, Sub-Librarian, *Bodl. Lib*, Aug. 21, 1884]. It was, however, printed from a copy by Fr. Junius by Jacob Grimm, at Gottingen, in 1830, as, *Hymnorum Veteris Ecclesiae XXVI. Interpretatio Theotisca* [Brit. Mus.].[41]

There is no letter from or reference to Shoults recorded in Madan's correspondence.[42] While Shoults obviously could not have used this particular manuscript, he must have visited the Bodleian on occasions, especially given the various sources he cites in his entries—for example, an eleventh-century manuscript at the Bodleian (*Liturg. Misc.* 3666 f. 21) cited in his entry on in *Crux benedicta nitet, Dominus qua carne pependit*.[43]

Other publications cited include the Rev. Digby S. Wrangham's edited and translated reprint of *The Liturgical Poetry of Adam of St. Victor*, published in 1881, in the entry on *Aeterni Festi gaudia*.[44] Wrangham was Vicar of Barrington, Yorkshire; Adam of St. Victor (c.1110–c.1180) was a liturgical poet, famed for his 'sequences', rhythmic pieces to be used in the liturgy of the Mass preceding the Gospel. Shoults's

---

[41] Julian (1892), 24.
[42] Thanks to Oliver House, Bodleian Library, personal correspondence, 20 December 2017.
[43] Julian (1892), 272).
[44] See 'Aeterni Festi gaudia', Julian (1892), 27.

meticulousness is evident in that he supplies cross-references to other works, such as *Oeuvres Poétiques d'Adam de St. Victor* (1859) by Léon Gautier (1832–97), the French historian, archivist, and palaeographer, John Mason Neale's *Medieval Hymns* (1867), and a work by the Flemish-born theologian, Jodorus Clichtoveus (1472–1543) published in 1517, probably his *Elucidatorium ecclesiasticum*. In the entry titled *Crux benedicta nitet, Dominus qua carne pependit* (272), Shoults gives another source, dated as late as 1881: the German philologist Friedrich Leo's edited version of Fortunatus's *Opera poetica*, published in Berlin in that year.

Many of the references he makes in his entries contain page or folio numbers, a practice that suggests that he had the books on hand to cite or knew them so well enough to leave such detailed referencing. He was obviously particular about the attention to detail, placing for any future reader the most correct and fullest information on the sources used. As already mentioned, he seemed to enjoy this sort of exact scholarship.

It is important to state that Shoults never saw the printed versions of his work. Julian's *Dictionary* was published in 1892; Shoults had died in 1887. It was left to Shoults's wife Eliza to reflect on her husband's achievement, which, while not a major contribution to the vast body of knowledge surrounding hymns and hymnology, is a significant part of his legacy.

11　A LOVING MARRIAGE AND TRAVEL

The death of Shoults's father in early April 1878 would have struck him hard. His sister Maria Susannah was certainly on hand to comfort and console him in what was a small tight-knit family. There was also another whom he could rely on for comfort and emotional support. This was his future wife, Eliza Katharine Ogle, whose father had died the previous year. Eliza could no doubt empathise with his loss.

Eliza had given him a book as early as September 1873: a copy of Joseph Marie Suares's *Praenestes antiqvae libri duo,* published in Rome in 1655. As revealed in the last chapter, she continued to give him books, a practice that indicates more than a passing relationship. On 28 March 1877, she gave him two Record Commission publications: *Nonarum inquisitiones in curia scaccarii* and *Placitorum abbreviatio*, published by Eyre and Strahan in 1807 and 1811. The detailed antiquarian nature of these large folios is daunting and relieved only slightly by the rather ornate inscription on the flyleaf of both: 'William Arderne Shoults. B. D. March XXVIII. A.D. MDCCCLXXVII. EKS'. (See pl. 15.) Given the use of 'S' rather than 'O', it was surely an inscription added after their marriage.

On 1 August 1878, William and Eliza were married at the parish church of St. Luke, Chelsea, an Anglican early Gothic Revival church designed by James Savage in 1819. Shoults's profession was registered as 'Clerk in Holy Orders'; he was 39, she was 36. They gave the same address for their residence: 71 Robert Street, near Regent's Park and the Royal College of Surgeons, and a one-hour walk to St. Edmund's on Lombard Street.[1] Witnesses to the wedding were Robert and Susannah Abbey. The officiating minister was the Rev. John Newenham Hoare, previously Chaplain to the Lord Lieutenant of Ireland and curate of Holy Trinity, Brompton, Kensington. Hoare was author of *The Old Catholic Movement in Bavaria* (1872), and, in the year that he married the couple, he had published *Pre-Christian Dispensaries and Hospitals* (1878) and *Buddhism as Known in China* (1878).

As an early Christmas present, Eliza gave her husband a copy of *The Liturgy, The Book of Common Prayer and Administration of the Sacraments and Other Rites and Ceremonies of the Church, According to the Use of the English Church*. This work, with a frontispiece of an angel holding a banner 'Liturgia Ecclesiae Anglicanae', was published in London in 1696. An inscription on the title page of this particularly appropriate present reads: 'W. A. Shoults. B. D. from his loving wife K. 23 Dec. 1878.'

---

[1] 1878: St. Luke, Chelsea, Parish register for marriage of William Arderne Shoults and Eliza Katharine Ogle, 1 August 1878, no. 58.

A few of Eliza's own books were incorporated into the new family collection. Those identified as hers point to a complementary seriousness in reading matter and perhaps an already-established leaning towards Anglo-Catholicism, if not Roman Catholicism. Her books include a copy of the fifth edition of John Gay's *Fables* (1737), a copy of the fourth edition of John Langhorne's *Letters That Passed Between Theodosius and Constantia; After She had taken the Veil* (1766), volume 2 of the short-lived *Monthly Register and Encyclopedian Magazine* (1803), a copy of Jeremy Taylor's *The Rule and Exercises of Holy Dying* (1853), and Richard Frederick Littledale's *Catholic Ritual in the Church of England Scriptural, Reasonable, Lawful* (1865). All have her inscription, marked either as 'E.K. Ogle' or 'E.K. S[hoults]'. A few contain evidence of purchase, as, for example, the Taylor, which was acquired by Eliza on 21 February 1871, and the *Monthly Register*, which was bought after her marriage, on 26 February 1881. The Gay book has the inscription 'Mrs Ogle', being once owned by her mother, Eliza Margaret.

ELIZA'S FAMILY BACKGROUND

Eliza was the eldest daughter of John Connell Ogle and Eliza Margaret Maplestone. She was born on 3 July 1842 and had seven siblings, four sisters: Cecilia Harriette (b.1844), Alice (b.1846), Isabel (b.1848), and Emily (b.1857), and three brothers: John (b.1850), David Montgomery Richards (b.1852), and Thomas Edgeworth (b.1854).[2] The three brothers were born overseas: in Corfu, Trieste, and Madras, respectively. In 1861, Eliza was living at 12 Seymour Terrace, Kensington (age 18); in 1871, she, along with her family, had moved to 16 Carlyle Terrace, Chelsea.[3] Eliza Katharine lived to 73, dying on 3 August 1914 at her residence, 50 Albany Road, New Malden, Surrey.[4]

Eliza's father was John Connell Ogle, born in Ongar, Essex, in 1813. He was a landscape and naval-maritime artist and a member of the Liverpool Water-colour Society, painting such items as 'Paddlesteamer off Corfu before the Palace' and 'Train passing over Maidenhead Bridge'.[5] Little is known about him. He lived mainly in

---

[2] 1861: England and Wales census, Brompton, under Eliza Katharine Ogle.
[3] 1871: England census, Kensington, under Eliza Katharine Ogle.
[4] *Times*, 7 August 1914, 1.
[5] Paintings and prints by Ogle include: 'Morning After a Gale' (no. 98, in the 1845 Liverpool Academy exhibition catalogue); 'Fishing Boats Returning' (154); 'Sunrise on the Thames' (576); 'Almost a Match for the Revenue' (654), and 'Troops Embarking' (720). Other pictures include 'View of Avlaki from Kassiopi Castle' (1849); 'Sinrades, Corfu' (1850); 'A Paddlesteamer lying off Corfu before the Palace' (1850); 'The Mill' (1853); 'Train passing over Maiden Bridge' (1876); and seven undated images: 'Gabbiani Sulla Scogliera'; 'Ulysses deriding Polyphemus'; 'Cathedral of Huy, Belgium'; 'After the Gale'; 'Bushey Park'; 'A Breezy day at the Harbour Mouth, Yarmouth'; and 'The Flying Dutchman'. Thanks to Dr Emma Roberts, Liverpool School of Art and Design, and Professor Glenda Norquay, Research Centre for Literature and

London and, in 1845, was resident at 12 Park Wall, Little Chelsea. He died on 19 August 1877 at the family home at 16 Carlyle Terrace, Chelsea, aged 64.[6] About 1849, he was living overseas in places such as Corfu, Rome, Trieste, and Madras. His family accompanied him, and they moved about, as the large expatriate community tended to do.[7] All this travel must have been a wonderful experience for young Eliza, experiencing some schooling, the excitement of the births of three brothers in three distinct places, the mixing with her father's artist friends, and assimilating, especially in Greece, the customs and languages of Venetian, Greek, and Jewish populations in the sunny climes of Corfu.

THE IONIAN ACADEMY AND EDWARD LEAR

The Ionian Academy was established by the fifth Earl of Guilford, Frederick North (1766–1827) in 1824. As early as 1811, Guilford had thought about establishing an institution on the educational lines of other European universities, cultivating scholars and teachers in the hope that they would disseminate their knowledge and skills to others. The Academy became a reality at Corfu, which, located within the Ionian Islands, was under British Protectorate rule. Guilford was the first chancellor and the prime financier of the Academy. Unfortunately, he died in 1827, and, with the disappearance of his enthusiasm and his financial backing, the Academy staggered on. Teaching positions were reduced, and schools such as the medical one was closed, although it did reopen in 1844. Successive administrators such as Andreas Moustoxydes and Antonios Polylas worked at keeping the Academy open. It was closed down in 1864, when the Union of the Ionian Islands melded with the Greek state.

It was at this institution that Shoults's future father-in-law was employed. Ogle was offered a position of drawing master (Professor) at the Academy.[8] His teaching duties are unclear, but he may have received an offer similar to that of the British artist Edward Lear, who, in 1856, was offered £100 *per annum* plus a house. (Lear did not take up the offer.)[9] Establishing Ogle's arrival at and departure from Corfu—and elsewhere—is not easy. Some of his paintings offer a hint of time and place. The watercolour 'View of Avlaki from Kassiopi Castle' is dated 1849, and one can imagine that he was in the northeast of the island in this year, busily sketching.[10] Other works

---

Cultural History, Humanities and Social Science, John Foster Building, Mount Pleasant, Liverpool. See Roberts (1997).

[6] Ogle's death is recorded in the *Liverpool Mercury*, 25 August 1877, 3.
[7] 'Edward Lear Diaries' (1858–9). Lear's descriptions of those he met are brief.
[8] Mallalieu (2002), 2, 82.
[9] Uglow (2017), 237.
[10] The painting was on display in 'Romanticism in Corfu', an exhibition curated by Megakles Rogakos at

have dates that help track his whereabouts in Corfu, give or take the time from sketch to completed work. These paintings include 'Sinarades, Corfu' (1850), 'A Paddlesteamer lying off Corfu before the Palace' (1850), and 'The Mill' (1853). His three sons were born in the respective towns of Corfu (1850), Trieste (1852), and Madras (1854). One can only presume that he was present at the birth of each one.

The British artist Edward Lear first visited Corfu in 1848, and over a period of some twenty years returned many times, especially during the winter seasons. In fact, in 1855, he set up residency in Corfu, which he called 'wonderfully lovely' and 'Paradise island'.[11] Lear's correspondence mentions Ogle, and the few references between 1858 and 1860 shed light on him and his family and with whom they mixed. Although they paint a scene of traffic to and from areas such as Corfu and 'home' by a busy expatriate community, Lear's references do not refer to Ogle at Corfu; they represent the before and after, and movements in between.

Ogle is first mentioned on 21 September 1858, when Lear was living at Portman Square, London, working on his Palestine watercolours. Lear went to the Oxford and Cambridge Club, Pall Mall, and had 'a very pleasant dinner' with 'Dr Ogle' and Charles Church, nephew to the Quaker Sir Richard Church. Lear added: 'wine, & smoking party—the like of wh. I have not enjoyed as much for a long time'.[12] Four months later, the Ogle family were in Rome, where they joined Lear in a pre-Christmas sing-song at his palazzo on the Via Condotti, at the foot of the Spanish Steps. On 4 February 1859, still in Rome, Lear entertained 'the Ogles'. Six days later, on 25 February, Lear makes reference to the 'Miss Ogles'—certainly Eliza (age 17) and sister Cecilia—and their acquaintance with Mrs Anna Maria Ruxton, widow of the Irish Member of Parliament William Parkinson Ruxton (1766–1847) of Red House in County Louth. On 10 May 1860, Ogle was at Livorno (Leghorn), catching a boat to Genoa. Lear was also on board and made the somewhat cryptic note: 'On board the [Canschipp] again —much greater crowd.—Ogle, & his confessions.' On 24 June 1860, Lear was back in England, as were the Ogles. Part of Lear's entry for that day reads: 'At 1.30 called on the Percys—out, Brights—where was Ogle. Grenfell, & Chapman,—seeing R. Cholmondeley & Gibbs:—Lady James, seeing Sir Walter;—then home.' Ogle was mixing with Richard Bright (1822–78), Conservative MP for East Somerset, Henry Riversdale Grenfell (1824–1902), a Liberal politician who was eventually MP for Stoke-upon-Trent, an unidentified B. Chapman, and

---

the Ionian Academy, Corfu (2–26 August 2018). It was displayed courtesy of the Derek Johns Family Trust, London.

[11] Lear (1907), 113, Edward Lear to Chichester Parkinson Fortescue, 18 June 1858.
[12] 'Edward Lear Diaries' (1858–9).

perhaps Reginald Cholmondeley, of Condover Hall, Shropshire, a Mr Gibbs, and the unidentified Lady James and Sir Walter. Four days later, on Thursday, 28 June 1860, Lear entertained more visitors, individuals that Ogle may also have known and mixed with: 'Dickenson [sic], R. Bright, Mrs. B. & Nephew, Mary Anne, & Catherine North, S. W. Clowes, Willie Nevill, Charles Wynne, Ogle ---, Beauclerk.' Dickinson was a partner in Foord and Dickinson, picture framers and dealers who framed work for Rossetti and Whistler; Richard Bright is already known; Mary Anne North was Marianne North, the traveller and noted botanical and landscape artist; her sister Janet Catherine North; Samuel William Clowes (a conservative politician); William (Bill) Nevill (one of Lear's earliest friends); Charles Wynn Griffith-Wynne (at one point MP for Caernarvonshire, Wales); and Beauclerk, who was William Amelius Aubrey de Vere Beauclerk, tenth Duke of St. Albans, a Liberal MP. Lear's last mention on his fellow artist's character was on 28 June 1860. He noted: 'Ogle is a singular fellow.'[13] This was the sort of social circles that Shoults's future father-in-law mixed.

Only one book from John Ogle's collection is in the Shoults Collection, a copy of George Percy Badger's *Description of Malta and Gozo*, published in Malta in 1838. It is inscribed 'J. Connell Ogle, 1839', and was surely obtained by him on an earlier visit to Malta, a British colony.[14] Artists of the time travelled to such places to sketch and paint; why not the twenty-six-year-old Ogle?

TRAVEL OVERSEAS

By the mid-nineteenth century, travel to Europe from Britain had become easier, with an increased frequency of ships and trains scheduled to cater to the increased flow of individuals eager to visit France, Italy, and the Mediterranean. There is no evidence that Shoults ever travelled to Europe to 'finish' his education, visiting cities such as Rome and Milan and their famed libraries. For some seventeen years he had worked in the poor parishes of London. By 1880, he had finished with his curacies and had more leisure time to indulge—in writing, reading, book collecting, and perhaps overseas travel. Importantly, he was now married and had someone to share his life with. It must be remembered that Eliza, at least in her youth, was already well travelled. She would have brought to the marriage reminiscences of past experiences and a wide variety of connections made possible through her father, an artist.

There is one book in Shoults's library that indicates the couple were in France in late 1880. It is *Conference Tenuë à Courtray, le 22. Septembre 1681. Entre les Procureurs*

---

[13] 'Edward Lear Diaries' (1858–9).

[14] Malta became a British colony through the Treaty of Paris, 1814. In 1956, integration with the United Kingdom was rejected.

des Roys de France & d'Espagne, published in 1682. Its contents cover the peace and land settlements handled by representative of Louis XIV, King of France, and Charles II, King of Spain, and could be considered outside Shoults's collecting interests. This book, however, was a gift from Eliza, inscribed: 'W. Arderne Shoults B.D. from his loving wife EKS Sept 28 1880, S. Omer, France.'

Saint-Omer, west-north west of Lille, is an important pilgrimage town. In the town stands Saint-Omer Cathedral, constructed during the thirteenth and fourteenth centuries. It contains paintings of Biblical scenes, a large statue of Christ seated between the Virgin Mary and St. John, and the tomb of Bishop Audomar (Saint-Omer) of Thérouanne, whom the town was named after and who presumably brought Christianity to the area. In addition, the Cathedral contains a number of ex-votos, those tangible records of devotional thanks given to a saint or a divinity by visiting pilgrims. Another attraction—and certainly one that would have interested Shoults—is the Abbey of St. Bertin, a Benedictine monastic establishment. It was already in ruins when Shoults and his wife visited it.[15]

Shoults was a bookman attracted to the minutiae inherent in bibliography and antiquarianism. From his reading, he may have known that the Abbey Library once held the 'Leiden Aratea', an astronomical manuscript written and illuminated in Lorraine around 816. This important surviving text (and with images) of the Greek work by the Roman general Claudius Caesar Germanicus (15 BC–AD 19) was based on the *Phaenomena* by the Greek didactic poet Aratus of Soli (fl. 3rd cent. BC). The text was supplemented by portions of a second Latin version of Aratus's poem, written by Rufus Festus Avienus in the fourth century. One can imagine that this was the sort of information that Shoults enjoyed. He may also have known that the manuscript was housed at Leiden Universiteitsbibliotheek, VLQ 79, obtained by the library in 1690.[16] Previous owners had been Hugo Grotius (1583–1645) and Isaac Vossius (1618–89), scholars with whom Shoults was familiar. In fact, he owned works by both these men.

ROME AND THE VATICAN

The one major reference to Shoults and his travels appears in the memoirs of Dame Paulina Bridges, where she writes:

---

[15] See 'St. Omer', in EB, XXIV, 33.
[16] After Grotius, the manuscript ended up in the library of Christina, Queen of Sweden. It then passed to her librarian, the Dutch scholar and manuscript collector Vossius. It was acquired by Leiden University Library as part of their acquisition of Vossius's library in 1690.

> When the Holy Father Pope Leo XIII opened the Vatican Library. Fr. Scholts [sic] and Mr. Worth were two of the first English clergymen to go there, and Mr. Worth used to tell a story of Fr. Scholts standing with a Syriac mss. in his hand and never moving for hours until someone found Mr. Worth and told him they wanted to close for the night and would he take his friend away. They thought he was deaf: they could not make him hear. Fr. Scholts told R. Mother afterwards the week he spent there was the happiest in his life, but oh for a lifetime there! He went several times after that and the next feast day would give us a conference on what he had seen and been doing there.[17]

Just prior to this entry, she had written:

> He [Shoults] was a wonderful man, a great scholar and linguist, knowing all modern languages and a great many Eastern ones, such as Syriac and Chaldean. He was in great request at the British Museum when Sir William Ramsey (sic) was exploring and excavating the buried cities of Nineveh and Babylon as he knew the characters of their writing and language.[18]

These notes by Dame Paulina were based on her recollections, and she made two small slips, the first concerning Shoults's involvement with Sir William Ramsay (1851–1939) through the British Museum. There is no evidence of any demand placed on Shoults by the institution to help Ramsay, who began his travels (and research) to Greek lands only in 1880, when he secured his first Oxford studentship.[19] The second was confusing the Vatican Library with the Vatican Archives, and the date of its opening.

The Vatican Library, which Shoults visited, was opened in 1475. By the 1580s, the Library was open to scholars for two to three hours in the day for consultation; the essayist Michel Montaigne used materials there in 1581.[20] By 1488, the Library had twenty-two Arabic manuscripts.[21] The Vatican Archives is the repository in the Vatican City for all the papers and acts published and put into law by the Holy See. It was opened on 1 January 1881, with a further relaxation of access to the papers passed on 18 August 1883. This opening up was at the instigation of Leo XIII.[22] Before the official opening of the Archives, there had been a few nineteenth-century users: G.H. Pertz (1821), the Rev. Joseph Stevenson (1872), and William Henry Bliss (1877).[23] These

---

[17] Cited in Bridges (1866–1936).
[18] Cited in Bridges (1866–1936).
[19] Anderson (2004).
[20] Chadwick (1978), 7, and in particular chapter 5, 72–109.
[21] Cited in Irwin (2007), 74.
[22] Chadwick (1978), 104.
[23] See Chadwick (1978). Stevenson was hired by the Vatican to transcribe documents.

men had to apply for permission to access the materials, which was given only by the Pope, on application to the Cardinal Archivist.[24]

In May 1809, Napoleon annexed Rome and the Papal States.[25] One part of Napoleon's vision for the French Empire was to have the best collections of manuscripts, books, and paintings. As a consequence, in February 1810 there began the first convoy of many of the Vatican Archives and Library treasures to Paris. The items were eventually returned, beginning in December 1815. The Library and the Archive faced huge long-term organisational problems, especially dealing with the large collections that were added to both after this time. In 1881, a guidebook commentator made the following remark of the situation at the Vatican Library:

> The library is open daily for study from 8 in the morning until noon, excepting during the recess, which begins on June 28th, and continues until Nov. on Thursdays, and on numerous feast-days, it is always closed to students, although generally open to visitors, and the accommodation is so limited that only those who wish to consult MSS. can find places. The printed books are little available for want of a catalogue.

and

> Visitors are hurried through it by a servant more intent on receiving his fee than anything else. The selected collections of the most valuable MSS. formerly exhibited to the public are seldom shown except by special permission; the sight of the Medals and Coins is still more difficult. As to the library of printed books and the Stanze Borgia, so interesting for their paintings by the great artists of the 16th century, they are closed.[26]

If one takes the 'occasion' of the opening given by Dame Paulina, it is quite possible that Shoults visited the Vatican Library just after the opening of the Vatican Archives in January 1881, or, more likely, just after August 1883. Shoults's friend the Rev. G. Henry Worth was present, and, although Eliza is not mentioned, she must have been with her husband in Rome, although not visiting the Library that day. Shoults had undertaken translation work for Father Ignatius and the Sisterhood.[27] He had also introduced Worth to the Feltham community. Worth was particularly

---

[24] *Handbook* (1881), 348.
[25] Pope Pius VII responded by excommunicating Napoleon, who in response held the pontiff prisoner, first in France and later in Savona, Liguria. The return resulted in great losses: the Archive material sent to Paris was despatched in 3239 crates; only 2450 were returned. See Chadwick (1978).
[26] *Handbook of Rome* (1881), 354.
[27] Cited in Bridges (1866–1936).

interested in liturgical music, and, in 1907, he would undertake similar translation exercises for the Abbess Scholastica (Mary Paulina) at Malling Abbey, which was supported by Shoults's friend, Charlotte Boyd.[28] It is certain that these two travelling companions had much to talk about.

It was in the Vatican Library that Shoults perused the Syriac manuscript, one of 459 Syriac manuscripts that the Library held at that time.[29] In the eighteenth century, the Vatican Library had taken the initiative to buy some Syriac manuscripts through the offices of Maronite scholars, thereby amassing, like the British Museum at the time, a formidable collection. Many of the manuscripts had come from Dayr al-Suryan (the Monastery of the Syrians) in the Wadi Natrum, Egypt. The particular manuscript that Shoults looked at that day may well have been one of those from Dayr al-Suryan.[30]

On his visit, he would not have escaped paying the entrance fee, one or two francs, given to the 'Custode' who monitored the use of the Library. There was also no such luxury for researchers as a reading room; the first was opened in 1892. One earlier visitor had been Lord Acton (1834–1902), the English Catholic historian and politician, who knew Rome well. In 1866, Acton wrote ecstatically about his bibliophilic ventures, which surely included the Vatican Library: 'My success in libraries and archives surpasses all expectation.'[31] His entrée was probably eased because of his name and position, and the fact that he was a Roman Catholic.

Shoults was not a Roman Catholic, although his friend Worth would later join the Roman Catholic Church in 1895, becoming a member of the Vatican Commission on Plainchant set up by Pope Pius X. The number of British readers visiting the Vatican Library in the 1880s is unknown, but it was surely small. Considering Dame Paulina's claim, it could well be that Shoults and Worth were two of the first English clergymen to visit the Library; certainly visiting Protestant clergy were a rarity.

Visiting the Vatican Library and the Archives was—and still is—a special privilege. Shoults or Worth must have known individuals—influential friends—who helped smooth the way for them to gain access. Shoults may have entertained the idea of visiting the Archives, but, firstly, it was more difficult to gain access, and, secondly, the materials were probably of little interest to him. In reality, it was the Library that

---

[28] In 1907, the Abbess asked Worth for advice, seeking changes to liturgical and ceremonial worship. Within four months he had completed the changes, including some translation. See Anson (1964), 426; see also Anson (1973), 208.
[29] *Handbook of Rome* (1881), 348.
[30] Thanks to Dr Sebastian Brock, Oxford, for the information on the Dayr al-Suryan monastery and the Syriac manuscripts. Personal correspondence, 12 July 2019.
[31] Dalberg-Acton (1906), 329–30.

offered greater interest, as documented by Dame Paulina, when he quite lost himself in 'manuscript reverie'. She states that he went back a number of times. It is a great shame that he did not write down any first-hand accounts of his visits to this great library.

12 THE COLLECTION I: CHURCH FATHERS AND THE SCRIPTURES

During the 1860s and 1870s, Shoults was attached to churches in London that had strong ritualistic, Anglo-Catholic leanings. Some were deemed ritualistic hotbeds, headed by men whom he knew and worked for. Although associated with many who were ritualistic, and who received criticism for such a stance, Shoults himself faced no controversies. He had no scandal attached to his name. He glided through life with little or no documentation, a minor Anglican clergyman playing out an extremely ordinary life. As a bookish intellectual, he obviously felt more comfortable with his growing library, reading, writing (evidenced at least by his work on Latin hymns), and buying books. There are no letters or papers surviving, and there is no evidence that he grappled with any of the major intellectual issues for Christians in his day, such as Darwinism and the rise of biblical criticism. In short, he knew what he liked and stuck to it. It was during the period of the late 1860s that he was associated with the revivalist Father Ignatius, whose 'Benedictine' monasteries and convents in London and Capel-y-ffin were tangible places with which he was involved. Although the charismatic Father Ignatius had a hold on him, a gradual disassociation, began about 1873 or 1874, when he was a curate at St. Michael's, Shoreditch, and at the beginning of his studies towards a Bachelor of Divinity degree. By 1878, he had married. Shoults worked as a curate for sixteen years, and he was described as a 'conscientious painstaking man desirous of doing his duty'.[1] St. Barnabas was termed 'a good man, and full of the Holy Spirit and of faith'.[2] Perhaps Shoults, certainly a quiet performer, was similar.

The writings and beliefs of the Church Fathers were fundamental to the formation of an Anglican clergyman in the nineteenth century. They permeated society in general, forming traditional precepts of a Christian society and an established Christianity. Their works—along with the Bible and the Book of Common Prayer—formed an essential triumvirate for the education of an Anglican, especially in relation to duty, family, doctrinal teachings, and rituals and observances, the last including baptism, prayer, and celebrating the Eucharist.[3] The message imparted was authoritatively orthodox, and, for one who had passed through St. John's College, in essence a

---

[1] 'St. Paul's Survey', Tait Papers, 145, ff. 175–6, Rev. F.G. Blomfield to Tait, 28 July 1866. LPL.
[2] Acts 11. 24.
[3] See Williams (2005), 30–1.

seminary for those heading towards Holy Orders, it would have resonated with a student like Shoults.

Interested professionally and personally in such matters, and, importantly, imbued with the collecting spirit, it was a matter of course for Shoults to collect the works of the Church Fathers, Church histories, and things ecclesiastical. However, as there is no documentation on the process of his collecting, it is necessary to apply a deliberately reconstructive approach to what he amassed in these fields. This exercise, a forensic one, enables a teasing out of the sort of books he collected and read, either for his professional requirements as a Church of England curate or for his own intellectual needs.[4] Hubertus R. Drobner's *The Fathers of the Church* (2007) has been used to provide a chronological guide for this approach.

What sort of books are in his collection relating to these fields? As will be revealed, the books noted below are not just contemporary nineteenth-century publications. There are also large sixteenth- and seventeenth-century folios closely-printed in Latin and Greek. The contents range widely from doctrinal and spiritual issues such as the Trinity, the place of the Eucharist, and Arianism (see below), topics embedded in the works of various writers, to rituals and practices associated with the Church, aspects of pastoral and community care, which as a curate Shoults was certainly involved in, and general histories of the Church.[5] There are also the scriptural essentials: Bibles, the Book of Common Prayer, breviaries. There are also some controversial publications, some deemed heretical. Many of them are seminal works.

It must be stressed that to collect in these fields was not unusual, and Shoults was no different from many other nineteenth-century book collectors, such as Nathaniel Phillips Simes (1805–62) and William E. Gladstone (1809–98), who amassed such collections, many much larger.[6] He was not systematic in his collecting, nor a completist, and so there are gaps. Despite the lacunae, the books that follow reflect something of his dedication to his calling, his strong intellectual inclinations, and, in essence, the sort of books he was happy to collect and immerse himself in.

THE CHURCH FATHERS

The eight preeminent Church Fathers are Ambrose of Milan (340–97), Hieronymus (Jerome) of Stridonium (347–420), Augustine of Hippo (354–430), Gregory the Great (540–604), Basil the Great (c.329–79), Athanasius of Alexandria (c.296–374), Gregory of Nazianzus (c.329–c.389), and John Chrysostom (347–407). Of the eight,

---

[4] Drobner (2007).
[5] See Linn (2009), chapter 33, 497–511. See 'Arianism', and 'Arius' in *ODCC* (1998), 99–100, 104.
[6] See Quaritch (1968), Parts IX and VIII.

five feature in the Shoults Collection: Jerome, Augustine of Hippo, Basil the Great, Gregory of Nazianzus, and John Chrysostom. There is one tentative association relating to Athanasius of Alexandria, the 'Father of Orthodoxy'.[7] Shoults owned a copy of Archbishop Theophylactus of Ochrida's *Enarrationes in epistolas S. Pauli*, a commentary on the epistles of St. Paul. It was printed by Ulrich Han (Udalricus Gallus) in Rome about 25 January 1477 and it contains a prologue that is ascribed to Athanasius.[8] He owned no works by or about Ambrose or Gregory the Great.

St. Jerome was a renowned classicist and a very strong advocate of monasticism, a practice that attracted Shoults. St. Jerome is best known for his revision of older Latin translations of the New Testament (and additional Greek manuscripts) that formed the Bible known as the Vulgate.[9] Shoults owned a copy of the third volume only of Nicolas de Lyra's commentary on the Vulgate: Isaiah-Maccabees.[10] It was published in Venice by Johannes Herbort de Seligenstadt for Johannes de Colonia, Nicolaus Jenson et Socii, completed about 31 July 1481. He also owned a Clementine edition of the Vulgate, published in Antwerp by Plantin in 1619.[11] Initiated by Pope Clement VIII (1592–1605), this edition was an improvement on the Sistine Vulgate and remained in use as the official Latin Bible of the Roman Catholic Church until well into the twentieth century. This publication, one of nine Plantins in Shoults's collection, has the names of previous owners: 'Johannis Smyth 1691', 'Marlin Gaven 1760', 'P. Kehoe, 1819', 'John Caldwell M.A., 1820', and 'George Arthur Smyth 1842.' Shoults deemed it somewhat special, inscribing it at front: 'very rare & beautiful copy.' He also owned the first volume only of a large folio edition of Jerome's *Epistolae, et libri contra haereticos*, published in Paris in 1578. A number of ink annotations are present at the beginning of Letters II, III and IV, which may well have been written by him. Letter II has a note: 'Contains a good deal of commonplace good advice to a young minister; together with much incipient monkery. He lashes the rich clergy of the day'; Letter III has: 'A letter of condolence, addressed to a clerical friend, on the death of his nephew, a hopeful young presbyter. Inflated in style, not unusually elevated in sentiment, much of it irrelevant; not the language of genuine feeling, so much as a piece of rhetoric. The view of Paradise p. 23 is curious. The brief view of the gratuitous deaths of so many Roman Emperors, p. 31, is well given'; and Letter IV

---

[7] For Ambrose and his hymns, see Drobner (2007) 307–18 (317).
[8] Theophylactus of Ochrida. Shoults Ic 1477 T. See *ISTC* it00156000; 100 known copies worldwide. There is one other copy in New Zealand: Alexander Turnbull Library, Wellington.
[9] See Drobner (2007), 339–51.
[10] Nicolas de Lyra. Shoults Ic 1481 B. See *ISTC* ib00611000; 237 known copies worldwide; see also Darlow (1911), II, 912, no. 6085.
[11] Darlow (1911), III, nos. 6181, 6184, 6191a, 6197.

has: 'In this letter it is very evident that there was the greatest difficulty in keeping the vow of chastity; that many, even then, broke it; a ridiculous artifice to preserve it is mentioned 45d. Useful cautions in the latter part, against flatterers, hypocrites, and slanderers. Pro-monkish argt [argument] from Scripture 43 a, b.' If in Shoults's possession about 1873 or 1874, the 'monkery' note may have reflected something of his dissatisfaction with Father Ignatius and his methods.

St. Augustine is one of the most important Church Fathers in Western Christianity, and certainly one of the most influential. Some 127 of his works survive, including his most important *De civitate Dei*, *De doctrina Christiana*, and *Confessiones*. It is understandable that Shoults owned five works by or about 'the greatest Father of the Latin Church'.[12] Firstly, he acquired a copy of Augustine's *Opus quaestionum*, a publication containing a number of exegetical and philosophical works, published in Lyon by Johannes Treschel on or about 25 April 1497.[13] Secondly, he owned an eleven-volume large folio edition of Augustine's works, published in Venice by Joseph Baptista Albrizzi Hieron between 1729 and 1730. Derived from the earlier Benedictine Paris edition of 1679–1700, this edition was compiled by the monks of St Maur (the Maurists), who produced numerous editions of the Patristics for the entire Roman Catholic Church. A small printed label gives the name of a previous owner: 'Ruggiero Falzacappa', the Italian collector who may have disposed of these particular volumes in 1843, when he gave other items to the Biblioteca Vallicelliana, Rome. The third title is a large folio edition of *Sermones X*, published in Rome in 1819 and once in the Biblioteca Conte di Aquila. The fourth is a standard trade Tauchnitz version of *De doctrina Christiana*, published in Leipzig in 1838. Lastly, Shoults owned a copy of Corneille Lancelotz's biography on Augustine entitled *Vita*. This book was published at the Plantin-Moretus press in Antwerp in 1616. And whether he knew it or not, Shoults had a copy of three pseudo-Augustinian texts, *Meditationes-Soliloquia-Manuale*, which are bound with St. Anselm's *De humani generis redemptione*, and a pseudo-St. Bernard text, *Meditations*.[14] This duodecimo edition was edited by Henri de Sommal (1534–1619), who thought the text was genuine.[15] It was published in Cologne by Cornelius van Egmond in 1631.

---

[12] Benedict XVI (2009), 136.
[13] St. Augustine. Shoults Gc 1519 H. See *ISTC* ia01297000; 122 known copies worldwide.
[14] Bernard's *Meditations* was probably written at some point in the thirteenth century. It circulated extensively in the Middle Ages under Bernard's name and was one of the most popular religious works of the later Middle Ages. Its theme is self-knowledge as the beginning of wisdom; it begins with the phrase 'Many know much, but do not know themselves.'
[15] There is some discussion on whether Soliloquia was written by Augustine. See Cleveland (1910).

Arianism is a doctrine named after Arius (c.256–336), a Christian priest in Alexandra, that, simply put, holds the belief that denied the divinity of Christ, Jesus Christ being subordinate to God the Father. The rise of Arianism was a divisive movement in the history of Christianity. Basil the Great was an influential theologian, who not only fought against Arianism, but also believed strongly in the importance of monasticism. Part of the Trinity controversy that he was involved in concerned the differences surrounding homoiousios (like in substance) and homoousios (of one substance).[16] Shoults owned three titles by Basil: a folio edition in Greek of his works, published by Johann Froben in Basel in 1551 (a stunning piece of printing), a Latin version of *Opera* (1596), and *Orationes XLIV* (1604). Many of his works were banned, deemed heretical, anti-clerical, or immoral to the Roman Catholic Church, and as a result they were placed in the *Index expurgatorius librorum*, the Church's banned list.[17]

Another who supported the Trinity was Gregory of Nazianzus, one of the Cappadocian Fathers, who is best remembered for his advocacy and defence of the God the Father, God the Son, and the Holy Spirit – 'a triple light gathered into one splendour'.[18] Because of this stance, Gregory is often called the 'Trinitarian theologian'. Shoults owned a copy of his *Opuscula quaedam*, a bilingual Latin and Greek edition published in Paris in 1575, and a copy of *Oratio apologetica*, published in Cambridge in 1712.

The last 'Doctor' is St. John Chrysostom, Archbishop of Constantinople, who was called 'silver-tongued' or 'golden-mouth' owing to his eloquent preaching and public speaking. This attribute is evident from an inscription in volume 3 of Shoults's *Opera* of Chrysostom's works, an ambitious eight-volume edition published at Eton in 1613 through the initiative of Sir Henry Savile. The note reads: 'The most eloquent of the Saints. Gibbon.'[19] Shoults's set is incomplete, lacking volumes 1, 7, and 8. Volume 2 contains the inscription of a former owner, 'H. S. Boyd, 1804', while volume 6 has a pencil note written at the colophon: '30 Dec 61, 76 Gower Street', indicating, at least, a date after which Shoults acquired these volumes, complete or not. Another inscription

---

[16] Drobner (2007), 267–77. The text of the Creed was drawn up to defend the orthodox faith against Arianism and included the word 'homoousios'. It was issued in 325 by the Council of Nicea. It contained as appendices four anti-Arian anathemas which came to be regarded as an integral part of the text. See entry on 'Homoousion' in ODCC (1998), 786; see also Drobner (2007), 218–22: Anomoeans; Homoousians; Homoiousians; and Homoeans.

[17] Early versions of the *Index librorum prohibitorum* began to appear in manuscript from 1529. It was first printed in 1557 under the direction of Pope Paul IV (1555–59) but withdrawn. In 1559, a new *Index* was published, banning the entire works of some 550 authors in addition to the individual proscribed titles.

[18] Cited in Benedict XVI (2009), 67.

[19] See Gibbon (1776–1789), chapter XXXII: Emperors Arcadius, Eutropius, Theodosius II. Part II.

marks the physical production, which is outstanding: 'This work has been considered by some Learned Men, as the most beautiful, & finished piece of Antiquity. The Learned Hughes of Jes. Coll. Camb. calls it, 'Scriptoris Elegantissimi, Opus omnium, Elegantissimum.'[20] The combination of a text by an important Church Father and its physical production would have made this set a very appealing purchase.

Shoults also owned a copy of Chrysostom's *De sacerdotio*, which also contains Gregory of Nazianzus's *Oratio apologetica*. His copy, an octavo edition published in Cambridge in 1712, was edited by the above-mentioned John Hughes (1682–1710).

THE APOSTOLIC FATHERS

The four prime Apostolic Fathers—those believed to have known some of the Twelve Apostles—are Clement of Rome (35–99), Ignatius of Antioch (35–c.107), Polycarp of Smyrna (c.69–c.155), and the lesser-known Papias of Hierapolis (c.60–163).[21] Clement of Rome's only extant writing is his letter to the Church at Corinth (*1 Clement*). Ignatius was responsible for the first known use of the Greek word 'katholikos' (catholic, meaning 'universal') and stressed in his epistles the value of the Eucharist.[22] Polycarp's only extant work is a letter to the Philippians. Shoults owned a two-volume edition that contained three of these Apostolic Fathers: *S. Clementis Romani, S. Ignatii, S. Polycarpi, Patrum Apostolicorum*, published in Oxford in 1840. He also owned a copy of an associated 'Clement' title, a Tauchnitz edition of *Recognitiones*, published in Leipzig in 1838. Originally in Greek, this work is now known only in the Latin, translated by the monk Rufinus of Aquileia (Tyrannius Rufinus; 344–411), who was better known for his translation of the works of Origen. This nineteenth-century version, narrated in the voice of Clement and detailing his religious questionings and his defence of the apostle Barnabas, was edited by Ephraim Gotthelf Gersdorf (1804–74), a German scholar-librarian famed for his work on the Latin Church Fathers. It is classed as a pseudo-Clementine, a forgery—a status that Shoults may have been aware of.[23]

THE GREEK APOLOGISTS

The Greek Apologists were men who were active in the period of persecution from the mid-second to the early-third centuries. Two representatives included are Justin

---

[20] Rev. John Hughes, of Jesus College, Cambridge, who was the editor of St. Chrysostom's *On the Priesthood*.

[21] See Drobner (2007), 46, for the full account of the Apostolic Fathers.

[22] Some of the epistles by Ignatius include *Ad Ephesios, Magnesios, Trallianos, Romanos, Philadelphenos, Srnyrnaeos*, and *Polycarpum*.

[23] Cited in Drobner (2007), 338; see also Ehrman (2013), 458–60.

Martyr (c.100–65) and Irenaeus of Lyons (c.130–c.202). Shoults owned a copy of a large folio edition of commentaries by (among others) Photius, Eusebius, St. Jerome, and 'moderns' such as Friedrich Sylburg (1536–96) on Justin Martyr, whose execution in AD 165 was documented in the *Chronicon Paschale*.[24] This bilingual Latin and Greek edition, published in Cologne in 1686, carries a superb engraved frontispiece of Justin by Wolfgang Kilian. Shoults also owned another bilingual Latin and Greek edition of the works of Justin, published in Venice in 1747. This large folio contains a reference to Tatian, a disciple of Justin, and his *Oratio ad Graecos*, his argument that pointed out the superiority of Christianity over the worthlessness of paganism.

Irenaeus of Lyons is known as the father of Catholic dogmatics. His major work was on the heresy of Gnosticism, a movement that appeared in the Church in the second and third centuries and, simply put, emphasised an unknown, altogether transcendent, God who had no involvement with creation.[25] It emphasised personal spiritual knowledge over the more orthodox teachings, traditions, and, importantly, ecclesiastical authority. The beliefs of Valentinus (100–c.160), an early Christian gnostic theologian, received much of Irenaeus's ire. Shoults owned a large folio copy of *Sancti Irenaei adversus Valentini & similium Gnosticorum haereses*, published in Paris in 1639 and edited by the Franciscan theologian Francois Feuardent (1539–1610). This bruised and now battered copy of the second edition was once in an Augustinian library.

THE CHRISTIAN SCHOOLS

The third century saw the foundation of episcopal schools that offered instruction for catechumens in the essential precepts of Christianity. One who established a Christian school was the Athens-born Clement (c.150–c.215), who settled in Alexandria as an independent Christian teacher. He advocated faith and knowledge (gnostics) as the way towards perfection, emphasising that man's ultimate end is to liken himself to God.[26] His main work was a trilogy: the *Protrepticus*, the *Paedagogus*, and the *Stromata*. Shoults owned a bilingual Latin and Greek copy edited by the Dutch theologian Daniel Heinsius (1580–1655), published in Paris in 1641. He also owned a Greek-Latin copy of *Klēmentos Alexandreōs logos tis ho sōzomenos plousios*, a

---

[24] *Chronicon Paschale* (the Paschal or Easter Chronicle), also called *Chronicum Alexandrinum*, *Constantinopolitanum* or *Fasti Siculi*, is the conventional name of a seventh-century Greek Christian chronicle of the world. This anonymous text was probably written about the last ten years of the reign of Emperor Heraclius (610–41). Its name comes from its system of chronology based on the paschal canon, or cycle of moveable feasts around Pascha (Easter). See *ODCC* (1998), 340.

[25] See Drobner (2007), 105–9.

[26] See Benedict XVI (2009), 19–22.

work covering subjects such as economics, wealth (the corrupting effects of money), and various moral and ethical issues. This octavo was published in Oxford in 1683 and edited by Dr John Fell (1625–86), the founder of the Oxford University Press.

Origen of Alexandria (c.185–c.254) started his school, one of the earliest, in Alexandria about 217. He stands tall in the history of Christian theology, and his principles (the first set out) of Christian theology remain very influential. His writings range from commentaries and biblical exegesis to textual criticism, especially his synopsis of the Hebrew text of the Bible (his *Hexapla*). Shoults surely knew and read his Origen. He owned four works relating to this 'true maestro', as Benedict XVI has called him, and one pseudo-Origen title.[27]

The first is Origen's *Opera*, edited by Josse Badius (1462–1535) and published in Paris in 1512. Shoults's copy, with its famed device of Badius and an image of a printing press on the engraved title page, is a two-volume edition which was once in the British Museum. Each volume is stamped as a 'duplicate'. The first, bound in marble boards, has the price of two guineas written inside, which may be what Shoults paid for the two. The second is a much grander copy, bound in brown blind-stamped calf with the remains of clasps and chapter/book guide-buttons present. Unlike the first volume, it is rubricated throughout.

Shoults's second Origen title is a copy of the first edition of *De Graeca Septuaginta*, published in London in 1655. This work was compiled by Archbishop James Ussher (1581–1656), who based it on Origen's work on the Septuagint and the Hebrew text of the Old Testament.

The third is Origen's *Contra Celsum*, his measured argument against Celsus, a pagan philosopher who severely attacked Christians and Christianity in his *Logos Alēthēs*. Shoults owned two copies of the second edition in Latin and Greek of *Origenis contra Celsum libri octo*, published in Cambridge in 1677. One copy has extensive manuscript notes in Greek and Latin at the back, most certainly by Shoults. The fourth is Origen's *Peri euches syntagma*, a title on prayer published in Oxford in 1686.

Finally, there is the pseudo-Origen title, printed in Greek as Ὁ κατὰ πασῶν αἱρέσεων ἔλεγχος (*Refutation of All Heresies*). Shoults's copy was published in 1851. Once claimed to have been written by Origen, it is now attributed to Hippolytus of Rome (c.170–235). It is impossible to ascertain from this distance whether Shoults knew of its true status.

Philo of Alexandria (c.20 BC–c.50 AD), or Philo Judaeus, was an early influence on Origen. Philo is regarded as an important synchroniser of Jewish and Hellenistic

---

[27] Benedict XVI (2009), 23.

traditions, blending Greek philosophy and education with critical Jewish thought (exegesis) and theology.[28] Some sixty works are attributed to him, including important commentaries on the Pentateuch in Greek, in Armenian, and in Latin. Shoults owned a copy of *Opera exegetica in libris Mosis*, a work on the life of Moses which, despite ongoing debate on its authorship, Philo is credited with writing.[29] Published in Cologny, Switzerland, in 1613, this second edition was translated and edited by the Greek scholar Sigmund Gelen (1497–1554). Shoults also owned a copy of the Greek-Latin edition of Philo's complete works, published in Paris in 1640 under the privilege of the Compagnie de la Grand-Navire, a Parisian association of printers formed in 1582 to promote the publication of works of the Church Fathers. The text of this folio is the second Vulgate edition. Shoults also acquired a few random volumes from sets of Philo's works published in the nineteenth century. He owned an interleaved copy of volume 3 only of *Opera omnia*, published in Leipzig between 1828 and 1830, and a copy of volume 4 only of Charles Duke Yonge's translation into English of *The Work of Philo Judaeus, the Contemporary of Josephus*, published by Bohn in his 'Ecclesiastical Library' series in 1854. Yonge (1812–91) was an inveterate debt-ridden student who made good, eventually being employed by Queen's University, Belfast, and writing histories and translating many of the classics, especially those by Cicero.[30]

TERTULLIAN AND OTHERS

Those who offered some of the earliest Latin translations of the Bible included Tertullian (c.155–c.222), Marcus Minucius Felix (d. c.250), Cyprian of Carthage (c. 200–58), and Lactantius (c.250–c.325). Tertullian has been called 'the father of Latin Christianity'. Not only is it claimed that he was the first in Latin to use the term *'trinitas'* (Trinity), but from all accounts he was a superb teacher, who fought hard with reason and good sense against heretics from within and heresies from outside aimed at the Christian church.[31] Shoults owned two works: a complete copy of Tertullian's *Opera*, published in Paris in 1616. A reprint of the 1584 edition, this folio contains the editorial work of Latino Latini (c.1513–93). The second is *Liber de Pallio*, edited by the French scholar Claude Saumaise (1588–1653) and published in Leiden by Johannes Maire in 1656.[32] This was Tertullian's (perhaps) tongue-in-cheek treatise

---

[28] See Drobner (2007), 126–30.
[29] See Sterling (2018), 31–46.
[30] The *Bristol Mercury* reported that 'His debts were of that description usually incurred by gentlemen without adequate means who aspire to the reputation of fashionable means.' See Jupp (2004).
[31] 'Tertullian', in *OCD* (1970), 1046–7; see also 'Tertullian', in *ODCC* (1998), 1591–2.
[32] McKechnie (1992), 44–66.

on the wearing of the pallium (philosopher's cloak) rather than the toga. It has been described as an anomaly in Tertullian's writings.

Marcus Minucius Felix was one of the earliest of Latin apologists for Christianity, and his *Octavius*, a dialogue on Christianity between the pagan Caecilius (representing Felix's prior state) and the Christian Octavius Januaris, is his only extant work.[33] Shoults owned a copy of a second edition of *M. Minucii Felicis Octauius et Caecilii Cypriani de vanitate idolorum liber*, which contains references to Cyprian's thoughts on the vanity of idols. Edited by the German historian Johan Gottlieb Lindner (1726–1811), it was published in Longosalissa, north Thuringia, Germany, in 1773.

Cyprian of Carthage was once a member of the senatorial nobility, who, in about 245 or 246, turned to Christianity. As a result, he gave much of his wealth away to the poor. In 248 or 249, he was appointed Bishop of Carthage.[34] Cyprian was a strong advocate of pastoral care and believed, as set out in his first work, *Ad donatum*, that prayer was 'the only refuge of the Christian'. He was also one of the first to write about the primacy of the Pope. Shoults owned four of his works, one being the aforementioned *De vanitate idolorum*. The second is an incunable, a copy of his *Opera*, printed by the Printer of the 'Erwahlung Maximilians' in Stuttgart about 1485 or 1486.[35] The third is a large, extremely-beautifully-printed copy of *Opera*, published in Paris in 1574 by Sebastian Nivelle, who had the reputation of being a printer who took time over his productions and, as recorded, always aimed for 'the beauty of his impressions'.[36] Shoults's final work by Cyprian is a Latin edition of *Sanctus Cyprianus ad martyrs & confsssores* [sic], which contains letters and details on church doctrine. It is published in London in 1794.

Lactantius was called 'the Christian Cicero' because of his classical style. As a distinguished rhetorician, he was appointed to teach by Emperor Diocletian and, later, became a tutor to Crispus, Constantine the Great's son.[37] His best-known work is *Divinarum institutionum libri septem*; his earliest surviving work is *De opificio dei*. Shoults owned a copy of his *Opera*, which contains these pieces. This octavo edition was published in Cambridge in 1685, and, according to the information in the preface, the unknown editor used various printed and manuscript editions to produce it.[38] Shoults may also have been aware that he owned a pseudo-Lactantius work, the attributed *De phoenice carmen* found in a copy of the second edition of the works of

---

[33] 'Minucius Felix', in *ODCC* (1998), 1091.
[34] See Drobner (2007), 166–72.
[35] Cyprian of Carthage. Shoults Gc 1485 C. See *ISTC* ic01014000. 85 known copies worldwide.
[36] Timperley (1839), 309.
[37] See Drobner (2007), 182–4.
[38] Lactantius, *Opera*. Cambridge, 1685, [2–3]. Shoults Eb 1685 L.

the Latin poet Claudius Claudianus, produced by Nicolaas Heinsius (1620–81) and published by Elzevir in 1665.

EUSEBIUS AND HILARY OF POITIERS

The first phase of the development of Arianism spawned major writers such as Eusebius, Bishop of Caesarea (c.260–c.340) and Hilary of Poitiers (c.300–c.368). While Eusebius accepted the Nicean Creed, he also acknowledged tenets within Arianism, especially those surrounding the notion of the Trinity. He was an admirer of Origen, who was a strong influence on Arius, the founder of the movement. Eusebius's most important work is his *Historia ecclesiastica*, which not only became a model for later church histories, but also earned him the title of the father of church history.[39]

It is thus understandable that some of the great chronologist's works are present in the Shoults Collection. He owned three different editions of *Historia 2cclesiastica*. The first is an incunable, the fourth edition printed in Mantua by Johannes Schallus, not before 15 July 1479.[40] The second is a large folio published in Mainz by Gerlach and Beckenstein in 1672. The last, a large well-printed folio, was published in Paris by Pierre Le Petit in 1678. Both the 1672 and the 1678 editions have the extremely detailed notes by Henri Valois (1603–76) on Eusebius and his works. They also have had different owners: the first edition of 1672 was owned by the Rev. Mark Aloysius Tierney (1795–1862), an English Catholic historian who, after 1850, became the first Canon Penitentiary of the Diocese of Southwark.[41] The second of 1678 was owned by Thomas Stevens (1809–88), Rector and Lord of the Manor of Bradfield, Berkshire, and founder of Bradfield College in 1850.

Shoults also owned copies of Eusebius's *Euangelicae praeparationis. lib. XV* and *Euangelicae demonstrationis lib. X*, published by Robert Estienne in Paris in 1544 and 1546. These two works constitute the *editio princeps* in Greek of Eusebius's 'Preparation for the Gospel'. The 'grecs du roi' font, commissioned by François I, is universally acknowledged as the finest cursive Greek types cut. This finely-printed copy, lacking its two covers, once belonged to 'Tho. Randolph, C.C.C. Dec 29, 1731', surely the Rev. Thomas Randolph (1701–83), President of Corpus Christi College and Lady Margaret's Professor of Divinity, Oxford.

The third work associated with Eusebius that Shoults owned is a copy of Joseph Justus Scaliger's *Thesaurus temporum*, a reconstructed edition of the Bishop's

---

[39] 'Eusebius', in *ODCC* (1998), 574.
[40] Eusebius. Shoults Fc 1530 M. See *ISTC* ie00127000; 218 known copies worldwide.
[41] See Cooper (2004).

Chronicle. Published in 1658, this is the second and best edition, carrying the results of Scaliger's demand for accuracy and rigour. There are notes in ink, quite possibly in Shoults's hand, that make reference to pages and passages in a work by George Synkellos (d. after 810), a Byzantine ecclesiastic who wrote a chronicle of world history, *Ekloge chronographias*, which first appeared in print in 1652. Shoults did not own a copy of Synkellos's work, and so he must have seen it elsewhere, perhaps at one of his visits to the British Museum.

Sometime between 311 and 313, Eusebius wrote a treatise called *Contra Hieroclem*, the response to *Philaletes*, a work by Sossianus Hierocles, Governor of Bythnia, that supported the superiority of Apollonius of Tyana over Jesus Christ. Eusebius's treatise is embedded in a work entitled *Ta ton Philostraton leipomena apanta; Philostratorum quae supersunt omnia*, at pages 411–69. The large folio bilingual Greek and Latin edition, which Shoults owned, was published in Leipzig in 1709. There is no indication of where and when he acquired it.

Hilary of Poitiers was called by Augustine of Hippo 'the illustrious doctor of the churches', and, in more modern times, in 1851, was recognised as the 'Universae Ecclesiae Doctor' at the synod of Bordeaux by Pope Pius IX.[42] Hilary's belief in 'justification by faith' and his stance on the Trinity, the divinity of Jesus Christ, son of God, and God as the father who generated him, are widely accepted.[43] *De trinitate* is regarded as his best work, and it is aimed specifically against the Arians. Shoults owned a four-volume edition of Hilary's *Opera*, published in Würzburg, Germany, in 1785. This set, bound in green buckram, has the price of 12s written inside, which may be what he paid for it.

CYRIL OF JERUSALEM AND EPIPHANIUS

The period after the synod of Alexandria in 362 represents the second phase of Arianism. Cyril of Jerusalem (c.313–86) attended the Council of Constantinople (381) and watched others work through issues concerning the Nicene Creed, the Constantinopolitan Creed (one, holy, catholic, and apostolic), and Arianism. The Biblical message (the scriptures) was so vital to Cyril in his personal theology that it has been claimed that he 'subscribed to a form of *sola scriptura* doctrine'.[44] He was exiled three times: by Emperors Constantius and Valens, and his bête-noire Acacius, a philo-Arian. Shoults owned a Greek and Latin edition of Cyril's works (*Opera*),

---

[42] 'St. Hilary of Poitiers', in *ODCC* (1998), 769–70; see also 'Hilarius', in *EB*, XIII, 458–59.
[43] See Drobner (2007), 253–61; Benedict XVI (2009), 91–4.
[44] Yarnold (2000), 56; see also Williams (1999), 89.

published in Paris in 1640. It contains the translation work by Johann Grodeck, who was the first to translate Cyril's catechetical discourses from the Greek.

Epiphanius, Bishop of Constantia (ancient Salamis, modern Famagusta) in Cyprus, was born in south Palestine between 310 and 320 and educated in monasteries in Egypt. As a pro-Nicean, this orthodox zealot wrote on the Trinity in his *Ancoratus*, and on heretical doctrines in *Panarion* (his so-called 'medicine chest' for the healing of those inflicted by heresies, especially Origenism.) Shoults owned two copies of works by Epiphanius. The first is a vellum-bound folio edition in Greek of *Panarion*, published in Basel in 1544. The second is a large folio edition of his works (*Opera*), published in Cologne in 1617. This blind-stamped calf-bound book contains Latin translations by Ponce De Leon (b.1530) and the Benedictine abbot and scholar Jacques de Billy (1535–81).

TRANSITIONAL YEARS

The years from the early fifth century onwards were transitional ones, with a gradual rise of church literatures, especially from the Latin West. Cyril of Alexandria (c.376–444) was an archbishop who was involved in a number of controversial political events throughout his career.[45] Shoults owned a small example of Cyril's work, a glossary that is in a copy of *Thesaurus utriusque linguae*, which contains various Greek texts edited by the Dutch humanist Bonaventura Vulcanius (1538–1614). Published in Leiden in 1600, this vellum-bound book was once in the library of the Duke of Sussex.[46] As related in chapter 8, Shoults was given the saintly honorific of 'Father Cyril' by Father Ignatius, probably because of Cyril's scholarly reputation and perhaps because of his association with the East.

One of the first writers of the Latin West was Salvian of Marseilles (c.400–70). Shoults owned a copy of the third edition of *Sanctorum presbyterorum Salviani Massiliensis et Vincentii Lirinensis opera*, a volume that combines the works of Salvian and Vincent of Lérins, a Gallic priest who died about 450. It was published in Paris in 1684. Salvian and Vincent shared the tutorial duties of Eucherius of Lyon's sons, Salonius and Veranus. Perhaps this common experience explains the fact that the works by these two Christian schoolmasters are often found bound together. Vincent of Lérins was the originator of the Vincentian Canon, the threefold definition of Catholicity as: 'quod ubique, quod semper, quod ab omnibus creditum est' (What is everywhere, what is always, what is by all people believed). Shoults would have known

---

[45] Especially the part Cyril played in deposing Nestorius as Patriarch of Constantinople and in the murder of Hypatia. See entry in *ODCC* (1998), 443–4; see also *OCD* (1970), 308.

[46] A Sussex bookplate is present with the old shelf no: IX M. g. 3.

about the importance of Vincent's Canon. As noted in chapter 4, this was one of the first books that he purchased while at St. John's College.

Although the Roman Boethius (c.477–524) had political posts as senator and consul, it is his philosophical writings that he is best known for, especially *De consolatione philosophiae*, written while he was in prison charged with treason. Boethius is regarded as a pivotal figure between Antiquity and the burgeoning new world of the Middle Ages (c.500–c.1400) and he is, as John Marebon writes, '*the* fundamental philosophical and theological author in the Latin tradition'.[47] Shoults owned two works by him: a copy of *De consolatione philosophiae*, published in Amsterdam by Blaeu in 1668, and a copy of a third edition of *In Topica Ciceronis Anitii Manlii Severini Boetii commentarius*, published in Paris by Robert Estienne in 1535. This work on topics such as free will, universals, and logical thought may have cost Shoults 4s 6d, the price noted on the front pastedown.

A near contemporary of Boethius was Benedict of Nursia (c.480–c.547), whose work shaped the Benedictine monastic movement and whose lasting influence has earned him the title: 'Father of the West.' Considering Shoults's involvement with Father Ignatius and the latter's drive to construct his own particular version of a Benedictine monastery and convent, it is understandable that Shoults should have books by and about Benedict and about Benedictine monasteries in general. He owned a number of breviaries: a *Breviaire monastique* (1690), and the already-mentioned *Specimen breviarii monastici ad mentem regulae S. Patris Benedicti. pars prima*, published in Nancy in 1771, and *Benedictionale romanum sive sacrae benedictiones in rituali Romano*, published in Regensburg in 1873. He also owned a copy of *Regula Santi Patris Benedicti*, specifically related to the congregation at Mons Casinus (modern-day Monte Cassino), published in 1857.[48] A number of other titles relating to various Orders included Christopher Hartmann's history of the monastery of the Order in Switzerland (1612), Paul Betschart's *D. Thaumaturga Einsidlensis* (1665), a work on Einsiedeln Abbey, a Benedictine monastery dedicated to Our Lady of the Hermits, Thierry Ruinart's biography of Jean Mabillon (1714), a French Benedictine monk and scholar of the Congregation of Saint Maur, *Hierarchia Augustana chronologica tripartita* (1707–1719), a three-volume text on the Diocese of Augsburg, covering

---

[47] 'Boethius', *OCD* (1970), 171; see also Drobner (2007), 493–9.
[48] The Abbey at Monte Cassino was the first house of the Benedictine Order, established by Benedict around 529. *Regula Santi Patris Benedicti* contains the prologue, and 73 Rule chapters. In relation to Father Ignatius and reports by those who knew him, it is interesting to note just one of many of his departures from one of St. Benedict's dictums: In qua institutione nihil grave, nos constituturos speramus—'By means of these instructions we trust that nothing oppressive and unbearable will be laid down'. See Drobner (2007), 504–11 (508). Constant travelling outside the monastery was another departure.

their Benedictine Order, and Abbot Gottfried Bessel's *Chronicon Gotwicense* (1732), an illustrated work on the history of Göttweig Abbey, a Benedictine monastery near Krems, lower Austria.

MAXIMUS THE CONFESSOR AND JOHN OF DAMASCUS

Catenas are continuous comments on biblical books in which the biblical text is not explained by means of actual and original theology but by verbatim excerpts from one or several older, proven commentaries, collated by a compiler.[49] The early seventh century saw the rise of Eastern literature—Syriac, Armenian, and Coptic catenas—that contained translations, either in whole or part, of Greek biblical commentaries. One representative of this period—and activity—is Maximus the Confessor (c.580–662), once a court civil servant who opted for monastic life at the monastery of Philippicus in Chrysopolis, otherwise Üsküdar (now Scutari), Turkey. He was eventually elevated to abbot.[50] His exegetical works, where he developed a Christ-centred theology, included *Opuscula theologica et polemica*, *ambigua* (on the ambiguities in the works of St Gregory of Nazianzus), and *Scholia*, which dealt with the nature of divinity. Shoults owned a work closely associated with Maximus: a copy of Johann van der Hagen's *Observationes in Heraclii imperatoris methodum paschalem*, published in Amsterdam by J. Boom in 1736. This work is based on the anonymous *Chronicum Paschale* (also known as *Chronicum Alexandrinum*), an outline of chronology from Adam to AD 629, accompanied by numerous historical and theological notes. This work also includes Maximus's *Observationes*.

John of Damascus (c.675–749) is generally regarded as the last great figure of Greek Patrology. He wrote works supporting the Christian faith, defended strongly the place of icons in services, and composed hymns, an activity which Shoults was surely aware of.[51] Like many other Church Fathers, John believed that the Blessed Virgin Mary was sinless, exempt from the curse of Eve. Shoults owned a vellum-bound copy of *Opusculum theophilosophicum de principatu, seu antelatione Marianae Gratiae*, published in Venice in 1755 and edited by the Jesuit Francisco Javier Lazcano (1702–62). This work contains John's notions on the immaculate conception.

SCRIPTURAL ESSENTIALS

Shoults also gathered together an assorted number of Bibles, individual copies of the Old and New Testaments, individual books of the Bible, commentaries and

---

[49] Drobner (2007), 530.
[50] See Drobner (2007), 536–42, and Bowers (2016).
[51] 'St. John of Damascus', in *ODCC* (1998), 891–2.

accompanying paraphrases, concordances, and a number of editions of the Book of Common Prayer. The ownership of such books, vital items for any practising Anglican clergyman, is of course understandable. They were essential, for both professional and personal use. Many of them represent the wide and varied range of scholarly attention given to the Scriptures from the sixteenth century onwards. They also offer a brief glimpse into what was available for someone like Shoults to collect. A selection follows.

The oldest English bible in the Shoults Collection is a copy of the Geneva Breeches Bible, published by Robert Barker in 1611.[52] As with earlier editions, this quarto volume has numbered verses to each chapter. While no previous ownership details are present, there is a printed cutting pasted on the front pastedown making reference to the sale of bibles once belonging to the Rev. Charles Pratt, Rector of St Margaret's, Ware, Hertfordshire. As Pratt's library was sold in September 1889, this label may have been pasted in by Eliza, Shoults's wife, or more likely by someone else after the volume arrived in New Zealand in 1893. Shoults also owned Barker's Authorised Version of 1613, which has bound in *The Book of Common Prayer* (1615) and Thomas Sternhold's version of *The Whole Booke of Psalmes* (1619).[53] He also owned the Authorised Version printed by John Baskett in Oxford in 1739, and the three-volume 'Wilson' Bible of 1785, one of the earliest books that he obtained (see chapter 2).[54]

GREEK TITLES

In 1565, the Reformation scholar Theodore Beza produced an edition of the Greek New Testament, which included in parallel columns the text of the Vulgate and a translation of his own making.[55] Shoults owned a copy of the second, revised version: *Iesv Christi, D.N. Nouum Testamentum,* published by Henri Estienne in 1582.[56] This large folio was once in the library of Thomas Edwards Hankinson (1805–43), the High Churchman and poet. Shoults also owned a copy of the first edition of *Tēs Kainēs diathēkēs apanta. Novi Testamenti libri omnes*, a work that was part-printed (title page and dedication) by Richard Whittaker in London and the rest by Bonaventure and Abraham Elzevir in Amsterdam in 1633.[57] This octavo was once owned by Archdeacon Henry John Todd (1763–1845), who wrote *Vindication of our Authorised Translation*

---

[52] Darlow (1911), English, 1611 (239), 133; see also Chamberlain (1991), 9. The newspaper clipping pasted onto paste-down endpaper reads 'Sale of Old Bibles: Two 'breeches' Bibles dated 1610, in an excellent state of preservation, belonging to the Rev. C. Pratt, late incumbent of St. Margaret's, Herts, were sold by auction'.
[53] Darlow (1911), English, 1613 (251), 142–3; see also Chamberlain (1991), 11.
[54] Baskett: Darlow (1911), English, 1739 (797), 273; Wilson: Darlow (1911), English, 1785 (937), 305–6.
[55] Baird (1899), chapter 13.
[56] Darlow (1911), II, 595–6, 4643.
[57] Darlow (1911), II, 606, 4680.

and Translators of Our Bible (1819). The next work is a significant one, albeit incomplete. Shoults owned one volume only of *Hē Kainē diathēkē tou Kyriou hēmōn Iēsou Christou*, published in Geneva by Pierre Aubert in 1638.[58] This is the earliest printed edition of the New Testament set in modern and ancient Greek, in parallel columns. A small reminder of the effort needed to use this work is present on the front endpaper: a pencil note, not by Shoults, that reads 'Perseverance'.

Shoults also owned two early eighteenth-century works. The first, a folio edition of *Hē Kainē diathēkē. Novum Testamentum, una cum scholiis Graecis, e Graecis scriptoribus*, was published in Oxford in 1703.[59] This edition has a superbly-engraved title page and frontispiece, and a list of subscribers at the back. The second is a copy of Ludolph Küster's revised, second issue of *Novum Testamentum Graecum*, published by the sons of Johann Friedrich Gleditsch in Leipzig in 1723. This work was based on John Mill's ground-breaking 1707 Oxford edition of the Greek New Testament and follows the first Amsterdam edition of 1710.[60] Shoults may have written the two-line inscription in Greek at the front. It reads in English: 'I give thanks to the one [or him] who gave me strength in [or filled me with the power of] Jesus Christ our Lord because he considered me a believer, placing me in service (the ministry).'[61]

The last four 'Greek' works were published in the United Kingdom: Robert Urie's *Kainē diathēkē Novum Testamentum* (1750),[62] Nathaniel Scarlett's *A Translation of the New Testament from the Original Greek* (1798), a three-volume *Novi Testamenti libri historici Graece* (1835), and Christopher Wordsworth's *The Acts of the Apostles in the Original Greek* (1857). This single volume (Part II of four) was a birthday present to Shoults from his mother in 1859.

COMMENTARIES AND CONCORDANCES

Shoults owned various sixteenth- and seventeenth-century works, some quite specific, that he no doubt found useful to help navigate his way through the complexities of scriptural studies and the many publications surrounding this vast field. He owned a large-folio copy of the commentary on Paul's Epistles by the medieval preacher Nicholas of Gorran (1232–95), which was published in Haguenau, France, in 1502. The second 'Pauline' item is the first collected edition of the 'Paraphrases' of the Epistles of Paul by Erasmus (1466–1536), the Dutch humanist. This book, part of

---

[58] Darlow (1911), II, 679–80, 4958.
[59] Darlow (1911), II, 619, 4721.
[60] Darlow (1911), II, 624, 4735.
[61] Special thanks to Rowan Gibbs, Wellington, for supplying the translation.
[62] Darlow (1911), II, 628, 4750.

the great scholar's notion of 'retelling', without fuss and complexity, the books of the New Testament, was published by Johann Froben in Basel in 1520. The Gospel of John was popular, and Shoults owned a large-folio edition of a commentary on John by the Jesuit Francisco de Toledo (1532–96), who was known for his rigorous and scholarly approach to his exegetical works. It was published in Cologne in 1611. Another scholar equally rigorous was the Dutch Daniel Heinsius (1580–1655), who applied his own standards to John, after having received instructions from the master, Joseph Scaliger.[63] Shoults owned a vellum-bound copy of Heinsius's commentary in Latin that includes ancient paraphrases by Nonnus of Panopolis, the Greek poet who was active in the fifth century. This book was published by Elzevir in 1627. He also owned a copy of Heinsius's *Sacrarum exercitationum ad Novum Testamentum libri XX*, published in Cambridge in 1640, and a copy of the large folio-edition of Hugo Grotius's *Annotationes in libros evangeliorum* (1641), published in Amsterdam by Joan and Cornelius Blaeu in 1641. Shoults also owned a large-folio edition of the Rome-based Jesuit Benedict Pereira's commentary on the Book of Genesis entitled *Commentariorum et disputationum in Genesim tomi quattuor*, published in Cologne in 1622. This was once in the Library of the College of Advocates in Doctors' Commons, portions of which were sold off in 1861 by Hodgson and Co., London.[64] He also acquired a copy of *Concordantiae Graecolatinae Testamenti Novi*, a concordance of the New Testament begun by Robert Estienne but completed (not without criticism for its errors) by Henri Estienne, Theodore Beza, and others. His copy was of the 1599 Geneva publication by Samuel Crisp, a reprint of the 1594 edition.

Eighteenth- and nineteenth-century publications were also obtained. Shoults owned a copy of the seventh edition of Henry Hammond's seminal *A Paraphrase and Annotations Upon all the Books of the New Testament*, published in London in 1702. The Royalist Hammond (1605–60) was a diligent scholar who, as the first Englishman to compare manuscripts of the New Testament, made a mark in the burgeoning field of biblical criticism.[65] Perhaps in an effort to gather a wider and more tolerant overview of this growing field, Shoults obtained a copy of the non-conformist Matthew Henry's three-volume folio *An Exposition on the Old and New Testament*, an exhaustive verse-by-verse study of the Bible. First appearing in 1707, with additional volumes following in 1708, 1710, and 1712, this work was popular, with some twenty-five editions published up to 1855.[66] Shoults's copy was published in 1786 and, like the

---

[63] 'Heinsius', in *EB*, XIII, 216.
[64] Satterley (2011), 46–7.
[65] De Quehen (2008).
[66] Wykes (2004).

Nouum Testamentum of 1582, was once part of T. E. Hankinson's library.

Shoults owned six copies of the Book of Common Prayer—not many in comparison to other book collectors. However, he obviously felt the need to obtain a copy of Francis Procter's seminal *A History of the Book of Common Prayer*, published in Cambridge in 1855. At the time of publication, it was a very useful reference book.

SCHOLARLY THEOLOGY

Scholarly books on the Church Fathers and significant theologians were certainly a natural fit for Shoults, considering his intellectual interests. One of the most influential titles that anyone interested in early church history and laws could consult was the 'Decretum Gratiani', a twelfth-century work compiled by Gratian, a Camaldolese monk, between 1139 and 1150. This primary source book on Church law is particularly strong on verifying the importance of the four ecumenical synods— Nicaea (325), Constantinople (381), Ephesus (431), and Chalcedon (451)—and the initiatives towards establishing a unified, orthodox canon in Christianity, grounded on the formalisation of the doctrine of faith.[67] As mentioned, Shoults acquired a copy on 28 March 1874 that had been published in Rouen in 1519. He also owned a dilapidated, broken-backed copy published in Lyon in 1555. He seemed to exhibit some tolerance towards differing opinions by purchasing a copy of Antonio Agustin's commentary on Gratian: *Dialogorum libri duo de emendatione Gratiani*, published by Étienne Baluze in Paris in 1760. Archbishop Agustin y Albanell (1516–86) was a major figure of the Counter-Reformation who, as one of the first to truly research canon law, was critical of Gratian's work, pointing out errors and discrepancies in the sources that he had used.[68]

The Jesuit (and Cardinal) Bellarmine (1542–1621) was another important figure in the Catholic Counter-Reformation, producing pioneering work that offered brief biographical and bibliographic information on ecclesiastical writers.[69] As mentioned in chapter 4, while a student at St. John's College in 1859, Shoults obtained a copy of Bellarmine's *De scriptoribus ecclesiasticis liber unus*, published in Paris in 1630.

Johann Albert Fabricius (1668–1736) was a German scholar and bibliographer who dedicated much of his career to collecting, compiling, and comparing books and manuscripts to form publications, many seminal, in the field of Christian literature. Shoults owned nine copies of his works, including a copy of his *Bibliotheca ecclesiastica*,

---

[67] See *ODCC* (1998), 700–1. Three other councils followed, of equal importance: the Second Council of Constantinople (553), the Third Council of Constantinople (680–1), and the Second Council of Nicaea (787).
[68] See Shahan (1907).
[69] For Bellarmine, see *ODCC* (1998), 181.

published in Hamburg in 1718, two copies of his *Bibliotheca Latina* (a London edition of 1703; a Leipzig edition of 1773), and eight volumes of G. C. Harles's edited and enlarged *Bibliotheca Graeca*, published in Hamburg between 1790 and 1809.[70]

Shoults also owned a copy of William Cave's *Scriptorum ecclesiasticorum historia literaria*, published in Geneva in 1720. First appearing in parts in 1688 and 1698, this literary history of ecclesiastical writers from the birth of Christ to the rise of Luther in 1517 was important in establishing a bio-bibliographical approach in church history and harked back to the works of Eusebius and Jerome.[71]

The last of this selection is Shoults's incomplete set of Samuel Parker's *Bibliotheca Biblia*. The first volume was published in Oxford in 1720 and the other four followed, published in London in 1722, 1725, 1728, and 1735. It was envisaged as a much larger project, but Parker (1681–1730) got only to the end of the Pentateuch. Shoults owned three volumes only—I and II (Genesis) and III (Leviticus)—of this work, which not only reflects Parker's wide learning in Church history and the scriptures, but also the scope and extent of publications on these subjects that had to be marshalled and codified. Shoults's copy once belonged to the parochial library of St. Nicholas, Deptford, Kent, and was given to that institution in 1833 by the 'Associates of the late Rev. Bray'. As a theologian, Parker, like William Cave, looked back to a better time, a so-called 'Primitive' period which surpassed the times in which he lived, termed by him a 'loose and vicious age'.[72] Parker's mantra was a simple one: 'Orthodox, Catholic, and Primitive.' Perhaps the sentiment attached to the phrase appealed to Shoults.

---

[70] See Verner (1966), 281–326.
[71] See Minton (2008).
[72] 'Life of Samuel Parker', *Bibliotheca Biblica* (1720-1735), V, preface, vii; see also Sharp (2004).

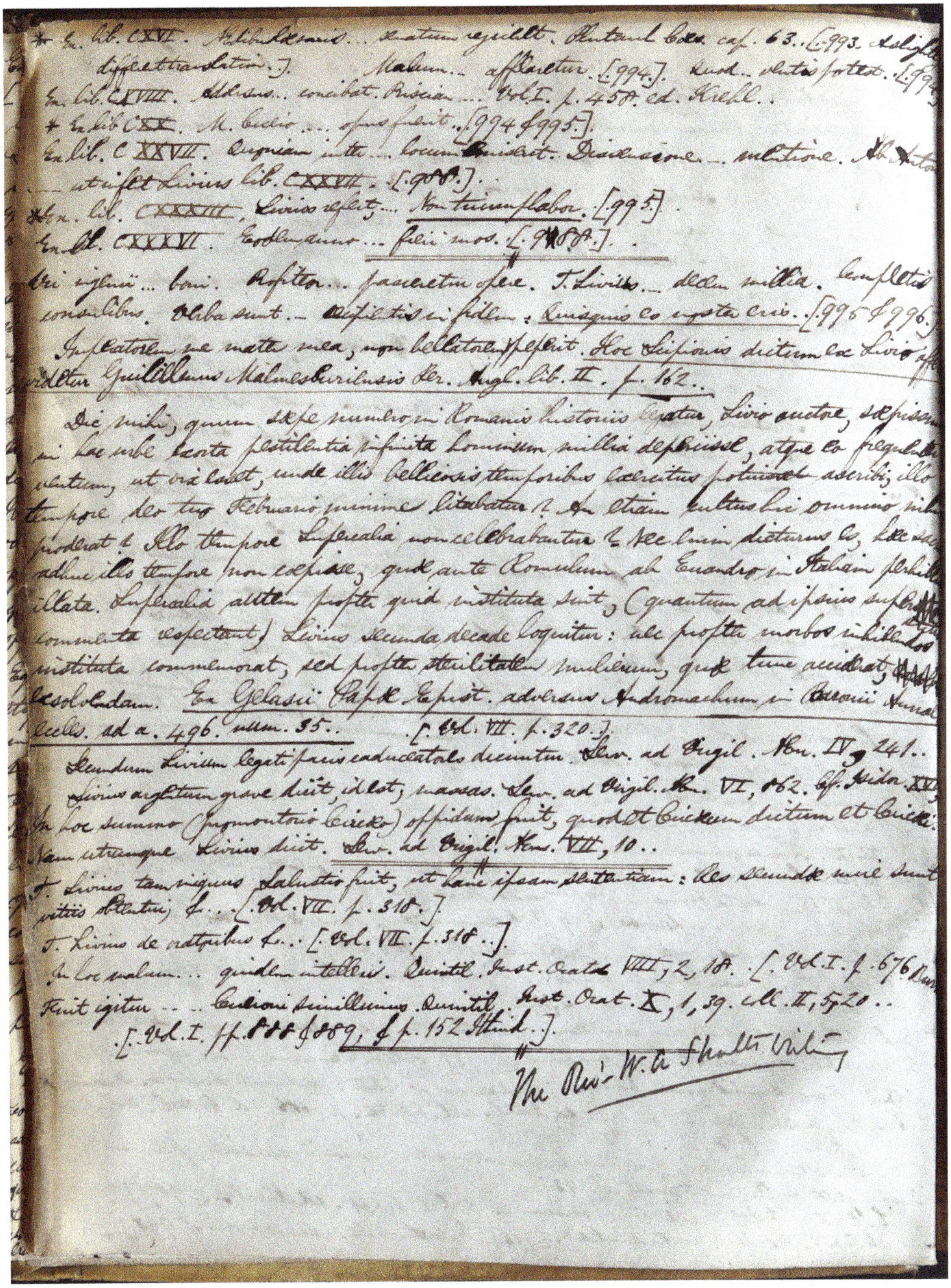

Imperatorem me mater mea, non bellatorem peperit. Hoc Scipionis dictum ex Livio affert Guillelmus Malmesburiensis Scr. Angl. lib. II. p. 162.

The Rev. W. A. Shoults Writing

Plate 17: Livy's *Historiarum ab urbe condita libri* (1738–1746), Vol. II.

Four hand-written sheets are tightly bound in Shoults's copy of volume two of Livy's Historiarum ab urbe condita libri *(Amsterdam, 1738–1746). The notes cover Perseus, the States of Greece, and the fragmentary nature of works by Livy. A contemporary hand has written at the end of the text: 'The Rev. W.A. Shoults's writing'.*

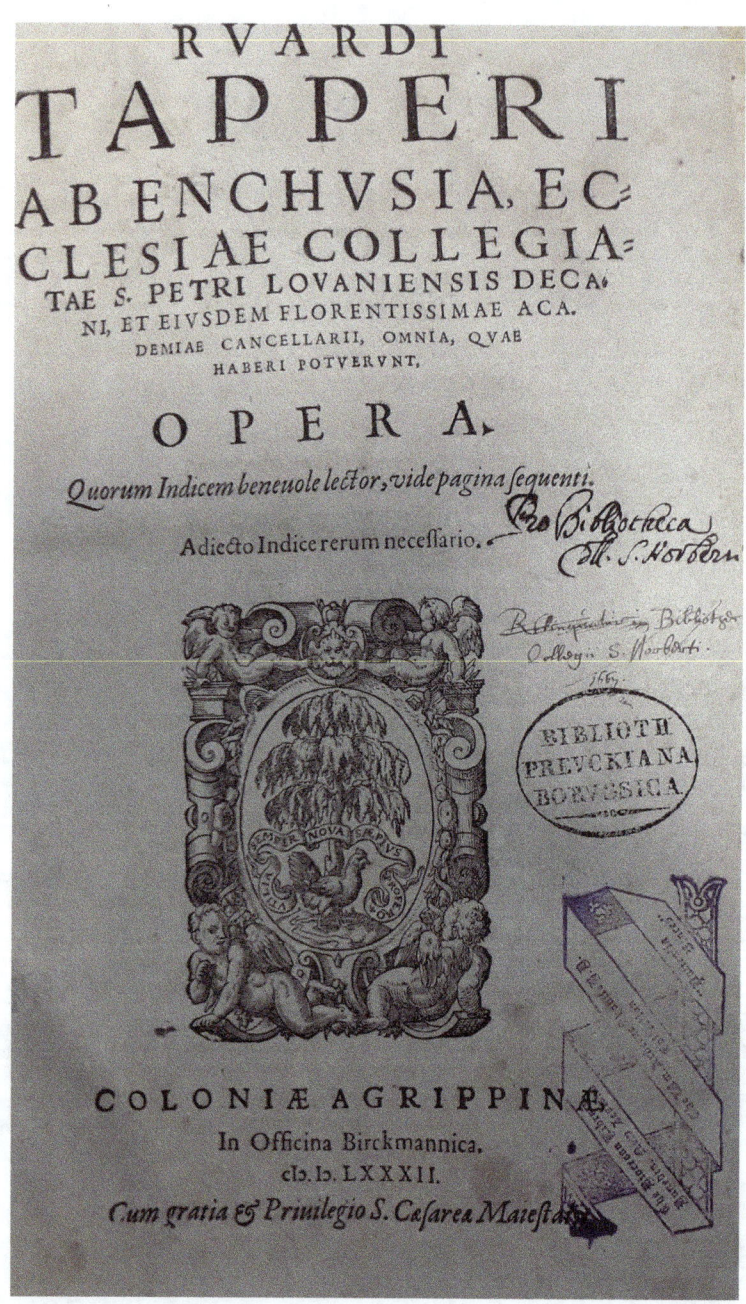

Plate 18. Ruard Tapper, Opera *(1582).*

Many of the books and manuscripts in Shoults's library contain provenance elements, offering evidence that they were once in monastic and institutional libraries, in the libraries of English and European book collectors, or in the hands of lesser-known individuals. This folio edition of the Dutch theologian Ruard Tapper's Opera *(1582) contains inscriptions such as 'Pro Bibliotheca Coll. S. Norberti' (a college of St. Norbert of Xanten, probably Steinfeld, near Cologne), an unidentified ink stamp: 'Biblioth. Prevckiana Borussica', and the purple 'Shoults' stamp, created about 1893.*

Plate 19. Vulgate Bible (1481).

Of the 28 incunables in Shoults's collection, this Venetian printing of the third volume of the Vulgate Bible (c. July 1481) with commentary by Nicolas de Lyra has three outstanding features: it is a typographic masterpiece; the text is bound in a rare Oxford Rood and Hunt binding, of only 26 world-wide; and it has four fragments of indulgences printed by William Caxton and John Lettou sewn in as binding guards.

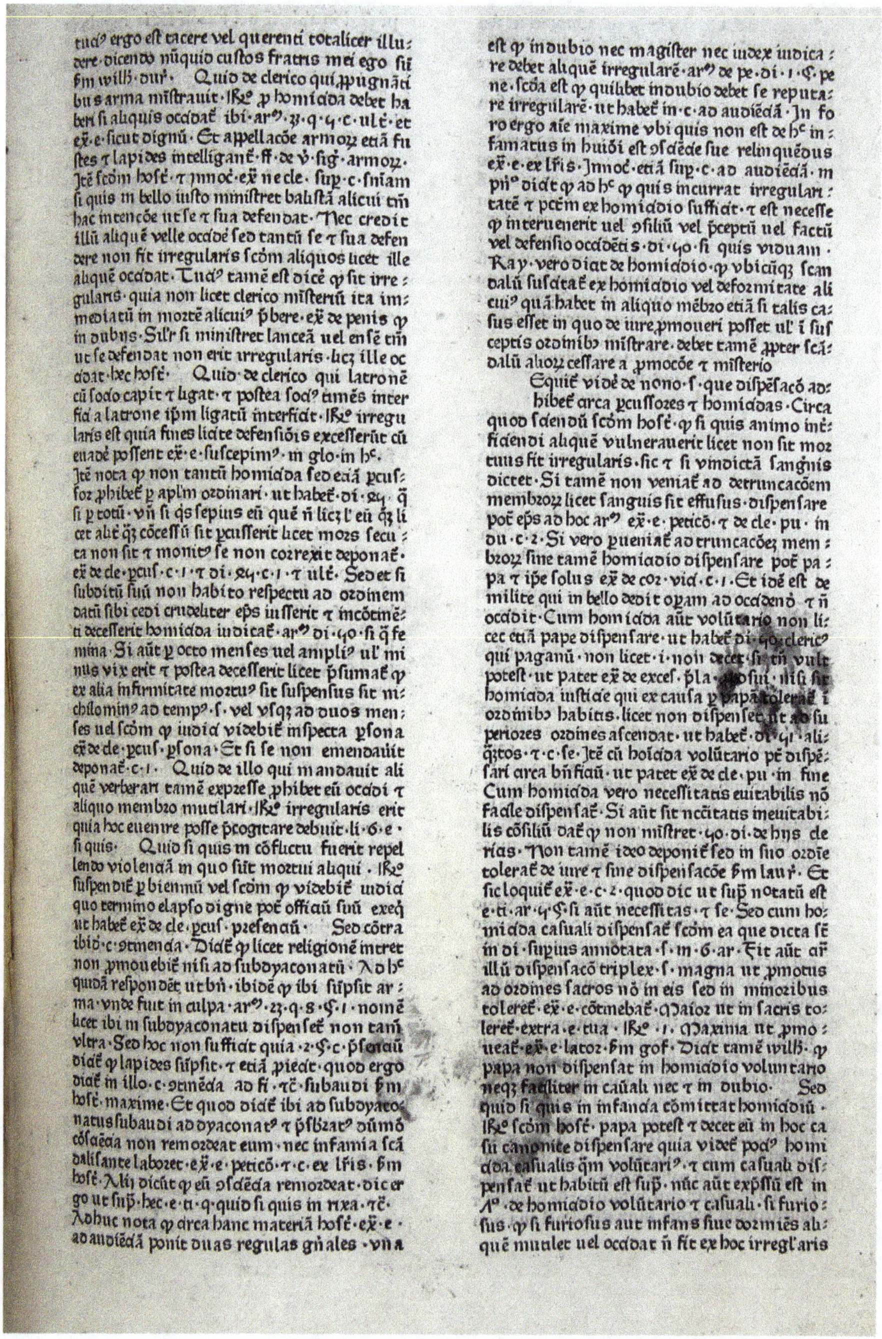

Plate 20. Astesanus de Ast's *Summa de casibus conscientiae* (c.1473).

Shoults owned Johann Mentelin's second printing of Astesanus de Ast's Summa de casibus conscientiae, *published about 1473. Mentelin owned a printing-house cat. On folio 252 there is a moggy's inky paw print on the text, evidence that it walked across the sheets before they were hung up to dry.*

Plate 21. Petronius's *Satyricon* (1693).

The family home at No. 37 Camberwell Grove provided Shoults with much-needed space and a degree of permanence to store his growing book collection. On the left of the title-page of his copy of Petronius's Satyricon *(1693), he has written: 'Brought up from 37 Camberwell Grove, where it had been for many years, last week, I think Thursday, May, 23rd. Thursday, May 30th, 1878.' He also notes a previous owner: Dr Edward Harwood.*

Assertionis Lu

THERANAE CON-
FVTATIO, IVXTA VERVM
ac etiam originalem archetypum, nunc
advnguem diligentissimè recognita,
per Reuerendissimum Patrem
Ioannem Roffensem E-
piscopum, acade=
miæ Canta=
brigien.
Cancellarium.

EZECH. XIII.
Væ Prophetis insipientibus, qui sequuntur spiri=
tum suum, & nihil uident.

PARISIIS
Apud Carolam guillard, sub sole aureo.
Via ad D. Iacobum.
M. D. XLV.

Plate 22 (left). John Fisher, *Assertionis Lutheranae confutatio* (1545).

Bishop John Fisher (1469–1535), was executed by order of Henry VIII for refusing to accept the king as the supreme head of the Church of England, and for upholding the Catholic doctrine of papal supremacy. Fisher's stand against Lutheranism was well-known, and Assertionis Lutheranae confutatio *was one of his many polemics. This Parisian edition of 1545 was printed by Charlotte Guillard, an important early French female printer.*

Plate 23 (above). Erpenius, *Rudimenta linguae Arabicae* (1628).

Amongst Shoults's Middle Eastern books and manuscripts is this Latin and Arabic edition of Rudimenta linguae Arabicae, *by Erpenius (1584–1624), published in Leiden in 1628. Someone has written out the missing text by hand.*

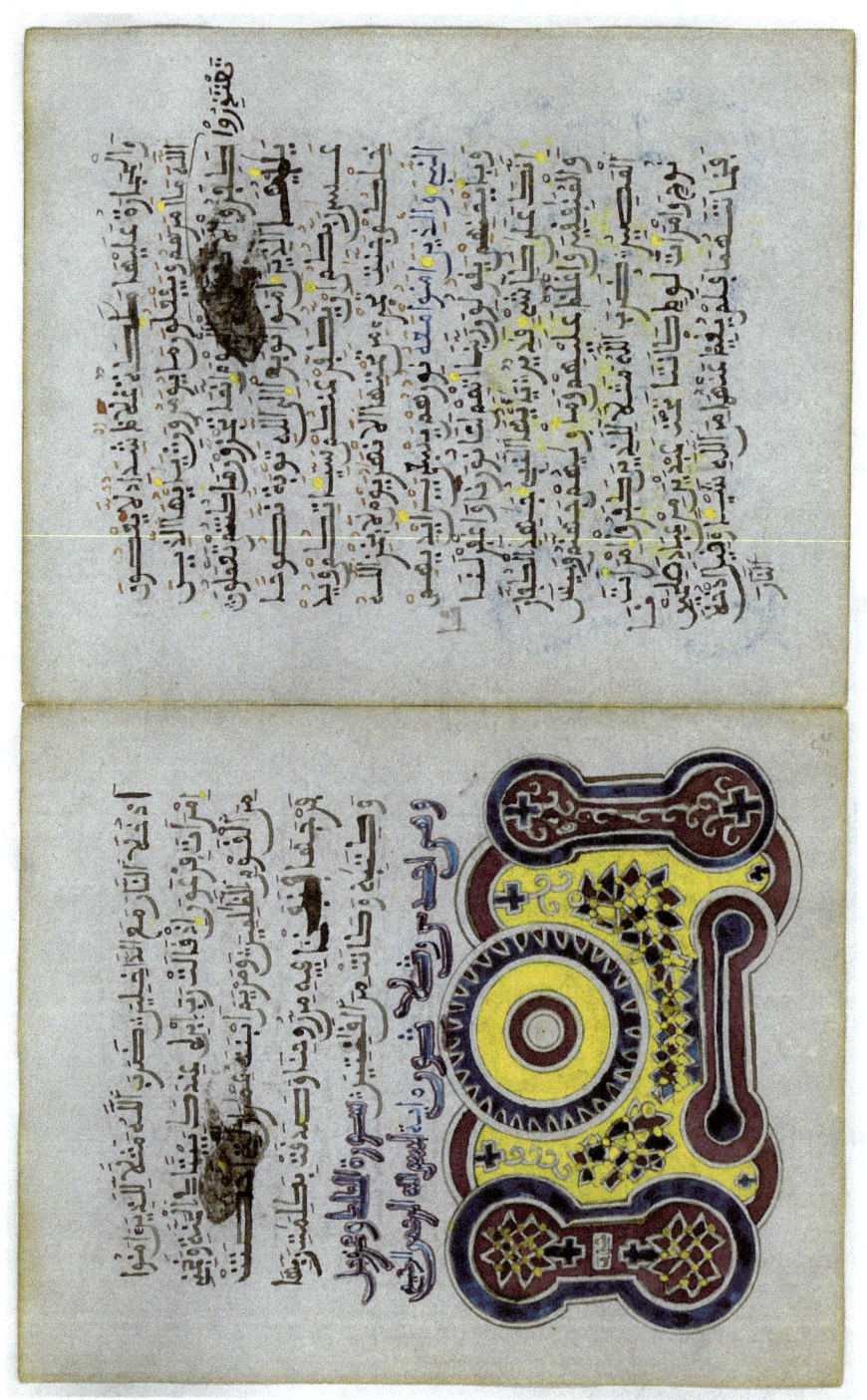

Plate 24. Qur'ān (Koran), c.1846.
One book gift given to Shoults by his wife Eliza is this Arabic language manuscript copy of the Qur'ān (Koran). It is an unusual manuscript of 103 folded, unbound leaves. It contains triangular signs evoking the Trinity, and circles, crosses and images that resemble Christian architectural elements. This 'Christianized' manuscript was written about 1846.

Plate 25.   Samuel Tarratt Nevill (1837–1921), Bishop of Dunedin.

In 1888, Samuel Tarratt Nevill (1837–1921), Bishop of Dunedin, was in London attending the Lambeth Conference. He met Eliza Shoults and convinced her to donate her husband's collection of some 5600 books and manuscripts to Selwyn College, Dunedin, as a foundation library. The entire collection arrived in Dunedin in 1893.

Plate 26. The Shoults Collection, Selwyn College, c.1900.

Esmond de Beer once wrote: 'At Selwyn I handled older books. With no instruction or guidance I could learn little about them, but I acquired freedom of approach to them and awareness that some of them invited study of a kind which I learnt later to know as bibliography.' He would certainly have sat in this room at Selwyn College, where the Shoults Collection was housed for a time. The photograph was taken about 1900.

SELWYN COLLEGE LIBRARY

WILLIAM ARDERNE SHOULTS COLLECTION

The bulk of the books in this collection were given by the widow of the Rev. W. A. Shoults, B.D. of Camberwell London, on the foundation of the college in 1893.

The books are to be used in the library and may not be removed from it.

Plate 27.   Printed notice of the Shoults Collection, c. 1893.

A printed notice created by the Trustees of the Shoults Collection at Selwyn College, Dunedin, c.1893.

13 THE COLLECTION II: THE MIDDLE EAST

Shoults visited Rome, and while there he visited the Vatican Library, losing himself momentarily through the experience of holding a Syriac manuscript in his hand. He may have been able to read Syriac, but, in truth, his expertise in reading this language, a variant of Aramaic, is not known. He could, however, read other languages. From notes written in some of his books, he had Arabic and Hebrew, and perhaps some familiarity with Persian and Chaldean. He was interested in such materials, and his collection contains seven Middle Eastern manuscripts (three Arabic, two a mix of Turkish and Persian, and two a mix of Persian and Arabic) and numerous printed books. In travelling to Italy, it is not inconceivable that he extended his travels to visit Egypt, Persia, and other Ottoman areas. However, this excursion, if taken, would have satisfied his personal interest only. In the main, book buying was done at the centre of the book collecting world, which was still London. Below is a brief description of the manuscripts and printed books that Shoults acquired, followed by publications that no doubt helped him contextualise the area we now call the Middle East. Although provenance details are scant, those that are present are given in the following descriptions.

MIDDLE EASTERN MANUSCRIPTS: ARABIC

The first Arabic manuscript is the text of Genesis 5. 32 to Exodus 19. 16. It consists of 87 leaves written in about 1808, probably for an English-based agency in the East (MS.10). Two aspects of the translation are interesting: one, that in contrast with common Arabic translations of the Bible, the term 'God' has been translated as 'Allāh' instead of 'Rabb'; two, that the use of the term *Raqīm* (Qur'ān (Koran) 18: 9) suggests that the translator was 'Islamicising' the Bible. There is a label of William H. Allen, a bookseller, publisher, and importer of Oriental works at 7 Leadenhall Street, London, from whom Shoults perhaps acquired it.

The second is an incomplete copy of the Qur'ān (MS.11). This manuscript, 103 unbound leaves wrapped in a blind-stamped calf binding, starts with *Sūrat Maryam* (Qur'ān 19), with the first page featuring an ornament of six crosses in red placed inside a circle surrounded by geometrical shapes. (See pl. 24.) Overall, the ornament resembles a flower. Triangular signs evoking the Trinity and circles and images that resemble Christian architectural elements are found throughout the manuscript. In addition, two wheels that look like flowers enclosing six white crosses are vertically positioned at Qur'ān 34: 30-33, surrounding verses that address disbelievers who reject the Qur'ān and earlier scriptures. The verses are directed to those arrogant enough to disbelieve: 'It was your scheming by night and day; as you instructed us to reject God, and to set up rivals to Him.' (Qur'ān 34: 33). This 'Christianised' manuscript, written about 1846, contains numerous scribal errors and omissions.[1] Shoults's wife Eliza seemed to have chosen well again. It was a gift from her, and has an inscription written inside: 'The Koran (Manuscript) in Native Binding. Very rare & curious (EKS).'

The final Arabic manuscript—Shoults MS.12—is a copy of *Dalā' il al-Khayrāt wa Shawāriq al-Anwār fī Dhikr al-Ṣalāt 'alā al-Nabī al-Mukhtār* (The Guide Book of Blessings and Enlightment [that comes from] Invoking the Chosen Prophet in Prayer) by Muhammad ibn Sulaymān al-Jazūlī (d.1465), written in 1804 or 1805. Bound in a blind-stamped leather wrap, with a gilt ornament on the flap and back cover, the manuscript consists of a number of sections with various supplications that address the beautiful names and attributes of God (*asmā' al-husnā*), prayer (*ṣalāt*), and supplication (*du'ā*) of *Istikhāra* (augury). There are notes about the qualities (*khawāṣṣ*) of some names that were used by Jesus to raise the dead and about the fact that he prayed *rak'atayn* (two units of prayer) before raising the dead. There is no evidence of when and from whom Shoults acquired the manuscript, but a later note clarifies the content of the work: 'It is not a Koran manuscript. It is a supplication book apparently written [copied] by 'Alī ibn al-Mabrūk al-Talghamtī on Thursday 21, Dhū al-Hijja/1219 A.H. [*Anno Hegirae*] March 1805 AD.'[2]

TURKISH MANUSCRIPTS

The first Turkish language manuscript (MS.08) is a copy of a commentary on the Preface (*dībācheh*) to the *Golestān* (The Rose Garden) by Sa'dī Shīrāzī (d. c.1292), with particular attention to its literal and grammatical aspects. The text is 69 leaves long and is written in an Ottoman Turkish and Persian script. Originally attributed to the scribe Sayyid Muhmmad (Mehmet) ibn Hāfiz Osmān (d. 1698), this copy has a commentary in Persian that gives the date 1790. Although a text primarily in Ottoman Turkish, it is replete with references to Persian poets, poems, and thinkers—among others, Hāfiz Shīrāzī (d. c.1390), Sanāī (d. c.1131), Firdowsī (d. c.1025), Kamāl Khojandī (d. c.1401), and Farrokhī (d. c.1037). It also has an appendix that contains a scarce Persian ethical and devotional instruction in which names such as Ishāq al-

---

[1] See Daneshgar (2017) for details on Shoults MS. 11 and all other Middle Eastern manuscripts and books mentioned in this chapter. See also the online link to the exhibition *A Middle Eastern Odyssey. From Constantinople to Palmyra* (2018).

[2] The Hijri year is the era used in the Islamic lunar calendar, which begins its count from the Islamic New Year in 622. In the West, this era is denoted as AH (*Anno Hegirae*), which is parallel to AD (*anno Domini*, 'in the year of our Lord').

Mūsilī (d. c.850), a famous Arab musician and thinker, and Jaʿfar al-Ṣādiq (d. c.765), the famous mystical figure and sixth Imām of Shīʿa, are mentioned.

The second Turkish manuscript (MS.09), with some Arabic alphabets and notes, is an untitled guide for writing letters and addressing petitions, written in the nineteenth century. The various sections, written in different hands, give advice on how to write letters offering full affection, respect, and kindness to authorities, and so on. Some parts of the Qur'ān are quoted, and various names occur throughout, such as Effendi Mustafā, Muhammad ibn Hasan, Hasan Çelebi, and Mawlānā ʿAbd al-Rahmān. On the front free endpaper there is an auction note ('Lot 466') and an inscription ('8/10/1879'), which hint at how and when Shoults acquired the manuscript.

ARABIC AND PERSIAN MANUSCRIPTS

The last two manuscripts are bound together in old half-bound board covers. The first text is *Mishkāt al-Daʿwāt* by ʿAbd al-Razzāq, the second *Munawwar al-Qulūb* by ʿAlī ibn Ahmad (MS.13a). The first is a traditional (*hadīthī*) book in Arabic and Persian phrases. It includes *tahlīl* (pronouncing loudly a formula), *tasbīh* (glorification), *tahmīd* (praising), *takbīr* (magnification of God), *hawqala* (expressing there is neither might nor strength but in God), and the names of God. Supplications of morning and evening are present, as well as topics such as the marriage sermon, *taʿwīdh* (amulet and incantation), pilgrimages, *tawāf* (circumambulation of the Kaʿba), the Day of ʿArafah,[3] and laying the deceased in a grave. Dated about 1722, the manuscript contains sources from Sunni *Hadīth* compendia.

The second text (MS.13b) is written in Persian with the title in Arabic. The Persian section begins with a note suggesting to Muslims a formula on how to ward off enemies through reciting Qur'ānic verses, twelve times being the magical number. The author, perhaps a Sufi, has prepared this treatise for those seekers of truth (*tālebān-e Haqq*), based on the advice of, seemingly, a Sufi ruler called Shaykh Mīranjīr. This mystical work also contains traditions from Jaʿfar al-Ṣādiq addressing how to fast and starve. This volume contains an unknown dealer's note that reads: 'Two Theological Treatises. The one in Arabic; the other in Persian. Indifferently written. Small folio; half-bound. 105 pp. 9s.' There is also an auction note of 'Lot 447' and date '8/10/79' that matches the inscription in the above Turkish manuscript on letter writing. Shoults surely secured both at auction in October 1879.

---

[3] One day before the festival of sacrifices (*ʿId al-Adhā*) during the pilgrimage.

PRINTED BOOKS

The seventy-one printed books relating to Middle Eastern languages are in Urdu (2), Persian (12), Ottoman Turkish (7), Arabic (30), Syriac (5), and Hebrew (15). The categories include grammars, dictionaries, student textbooks, scriptures, history, literature (mostly poetry), philosophy and ethics, and science. Many of the works are bilingual—for example, Latin and Arabic, Latin and Persian, and English and Turkish.

URDU

The first book in Urdu is a copy of *Durrat al-Tāj* (*The Crown Jewel*) by Muzaffar ʿAlī Khān (also known as Asīr), Captin Maqbūl al-Dawlah, and Ihān al-Mulk Muhammad Mahdī-ʿAlī-Khān. This battered and torn copy of this Shiite prayer book contains rhyming couplets (*mathnavī*) and odes (*ghazal*s) that make special reference to the praise of the Prophet Muhammad and his ascension night, 'the Isra' and Miʿraj'. Historical events and periods are also mentioned. The book was published in India, perhaps Delhi, in 1853.

The second Urdu text is a copy of a translation of a treatise by Ikram ʿAli called *Ikhwan al-Safa'* ('Brethren of Purity'), published at Fort William College, Calcutta, around 1810. As a textbook for civilians and interpreters, it shows evidence of use. There are English glosses in pencil running throughout the text, suggesting that they were done by an English speaker learning Urdu.

PERSIAN GRAMMARS

Shoults had four Persian works relating to grammar, vocabulary, and the like. The first is a copy of the first edition of Sir William Jones's classic *A Grammar of the Persian Language*, published in 1771. This seminal work lacks the title page and all the preliminary leaves before page [iii]. Jones (1746–94) was an Anglo-Welsh philologist, particularly known for his work on Sanskrit, his demonstration of the existence of a relationship among European and Indian languages (thus Indo-European languages), and his formation of the Asiatic Society of Bengal in 1784. Shoults also owned a copy of the fourth edition of the *Grammar*, published in 1797, which, according to an ink inscription, was probably acquired by him on 7 February 1877.

The third title is a copy of the second edition of Francis Balfour's *The Forms of Herkern Corrected from a Variety of Manuscripts*, published in 1804. This Persian-English version of *Insha-ye Herkern*, translated by Balfour (c.1744–1818) and dedicated to Warren Hastings, includes various sample letters with their replies, some verse, and a comprehensive index. Shoults's copy contains the bookplate of Sir Henry Miers Elliot (1808–53), an English civil servant who worked for the East India Company and is best known for his posthumously-published *The History of India* (1867–1877).

The last title is Arthur Henry Bleeck's *A Concise Grammar of the Persian Language, Containing Dialogues, Reading Lessons, and a Vocabulary: Together with a New Plan for Facilitating the Study of Languages. And Specimens in Arabic, Armenian, Bengali, Greek, Georgian, Hindustani, Hebrew, Latin, Persian, Russian, Sanskrit, Swedish, Syriac, and Turkish*. This publication, which makes reference to important Persian literary works, contains various sections on the alphabets, pronouns, verbs, adverbs, and so on. It was published by Bernard Quaritch, 'Oriental and Philological Publisher', in 1857.

PERSIAN HISTORIES

The first Persian history (of four) is a version of *The Life of Sheikh Mohammed Ali Hazin*, translated and edited by Francis Cunningham Belfour (fl. 1829–47) from two Persian manuscripts. It was printed for the Oriental Translation Fund in 1831 and dedicated to King William IV and members of the Royal Asiatic Society (RAS), an organisation established by Royal Charter on 11 August 1824 with the aim of investigating 'subjects connected with and for the encouragement of science, literature and the arts in relation to Asia'.[4]

The second is a geographical publication that gives the names of various countries, cities, villages, rivers and mountains derived from two Persian manuscripts in the collection of Sir William Ouseley (1767–1842), a British orientalist and prolific author of Persian-related materials. Originally titled *Tahkik al-'Irab*, this work is translated as *Geographical Works of Sādik Isfahani*, a famous map-maker at the Mughal Court, for the emperor of India, Shah Jahan (1628–58). The identity of the translator—one J.C.—remains unknown. Although somewhat pedestrian in content, the work is a complex piece of printing that had the inherent purpose of instilling in readers the proper pronunciation of Middle Eastern locales. It was published for the Oriental Translation Fund in 1832.

The third is a copy of David Shea's translation of *Rawdatu 's-safa*, the Persian-language history of Islam and Persian history by Mirkhvand (1433–98). Sometimes translated as *The Gardens of Purity in the Biography of the Prophets and Kings and Caliphs*, Shea's version is titled *History of the Early Kings of Persia*. Shoults's copy was published in 1832 for the Society for the Publication of Oriental Texts.

---

[4] 'Charter of Incorporation', *Royal Asiatic Society*, 1 (1824), xi.

The final history title is Mir Hussain Ali Khan Kirmani's *The History of the Reign of Tipu Sultan*, which was translated into English by Colonel William Miles and also printed for the Oriental Translation Fund in 1844. Taken from a Persian manuscript owned by Queen Victoria, it is a contemporary account of Tipu (1750–99), a military strategist and freedom-fighter, known as the 'Tiger of Mysore'.

PERSIAN POETRY

Shoults acquired two books of Persian poetry. The first is a copy of the first edition of Aleksander Borejko Chodzko's *Specimens of the Popular Poetry of Persia*, published in 1842. It was the Polish poet's first foray into Persian folklore and traditions.[5] The second is a copy of Nizami Ganjavi's *Makhzan Ul Asrar, The Treasury of Secrets: Bring the First of the Five Poems, or Khamsah, of Sheikh Nizami, of Ganjah* (d.1209), printed for the Society for the Publication of Oriental Texts in 1844. It contains the bookplate of John Lee (1783–1866), born John Fiott, an English philanthropist, astronomer, mathematician, and antiquarian. Lee was also a member of the Oriental Translation Committee, which was established in 1828 as an initiative of the RAS. According to a note inside, Lee received this copy on 18 January 1848 as part of his duties for the Committee. More details on Lee will be covered in chapter 16.

PHILOSOPHY AND ETHICS

Shoults acquired a few books dealing with social and moral practices. One is a copy of *Practical Philosophy of the Muhammadan People, Being a Translation of the Akhlak-i-Jalaly, the Most Esteemed Ethical Work of the Middle Asia*, from the Persian of Fakir Jāny Muhammad Asäad, with references, notes, and English translation by W. F. Thompson. It was published for the Oriental Translation Fund in 1839. Another is a copy of a translation by the polymath Hosayn Wa 'Ez Kāšefi called *Akhlak-i Muhsini, or The Morals of the Beneficent*. Published in 1850, this work on ethics and statecraft had been translated by the Rev. Henry George Keene (1781–1864), a student at Fort William College who gained high honours as a scholar in Persian and Arabic studies.[6]

TURKISH BOOKS

Shoults was interested enough in the Ottoman Turkish language to acquire six grammars, some of them quite scarce. The first is a copy of the second edition of Franciscus (Franciszek) à Mesgnien Meninski's *Institutiones linguae Turcicae*, published in Vienna in 1756. First published in 1680, it was ground-breaking, as it offered historians

---

[5] Calmard (1990).
[6] Subtelny (2011).

and linguists valuable information on the Turkish language of the early modern period. Shoults's two-volumes-in-one copy was a greatly improved edition, offering, in Latin, instruction on the Ottoman Turkish language and samples of romanised and transliterated versions of various terms and phrases.[7] The book has the price of '£1.1.0 2 vols in one' written inside, which may have been what he paid for it.

The second is a copy of the first edition of Arthur Lumley Davids's *Grammar of the Turkish Language* (*Kitab al-'ilm al-Nafi' fi Tahsil Sarf wa Nahw Turki*), published in London in 1832. It was regarded as a significant publication, covering the language in four parts: Grammar, Vocabulary, Dialogues, and Extracts.[8] Tucked between pages 66 and 67 is a loosely-inserted map of 'Plan of the Bombardment of Odessa, 22 April 1854'. The third is a copy of the first edition of William Burckhardt Barker's *A Practical Grammar of the Turkish Language*, published by Bernard Quaritch in 1854. This elementary guide contains the usual alphabets, parts of speech, and simple dialogue with conversation samples. It also contains a vocabulary of English-Ottoman Turkish words.

The fourth, of which only the second volume of two is present, is a copy of an *English and Turkish Dictionary* by Sir James William Redhouse (1811–92), who was secretary of the RAS from 1861 to 1864. This title was published by Bernard Quaritch in 1857. The fifth is a copy of a Turkish-English textbook for foreign speakers, entitled *Ingilizcenin Mubtediye Mahsus olarak Imla ve Telaffuz Risalesidir*, published in London in 1858.

The last is a copy of *Dialogues in English and Turkish* by Mahmoud Effendi, who, according to the title-page, was a mining engineer. This grammar, prepared for the Sultan and those students interested in learning English, is divided into two parts: 'Easy Dialogues' (47 conversations) and 'Familiar Dialogues' (50 conversations covering topics such as visiting and going to school). The title-page has an embossed stamp from the Protestant College of Malta. John Connell Ogle, Shoults's father-in-law, travelled through this area in the 1850s, and perhaps he acquired this volume on his travels, it being one of those titles passed to his daughter Eliza and eventually to William.

The only Scriptural work in Ottoman Turkish that Shoults owned is a copy of *Kitab al-'Ahd al-Jadid*, the New Testament, published by the British and Foreign Bible Society in 1853. This is a provisional revision of the *editio princeps* of the Bible in Osmanlı (Turkish), published in Paris in 1827.[9]

---

[7] Entry of 'Meninski or Menin' in Chalmers (1815b), XXII, 52–4.
[8] See Davids (1882), 353–6.
[9] See Darlow (1911), 9468.

PRINTED ARABIC BOOKS: GRAMMARS

Thirty 'Arabic' books form a large percentage of Shoults's Middle Eastern cache. He owned 14 grammars, lexicons, and the like. Some are seminal titles. The first is a copy of the first edition of Franciscus Raphelengius's *Lexicon arabicum,* an Arabic-Latin dictionary posthumously published in Leiden in 1613. Raphelengius (1539–97), a Flemish-born scholar who later became Professor of Hebrew at the University of Leiden, was the first to compile such a dictionary.[10]

The Dutch scholar Thomas van Erpe (1584–1624) was responsible for seeing the above *Lexicon* through the press, and, somewhat fittingly, his own *Observationes in lexicon arabicum* is bound in. In 1613, Erpenius, as he was known, Professor of Arabic and Oriental (not Hebrew) Studies at the University of Leiden, was the first European to publish an accurate book of Arabic grammar.

Shoults owned three other works by Erpenius, who has been called 'the first great Protestant Orientalist'.[11] He acquired a copy of the rare second corrected edition of Erpenius's *Rudimenta linguae arabicae,* an abridged version of his famed *Grammatica arabica,* published by Elzevir in Leiden in 1628. (See pl. 23.) Six leaves of the original printed text are missing (pages 121 to 132), but they have been replaced in manuscript. The book has extensive annotations, especially in the chapter on verbs. It also has an index written in black ink at the front, quite possibly in Shoults's hand. It also has a presentation inscription: 'Liber Francisci Ffox Ex Dono Michaelis Payn, Dec 10th out of his prison chamber in the Princes Hostle in Sycamore Court, 1663.'

The second is a copy of the 'third' edition of Erpenius's *Grammatica arabica* incorporated into *Arabicae linguae tyrocinium,* a chrestomathy published in Leiden in 1656, edited by Jacob Golius (1596–1667), Erpenius's most distinguished student. This book contains a later printing of *Locamani sapientis fabulae,* a collection of proverbs and fables attributed to Luqman (Lokman) the sage. Shoults's copy was once owned by J. B. Hollingsworth, Fellow of Peterhouse, Cambridge, who presented it to George Cecil Renouard (1780–1867), Lord Almoner's Professor of Arabic at Cambridge.

Finally, Shoults acquired a copy of Leonard Chappelow's revised and augmented edition of Erpenius's standard Arabic grammar *Elementa linguae arabicae,* published in London in 1730. Chappelow (1692–1768) was an orientalist, appointed in 1720 as Professor of Arabic and in 1729 as Lord Almoner's Reader in Arabic.

In collaboration with his brother Everard Scheidius (1742–94), professor of Oriental Languages at the now defunct University of Harderwijk, Jacobus Scheidius

---

[10] See Irwin (2007), 101–2.
[11] Irwin (2007), 102.

(1754–1801) re-edited Jacob Golius's *Lexicon arabico-latinum*. The result, which Shoults owned, was *Glossarium arabico-latinum manuale*, published in Leiden in 1769. His copy contains a rather long pencil note at the bottom of the rear pastedown, which ends with: 'L. B. (1787) [indecipherable squiggle] Br. d. Ogle 136', a hint that it may have belonged to Shoult's father-in-law.

The next Arabic publication is a copy of Claude-Étienne Savary's *Grammaire de la Langue Arabe Vulgaire et Litterale,* published in Paris in 1813. This posthumous publication by Savary (1750–88), an orientalist and pioneer of Egyptology, is important because it contains for the first time in print a substantial part of *One Thousand and One Nights* in Arabic.

Shoults also owned a copy of the first and only edition of Ernest Friedrich Karl Rosenmüller's *Institutiones ad fundamenta linguae arabicae*, published in Leipzig in 1818.

There are six remaining grammars. They are *Grammatica generale della lingua araba* by Archbishop Maksimus ibn Jurjis Mazlum (1779–1855), published in Rome in 1830, an Arabic and English textbook containing grammatical exercises and dialogues, published in Malta in 1840, *Marah al-arwah*, an extensive work on Arabic morphology and phonology by Ahmad ibn 'Ali ibn Mas'ud, published in Istanbul in 1852, and a copy of the second edition of *A Practical Grammar of the Arabic Language* by Faris El-Shidiac, or Fares Chidiac (1805–87), Professor of Arabic at the University of Malta, published by Bernard Quaritch in 1866. The final two grammars have dates pencilled inside that indicate when they were acquired. *The Eastern Traveller's Interpreter; or, Arabic without a Teacher* is an Arabic-English guide book by Assaad Yacoob Kayat (c.1811–70), published in London in 1844.[12] Written inside is '8 October 1879', the date that matches those written in the Turkish and Persian manuscripts mentioned above. The last is a copy of the first edition of *Cours Synthétique, Analytique et Pratique de Langue Arabe*, a textbook for students by Jean-François Bled de Braine, published in Paris in 1846. Here Shoults wrote firmer acquisition details: 'Bought 27/6/78'.

SCRIPTURES IN ARABIC

Scriptural works in Arabic number four. The first is a copy of *Kitab Ta'lm al-Mas*, a translation of *L'Instruction du Chrétien*, a catechism composed by Cardinal Richelieu (1585–1642) and translated into Arabic by Juste de Beauvais, one-time head of the Capuchin mission in Baghdad.[13] Shoults's copy was published in Paris in 1640.

---

[12] Zachs (2014), 21.
[13] See Ayalon (2008), 151–65.

Shoults owned a first edition of the *Holy Bible* in Arabic, printed and published by Sarah Hodgson at Newcastle-upon-Tyne in 1811. First supervised by Joseph Dacre Carlyle (1759–1805), professor of Arabic at Cambridge, it was seen through the press by Henry Ford, Lord Almoner's Reader in Arabic at Oxford. Hodgson's Bible has an English title-page, with the remaining text in Arabic, based on the *naskh* calligraphy.[14] This publication, an outstanding achievement in printing, was supported financially by the Society for the Propagation of the Gospel and the British and Foreign Bible Society.[15]

The third is a copy of the Four Gospels in Coptic and Arabic, published by the British and Foreign Bible Society in 1829. The Coptic text was edited by the Coptic scholar Henry Tattam (1788–1868), the Arabic by Samuel Lee (1783–1852), Professor at Cambridge, first of Arabic and then of Hebrew.[16]

The last scriptural work is Shoults's second *Qur'ān*, a lithographed edition published in Bombay in 1850, according to a note in Persian which reads in English: 'the divine Word of God and heavenly revelation finished and designed in the manufacture (the publisher/ printer) of Mīrzā Hasan Kāshānī in Bombay in Safar of 1266 AH (1850 AD).' This work is wrapped in a conventional Middle Eastern cover of red calf, with the front flap gilt stamped. The *Qur'ān* ends with the supplication of 'the Completion of Qur'anic Recitation'.

ARAB HISTORIES

Shoults owned five history titles. The first is a copy of the second edition of Muwaffaq al-Din 'Abd al-Latif al-Baghdadi's *Abdollatiphi historiae Aegypti compendium*, published in Oxford in 1800. Compiled and amended by Joseph White (1745–1814), Laudian Professor of Arabic and Regius Professor of Hebrew at Oxford, this Arabic and Latin version was based on an Arabic manuscript discovered by Edward Pococke in 1665.

The second is a copy of *Selecta ex historia Halebi*, a Latin and Arabic translation of a selected history of Aleppo by the historian Kamal al-Din 'Umar ibn Ahmad ibn al-'Adim (1192–1262). Published in Paris in 1819, the Latin translation is by Georg Wilhelm Friedrich Freytag (1788–1861), a German philologist who was Professor of Oriental Languages at the University of Bonn. This copy once belonged to Frederick North, fifth earl of Guilford, who, as described in chapter 11, founded the Ionian

---

[14] Darlow (1911), 1650.
[15] Each contributed £250. See Darlow (1911), 1650.
[16] Darlow (1911), Arabic, 1829.

Academy in Corfu. It was then passed to John Lee, whom we will meet further in chapter 16.

The third is another publication financed by the Oriental Translation Fund. It is Husayn ibn 'Alī al-Mas 'Udī's *Muruj adh-Dhahab wa-Ma 'adin al-Jawhar*, a world history translated into English as *Meadows of Gold and Mines of Gems*, published in 1841. This seminal work, a historical encyclopaedia by one who was termed the 'Herodotus of the Arabs', was translated by the Austrian orientalist Aloys Sprenger (1813–93).[17]

The fourth is another RAS publication, published in Paris in 1842. This is Taki-Eddin-Ahmed-Makrizi's *Histoire des Sultans Mamlouks, de L'Egypte*, edited and translated into French by Étienne Marc Quatremère (1782–1857), the French orientalist and student of Silvestre de Sacy (1758–1838). The Egyptian Al-Maqrizi or Makrizi (1364–1442) was a Sunni Muslim historian. Shoults's copy—the second volume only of four—is uncut, and thus not read.

The final history title is by Ibn Qutaybah (Ibn Coteiba; 213–15 Rajab 276 AH; 828–89), who was a renowned Islamic polymath. Qutaybah's *Handbuch der Geschichte (Kitāb al-Ma 'ārif)* covers the creation of, and facts about, the period before the appearance of Islam (*jāhiliyyah*), the names of the companions of the Prophet Muhammed, and of famous jurists and masters of the oral tradition (*hadīth*) associated with the Prophet. Shoults's copy, with its German translation by the orientalist Heinrich Ferdinand Wüstenfeld (1808–99), was published in Göttingen in 1850.

ARABIC LITERATURE

Shoults owned three literary works. Perhaps the greatest orientalist of the seventeenth century in England was Edward Pococke (1604–91).[18] Shoults owned a copy of the first edition of Pococke's Latin translation of al-Tughrai's *Lamiato 'l Ajam*, published in Oxford in 1661. The ode (*qasida*) decries the corrupt times which the author lived in and has been called 'a tour de force'.[19] The second title is bound in with Pococke's text: Samuel Clarke's *Scientia metrica & rhythmica, seu tractatus de prosodia Arabica* (1661), one of the first European treatises on the metrics of Arabian poetry. Samuel Clarke (1624–69) was one of Pococke's students, and it was he that saw the work through the press. There are manuscript notes aplenty in this rather broken book. Shoults created a small index headed 'Proverbia'. He also made a note on a preliminary page that reads:

---

[17] Irwin (2007), 207–8.
[18] 'Pococke', in *EB*, XXI, 873.
[19] Irwin (2007), 96.

'Proverbia Index. D. Castelli p. 2253 iii.' He did not own any of David Castelli's works and must have sourced the Italian scholar's work from elsewhere. Also noted are the names of previous owners—one Kilvert and an R. Howell (1791)—and a number of unidentified booksellers' catalogue entries accompanied by prices such as 3s and 3s 6d.

The last literary work is a copy of the first edition in Arabic and Latin of the Cambridge scholar Henry Sike's *Evangelium infantiae vel liber apocryphus de infantia servatoris*, a version of *Injil al-Tufuliyya* that originates from Syriac sources of the fifth and sixth centuries. Published in Utrecht in 1697, this apocryphal piece concerns the childhood of Jesus: his birth, based on the Gospel of James; miracles performed during the flight into Egypt; and miracles that Jesus performed as a little boy, based on the Infancy Gospel of Thomas. Some of the claims are amusing: a magic diaper that heals people, the sweat of Jesus that turns into balm and cures leprosy, and an early encounter between Jesus and Judas Iscariot.[20] A front endpaper has the note 'very curious' written on it.

PHILOSOPHY

Philosophy-related texts follow. Shoults owned a copy of the parallel Greek and Latin edition of Simplicius of Cilicia's *Commentarius in enchiridion Epicteti*, published by Johan Maire in Leiden in 1640. Amendments to Simplicius's commentaries on Epictetus's *Enchiridion* are by Hieronymus Wolf (1516–80) and Claude de Saumaise (1588–1653). Bound with this work is the parallel Greek, Latin, and Arabic *Tabula Cebetis Graece* and the golden verses of Pythagoras (*Aurea carmina Pythagorae*) translated by Johan Elichman (c.1601–39), the gifted Silesian linguist famed for his 'Scythian' theory, establishing similarities between Persian and Germanic languages.[21] The presswork and typography by Maire is excellent.

The other 'philosophical' work is a copy of the first Latin and Arabic edition of Burhan al-Islam al-Zarniji's *Ta 'lm al-Muta 'allim-arq at-Ta 'allum*, entitled *Enchiridion studiosi Arabice conscriptum*, a short introduction to the secrets of attaining knowledge, originally composed about 1200. Published in Utrecht in 1709, this edition is the work of Adrian Reeland (1676–1718), the noted Dutch orientalist. Shoults also owned a later edition of Reeland's *De religione Mohammedica*, published in Utrecht in 1717. This work is considered the first objective survey of Islamic beliefs and practices and as a consequence was quickly translated into numerous European languages.[22]

---

[20] See Elliott (1993).
[21] Van Hal (2010), 70–80.
[22] Irwin points out that despite all his good work, Reeland (or Reland) regarded Arabic as a handmaiden to

SCIENCE

The one scientific work that Shoults acquired is a copy of the Latin and Arabic edition of Muhammad ibn Kathir al-Farghani's *Elementa astronomica, Arabice & Latine* (*Kitab fi l-Harakat al-Samawiya wa Jawami' 'Ilm al-Nujum*), published in Amsterdam in 1669. Al-Farghani (known as Alfraganus in the West) was a Sunni Muslim and one of the most famous astronomers of the ninth century. This rather battered copy was once owned by Dr Thomas Robinson (1790–1873), Lord Almoner's Professor of Arabic at Cambridge. A label of the London booksellers Ogles, Duncan, & Cochran, a firm that specialised in theological books, is pasted inside. Robinson could have purchased the book from their Holborn Road premises, or perhaps Shoults acquired it from them sometime after the death of Robinson.

SYRIAC BOOKS

The Bible was translated into Syriac, a Semitic language, in about the second century. This translation process was instrumental in aiding the expansion of the Christian faith in the Middle East. Indeed, for scholars Syriac was a way through to understanding biblical Aramaic, the language that Christ spoke.[23] While Shoults did not own a Syriac manuscript to lose himself in, he did possess a copy of a printed Syriac New Testament, a *Peshitta* in Serto script, edited by the orientalist Samuel Lee, published in London in 1816.[24]

Shoults possessed four other Syriac-related titles. One is a copy of Henry Noris's *Annus et epochae syromacedonum in vetustis urbium Syriae nummis praesertim mediceis expositae*, a work on the Syro-Macedonian calendar, published in Leipzig in 1696. The research that Noris (1631–1704), an Italian church historian, undertook was valued for its accuracy and thoroughness. The second is a copy of the German biblical scholar Johann August Dathe's Latin and Syriac *Psalterium Syriacum*, published in Halle in 1768, based on the work by Erpenius. Of the final two one is the already-mentioned second edition of Theodore Beza's Greek and Latin New Testament (1582), which contains his collation from the Syriac New Testament. The other is a copy of Samuel Bochart's *Hierozoicon sive bipertitum opus de animalibus s. scripturae*, published in

---

Hebrew and biblical studies, and thus slanted his work too heavily on philology. Irwin (2007), 126.
[23] See Larsen (2011), 47–8.
[24] The Peshitta is the standard version of the Bible for churches in the Syriac tradition. It originally excluded disputed books such as 2 Peter, 2 John, 3 John, Jude, and Revelation, all of which were added into the Harklean Version of Thomas Harqel, c.616. The Harklean Version is the only translation of the complete text of the New Testament in Syriac.

Frankfurt in 1675. While much of the text of this zoological treatise on the animals of the Bible is in Latin, it does contain Syriac references, as well as those in Hebrew, Arabic, and Greek.

HEBREW

Hebrew, another Semitic language, was a mainstay for Biblical theologians and scholars, especially for those needing to establish the truths of Christianity by utilising the original literature of the Jews. A small selection of works owned by Shoults follows.

Shoults owned a copy of the Hebrew Bible, published in Leiden in 1611. This publication was the result of the work by the already-mentioned Franciscus Raphelengius, a pioneer of Hebrew typography in the Netherlands, who collaborated on the Plantin Polyglot Bible (Hebrew, Aramaic, Syriac, Greek, and Latin) published in Antwerp between 1569 and 1573. Shoults has three of the four volumes in his collection, each inscribed: 'E. K. S. Dono dedit W. A. S. II Kal. Hirst. A.D. 1886', with a pencil note of 11s on the rear pastedown. This may have been the price his wife paid for them.

Thirteen other titles warrant mention. Shoults owned a copy of *Sefer tehillim = psalterium hebraicum* (*Psalms*), published in Basel in 1547 by Hieronymus Froben; a copy of *Dictionarium Hebraicum*, a collaborative work by Sebastian Münster and Johann Froben, published in Basel in 1564; a copy of Leo Cappel's *Diatriba, de veris et antiquis Ebraeorum literis* (1645), published by Elzevir in 1645; two copies of the lexicographer Johann Buxtorf's *Lexicon Hebraicum et Chaldaicum*, a first edition published in London in 1646, and a later publication of 1710; a copy of the Dutch Hebraist Johannes Leusden's *Hebraica Veteris Testamenti*, published in Utrecht in 1683; a copy of Solomon b. David de Oliveyra's *Livro de grammatica Hebrayca & Chaldayca*, a grammar in Portuguese and Hebrew, published in Amsterdam in 1689; a copy of the German biblical scholar Salomon Glassius's *Philologiae sacrae*, published in Amsterdam in 1711; an incomplete copy of *Psalmorum liber*, published in 1736; a copy of the first edition of Johann Christian Clodius's Latin-Hebrew-Arabic *Lexicon Hebraicum selectum*, published in Leipzig in 1744; a copy of Gottlieb Immanuel Dindorf's *Novum lexicon linguae Hebraico-Chaldaicae commentario in libros veteris testamenti*, published in Leipzig in 1801; a copy of Bishop Robert Lowth's *De sacra poesi Hebraeorum*, a commentary on Hebrew poetry, published in London in 1787; and, finally, a copy of Wilhelm Gesenius's *Hebrew and Chaldee Lexicon to the Old Testament Scriptures*, published by Samuel Bagster in London in 1853. Gesenius (1786–1842) was a German orientalist credited with the reconstructed pronunciation of the Tetragrammaton 'Yahweh'. This work was translated by Samuel Prideaux Tregelles (1813–75), an English biblical scholar, textual critic, and theologian.

CONTEXTUALISING THE MIDDLE EAST

As a complement to the language materials, Shoults gathered a number of publications that offered information on a variety of aspects on the Middle East. The works range from histories, memoirs, and travel writings to more specialised bibliographies. What follows is a selection of these publications.

Shoults owned a copy of Pierre Belon's *Plurimarum singularium & memorabilium observationes*, published in Antwerp by Plantin in 1589. This is an account of the author's travels through Greece, Crete, Egypt, Arabia, and Palestine between 1546 and 1549. As a naturalist, he introduced many new Middle Eastern plants to France.

Shoults also owned a copy of *Arabia, seu Arabum vicinarumque gentium Orientalium leges*, published by the famed Dutch cartographer Jan Jansson (1588–1664) in Amsterdam in 1633. This work, one of the earliest guides containing descriptions of cities such as Baghdad, Damascus, Medina, and Mecca, is by Gabriel Sionita (1577–1648), a Maronite scholar who at one time was based in Paris. It also includes Wolfgang Drechsler's 'Historia Arabum' and an appendix on the Arabic calendar.

Athanasius Kircher (1602–80) was a Jesuit-trained polymath, whose interests covered almost everything, from magnetism and the plague to dragons and hieroglyphs (especially the last). He has been described as a one-man intellectual clearing house.[25] Shoults owned copies of three of his works: a duodecimo edition of his *Magneticum naturae regnum, sive, disceptatio physiologica*, which dealt with magnetic phenomena observed in nature, published in Amsterdam in 1667, and two important 'Egyptian' titles: *Prodromus Coptus sive Aegyptiacus* and *Obelisci Aegyptiaci*. *Prodromus Coptus* was his first venture into the field of Egyptology, and, a product of his learning of Coptic, it contains the first grammar of that language. Shoults's copy is the first edition, published in Rome in 1636, and once belonged to 'R. W. Hay, Rome, 2 April 1846', as inscribed within. *Obelisci Aegyptiaci* is perhaps Kircher's best known work, a vast study of Egyptology and comparative religion, in which he posited that ancient Egyptian was the language spoken by Adam and Eve and that hieroglyphs were occult symbols (this was before Thomas Young and Champollion). Shoults's copy is of the first edition, published in Rome in 1666. It was a gift from the above-mentioned Robert William Hay (1786–1861), Under-Secretary for the Colonies, to one Professor S. Marmora, 1851. Shoults may have questioned some of Kircher's theories: some remain simply bizarre; others have gained credence, such as the link between Coptic and ancient Egyptian.

---

[25] Paula Findlen's edited work on Kircher is subtitled: '*The Last Man Who Knew Everything*'. See *Kircher* (2004).

Shoults had a small clutch of works written by Humphrey Prideaux (1648–1724), the Dean of Norwich. These include a copy of *Marmora Oxoniensia*, a catalogue and chronology of the Arundel marbles and related collections (1676; previous owner Edmund Chishull (1671–1733), an English clergyman and antiquary attached to the Turkey Company at Smyrna); a copy of the corrected second edition of *Ecclesiastical Tracts Formerly Published* (1716); a copy of the fifth edition of *The Old and New Testament Connected, in the History of the Jews* (1718); and a copy of the second, revised, and augmented, edition of *The Original and Right of Tithes* (1736), previously owned by one J. Berriman and the Rev. Mark Aloysius Tierney (1795–1862).[26] Shoults also owned a copy of the third, corrected, edition of Prideaux's *The True Nature of Imposture Fully Display'd in the Life of Mahomet*, published in London in 1698. This polemic was extremely popular, being reprinted many times and influencing later scholars. The author and his work, however, was attacked—for example by George Sale—who proved *The True Nature of Imposture* to be a shoddy, error-ridden work, written by one who maintained that Arabic was like English and whose grasp on the language was minimal.[27]

One publication that Shoults owned has a visual and architectural focus. He owned a copy of *Relation Nouvelle d'un Voyage de Constantinople* by the French painter Guillaume-Joseph Grelot (c.1630–80), who, among other experiences, was the first to delineate Haghia Sophia in detail. This now badly battered copy was published in Paris in 1680.

The above-mentioned Edmund Chishull owned a copy of *Marmora Oxoniensia* which Shoults acquired. Chishull wrote his own *Antiquitates Asiaticae*, published by Bowyer in London in 1728, a copy of which Shoults also owned.[28] His copy of this once-handsome publication is now in poor condition: it has a broken spine and is incomplete, lacking various leaves.

Charles Perry's *A View of the Levant* is another work that Shoults obtained. This first edition, published in London in 1743, contains 33 superb engravings by George Bickham Junior. Perry (1698–1780) travelled through France to Egypt, Palestine, Constantinople, and Greece between 1739 and 1742, and, as listed in the subtitle, his coverage is wide: antiquities, government, politics, maxims, manners, and customs.

The poverty-stricken, manuscript-hungry Johann Jakob Reiske (1716–74) has been called 'the greatest Greek and Arabic scholar of the eighteenth century', a

---

[26] See Cooper (2004).
[27] See Irwin (2007), 100.
[28] See Gibson (2004).

pioneer in Arabic and Byzantine philology and Islamic numismatics.[29] Shoults owned one only of Reiske's five volume *Animadversionum ad Graecos auctores*, published in Leipzig in 1757, along with his valuable *Abilfedae annales moslemici*, published in Leipzig in 1754. The latter publication, dealing with Arabic history and coinage, was once in the library of Dr Benjamin Heath (1739–1817), headmaster of Harrow and rector of Walkerne, Hertfordshire. It was then acquired by the classical scholar the Rev. Henry Drury (1778–1841), who collated the book as perfect.[30]

Simon Ockley (1678–1720) was a British orientalist who advocated the presentation of Islam in a vernacular tongue—that is, Arabic.[31] Shoults owned two copies of what is regarded as his most important work, *The History of the Saracens*: one only of the two-volume third edition, published in 1757, and the revised, improved, and enlarged one-volume fifth edition, published by Bohn in London in 1848.

As travel to the Middle East increased markedly in the nineteenth century, there was a plethora of books published that not only related to the experiences encountered by the travellers, but also offered a wide variety of descriptions of places visited and of the people and their customs. Many of the travellers were attached to commercial companies, others to official government stations. Shoults owned copies of a number of them, including the second edition of British merchant Thomas Thornton's *The Present State of Turkey* (1809); Edward Upham's *History of the Ottoman Empire* (1829); the journalist Jaochim Hayward Stocqueler's *Fifteen Months Pilgrimage through Untrodden Tracts in Khuzistan and Persia* (1832); the second edition of Admiral Sir Adolphus Slade's *Records of Travel in Turkey, Greece, &c., and of a Cruise in the Black Sea with the Capitan Pasha* (1833); the Rev. Robert Walsh's *A Residence at Constantinople* (1836); the Rev. Horatio Southgate's *Narrative of a Tour through Armenia, Kurdistan, Persia and Mesopotamia* (1840); and Arthur J. Joyce's *The Cossack and the Turk* (1853).

COMPILATIONS

Perhaps one of the most important publications pertaining to travel in the area is a copy of Thomas Wright's *Early Travels in Palestine*, first published by Bohn in his 'Antiquarian Library' series in 1848. Wright assembled narratives of early travellers, such as Bishop Arculf, Willibald, Rabbi Benjamin of Tudela, Mandeville, and Henry Maundrell, and, even though the publication suffered from errors and misreadings,

---

[29] Cited in Irwin (2007), 127.
[30] For Heath, see Fletcher (1902), 253–56; for Drury, see De Ricci (1969), 98.
[31] See Irwin (2007), 118-20. It was Ockley's *History* that got Gibbon interested in Islam, inspiring him to study Arabic at Oxford.

it was a very popular source book. Shoults owned a copy of the Bohn edition, and he may have known that Wright (1810–77) had never travelled to the East.

The English historian Richard Knolles (c.1545–1610) was another who did not visit the Middle East. He produced for 'Christian Readers' *The General History of the Turkes*, the first English-language description of the Ottoman Empire, which first appeared in 1603.[32] Shoults owned a copy of the fifth edition of 1638, which, as evidenced by a stamp, once belonged to a 'N. Snow, Pamphilon's Coffee House, Sherrard Street'.[33] The work's popularity, 'a masterpiece of narrative synthesis', meant that it was reworked numerous times, with one edition (1700) edited by Sir Paul Rycaut (1629–1700), one-time secretary to the ambassador in Constantinople.[34] While Shoults did not own that particular edition by Rycaut, he did own other works by Rycaut that complemented Knolles's 'general histories'. They include a copy of the first edition of *The History of the Turkish Empire from 1623 to 1677*, published in 1680, a copy of the fifth edition of *The History of the Present State of the Ottoman Empire*, published in 1682, and a French language edition published in Paris in 1709.

Three important works complete this overview. Shoults owned a copy of the British orientalist Edward William Lane's *The Thousand and One Nights*, which was originally published in monthly parts between 1838 and 1840. It was first published in book form (three volumes) in 1840; Shoults owned a later edition of this classic, albeit bowdlerised, version, published in 1865.

The last two titles are bibliographies, one specific, the other all-encompassing. The above-mentioned Silvestre de Sacy (1758–1838) was head of the École Spéciale de Langues Orientales Vivantes, and co-founder of the Société Asiatique. This little-travelled scholar knew a number of Middle Eastern languages, such as Arabic, Persian, and Syriac. It was through his dedication to the field that he established 'Orientalism' as a more disciplined study, and, as first editor of the multi-volumed *Notices et Extraits des Manuscrits de la Bibliothèque Impériale et Autres Bibliothèques* (1799–1895), he was able to make his readers aware of the location and availability of Middle Eastern texts throughout Europe.[35] Shoults owned the ninth volume (1813) only of this work, once part of Frederick North's library.

The last book is a copy of Barthélemy d'Herbelot's *Bibliothèque Orientale*, a very influential alphabetically-arranged encyclopaedic work that introduced readers to new information on Arabic, Persian, and Turkish matters. Herbelot (1625–95),

---

[32] See Woodhead (2004).
[33] Once a cultural oasis in London as cited by Chapman (1940), 107–8.
[34] Cited in Woodhead (2004).
[35] See Irwin (2007), 141–6 (146).

professor of Syriac at the Collège de France, did not finish what is considered his most important publication, the precursor to the twentieth-century *Encyclopaedia of Islam*.[36] It was completed in 1697 by Antoine Galland (1646–1715), the first European translator of *The Thousand and One Nights*. Shoults owned a copy of the edition published in Maastricht in 1776.

The descriptions of the books presented above confirm the fact that Shoults had a very keen interest in the Middle East. They were gradually acquired through auction houses and booksellers, and despite the scant details of how much was paid for them and when they were acquired, they sit together as a significant collection of books and manuscripts in the field.

---

[36] See Irwin (2007), 114.

14 THE COLLECTION III: EUROPEAN MANUSCRIPTS, INCUNABLES, AND TOOLS OF THE TRADE

While the focus in the last chapter was specifically on Shoults's Middle Eastern materials, it is instructive to examine his collection of 'European' manuscripts and incunables (those books printed before 1501). At the time that Shoults was collecting, these two areas were the benchmark of what to collect, the determiners of what was rare and scarce, and the focus of much attention by booksellers, bibliographers, and librarians, who, especially in the case of the printed books, documented them in list after list, each time adding new information about issues, states, condition and production.[1] Shoults acquired ten manuscripts, of which seven are medieval, and 38 incunables. As will be discussed in chapter 18, some of the manuscripts and incunables were sold after their arrival in Dunedin in 1893.

MEDIEVAL MANUSCRIPTS

Although at one time Shoults owned seven medieval manuscripts, there are currently only three in the collection, all paper copies from Germany.[2] The first contains a copy of Conrad of Halberstadt's *Liber tripartitus moralium* and the anonymous *Moralium dogma philosophorum*, dating from the fifteenth century (MS.01). The manuscript of 52 leaves is written in brown ink, and a few capitals are touched in red. It is water-stained and bound in a very worn and defective nineteenth-century blue and black marbled paper over pasteboards. Although somewhat unprepossessing, the manuscript is significant in that it is made up of some of the oldest paper to be found in New Zealand.[3] One visible watermark, no.3226 in Briquet, classified under CERCLE, has been identified as in use at fifteen different places in western Germany between 1353 and 1391. A provenance note in pencil reads: 'From Dr Kloss's library.'

---

[1] See Taylor (1987) and McKitterick (2018).
[2] There were four other medieval manuscripts, but these fifteenth-century works are no longer in the collection: *Breviarium Romanum*, St. Jerome, *Epistolae*, and Bonaventura's *Sermones* and Augustine's *Liber soliliquiorum* (once belonging to the Celestine convent at Amiens). See chapter 18 for their disposal.
[3] The Bible Society in New Zealand collection at the Alexander Turnbull Library, Wellington, has a Qur'ān on paper, with a suggested date of the twelfth century. Thanks to Anthony Tedeschi, Rare Books Librarian, Alexander Turnbull Library, Wellington. See Briquet (1968), II, 217.

Dr Georg Franz Burkhard Kloss lived in Frankfurt, and one sale of his books and manuscripts occurred at Hodgson's, London, on 20 October 1828.[4]

The second is another fifteenth-century manuscript (MS.02), entitled *Malogranatum*, by Gallus, Abbot of Aula Regia (that is, Königssaal (Zbraslaw) on the Moldau in Bohemia, near Prague). The work's title means a pomegranate, which is interpreted in the preface as a fruit that contains many grains or pips—thus many little grains of wisdom from great doctors. The text of 244 leaves is written in a cursive hand in brown ink, with rubrication of some headings and capitals. At the end of Book II, a page is filled with verses and prayers by a later hand, and the rear free endpaper has a drawing of a tree, with the name Adam at the root and other names (e.g. Christ) on the branches. It is bound in vellum-covered boards, and there are the remains of clasps and bosses. Its provenance is unknown, despite the presence of sale and auction notations on the front pastedown.[5]

The last is a copy of Conrad of Brundelsheim's *Sermones de tempore* of the fourteenth or fifteenth century (MS.03). The text of 153 leaves is written in brown ink in a gothic cursive bookhand, with headings in red. It is bound in pigskin over bevelled wooden boards, and blind ruled with a pattern of lozenges and rectangles on both covers. There are the remains of clasps, and a medieval manuscript fragment has been sewn in as a guard at the front. A note on a label pasted on the spine and repeated inside reads: 'Sermons manuscript circa 1385. Injured by water in Great Fire of London.' The provenance of this manuscript is unknown, but, like the copy of Halberstadt's *Liber tripartitus moralium* above, it may have come from the Kloss Library.[6]

LATER MANUSCRIPTS

The remaining four manuscripts are later productions from the seventeenth and eighteenth centuries. The first is 'Thirteen sermons preached at Dudliston Chapel, Shropshire, by the Rev. Mr John Sherratt, B.A. of Sidney Sussex College in Cambridge, 1732–1745' (MS.04). The sermons are of various lengths. Bound in mottled-calf, this volume was once in the library of the Rev. Thomas Fell, whose bookplate is present. This work, like other books from Fell's library, came into the Shoults Collection after its arrival in Dunedin (see chapter 18).

The second manuscript (MS.05) is a log of 44 leaves of the voyage of the *York* travelling from London to Madras, then China to St. Helena, and then back to

---

[4] See Taylor (1955), 58–9; Manion (1989), 114–15, no. 129. A Kloss sale of books and manuscripts occurred at Hodgson's on 20 October 1828; another occurred at Sotheby's in 1835.
[5] Taylor (1955), 57–8; Manion (1989), 114, no. 128.
[6] See Manion (1989), 115, no. 130.

London between 9 November 1779 and 2 November 1781. Bound in light suede-covered boards, the log contains lists of those people who boarded in India, and of passengers and army recruits bound for Madras. As expected, there are entries on winds, the distance travelled, the weather, observations of latitude, and sundry daily comments. A red calf label is pasted on the front cover reading: 'Ship York' and 'William Stanton Stationer at the Boar's Head, No. 5 Cornhill, near the Mansion House, London.' It is unknown how or why Shoults obtained this volume.

The last two manuscripts are in Latin. The first is headed (as written): 'Tractatus de actibus crearo raalis ordinato ad beatitudinem', a three-part religious work of 249 leaves written in ink. (MS.06). The date of 1700 is present in the text, giving an indication of when it was created. A succinct colophon reads: 'Finis. Demetrius Mahony sacerdos indignus.'

The second is a philosophical work headed 'Sumulae seu Introductio ad universam logicam articam proemium' and is written in a seventeenth-century book-hand (MS.07). Bound in brown calf, there is an inscription at the end: 'R. C. Anno Dom. 1662.' The names of previous owners are scribbled throughout: 'Will Nisbet, 1665', 'Robert Paterson', 'Joannis Nisbet', 'Gilbertus Lorimer', and 'Nov. 8 1768 Sam: Baker, Bibl. d.d.'.

INCUNABULA

Shoults owned 38 incunables, and, in 1893, when the library arrived in Dunedin, the collection was the one that held the greatest number of pre-1501 printed books in New Zealand. It has since been surpassed by the Sir George Grey and Henry Shaw Collections at Auckland City Library and by the Alexander Turnbull Library, part of the National Library of New Zealand, Wellington. Today there are only 28 incunables in the Shoults Collection: six German, four French, five Swiss, and thirteen Italian. Ten were sold after the collection arrived in Dunedin. The disposal of these books is covered in chapter 18.

GERMAN IMPRINTS

The oldest printed book in the Shoults Collection is a copy of Matthaeus de Cracovia's *De modo confitendi et puritate conscientiae*, printed by the Printer of the *Gesta Christi* in Speyer and dated 1472 or 1473.[7] Bound in vellum-covered boards, the text of 36 leaves is printed in a rounded Roman type. There are manuscript annotations throughout

---

[7] Matthaeus de Cracovia. Shoults Gb 1472 T. See *ISTC* im00371850: 13 known copies worldwide. *Gesta Christi*, a work of 12 leaves, was printed in Speyer about 1472 by an unidentified 'Printer', who has been assigned 12 other works.

the text, which has a short contents page (f.1b). Often attributed to Thomas Aquinas, this work received attention sometime after its arrival in Dunedin. A tipped-in letter from A.W. Pollard, of the British Museum, explains:

> 5 April 1924. Dear Sir, I am glad you are getting some specimens of 15th century printing. I wish the Dominion Libraries would acquire more early English books instead of letting Dr Rosenbach convey all the best of them to the United States as he has been doing at the Christy [sic] Miller sale this week. I am sorry not to be able to confirm your hope that the edition of Aquinas *De modo confitendi et de puritate conscientiae* of which you have sent me photocopies is a Caxton. It was probably printed about the time Caxton was learning his craft. The printer's name is unknown, but he is quoted as the Printer of the Gesta Christi (the title of one of his books), and worked at Speyer in 1472 and 1473. We have two copies of this edition in the Museum, press marked IA 8456 and IA 8457, and described on p.483 of the German section of our Catalogue of Books printed in the XVth century in the British Museum. Faithfully yours, A.W. Pollard. Keeper.

It was once part of the Benedictine Abbey library of St. Alexander and Theodor in Ottobeuren, near Memmingen, Germany.

Johann Mentelin (c.1410–78) was the first printer in Strasbourg. A former illuminator (*Goldschreiber*) and episcopal notary, he set up a printing press about 1458, producing, in 1461, the 'Mentelin Bible', the first printing of a Bible in the German language. Shoults owned a copy of the second edition of Astesanus de Ast's *Summa de casibus conscientiae*, printed by Mentelin in 1473.[8] This large volume, with leaves measuring 396 x 255 mm, is printed in Gothic type. Divided into eight books, it deals with topics such as the Ten Commandments, virtues and vices, questions of civil law, the Sacraments, the ordination of priests, and matrimony. The first leaf of Shoults's copy has been restored, mounted onto a later paper. This edition has a curious reminder of life within a fifteenth-century printing house: on f.252a there are the inky paw prints of a cat that had obviously walked across the paper before the ink was dry. (See pl. 20.)

Another Speyer production that Shoults owned was a copy of Leonardus Matthaei de Utino's *Sermones de sanctis*, printed by Peter Drach and completed, according to the colophon (f.349a), on 9 February 1478.[9] Drach often used a heavy Gothic type and adapted his printer's device (which is present) from the well-known

---

[8] Astesanus de Ast. Shoults Gd 1472 A. See *ISTC* ia01161000: 68 known copies worldwide.
[9] Leonardus Matthaei de Utino. Shoults Gc 1478 L. See *ISTC* il00160000: 49 known copies worldwide.

14 THE COLLECTION III: EUROPEAN MANUSCRIPTS, INCUNABLES, TOOLS 223

Fust and Schoeffer shield. The book is complete (350 leaves), and much of the text is rubricated. A hand-coloured initial and flourish are present at f.16a. It is bound in calf-covered oak boards, and there are the remains of an unidentified manuscript sewn in to reinforce the binding. This folio, with its leaves measuring 280 x 200 mm, was once in the Franciscan library in Amberg, Bavaria.

The next German incunable is a copy of Saint Cyprian's *Opera*, printed by the Printer of the 'Erwahlung Maximilians' in Stuttgart between 1485 and 1486.[10] The text of this folio, with its leaves measuring 275 x 195 mm, is printed in gothic type in two columns. There is an example of an early contents page (f.2a) that covers some of the book's content, from the application of the Roman juridical tradition to the governance of church affairs. Bound in a nineteenth-century binding of mottled calf over paper boards, there are annotations throughout. Included are prices such as '4/-' and '24/-'; perhaps Shoults bought this copy for the cheaper price.

Peregrinus of Oppeln was Prior of the Polish Dominican province. His sermon sequences for the temporal and sanctoral liturgical cycles circulated widely in Germany and eastern Europe. Shoults owned a copy of his *Sermones de tempore et de sanctis*, completed in Strasbourg by Johann Prüss in 1493.[11] This quarto, with its leaves measuring 178 x 130 mm, is printed in gothic type in double columns. It is an incomplete copy, lacking leaves 62, 74, 78-85, and 201-6. Bound in brown mottled-calf boards, the book has some dealer notations, writings by an early reader, and the name of a previous owner: 'Father Nicolaus Maignaut.' Shoults was obviously aware of past book sales, as he linked his copy to the sale of the library of the Louis César de La Baume Le Blanc, duc de Vaujours, duc de La Vallière (1708–80), 'one of the greatest private libraries of all time', and to a catalogue issued by bookseller André-Charles Cailleau (1731–98).[12] Opposite the title information is his note that gives the sale price realised: '17 francs', and reference to the catalogue: 'Cailleau page 354 tom.2.'

The final German incunable that Shoults owned was a copy of Saint Bonaventura's *Opuscula, pars I.*, completed by Georg Husner in Strasbourg about 1495.[13] Printed in gothic type, its leaves measure 275 x 190 mm. Shoults's copy is incomplete, wanting the first two preliminary leaves, the whole of signature d, and the final three leaves, including the colophon. It is also in poor condition: the nineteenth-century buckram boards are detached.

---

[10] Saint Cyprian. Shoults Gc 1485 C. See *ISTC* ic01014000: 86 known copies worldwide.
[11] Peregrinus. Shoults Gb 1493 P. See *ISTC* ip00268000: 42 known copies worldwide.
[12] Cited in McKitterick (2018), 209. Sales occurred in 1768, 1773, 1777, and twice in 1784.
[13] Saint Bonaventura. Shoults Gc 1495 B. See *ISTC* ib00928000: 235 known copies worldwide; one other in New Zealand: one part in the Sir George Grey Special Collections, Auckland City Library.

FRENCH IMPRINTS

The oldest printed French book owned by Shoults is a copy of Bartholomaeus Anglicus's *De proprietatibus rerum*, a popular work during the Middle Ages that was designed to help preachers and members of mendicant orders prepare sermons. This folio, with its leaves measuring 275 x 185 mm, was printed in gothic type in double columns by the Lyon-based Petrus Ungarus (Pierre Hongre), completed on 21 November 1482.[14] Guide letters have not been embellished, and the inscriptions of previous owners (f.2a and f.3a) have been blacked out. The book has suffered: its spine is cracked and broken. The second French incunable that Shoults owned is a copy of *Epistolae familiares* by Pope Pius II (1405–64), formerly Aeneas Sylvius Piccolomini. This quarto edition, with its leaves measuring 255 x 170 mm, was completed by Jean de Vingle in Lyon on 8 November 1497.[15] Printed in gothic type, this publication contains a good example of an early title-page, printed in red (f.1a). It also has woodcut capitals throughout. Re-bound in suede-covered boards, the binder has used an unidentified manuscript fragment to strengthen the binding within, and an unidentified printed black-letter leaf as an endpaper. It has an engraved book label of W. Jones with the motto: 'Studio Fallente Laborem,' which was that of The London Institution, established in 1806, with the aim 'to promote the diffusion of Science, Literature and the Arts'.[16]

The final two French books were both printed by Johannes Trechsel in Lyon in April 1497. The first is a copy of the English Dominican Robert Holcot's commentary on Peter Lombard's *Sentences* titled *Quaestiones super IV libros sententiarum*, completed between 5 and 20 April 1497.[17] Written about 1150, Lombard's 'Book of Sentences' covers topics such as notions of the Trinity, predestination, the creation, the Ten Commandments, and the Sacraments. Printed in gothic type in double columns, this folio, with its leaves measuring 285 x 205 mm, was edited by Josse Badius (his dedicatory letter is at f.1b) and Augustinus de Ratisbona. It is rubricated (mostly red, with some blue and yellow), contains a printer's device on the colophon page, and has an inscription on the title-page (f.1a): 'Ex bibliotheca collegij montisancti'. The volume is half-bound in calf, with buckram sides.

Almost immediately, or perhaps simultaneously, Trechsel had on his press St. Augustine's *Opus quaestionum*, which he completed on 25 April 1497 (f.285b).[18]

---

[14] Bartholomaeus Anglicus. Shoults Fc 1482 B. See *ISTC* ib00134000: 61 known copies worldwide.
[15] Pope Pius II. Shoults Fc 1497 P. See *ISTC* ip00722000: 56 known copies worldwide.
[16] See London Institution (2021), https://en.wikipedia.org/wiki/London_Institution
[17] Robert Holcot. Shoults Fc 1497 H. See *ISTC* ih00287000: 127 known copies worldwide.
[18] St. Augustine. Shoults Gc 1519 H. See *ISTC* ia01297000: 123 known copies worldwide.

This folio, with its leaves measuring 270 x 190 mm, is printed in gothic type in two columns. It was edited by Badius and Ratisbona. On acquiring the blind-stamped calf bound volume, Shoults may have been surprised to find another title bound in: a copy of Bishop Haymo of Halberstadt's *In divi Pauli epistolas*, published by Renatus Beck in Strasbourg in 1519.

SWISS IMPRINTS

The first of five Swiss incunables that Shoults acquired is a copy of Bishop Alphonsus de Spina's *Fortalitium fidei*, completed in Basel by Bernard Richel, sometime before 10 May 1475.[19] This work, a folio of 240 leaves, which measure 390 x 285 mm, deals with the different kinds of spiritual armour to be used by preachers (and others) in their warfare against the enemies of the Christian religion. The text is rubricated throughout and has at f.10a a coloured woodcut image depicting a devil and a number of men blindfolded. Bound in wormed vellum-covered blind-stamped boards, it has a painted red 'I' on the front cover. There is a long note written in Latin on Spina on the front free endpaper.

The second is a publication on canon law titled *Formularium procuratorum et advocatorum Curiae Romanae*, supposedly completed by printer Michael Furter in Basel on 10 March 1493.[20] This quarto of 230 leaves, which measure 200 x 140 mm, is in poor condition with some leaves and gatherings loose and the spine broken. The text is rubricated, and there is a hand-coloured initial on f.7a. Bound in brown calf over paper boards, this volume was once in a monastery library (inscription indecipherable) and then owned by Joseph Pratten, Upper Easton, Bristol, who dated his signature '30 November 1828'.

The last three Swiss incunables were printed by the German-born Johann Amerbach (c.1430–1513), who studied at the Sorbonne under Johann Heynlin before working in Nuremberg as a press corrector for Anton Koberger. He established a press at Basel about 1475 and became the city's leading printer, issuing some seventy works.

The first is a copy of Johannes de Turrecremata's *Quaestiones evangeliorum de tempore et de sanctis*, printed before 28 September 1481.[21] Rubricated throughout, the folio, with its leaves measuring 290 x 200 mm, is incomplete, lacking gatherings before D and the final leaves, including the colophon. Its calf-covered oak boards are detached and the back-strip of the spine is badly ripped, exposing the remaining gatherings.

---

[19] Alphonsus de Spina. Shoults Swe 1475 E. See *ISTC* ia00540000: 69 known copies worldwide.
[20] *Formularium procuratorum et advocatorum Curiae Romanae*. Shoults Swb 1493 F. See *ISTC* if00268000: 37 known copies worldwide.
[21] Johannes de Turrecremata. Shoults Fc 1485 T. See *ISTC* it00553000: 83 known copies worldwide.

The second is a copy of Petrarch's *Opera latina*, published in 1496.[22] This folio contains 360 leaves that measure 275 x 190 mm. Printed in Roman type, it is rubricated throughout with blue and red initials. It is also in poor condition: its calf boards are detached and the spine is cracked and disintegrating. Edited by Sebastian Brant, it is a significant edition: the only collected edition published in the fifteenth century and the first collected edition of the Latin poetry and prose works by Petrarch.

The last Swiss incunable is a copy of Johannes Cassianus's *De institutis coenobiorum*, a work on monasticism and religious orders in the early church, completed by Amerbach in 1497.[23] The text of this quarto of 205 leaves, which measure 185 x 135 mm, is printed in gothic type in two columns. Guide letters are present; very few capital spaces have been added. There are three annotations on the title-page (f.1a): the first quoting a sentence from St. Augustine's *City of God*, beginning: 'Naviganti uita mea similis est sive dormiam siue uigilem semp[er] uado festinus', the second describing the fifth-century hermit Cassian, and the third an extract from chapter 5 of *Liber de institutione et regimine praelatorum* by Laurentius Justinianus, part of which reads in English: 'Very beneficial is discipline by the faithful by which they purge their crimes, and are moved towards virtues, and removed from carnal pleasures.' The half-bound calf and marbled boards are detached from the text block. An inscription on the title-page reveals that this book was once in a library in Vivajo, Tuscany.

ITALIAN IMPRINTS

The earliest Italian incunable that Shoults owned is a copy of Archbishop Theophylactus of Ochrida's *Enarrationes in epistolas S. Pauli*, a commentary on the epistles of St. Paul, with a prologue attributed to St. Athanasius. This folio of 278 leaves, which measure 320 x 225 mm, was printed in Roman type by Ulrich Han (Udalricus Gallus) in Rome about 25 January 1477.[24] Shoults's copy is incomplete and in poor condition: it wants the first ten leaves, the next twenty-five leaves are badly ripped, and the marbled boards are detached. This battered book was once owned by one T. Kershaw, in 1811.

As mentioned in chapter 12, Shoults owned a copy of the fourth edition of *Historia ecclesiastica* by Eusebius. This folio, with its leaves measuring 280 x 185 mm, was printed in Roman type by Johannes Schallus in Mantua, sometime before 15 July 1479.[25] Apart from lacking the first leaf, the text is complete. This vellum-bound

---

[22] Petrarch. Shoults Swc 1496 P. See *ISTC* ip00365000: 277 known copies worldwide.

[23] Johannes Cassianus. Shoults Swb 1497 C. See *ISTC* ic00235000: 149 known copies worldwide.

[24] Theophylactus of Ochrida. Shoults Ic 1477 T. See *ISTC* it00156000: 100 known copies world-wide; one other in New Zealand: Alexander Turnbull Library, Wellington.

[25] Eusebius. Shoults Fc 1530 M. See *ISTC* ie00127000: 219 known copies worldwide.

volume also contains a copy of P. Mela's *De orbis situ*, printed in Paris in 1530. An inscription reveals that it once belonged to Colonel Thomas Stanley (1749–1818), whose library was sold by Evans in London between 30 April and early May 1813.[26]

Shoults owned four incunables printed in Venice. The first is a copy of the third volume only of the Vulgate Bible with commentary by Nicolas de Lyra.[27] This volume, of four, contains the text of Isaiah-Maccabees. This folio, with its leaves measuring 322 x 220 mm, was printed by Johannes Herbort de Seligenstadt for Johannes de Colonia, Nicolaus Jenson et Socii, completed about 31 July 1481. This particular volume is significant on four levels. First, it is the earliest edition with de Lyra's commentary surrounding the text. Second, with the biblical text surrounded left and right by de Lyra's commentaries, the result is an intricate hand-set layout. It is a typographic masterpiece. Third, the volume is bound by the Rood and Hunt binders, active in Oxford c.1478–c.1483, and is one of their 26 bindings extant. (See pl. 19.) Lastly, there are four fragments sewn in as binding guards which are the remains of indulgences printed by William Caxton (Westminster, after 9 August 1480) and John Lettou (London, after 1480).[28] These slivers were discovered by Dr Christopher de Hamel in the 1980s when he was researching for his book on medieval manuscripts in New Zealand. It is not known whether Shoults owned the other three volumes or when he obtained this particular volume.

The second Venetian volume is a copy of Boccaccio's *Genealogia deorum*, an encyclopedia of classical mythology, tracing the genealogy of the pagan gods. This folio, with its leaves measuring 298 x 205 mm, is a page-for-page reprint of the earlier edition printed by Locatellus for Scotus in Venice in 1494–1495. Set in Greek and Roman type in double columns by Manfredus de Bonellis de Monteferrato, it was completed about 25 March 1497. It has the usual illustrative genealogical tables.[29] At the foot of the title-page there is a black ink oval stamp containing a plant with three lilies and the letters 'D.S.A.' (representing 'Domus Sanctissimae Annuntiatae', the

---

[26] De Ricci (1969), 88; Kerney (1968), II, on Stanley. There is no listing of Eusebius or Mela in the 1813 Evans catalogue.

[27] Nicolas de Lyra. Shoults Ic 1481 B. See *ISTC* ib00611000: 237 known perfect/imperfect copies worldwide. See also Darlow (1911), II, 6085. For further details on the binding: see Pingree (2003), 371–401. On the indulgence fragments Dr de Hamel has reported his findings in an unpublished paper read to the Oxford Bibliographical Society on 1 December 1982, and in his Lyell Lectures, 'Fragments in Book Bindings', 2009. See De Hamel (2009).

[28] For further details, see Pingree (2003), 371–401; see also Duff (2009), 248.

[29] Boccaccio. Shoults Ic 1497 B. See *ISTC* ib00754000: 172 known copies worldwide; two others in New Zealand: Alexander Turnbull Library, Wellington and the Sir George Grey Special Collections, Auckland.

Order of Servites, Florence).³⁰ There are also two indecipherable inscriptions. This volume is bound in vellum-covered boards.

The third Venetian publication is a copy of *Opera medicinalia* by Joannes Mesuë (Yuhanna Ibn Masawayh), one of the first medieval Arabic physicians, who composed a number of medical monographs on topics such as fevers, leprosy, melancholy, dietetics, and eye diseases. Many of Mesuë's Arabic texts were among the earliest texts translated into Latin and disseminated throughout Europe. Shoults's copy, a folio of 294 leaves, which measure 300 x 210 mm, was completed by Peregrinus de Pasqualibus Bononiensis for Dionysius Bertochus about 21 December 1484 (colophon: f.294a).³¹ It is rubricated throughout. The blind-stamped pigskin-covered boards are wormed and the clasps are no longer present.

The last Venetian printing is of particular interest: the first edition (*editio princeps*) of Ubertino de Casale's iconoclastic *Arbor vitae crucifixae Jesu Christi*, completed by Andreas de Bonetis about 12 March 1485, (colophon, f.48b).³² Ubertino of Casale (1259–c.1330) was leader of the Spirituals in Tuscany, a strict branch of the Franciscan Order. This folio of 250 leaves, which measure 285 x 200 mm, is his chief work, a collection of allegorical, theological, and political pieces aimed at civil society and the Church—for example, his attack on the popes and the Church (for their abuses) and the Franciscan Order (for not practising extreme poverty).³³ Guide letters are present, but they lack embellishments. The volume is quarter-bound in red calf with green paper sides. A large bibliographical note on the front flyleaf makes reference to this very rare ('rarissima') work in Guillaume-François De Bure's catalogue of the library of Louis-Jean Gaignat (1769; No. 4549) and volume five of the catalogue of the Biblioteca Magliabechiana in Florence.³⁴

The last seven incunables are North Italian productions, from Parma, Milan, Pavia, Reggio Emilia, and Brescia. The first is a copy of Nicolas d'Orbellis's *Expositio logicae*, completed in Parma by Damianus de Moyllis and Johannes Antonius de Montalli on 30 April 1482 (colophon, f.108a).³⁵ This quarto, with its leaves measuring 200 x 145 mm, is a commentary on the *Summulae logicales* of Petrus Hispanus (Pope

---

30   See Rhodes (1975), 417–20.
31   Joannes Mesue (Yuhanna Ibn Masawayh). Shoults Ic 1484 M. See *ISTC* im00514000: 54 known copies worldwide; one other in New Zealand: the Sir George Grey Special Collections, Auckland.
32   Ubertino de Casale. Shoults Ic 1485 U. See *ISTC* iu00055000: 245 known copies worldwide.
33   See 'Ubertino of Casale' in *ODCC* (1998), 1651.
34   This item is deemed 'premiere et seule edition' in the *Catalogue de Livre de la Bibliothèque de M. Pierre-Antoine Bolongaro-Crevenna* (1789), 4, no. 5996. See Taylor (1987), 242.
35   Nicolas d'Orbellis. Shoults Ib 1482 O. See *ISTC* i00077700: 59 known copies worldwide.

John XXI). There are a few annotations throughout in several hands. It is bound in faded red buckram.

The second is a copy of Bernardinus de Busti's *Mariale*, completed by Leonardus Pachel in Milan on 21 May 1493.[36] This quarto of 388 leaves, which measures 200 x 135 mm, contains sermons on the Virgin Mary. It also contains an early example of a title-page (f.1a). Printed capitals are present throughout, and there is a good impression of Pachel's distinctive device, an example of an early trademark.[37] There are inscriptions by past owners: 'Nicolai Landei' (?) and 'Father Paulus'.

The third Northern Italian volume contains three relatively scarce titles, all by Jason de Mayno (1435–1519), the Italian jurist. One is published in Milan; the other two in Pavia. The Milan publication is a copy of de Mayno's *Epithalamion in nuptiis Maximiliani et Blancae Mariae*, a quarto of 8 leaves, which measures 215 x 145 mm. It was printed by Philippus de Mantegatiis, Cassanus, sometime after 8 September 1494 (colophon, f.8a).[38] The two Pavian titles are *Oratio apud Alexandrum VI habita pro Mediolanensium principe* and *Oratio in funere Hieronymi Torti habita*. The *Alexandrum*, a text of 8 leaves, was printed by one of three possible candidates: the Printer of Butigella about January 1493, Franciscus Girardengus, about 1494, or the Pavian-based Antonius de Carcano (fl. 1472–97).[39] The *Hieronymi*, a text of 24 leaves, was printed by Johannes Andreas de Boscho and Michael and Bernardinus de Garaldis, about 1495.[40] These three titles are bound in scuffed and wormed paper-covered boards. On the front pastedown there are the remains of an unidentified sale and catalogue number.

The sixth is a copy of *Scriptores rei rusticae*, completed by Dionysius Bertochus in Reggio Emilia about 18 September 1496.[41] It is a collection of works by four agricultural writers—Columella, Varro, Cato, and Palladius—and was edited by Philippus Beroaldus, after Georgius Merula and Franciscus Colucia. Shoults's copy of this folio, with its leaves measuring 305 x 205 mm, is printed in Roman and Greek type and bound in a scuffed calf binding. On the title-page is pasted a triangular-shaped piece of paper with *Opera agricolationum* printed on it. The purple Selwyn

---

[36] Bernardinus de Busti. Shoults Ib 1493 B. See *ISTC* ib01333000: 114 known copies worldwide.
[37] Printer's or publishers' devices were often found at the back of a publication, usually near the colophon. They were useful tools aiding identification, often containing a simple symbol, a vignette, or an abbreviated reference – such as initials – to the printer or publisher's name.
[38] Jason de Mayno. Shoults Ib 1494 M. See *ISTC* im00402000: 14 known copies worldwide.
[39] Jason de Mayno. Shoults Ib 1494 M. *Alexandrum VI*, see *ISTC* im00412500: 5 known copies worldwide. See *ISTC* entry for other attributions.
[40] Jason de Mayno. Shoults Ib 1494 M. *Hieronymi*. See *ISTC* im00412300: 19 known copies worldwide.
[41] *Scriptores rei rusticae*, Shoults Ic 1496 S. See *ISTC* is00349000: 89 known copies worldwide.

College stamp made for the Shoults Collection is stamped below. The book has woodcut initials throughout, and there are some manuscripts annotations within. This popular work on husbandry, frequently published during the Renaissance, once belonged to Christopher Tower, Esq. (1775–1867) of Weald Hall, M.P. for Harwich between 1832 and 1837.[42] There is no indication of when and from whom Shoults acquired it.

The last is a copy of Johannes de Turrecremata's *Questiones super euangeliis totius anni*, published by Angelus Britannicus and completed in Brescia about 2 June 1498 (colophon with device, f.166b).[43] This quarto of 166 leaves, which measure 190 x 135 mm, is bound in vellum and contains woodcut initials and two unknown dealers' catalogue entries on the marbled front pastedown. There is a pencil note of 'Damaged' on the front pastedown and the price '7s 6d' beside it. Shoults may have paid this amount for it.

Of the incunables described, 24 are on religious topics such as spiritual affairs, assistance and advice to clergy, historical information on religious orders, canon law, sermons, and Biblical commentary. Only two are first editions (Casale and Mayno), the others later editions which carry some specific-copy interest. Many of the books are in poor condition: water-stained, ripped leaves, wormed, incomplete, and broken-backed with detached covers. It is not known whether Shoults acquired them in the conditions described, or whether over time they suffered at the hands of students at Selwyn College. One thing is evident: the books are not fine copies. Shoults seemed to prefer content over condition. Cost may also have been a consideration at the time of purchase.

Given Shoults's educational background and personal interests as well as the times in which he lived, acquiring these books is understandable. It was fashionable to collect incunables, and many respectable book collectors in the nineteenth century had one or two on their shelves. The answer to one question remains unknowable: how much did he use or refer to these books, either for personal interest or for some

---

[42] Columella's 'De Re Rustica' deals with 'the cultivation of fields, trees, and vines, the raising of large animals and barnyard animals, the raising of bees, vegetables, and flower gardens, and the duty of the bailiff and his wife'; Varro's 'De Re Rustica' deals with agriculture, livestock and raising barnyard animals, bees and fish; Cato's 'De Agri Cultura' is 'a collection of general precepts on how the land owner should behave'; and Palladius' 'Opus Agriculturae' presents 'the point of view of the landed proprietor in the West, facing rapid technological innovation and social change that would lead to a different organization of work.' Cited in Conte (1999).

[43] Johannes de Turrecremata. Shoults Ib 1498 T. See *ISTC* it00548000: 83 known copies worldwide.

professional requirement as a curate? He did make cursory notes in some, but on the whole they do not lead to any firm conclusions on use.

The remaining four incunables raise some intriguing questions to which there are again no ready answers. Shoults had no other work by Boccaccio in his library, yet for some reason he acquired the copy of *Genealogia deorum*, a work that deals with the genealogy of pagan gods. His copy of *Opera medicinalia* by Mesuë is one of the few medical texts in his collection. The area of *materia medica* was outside his normal collecting interest, and the most likely explanation for his purchase—if needed at all—is his interest in the Middle East.

Scriptores rei rusticae is another important work that Shoults obtained. No other example exists in his collection, and agriculture was certainly not a field that he concentrated on. The last incunable is his copy of Petrarch's *Opera latina*, published in 1496. Shoults owned copies of two editions: one published in Venice in 1564 with notes by Pietro Bembo, and the other a fifth edition, published in Basel in 1581. Although significant in their own right, the small number held does not reflect a strong interest in the works of this Italian humanist.

There is no clear reason why Shoults collected the incunables he did, nor the disparate manuscripts. Book collecting is a highly individualistic activity, and one is left with A.W. Pollard's notion that these works captured Shoults's eye, mind, or imagination, certainly enough for him to buy or accept into his library.

TOOLS OF THE TRADE

Shoults was a scholar-collector who seemed to like his own reference books within easy reach. Complementing the above works, he gathered a number of significant publications in the area of bibliography, the formation of libraries (institutional and private collections), classical scholarship, ecclesiastical scholarship, and general literature.[44] They not only reflect his scholarly interests, but also no doubt supported his collecting. Many of the publications are seminal, and the names of the authors and the associated libraries read like a Who's Who in bibliography. They include Angelico Aprosio, Francesco Barberini, William Beloe, Friedrich Benedict Carpzov, Léopold Auguste Constantin Hesse, François Xavier Laire (de Brienne Library), William Oldys (Harleian Library), Maffeo Pinelli, Joseph Justus Scaliger, Burkhard Gotthelf Struve, and a number of individual catalogues of sales and libraries including Hassill Hutchins's Jonathan Blackburne sale (1785), the Doctors' Common (College of Civilians) Library (1818), and the Townley Gallery Library (1836).

---

[44] See Taylor (1987) and McKitterick (2018).

A few stand out as establishers of the canon, those who provided essential reference books for the shelves of many respected book collectors. They are Maittaire, De Bure, Renouard, Dibdin, Peignot, and Brunet.

Michel Maittaire's *Annales typographici* (1719–25) was an essential tome for anyone interested in the history of printing before 1600, a standard source for information on incunables and editions of the classics. Shoults acquired the first volume, published at the Hague in 1719. He did not acquire the other four volumes.

Shoults was much more successful with the works of the French printer and bibliographer Guillaume-François De Bure (1731–82), who produced his *Bibliographie Instructive, ou, Traité de la Connoissance des Livres Rares et Singuliers*, a bibliographer's and dealer's list of best books, which broke new ground for the extensive bibliographical data and notes on them. Shoults owned the full set: the two-volume *Belles-Lettres*, the three-volume *History, Theology,* and *Jurisprudence-Science*, and the two-volume *Supplement à la Bibliographie Instructive (1769)* by Louis Jean Gaignat.[45]

Shoults owned only three Aldines, yet he acquired a copy of Antoine-Augustin Renouard's *Annales de l'Imprimerie des Alde* (1803), a work that established his reputation. If anything, this specifically-focused publication stood as an exemplar of what could be achieved by others if they contemplated undertaking a similar endeavour in the field of bibliography.

The reputation of Thomas Frognall Dibdin (1776–1847) centres on his bibliomaniac enthusiasm, matched by the many inaccuracies and errors in his books. Shoults owned a copy of the expanded third edition of *Introduction to the Knowledge of Editions of Rare and Valuable Editions of the Greek and Roman Classics*, published in London in 1808. No doubt it offered him useful information on the early Greek editions of the Holy Scriptures and the Classics.

Although Shoults did not own the French librarian and bibliographer Gabriel Peignot's handbook *Dictionnaire Raisonné de Bibliologie* (1802; supplement 1804), he did own four other Peignot titles: *Répertoire Bibliographique Universel* (1812), a bibliography of bibliographies with critical commentaries, listing selected subject bibliographies and nearly 500 private library catalogues, *Dictionnaire Historique et Bibliographique, abrégé des Personnages Illustres Célèbres ou Fameux* (1821), an abbreviated historical and bibliographical dictionary of nearly 20,000 famous people, *Catalogue d'une Partie des Livres composant la Bibliothèque des ducs de Bourgogne*, au

---

[45] The Supplement contain the bookplate of N. Vansittart, perhaps Nicholas Vansittart, first Baron Bexley (1766–1851), an English politician and one of the longest-serving Chancellors of the Exchequer in British history.

XVe siècle (1841), and *Le Livre des Singularités* (1841), Peignot's light-hearted work on philological amusements.[46]

The publication of Jacques-Charles Brunet's *Manuel du Libraire et de l'Amateur de Livres* (3 vols, 1810) led to an international reputation lasting long after the author's death. Shoults owned the expanded second edition of 1814, which contained in one volume numerous bibliographical details on books, mainly Continental. It was an essential tool for any serious book collector.

There are other 'tools of the trade' in Shoults's library. However, the fact that most are specialised publications does raise a few questions. It is a truism that many books are owned but not read: they sit on bookshelves patiently waiting to be used. It is also true that books can be accumulated randomly, by presentation or purchase, with the desire to read them fluctuating from a euphoric 'must read' to a later dull indifference. How much did Shoults actually use his books? And what does owning a single volume of Brunet or Gesner actually mean? Given the specific nature of these works, one can imagine referral and a dipping into—reading from cover to cover, perhaps not. Used or not, Shoults obviously felt he had to have such items on hand—just in case. The titles mentioned below cover bibliographies of bibliographies, more specialised publications, catalogues recording collectors and their collections, some institutional catalogues, and a few works on the burgeoning profession of librarianship.

Conrad Gesner (1516–65) was a Swiss botanist, physician, and classical linguist, whose *Bibliotheca universalis* (1545–49) was the first truly comprehensive 'universal' listing of all the books of the first century of printing, an alphabetically-arranged bibliography of about 10,000 titles printed in Latin, Greek, or Hebrew. This mammoth undertaking, by the 'father of bibliography', was 'a work of universal biography, a lexicon of writers', which 'had never previously existed'.[47] Shoults owned a vellum-bound copy of the second edition, published in Zurich in 1574, greatly expanded to include a further 35,000 titles.

The French scholar Philippe Labbé (1607–67) was a Jesuit Professor of Philosophy, who produced a wide range of publications on history, theology, and philology. Shoults owned two of his works: an extremely battered copy of the third edition of *Bibliotheca bibliothecarum*, a bibliography of bibliographies that included information on antiquities such as medals and coins, published in Rouen in 1678, and a copy of the first edition of *Nova bibliotheca manuscriptorum librorum*, published in Paris in 1653.[48]

⁰ See Breslauer (1984), 120; Taylor (1987), 187.
⁴⁷ Fischer (1966), 269–81; see also Breslauer (1984), no. 14. Ironically Gesner, a physician, did not complete the intended medical section of his *Bibliotheca universalis* (Liber xxi) and it was never published. See Besterman (1940), 15–18.
⁴⁸ Philippe Labbé. Shoults Eb 1678 L; Fb 1653 L.

Labbé not only listed in this work many of the incunables from the Bibliothèque du Roi, but also promoted the term 'incunabula' as applied to fifteenth-century books.

Shoults acquired copies of two works by the Church historian Louis Ellies du Pin (1657–1719). The first is a copy of *De antiqua ecclesiae disciplina dissertationes historicae*, published in Paris in 1686. Du Pin spent his last years working towards a reunion between the Church of England and the Roman Catholic Church. However, in this work, a controversial one, he focused on supporting the independence of the Gallican Church from Rome. Meeting with papal disapproval, it was banned and placed on the Roman Catholic Church *Index of Forbidden Books*, where it remained until 1948.[49] The second title was a copy of one volume only of the second, corrected edition of *Nouvelle Bibliothèque des Auteurs Ecclésiastiques*, published in Paris in 1688. This multi-volume publication of 58 volumes, published between 1686 and 1704, comprised biography, literary criticism, and bibliographies of the works by Church notables. It broke new ground because it was printed in French rather than Latin; it too was placed on the *Index*, in 1757. The Jesuit Thomas Baker was a previous owner, who wrote a note on a preliminary page: 'This with the three following volumes affords us all what is very valuable, or of good authority, amongst our ecclesiastical writers, concluding with cinquieme siècle. For this reason I have not extended my collection further.'

Shoults owned five works by the German scholar and bibliographer Johann Albert Fabricius (1668–1736). The first is a copy of *Bibliotheca latina*, a comprehensive biographical and bibliographical publication that contains all the known authors of the classical period with their works listed in all available editions. This vast undertaking established his reputation. Shoults owned three copies: an edition published in London in 1703, a 'Supplementum' edition published in Hamburg in 1712, and an edition published in Leipzig in 1773. The second title is a copy of *Bibliotheca ecclesiastica*, a compilation that contained short sketches on various ecclesiastical writers, published in Hamburg in 1718. The third is a copy of the first edition of *Historia bibliothecae*, a list of books owned by Fabricius, with brief but very valuable accounts of the life and writings of the various authors. Published by Gottfried Freitag in Wolfenbüttel between 1718 and 1724, Shoults's copy is complete, with the six volumes bound in three. The fourth work is a copy of the first edition of *Opusculum historico-critico-literariorum*, published in Hamburg in 1738. The last is a copy of Fabricius's masterpiece, *Bibliotheca Graeca*, extending from pre-Homeric times to 1453. Shoults's copy is of the revised, extended, edition by G.C. Hales, published in

---

[49] Shoults owned three versions of the *Index: Index expurgatorius librorum* (1586), *Indicis librorum expurgandorum* (1607), and *Index librorum prohibitorum* (1855).

14 THE COLLECTION III: EUROPEAN MANUSCRIPTS, INCUNABLES, TOOLS

Hamburg in 1790. Fabricius's achievement was recognised with this work designated: *maximus antiquae eruditionis thesaurus*: the greatest repository of ancient learning.[50]

ENGLISH PUBLICATIONS

At the end of his career, the busy academic Edward Bernard (1638–97) compiled his *Catalogi librorum manuscriptorum Angliae et Hiberniae*, a large folio catalogue of manuscripts in British and Irish libraries, published in Oxford in 1697. Assisted by Humfrey Wanley (1672–1726), palaeographer, and first keeper of the Harleian Library, Bernard included a life of Thomas Bodley, a description of the Bodleian Library, lists of various collections of manuscripts contained in the libraries of Pembroke, Cromwell, Digby, and Ashmole, lists of manuscripts in Oxford and Cambridge colleges, manuscripts in public, cathedral, and school libraries, and the holdings in some fifty private collections and various Irish libraries. Shoults owned a copy of the first edition, which has been described by de Ricci as 'one of the most notable achievements of early English bibliographers'.[51]

William Nicolson (1655–1727), Dean of Carlisle, wrote the *English Historical Library*, a bibliography of printed and manuscript materials on English history, first published between 1696 and 1699. Its focus is on topographical and geographical matters, ecclesiastical history, and the contents and locations of public records. Shoults owned a copy of the one-volume second edition, published in London in 1714.

Edward Harwood (1729–94) was a controversial biblical critic and writer of numerous works on the classics. His *A View of the Various Editions of the Greek and Roman Classics* was published in 1775. Shoults owned a copy of the second edition, published in 1778. His copy is an interleaved one with numerous annotations on the various editions mentioned, and including prices realised at various auction sales. Some of the notes may have been made by Shoults.

CATALOGUES

Shoults collected a number of catalogues devoted to individual collectors and their books. The following six give an idea of the sort of catalogues that he was interested in.

The first is a copy of the famed *Index bibliothecae qua Franciscus Barberinus*, which details the collection of more than 60,000 books and ancient Greek and Roman manuscripts amassed by Cardinal Francesco Barberini (1597–1679).[52] Compiled by

---

[50] 'Fabricius', in *EB*, X, 119; see also Verner (1966), 281–326.
[51] De Ricci (1969), 9; McKitterick (2018), 105–6.
[52] In 1902, the large Biblioteca Barberina was purchased by Pope Leo XIII and became part of the Vatican holdings. See Magnuson (1982), I, 239.

Lukas Holste and Carlo Moroni, both custodians of the Vatican Library, the two-volume catalogue is an important work in bibliographical history.[53] It contains one important feature and one significant inclusion: items are arranged under the author's surname, which at that time was a revolutionary system, and volume 2 of Shoults's copy has the scarce one-leaf 'Motu Proprio' by Pope Clement IX, allowing the Barberini Library to own, with certain restrictions on their use, heterodox works.

The second is a copy of the *Bibliotheca Carpzoviana, sive, catalogus librorum*, an auction sale catalogue of 1022 pages published in Leipzig in 1700. It was compiled by the German lawyer Friedrich Benedict Carpzov (1649–99), who was co-editor of the scientific journal *Acta Eruditorum*. While Shoults's copy is clean, with no marginal marks, there is a loosely inserted leaf that has a note by a previous owner, 'Radulphi Emmerson, A.M.', that gives the numbers of folios, quartos, octavos, and duodecimos in the various sections of the catalogue (Theology, Philosophy and Mathematics, Literature, and so on). The total given is 15,670 titles.

The third is a copy of *Bibliotheca Pinelliana*, published in London in 1789. This important antiquarian sale catalogue was based on the earlier *Bibliotheca Maphei Pinelli* (1787), a catalogue edited by Jacob Morelli that detailed some 12,859 items owned by the book collector Maffeo Pinelli (1736–85). The entire collection had been bought by booksellers Robson & Clarke (New Bond Street) and James Edwards (Pall Mall), who undertook the production of the catalogue. The Pinelli sale began on 2 March 1789, attracting much attention because of the inclusion of many rare and scarce items. Shoults's copy is clean.

Étienne Charles de Loménie de Brienne (d.1784) was the Archbishop of Sens, finance minister under Louis XIV, and a book collector. He owned well over 1300 incunabula, including two copies of the Gutenberg Bible, a copy of the 1459 Fust and Schöffer *Psalter*, and a copy of the first Durandus (1459) on vellum. His librarian, François-Xavier Laire, compiled a two-volume sale catalogue of the collection, the *Index librorum ab inventa typographia ad annum 1500*, published in Sens in 1791. Shoults owned a copy of this work, the first such to describe fifteenth-century printed books in bibliographical details, such as composition, collation, and so on. Shoults also owned a third volume, *Catalogue des Livres de la Bibliothèque de M**** (1792), which was a continuation of this famed work. His copies are all marked up, but by an earlier hand.

Shoults also collected catalogues that reveal specific treasures within individual institutional libraries. On 11 December 1880, he acquired one volume only of the eight-volume folio *Commentariorum de augustissima bibliotheca Caesarea Vindobonensi*,

---

[53] 'Virtually unobtainable', see Taylor (1987), 228–9.

compiled by Peter Lambeck (1628–80), a German historian and librarian to Emperor Leopold (1640–1705) in Vienna. Published between 1665 and 1679, this work details the treasures of the Royal Library. One wonders whether, on this day, Shoults purchased the other seven volumes, which are now lost, or was attracted to this volume only.

In 1674, Thomas Hyde (1636–1703), an English orientalist and librarian, and Thomas Hearne, assistant-keeper at the Bodleian Library, published their two-volume *Catalogus impressorum librorum bibliothecæ Bodlejanæ in academia Oxoniensi*, the third catalogue of the Bodleian Library. This catalogue became very influential throughout Europe, placing greater emphasis on cataloguing practices of the day and establishing itself as a valuable reference work.[54] Shoults's copy was once owned by John Robertson, who gave it (donor inscription) to the Rev. Archibald Seton. It was then passed to John Hunt of All Souls College, Oxford. It has a pencil note on the front pastedown reading: 'useful work.'

THE LIBRARY PROFESSION

In 1669, Johannes Lomeier (1636–99), Professor of Philosophy at Zutphen, Gelderland, Netherlands, produced his *De bibliothecis liber singularis*, a work that deals with the origin of libraries, the conservation of records in Biblical times, the role and duties of librarians, library fittings, enemies of books, and other library matters. Shoults obtained a copy of the second edition, published in Utrecht in 1680. This updated work has the delightful frontispiece engraving of Lomeier at his desk reading, which is not in the first edition.

Another title related to the library world that Shoults acquired was a copy of Léopold Auguste Constantin Hesse's *Bibliothéconomie, ou Nouveau Manuel Complet pour l'Arrangement, la Conservation et l'Administration des Bibliothèques*, which was first published in 1839. Shoults's copy is the second edition of 1841. In this work, Hesse (1779–1844) discusses all aspects of establishing and running a library, including bibliography, collecting, displaying books, descriptions of old and rare books, and manuscripts. One wonders what precepts Shoults took from this handbook towards the care and development of his own growing collection.

The books described briefly above are remarkably clean, and there is no evidence of use by Shoults. He was, as already mentioned, a reader who left very few signs of use. Nevertheless, the books discussed above—his manuscripts, incunables, and reference

---

[54] Taylor (1987), 158–9.

books—represent a significant personal library, all acquired by the age of 48. They are a tangible reminder of what a curate with wide intellectual interests and some discretionary funds could amass in London during the mid-nineteenth century.

15 THE COLLECTION IV: LAST READINGS AND CONTEMPORARY MAGAZINES

Number 37, Camberwell Grove, Camberwell, south of the Thames, was the Shoults family home, acquired by William Shoults Senior in 1863. When he died in 1878, he bequeathed the house to his only daughter, Maria Susannah. After ending his curacy duties in 1880, Shoults also settled at No. 37. He was married and, as discussed, had travelled. After the death of her husband, Eliza Katharine stayed on at No. 37, eventually moving in 1901.[1]

No. 37 Camberwell Grove still stands, an imposing brick four-storey Georgian house.[2] (See pl. 16.) While Shoults was moving about, either during his curacies and visiting Father Ignatius's monastery at Capel-y-ffin or while overseas, he used No. 37 as a place to store his book and manuscript collection. He was fortunate, because by the 1880s his collection numbered about 5000-plus volumes, including 160 large, heavy folios. This number of books requires space for storage, and he must have been pleased to see them so housed, no doubt in alcoves and beside casement windows, all likely places for bookshelves.

The books were always available to read and consult. While at St. Edmund the King and Martyr on Lombard Street, he needed to use his copy of Petronius's *Satyricon*, an edition that had been published in Rotterdam by Leers in 1693 but has a title page containing the imprint of the London publishers A. and J. Churchill. He wrote inside this book, the first Latin edition published for the English market: 'Brought up from 37 Camberwell Grove, where it had been for many years, last week, I think Thursday, May, 23rd. Thursday, May 30th, 1878.'[3] (See pl. 21.)

FINAL ACQUISITIONS

A physical examination of Shoults's collection has revealed that he acquired very few books between the years 1880 and 1887. While there may be some that remain unidentified, the total located number seven only: three are dated by him, and four are gifts. One possible reason for the diminishing activity was that he may have started to experience ongoing health issues, problems that may have shifted his priorities away from collecting.

---

[1] 1901: England and Wales census, Camberwell, under Eliza Katharine Shoults.
[2] Many thanks to Alan Bell, current owner of 37 Camberwell Grove, London.
[3] Petronius, *Satyricon* (1693). Shoults Eb 1693 P.

On 5 June 1881, Shoults acquired a copy of an English translation of Jean-Baptiste Cléry's *Journal of What Took Place at the Tower of the Temple during the Captivity of Louis XVI, King of France*, published in London in 1828. First appearing in French in 1798, this edition was translated into English by John Bennett. He inscribed the date of acquisition on the title page. Sometime that year, he acquired a copy of John Gay's *Poems on Several Occasions,* which also includes the poet's somewhat cryptic farce, *The What D'ye Call It*. Published in Glasgow by the brothers Foulis in 1751, this volume, one of two, carries his inscription: 'W. A. Shoults. B. D. 1881.' The final book so inscribed is a copy of the *Memoirs Illustrative of the History and Antiquities of Norfolk and the City of Norwich*, published by the Royal Archaeological Institute of Great Britain and Ireland. Appearing in 1851, this volume contains copies of papers given, a general report of proceedings, and a catalogue of antiquities exhibited at the annual meeting of the Institute in Norwich in July 1847. Why he acquired this rather specialised item at the time is particularly intriguing, and one wonders whether it was the information and plates on church architecture that captured his attention. He wrote in it: 'W. A. Shoults B. D. Feby 26th 1883.'

As noted in chapter 11, Eliza presented him with a copy of *Conference Tenue a Courtray, le 22. Septembre 1681. Entre les Procureurs des Roys de France & d'Espagne* (1682) while at Saint-Omer in September 1880. Among the three other books that she gave him is a copy of Walter Raleigh's *A New History of England, Ecclesiastical and Civil*, published in London in 1756. Only one volume of two is present of this octavo edition, which is enhanced by 32 engravings. He inscribed it: 'W. A. Shoults. B. D. from his loving wife EKS, 3/1/1881.' The second, as mentioned in chapter 13, is three of the four volumes of the *Biblia Hebraica*, published by Plantin in Leiden in 1611. Each volume is inscribed by Shoults: 'E. K. S. Dono dedit W. A. S. II Kal. Hirst. A.D. 1886.' The final is a copy of the fourth edition of John Gregory's *Works*, published in London in 1684. Inscribed by Shoults, 'Wm Arderne Shoults B. D. from his loving wife EKS, 14th December 1886', it may have been the last book that she gave her husband. Gregory (1607–46) was an English orientalist, fluent in Latin, Greek, Syriac, Arabic, Ethiopic, Samaritan, and Saxon. He made some significant contributions to biblical scholarship, being the first to realise that most of the Old Testament Apocrypha had originally been written in Hebrew or Aramaic.[4] Unless Eliza got this purchase completely wrong, it does indicate that she knew what her husband was interested in. She may have known of Gregory's reputation and abilities, envisaging that he was the perfect model for her husband to emulate.

[4] See Hamilton (2006).

LAST BOOKS

Shoults's collection at the University of Otago is arranged by imprint and place of publication. He owned only eight titles published between 1880 and 1887, strong proof that there was a marked reduction in buying new books. They are a motley band, revealing something of the heterogeneity of his collection. Six of the eight titles include a Basque language edition of the Gospel of John entitled *Jesu Cristoren evanjelioa Juanen araura* (1880); a Chinese language edition of the New Testament entitled *Hsin Yueh Ch'uan Shu* (1880); a copy of the 'Syntax' volume only of the fifth edition of William Edward Jelf's *Grammar of the Greek Language* (1881); a copy of the abridged edition of William Smith's *Smaller Classical Dictionary of Biography, Mythology & Geography* (1882); a copy of Daniel Defoe's classic *Journal of the Plague Year* (1884); and a two-volume set of 'Tracts', containing between them thirty-nine titles published between 1848 and 1886.

MAGAZINES AND PERIODICALS

Shoults carved out for himself a small, undistinguished career in Holy Orders and was plainly a High Church Anglican with a strong preference for ritualistic services. By 1880, he had formed a reasonably substantial book collection, and, before his marriage at least, he was a solitary, private reader who not only had leisure to read, but also some spare money to spend on books and magazines. He was certainly an intellectual, and, as an educated gentleman (so classified), he was in a very privileged position to indulge in his bookish activities.

It was good for someone like Shoults to grow up in the 1850s. There was a significant growth of establishments such as mechanics' institutes and public libraries that promoted learning and self-education.[5] There was a significant increase in book publication, and there was a profusion of periodicals and ephemeral tract publications, many of which promoted useful knowledge in their pages. Importantly, the periodicals fostered the habit of reading, with many a subscriber eagerly looking forward to the next issue to reappear and be read (for example, Charles Dickens and his successful *The Pickwick Papers*, issued in monthly parts between 1836 and 1837). Periodicals also formed an extension to the collecting of books, with the dedicated collector often binding up the cumulated issues into a single volume, thereby solving storage problems inherent in individual issues of periodicals. With some 18,000

---

[5] See Bell (1993), 124–44.

periodicals of different titles published in the Victorian period, the reader had much to choose from.[6]

The two remaining publications are *The Antiquary: A Magazine Devoted to the Study of the Past* (4 volumes covering January 1880 to December 1881) and *Knowledge: An Illustrated Magazine of Science* (7 volumes covering 4 November 1881 to 26 June 1885). These periodicals are shelved at '1880' and '1885' respectively, and form almost perfectly-placed book-ends to the above six titles.

In addition to the above two titles, Shoults owned a further 48 periodicals, the contents of all of them covering almost every imaginable topic. The nineteenth-century literary critic George Saintsbury wrote in 1896: 'Perhaps there is no single feature of the English literary history of the nineteenth century, not even the enormous popularisation and multiplication of the novel, which is so distinctive and characteristic as the development in it of periodical literature.'[7] The nineteenth century is deemed the century of periodicals, and Shoults owned 30 titles from that period.[8] His holdings of periodical titles from the eighteenth century number 20. Forty-six were published in England; three were published in France; and one was published in Jamaica. There are no complete runs, with often only one or two single issues of a title present. They are all bound into sturdy volume formats.

EIGHTEENTH-CENTURY PERIODICALS

A breakdown of Shoults's eighteenth-century periodical holdings is as follows: 15 are of general content; four cover politics and history; and one geared towards female readership.[9] Some of the general periodicals are *The British Magazine and General Review of the Literature, Employment and Amusements of the Times*, *The European*

---

[6] Wolff, cited in Scott (1975), 325.

[7] George Saintsbury, cited in Brake (1993), 83–102 (86).

[8] Wolff, cited in Scott (1975), 325–39 (325).

[9] The titles of Shoults's eighteenth-century periodicals are as follows: *Annual Register, or, A View of the History, Politics, and Literature for the Year* (1762); *British Apollo, or, Curious Amusements for the Ingenious* (1708); *British Magazine and General Review of the Literature, Employment and Amusements of the Times* (1772); *Columbian Magazine, or, Monthly Miscellany* (1796–1797); *Complete Magazine of Knowledge and Pleasure* (1764); *Court Magazine* (1761); *Critical Review, or, Annals of Literature* (1790); *European Magazine, and London Review* (1782); *Gentleman's Magazine* (1731); *Grand Magazine of Magazines, or, Universal Register* (1758); *London Magazine and Monthly Chronologer* (1736); *London Magazine, or, Gentleman's Monthly Intelligencer* (1747); *Political Magazine and Parliamentary, Naval, Military, and Literary Journal* (1780); *Present State of Europe, or, The Historical and Political Mercury* (1690); *Quarterly Review*; *Royal Female Magazine; or the Ladies General Repository of Pleasure and Improvement* (1760); *Sentimental Magazine; or, General Assemblage of Science, Taste, and Entertainment* (1773); *Town and Country Magazine, or, Universal Repository of Knowledge, Instruction, and Entertainment* (1769); *Universal Magazine of Knowledge and Pleasure* (1747); and *Westminster Magazine* (1773).

Magazine, *The Gentleman's Magazine*, *London Magazine*, *The Town and Country Magazine*, *The Universal Magazine of Knowledge and Pleasure*, and *The Westminster Magazine*, subtitled 'The Pantheon of Taste'.

Two from the general category are of particular note. He owned the first volume of *The British Apollo*, started by poet Aaron Hill (1685–1750) on 13 February 1708. As a precursor to *Notes & Queries*, the stated aim of this periodical was to 'endeavour to answer all questions in Divinity, Philosophy, the Mathematicks, and other Arts and Sciences'.[10] It also included poetry (serious and comical), a foreign news column, and advertisements. It ended on 11 May 1711, and at its height reached between 1000 and 2000 subscribers.[11] Shoults may have had a general curiosity about the contents, which are wide in coverage, informative, and in some instances very amusing: for example, two sample 'Queries': 'Why did not God make the World in a Moment as well as in six Days?' and 'Why are Cuckholds said to wear Horns, and not their Wives?'[12] This volume was subjected to rudimentary collation, perhaps by Shoults. A scrap of blue paper is loosely tipped in, reading: 'Supernumerary Papers Nos 10 & 11 wanting & No.12 misplaced.'

The Columbian Magazine, or, Monthly Miscellany was published in Kingston, Jamaica, between June 1796 and June 1800, and has the distinction of being one of the oldest magazines published in the colony. Its contents are wide-ranging, from foreign and domestic events, letters to the editor, and articles on the slave trade, to duelling, curing dry-rot, and poetic extracts from 'luminaries' such as Dr John Wolcott (Peter Pindar), who was once a resident in Kingston. This one volume, containing an incomplete run from June 1796 to May 1800, may have been passed to Shoults by a family member, or perhaps was a pure happenstance purchase.[13]

HISTORICAL MAGAZINES

Periodicals of a political and historical nature number four. The first is copies of two volumes of *The Present State of Europe, Or, The Historical and Political Mercury* (April 1691 and January 1692), a scarce monthly newsletter that offered readers information on political and military events in Europe; the second is a copy of the *Annual Register* for 1762; the third a copy of the volume for 1780 of the Tory *Political Magazine and Parliamentary, Naval, Military, and Literary Journal*, with its reputation for maps,

---

[10] *British Apollo*, 13–18 February 1708, [1]. Shoults Ec 1708 B.
[11] Cited in Gerrard (2003), 16; see also Gerrard (2007).
[12] *British Apollo*, 13–18 February 1708, [1–2]. Shoults Ec 1708 B.
[13] The *Columbian Magazine* is a scarce publication, with incomplete holdings at the National Library of Jamaica, the American Antiquarian Society (Massachusetts), and the Shoults Collection: Eb 1796 C.

especially military; and the last, five issues of volume 70 (July–December 1790) of the Tory-based *Critical Review*.

FEMALE READERSHIP

The one periodical geared towards a female readership is the *Royal Female Magazine; Or the Ladies General Repository of Pleasure and Improvement* (1760). This work was compiled by 'Charles Honeycombe', a pseudonym for Robert Lloyd (1733–63), a poet who dedicated the work to Augusta of Saxe-Gotha-Altenburg (1719–72), the Princess-Dowager of Wales. His aim for it was well intentioned: 'I shall always select such subjects as may be immediately and interestingly conducive to their [the ladies'] improvement; but as such studies, if pursued too closely, might be in danger of giving disgust, or fatigue, I shall intersperse topicks of entertainment, to ease the attention and exercise the fancy.'[14] This title is outside Shoults's normal collecting interests, and perhaps it belonged to Eliza, or his mother, who, as revealed, was registered as a school mistress in Margate.

NINETEENTH-CENTURY PERIODICALS

Shoults's nineteenth-century periodicals are an eclectic lot. There are three general ones; eleven that have an antiquarian and archaeological focus; one with a manufacturing and industry emphasis; one historical; two of popular science; one specifically on book collecting; one emanating from St. John's College (the *Eagle*, see chapter 4); and ten with a definite religious focus. Twenty-seven are in English, three in French.

The three general periodicals are the *British Almanac*, the *Penny Magazine*, and the *Quarterly Review*. The first two were sponsored by the Society for the Diffusion of Useful Knowledge (SDUK), established by the co-founder of the *Edinburgh Review* (1802), Henry Peter Brougham, first Baron Brougham and Vaux (1778–1868). The aim of this Society was to give the growing number of readers inexpensive texts that were both informative and useful. They were 'opposed to works of imagination'.[15] The *British Almanac* fulfilled its function admirably, and, as the title implies, each issue contained a calendar of events, dates, and days that were deemed important to celebrate. Weather and astronomical information was included, as well as garden and farming hints, along with news domestic and foreign. With some gaps, Shoults owned 28 volumes, ranging from 1829 to 1861.

---

[14] *Royal Female Magazine*, 1 (1760), vi. Shoults Eb 1760 R.
[15] Altick (1957), 333.

The other SDUK periodical is the *Penny Magazine*, which began on 31 March 1832 and at its height had a circulation of 200,000.[16] As mentioned in chapter 2, the twelve issues (1834–41) of this landmark publication, cheap (a penny), packed full of information (of the useful sort), and profusely illustrated, were 'hand-me-downs', volumes that were once owned by Shoults's father, whose book label is pasted in each.

The last general periodical Shoults owned was the *Quarterly Review*, which at its peak reached sales of about 12,000 to 13,000.[17] First published by John Murray II in February 1809, it was aimed at countering the Whig-supported *Edinburgh Review*. Its long articles and book reviews represent some of the best writing for the times in politics, literature, science, and religion. Shoults owned a long but broken run of 41 volumes, from January 1815 to July 1877. Many of his copies have broken spines and appear well used, but they are clean, with no marginalia or notes within.

ANTIQUARIANISM

Shoults owned eleven periodicals that have antiquarianism and archaeology as their focus. His interests certainly encompassed ancient, classical, and ecclesiastical history, and, although he was not a member of any archaeological society, this discipline, a burgeoning one that developed from fields such as antiquarianism, obviously held enough fascination for him to purchase items related to it.[18] In fact, as already mentioned, he acquired in 1883 a copy of the Royal Archaeological Institute of Great Britain and Ireland's *Memoirs Illustrative of the History and Antiquities of Norfolk and the City of Norwich* (1851).

The first is a copy of *The Oriental Annual, or, Scenes in India*, published in 1834 and 1835. This work details the history of India and towns such as Madras, Calcutta, and Bombay and is illustrated with engravings by the landscape and maritime painter William Daniell (1769–1837). However, this well-produced publication, with its gilt edges and ornate covers, may not have been purchased by Shoults. Although the content may have interested him, the volumes, especially with their illustrative emphasis, seem like items that were possibly acquired by his father-in-law, John Connell Ogle, who, as an artist, may have known Daniell, a successful artist in similar fields.

The second is *The Archaeologist and Journal of Antiquarian Science*, started jointly by Thomas Wright (1810–77) and James Orchard Halliwell (1820–89), which

---

[16] Altick (1957), 335. He writes: 'The *Penny Magazine* at best was never light reading.'
[17] Altick (1957), 319.
[18] The *Oxford English Dictionary* cites the first use of 'archaeologist' as in 1824, and the modern meaning of 'archaeology' (rather than wider 'ancient history') from 1837.

ran from September 1841 to June 1842.[19] Its coverage is wide: architecture, historical literature, philology, bibliography, topography, and reviews of recent works. Shoults owned all ten issues, and all are clean copies, except for a very small ink annotation at the beginning of the review of J.K. Walker's *Some Observations on the Antient Language of the Etruscans*. Shoults had a strong interest in languages, yet it is hard to determine if this note was made by him.

The third is the *Transactions of the Royal Society of Literature of the United Kingdom*. Shoults owned two volumes, 1 (1843) and 4 (1853), each with an antiquarian focus that followed the first aim of the Society, instituted under George III in 1821: 'to promote the publication, and, in some cases, the translation, of valuable Manuscripts, discovered in any public or private Collection.'[20] These particular volumes contain contributions by book collectors and antiquarians such as Sir Thomas Phillipps and the above-mentioned James Orchard Halliwell. Shoults's copy of volume 1 is unopened, and thus not read. The leaves of volume 4 have been opened; Shoults may have read parts of it.

The fourth is the *Archaeological Journal* (1846–67), a quarterly established in 1844 by members of the British Archaeological Association (BAA). Shoults owned five volumes: the second edition of volume 1 (1846), and first editions of 2 (1846), 4 (1847), 5 (1848), and 14 (1867). The topics within were wide-ranging: numismatics, Anglo-Saxon architecture, bell turrets, English medieval embroidery, a Norman tombstone at Coningsborough, descriptions of a chamber in a castle, and so on.[21] Co-founder and first secretary Albert Way (1805–74) summed up the Society's *raison d'être* in the first issue: 'the encouragement of intelligent researches into British antiquities.'[22]

The fifth is a single issue of the *Proceedings* of the Archaeological Institute, published in September 1846. The Institute, eventually becoming the Royal Archaeological Institute (RAI), was founded by Way in 1845 as a rival to the BAA. This issue was once owned by a RAI member, the Rev. Thomas Jessop, D.D.

The sixth is volume 2 of the *Reports and Papers read at Meetings of the Architectural Societies of the Archdeaconry of Northampton, the County of York, and the Diocese of Lincoln, and of the Architectural and Archaeological Society of the County of Bedford during the Years [1852–1853]*, published by the Architectural Society in 1854. Perhaps Shoults was attracted by some of the contents such as the antiquarian information on Southwark, his birthplace, or by Henry E. L. Dryden's article 'On Church Music

---

[19] Vol.1, 8 (April 1842), 73. Shoults Eb 1842 A. See Thompson (2015); see also Freeman (2004).
[20] *Transactions of the Royal Society of Literature of the United Kingdom*, 1 (1829), vii. Shoults Eb 1829 R. The publication ceased in 1919.
[21] Cited in *Archaeological Journal*, 1 (1845), title and contents pages. Shoults Eb 1845 A.
[22] *Archaeological Journal*, 1 (1845), 1.

and the Fitting of Churches for Music', which was originally read at a meeting of the Architectural Society at Northampton in 1853.

The seventh is the *Journal of Classical and Sacred Philology* (1845–59), which has a strong antiquarian emphasis. Shoults owned the parts for March and June of volume 1, 1854, which contained topics and articles such as 'The "Birds" of Aristophanes', 'Value of Roman Money', Bishop Pearson's 'Marginalia on Eusebius', and E. M. Cope's 'The Sophists'. The periodical had strong links with the University of Cambridge. It was started by Joseph Barber Lightfoot, Fenton John Anthony Hort, and John Eyton Bickersteth Mayor, with one contributor being the Rev. Churchill Babington. As revealed in chapters 3 and 6, Shoults certainly knew these men.

The eighth is *Surrey Archaeological Collections: Relating to the History and Antiquities of the County*, issued by the Surrey Archaeological Society. Shoults owned five volumes: 1 (1858), 2 (1864), 3 (1865), 4 (1869), and 5 (1871). All are clean copies, with volume 5 unopened.

The ninth is another single copy, a Report of the *Antiquarian Communications*, published by the Cambridge Antiquarian Society in 1859. The Society was established in 1840 for the 'encouragement of the study of History, Architecture and Antiquities', especially around the Cambridgeshire region.[23] Many of its core members, such as Churchill Babington and John E.B. Mayor, were known to Shoults. He was not a paid-up member, and one can only presume that it was his interest in the field, spurred on by College associations, that led him to acquire this volume.

The tenth is the only French publication specifically dedicated to antiquities that Shoults owned: volume 8 of *Mémoires de la Société des Antiquaires de Picardie*, published in 1861. Formerly the Musée Napoléon in Amiens, the Society became the Musée de Picardie, which housed collections of manuscripts, art, archaeological relics, and rare books. There were a number of English associations attached to the Musée de Picardie, including the Society of Antiquities of London and the BAA. These associations may have been a catalyst for Shoults to purchase this one volume, or he may well have visited Amiens at some time, it forming a keepsake of that journey.

The last periodical in this field is, as already mentioned, *The Antiquary*, which had as its first editor Edward Walford (1823–97). The contents of this publication, which ceased in 1915, covered architecture, painting, design, furniture, and literary works of antiquarian interest. Shoults owned four volumes: 1 (January–June 1880), 2 (July–December 1880), 3 (January–June 1881) and 4 (July–December 1881). The May issue of 1880 bears testimony to the variety of subjects, all packed into 47 pages: 'The History of Jade'; 'Notes on some Northern Minsters: Bolton Priory'; 'Church

---

[23] *Antiquarian Communications* (1860), 11. Shoults Eb 1851 C.

Restoration with Experiences and Suggestions'; and 'Celtic Superstitions in Scotland and Ireland'. Regular columns include 'Reviews'; 'Meetings of Antiquarian Societies'; 'The Antiquary's Note-book'; 'Antiquarian News'; 'Correspondence'; 'Books Received'; and 'The Antiquary Exchange'. His four volumes are clean.

INDUSTRY

As mentioned in chapter 2, there is a small run of *The Builder. An Illustrated Weekly Magazine for the Architect, Engineer, Archaeologist, Constructor, & Artist* in Shoults's collection: volumes 16 to 18 (1858–60). Started by Joseph Aloysius Hansom, architect and designer of the Hansom cab, in 1843, this publication was aimed at those in the trade. The architect George Godwin (1813–88) took over the editorship in 1844, expanding its coverage and scope.[24] Like the *Penny Magazine*, this periodical belonged to Shoults's father William. While the younger Shoults may have evinced some interest in his father's trade (and his business successes), he merely took these publications in when his father died.

HISTORY

Shoults owned volume 2 only of *The Portfolio, or, A Collection of State Papers: Illustrative of the History of Our Times* (1836), edited by the Scottish diplomat David Urquhart (1805–77).[25] The reason why Shoults acquired this single volume on secret Russian despatches is unknown. Urquhart was at one time a Philhellene, who subsequently switched to being a Turcophile. Shoults was interested enough in the Middle East to collect books in the field, and he donated money towards war-wounded Turkish soldiers in July 1878.[26] Empathy and interest may have induced him to acquire it. However, even the best intentions of book collectors are often thwarted; the leaves remain unopened.

SCIENCE

The Magazine of Science, and School of Arts began as 'a cheap and useful publication', those behind it having recognised an 'increasing desire among all classes for rational and scientific amusement'.[27] Shoults owned ten issues, published between April 1839 and June 1842. The editors were enthusiastic in their claims: 'we have recorded

---

[24] See Richardson (1989), 121–40.
[25] See Taylor (2004).
[26] Shoults is listed among '23rd List of donors to "Stafford House Committee for the relief of sick and wounded Turkish soldiers"', *The Times*, 27 July 1878, 8.
[27] *Magazine of Science, and School of Arts*, 1 (6 April 1839), [1]. Shoults Eb 1840 M.

every thing new and valuable—explained numerous most important Philosophical Instruments—have ourselves written nearly Two Hundred Original Papers on Scientific Manipulation, or explanatory of interesting Processes, (some of which were never before made public)—have answered One Hundred and Seventy Queries, and conducted, we trust with courtesy and attention, an extensive Correspondence.'[28] Bound at the back of the second volume are a few leaves of the *Penny Mechanic and Chemist*. The name of a previous owner on the title page of the *Penny Mechanic* has been scratched out.

The other science-based periodical is the already-mentioned *Knowledge: An Illustrated Magazine of Science*, with its subtitle 'Plainly Worded-Exactly Described'. Shoults owned seven volumes, 1 (4 November 1881–26 May 1882), 2 (2 June–29 December 1882), 3 (5 January–29 June 1883), 4 (6 July–22 December 1883), 5 (4 January–27 June 1884), 6 (4 July–26 December 1884), and 7 (2 January–26 June 1885).[29] It was edited by Richard A. Proctor (1837–88), who aimed to give his readers less confusion and more clarity: 'to bring the truths, discoveries, and inventions of Science before the public in simple but correct terms—to be, in fact, the minister and interpreter of Science for those who have not time to master the technicalities.'[30] Each weekly issue of 20 pages is packed with information, information that would satisfy any keen, curious reader. It differs markedly from *The Antiquary* in that it contains illustrations, including images of comets, the night sky, flora and fauna, and line drawings of machinery. There is no evidence of whether Shoults paid 2d for each weekly issue, and the sixpenny charge for monthly parts adopted in 1885. There is also no evidence as to whom he paid to have them bound.

BOOK COLLECTING

In March 1866, Antoine Bachelin (b.1835) opened a bookselling outlet at 26 Garrick Street, Covent Garden, claiming that the 'main purpose will be the commission between France, England and America, for all ancient and modern works published in these countries'.[31] With financial support from his wife, Madame Deflorrene (c.1813–67), Bachelin had started *Le Bibliophile*, a Parisian-based periodical on book collecting in June 1862. He later produced a grander version in May 1868.[32] Shoults owned 13 issues of the lesser '*Little Bibliophile*', as the smaller publication was called,

---

[28] *Magazine of Science, and School of Arts*, 1 (1 April 1840), [1].
[29] *Knowledge*, 1–7 (1881–85). Shoults Ec 1881 K.
[30] Proctor (1881), 3. Proctor's brother, William Addy Proctor, was one of Shoults's classmates at St. John's College.
[31] See Jimenes (2009), 60.
[32] Jimenes (2009), 59–64. *Le Bibliophile* ceased in 1873; the '*Little Bibliophile*' ceased in 1876.

from January 1863 to January 1865. The title page of this thin volume, which offered bibliophiles information on new and antiquarian books, and continental sales and auctions, has a London address printed within: 'E. Rascol, Libraire-Éditeur, 4 Brydges Street, Convent Garden.' Shoults may have acquired his copies directly from the shop, or they could well have been retrospective purchases, obtained from someone else.

RELIGION

In his classic *The Victorian Church*, Owen Chadwick writes a truism: 'Victorian England was religious.'[33] The historian G. Kitson Clark commented earlier that 'probably in no other century except the seventeenth [...] did the claims of religion occupy so large a part in the nation's life, or did men speaking in the name of religion contrive to exercise so much power'.[34] In 1804, the Religious Tract Society issued 314,000 copies of tracts; by 1861 annual output was about 20 million, in addition to 13 million copies of periodicals.[35] The Society for the Promotion of Christian Knowledge (the oldest evangelical society, founded 1699) raised its yearly production of periodicals from 1.5 million in 1827 to 8 million in 1867. In 1832 its Committee began the *Saturday Magazine* in response to the 'useful knowledge' *Penny Magazine*, which at its height had a circulation of 200,000.[36] The *Saturday Magazine* was priced at a penny, and claimed a circulation of 70,000.[37]

Shoults owned ten periodicals that were religious in nature, each with their High Church, Anglo-Catholic, or Roman Catholic leanings. The first is the *British Critic*, which was founded in 1793 by Archdeacon Robert Nares with assistance from William Beloe. It was later run by Joshua Watson (1771–1855) and the Rev. Henry Handley Norris (1771–1850), both representatives of the Hackney Phalanx, a group of clergy and laymen who defended Anglican orthodoxy.[38] In 1825, it became a quarterly, and, two years later, merged with Francis and Charles Rivington's *Quarterly Theological Review*. Shoults owned eight volumes: 33 (January 1809), 38 (July 1811), 24 (1838), 30 (1841), 31 (1842), 32 (1842), 33, (1843), and 34 (1843).

On the face of it, these volumes had passed their use, no longer providing the reader with current news and views of the world about them.[39] Yet the volume for

---

[33] Chadwick (1987), I, 1.
[34] Clark (1962), 20.
[35] Altick (1957), 101. The RTS did not just focus on religious publications. They also published books on useful knowledge and some general travel books.
[36] Altick (1957), 335.
[37] Altick (1957), 40.
[38] See Houghton (1991), 111–18.
[39] See Altick (1957), 318, but generally chapters 5 (99–128), 14 (318–47), and 15 (348–64).

15 THE COLLECTION IV: LAST READINGS & CONTEMPORARY MAGAZINES 251

January 1809 proved useful to Shoults. Under the heading of 'British Catalogue. Divinity', there is a review of the second edition of the Rev. Josiah Thomas's *Strictures on Subjects Chiefly Relating to the Established Religion and the Clergy* (1807).[40] Shoults obviously read the review and answered the unknown reviewer's question: 'Who is to receive the tenth part of the produce of your estates, when the usufructuary priest shall be allowed to collect or compound for it no longer? Do you mean to take it to yourselves? That would be hardly honest.'* The asterisk refers to Shoults's response, which he wrote on an outer margin of the leaf (p. 308), which had been folded in and thus missed the binder's cropping: *'Few landlords take the consideration of tithes into their valuation unless the lands are quite tithe free. Therefore the farmer is in general being feted by what sum he can get the propensity of the tithe to take cap.[capital] than the real value.' As mentioned in chapter 10, in 1878, Shoults acquired some books on tithing. He may also have read his copy of Peter Heylyn's 'The Undeceiving of the Peoples in the point of Tithes' in his *The Historical and Miscellaneous Tracts of the Reverend and Learned Peter Heylyn, D.D.* (1661), which he had acquired in 1859. By 1878, he was a property owner. It is quite possible that he made the note in the volume then, when this topic was uppermost in his mind. Although it is a small note, it does reveal an aspect to his character that is hidden behind his more tangible intellectual and theological activities.

The second is *The British Magazine and Monthly Register of Religious and Ecclesiastical Information, Parochial History, and Documents Respecting the State of the Poor, Progress of Education*, of which Shoults owned volumes 2 and 3, published in 1832 and 1833.[41] Started by the Rev. Hugh James Rose (1795–1838) in 1832, this was a monthly journal for clergy, with a clear aim to provide a middle ground between the more conservative High Church faction and those younger men in or influenced by the Oxford Movement.[42] Rose was an advocate of the early Tractarians, and, as editor, he accepted some of their works into the periodical's pages.[43] Shoults acquired his copies sometime after 1869, as James Mead, a previous owner, has inscribed his name with the date '1869' in volume 2.

The third is the *English Review, or Quarterly Journal of Ecclesiastical and General Literature*, published by the Rivingtons, who not only published the *Tracts for the Times* (which Shoults also owned), but also were the undisputed publishers of the

---

[40] See *British Critic* (1809), 307–9. Shoults Eb 1793 B.
[41] *British Magazine* (1832 and 1833). Shoults Eb 1832 B
[42] See Nockles (2014).
[43] Some of the contributors to the magazine included William Palmer, A.P. Perceval, Hurrell Froude, John Keble, and J.H. Newman, whose sacred poetry *Lyra Apostolica* first appeared in its pages. See Altholz (1989), 25, and Nockles (2014).

Established Church.⁴⁴ Shoults owned five volumes of the *English Review*: 1 (2 April 1844), 2 (July 1844), 3 (June 1845), 4 (October 1845), 5 (March 1846), and 9 (June 1848). A reincarnation of the failed *British Critic*, this conservative anti-Rome magazine represented the Old 'High and Dry' School.⁴⁵ Like the *Church Remembrancer* (see below), its content is heavily textual, with long erudite articles and reviews. It ceased publication in 1853.

The fourth is one volume of *The Theologian: A Review of Ancient and Modern Divinity, and Universal Christian Literature*, No. 8 (October 1845). *The Theologian* was a monthly aimed at parish clergy, specifically those associated with the Oxford Movement, post-Newman. It did not last, merging with the *Ecclesiastic* (1846) to form *Theologian and Ecclesiastic*. It is a clean copy.

The fifth is the *Christian Remembrancer*, started by Frederick Iremonger at the instigation of the owners of the *British Critic*, Joshua Watson and the Rev. Henry Handley Norris, 'to maintain the character and pretensions of the Establishment, upon popular arguments'.⁴⁶ This High Church periodical, which ran from 1819 to 1868, was dominated by Norris, with its editors including William Scott and J. B. Mozley. Contributors included John Armstrong, Richard William Church, John Mason Neale, and Mark Pattison. Shoults owned twelve volumes: 42–51 (January 1862–April 1866), 53 (January–April 1867), and 55 (January–April 1868). The articles and reviews within are no easy read; they are dense, erudite pieces. Shoults's blue buckram-bound volumes are clean.

The sixth is a bound volume of the *Church News*, a London-based Anglo-Catholic magazine, with issues covering 13 March to 24 December 1867. Complementing the *Church Times*, a much-longer-lived Anglo-Catholic periodical founded in February 1863 by George Josiah Palmer (1828–92), this short-lived periodical (as mentioned in chapter 7) contains chatty notes, queries, articles on ecclesiastical matters, correspondence, and book reviews.⁴⁷ At one point the ritualist Frederick George Lee (1832–1902) edited it.⁴⁸ Shoults's copy is an extremely battered one, with its binding almost detached from its text block.

The seventh is the *Union Review: A Magazine of Catholic Literature and Art*, of which Shoults owned two volumes: 1867 and 1872. This periodical started as *The Union* in 1857, its chief aim being to bring about the reunion of the Church of England, specifically the Tractarian branch and the Roman Catholic Church. It eventually

---

⁴⁴ See Rivington (1894); Fitzpatrick (1995).
⁴⁵ See Houghton (1991), 111–18.
⁴⁶ 'Introduction', *Christian Remembrancer* (January 1819), 2. Shoults Eb 1819 C.
⁴⁷ See Palmer (2004).
⁴⁸ See Pawley (2009).

morphed into the *Union Review*, and at one stage was edited by the already-mentioned ritualist F.G. Lee. The articles and literary notices are textually dense. Both volumes are clean.

The eighth is *The Literary Churchman and Critical Record of Current Literature*, of which Shoults owned three badly-damaged blue-buckram volumes for the years 1871, 1873, and 1874. This fortnightly publication offered readers like Shoults notices on recently published religious books and general literature titles. One of its frequent reviewers was Thomas Thellusson Carter (1808–1901), 'one of the most venerated and the last of the Tractarians', who re-introduced some Catholic practices into the Church, was the founder of the Confraternity of the Blessed Sacrament (a devotional society within the Church), and established the Clewer House of Mercy, a sisterhood convent which later became the Community of St. John Baptist.[49] Given his own personal experiences, especially with Father Ignatius and the Sisterhood at Feltham, it is hard to imagine Shoults not knowing of the activities of this extraordinary ritualist as he perused the pages of this periodical.

ROMAN CATHOLIC PERIODICALS

It has been calculated that there were 67 Roman Catholic periodicals founded in the first half of the nineteenth century.[50] One 'Catholic' periodical that Shoults owned was the *Catholic Magazine,* started in 1838 by Charles Dolman (1807–63), who was the publisher of the *Dublin Review*, an aggressive pro-Catholic quarterly journal.[51] The *Catholic Magazine* aimed to bridge the gap between Catholics and Protestants and to promote the Roman Catholic faith to a wider audience: 'our sole object and aim is to simply to advance the cause of the ONE, HOLY, CATHOLIC and APOSTOLIC FAITH, in our beloved country; and in so doing, to promote as far as our feeble endeavours can, the greater glory of our good GOD.'[52] Shoults owned three volumes: 2 (1838), 3 (1839), and 4 (1840), with issues for January to April 1841 bound in volume 3. All his volumes are clean.

The last religious periodical is *L'Union Chrétienne*, edited by René-François Guettée (1816–92), later known as Father Vladimir or Wladimir Guettée. Ordained a Roman Catholic priest in 1839, Guettée converted to Eastern Orthodoxy, convinced that the Orthodox Church (the Russian Church) was the true one. In 1854, he established the *Catholic Review*, only to change it to *L'Union Chrétienne*, a vehicle

---

[49] See Anson (1964), especially 304–16; see also Bonham (2004).
[50] See Altholz (1989), 99.
[51] See Mitchell (2012).
[52] *Catholic Magazine*, Third Series, 1 (January 1843), 1. Shoults Eb 1838 C.

for him to promote Orthodoxy.⁵³ Shoults owned four volumes: 1(4 November 1860–27 October 1861); 2 (January–December 1868); 3 (March 1869, January–December 1870); and 4 (January–December 1872).⁵⁴ A tipped-in leaf in volume 1 for April 1870 has a note written by Shoults, representing the issue and debate by early Christians on 'Theotokos' versus 'Christokotos'. It reads:

> As to <u>Bright's</u> assertion that to scruple at THEOTOKOS <u>must</u> imply heresy, just as to deny HOMOOUSIOS is heresy. But JHN [Newman] says (S. Ath. [Athanasius] Treatise agᵗ Arianism, part 1, note p.157.) 'It shᵈ be observed how careful the Fathers of the days were not to mix up the qⁿ· of doctrine, whʰ rested on Cathᶜ tradⁿ w that of the adoption of a certain term wʰ rested on a Cath. injunction. Not that the term was not in duty[?] to be recᵈ., but it was to be recᵈ on accᵗ of its Cath. sense, & where the Cath. sense was held, the word mᵗ even by a sense of desperation be waived Christokotos.⁵⁵

SUMMARY

The preceding notes on Shoults's periodicals raise a few questions. The periodicals are in his collection, but there is no clear-cut reason why. Some of them were published before his birth and some were published when he was quite young. The remainder were published when he was active as a curate in London. There are certainly a number of periodicals that are pertinent to his profession, while others match perceived personal interests. There are others that appear outside his normal collecting fields and that more than likely fell into his hands quite randomly—a scenario quite common for book collectors. There are no invoices or letters that document any conscious effort to purchase them, and only the occasional hint of when any were obtained, witness his acquisition of *Memoirs Illustrative of the History and Antiquities of Norfolk*, which was published in 1851 but acquired in 1883. What drove him to focus on this particular item at that time? Some of course belonged to family members, and they came to him—as head of the family and as the collector in the family. There is no certainty as to why he acquired them. With this uncertainty, one falls back on Pollard's justification for collecting: that an item acquired appealed to the mind, to the eye, or to the imagination.

---

⁵³ Kirwan (1999).
⁵⁴ *L'Union Chrétienne*. Shoults Ec 1859 U.
⁵⁵ The 'Bright' mentioned was certainly William Bright (1824–1901), an English ecclesiastical historian and Anglican priest, who not only wrote hymns, but also, especially in reference to Father Ignatius's early education, was founder of Trinity College, Glenalmond. THEOTOKOS θεοτοκος = 'one who gave birth to God', the standard honorific in the Orthodox Churches for the Blessed Virgin Mary; HOMOOUSIOS ‛ομοουσιος = 'of one substance', as used in the Nicene Creed since 325.

The second point is the type he collected. He did not have any samples of the cheap, popular serialised fiction magazines such as Charles Dickens's *Household Words* (1850) or *All the Year Round* (1859), nor any of the popular, sensational, publications such as penny dreadfuls, which often contained reprinted stories of detectives, criminals, or vampires. The sensational, the trifles, were not for him. He had no annuals such as the *Keepsake*, nor works that were heavily illustrated, except for his father's *Penny Magazine* and his run of the science magazine *Knowledge*. Overall, the periodicals he owned were serious reads, brimming with practical, useful information, packed full of intellectual content that he obviously enjoyed. His predilection for the ritualistic and his leanings towards Anglo-Catholicism meant that there were no Low Church periodicals such as the *Christian Observer* or *The Record*, no temperance periodicals such as the *Church of England Temperance Magazine*, no Evangelical periodicals such as the *Evangelical Magazine* or the *Spiritual Magazine*, no nonconformist ones such as the *Eclectic Review* or the *British Quarterly Review*, or later magazines such as *Macmillans*, *The Cornhill Magazine*, or *The Fortnightly Review*.

Richard Altick aptly describes a stereotypical Bible-reading Victorian reader as 'a person of inflexible seriousness, shuddering at the thought of worldly amusement'.[56] Although this might be too harsh to apply to Shoults, the description matches him somewhat, especially given the serious nature and content of his library. It can be hoped that at some stage throughout his short life, he occasionally broke this mould and became a little less earnest.

---

[56] Altick (1957), 115.

16 PROVENANCE AND THE TRAFFIC OF BOOKS

Provenance is the study of the chronology of the ownership, custody, or location of a historical object. In the case of the book and its pedigree, evidence of provenance is obtained through a few tangible markers: bookplates, book labels, stamps, inscriptions, and notes.

Bookplates are small, printed sheets that are usually pasted onto the inside front cover (pastedown) of a book. They often contain the Latin phrase *Ex libris*, which means 'from the books or library of', followed by the name of the owner and sometimes a family motto and/or date. They display a marked individuality in their design, ranging from the heraldic to the pictorial, which can include, in these modern times, photography. Printed labels are a much simpler form of ownership, comprising the owner's name and sometimes a little ornamentation. Ink stamps, using rubber, or engraved metal or wood, usually have the full name of the owner and perhaps a date.

Palaeography is the study of ancient and historical handwriting, and correctly reading inscriptions in books is an obvious skill needed for any student of book history. Inscribing one's name in a book is the easiest way to indicate ownership, and it can be accompanied by other evidential material important to the book historian: place of residence, price paid, 'ex dono' presentations, date acquired. Sometimes there is a warning attached, as in Shoults's copy of Edmund Waller's *Works* (1730), which was once owned by Samuel Daniel, who wrote in it 3 March 1828: 'Steal not this book.'

Almost all of Shoults's books and manuscripts have the purple 'Selwyn College' stamp inside them. About 600 to 700 have provenance markers such as those described above. Their presence is useful to the book historian, who, on examining them, can gain some impression of the traffic of a book, the movement from a previous owner (through dispersal) to the shelf of a book collector or an institution. When further provenance information from other books is added together, the result can often provide a firmer picture or pattern of the formation of a library collection. Book sales and auctions can offer precise dates of purchase, if the book is sold directly to the owner. However, not every sale provides such certainty, especially when the book is sold to an agent or bookseller, who then sells it on. This process, the traffic of a book's progress from the shelves of the bookseller (or other agent) to the shelves of a book collector, can have many stages and can take time.

There are some 51 books in Shoults's collection that contain inscriptions and specific dates (day, month, year) that offer certainty of when they were acquired by him. For the remainder, there is no such certainty. These others have markers that record ownership details only. Occasionally, a year is added, but this offers nothing definite on when they were actually acquired. For these books, it is a matter of approximation. The difficulty of determining a firm date of acquisition is highlighted by one example. Shoults owned a copy of Richard Hooker's *Of the Lawes of Ecclesiastical Politie*, published in London in 1622. This book passed through five hands, finally resting with the Rev. Mr Waite, who, as recorded on the title page, gave the book to one Thomas Barnes in 1877. Before Waite owned the book, previous owners were 'Robert Hydeste' (initials stamped in gilt on the cover and name inscribed on the title page); 'J. Crouchley' (flyleaf); and 'Hen. Dickenson' (title page).[1] It is difficult to ascertain when the book came on to the open market, but it was obviously acquired by Shoults sometime after 1877.

Richard Hooker's work also represents a feature of the Shoults Collection. Many of his books were owned by individuals who occupied the next stratum down from those prominent, well-known book collectors such as the Duke of Devonshire or Sir Thomas Phillipps. Increasingly, especially in the nineteenth century, libraries were formed by middle-class men and women who were genuinely interested, for whatever reason, in increasing their knowledge and education. Whether for leisure or work purposes, men such as Richard Betton and Robert Spencer, and women such as Eliza Cosway and Sarah Godschall obviously enjoyed possession of a book enough to leave their mark inside.[2]

MONASTIC AND INSTITUTIONAL LIBRARIES

Strife in Europe from the Reformation onwards led to the dispersal of books from monastic libraries, the closure of some one hundred Jesuit libraries in Germany in 1773, further confiscation of books from some 1300 monastic libraries—hundreds secularised in 1803—and the dissolution of libraries during the French Revolution and the Napoleonic Wars (Napoleon is said to have looted 10,000 incunabula on the west bank of the Rhine).[3] As a consequence, a huge number of books found new homes at court and in university libraries, as well as flooding onto an open market, booty for eager book collectors. And one cannot forget the removal of duplicates by various institutions—the sale of which no doubt alleviated space issues.

There are a number of books from monastic and institutional libraries in the Shoults Collection. Of the 28 incunables in his library, four carry legible inscriptions

---

[1] Hooker, *Of the Lawes of Ecclesiastical Politie*. Shoults Ec 1622 H.
[2] David Pearson has done much to promote provenance as a study in book history, with a special focus of the British scene. See Pearson (1994), (2011), and (2019). I am also much indebted to Dr Christopher de Hamel for teasing out various inscriptions.
[3] Flood (2010), 223–36 (232).

that record their pedigree. The first is his copy of Matthaeus de Cracovia's *De modo confitendi et puritate conscientiae*, published in Speyer by the 'Printer of the "Gesta Christi"' about 1472. It was once in the Benedictine Abbey Library of St. Alexander and Theodor in Ottobeuren, near Memmingen, Germany. The Abbey, known as the 'Swabian Escorial', was secularised in December 1802 and became the property of the Electorate of Bavaria. It was later restored as a Benedictine priory by King Ludwig I of Bavaria in 1834. Even though the library remained in place, it did suffer losses, as is evidenced by this one volume.[4]

The second is his copy of Leonardus Matthaei de Utino's *Sermones de sanctis*, published by Peter Drach in Speyer in February 1478. From the inscription on the title page, this work was once on the shelves at the Franciscan Monastery at Amberg, Germany, which was dissolved in 1555 during the Reformation.

The third is his copy of Bernardinus de Busti's *Mariale*, completed in Milan by Leonardus Pachel, 21 May 1493. This copy was once in the church library in Piacenza, as shown by the note: 'Conventus sancti Laurentii de Placentia ex subscripto fratre defuncti' and, below, 'fr. Paulus placentiae prior'—translated as 'Given to San Lorenzo in Piacenza, [Emilia-Romagna, Italy] by its late prior Paolo.'

The last incunable is a copy of *Formularium procuratorum*, a work of canon law pertaining to the Roman curia. Published in Basel in 1493, it has been attributed to printer Michael Furter. Two previous owners were the 'Bibliothecae Gorlicensis', which is today the Stadtbibliothek at Görlitz, eastern Germany, and Joseph Pratten of Bristol, who dated his inscription '1828'.

LATER PRINTED BOOKS AND THEIR OWNERSHIP

Books printed after 1501 also feature. The following fifteen examples offer an idea of past ownership and the traffic of books from Europe to England.

Shoults owned a copy of Pietro Colonno Galatino's *De arcanis Catholicae veritatis*, which contains a discussion involving Capnio (the Hebraist Johann Reuchlin), the Dominican Inquisitor Jacobus van Hoogstraten, and the author in defence of Reuchlin in the controversy over the confiscation of Jewish books. Published in Basel in 1550, it was once in the 'Bibliotheca Regia Monacensis', which is now the Bavarian State Library (Bayerische Staatsbibliothek) in Munich. In 1856, the book was in the possession of the Rev. Richard Wilson of Carlton Hill, Leeds, who may have been the Cambridge student Richard Bassett Wilson, who died in 1867.[5] If

---

[4] The Bibliotheca Ottenburana still contains a number of medieval manuscripts, 457 incunables, and some 15,000 folios. See Hubay (1970).
[5] Wilson, *AC* (1954), VI, 527.

they are one and the same, the book may well have been part of a general library sale that allowed Shoults to eventually acquire it sometime after that date.

Shoults also owned a copy of the second edition of Giovanni Battista Cipelli's *De exemplis illustrium virorum Venete ciuitatis*, published in Paris in 1554. This work by Egnazio, as Cipelli (1478–1553) was known, is a collection of episodes dealing with the lives of famous Venetians and other historical figures.[6] It has an inscription on the title page 'Ex biblioth. Ff. Minorum', but a later owner, a doctor in Lyon, has altered it to read: 'Ex biblioth: A. Moroud chirurgien de Lyon.'

Shoults owned a copy of Nonnus of Panopolis's *Metabole*, published in Paris in 1561, which is bound with a copy of St. Prosper's *Opera*, published in Cologne in 1565. This volume carries the inscription 'Bibliothecae Academicae Ingolstadii, 1582', which is now the University Library, Ingolstadt. Stamped as a duplicate, this book eventually found its way to England, ending up on the shelves of Henry Nelson Coleridge (1798–1843), nephew of the poet Samuel Taylor Coleridge.

Ruard Tapper (1487–1559) was a Dutch theologian of the Catholic Reformation and chancellor of Leuven University. Shoults owned a copy of his *Opera*, published in Cologne by Birckmann in 1582. With inscriptions on the title page reading 'Pro Bibliotheca Coll. S. Norberti' and 'Relinquatur Bibliotheca Collegii S. Norberti, 1667', the folio more than likely came from one of the colleges of St. Norbert of Xanten, probably Steinfeld, near Cologne.[7] In 1802, Steinfeld Abbey was abolished by Napoleon, and buildings and effects, which no doubt included the library, were sold. This book also has a round ink stamp of 'Biblioth. Prevckiana Borussica' on the title page, an institution as yet unidentified, but perhaps somewhere in former Prussia. (See pl.18.)

Sidonius Apollinaris (431–87) was a statesman, poet, and bishop, who has been called the 'last representative of classical Roman culture'.[8] Shoults owned a copy of his *Opera*, published in Paris by Hadrian Perier in 1598. This book was once in the library of the famed Italian family of Bonclerici.

The Jesuit Nikolaus Serarius (1555–1609) was a commentator on books of the Bible. Shoults owned a copy of his *In Sacros divinorum Bibliorum libros, Tobiam, Ivdith, Esther, Machabaeos commentarius*, published in 1599. Once on the shelves of the Franciscan library at Roermond, Limburg, an old Dutch monastery established about 1309, its dispersal was probably in the 1820s, when it was converted to a Protestant

---

[6] It is divided into nine books within which each of the numerous chapters is devoted to a topic (either virtue or vice). F.301v includes a note on Columbus.

[7] Norbert (1080–1134) was the founder of the Norbertine or Premonstratensian order of canons regular, and Archbishop of Magdeburg. See Staikos (2000), 465–6.

[8] Cited in Starr (2013), 45.

church. The book survived the looting and closures bought about by the Reformation, the religious wars, and the occupation by the French in 1796. In 1883 the monastery was demolished.

In 1619, the Antwerp-based Jean-Gaspard Gevaerts (1593–1666) had his own *Electorum libri III* published in Paris. Shoults owned a presentation copy, given to the library of the Holy Augustinian Fathers in Antwerp, which stayed on the shelves until 1797, when the monastery, church, and school were shut down. Its effects, which no doubt included the library, were sold at a public auction. Another presentation copy that Shoults owned is a copy of Gerrit Janszoon Vos's *Dissertatio gemina: una de Jesu Cristi genealogia*, published in Amsterdam by Blaeu in 1643. This work, for which the Dutch scholar Vossius (1577–1649), 'the greatest Polyhistor of his time', became famous, concerns the genealogy of Jesus Christ, his birth, baptism, and death.[9] It was given by Vossius to the library of la Congrégation de la doctrine Chrétienne in Milan, which was then under the patronage of Saint Charles Borromeo (1538–84).

Leo Allatius (c.1586–1669) was a Greek scholar, theologian, and librarian to Cardinal Francesco Barberini, and keeper of the Vatican Library. He was an advocate of the reconciliation of the Greek Church with that of Rome. Shoults owned a copy of his *Symmicta*, a compilation of works by earlier Latin and Greek writers published in Cologne in 1653. It was once in the University of Paris Library.[10]

In July 1773, Pope Clement XIV issued a decree that suppressed the Society of Jesus, a move following expulsions from Portugal, Spain, and France.[11] Retrenchment and re-consolidation saw the Society's eventual restoration by Pope Pius VII in August 1814. During the period of suppression, many College libraries were dissolved or incorporated into others. One book that found itself on a shelf in Camberwell is Antoine Bonnet's biography of Jean-François Régis (1597–1640), a priest whose tireless devotion to his ministry led to his beatification by Pope Clement XI in 1716 and canonisation by Pope Clement XII in 1737. The Society commissioned the work, and Bonnet (1634–1700), himself a Jesuit priest, completed it in 1692. Shoults's copy was a presentation to a Jesuit library, certainly in Toulouse, from the poet Jacques Vanière (1664–1739): 'Biblioth Scriptorum Collegii Colosani Societatis Jesu Catalogo Inscriptitus. Dono P. Jacobi Vaniere Soc Jesu.'

Another duplicate is from the University Library of Freiburg im Breisgau, a copy of Prince-abbot Celestino Sfondrati's three-volume edition of *Cursus philosophicus monasterij S. Galli*, published by Joseph Sam in the monastery print-shop at St. Gall,

---

[9] Sandys (1908), II, 307.
[10] *International Dictionary* (2001), 881.
[11] See Comerford (2015), 179–88.

Switzerland, in about 1695. Shoults also owned copies of Sfondrati's *Legatio Romam marchionis Lavardini* (1688) and a second edition of *Nodus praedestinationis ex sacris litteris* (1699).

Vossius Esprit Fléchier (1632–1710) was Bishop of Nîmes from 1687 to 1710. In 1711, a posthumous edition of *Lettres de Mr. Fléchier* was published in Paris. Shoults owned a copy which was once in the 'Bibliotheca Ecclesia' of Rothomagensis—that is the library of Rouen Cathedral. After the French Revolution of 1789, the building was nationalised and its effects sold to support the war effort. It may have been then that this book disappeared from the shelves, ending up on 15 June 1802 in the hands of one William George Burgess, who then presented it to a close friend, perhaps his wife: 'For ma chere Caroline WGB 15 Mar 1814.'

Shoults owned a copy of the first edition of *Corpus historicum medii aevi*, a medical resource compiled by the German historiographer Johann Georg von Eckhart (1674–1730), published in Leipzig in 1723. It contains a large book label that reads 'Ad Bibliothecam Principalem Aravsio-Nassaviensem Dillenburgicam', indicating it was once in the library of the princes of Nassau-Orange at Dillenburg, in the Lahn-Dill-Kreis region, Germany. There is also an inscription by 'Wm Grylls', who may be the William Grylls who died in 1863 and who bequeathed some 9000 books to Trinity College, Cambridge.[12] The residue of his library, which may have included this copy of *Corpus historicum medii aevi*, was sold at auction in London.

A second edition of Jacob Wilhelm Imhof's chief genealogical work, *Notitia sacri Romani Germanici imperii* was published in Tübingen in 1732. A copy of this book was acquired by the Oldenburg State Library, Germany, who stamped it: 'Ex Bibliotheca Oldenburgensi'. Somehow it ended up in England, and eventually on one of Shoults's bookshelves.

The polymath Burkhard Gotthelf Struve (1671–1738) wrote his *Introductio ad notitiam rei litterariae* in 1704. This seminal work on scholarship was revised by J. C. Fischer in 1754, and again by J.F. Julger, who not only made significant changes but also changed the title of this three-volume work to *Bibliotheca historiae litterariae selecta* (1754).[13] Shoults owned copies of volumes one and three of Jugler's edition, which were once in the Royal Library, Berlin; they carry the black stamp 'Ex Biblioth. Regia Berolinensi' and a red stamp: 'Vend Ex Bibl. Reg Berol.'

---

[12] In reference to Grylls, see Adams (1954), 50–4.
[13] See Taylor (1987), 180–2.

COLLEGE OF DOCTORS' COMMONS LIBRARY

One institution that features prominently in the Shoults Collection is the College of Doctors' Commons, which represented the College of Advocates of the Court of Arches, the Archbishop of Canterbury's Prerogative Court, the Court of Faculties and Dispensations, the Consistory Court of the Bishop of London, and the High Court of the Admiralty. This august association or college of ecclesiastical lawyers (with library) was founded about 1494.[14] Although dissolved through the Court of Probate Act in 1857, the buying of books for the library continued, finally stopping on 9 March 1860.[15] About one third of the books were bought by the Government; the rest were sold at auction by John Hodgson in London on 22 April 1861 and the seven following days.[16] Shoults acquired five items, each containing the book label: 'Ex Bibliotheca Hospitii Dominorum Advocatorum de Arcubus Londini.'

The first is a copy of *Practica* by Giovanni Pietro Ferrari. Originally appearing in manuscript in 1416, this large folio, with amendments and improvements, was published in Cologne in 1590. On the front pastedown is written 'E 147', its old shelf position in the Doctors' Commons Library, as is confirmed in the entry for the book in the *Catalogue of the Books in the Library of the College of Advocates in Doctors' Commons*, published in 1818.

The second is another legal work, the jurist Vincenzo Carocci's *Novi tractatus et practicabiles*, published in Cologne in 1594. This small octavo has the inscription on the title page 'Tho. Crashawe Esq' and the number '276' circled in pencil. Although a copy of Carocci's work is described in Hodgson's sale catalogue, it is listed as number '476', not '276', and is a Venetian printing dated 1604. The College obviously had a second copy for disposal.

The third is a copy of Benedictus Pererius's *Commentariorum et disputationum in Genesim tomi quatuor*, an exegetical work concerning the book of Genesis, published by Anthony Hierat in Cologne in 1622. The title page of this folio has been repaired and there is a pencil note on the front free endpaper: 'Valuable & beautiful copy.'

The fourth is a copy of Thomas Stanley's edition in Greek and Latin of Aeschylus's seven plays and fragments, published by Jacob Flesher in London in 1663. This battered folio, without its front cover, has an additional inscription of 'Caroli

---

[14] See Squibb (1977), 5–8.
[15] Squibb (1977), 96.
[16] Hodgson (1861). See also Squibb (1977), 90, and fn 8, 96, who states there is an annotated copy in the British Library (General Reference Collection S.C.2418), detailing prices only and not purchasers.

Bernard' on the title page, certainly the English surgeon Charles Bernard (1652–1710), a Fellow of the Royal Society.

These four volumes are recorded in the *Catalogue of the Books in the Library of the College of Advocates in Doctors' Commons*. Shoults owned an interleaved, annotated copy (see below) of this work.[17] The last title, which is not recorded in the *Catalogue of the Books in the Library*, is a two-volume vellum-bound copy of Giovanni Graziani's *Historiarum Venetarum libri XXXII*, published in Passau in 1728.

DR JOHN LEE

One who was an active member of Doctors' Commons was Dr John Lee, otherwise John Fiott (1783–1866). On 4 October 1815, Fiott changed his name by royal licence to Lee under the will of William Lee Antonie of Colworth House, Bedfordshire, his maternal uncle. He acquired the estates of Colworth, as well as Totteridge Park and other lands, and, in 1827, he inherited from the Rev. Sir George Lee the estate of Hartwell in Buckinghamshire. He was a polymath: philanthropist, astronomer, mathematician, antiquarian, and barrister, belonging to groups such as the Royal Astronomical Society, the Society of Antiquaries, the Royal Society, and the British Archaeological Association.[18] In 1816, Lee became a member of the College of Advocates and was at one time its treasurer and librarian. He strongly opposed the closing of Doctors' Commons, and, when the sale occurred, he bought a number of books. It was ten years after his death that the sale of his books occurred through Sotheby's, on 7 April 1876.

In all, Shoults acquired fourteen 'Lee' books, and it is more than likely that he acquired them from the same bookseller who supplied the five Doctors' Commons Library books. Lee's bookplate is an armorial one with the family motto etched below: 'Verum atque decens' (True and becoming). It also carries the engraver's name and an address: 'Mutlow sculp York'—that is, Henry Mutlow (1756–1826), who, at one time, operated in York Street, London. Nine of the fourteen books contain Lee's bookplate.

The first is Lee's interleaved copy of the *Catalogue*, which he has inscribed: 'J Lee, Doctor's Commons my private copy'. It contains numerous additions in his hand, including a manuscript bound at the back entitled 'List of Books deficient in the Catalogue of the Library Doctors Commons'. Shoults added his own name to this catalogue: 'Wm Ardene Shoults B. D.'

---

[17] Ferrari, 83, E 147; Carocci, 42, D 46; Benedictus Pererius, 164, B 192; and Aeschylus, 6, H 145. See College of Advocates (1818). Shoults Eb 1818 L.

[18] See McConnell (2014).

The second is a copy of Euclid's *Opera*, published in Paris in 1578. Along with Lee's bookplate there is his inscription, 'J. Lee, Colworth', and a note by him on annotations made on pages 109 and 131 by a previous owner. Of these annotations, Lee writes: 'A practice much to be avoided.'

The third is Pierio Valeriano Bolzani's *Hieroglyphica, seu de sacris Aegyptiorum aliarumque gentium literis commentarii*, published in Lyon by P. Frellon in 1626. This copy is a British Museum duplicate, and its title page and some preliminary leaves are wanting. Alongside Lee's bookplate is his note: 'J. Lee. Doctors' Common, repaired August 1832.' It is now a rather battered copy, with both covers detached.

The fourth is a copy of Edmund Chishull's *Travels in Turkey and back to England*, published in 1747. It too has a 'repaired' note, Lee's bookplate and his inscription: 'J. Lee, Doctors' Commons 1828.' Someone has pencilled on a preliminary leaf: 'A valuable work.'

The fifth is a copy of *Makhzan Ul Asrar, The Treasury of Secrets: Being the First of the Five Poems, or Khamsah, of Shaikh Nizami, of Ganjah*, published for the Society for the Publication of Oriental Texts in 1844. Lee had a personal interest in the Middle East, and, as revealed in chapter 13, so did Shoults. Edited by Nathaniel Bland, this work in Persian carries Lee's bookplate and the inscription: 'J. Lee, Hartwell. Received January 18th 1845 as a member of the Oriental Translation Committee.'

GUILFORD CACHE

The sixth is a copy of *Notices et Extraits des Manuscrits de la Bibliothèque Nationale et Autres Bibliothèques*, volume 9. Published in 1813, this work features printed Arabic texts edited by the Arabic and Persian scholar Antoine Isaac Silvestre de Sacy. This volume carries Lee's bookplate and his inscription dating its acquisition: 'J. Lee. Doctors' Commons 28 February 1829.' It was once owned by Fredrick North (1766–1827), fifth earl of Guilford, as confirmed by Lee in a note opposite the beginning of 'Table des Notices': 'No. 564/9. Lord Guilford's Library, 28 February 1829' and 'No. 562/9 besides pamphlets &c manuscripts.' Lee attended a few of the sales of Guilford's library, which was sold by auction by Evans in London between 1828 and 1835.[19] He obtained three, perhaps four, books which would later become Shoults's.

The seventh 'Lee' and second 'Guilford' book Shoults owned is a copy of Samuel Bochart's *Geographiae sacrae pars prior*, published at Caen by Pierre de Cardonnel in 1646. It not only contains Guilford's large bookplate with his motto: 'La Vertue est La Seule Noblesse' (Virtue is the only nobility), but also Lee's, with his additional

---

[19] The fifth earl of Guilford's library was sold by Evans in seven parts in the years 1828, 1829, 1830, and 1835. In total, there were forty days and 8511 lots; the total amount realised was £12,175.

note on when it was acquired: 'John Lee, Doctors' Common No. 435 Lord Guilford's Library 20 December 1830.'

The eighth 'Lee' and the third 'Guilford' book is a copy of *Selecta ex historia Halebi*, a history of Aleppo edited by G. W. Freytag and published in Paris in 1819. This Arabic and Latin primer contains Lee's bookplate and his inscription: 'J. Lee. Doctors' Commons. Bound Dec. 1838 No.5/114. A duplicate at Hartwell. Lord Guilford's copy.' A bookseller's note opposite Lee's inscription reads: 'A valuable and learned work.'

The ninth 'Lee' book is a copy of Thomas Baker's *Reflections Upon Learning, wherein is shewn the Insufficiency Thereof*, published in London in 1714. Once owned by John Griffies (his inscription on the title page), it was acquired by Lee in 1828, as evidenced by his inscription: 'J. Lee Doctors' Commons, 1828.' There is a large rectangular cut in the front pastedown, where a bookplate had been placed. The excision matches the size of Guilford's bookplate, suggesting that the book—the presumed fourth one—may have come from his collection.

SIR WILLIAM LEE

Shoults owned two volumes that were purportedly owned by Lord Justice Sir William Lee (1688–1754), ancestor of Dr John Lee, and two that were definitely owned by him.[20] All four book came from John Lee.

The tenth 'Lee' book and the first purportedly owned by Sir William, is a copy of John Collinson's *A Letter to Andrew C. Dick, Esquire, Scotch Advocate: on his Dissertation on Church Polity*, published by J. G. and F. Rivington in London in 1836. Extensively annotated by John Lee, it was a presentation copy, presumably from George Charles Rivington (1801–58), son of publisher Charles Rivington: 'For Dr Lee's use & acceptance. A more active & worthy minister than the author. Cannot easily be found. G. C. R.' Its title page carries a note: 'J. Lee. Doctors' Commons. Finished 21 February 1837.' Also present is an armorial bookplate of Sir William Lee with the family motto: 'Verum atque decens.' Collinson's work, however, was issued well after Sir William's death, indicating that he could not have owned this book. In fact, Sir William's bookplate also contains the engraver's details: 'Mutlow sculp. York'—that is, the same nineteenth-century engraver responsible for Dr John Lee's bookplate. This case of misrepresentation has already been noted. David Pearson has called the judge's bookplate a fake, or, putting it more charitably towards John Lee, 'a deliberate recreation'.[21] Pearson has offered a plausible reason why this recreation

---

[20] See Lemmings (2004).
[21] Pearson (2014), 103–23, especially 112–13, and pl. 9. None of Shoults's Lee books contain the bookplate of

occurred: Dr John Lee was 'someone sufficiently interested in marking the previous ownership of the book to have an imitation bookplate made. Family piety, a wish to demonstrate distinguished ancestry, an additional act of homage beyond the changing of his name, or [perhaps] something more purely antiquarian?'[22]

This 'doctoring' also occurs in the eleventh book: a copy of Pierre Peck's *Opera omnia*, published in Antwerp by Hieronymus and Ioan. Bapt. Verdussi in 1666. It has the recreated bookplate of William Lee Esq. of Hartwell and an inscription by John Lee at the front: 'Hartwell Library. repaired June 1837 No.10/108.'

The twelfth title is a copy of Virgil's *Opera*, published in Basel by Sebastian Henripetrus in 1586. Although this book has the recreated bookplate of William Lee, it also has two inscriptions that confirm Sir William's ownership: an indecipherable note on the title page with 'Oriel College, Oxon, 1734' and 'Ex Libris W. Lee, Oct 29 1744'. John Lee has added a further inscription: 'Colworth Library. Rebound 1826.'

Aside from the recreated William Lee bookplate, the judge actually had two other bookplates, both created at different stages of his life: 'William Lee Esq., of Hartwell, Bucks.' and 'Sir William Lee, Bart. Hartwell'. The thirteenth book is a copy of the twelfth edition of William Melmoth's *The Great Importance of a Religious Life Consider'd*, published in London in 1748. It contains the full array of Lee bookplates: the two armorial ones that belonged to the judge (thus proving definite ownership) and the recreated one. Dr John Lee has added a note: 'Hartwell Library. Repaired April 1841, Aylesbury. No.24/U.'

The last 'Lee' book is a two-volume edition of Cicero's *Opera*, published in Amsterzam in 1724. Lee was obviously pleased with the purchase. He noted in pencil: 'Excellent edition. T. F. Dibdin', and, while his bookplate is not present, there is an inscription that reveals a London address: 'J. Lee Esq., 4 Saville Row, London. Jan. 2nd 1860.'

The Shoults Collection contains a number of books that were once owned by prominent English and Continental collectors. Some of these individuals include Jean-Baptiste Colbert, Maffeo Pinelli, Antonio Baldigiani, the Duke of Sussex, and Richard Heber. One example from among the many is Shoults's copy of the first edition of Celio Calcagnini's *Opera aliquot*, a proto-Copernican treatise advocating the concept of movement of the Earth, published in Basel in 1544. After passing through the hands of Iippolito Bocci and Francesco Angolia (as evidenced from

---

Lee's uncle, William Lee Antonie, whom Lee inherited the estates from in 1815. Lee Antoine was grandson to Sir William Lee. Thanks to David Pearson for this information. Personal correspondence, December 2019

[22] Pearson (2014), 113.

inscriptions), it ended up in the Bibliotheca Pinelli, a library formed over many years by this Venetian family, especially Maffeo Pinelli (1736–85). After the death of Pinelli, the library was bought *en bloc* by the two London bookselling firms of Robson & Clarke and James Edwards.[23] A sale catalogue was published on 25 February 1789 with Calcagnini's *Opera* as lot 12586.[24] One person who attended the sale was Thomas Taylor (1758–1835), the scholar who was the first to translate into English the complete works of Aristotle and Plato.[25] He made a note in the copy in 1835, the year of his death. It reads: 'This very rare book was bought by me at the sale of the Pinelli Library between 40 & 50 years ago. The commentary *De Rebus Aegyptiacis* p. 229 is for the most part a translation of Plutarch's Treatise respecting Isis & Osiris. But this is not noticed by Fabricus in his Bibliotheca Graeca. T.T.' The sale of Taylor's 'singularly curious library' by Sotheby's in London on 2 and 3 February 1836 ultimately led, over time, to Shoults acquiring it.

The names of three book collectors feature strongly in the Shoults Collection: James Veitch, Lord Elliock; Samuel Parr; and William Henry Black. Although W. C. Hazlitt gives a one-line entry to Lord Elliock in his list in *Contributions towards a Dictionary of English Book-collectors*, there is no mention of Parr or Black.[26] The brief detail and the omission are important. These men were well-known in their own fields, yet they are not regarded as comparable with those wealthier book collectors such as those mentioned in chapter 5. Even though not widely recognised, they belonged to the majority who, as Hazlitt himself wrote, 'serve to establish the unbroken succession of interest in books of some kind or other on some principle or scale'.[27] Examining the books that Shoults obtained from the libraries of these men is useful on two levels. It not only reveals the type of books that these men collected, but also emphasises again the type that Shoults was interested in.

JAMES VEITCH, LORD ELLIOCK

James Veitch was born in Edinburgh, 25 September 1712, and, after training at Edinburgh, Leiden, and Halle universities, he began his legal career as an apprentice to his father, a writer to the Signet, a private society of Scottish solicitors and part of the College of Justice, Edinburgh. Veitch was called to the Scottish bar in 1738. After experiencing European travel, including life at the court of Frederick the Great, he returned to Scotland and entered on a long career as a parliamentarian and jurist. In

---

[23] For details of the Pinelli sale see Taylor (1987), 97–8, and McKitterick (2018), 218–22.
[24] *Bibliotheca Pinelliana* (1789), 519.
[25] See Louth (2004).
[26] Hazlitt (1968), XII, 12.
[27] Hazlitt (1968), XII, 2.

1761 he was elevated as Lord Elliock.[28] On this occasion, he had a bookplate designed that reads 'Lord Eliock' [sic] along with the family motto: 'Famam extendimus factis' (We extend our fame by our deeds). Elliock died in July 1793. The estate was entailed, and it eventually passed to his nephew, Colonel Henry Veitch, who died in 1838. The estate then passed to his son James, who died in 1873.

As 'one of the most accomplished scholars of his time', it was natural that Elliock had a library.[29] In James Brown's *The History of Sanquhar* (1891), there is an anecdote surrounding the fitting out of a room as a library:

> The workmen's conception of a library that would be suitable for Lord Elliock was that its greatness should correspond with the greatness of the man who was to occupy it, and so they constructed an enormous room with a gallery on all four sides, guarded with a plain railing, and reached by a spiral stone stair at the corner of the room. At Lord Elliock's next visit he was taken in to be shewn his new library. He no sooner entered, and saw this huge, cold, draughty room, with its over-hanging gallery, the whole destitute of the slightest attempt at architectural decoration, and conveying not the slightest suggestion of comfort, that he threw up his hands and exclaimed, in a scornful tone, "Good Heavens," and fled, never to enter it again.[30]

Shoults acquired nine books that were once in Elliock's library. All of them have the 'Lord Eliock' bookplate pasted in.

The first is a copy of a two-volume edition of the works of Apuleius (c.124–70), famed for his novel *Metamorphoses*. Published in Leiden in 1614, this work contains not only commentaries by Philip Beroaldi and Gottschalk Stewech, but also the well-known tale of *Cupid and Psyche*. If one were looking for light reading within Shoults's collection, these magical, often bawdy, tales fit the bill.

The second is a vellum-bound copy of the first edition of the Frisian historian and chronologist Ubbo Emmius's *Opus chronologicum novum*, a folio published in Gröningen in 1619. Elliock's bookplate is pasted over his inscription, which reads in part 'Leiden', where, in 1733, he presumably obtained this book.

The third is a copy of Johannes Meursius's *Danica pariter, & Belgica*, a history

---

[28] James Veitch, Lord Elliock (or Eliock), was not a member of the House of Lords. He was a Senator of the College of Justice, the equivalent in the Scottish Legal System of a High Court judge. These are called Lord and take titles but are not peers. After 1873, the estate was transferred to a younger brother, the Rev. William Douglas Veitch, who died at Elliock, Dumfries, in 1884. The seat was then transferred to William's son, the Rev. Henry George John Veitch. See Scott (2004) for spelling variation of Eliock/Elliock.

[29] Cited in Brunton (1832), 525–6; see also Scott (2004).

[30] Brown (1891), especially chapter V: 'The Elliock Family'.

of Denmark published by Willem Blaeu in Amsterdam in 1638. A striking engraving of Van Meurs (1579–1639) is contained in this work. Van Meurs was called a patchy historian, an 'ignoramus', by Joseph Justus Scaliger (1540–1609).[31] As will be seen in the next chapter, Shoults owned copies of a number of works by Scaliger and was no doubt aware of his rigorous approach to scholarship. He may not, however, have known of this antiquarian 'dust-up'.

The fourth is a copy of Marcus Minucius Felix's *Octavius*, an early Christian Latin dialogue between Caecilius (a pagan) and Octavius Januarius (a Christian). This vellum-bound octavo was published in Leiden in 1672. The price of one shilling and sixpence is written on the front pastedown, the amount that Elliock or Shoults could have paid for it.

The fifth is a copy of the geographical dictionary originally written by Vibius Sequester (c.4th or 5th century): *De fluminibus, fontibus, lacubus, nemoribus, paludibus, montibus, gentibus*.[32] This edition, published in Rotterdam in 1711, contains extracts from classical authors such as Virgil, Silius, Lucan, and Ovid. It was compiled by the Dutch jurist and philologist Franz Hessels (1680–1746).

The sixth is a copy of *Opusculorum variorum sylloge* by Johann Gottlieb Heineccius (1681–1741), a German jurist who adopted a rational approach to law. It was published in Halle (Saale) in 1735. James Veitch spent some time in Halle, and his acquisition of this legal work not only gives evidence of his staying abreast with contemporary legal issues, but also places him in the city at a particular time. On the upper right-hand corner of a preliminary leaf he has written 'Halle, 30 April 1735', with an indecipherable sum that he paid for this weighty book of over 1000 pages. It contains his 'Lord Eliock' bookplate, indicating that he pasted it into the book at least some twenty-six years after acquiring it.

The seventh is another large folio, a veritable doorstop running to well over 3000 pages. It is a vellum-bound copy of Basil Faber's *Thesaurus eruditionis scholasticae*, published in Leipzig in 1735. Faber (c.1520–75) was a German schoolmaster and theologian who advocated and strongly promoted the works of Martin Luther, and this Latin-German dictionary, first published in 1571, is his best-known work.

The eighth is a copy of Johann Joachim Becher's *Physica subterranea*, published in Leipzig in 1738. This alchemical treatise by Becher contains additional notes by his disciple Georg Ernst Stahl (1659–1734). There is a curious emblematic engraved frontispiece in the book, which may have attracted Shoults's attention. There is no

---

[31] 'Meursius', in *EB*, XVIII, 315.
[32] The lists are: 1. *Flumina* (rivers/waterways); 2. *Fontes* (springs); 3. *Lacus* (lakes); 4. *Nemora* (forests); 5. *Paludes* (marshes); 6. *Montes* (mountains); and 7. *Gentes* (peoples).

indication when he acquired this and the seven 'Lord Eliock' books so far considered. They may have been acquired individually over time, or perhaps purchased en bloc.

The date of the acquisition of the ninth and final 'Lord Eliock' book is definite. Shoults owned a copy of Anton van Dale's *Dissertatio super Aristea, de LXX interpretibus*, an epistolary composition written in Greek by an unknown Jew to one Philocrates, which contains the legend of how the Septuagint was created. Published in Amsterdam in 1705, this copy, as already noted, was a gift to Shoults from his wife. Although he inscribed the gift 'The Rev. W. A. Shoults B. D. from K, Nov. 7th 1874', it did not get his full attention, nor Elliock's. Only the first eight of the 250-plus leaves have been opened. The date of the gift, however, is of some importance, in that it points to the availability of some Elliock books on the open market in late 1874. Elliock's son James died in 1873, and with the transfer of the estate to a younger brother, the Rev. William Douglas Veitch, there was some books disposed of from the library. This allowed Eliza to secure this title for her husband.

SAMUEL PARR

Samuel Parr (1747–1825) was an English schoolmaster and Anglican minister who counted as his friends the orientalist William Jones, the radical minister Joseph Priestley, and the poet Walter Savage Landor, who owned the Llanthony estate that figures so strongly with Father Ignatius and Shoults. Parr modelled himself on Samuel Johnson, although 'The Whig Johnson', as he was termed, did not match the Great Cham's wit and authority. Parr was employed as a curate at Hatton parsonage, near Warwick, and amassed a library there of some 10,000 books.[33] In 1827, John Bohn compiled *Bibliotheca Parriana* (1827), a catalogue of Parr's collection, which was described as 'though chiefly consisting of useful books, nevertheless contains many articles of the greatest curiosity'.[34] Bohn tried to sell the collection en bloc, but the attempt was unsuccessful. As a result, the library was sold at auction by Evans, beginning in May 1828.[35] Parr's ownership is marked with a printed label, found in most of his books. Shoults obtained ten 'Parr' books.

The first book is a copy of Latino Latini's *Epistolae*, published in Rome in 1659. It contains Parr's signature on the title page, but lacks the book label because the front cover is also missing. This book is listed in Bohn's catalogue and was one of

---

[33] See Cowie (2004b); *Bibliotheca Parriana* (1827); Evans (1828); and Sparrow (1956), 63–72.
[34] *Bibliotheca Parriana* (1827), preface, v.
[35] The sale of Parr's library occurred on 16 May 1828 (and six following days) and 31 October 1828 (and six following days), a total of 3561 lots. For details see Sparrow (1956), 71.

3561 volumes sold at the two sales in 1828.³⁶ *Epistolae* was purchased by Edmund Henry Barker (1788–1839), who was not only a good friend of Samuel Parr's, but also produced his own *Parriana*, a hotch-potch of biographical and critical matter on and by Parr, in 1828–29.³⁷ As mentioned in chapter 5, Barker gave this book to John Mitford on 21 February 1835. The provenance of this book by Latini is thus: Parr-Barker-Mitford-Shoults.

The second is a folio edition of Themistius's *Orationes XXXIII*, published in Paris in 1684. This particular Latin and Greek text by the pagan philosopher (317–90) contains editorial work by the French chronologist Denis Pétau (1583–1652).

The third is a vellum-bound copy of *Curae posteriores de barbarismis et idiotismis sermonis Latini* by the German philologist Christoph Cellarius (1638–1707), famed for his work on chronology (among other things) and credited with coining the term 'Middle Ages'. The contents of this book, which was published in Jena in 1700, detail his observations on the Latin language, particularly on prevalent spoken distortions and barbarisms. Shoults also owned a copy of his *Smalcaldensis geographia antiqua recognita denuo*, a book on geography designed as an aid to the study of the Old and New Testaments, published in London in 1745.

The fourth is a copy of Nikolaos Maurokordatos's *Peri Kathēkontōn biblos syngrapheisa para tou Eusebestatou*, a work about conduct in life. Published by Samuel Palmer in London in 1724, the Greek text was edited by Gysbertus Dommer and the Latin supplied by Stephen Bergler.

The fifth is a copy of Johann Benedict Carpzov's *Observationum philologicarum in palaephatum*, a work on the philology of Greek myths, published in Leipzig in 1743. Carpzov (2720–1803) belonged to the famed Carpzov family that boasted jurists, statesmen, and theologians; he was Professor of Philosophy at the University of Leipzig and Professor of Poetry and Greek at the University of Helmstedt. This calf-bound copy contains both Parr's signature and his book label.

The sixth is another Leipzig imprint: a copy of Marcus Junianus Justinus's *Historiae Phillipicae*, published in 1757. An important source book for historians of the Hellenistic age, this edition was edited by the scholar Johann Georg Graevius.³⁸ Like the Carpzov title above, it contains Parr's signature and book label.

---

36   The Latini entry is in *Bibliotheca Parriana* (1827), 310.
37   See Sparrow (1956), 63–72 (71).
38   The Hellenistic Period (or Age) is usually described as from the death of Alexander the Great in 323 BC to the conquest of the last Hellenistic kingdom by Rome at the Battle of Actium in 31 BC.

The seventh is a copy of Johannes Leusden's *De dialectis N.T. singulatim de eius Hebraismis libellus singularis*, published in Leipzig in 1792.[39] Leusden (1624–99) was a renowned Biblical scholar who produced *Biblia Hebraica*, the first edition of the Hebrew Bible with numbered verses. Shoults also owned copies of other books by him: *Clavis Hebraica Veteris Testamenti* (1683), the Hebrew Old Testament with criticism and interpretations, and *Torah, Nevi'im u-Khetuvim*, published in 1831 and based on an edition by Everardus van der Hooght, the eminent Dutch scholar.

The eighth is a copy of a selection of lyrical poems by the Greek poet Archilochus (680–645 BC) entitled *Archilochi iambographorum principis reliquiae*, published in Leipzig in 1812. It is not often that Shoults had duplicate copies of a book. Beside his Parr copy sits a second, once owned by Philip Smith, whose armorial bookplate is on the front pastedown.

The ninth volume contains a number of works by Gottfried Hermann (1772–1848), the German classicist and philologist. Hermann was a rigorous scholar who maintained that Greek and Latin were essential for understanding the intellectual life of ancient times. Shoults obtained two of his scholarly dissertations—*De poeseos generibus* (1794) and *Solemnia magistrorum creandorum inaugurandorumque* (1814)—in a sammelband of eleven titles. Parr thought sufficiently well of this volume to inscribe in it: 'A most precious book SP.' Shoults also thought highly of this German scholar, as his collection contains other Hermann and Hermann-related publications: *De emendanda ratione Graecae grammaticae* (1801), *Elementa doctrinae metricae* (1817), *Euripidou Medeia* (1822), *Pindari carmina* (1824), *Sophoclis Philoctetes ad optimorum librorum fidem* (1825), and *Draconis Stratonicensis Liber de metris poeticis* (1812), which, when Hermann worked on it, was ascribed to Dracon but later shown to be a sixteenth-century forgery.[40]

The tenth and final book from Parr's library is a volume containing two further scholarly dissertations. The first is Frideric August Menke's *Observationes criticae in Statii Achilleida et alios passim scriptores*, published in Göttingen in 1814, and August Boeckh's *Commentaries* on the metres of Pindar, published in Leipzig in 1821.

In addition to the ten books from Parr's library, Shoults owned a copy of the Rev. William Field's two-volume biography of Parr, published in 1828. A previous owner has not only made numerous remarks on the solidity and soundness of the biography by this dissenting minister (Field), but also has pencilled in the date of '29 March 1869'.[41] Shoults thought enough of this controversialist to secure the set for his

---

[39] See *Bibliotheca Parriana* (1827), 67.
[40] 'Dracon of Stratonicea', in *OCD* (1970), 364.
[41] Field (1828). Shoults Eb 1828 F.

library sometime after this date. It was either a catalyst for him to search for the other 'Parr' books, or a natural complement to those that he already held.

WILLIAM HENRY BLACK

The final book collector represented in the Shoults Collection is the antiquary and Seventh-Day Baptist leader William Henry Black (1808–72), who compiled a number of catalogues, such as those of the Arundel manuscripts at the College of Arms (1829) and of Colfe's Library at Lewisham (1831). While working in Oxford between 1831 and 1833, he compiled the catalogue of Elias Ashmole's manuscripts, published in 1845.[42] At one point, he was assistant keeper of the newly-established Public Record Office. Black was elected a Fellow of the Society of Antiquaries of London in 1858, and he belonged to various archaeological or antiquarian groups, such as the British Archaeological Association, and the Surrey, London, and Wiltshire Archaeological societies. His library was sold in London by Sotheby's, Wilkinson and Hodge in July–August 1873.[43] Shoults owned seven books once in Black's library.

The first book is a copy of a sextodecimo edition of *Politicorum sive civilis doctrinae libri sex* by the Flemish humanist scholar Justus Lipsius (1547–1606), published by the Plantin Press in Antwerp, 1605. A reprint of one of Lipsius's most important works, it covers civil doctrine and Christian principles and precepts for good government.[44] Black acquired his copy in 1823, and yet it was seven years later that he made comments on the work. Four leaves of manuscript notes by him are tipped in and dated '14 January 1830'.

The second is a copy of *Marmora Arundelliana*, a catalogue compiled by the polymath John Selden (1584–1654), published in London in 1628. The Greek marbles (known as the Arundel or Oxford Marbles) were in the collection of Thomas Howard, 21st Earl of Arundel, and then given to the Ashmolean Museum, Oxford, in 1667 by Arundel's grandson, Henry Howard, 6th Duke of Norfolk. This slim quarto, containing 29 Greek and 10 Latin inscriptions deciphered and illustrated, was once in the Colbert Library, a collection amassed principally by Jean-Baptiste Colbert (1619–83), Finance Minister to Louis XIV. The library was sold by his descendants in 1728.[45] Black obtained this copy in 1824. While Shoults gives no hint at liking association copies, he surely appreciated its strong pedigree: Colbert-Black.

---

[42] See Nurse (2004).
[43] See Sotheby, Wilkinson (1873).
[44] When *Politicorum* was first published in 1589, it was placed on the *Index*. After some adjustments to the text concerning non-Catholics and Machiavelli, the revised edition was allowed to stand. See Shuger (2006).
[45] *Bibliotheca Colbertina* (1728), 3, 1210, joint lot no. 16056, and listed as sold for 1s 6d. See also Taylor (1987), 108.

The third is a copy of *Chronologica sacra* by Archbishop James Ussher (1581–1656), famed for establishing the time and date of Creation, that is, 22 October 4004 BC, in his last works, *Annales veteris testamenti* (1650) and its continuation, *Annalium pars posterior* (1654).[46] Published in London in 1660, Shoults's copy is bound with a copy of *De Romanæ Ecclesiæ symbolo apostolico vetere* (1660), which contains Latin and Greek texts of the Apostles' Creed. And although not a 'Black' book, Shoults also owned a copy of Ussher's *De Graeca Septuaginta, interpretum versione*, the first serious examination of the Septuagint, discussing its accuracy as compared with the Hebrew text of the Old Testament.[47]

The fourth is a copy of *Liber de nummis*, a work on ancient numismatics published in London in 1675. First published in 1579 as the work of Alessandro Sardi, it has, in this reprint, been mistakenly attributed to John Selden. Black has inscribed the date of acquisition on the front pastedown: '13/3/1862.'

The fifth is the only one published in English that Shoults acquired with a Black provenance. It is a copy of John Marlow's epistolary *Letters to a Sick Friend*, published in London in 1682. Previous owners include 'H. Scott, clerk' and 'J. Conder', who may have been the Congregationalist hymn writer, author, and anti-slavery activist Josiah Conder (1789–1855). A passionate and rudimentary bibliographical note written on the front free endpaper reads: 'Some copies have but 160 pages. Some 202, & 250. This has 263 pages only one I have met with; which I would not be without for 5d.' Black himself commented on this work: 'Picked up this quaint but sensibly written book in Oxford Jan 13th 57 WHB.' Marlow's most unusual medically-orientated work captured Black's attention; it also attracted Shoults's.

The sixth is a copy of the three-volume first edition of Giovanni Poleni's *Exercitationes Vitruvianae primae*, published in Padua between 1739 and 1741. Volume three also includes the second printing of mathematician Bernardino Baldi's *Scamilli impares Vitruviani* (1739). Poleni (1683–1761) was an expert in hydraulics and architecture and this work contains his bibliographical notes on Vitruvio's 'Ten Books'. This large, impressively-printed folio is inscribed by Black '2/10/68'.

The final book is a copy of Fulvio Orsini's *Virgilius collatione scriptorum Graecorum illustratus*, published in Leeuwarden, Netherlands, in 1747. This work by Orsini (1529–1600), a librarian and classicist, is a reprint of his comparative study on Virgil and other Greek writers. Black acquired this book on 4 February 1862.

---

[46] Thomas Barlow, an Oxford scholar, has also been credited with establishing the time and date of Creation, four years after the death of Ussher. See McCarthy (1997), 73–82 (77).

[47] See Ford (2004).

The very brief examination of the above books confirms Shoults's taste and interests. There is the serious nature to them that points to his specific intellectual needs. If anything can be said about his intellectual predilections, it is that he preferred an older, richer past represented by scholars such as Scaliger, Latini, Cellarius, and Selden and of course what they produced.

There is no surviving evidence on what Shoults felt about the provenance association of his books. Although he was seemingly content-driven, it must have pleased him that a particular book in his library was associated with individuals such as the Duke of Sussex or W.H. Black.

The traffic of books through sales, auctions, and booksellers is a fascinating aspect of book history. In this case, it is made more interesting by the fact that these books, almost all European in origin, have ended up in Dunedin, New Zealand, thousands of miles from their place of production and from their former homes. These books, once dispersed from monastic libraries or owned by Sussex, Harley, or Elliock, now add to the larger store of resources that make up New Zealand's own book history. It is rich indeed.

17 LISTS AND JOTTINGS: EVIDENCE OF USE

A large number of books in Shoults's collection show no signs of use, let alone of having been read. This sentence suggests that Shoults did not read his books, but merely amassed them. Such a suggestion does him an injustice. He was a reader, but he left little evidence of his reading. However, while most of his books show no evidence of use, there are some that do. This chapter focuses on the notes and annotations that he left in these books, some of them brief, others quite lengthy. There is nothing creative about them. In fact, they confirm his scholarly, often esoteric, interests. Understandably, some of them are perfunctory aides or prompts that on occasion reflect his thoughts about the Church, philosophical matters, or a particular author's works. They smack of the useful and practical.

These tangible traces are important on two levels. They reflect use, and they give some idea of the themes or subjects that Shoults was obviously concerned with, certainly enough for him to tabulate or record them in his books. There is a caveat about them: the notes reveal *only something* of Shoults—they do not in any way determine the whole man.

In 1859, when Shoults was 20, he made reference to Caelius Rhodiginus's *Lectionum antiquarum libri triginta* (1599) in his three-plus page article 'On Cupid's Blindness', published in the *Eagle*, St. John's College newly-established journal.[1] While there are no written notes in his copy, his bookmark with a small inky scrawl is still there, marking the page and text that he made reference to in the article. As already mentioned in chapter 4, the article is impressively erudite for a 20-year-old, and it establishes from a very early stage a serious scholarship. His later contributions on Latin hymns in John Julian's *Dictionary of Hymnology* represent a further predilection for detail and accuracy (see chapter 10).

Shoults owned a copy of *Sermones prope omnes continens*, the second volume of *Eclogae Horatianae*, published in London in 1843. This volume, which contains the satires of Horace, was edited by Thomas Kerchever Arnold. There are notes in pencil and ink in four parts: Satira IV, Satira V, Satira VI, and Epistola XVII. The pencil notes are not Shoults's; the ink ones are written in his familiar spiky script. He has underlined Latin words and added English translations, glosses that are examples of the learning process of a young student—that is, Shoults—coming to terms with additional vocabulary and grammar. Selected samples in Satira IV, a dialogue

---

[1] 'On Cupid's Blindness', *Eagle*, 3 (November 1858), 168–71.

between Horace and Catius, are (as written, with definitions in parentheses): Caule (Cabbage), Mitulus (Muscle), Curvat (flabby), and muriaque (pickle). Some examples in Satira V are: Persta (persevere), Adrepe (steal gently), limis (side glances), and Captatorque dabit risus (become the dupe). Some in Satira VI are: Interiore diem gyro (narrow circle), De re communi (their common interest), nugas (trifles), lardo (bacon), usus rectumne (expediency or uprightness), Frusta (raisin) with 'nibbled scraps' at the end of the line (l.86), and canistris (baskets). At the foot of the page Shoults has written: 'Ventum est Esquilias, aliena negotia centum (A formula wh. is hurtful to myself).' In Epistola XVII, an address to Scaeva, he not only underlined numerous words such as the above samples, but also provides a translation: 'Since mine is the better way & far more honorable' to 'rectius hoc et splendidius multo est' at lines 19 and 20. Finally, in reference to 'dante minor' on line 22, he has written: 'A dependent on the giver.'[2] These notes are but small beer, but they do give evidence of the use of a textbook by Shoults.

Shoults seemed to like lists and completeness. He owned a defective copy of Vossius's *Etymologicon linguae latinae*, published by Elzevir in 1662. In the back of this folio, there is a folded leaf of blue paper tipped in. On each of the sides of the leaf there is a long list of phrases written by Shoults that run alphabetically from S to Z. This sequence makes good the final leaves of the printed 'Index Vocabulorum Extra Seriem', which ends at 'seu, in Si'. He has written out the first line of many hundreds of phrases, starting with 'Severus mons, in teter' and ending at 'Zygia'. To some, the writing out of a missing index such as this would be a tedious task, but Shoults obviously felt strongly enough to complete the sequence. He would have had to have had access to a second copy to finish the task.

Another practical listing is found in his copy of Cellarius's *Smalcaldensis geographia antiqua recognita denuo* (1745). He constructed another index of the twenty-five 'antiqua' maps in the book: 'Hispania Antiqua p.17', 'Gallia antiqua transalpin p.18', 'Insulae Britannicae p.22', and so on through to 'Africa interior p.121.' While there is an elaborate and detailed printed index of towns and places in the book, it was obviously not enough for him.

Further simple tabulations occur in Shoults's copy of *Correspondence of the Late Gilbert Wakefield, B.A., with the Late Right Honourable Charles James Fox*, published in London in 1813. Gilbert Wakefield (1756–1801) was an English biblical scholar who at one stage earned his living as a classical tutor in dissenting schools

---

[2] 'My conduct is better and nobler by far. I do service that I may have a horse to ride and be fed by a prince: you sue for paltry doles; but you become inferior to the giver, though you pose as needing no man.' English translation, giving context to Shoult's notes. Horace (1942), l. 2-6, 363 to the original, l.19-22, 362.

such as Warrington and Hackney Academies. He was a controversial writer, deemed by Henry Crabb Robinson to be a political fanatic.[3] Shoults created an index on a leaf at the back of the book, writing out the names of various classical writers: Anacreon, Apollonius, Aratus, Aristophanes, Euripides, Nicander, Nonnus, and Ovid. To his note on Virgil, he adds a little more than the page number: 'Virgil 97, 190, 197 "his most beautiful passage" 192, 210.' This addition is a paraphrase of Fox's own celebratory note of Virgil's *Aeneid*, particularly Book 8 with its passages on the Rites of Hercules, the story of Cacus, the shield made for Aeneas by Vulcan, the description of King Evander's town, and the infancy of Rome.[4]

In the 1860s, Shoults acquired a volume of eleven tracts that once belonged to John Mitford, whom we have met in chapter 5. While on the surface most of the tracts appear to fall outside Shoults's collecting interests, one is a copy of the second edition of William Vincent's *Considerations on Parochial Music* (1790), which, because of Shoults's interest in hymns, may have been the reason why the volume was acquired. However, two of the other tracts did capture his attention: Benjamin Buckler's *A Complete Vindication of the Mallard* (1793) and J. Friend's [sic] *Epistle to Dr Mead* (1719). To Mitford's own tabulation, Shoults added a manicule with the note below it: 'The Vindication of the Mallard of All Souls was written by Dr Buckler of All Souls. The complete history of the Mallardians was by Mr Rowe Mores and Mr Bilson. See Chalmers Oxford 1 189.'[5] And to the physician John Freind's epistle to his friend and rival Dr Mead, Shoults added a small note: 'Lucerne by St. Andre? See Nicholls Hogarth, p.480.' This note is a reference to appendix 1 of the third edition of John Nichols's *Biographical Anecdotes of William Hogarth* (1785), which mentions Dr Mead, Nathaniel St. André, rabbits, and Mary Tofts.[6] It is too hard to discern why Shoults made this reference, but one fortunate outcome is that it proves that he was aware of the then authoritative biographical work by Alexander Chalmers, and Nichols's editions of and comments on Hogarth's work.

---

[3] Cited in Robinson (1869), I, 56; see also Graver (2004).

[4] See C. J. Fox to Wakefield, 13 April 1801, in Wakefield (1813), 192–8 (197).

[5] In his *Oxoniensis Academia, or the Antiquities and Curiosities of the University of Oxford* (1749), John Pointer downgraded the famous mallard of All Souls to a goose. Benjamin Buckler responded with *A Complete Vindication of the Mallard*, first published in 1750. Bilson and Rowe Mores continued the fracas with their *History of the Mallardians*, of which Shoults mentions. See Chalmers (1815a) on 'Buckler', who makes the claim that Pointer's was 'a superficial and incorrect work'.

[6] St. André was Nathaniel St. André (c.1680–1776), a Swiss physician who, in 1726, examined Mary Toft or Tofts (c.1701–63), an English woman who tricked doctors into believing that she had given birth to rabbits. St André was convinced, publishing his own *A Short Narrative of an Extraordinary Delivery of Rabbets* in December 1726.

Readers often use any scrap of paper to make jottings on what they are reading, or leave small 'notes to self' as reminders. Shoults was no exception. In his copy of Frontinus's *Strategematon*, published in Leiden in 1779, is a remnant of a letter addressed to one Thomas Sheppard, Southville, Wandsworth, franked December 1860. The loosely-inserted sheet has 16 lines of text, a mix of Greek, Latin, and English words and phrases in Shoults's hand. Surrounding the post-mark and the seal are examples such as: 'Chronical/Chronic', bracketed with the following: 'a cronical distemper is of length—opposed to acute'; 'Chronogram', followed by 'an inscription including the date of any action as VIXI I have had 2 [?]'; and 'Lizan', followed by 'lay to rest horizontally'. As the sheet is loosely inserted, it may well have belonged and related to a work in his library, and not this treatise on military strategy, which seems a most unlikely read for Shoults. Perhaps it just became a simple bookmark.

Shoults had a strong interest in language and philology. One book he owned was a copy of *Dictionarium Armeno-Latinum*, an important first work on the Armenian language by Francesco Rivola, published in Paris in 1633. Shoults's copy is defective, having the title-leaf of Petro Paulo's *Doctrina Christiana* (1634) and its preface and imprimaturs bound in. Someone, and certainly not Shoults, has put a line through the printed title of *Doctrina Christiana* and added at top of the title page written: 'Dictionarium Armeno Latinum.' Loosely inserted is an invoice dated January 1860 from the Rev. Oswald Cockayne (1807–73), a philologist, to one Ashcroft. The invoice was useful to Shoults because he created two columns on it. The left-hand side contains the Armenian alphabet. On the right-hand side, opposite each letter, he has written the corresponding Roman letters and hints on pronunciation—for example, the third letter down, a distorted capital E that equates to 'CH "soft as child"' and an upside down 'm' with a descender equating to 'P gentle'. This basic alphabet listing represents a first start for Shoults at coming to terms with the Armenian language. The rest of the book is clean, and there is no further evidence that he persisted with his Armenian studies.

As mentioned in chapter 12, Shoults owned a copy of three pseudo-Augustinian texts, *Meditationes-Soliloquia-Manuale* (1631), which are bound with St. Anselm's *De humani generis redemptione* and a pseudo-St. Bernard text, *Meditations*.[7] The pseudo-Augustine text runs to page 257, the Anselm text from page 258 to 294, and the pseudo-Bernard from page 295 to 410. Shoults was interested in the works of all

---

[7] Bernard's *Meditations* was probably written at some point in the thirteenth century. It circulated extensively in the Middle Ages under Bernard's name and was one of the most popular religious works of the later Middle Ages. Its theme is self-knowledge as the beginning of wisdom; it begins with the phrase 'Many know much, but do not know themselves.'

three, making extensive ink notes in each. He noted 15 references to both Augustine and Bernard, and six to Anselm. His references to the pseudo-Augustine text are in Section 4, specifically chapter 19, 'The souls of the righteous are the house of God'; chapter 24, 'A prayer for succour in trouble and danger'; chapter 28, 'Most great, most gracious, most mighty, most just'; and chapter 40, 'Devout reflections upon the sufferings of Christ'. As to the Anselm text, he noted four page references (268, 269, 270, 271) to chapter 6, 'De beneficiis homini a Christo exhibitis', and two (286, 287) to chapter 7, 'Redemptoris innocentis, & perditi nocentis, inter se comparatio; ac hujus renovatio'. Finally, there is the pseudo-Bernard text, with 15 page references written by Shoults: 320, 321, 322 (chapter 7, mortis consideratio); 323, 324 (chapter 8, Qualiter homo debeat intente orare); 325, 330, 331, 376, 377 (chapter 32, Contra amorem mundi); 406, 407, (chapter 34, Contra amorem perversum mulierum); and 408, 409, and 410. Underneath the references to these works, someone has written an undated note: 'the Rev. W. A. Shoults's writing.'

Shoults owned a large-paper copy of John Caius's *De canibus Britannicis*, published in London in 1729. There is a note by Shoults on the front free endpaper that reads: 'The small paper in 12mo is marked '7/6' in Bohn's Catalogue. The large paper is extremely rare.' This bibliographical note reveals at least some knowledge of formats and the pleasing fact that Shoults consulted some of the famed bookseller's catalogues.

As mentioned in chapter 12, Shoults owned two copies of the second edition of Origen's *Contra Celsum*, published in Cambridge in 1677. *Contra Celsum*, Origen's last work, was significant in that it was an orthodox defence of Christianity against the pagan philosopher Celsus, who was, during the second century, Christianity's foremost opponent. Origen was orthodoxy personified, and his notion of Christ as human and divine and the perfect unity of God the Father seemed to resonate with Shoults. He was certainly familiar with Origen's works, knowing that the text of *Contra Celsum* was repeated in Origen's *Philokalia*, an anthology of chapters that had been assembled by Basil the Great and Gregory Nazianzus, which he also owned. In what is a small sample of comparative textual work for his own private use, Shoults compared the two texts and identified the passages that occur in both, making extensive notes in Greek and Latin. Too many to cite, the following three are examples, as written: 'Lib.1 p. 5 l. 37 to line 47 in Chapter 15 Philokalia'; 'p. 32 lin 3, ad lin 40 ibid. in Cap 15'; and 'E Lib 7, p. 370 l. 37 ad p. 373 l.14 ibid [Chapter 15, Philokalia]'.

William Beveridge (1637–1708) was interested in Middle Eastern and Asian languages and the history of the early Church. He was also an advocate of Anglican voluntary religious societies. As recorded, Beveridge was styled in his day 'the great reviver and restorer of primitive piety'. There was also a marked seriousness to this future bishop of St. Asaph: it was said that he was 'very rarely if ever' to be seen in 'places of diversion', but normally spent his leisure hours 'either at a bookseller's shop, in useful conversation, or in his chamber at his study'.[8]

Shoults owned a copy of the first edition of Beveridge's *Codex canonum ecclesiae primitivae vindicatus ac illustratus*. Published in London in 1678, this work was a response to Matthieu de Larroque's *Observationes*, an attack on the canons published in Rouen in 1674. In his copy, Shoults made some simple textual notes, comparing Beveridge's text with a copy of *Collectiones canonum Dionysianae*, a collection of ancient ecclesiastical canons translated from Greek into Latin by the monk Dionysius 'the humble' (470–c.544). Sourcing a copy of Dionysius's *Collectiones*, which he did not own, he went through each chapter and compared the two. In most cases the matches are exact; in other instances, there are small discrepancies, which he noted down—for example, chapter 6 in Dionysius equated with chapter 5 in Beveridge; chapter 33 in Dionysius to chapter 32 in Beveridge; and chapter 39 in Dionysius to chapter 38 in Beveridge. To some the result of this activity may seem small and inconsequential, yet to Shoults the details surrounding canons and decretals were obviously important. This exercise certainly reveals a deep familiarity with the content of both books.

Shoults may have warmed to the serious-minded Beveridge. He certainly had a high regard for his writings, owning four titles, all published in London: his treatise on chronology, *Institutionum chronologicarum libri II* (1705), third edition copies of his sermons *The True Nature of the Christian Church* (1716) and *The Being, Love and Other Attributes of God, as Our Creator* (1716), and a two-volume copy of *Ecclesia Anglicana Ecclesia Catholica; Or the Doctrine of the Church of England, Consonant to Scripture, Reason, and Fathers, in a Discourse upon the Thirty-nine Articles, agreed upon in the Convocation held at London MDLXII* (1840). He also owned a copy of Vincent of Lérins's *Against Heresy*, published in London in 1841, that contains the preface from Beveridge's *Codex canonum ecclesiae primitivae* (1678) in the introduction.

In 1691, Peter King, first Baron King (c.1669–1734), published his *An Enquiry into the Constitution, Discipline, Unity & Worship of the Primitive Church*, an anonymous treatise arising out of the Toleration Act (1689) that granted freedom of worship to Protestant nonconformists (after pledging oaths of Allegiance and Supremacy), but not to Roman Catholics. King, a fiercely independent politician, completed a second part, which was not published until 1713. William Sclater, Schlater, or Slater (1638–c.1717) compiled a rejoinder, a refutation of King's thesis that the primitive church was organised upon congregational principles: *An Original*

---

8 Said by a contemporary, Isaac Milles, and cited in Cowie (2004a).

Draught of the Primitive Church in Answer to a Discourse Entituled, An Enquiry into the Constitution, Discipline, Unity, and Worship, of the Primitive Church, published in London in 1717. Shoults owned a copy of this publication, and at the front he wrote a note on the Rev. Sclater, which reads (in part):

> The author of this Book was the Revd W. Sclater. He was not the only Answer of Ld King's Primitive Church but probably the most successful one as he made of convincing of Ld King than Mr King himself. Ld King better known as Sir Peter King appears to have been a remarkably candid man who wrote proper history but to arrive at the truth & he solicited answers & conclusions of his opinions as expressed in his work & received this in return. But while he was so pleased that he became a friend of his opponent thro' lip service [?] when he arrived at the office of Chancellor of England & had an opportunity of giving him consent [?] he availed himself of the opportunity.

Shoults did not own any of King's works, and yet in order to pass judgement, he must have been familiar with his life and works.

Another publication that Shoults did not own was Samuel Taylor Coleridge's *Table-Talk*, first published in 1836. At one point, he accessed a copy and transcribed a small quote from it into his copy of the Rev. William Orme's *Memoir of the Controversy Respecting the Three Heavenly Witnesses, I John V. 7: Including Critical Notices of the Principal Writers on Both Sides of the Discussion*, published in London in 1830. The quote on the front pastedown reads:

> I think the verse of the three witnesses (1 John, V.7) spurious, not only because the balance of external authority is against it, as Porson seems to have shown; but also, because in my way of looking at it, it spoils the reasoning. Coleridge, Table Talk. 1. 20.

Orme (1787–1830) was a Scottish Congregational minister who used I John 5: 7, 'For there are three that bear record in heaven, the Father, the Word, and the Holy Ghost: and these three are one', as the basis for his work. 'Porson' was Richard Porson (1759–1808), an English classical scholar who wrote *Letters to Archdeacon Travis* (1790), which deals with the debate of the biblical verse 1 John 5: 7 (*Comma Johanneum*). Shoults owned fourteen Porson titles, including *Tracts and Miscellaneous Criticisms of the late Richard Porson* (1815), and *A Vindication of the Literary Character of the late Professor Porson, from the Animadversions of the Right Reverend Thomas Burgess, in various publications on 1 John v. 7* (1827).

Shoults owned a vellum-bound copy of Julius Caesar Scaliger's *Exotericarum exercitationum*, published in Hanover in 1620. From another book that he did not own, John Evelyn's *Diary*, which first appeared in 1818, he wrote inside Scaliger's work: 'At Leyden the Churches are very fair; in one lies buried that prodigy of learning Joseph Scaliger, without any extraordinary inscription, as having himself left so many monuments of his worth behind him, more lasting than marble, besides giving his library to the university.' Evelyn's Diary. 1 p. 33. 8vo.'[9] Although not strictly evincing use, this note does represent a high regard that Shoults had for the Scaligers: Julius Caesar Scaliger (1484–1558) and his son Joseph Justus (1540–1609). Joseph Scaliger was an important figure in the development of the science of historical criticism. Shoults owned some 28 works, either by him or those containing his commentaries and editorial notes. Significant publications include a copy of Scaliger's edition of Marcus Manilius's *Astronomicon* (1600), his *De emendatione temporum* (1629), which posited his ground-breaking notion that ancient chronology was not confined to Greeks and Romans, but also known to Persians, Babylonians, Egyptians, and Jews, and *Thesaurus temporum* (1658), which contains the lost *Chronicle* of Eusebius. Other holdings include a copy of *Scaligerana ou Bons Mots, Rencontres Agréables, et Remarques Judicieuses et Sçavantes de J. Scaliger*, published in Cologne in 1695, and the Greek Bible, published by Elzevir in Leiden in 1633 for Richard Whittaker of London. This last publication contains notes by Scaliger.

Shoults owned a rather battered copy of an edition of Simplicius's commentaries upon *Epicteti enchiridion*, a manual of ethical and moral advice originally compiled in the second century, published in Leiden in 1640. Simplicius of Cilicia (490–c.560), a pagan philosopher, expanded the work greatly, apparently to ten times the original text. On the front free endpaper Shoults wrote down a slight variant of Edward Gibbon's note on Simplicius from his *Decline and Fall of the Roman Empire*: 'Simplicius' moral interpretation of Epictetus is most excellently calculated to direct the will, to purify the heart, & to confirm the understanding, by a just confidence in the nature both of God & man. Gibbon's Comp. Hist. IV, p. 119.'[10] There is no copy of Gibbon in the Shoults Collection.

---

[9] The entry for Tuesday 24 August 1641 in Evelyn's *Diary* reads: 'The churches are many and fair; in one of them lies buried the learned and illustrious Joseph Scaliger, without any extraordinary inscription, who, having left the world a monument of his worth more lasting than marble, needed nothing more than his own name; which I think is all engraven on his sepulchre. He left his library to this University'. See Evelyn (1955). Of the father, Julius Caesar Scaliger, Jacques Auguste de Thou claimed that none of the ancients could be placed above him and that he had no equal in his own time. See 'Scaliger', in *EB*, XXIV, 283–6.

[10] The exact wording in Gibbon's work is: '[Simplicius's] moral interpretation of Epictetus, is preserved in the library of nations, as a classic book, most excellently adapted to direct the will, to purify the heart, and to confirm the understanding, by a just confidence in the nature both of God and man.' Gibbon (1776–1789), IV, 119.

There are some notes in Shoults's books that indicate where he was at a particular time. While working at St. Michael's in Shoreditch between 1873 and 1875, he made a rudimentary note in his copy of Charles J. Blomfield's *Aeschyli Prometheus vinctus*, published in London in 1846. On a blank page at the back he wrote the names of four Classical writers, the first three being outstanding representatives of Old Attic Comedy and the fourth a Roman satirist. His note reads: 'Eupolis – born B.C. 446 / Cratinus born B.C. 519 / Aristophanes from (circa) B.C. 445 / Lucilius (a Roman Knight) born at Suessa a town in the Auruncan territory. B.C. 249.' His copy once belonged to the Rev. Henry David Nihill, who had hired him as a curate at St. Michael's. As evidenced by the inscription inside, Nihill had received the book from his father, the Rev. Daniel Nihill. Shoults must either have borrowed it from Henry David or was given it.

Another example of note-taking provides a firmer date. On 30 June 1876, Shoults was still employed as a curate at St. Edmund the King and Martyr. At this time, he owned a copy of the two-volume edition of Richard Newcourt's *Repertorium ecclesiasticum parochiale Londinense*, published in 1710. Volume 1, which deals with the parochial histories of London, Middlesex, and Buckinghamshire, was seemingly of no interest to him. He wrote no annotations within it. Volume 2, however, which covers the parochial history of Essex, was of special interest. He wrote nine pages of notes and amendments to the text, dating them on the first page '30 June 1876'. In the main they concern Church dedications and corrections to the record on certain rectors.

On page 10 of volume 2 there is an entry for 'Ardley, Vicarage'. Line 5 has a gap in the printed information on the Church, reading: 'The Church here, dedicated [gap], in the reign of K. Stephen.' Shoults added by hand 'dedicated to St. Mary', thus completing the sentence. On page 44, he added 'St. Mary' to the dedication gap in the printed text for 'Belchamp-Walter, Vicarage'. The printed entries for 'Bocking, Deanry' (p. 67) and 'Buers and Monton rectory' (p. 102) get similar treatment with his note 'dedicated to ye B. Virgin S. Mary' added to both. Some of his additions are made from memory—for example, the 'Bocking' entry has an afterthought in square brackets: '[I think, W.A.S.]'. This use of square brackets and 'I think' is repeated elsewhere. Some, like 'Bardfield-Saling, Chappel' (p. 30), are given a longer note, indicating a familiarity with specific documents: 'This Chappel is dedicated to St. Margaret as I find in the will of Kath. Downham dated 1425—she was lady of Old Hall in Kayne.'

Shoults's concern for past rectors begins at page 63 at the entry for 'Birdbroke, Rectory'. His note reads: 'In list of Rectores, after 'Sim. Collyson' [20 June 1430] insert 'Hen Dalham, 1436' p. Rev Collyson 6 [I think 6 W.A.S.].' He then adds: 'Collyson

& Dalham exchanged for Dalham Suffolk. L. M IX 86 [I think 6 W.A.S.]' and 'Line 7 is Hen Dalham the same as Hen Deke (as printed). Dalham being merely the name of dwelling place (W.A.S.).' On page 76, in the entry for 'Borley, Rectory', he expands a little on rectors Robert De Stokes and William Hyndele. On page 88, in the entry for 'Braintree, Rectory, Vicarage' he writes: 'J. Kendale, 1356 and Thomas de Messton [I think this is same, W.A.S. Dec 1359]'. On page 105, in the entry for 'Bulmer', there is his note: 'After text proper add in Rectors, including Thomas Grimesby 25 Aug 1410.' These small amendments continue through to page 690, ending on the entry for 'Yelham-parva, Rectory', where he adds 'Rector John Wilde'.

All of the notes that Shoults makes in this volume are extremely detailed, and one wonders why he worked through it at all, making such small changes to dedications and adding in information on certain rectors. At the end of volume 2, he made a final note, which raises more questions, especially about who was the unidentified annotator, and who was 'D.K', whom he may have known. He wrote: 'No notes appear to have been made in Vol. I. It was looked through this volume by D.K. W.A.S.', and 'There is no note as to who the copy belonged. One or two of short marginal notes appear to be in a different hand to the interlineations. All in all waiting.'

Almost a year later, on '20/4/77', Shoults acquired a copy of André Rivet's *Instruction Préparatoire á la Saincte Cene*, published by Elzevir in Leiden in 1634. On the front free endpaper he has written a long note, but, because of the purple 'Selwyn College' stamp applied after it was received in Dunedin, much of it is now difficult to decipher. It reads (in part):

> Of Sanctification of the new creature. / It is no less than for a man to be brought to an [?] resignation of his will to the Will of God (to live in the offering up of his Soul continuously in the hands of [?] as a whole burnt offering to Christ). Bt just then and how little are many of those who profess Xianity, experientially are acquainted with this work on their souls.

This work, by the French Huguenot, was dedicated to one of his correspondents, Anna Maria van Schurman (1607–78), known as the 'Star of Utrecht' and famed for being the first female to attend a Dutch University, in 1636.

Another example of Shoults's lengthy note-making is found in his copy of the three-volume quarto edition of Celestino Sfondrati's *Cursus philosophicus monasterijs Galli*, published in 1696. These notes are copied from some unknown work, and even though part of the text refers to a movement away from the Protestant camp to another, this was not Shoults's experience. He may have had some doubts about his allegiance to the Anglican Church, but the fact is that he remained an Anglican priest. The text is interesting in that it prompted him to note down authors and books that he wanted to read and in fact owned. They confirm the type of books that he enjoyed and liked to immerse himself in.

A tipped-in ripped leaf between pages 58 and 59 of volume one (Logica) reads in part:

> . . . to the distinction (or difference) between the [?] Civil Law, whether the Council of Trent has been received in France, whether a Papist cannot in some cases absolve prospectively; the doctrine of intention [perhaps intuition?]; the <u>opus operatum</u>, in what sense knows one called Lectus [?]; (I am not sure if this quotation being written correctly. W.A.S.). A letter, reverential confession be required in each to obtain forgiveness; whether we deny the reality of natural virtue, & what worth we assign to it. (This I copied exactly W.A.S.). On these sacred subjects Catholics should be able to return a prompt & clear answer: A few words may perhaps furnish most serious inconveniences to the Catholic body. Half the controversies with Catholics arise from ignorance of the facts of the case; half the prejudices against Catholicity arise from misinformation of the prejudiced parties. Candid persons are set right, & enemies silenced, by the mere statement of what it is that we believe. People that speak against Catholicity, nevertheless like to hear something of it; and if only Catholic can only give information by will but perhaps be asked for arguments. When I was a protestant, three friends of mine, then Clergymen of the Church of England, travelling on foot to the W. or S. part of Ireland, took for their guide a boy of twelve or thirteen, & amused themselves by asking him questions about his religion, but they afterwards confessed that the child had put them all to silence, of course not by arguments, but merely by knowing & understanding his Catholicity thoroughly, and being able to answer questions correctly.

Underneath this text he has asterisked two footnotes:

> *Secular power, influence, & resources, are never so well employed, as when they are in the hands of Catholics.

> ** Read Apologies, defences Origen against Celsus, Tertullian's Apol.; St Augustine's City of God (Some books I own I think. W.A.S.) Vincentius Livinsis; Bellarmine's Controversies; Senarius de Legibus; Melchior [sic] Canne de Locis Theologia.

Shoults was correct in his bracketed guess. He owned works of all of those mentioned: Origen, Tertullian, St. Augustine, Vincent of Lérins, Robert Bellarmine, Christopher Wase's *Senarius, sive, de legibus & licentia veterum poetarum* (1687), a treatise on

Greek and Latin metrics and rhythmics, and the Spanish theologian Melchor Cano's *Opera* (1776).[11]

The second page of the insert is not completely legible because of Shoults's often hard to read writing, and because the leaf is tightly tipped-in. It reads in part:

> ... eloquence [?] (still worse) should be the object in view; but effect. (I think I have written this rightly. W.A.S.). In England & Scotland it is the practice to read sermons. But the Irish, & foreign custom (& the use of the Church from the first) is to preach without the book. To read <u>without</u> book is much better than to read a sermon. Protestants often say to those who urge them to go to Church, that they can read their prayers & book of sermons as well at home, & those who urge them are puzzled for an answer. There is an earnestness in a sermon delivered, which is wanting in the private reading, that a sermon preached has more effect than a better sermon read privately. A sermon delivered from book has less & less effect the more the delivery approaches the reading. The book may be left at hand. The French practice is to write the sermons & then learn them by heart, so as to deliver them without book. This is in evidence, it would seem, with the practice of S. Ser. [?] & St. Chrystomo [John Chrysostom, the 'golden-mouthed'] (the reasons being furnished by the style of the sermons peculiar to the writers, which being consistent in minute particulars, the sermon cannot have been published from reprinted notes.) Peculiarities of S. Chrystomo noticeable in the Latin. On the other hand, from the number of homilies ascribed to S. Augustine, & some other Fathers, they cannot all have been written. Cicero's Orationes against Celsus written but not delivered; & yet have all the appearance of real Matins so others may be written & then delivered. Cicero mentions memory as one of the qualifications of a good orator.

Shoults again adds a footnote under the text:

> # Pastoral letters of Henry, Bishop of Exeter, about 1851 I think about the middle. The Bishop mentions stand of the Archbishop of Canterbury 'that the clergy would not desert protestant faith or something such' [?] the Bishop then mentions that the object of faith is divine truth, & the object of predestination is ever.

---

[11] Wase, *Senarius, sive, de legibus & licentia veterum poetarum* (1687). Shoults Eb 1687 W; Cano, *Opera* (1776). Shoults Itb 1776 C.

He ends this written sample with a note in square brackets: '[Notice this well. I copy the passage. W.A.S.]'

It is a long passage to copy out, and one wonders how much Shoults was interested in the notion of the habit of the Irish and the French to memorise sermons. His recall, however, was moderately good on the placement of the Lord Bishop's mention of the Archbishop of Canterbury and the clergy. This particular paraphrased passage is found on page 65 in Henry Phillpotts, Lord Bishop of Exeter's *A Pastoral Letter to the Clergy of the Diocese of Exeter on the Present State of the Church*, published in London in 1851. The pamphlet—a copy of which Shoults owned—is 126 pages long.

A physical examination of a collection reveals surprises. Shoults owned a copy of Francesco Redi's study on intestinal worms, *De animalculis vivis quae in corporibus animalium vivorum reperiuntur observationes ex Etruscis latinas fecit Petrus Coste*, published in Amsterdam in 1708.[12] It is a pioneering work on parasitology. For some unknown reason, Shoults made a few brief notes in it: 'Peel's Museum at Philadelphia contains specimens of snakes with 2 heads' and, at the back (incomplete because of a tear), '. . . of Noothe were Baskets of Bark, so curiously wrought as to contain Water like an earthern vessel, without leakage or drips.' The Peale Museum, named after Charles Willson Peale, was established in Philadelphia in 1786 but later moved to Baltimore in 1814. Shoults may have read some information about this natural history and art museum from general reading, including the details of the two-headed snake. Previous owners of this volume include a 'J. Buckland', and 'Bourdillon V.D.M., 1763', most certainly the Rev. Jacob Bourdillon (1704–86), pastor of the Artillery Church, Spitalfields, London, and Verbi Dei Minister (V.D.M), a Preacher of God's Word.

After seven years spent in research and writing, Cardinal Giovanni Bona (1609–74) saw his *Rerum liturgicarum libro duo* published in Rome in 1671. This work is his most famous, the first comprehensive publication on the history of the Eucharist and its parts, including subjects such as rites, churches, and vestments. Tipped in at the front of this vellum-bound copy is a two-page note by Shoults. Too long to quote in full, it begins: 'In a copy of Card. Bona's *de Rebus Liturgicis* (Parisii, Apud Ludovicum Billaine in Palatio Regis MDCLXII Cum Privilego Regis Christianiss), after the preface to the reader, & before the Index Librorum et Capitum, occurs the following.' Under the heading 'MONITTO' (sic), he writes 'Vix emersit e praedo hic Liber, cum statum intelleci displicinisse' through to the last underlined sentence overleaf: '<u>Felices artes, si de iis soli artifices judicarent.</u>' The text he copied, usually headed 'Montio ad Lectorem', is found in later editions by Bona such as the Paris publication of 1672. He

---

[12] The first Italian edition was published in Florence in 1684.

thought well enough of what was copied to have it tipped into his own copy. Someone has written underneath the text: 'The Rev. W. A. Shoults's writing.'

Livy's only surviving work is his *Historiarum ab urbe condita libri*, a history of Rome that survives in fragments: about twenty-five percent, with some 35 books out of the original 142. Shoults owned various copies of this classic work, including the seven-volume edition of published in Amsterdam between 1738 and 1746, and three nineteenth-century editions (1813; 1821; 1842). He also owned a copy of Johann Friedrich Gronovius's edition of Book XXXV, *Superstites*, published by Elzevir in Leiden in 1645, a copy of Arnold Drakenborch's *T. Livii Patavini Singularum quae supersunt, decadûm liber prior*, published in London in 1787, and a copy of *Commentarius perpetuus in T. Livii Patavini historiarum libros*, published in London in 1825.

In the above Amsterdam edition, Shoults copied out a large section of text onto four leaves and tipped it into volume 2. The transcription, too long to reproduce here, is a long extract from volume 3 of *T. Livii Patavini Historiarum libri qui supersunt cum deperditorum fragmentis et epitomis omnium,* published in Hanover in 1828. It starts: 'After the Epitomo Libri XLI in the Tauchnitz edition, follows: Adustatio Quinque Livii historarium libri, qui superscent, hoc est [. . .] minsiubius litteris distinctae.'[13] Throughout the text, he makes mention of the fragment of the 91st Book that was discovered in the Vatican Library in 1772, *La storia Romana di T. Livio*, published in Brescia between 1804–1818, William of Malmesbury, and cites various authors and their works that refer to the fragmentary nature of the text. Shoults also mentions 'Laurentianus', the Laurentian Library, containing 11,000 plus manuscripts (some pertinent to Livy), which is now part of the Biblioteca Medicea Laurenziana in Florence. At the end of the text on leaf four, he cites the Roman historian Quintilian and his *Institutio Oratoria* and a reference: 'X, 1, 39. coll. II, 5, 20', followed by a final '[Vol. I. pp. 888–889 & p. 152 I think]'. Again, after the text, in the same hand of that in the Bona edition above, is written: 'The Rev. W.A. Shoults's writing.' (See pl. 17.)

It is not possible to truly answer the question of why Shoults copied the text and all the other portions out, except for the obvious, that he was interested in Livy's history and its fragmentary nature. It is a lengthy piece of note-taking, and it certainly involved familiarity with various editions of Livy's history, including some of the manuscript discoveries, and an inclination to undertake close textual collations. It was done for his own private use, and he made it permanent by tipping it into the volume.

---

[13] See 'Livius (Livy)', in *OCD* (1970), 614–16.

Finally, Shoults owned a copy of a *Breviaire monastique*, published in Paris in 1800, which is bound with a copy of *Supplementum novum ad Breviarum monasticum*, published in Paris in 1832.[14] Loosely inserted in this volume are two sheets that contain in Shoults's hand a Latin hymn for Vespers on the Friday after the First Sunday in Lent, dedicated to the spear and nails of Christ. He has included musical notations with the text. However, what he has written is incomplete. The text of the first sheet reads: 'Quænam lingua tibi, O Lancea, debitas. Grates pro merito est apta rependere? Christi vivificum namque aperis latus, Unde Ecclesia nascitur'. The second sheet has the third verse: 'O Clavi! æqua manet vos quoque gratia, Christi quando sacris artubus insiti, Deletum Domini sanguine figitis Mortis chirographum Cruci.' The sheets are small in size, and it is perhaps the consequent lack of space that made him omit parts of the hymn, which he surely would have known through his own parish work. He has included an 'Amen' after 'nascitur' in the first verse.[15]

Shoults was a reader who left very few notes or evidence of use in his books. The lists and jottings above are admittedly few, considering the size of the collection. However, what is presented does provide a small glimpse into his thoughts, interests, and bookish activities.

---

[14] Shoults Fb 1800 C.

[15] The full text of the hymn is: 'Quænam lingua tibi, O Lancea, debitas. Grates pro merito est apta rependere? Christi vivificum namque aperis latus, Unde Ecclesia nascitur. / Hæc est Heva viri de latere exiens, Olli membra gravis dum sopor occupat; Hanc quippe alter Adam corde scatentibus Unda, et sanguine procreat, / O Clavi! æqua manet vos quoque gratia, Christi quando sacris artubus insiti, Deletum Domini sanguine figitis Mortis chirographum Cruci. / Te, Iesu, superi laudibus efferant, Qui Clavorum aditus, signaque Lanceæ In Cælo retines, vivus ubi imperas Cum Patre, atque Paraclito. Amen.' This has been translated as: 'What tongue, illustrious Spear, can duly sound Thy praise, in Heav'n or earth? Thou, who didst open that life-giving wound, From whence the Church had birth. / From Adam, sunk in an ecstatic sleep, Came Eve divinely framed; From Christ, – his Spouse; when from that wound so deep The Blood and Water stream'd. / And equal thanks to you, blest Nails, whereby, Fast to the sacred Rood, Was clench'd the sentence dooming us to die, All blotted out in blood. / To Him who still preserves in highest Heaven The wounds which here He bore, Be glory, with th'eternal Father, given, And Spirit evermore. Amen.' Translation by Fr. Edward Caswall, 1849. See St. Augustine's Lyre (c.2020), https://tosingistopraytwice.wordpress.com/

18 TREASURES TO NEW ZEALAND, AND SHOULTS'S LEGACY

On 14 June 1887, William Arderne Shoults died at the family home at 37 Camberwell Grove. He was 48 years old. His death certificate states that the cause of death was 'Phthisis Pulmonatis (left)'—that is, pulmonary tuberculosis. He was buried in the family catacomb (no.40) in South Metropolitan Cemetery, West Norwood, on 18 June.[1] His estate was valued at £290 3s 9d, and Eliza, 'his dear wife', was the sole beneficiary and executrix.[2] The will, dated one month earlier, on 11 May 1887, does not mention his books. William Bramley Taylor, M.R.C.S., a 'valued and esteemed' family friend, witnessed the will.[3] Taylor had been a student at Guy's Hospital, and he may have looked after Shoults in his last years, using facilities at the hospital to provide care and assistance to his patient.

When Shoults died, Eliza was living at the family home. She resided at No. 37 with her sister-in-law Maria Susannah. Also resident at No. 37 was Eliza's sister, Emily and her husband Henry Taylor White, a printer. Eliza's later movements are recorded through the census records and one newspaper account.[4] In 1891, she is recorded as 'living by her own means' at No. 37, and in June 1895, according to the *Morning Post*, she helped out at the Hampstead Stalls at a bazaar for the National Society of Prevention of Cruelty to Children. In 1901, she was living at 23 Crawford Street, Camberwell, and in 1911 she moved to 5 Cavendish Street, where she is described as 'widow, 69'. In 1912, she moved to Glentamer Mansions, 108 Kingston Road, New Malden, and, on 3 August 1914, she died at 50 Albany Road, New Malden, aged 72.[5] After her effects were affirmed, the sum of her estate amounted to £1624 18s 6d.

In her will she left the sum of £50 to Taylor. And it may have been through his association with Guy's Hospital that Eliza included the hospital in her will of December 1912. She set aside an unknown sum of money to establish a bed called 'The William Arderne Shoults Bed', 'in loving memory of my beloved husband'. The residue, after costs, was directed to the President and Governor of the Hospital.

---

[1] The family catacomb is no longer there; it is now (2018) a grassed area.
[2] 1887: England & Wales, National Probate Calendar (Index of Wills and Administrations), 1858-1995, England: will of William Arderne Shoults, 11 May 1887, 646.
[3] Taylor was also a bookman and in post-career, a librarian who compiled the *Catalogue of the Library of the Society of Apothecaries* (1913). Obituary, *British Medical Journal*, 27 February 1937, 475.
[4] 1891: England census, Camberwell; 1901: England and Wales census, Camberwell; 1911: England and Wales census, Camberwell; and *Morning Post*, 27 June 1895, 4.
[5] *The Times*, 7 August 1914, 1.

W. Palmer, a solicitor based at Three Crown Square, Southwark, London, was a witness to her will.[6]

BISHOP NEVILL AND SHOULTS'S LIBRARY

Samuel Tarratt Nevill (1837–1921) was the Anglican bishop of Dunedin from 1871 to 1919. He was described by the historian W.P. Morrell as 'a bishop of long views, abounding energy and tenacious purpose'.[7] (See pl. 25.) In 1888, Nevill was in London attending the Lambeth Conference, beginning on 30 June.[8] While in England, he had another mission in mind, to found a theological college in Dunedin to rival that of St. John's College in Auckland. There had already been some beginnings at realising his dream. In 1873, he had been successful in receiving from the Syndics of the Cambridge University Press a number of books, and he owned a Prayer Book that had been given to a Māori preacher by Bishop Selwyn in 1844. These gifts were the first recorded benefactions to the Selwyn College Library.

While in London Nevill met Eliza Shoults. There is no evidence of any prior association, but he may have known Shoults through the Synod or through University of Cambridge networks. He certainly knew of Shoults's book collection because, when he met Eliza sometime in August or early September 1888, the notion of donating it as a founding library to Selwyn College was discussed. Her original intention was not to part with the library in her lifetime, bequeathing it to St. John's College, or Cambridge University, her husband's *alma mater*. Nevill was obviously persuasive in their discussions, because Eliza 'eventually yielded', admitting that the needs of a young colony such as New Zealand were more pressing.[9] On agreeing to donate the library to the College, she made one stipulation: that it was to be known as the 'Arderne Shoults Library'. The library was in Nevill's hands by 20 September 1888, when the *Morning Post* published his letter, which was reprinted for New Zealand readers in the *Otago Daily Times*, 14 November 1888.[10] His report in the letter was enthusiastic:

> I have recently had the happiness of receiving a most valuable benefaction to my diocese in the shape of a library of over 3000 volumes, embracing a wide

---

[6] 1912–1914: England & Wales, National Probate Calendar (Index of Wills and Administrations), 1858-1995: will of Eliza Katharine Shoults, 31 December 1912; 16 May 1914 (Codicil).

[7] Morrell (1969), 197; see also Hargreaves (1993), 9.

[8] Of the 145 members who attended, three others were from New Zealand: the Bishop of Nelson, the Rev. Dr Suter; the Bishop of Auckland, the Rev Dr Cowie; and the Bishop of Waiapu, the Rev. Dr Stuart.

[9] 'Selwyn College', *Otago Witness*, 24 May 1894, 16.

[10] 'Bishop Nevill's Appeal', *Otago Daily Times*, 14 November 1888, 3, citing 'Diocesan Library for Dunedin', 26 September 1888, in *Morning Post*, 28 September 1888, 5.

scope of subjects: theology (ancient and modern), Greek and Roman classics, natural science, and modern literature (English and foreign) are represented. There are, besides, many curiosities of manuscript and printing, the like of which are not to be seen in New Zealand. I am very anxious to make this gift as useful as possible, not only to my clergy and students of theology, but the students of the Otago University, or others generally.[11]

Nevill also realised that an acquisition such as this involved some financial outlay on the part of the diocese, and he admitted to the *Morning Post* readers that it was poor and could not met any anticipated expenses. His letter included an appeal 'to well-wishers of New Zealand' and to those 'who sympathise with the advancement of learning and culture'.[12] He admitted that there were challenges: 'The expense [. . .] of this acquisition will be very great.' He continued: 'I shall first have to enlarge a room in my small theological institute to receive it, then there will be the necessary carpenter's work for shelves, the packing and freight', and then, reflecting on the state of some of the books, 'a considerable outlay for the binding of books not in a good condition'. It was not all doom, and he listed one success: 'I have already £800 to raise to pay for the site and building of my theological college.' He ended his letter thus: 'I should be thankful if I were enabled to go back with my books and £1000, but any cheques marked 'Library' would be devoted solely to the expenses incident to its establishment.' The Colonial Bank of New Zealand in Moorgate Street, London, was given as the address to receive any subscriptions.

On his return to Dunedin, Nevill reported his successes at the second session of the Eighth Synod of the Diocese of Dunedin in November 1889, repeating them in an address in November 1890, and again in another address on 30 October 1893.[13] In the last, he was much more explicit on the help that he had received. Apart from giving special thanks to Eliza Shoults, he mentioned Elizabeth Georgina Palmer, of 56 Cromwell Road, London, who may have been a friend of Eliza's.[14] Miss Palmer was the daughter of John Horsley Palmer (1779–1858), a director of the Bank of England, and owner of Hurlingham House in Fulham. She never married and lived at Cromwell Street until she died on 3 March 1900, aged 83. According to Nevill, Miss Palmer heard of his plight and asked him how much the costs would be to convey the library to New Zealand. Nevill's estimate—putting books in good order, packing

---

[11] As cited in 'Bishop Nevill's Appeal', *Otago Daily Times*, 14 November 1888, 3.
[12] 'Bishop Nevill's Appeal', *Otago Daily Times*, 14 November 1888, 3.
[13] Bishop Nevill, 'History of the College, c.1889–1893', Selwyn College Papers, 84–086, 47, Hocken Library.
[14] Cited in Cox (1977).

and carriage—was 'hardly less than £200'.[15] Miss Palmer promptly donated that sum for the purpose. Assistance came also from another benefactor in England: the Rev. Dr Frederick Schiller May (1831–1909), who not only provided his time and money to put the books in good repair, but also created some preliminary inventories.[16] In 1878, when Nevill was in England attending the Bishops' Conference at Lambeth, he engaged May as his chaplain. The two had obviously kept in contact and when it came to dealing with Shoults's books in 1888, Nevill was fortunate to be able to call on May and utilise his services again.

THE COLLECTION IN DUNEDIN

By early November 1893, the Shoults Collection was in Dunedin, housed in a newly-dedicated building on Castle Street.[17] A committee had been formed to assist Nevill in preparing for its arrival, and there were formalities, such as a vote of thanks to Mrs Shoults and other library benefactors, including the Trustees of the estates of the late Rev. Dr Fell and the Rev. Edward Bulkley.[18] At the Synod meeting, it was recognized that 'the donation of 7000 volumes was a public benefaction, and a library of that kind coming out to this colony ought to have an enormous influence on the culture, literary life, and enlightenment of the town'.[19] One who was quick to peruse the collection was Dr T.M. Hocken, himself a book collector. He delivered an address on the library, commenting, 'as one who knew something about old books', that 'the library was worth many thousands of pounds, while some of the volumes were quite priceless'. Hocken also remarked that Mrs Shoults 'still took a keen interest in the progress of the library'.[20]

In 1893, there were six students at Selwyn, five of whom were studying theology. Their use of the collection is not known. In Ray Hargreaves's *Selwyn College's First Century* there is a photograph of the Library taken about 1900. The two-and-a-half

---

[15] Bishop Nevill, 'History of the College, c.1889–1893', Selwyn College Papers, 84–086, 47, Hocken Library.

[16] 'The Philosophy of Christianity. Bishop Nevill's Address at the Anglican Diocesan Synod', *Otago Witness*, 2 November 1893, 14, contains, in relation to Dr May's work, the phrase 'to the working out of catalogues, some 23'. See also Bishop Nevill, 'History of the College, c.1889–1893', Selwyn College Papers, 84–086, 47. Hocken Library. According to Dr Stephen Gamble (London), an inventory was made prior to shipment of Shoults's books by Dr May, but it, the so-called 'catalogues', have not been found. Email correspondence with Dr Stephen Gamble, 18 September 2002. For May, see *AC* (1947), IV, 373.

[17] The foundation stone was laid on 31 October 1891 and the new building dedicated on 25 January 1893. See Hargreaves (1993), 11.

[18] See 'Library for College', 5 November 1893, 183, and 'Vote of thanks to Donors of Library', 6 November 1893, 187. Synod Minute Book 1887–1902, AG–349–003/003, Hocken Library.

[19] 'Donation of a Library', *Otago Daily Times*, 7 November 1893, 4.

[20] 'Selwyn College Library', *Otago Witness*, 6 June 1895, 12.

walls visible are covered with shelves, and one can only presume that many of the books tidily arranged were from the Shoults Collection, especially the large folios on the lower shelves. A framed portrait of Bishop Nevill is mounted on a shelf, covering some of the books. A reading table is in the centre of the room, on it a few books and a vase of flowers. (See pl. 26.)

There is one early positive response to the collection: Esmond de Beer (1895–1990), who attended the Selwyn Collegiate School between 1903 and 1910, was allowed access to the collection. He remembered it fondly: 'At Selwyn I handled older books. With no instruction or guidance I could learn little about them, but I acquired freedom of approach to them and awareness that some of them invited study of a kind which I learnt later to know as bibliography.'[21]

In 1904, there were six resident students. By 1909, there were twenty-five, the number dropping to sixteen in 1917.[22] Over this period, a constant refrain was the need for more money—funds for maintenance, building projects, and book purchases. Hargreaves paints a sombre picture: 'After about 1914, the collection was shamefully neglected. Students and clergy appear to have been uninterested in, or unaware of, its great historical worth.'[23] During the First World War, the College closed its doors. On the College re-opening, the collection faced the first of many moves. In 1925, it was moved to an old classroom block, and then into an old dining room. It was then next moved to the old billiards room and then to a run-down building in the north ground, which had once been the Warden's residence. The Depression followed, and the Second World War compounded financial difficulties. Over the post-Second World War period there was also a marked change in fields of study. According to enrolment registers, the number of students studying theology plummeted, with a corresponding rise in the number of students studying in the fields of medicine and health sciences.

As a consequence of all these moves, exposing the books to damp and dusty conditions, overall neglect, and misuse, many of them suffered. Jean Klemp, a librarian at the University of Otago, mentioned that some books found in an old chest crumbled to dust on handling, and others suffered wanton vandalism from theological students, who used some of them as missiles. Others faced a worse fate: a copy of Augustin Calmet's *Histoire Ecclésiastique et Civile de Lorraine* (1728) has a note recorded in volume 4: 'This book was peed on in the Year of Our Lord Nineteen Hundred and Forty One at the 24th hour of the sixteenth day of the month of

---

[21] Strachan (1995), 14.
[22] Selwyn College Minute Book, 1914–1926, Box 1, Selwyn College Papers, 84–086, Hocken Library.
[23] Hargreaves (1993), 48.

November.' In 1947, when David M. Taylor was carrying out research for *The Oldest Manuscripts in New Zealand* (1955), he noted that conditions were not suitable for the books. He noted one exception: 'In an upstairs room at Selwyn College, Dunedin, in 1947 was a zinc-lined chest in which were preserved the oldest possessions of the College Library.'[24]

THE GIFTS OF OTHERS

Although Bishop Nevill's dream for a diocesan theological library available to students, clergy, and the wider community was not fully realised, his enthusiasm attracted others. Aside from the Shoults Collection, there was a large donation of books from the Trustees of the late Dr Thomas Fell (1809–67).

The Trustees of Dr Fell's estate felt that Nevill's appeal was important enough to respond generously. Their donation numbered 62 books, each containing Fell's bookplate and the family motto: Suum Cuique ('to each, his own').[25] The donation included copies of Arthur Hildersam's *CVIII Lectures upon the Fourth of John: Preached, at Ashby-Delazouch in Leicester-shire* (1632), William Cave's *Primitive Christianity: or, The Religion of the Ancient Christians in the First Ages of the Gospel* (1676), Edward Stillingfleet's *A Discourse Concerning the Idolatry Practised in the Church of Rome* (1676), John Locke's *Works* (1714), Gilbert Burnet's *The History of the Reformation of the Church of England* (1715), Humphrey Prideaux's *The Old and New Testament connected in the History of the Jews and Neighbouring Nations* (1725), Thomas Stackhouse's *The New Sacred History of the Bible* (1749), Samuel Shuckford's *The Creation and Fall of Man* (1753), and John Bird Sumner's *Apostolical Preaching Considered in an Examination of St. Paul's Epistles* (1817). They were all incorporated into the Shoults Collection.

A few other titles also found their way to the Shoults Collection. These included two volumes from the estate of the Rev. Edward Bulkley, namely George Bancroft's translation of Arnold Hermann Ludwig Heeren's *Ancient Greece* (1845) and William Mitford's *The History of Greece* (1838). There were also six books from the library of the already-mentioned Rev. Thomas Edward Hankinson (1805–43), a student of Corpus Christi College, Cambridge, and at one stage, Minister of St Matthew's Chapel,

---

[24] Taylor (1955), 56. The cumulative deterioration is evident in the Shoults Collection today, with detached covers, worm-holes, brittle leaves, tears, evidence of water damage, and foxing. It is pleasing to note that environmental conditions in Special Collections, University of Otago, are such that any deterioration has been arrested. Books with detached covers are now placed in purpose-made archival boxes or folders.
[25] Fell, *AC* (1944), II, 475.

Denmark Hill, Camberwell.[26] There are two pamphlet volumes, which were bound together by someone at the College Library much later.[27]

DISPOSAL

In the early 1920s, despite the apparent neglect, there was an air of optimism surrounding the Shoults Collection. In November 1923, certain individuals at the Dunedin Public Library, in association with the Trustees of Selwyn College, took the initiative in planning a display of some of the books and manuscripts from the collection. It was a significant project for the library, which included setting a budget for the making of purpose-built cabinets with glass fronts to display the items. A loan period of ten years was mentioned. By 1924, twelve manuscripts, twenty-nine incunables, and a number of Persian, Turkish, and Arabic items were chosen. Two of the manuscripts were a *Breviarium Romanum* (1464) and Jerome's *Epistolae* (c.1439–40). While no individual printed books were named for display, it was reported that it was sad to leave out other choice sixteenth-century items.[28] The writer of the Dunedin Public Library's *Annual Report* for 1924 was enthusiastic about the prospect: 'It may be added that the Public Library is exceedingly fortunate in obtaining possession of these records of a past age, for exhibition to the public.'[29]

By the early 1930s, with the full effects of the Depression affecting the College, the optimism had diminished. In order to raise money for the College, there was a move to sell off a few books from the Shoults Collection. Someone at this time wrote to Sotheby's in London supplying a list of books for appraisal and possible sale. On 17 February 1932, the Trustees heard back from the firm, and the proposed sale was discussed at their February meeting. The motion of consent to send the books to auction was moved by Sir James Allen (1855–1942) and seconded by Dr William Alfred Robertson Fitchett (1872–1952).[30] However, Isaac Richards (1859–1936), the then Bishop of Dunedin (1920–34), and Nevill's immediate successor, stepped in and stopped any action on the proposal.

In 1938, the issue of selling off books from the Shoults Collection was raised again, this time at the instigation of Louis Grenville (Algy) Whitehead, Warden of Selwyn, who, ironically, was a book collector. This time permission was granted by the new Bishop, Dr Fitchett (1934–52). The success of this request was due to the fact that

---

[26] Hankinson, *AC* (1947), III, 226.
[27] 'Tracts'. Shoults Eb 1880 N; 'Tracts on Various Subjects'. Shoults Eb 1880 T.
[28] *Evening Star*, 2 November 1923, 6.
[29] Dunedin Public Library (1924), 128.
[30] Minutes of Selwyn College Meeting, 17 February 1932, Minute Book, February 1927–April 1948, Box 2, Selwyn College Papers, 84-086, Hocken Library. See also Hargreaves (1993), chapter 'The Library', 48–51.

Whitehead was going to England on leave and was willing to transport the rare books and manuscripts to the auction house. The Board were furthermore convinced that there was no legal impediment to disposing of any of the Shoults books and that the sum raised would assist in easing the College's straitened circumstances.[31]

Whitehead sailed off with 16 books: two medieval manuscripts, eight incunables, and six early printed books.[32] The items were given to Sotheby's and advertised for sale in their *Catalogue of Valuable Printed Books*, June–July 1938, lots 511 to 522. Each of the entries refer to the presence of a 'library stamp', which is no doubt the very distinctive purple 'Selwyn College' stamp.

The first medieval manuscript was a copy of *Breviarium Romanum*, written on 464 vellum leaves at Lucca, Tuscany, by Karolus de Blanchis de Bordone in 1464. This item, lot 512, 'Sold by Order of the Selwyn College Board, Dunedin, N.Z.' went to Marks and Co, the antiquarian bookseller located at 84 Charing Cross Road, London.[33]

The second manuscript was a copy of Jerome's *Epistolae*, written on vellum in France by Johannes de Carnago, c.1439–40. Bound in old panelled calf, this manuscript of 304 leaves had two historiated initials, both of Jerome, at fol. 1 and 25. Two colophons were reported: fol. 249 recto, and fol. 257 verso. According to Christopher de Hamel, this manuscript (lot 513) was sold to the bookseller Maggs of London.[34] It later appeared in a catalogue, *Text Manuscripts of the Middle Ages and Renaissance* (No.15), issued by the art dealer Sam Fogg in London in 1992, lot. 18.[35] The current location of these two manuscripts is unknown.

At one stage Shoults owned 38 incunables. Eight were identified as saleable. Three were printed in Venice, two in Strasbourg, and one each in Cologne, Rome, and Bologna. They ranged in date from 1475 to 1499.

The first Venetian publication was a copy of Lactantius's *Opera*, completed by Andreas de Paltasichis & Boninus de Boninis on 12 March 1479. According to the catalogue, this vellum-bound folio had 212 leaves, wanting fol. 1 and 214 (both blank).[36] The second was a copy of Ovid's *Metamorphoses*, completed by Simon

---

[31] See Minutes for meeting, 24 January 1938, Minute Book, February 1927–April 1948, Box 2, Selwyn College Papers, 84–086, Hocken Library.

[32] The Atlas insurance documents for the transported books still exist and they list fifteen items rather than the sixteen. The list lacks details on the pigskin bound copy of Conrad Koellin's *Adversus caninas M. Lutheri nuptias* (1530). Miscellaneous Papers, 1884–1930s, Selwyn College Papers, 84–086, 18, Hocken Library.

[33] *Breviarium Romanum*. Sotheby (1938), 66, lot 512.

[34] St Jerome, *Epistolae*. Sotheby (1938), 66, lot 513. See de Hamel, in Manion (1989), 80, note 2.

[35] Thanks to Mitch Fraas, Senior Curator, Special Collections, Kislak Center for Special Collections, Rare Books and Manuscripts, University of Pennsylvania Libraries, Philadelphia. Correspondence 14 May 2021.

[36] Lactantius, *Opera*. See *ISTC* il00008000: 108 known copies worldwide. Sotheby (1938), 67, lot 518.

Bevilaqua on 8 July 1497. This folio of 168 leaves was bound in half-stamped pigskin over wooden boards, with the remains of a few brass clasps and catches. It contained numerous hand-written notes.[37]

The final Venetian publication was a copy of Plautus's *Comoediae*, with the commentaries of J. P. Valla and Bernadinus Saracensus. Completed by Simon Bevilaqua on 17 September 1499, this copy comprises 348 leaves and was once part of the Kloss Library, from which Shoults secured other books. Its provenance is enhanced by the recorded fact that the first eight plays in it have interlinear glosses and notes by Philip Melanchthon, the German reformer and collaborator with Martin Luther. This incunable is now in the Rare Book & Manuscript Library at the University of Illinois at Urbana–Champaign, purchased on 11 October 1938 from a bequest in memory of Charles A. and Charles N. Denison. The catalogue description in Marion Harman's *Incunabula in the University of Illinois Library at Urbana-Champaign* (1978) erroneously advances Shoults to a 'D.D.', Doctor of Divinity.[38]

The first book from Strasbourg was a copy of Jacobus de Voragine's *Legenda aurea sanctorum*, completed by Georg Husner on 16 August 1490. This folio of 251 leaves has the signature of Francis Palgrave in it—either Sir Francis Palgrave [*formerly* Cohen] (1788–1861) or his son, Francis Turner Palgrave (1824–97), compiler of the *Golden Treasury of English Songs and Lyrics* (1861). According to the catalogue details, the wooden boards are bound in calf.[39]

The second was headed by Sotheby's as *Mariale, sive de laudibus beatae Mariae Virginis*, completed by Martin Flach in Strasbourg in 1493. This folio, actually a copy of *De laudibus Mariae*, a Pseudo-Albertus Magnus work, is comprised of 299 leaves (wanting fol. 300) and is bound in pigskin. It carries an inscription by one Sebastian Honneffinger and the bookplate of the Duke of Sussex. It is now in the Francis A. Countway Library of Medicine, Boston, carrying a note about the donor, Frederic Thomas Lewis.[40]

The one Cologne publication was a copy of Guilielmus Durandus's *Rationale divinorum officiorum*, which may have been completed by Ulrich Zel about 1475. A folio of 474 leaves, it has a note in the Sotheby's catalogue: 'A large copy' with the

---

[37] Publius Ovidius Naso, *Metamorphoses*. See *ISTC* io00193000: 81 known copies worldwide. Sotheby (1938), 67, lot 519.

[38] Titus Maccius Plautus, *Comoediae*. See *ISTC* ip00784000: 150 known copies worldwide. Sotheby (1938), 68, lot 521. University of Illinois Library at Urbana-Champaign call number: Incunabula Q.871 P51499), see Harman (1978), 139.

[39] Voragine, *Legenda aurea sanctorum*. See *ISTC* ij00124000: 58 known copies worldwide. Sotheby (1938), 66, lot 514.

[40] See *ISTC* ia00248000 with a note: 'Although attributed to Albertus Magnus, the probable author is Richardus de Sancto Laurentio (Sack (Freiburg))'. Sotheby (1938), 66, lot 515. See Walsh (1991), no. 280.

heading: 'RARE'. With only 24 copies recorded on the *ISTC* database, this is certainly so. According to the catalogue, it is bound in old goatskin and has the collation mark (a complete copy) by the book collector Thomas Rawlinson (1681–1725).[41]

The book printed in Rome is far less rare, although an *editio princeps*. This was a copy of Johannes Antonius Campanus's *Opera*, completed in Rome by Eucharius Silber on 31 October 1495. According to the *ISTC* database, 221 copies exist worldwide of this folio of 304 leaves. The vellum-bound Shoults copy was incomplete, lacking fols. 291–304. It is now at the Francis A. Countway Library of Medicine, Boston.[42]

The last incunable is Matthaeus Bossus's *Recuperationes faesulanae*, completed in Bologna by Franciscus de Benedictus on 20 July 1493. Described in the catalogue as 'Part II (Epistles)', this small folio, bound in 'old sheep gilt', lacks some 72 leaves, being described as '112 (should be 184) leaves.'[43] As detailed, the final whereabouts of only three of these incunables have been identified.

The six sixteenth-century publications included copies of three anti-Luther works, namely: a copy of Erasmus's *Hyperaspistes diatribae adversus servum arbitrium M. Lutheri* (1526), a vellum-bound copy of Johann Eck's *Enchiridion locorum communium adversus Lutheranos* (1527), and a pigskin-bound copy of Conrad Koellin's *Adversus caninas M. Lutheri nuptias* (1530). These three were put together with Paulus Manutius's publication of *De legibus Romanis* (1569) as lot 511. Lot 522 comprised two books: an Aldine edition of Johannes Bessarion's *In calumniatorê Platonis lib IV*, published in Venice in 1516, and a vellum-bound copy of Virgil's *Opera*, published in Antwerp by Plantin in 1575.[44]

The above printed books and manuscripts realised at sale the sum of £65 2s 3d, not enough to straighten out finances, but just enough to pay for a new boiler.[45]

❧

At some stage, two other incunables were removed from the collection, either kept back from the transfer in 1893 or disposed of quietly just after they had arrived in Dunedin.

---

[41] Guillelmus Duranti, *Rationale divinorum officiorum*. Possibly *ISTC* id00410000: 24 known copies worldwide. Sotheby (1938), 67, lot 516.

[42] Johannes Antonius Campanus, *Opera*. See *ISTC* ic00073000: 221 known copies worldwide. Sotheby (1938), 67, lot 517. The Francis A. Countway Library catalogue records the presence of the purple 'Selwyn College' stamp and the donor collection: the Solomon M. Hyams Collection.

[43] Matthaeus Bossus, *Recuperationes faesulanae*. See *ISTC* ib01045000: 118 known copies worldwide. Sotheby (1938), 67, lot 520.

[44] Johannes Bessarion, *In calumniatorem Platonis lib. IV* (Aldus, 1516); Virgil, *Opera* (Plantin, 1575). Sotheby (1938), 68, lot 522.

[45] Minutes of Meeting, 9 December 1938, Box 2, Selwyn College Papers, 84–086, Hocken Library. See also Hargreaves (1993), 49.

In the Cambridge University Library, there is a copy of Bartholomaeus Platina's *De flosculis linguae latinae; de amore ad Ludovicum Agnellum*, completed in Milan by Antonius Zarotus, for Johannes de Legnano, on 18 August 1481. This large folio has the Latin inscription 'Collegij Ste Maria Seculte Mli' on fol.1, identifiable with the Padri Somaschi of Santa Maria Segreta at Milan, Italy, and Shoults's inscription 'W. A. Shoults B.D'.[46] The fact that it does not have the purple 'Selwyn College' stamp and was sold through Leighton in London in May 1895 (lot 1238) means that it was most likely left with Eliza Shoults, who sold it on.

The other missing incunable is a copy of Boethius's *De disciplina scolarium*, completed by Georg Husner in Strasbourg in 1491. Now in the Folger Shakespeare Library, Washington, D.C., it carries Shoults's inscription 'W. A. Shoults B.D.' and, on the front flyleaf 'Ex lib. Joh: Edgar Ker, Willoughthorpe, Herts, 24. Ap. 95'. Further sale details are found at the back of the book: 'Willoughthorpe 24 Ap. 94 Lot 691' and 'Sotheby 24-4-95.'[47] Ker (1818–1904) was a book collector, who had an administrative career with the São Paulo Railway Company and lived at Willoughthorpe (now a care facility), Stanstead Abbotts, Hertfordshire. The Boethius lacks the purple 'Selwyn College' stamp, meaning that this book too was kept and later disposed of by Eliza.

D.G. ESPLIN

David G. Esplin was a reference librarian at the University of Otago Library and honorary librarian at Selwyn College. For this latter position he was paid an honorarium of £50 per annum. Esplin had a deep interest in early printing and spent evenings and weekends cataloguing the Shoults Collection. He also identified many of the English books printed before 1701 in the collection for inclusion in Pollard and Redgrave's *Short-title Catalogue* (1475–1640), and Donald Wing's *Short-title Catalogue* (1641–1700). As he wrote in one of his articles published in *New Zealand Libraries*: 'The purpose of this article is twofold, to make known the holdings of English books published before the year 1701 in some Dunedin libraries, and to supply additions and corrections to extant catalogues.'[48] Esplin left New Zealand in May 1962, taking up a library position at UCLA. He later moved to the University of Toronto Library, playing a large part in building up its fine collection. He died in 1983.

In 1951, Esplin noted the parlous state of the Shoults Collection and arranged

---

[46] Bartholomaeus Platina, *De flosculis linguae latinae*. See *ISTC* ip00760000: 30 known copies worldwide; Inc.4.B.7.1[1879], Cambridge University Library, Cambridge.

[47] Boethius (Pseudo), *De disciplina scolarium*. See *ISTC* ib00822000: 41 known copies worldwide; INC B737, Folger Shakespeare Library, Washington, D.C.

[48] Esplin (1960), 229–32 (229).

for the transfer of the incunables to the University Library.⁴⁹ The transfer was short-lived, because, in about 1956, these books were returned to Selwyn, facing again less than satisfactory conditions. In May 1955, just prior to the move back, Esplin had been delegated to catalogue the collection. In 1957, he submitted a report to the Trustees stressing three important aspects: to complete the cataloguing, to keep the library collection up to date, and to better house it.⁵⁰

Apart from improving the bibliographical records of some of the books, Esplin did manage to promote the collection. A large full-spread article in the *Evening Star* of 15 October 1960 was headed 'Selwyn College Can Be Proud Of Its Library'. This illustrated overview was aimed at general readers, and the catalyst for it, as stated by the newspaper reporter, was that an honours student from Canterbury University had written to Selwyn College asking to see the first Greek edition of Zosimus. The Shoults Collection had the only copy in New Zealand, and Esplin (as custodian) was happy to assist. A few books from the collection were mentioned in the article: *Summa de casibus conscientae* completed by Mentelin in 1472 that contains an inky cat-paw print; the first English translation by James Mabbe of *The Rogue* by Mateo Aleman, published in 1623 for Edward Blount, one of the publishers of Shakespeare's First Folio (1623); John Speed's *The Theatre of the Empire of Great Britain* (1627); the bedside book by John Marlow entitled *Letters to a Sick Friend* (1682); and *Great Britain's Coasting Pilot* (1749), which reproduced on plates the original maps of Captain Grenville Collins, Hydrographer Royal to Charles II. The article ended on a high note: 'Selwyn is aware that it is certainly favoured in owning the Shoults Collection. Never again will it ever suffer from neglect or disuse.'⁵¹

In 1962, another cull took place: a manuscript comprising Bonaventura's *Decem sermones Nominus Ihesus* and Augustine's *Liber soliliquiorum*, written by a scribe in the convent of Celestines of Amiens, c.1460. This volume was sold through the bookseller Maggs in London, appearing in their catalogue 890, *Early Presses and Monastic Libraries of North-west Europe* (1964), no. 117 (and plate XXXVI).⁵² The text of this manuscript, mainly on paper, with a vellum title-page, occupies 82 leaves. It was priced at £25. Previous owners include Edmund Gill Swain, M.A., Emmanuel and King's College, Cambridge (bookplate), and Shoults, who is named 'Shoulto'. His distinctive inscription 'Wm Arderne Shoults, B.D.' runs across the head of the title page.

There were other books disposed of, but they can no longer be identified. They

---

⁴⁹ See Taylor (1955), 57, where he states: 'the incunabula are now lodged'.
⁵⁰ Minutes from Meeting, 5 May 1955 and 5 June 1957, Minute book, September 1948–July 1975, Box 2, Selwyn College Papers, 84–086, Hocken Library.
⁵¹ 'Selwyn College Can Be Proud Of Its Library'. *Evening Star*, 15 October 1960, 3.
⁵² Maggs (1964), 117; see also de Hamel, in Manion (1989), 80.

may have been part of a consignment sent to a Chicago book dealer in 1962, who forwarded the sum of $95.68 to the College for sales realised. This time the money was earmarked for the purchase of new books.[53]

TRANSFER AND LEGACY

Fortunately for the Shoults Collection, the Esplin spirit and enthusiasm were passed to the new University Librarian W. J. (Jock) McEldowney, who began his term in 1961 (ending 1987), and the then reference librarian Don G. Jamieson. McEldowney realised the usefulness to the University of a fully-catalogued collection. He delegated Jamieson to organise the cataloguing of it and to ensure that there was reasonable access to the books. McEldowney also assured Canon (later Archdeacon) Douglas Stewart Millar, Warden of Selwyn College from 1955 to 1969, that 'this is not a take-over bid'.[54] The honorarium allocated to Esplin was to be added to a fund for the purchase of books for the College Library. By November 1962, the English books published between 1573 and 1700 and the Italian books published between 1501 and 1600 had been catalogued. The uncatalogued remainder—the German, Swiss and Low Countries publications—were filed by their imprint date.

By June 1965, McEldowney raised the possibility of housing the collection in the University Library, voicing his concern that it was 'of very great scholarly value' and that it should be protected from the possibility of damage and deterioration. As he wrote to Canon Millar, there was the added advantage: 'that the two largest collections of early printed books in Dunedin could be consulted in one building, and that our Reference Librarian [Jamieson], who already has general supervisory function in co-operation with you will be able to carry out these functions more expeditiously.'[55] Notice was given confirming that ownership of the collection was to remain with Selwyn College; that the collection was to be placed at the University on long-term loan; that the Selwyn Board could revoke the loan at any time; and that the University would continue to house the collection, which would be in a closed-stack area and kept separate from the other rare book collections. Standard rare book rules were drawn up governing use by readers.

---

[53] Hargreaves (1993), 49.
[54] W.J. McEldowney to Canon D.S. Millar, 31 August 1962, Shoults Collection Archive, 708/2, MS–3910/019, Hocken Library.
[55] W.J. McEldowney to Canon D.S. Millar, 1 June 1965, Shoults Collection Archive, 708/2, MS–3910/019, Hocken Library.

By 28 July 1965, the Selwyn College Board had ratified the proposal. The Shoults Collection was on the move again, but this time to a more stable home. The entire collection was valued for insurance purposes at £31,200, some £6 per volume. The Board decided to distinguish the Shoults books from other rare books held at the University Library. They therefore delegated someone in the library (perhaps Jamieson) to engage Stantons on King Street to make one large and one small rubber stamps, which read: 'William Arderne Shoults Collection, Selwyn College, Dunedin.'[56] These new stamps complemented the older, less-than-aesthetically-pleasing larger purple 'Selwyn College' stamp.

The *Evening Star* was again called on to announce the good news. Under the heading 'Around the University', an article began: 'One of New Zealand's outstanding literary treasures has been transferred for safe keeping to the new University Library this week, by its owners, Selwyn College.'[57] It was deemed 'a satisfactory close [to] the long chapter of events in the story of the collection since its arrival in New Zealand'. Much of the information on books from the 1960 article was repeated, along with a succinct account of how the collection had made it to New Zealand. Esplin was again congratulated on his achievement. The article ended on a high: 'This is a rich fund of material which scholars at the University and in the community will rejoice to see in good keeping and available for study under appropriate conditions.'

Don Jamieson also provided a breakdown of the Shoults Collection in *New Zealand Libraries*. His article gave a brief history, focusing on the magazines in the collection, such as the *London Magazine*, the *Universal Magazine*, the *European Magazine*, and the *Royal Female Magazine*. He also gave members of the library profession an idea of use of the material to date, noting D.H. Borchardt's article on the incunables and manuscripts published in *New Zealand Libraries* (1948), David Taylor's *The Oldest Manuscripts in New Zealand* (1955), Esplin's work on the short-title catalogues of Pollard and Wing, and Keith Maslen's article on books printed by the Bowyers, in *New Zealand Libraries* (1962).[58]

MODERN TIMES

In January 2002, the new University of Otago Library was opened, featuring a new Special Collections area. This newly-formed space encompassed an environmentally-

---

[56] W.J. McEldowney to G.M. Broad, Registrar, University of Otago, 16 September 1965. See accompanying note to McEldowney by Jamieson on the stamp. Shoults Collection Archive, 708/2, MS–3910/019, Hocken Library.

[57] Phineas, [R.G. Lister], 'Around the University', *Evening Star*, 5 October 1965, 2.

[58] Jamieson (1965), Borchardt (1948), Taylor (1955), Esplin (1960), and Maslen (1962).

controlled stack area to house all the rare books and manuscripts, a reading room, and a display area, called the de Beer Gallery, after benefactor Esmond de Beer. A quarterly programme of exhibitions was established. As part of the new Library celebrations, Michael Wooliscroft, the University Librarian, established the position of Special Collections Librarian. Maintenance of the rare book collections (De Beer, Charles Brasch, Shoults, and others), collection development, and promotion were the key goals. A Special Collections booklet was published, giving a succinct outline of the various collections.[59]

Prior to these developments, the rare book collection had been supervised by successive reference librarians, Elizabeth Tinker and Jean Klemp. Over this period, use of the Shoults Collection was confined to individual researchers, small, themed exhibitions, and initiatives such as a 'Shoults Evening' on 19 April 2001, attended by twenty people, who viewed some forty-six items from the collection.[60]

Register books record past use of the Shoults Collection in the old University library. In November 1993, a lecturer from the Classics Department consulted a copy of Johan Jakob Wettstein's *Prolegomena ad Novum Testamentum* (1764). In August 1994, a reader used copies of William Beveridge's *Codex canonum ecclesiæ primitivæ vindicatus ac illustratus* (1678), Justini's *Opera* (1686), St. Augustine's *Operum* (1729–1735), and Cavalieri's *Opera omnia liturgica* (1758). In September 1994, a small display was mounted at St. Paul's Cathedral, Dunedin. This event featured five books, comprising the Cranmer-associated *Reformatio legum ecclesiasticarum* (1640), Isaac Barrow's *Works* (1683), Justini's *Opera* (1686), Richard Hooker's *Works* (1723), and an unrecorded Beveridge title.

The St. Paul's Cathedral display sparked a much larger exhibition in Special Collections, entitled 'Reconstructing the Canon'. Curated by Elizabeth Tinker and assisted by Dr Stephen Gamble, a London-based scholar related to Shoults's great-grandfather, Peter Martin Shoults (1747–1812), this exhibition began in February 1995.[61] Some 23 books featured, including copies of Hesychus of Alexandria's *Dictionarium* (1514), Cesare Baronio's *Annales eclesiastici ex XII tomis* (1618), Isaac Casaubon's *Exercitationes XVI* (1663), and Thomas Salmon's *An Impartial Examination of Bishop Burnet's History of His Own Times* (1724). It is difficult to ascertain how much of an impact the 'Canon' exhibition had on use, but 1995 proved

---

[59] *Special Collections at the University of Otago* (2011).
[60] Special Collections Register, May 1996 to December 2001. Special Collections, University of Otago.
[61] In 1995, Dr Stephen Gamble compiled his 'Secondary literature on Shoults's library, with additional mention of other antiquarian collections in the University and other libraries at Dunedin', much of which was used for caption information in the exhibition. See Charmian Smith, 'Clergyman's personality sought through his books', *Otago Daily Times*, 7 March 1995, 15.

a productive year. An exhibition centring on Tycho Brahe was also mounted, with Shoults's copies of Brahe's *Astronomiae instauratae mechanica* (1602) and Christiaan Huygens's *Opuscula postuma, quae continent dioptricam* (1703) displayed. There was also a small flurry of interest from the Classics Department in Shoults's holdings of Cicero, and lecturers from the English Department used his holdings of Tasso, Dante, and Petrarch for teaching purposes. In February 1996, Elizabeth Tinker mounted an exhibition devoted to the incunables that the University of Otago held, displaying 22 from the Shoults Collection. And occasionally there was an overseas enquiry. One scholar from Germany wrote asking for information on Shoults's copy of Conrad of Halberstadt's *Liber tripartitus moralium*, one of the three medieval manuscripts in the collection.

Over the following years, there was a slight increase in use, but the numbers have never matched those from the de Beer Collection, a much more accessible collection of rare books, especially in the fields of garden history (John Evelyn) and philosophy (John Locke). In 1996, 28 Shoults books, aside from those displayed, were used, while 141 were used from de Beer; in 1997, 19 from Shoults, 135 from de Beer; in 1998, 11 from Shoults, 100 from de Beer; in 1999, 5 from Shoults, 33 from de Beer; and in 2000, 28 from Shoults (including sixteen enquiries from the Early Imprint Project (EIP) at the British Library), and 83 from de Beer. In 2001, the rare book collections were temporarily housed in a building in Leith Street during the rebuilding of the University Library. Use in that year was 24 Shoults books, 136 de Beer. In 2002, with the new Special Collections area established in the new library, use was 15 Shoults books, 179 de Beer. In 2003, 20 Shoults books, 119 de Beer; in 2004, 25 Shoults books, and 95 de Beer.[62]

The year 2005 was a bumper one, with 102 Shoults books used. This increase was largely through the 2005 Rare Books Summer School, which featured courses run by Dr Christopher de Hamel, Dr Brian McMullin, Professor Wallace Kirsop, and Keith Maslen. In addition, an Arabic Summer School programme led by Princeton scholar Dr Justin Steams saw some 20 Middle Eastern books and the manuscripts from the Shoults Collection being used. In 2006, 45 Shoults books were used, 183 de Beer; in 2007 17 Shoults, 95 de Beer; and in 2008 15 Shoults, and 93 de Beer. In 2009, the Rare Books Summer School returned, with David Pearson (City of London) running a Provenance course, and Eric Holzenberg (Grolier Society) and Donald Kerr running

---

[62] The Brasch Collection, a twentieth-century book collection at Special Collections, registered 115 in 2003 and 267 in 2004. These relatively high figures were due to the increased interest in Charles Brasch, especially given that in 2003 the embargo was lifted on his personal papers at the Hocken Library. For further details, see the *Annual Report* issued by the University of Otago Library (2003).

an Exhibitions course. Some 21 Shoults books were used for these two courses. In 2010, 22 Shoults books were consulted and 45 from the de Beer collection. After 2011, to simplify registration, the collection field (Shoults, de Beer, Brasch, etc) was dropped from the Special Collections Register, making it very difficult to identify use from any one of them. In 2016, a Book History course was run through the Rare Books Summer School. Instructor David McKitterick used numerous books from the Shoults Collection as teaching examples.

It is fair to say that the use of the Shoults Collection by readers and scholars has been patchy. There are a number of reasons that contribute to the low use. The first is the aspect of language. Even though the majority of the books in the collection are in English, there are others in Latin, French, and Hebrew that pose a barrier, especially to present-day students, who tend to be monolingual. The second is subject matter. Despite the strong showing by staff and students of the Theology and Religious Studies Departments at the University, there seems to be little interest in ecclesiastical history, issues surrounding Anglo-Catholicism, and early printing, at least in Dunedin. This aspect is closely allied to the last reason: the promotion and awareness of what is in the collection. Many researchers, University staff, and students do not know what the Shoults Collection is and what it offers. Exhibitions and subject inventories have increased its visibility, but there is still much to do to increase engagement, to reveal the strengths of the collection, and to make them useful to readers. Promotion to increase the awareness of this under-utilised resource continues.

Research trends come and go, and scholars who want to see and touch the physical item, as opposed to virtual versions, request books or manuscripts from the collection, which is now fully catalogued. Requests are often made for one or two items only, and usually not for any sustained length of time. Some more recent users have examined a copy of Johannes Wolleb's *Compendium theologiæ Christianæ* (1642), in connection with John Milton and *De doctrina Christiana*, while another, writing a book on time, dipped into the many Scaliger books in Shoults, especially *De emendatione temporum* (1629). One perennial favourite with English Department lecturers (Drs Shef Rogers and Paul Tankard) is Shoults's copy of Dr Johnson's *The History of Rasselas, Prince of Abissinia*, published in London in 1799. The two publications that have highlighted the Shoults holdings of manuscripts have already been mentioned: David M. Taylor's *The Oldest Manuscripts in New Zealand* (1955) and Margaret M. Manion, Vera F. Vines, and Christopher de Hamel's *Medieval and Renaissance Manuscripts in New Zealand Collections* (1989). The latter is a significant contribution from de Hamel, a former Dunedin-based resident and Otago graduate, and it has done much to spread the word of the University of Otago's medieval manuscript holdings.

EXHIBITIONS

One particular avenue for highlighting items in the Shoults Collection has been the exhibitions organised and mounted four times a year in a dedicated space in the new library. Since 2002, there have been 72, each with its own distinctive theme. Esmond de Beer is recognised as the prime benefactor of Special Collections, and many of the first displays focused on his collection: travel, architecture, John Locke, and garden history. One of the exhibitions that displayed a number of Shoults books was *Initials: In the Beginning*, which ran from 17 October to 14 December 2007.[63] The elements of this exhibition were not text-reliant, and so samples of manuscript, coloured, historiated, floriated, inhabited, and arabesque initials within the books were shown. Another exhibition had a bibliopegic focus, *From Pigskin to Paper: The Art and Craft of Bookbinding*, which ran from 20 December 2012 to 22 March 2013.[64] Curated by Romilly Smith, Special Collections assistant and a trained binder, this exhibition allowed many of the original pigskin and vellum bindings from the Shoults Collection to be shown. Of particular note was the rare example of the Rood and Hunt binding in de Lyra's *Commentaries* (1481; see chapter 14). And there have been displays that have been a perfect fit for the materials in Shoults: a Classics-related exhibition entitled *Maths, Politics, and Concrete: The Legacy of the Classical World*, which ran from 28 June to 20 September 2013, numerous Shoults books were displayed.[65] Four years later, Special Collections celebrated the quincentenary of the posting of the Ninety-five Theses on the door of All Saints' Church, Wittenberg, in 1517. The exhibition, *500 Years On. Martin Luther and the Protestant Reformation*, ran from 24 March to 9 June 2017 and featured many books from the Shoults Collection.[66] In 2018, an exhibition entitled *A Middle Eastern Odyssey: Constantinople to Palmyra* ran from 16 March to 1 June 2018.[67] The vast majority of items on exhibition were from Shoults, many of them the Turkish, Persian, Urdu, and Arabic books and manuscripts discussed in chapter 13. One additional result from this exhibition was the compilation of an inventory of Middle Eastern materials in Special Collections, produced by Drs Majid Danesghar and Donald Kerr.[68]

---

[63] *Initials. In the Beginning* (2007). Curated by Catherine Robertson.
[64] *From Pigskin to Paper: The Art and Craft of Bookbinding* (2013). Curated by Romilly Smith.
[65] *Maths, Politics and Concrete: The Legacy of the Classical World* (2013). Curated by Romilly Smith.
[66] *500 Years On. Martin Luther and the Protestant Reformation* (2017).
[67] *A Middle Eastern Odyssey: Constantinople to Palmyra* (2018).
[68] Daneshgar (2017).

Importantly, since 2002, almost all of the physical exhibitions mounted have been put online. Freely available to all, they remain an excellent resource for students, staff, and the wider community, and further promote the holdings of the Special Collections.[69] Inventories of the manuscripts and the incunables have also been put online.[70] These too promote the holdings of Special Collections, especially those of the Shoults Collection.

CODA

The arrival of the Shoults Collection in Dunedin was a significant event, especially for those at Selwyn College. Indeed, it was the second-largest collection of rare book materials in the country, exceeded only by the Grey Collection, which had been given to the Auckland Free Public Library by Governor Sir George Grey in 1887. The Shoults Collection was heralded as a rich resource for theological students and interested clergy; there was promise of bright beginnings.

It is true that the Shoults Collection is a significant library not just in Dunedin, but also in New Zealand. It remains a fine example of what would have been possible to collect at that time in those particular subject fields. However, it is not a deluxe library filled with high-spot items: it is a working library formed gradually over the years by a nineteenth-century cleric who had predilections for ecclesiastical history, patristics, philology, and Anglo-Catholicism.

Shoults was a bookish intellectual who passed through a very short life with no known scandal or controversy attached to his name. He would have remained an unremarkable curate were it not for the generosity of his wife and the timely initiative by Bishop Nevill in acquiring his library for the colony. It is amazing that it is in Dunedin, let alone that it has survived virtually intact.

In 1986, Jim Traue, the then Alexander Turnbull Librarian, included Shoults in a list of thirty-two private book collectors whose collecting had enriched New Zealand's public institutions by bequest, gift, or sale. To him they were all 'patriots', their collections contributing to the pool of books and manuscripts available in New Zealand. As he wrote, 'Without them the resources for scholarship and research in our libraries would be pitifully weak and our ability to understand our distinctively New Zealand experience would be greatly hindered'.[71] Even though Shoults never visited New Zealand, his collection is here—his more tangible and lasting legacy.

---

[69] General Link: www.otago.ac.nz/library/specialcollections/exhibitions.html.
[70] *Incunabula. Special Collections* (2009); *Manuscripts in Special Collections, University of Otago* (2011).
[71] Traue (1991), 28–42.

The field of book history, especially research encompassing the artefactual, means that the Shoults Collection stands as an important physical resource for students and scholars, both in New Zealand and overseas. This fine resource, permanently placed at the University of Otago, waits patiently for readers and greater use. A prelate is reported to have said many years ago: 'Spare me from the English clergyman of wide and miscellaneous learning.'[72] Selwyn College in Dunedin, the University of Otago, and the wider research community will not (and should not) cease to be grateful to just such a clergyman and book collector as the Rev. William Arderne Shoults.

---

[72] 'Selwyn College Can Be Proud Of Its Library', *Evening Star*, 15 October 1960, 3.

BIBLIOGRAPHY

The primary source used in writing this book on William Arderne Shoults has been his books and manuscripts themselves, along with associated Reader registers, held at Special Collections, University of Otago, Dunedin, New Zealand.

CAMBRIDGE, ENGLAND
    Archives, St. John's College
    DS3.2-6, Junior Dean's Register
    DS4, Senior Dean's Register
    Parkinson/3/2/1 Address Book
    SJAC/1/2/France Tutorial Files
    SJAR/1/2/Parkinson/2/1/1 Examination Books 1848-1895
    SJAR/1/3/1/2 Parkinson, 2/3
    SJAR/6/1/4 Admission Registers
    SJAR/6/1/5/1-5 Register of terms kept and residence book
    SJAR /6/1/6/2 College Admission and Register
    SJAR 6/1/13/8 Rediit Register
    SJAR/8/1/1/1/4-6 Senior Dean's Records 1852
    SJCS/15 Records of the Debating Society
    SJHR/1/22 List of Scholarships and Exhibitioners
    St. John's College Biography Card Index

Special Collections, St. John's College Library
    Examination Papers collected by Parkinson, CA Exam.L.9 1824–1883 and Exam.L.68
    Parkinson, Notebooks (19)
    Parkinson Papers, GBR/0275/Parkinson

Cambridge Public Library
    Cambridgeshire Collection, local histories, directories

Cambridge University Library
    Bachelor of Divinity Class Catalogue
    Ely Diocesan Records, Visitation Packets, GBR/0012/MS EDR
    Charles Wisbey's Auction Sheet, November 1859. Map Room, Maps.PSQ.bb.18.210

LONDON

British Library
    John Julian, Music Collections Add MS 57496-57520, Add MS 69037
    James Mearns, Music Collections Add MS 69438
    John Mitford sale catalogue, Shelfmark S.C.S. 475

British Museum
  Reader Card Indexes, Reading Room

Lambeth Palace Library
  E. W. Benson Papers, Vol. 48, 1887: Home J. 79–M.90
  Burial registers, 1837-1961, IV/100/51–90
  Archbishop Sir Henry Longley Papers, 4
  Ollard Papers, MS 3388
  Tait Papers, Vols. 121–290

London Metropolitan Archives

  . *St Peter's Walworth*
  Clerical Register, P92/PET1/97: January 1850–January 1864
  Clerical Register, P92/PET1/98: January 1864–December 1870
  London Diocese Ordination Papers, St. Peter's Walworth, 1863–1865, Deacon and Priest Folder, 9651–10390 no.12: DL/A/B/004/MS10326/269 – 2751863. December 1863–November 1864
  Minute Book, April 1849–July 1882. P92/PET1/124/1
  Walworth Schools, 1846–1870, P92/PET1/137

  . *St. Paul's, Bunhill Row*
  Bunhill Row, Islington, P76/PAU1/008

  . *St. Edmund the Martyr, City of London*
  Preachers' Book for the United Parishes of St. Edmund the King and Martyr with St. Nicholas Acons, 1866–1883, P69/edk/a/015/Ms 18495/003
  Vestry Book for the United Parishes of St. Edmund the King and Martyr with St. Nicholas Acons, 1871–1930, P69/edk/b/004/Ms 11261/001

Southwark
  Southwark Local Studies Library: Vine Yard, Southwark Indenture, 23 January 1858. Covenant between William Shoults of Maddingley Road, Cambridge, gentleman and Elizabeth his wife, and the Board of Works of St. Olave. MS 40638

OXFORD

Bodleian Library
  Correspondence of Falconer Madan, Bodleian Librarian, 1912–1919, ME–MY, dated 1882–1900 Library Records d.302

NEW ZEALAND

Dunedin

Hocken Library

Anglican Diocese of Dunedin Records, ARC-0142
Bishop Nevill Family Papers, MS-0876
Bishop Nevill Papers, AG-349-010/009, ARC-0209, MS-0161-0164
Selwyn College Library, MS-3910/020
Selwyn College Papers, 84-086
Shoults Collection Archive, 708/2, MS-3910/019
Synod Minute Book 1887-1902, AG-349-003/003

Special Collections

Reader registers (uncatalogued)

ANCESTRY.COM SEARCHES

(from Public Record Office (PRO), now The National Archives).

William Shoults (1777-1846), carpenter and builder
England & Wales, Prerogative Court of Canterbury Wills, England: will, December, PROB 11/2047/19/901-950 (1846)/ 254

William Shoults (1812-1878), carpenter, builder, gentleman
Deed Reference SLS 4638, Southwark, England: will, 20 August 1878. no. 349
COW249612

William Arderne Shoults (1839-1887), cleric
Bermondsey, St. Olave, Southwark baptisms: William Arderne Shoults, 24 April 1839, no. 1100
1841: England and Wales census, St. Olave, Surrey, England, United Kingdom, citing PRO HO 107/1087/11/ 12
1851: England census, Thanet St. Lawrence, England, United Kingdom, citing PRO HO 107/1630/128/28
1861: England and Wales census, Camberwell, London, England, United Kingdom, citing PRO RG 9/378/101/6
1871: England census, Islington, St. John, London, England, United Kingdom, citing PRO RG 10/275/39/13
1881: England and Wales census, William Arderne and Eliza Shoults: Camberwell, London, England, United Kingdom, citing PRO RG 11/673/73/12
1887: England and Wales, National Probate Calendar (Index of Wills and Administrations), 1858-1995, England, will of William Arderne Shoults, 11 May 1887, 646

Eliza Katharine Shoults, née Ogle

1842: St. Luke, Chelsea, Parish Register for baptism of Eliza Katharine Ogle, 15 Jan 1843, no. 1012

1861: England and Wales census, Brompton, London, England, United Kingdom, citing PRO RG 9/22/11/14

1871: England census, Kensington, London, England, United Kingdom, citing PRO RG 10/56/22/35

1881: England and Wales census, William Arderne and Eliza Shoults: Camberwell, London, England, United Kingdom, citing PRO RG 11/673/73/12

1891: England census, Camberwell, London, England, United Kingdom, citing PRO RG 10/465/74/10

1901: England and Wales census, Camberwell, London, England, United Kingdom, citing PRO RG 13/493/121/13

1911: England and Wales census, Camberwell, London, England, United Kingdom, citing PRO RG 14/3453/249

1912–1914: England and Wales, National Probate Calendar (Index of Wills and Administrations), 1858–1995, will of Eliza Katharine Shoults Last Will and Testament, 31 December 1912; 16 May 1914 (Codicil)

1914: Surrey Church of England Parish Registers, Woking, England, Burial Eliza Katharine Shoults, EKS no. 2391, reference: P33/1/42

Marriages

1841: St. Luke, Chelsea, Parish Register for marriage of John Connell Ogle and Eliza Margaret Maplestone, 7 October 1841, no. 248

1878: St. Luke, Chelsea, Parish Register for marriage of William Arderne Shoults and Eliza Katharine Ogle, 1 August 1878, no. 58

Joseph Leycester Lyne 'Father Ignatius'

1861: England and Wales census, St. Andrew Parish, Plymouth, England, United Kingdom, citing PRO RG 9/1439/30/53

✤

PRINTED BOOKS AND ARTICLES

Adams (1954). H.M. Adams, 'The Shakespeare Collection in the Library of Trinity College, Cambridge', in *Shakespeare Survey*, 5, 50–4

Allchin (1958). A.M. Allchin, *The Silent Rebellion: Anglican Religious Communities 1845–1900*. London: SCM Press

Allen (2016). Hugh Allen, *New Llanthony Abbey: Father Ignatius's Monastery at Capel-y-ffin*. [Oxford]: Peterscourt Press

Alphabetical List (1871). *Alphabetical List of the Signatures to a Remonstrance addressed to the Archbishops and Bishops of the Church of England on occasion of the Report of the*

Judicial Committee of the Privy Council In Re Herbert v. Purchas. London: Sold by Messrs. James Parker

Altholz (1989). Josef L. Althoz, *The Religious Press in Britain, 1760–1900.* New York: Greenwood Press

Altick (1957). Richard D. Altick, *The English Common Reader: A Social History of the Mass Reading Public 1800–1900.* Chicago: The University of Chicago Press

Alumni Dublinenses (1924). *Alumni Dublinenses.* London: Burtchaell & Sadler

Alumni Oxonienses (1888). *Alumni Oxonienses: The Members of the University of Oxford 1715–1886.* Compiled by Joseph Foster. Oxford: Parker

Anderson (1991). Patricia Anderson, *The Printed Image and the Transformation of Popular Culture 1790–1860.* Oxford: Clarendon Press

Andrews (2017). Robert M. Andrews, 'High Church Anglicanism in the Nineteenth Century', in *The Oxford History of Anglicanism, III: Partisan Anglicanism and its Global Expansion 1829–c.1914.* London: Oxford University Press

Annan (1984). Noel Annan, *Leslie Stephen. The Godless Victorian.* London: Weidenfeld and Nicolson

Anson (1964). Peter F. Anson, *The Call of the Cloister: Religious Communities and Kindred Bodies in the Anglican Communion.* London: SPCK

Anson (2015). ——, *Building up the Waste Places: The Revival of Monastic Life on Medieval Lines in the Post-Reformation Church of England.* Eugene, Oregon: Wipf & Stock

Attwater (1931). Donald Attwater, *Father Ignatius of Llanthony.* London: Cassell

Ayalon (2008). Yaron Ayalon, 'Richelieu in Arabic. "The Catholic Printed Message to the Orient in the Seventeenth Century"', in *Islam and Christian-Muslim Relations*, 19, 151–65

Bagshaw (1847). Samuel Bagshaw, *History, Gazetteer & Directory of Kent*, II. Sheffield: For the Author

Baird (1899). Henry Martyn Baird, *Theodore Beza: The Counsellor of the French Reformation.* New York: Putnam

Bamford (1967). T. W. Bamford, *Rise of the Public Schools: A Study of Boys' Public Boarding Schools in England and Wales from 1837 to the Present Day.* London: Nelson

Barker (1978). Nicolas Barker, *Bibliotheca Lindesiana.* London: Bernard Quaritch

Barnett (1921). Henrietta Barnett, *Canon Barnett: His Life, Work, and Friends.* London: John Murray

Bayle (1737). Peter Bayle, *Dictionary Historical and Critical.* Second edition. 4. London: Printed for D. Midwinter [and others]

Beard (1982). Geoffrey Beard, *The Work of Christopher Wren.* Edinburgh: John Bartholomew & Son

Begheyn (2014). Paul Begheyn, *Jesuit Books in the Dutch Republic and its Generality Lands: A Bibliography.* Leiden: Brill

Bell (1993). Bill Bell, 'Fiction in the Marketplace: Towards a Study of the Victorian Serial', in *Serials and their Readers, 1620-1914*. Edited by Robin Myers and Michael Harris. Winchester: St Paul's Bibliographies

Benedict XVI (2009). Benedict XVI, *The Fathers of the Church: From Clement of Rome to Augustine of Hippo*. Grand Rapids, Michigan: William B. Eerdmans Publishing Company

Besant (1902). Walter Besant, *Autobiography*. London: Hutchinson

Besterman (1940). Theodore Besterman, *The Beginnings of Systematic Bibliography*. Second edition. London: Oxford University Press

Bibliotheca Biblica (1720–1735). *Bibliotheca Biblica*. Oxford: Printed at the Theater, for W. and J. Innys

Bibliotheca Colbertina (1728). *Bibliotheca Colbertina*. Paris: Gabriel Martin and François Montalant

Bibliotheca Heberiana (1834). *Bibliotheca Heberiana: Catalogue of the Library of the Late Richard Heber: Part the First*. London: Sotheby

Bibliotheca Parriana (1827). *Bibliotheca Parriana. A Catalogue of the Library of the late Reverend and Learned Samuel Parr*. Compiled by John Bohn. London: C. Richards for John Bohn and Joseph Mawman

Bibliotheca Pinelliana (1789). *Bibliotheca Pinelliana: A Catalogue of the Magnificent and Celebrated Library of Maffei Pinelli, Late of Venice*. London: Robson and Clarke

Birrell (1991). T. A. Birrell, 'Reading as pastime: the place of light literature in some gentlemen's libraries of the 17th century', in *Property of a Gentleman: The Formation, Organisation and Dispersal of the Private Library 1620–1920*. Edited by Robin Myers and Michael Harris. Winchester: St Paul's Bibliographies

Bolton (1973). Diane K. Bolton and G. R. Duncombe, 'Parishes: Shepreth', in *A History of the County of Cambridge and the Isle of Ely*, 5. London: Oxford University Press

Bonney (1909). T.G. Bonney, 'A Septuagenarian's Recollections of St John's', in the *Eagle*, 30, 294–310

Bonney (1921). ——, *Memories of a Long Life*. Cambridge: Metcalfe

Booth (1902–1903). Charles Booth, *Life and Labour of the People in London*. Third edition. 7 vols. London: Macmillan

Borchardt (1948). D.H. Borchardt, 'Incunabula and Medieval Mss in Dunedin', in *New Zealand Libraries*, 11, 98–103

Bowers (2016). Paul M. Bowers, *Maximus the Confessor: Jesus Christ and the Transformation of the World*. Oxford: Oxford University Press

Brake (1993). Laurel Brake, '"The Trepidation of the Spheres": The Serial and the Book in the 19th Century', in *Serials and their Readers 1620–1914*. Edited by Robin Myers and Michael Harris. Winchester: St Paul's Bibliographies

Breslauer (1984). Bernard H. Breslauer and Roland Folter, *Bibliography: Its History and Development*. New York: The Grolier Club

Briquet (1968). C. M. Briquet, *Les Filigranes,* II. Amsterdam: The Paper Publications Society

Bristed (1852). Charles Astor Bristed, *Five Years in an English University.* London: Putnam

Brooke (2004). Christopher N. L. Brooke, *A History of the University of Cambridge,* IV: 1870–1990. Cambridge: Cambridge University Press

Brown (1891). James Brown, *The History of Sanquhar.* Dumfries: J. Anderson & Son

Brunet (1842). Jacques-Charles Brunet, *Manuel du Libraire et de l'Amateur de Livres.* Paris: Silvestre

Brunton (1832). George Brunton and David Haig, *An Historical Account of the Senators of the College of Justice.* London: Thomas Clark

Burrows (2007). J. Burrows, J. Edelman, and E. McKendrick, *Cases and Materials on the Law of Restitution.* Second edition. Oxford: Oxford University Press

Butler (1970). Samuel Butler, *The Way of All Flesh.* London: Heron Books

Calder-Marshall (1962). Arthur Calder-Marshall, *The Enthusiast: An Enquiry into the Life Beliefs and Character of the Rev. Joseph Leycester Lyne alias Fr. Ignatius, O.S.B., Abbot of Elm Hill, Norwich and Llanthony, Wales.* London: Faber & Faber

Calmard (1990). Jean Calmard, 'Aleksander Borejko Chodźko', in *Encyclopædia Iranica*, 5. Costa Mesa, California: Mazda Publishers, 502–4

Cambridge Antiquary Society (1860). Cambridge Antiquary Society, *Report*, General Meeting, 14 May 1860. Cambridge: Deighton, Bell

Cambridge Examination Papers (1858). *Cambridge Examination Papers: Being a Supplement to the University Calendar for the Year 1858.* Cambridge: Deighton, Bell

Cambridge University Calendar. *Cambridge University Calendar: 1858, 1859, 1860.* Cambridge: Deighton, Bell

Chadwick (1977). Owen Chadwick, 'Lord Acton at the First Vatican Council', in *Journal of Theological Studies*, New Series, XXVIII, Part 2, 465–97

Chadwick (1978). ——, *Catholicism and History: The Opening of the Vatican Archives.* Cambridge: Cambridge University Press

Chadwick (1987). ——, *The Victorian Church: I 1829–1859; II 1860–1901.* London: SCM Press

Chalmers (1815a). Alexander Chalmers, entry for 'Buckler', in *The General Biographical Dictionary Containing an Historical and Critical Account of the Lives and Writings of the Most Eminent Persons*, VII. London: J. Nichols, 240

Chalmers (1815b). ——, entry for 'Meninski, or Menin', in *The General Biographical Dictionary Containing an Historical and Critical Account of the Lives and Writings of the Most Eminent Persons*, XXII. London: J. Nichols, 52–4

Chamberlain (1991). William J. Chamberlain, *Catalogue of English Bible Translations.* New York: Greenwood Press

Chapman (1940). Guy Chapman, *Culture and Survival.* London: Jonathan Cape

Christie, Manson (1897). Christie, Manson & Woods, *Catalogue of the Collection of Pictures by Old Masters of the Late Reginald Cholmondeley, Esq.* London: Christie, Manson & Woods

Clark (1962). G. Kitson Clark, *The Making of Victorian England.* Cambridge, MA: Harvard University Press

Clarke (1966). Basil F.L. Clarke, *Parish Churches in London.* London: Batsford

Clarke (1974). M.L. Clarke, *Paley. Evidences for the Man.* London: SPCK

Cleveland (1910). Rose Elizabeth Cleveland, 'Preface', in *The Soliloquies by St Augustine of Hippo.* Boston: Little, Brown

College of Advocates (1818). College of Advocates, *Catalogue of the Books in the Library of the College of Advocates in Doctors' Commons.* London: Baldwin

Comerford (2015). Kathleen M. Comerford, 'Jesuits and their Books. Libraries and Printing around the World', in *Journal of Jesuit Studies,* 2, 179–88

Conte (1999). Gian Biagio Conte, *Latin Literature: A History.* Second edition. Baltimore: Johns Hopkins University Press

Cox (1997). K.F.S. Cox and W.R. Morris, *Archdeacon L. G. Whitehead: A Biography.* Christchurch, NZ: Pegasus

Craven (1855). *Craven and Co's Commercial Directory.* Cambridge, England

Crevenna (1789). *Catalogue de Livre de la Bibliotheque de M. Pierre-Antoine Bolongaro-Crevenna,* 4. Amsterdam: D. J. Changuion and P. Den Hengst

Crockford's (1865, 1868, 1879, 1884, and 1888). *Crockford's Clerical Directory.* London: Horace Cox

Dalberg-Acton (1906). John Dalberg-Acton, 1st Baron Acton, to an unknown correspondent, 10 December 1866. Letter CLVII, in *Lord Acton and his Circle.* Edited by Abbot Gasquet. New York: Longmans, Green, & Co

Daneshgar (2017). Majid Daneshgar and Donald Kerr, *Middle Eastern and Islamic Materials in Special Collections, University of Otago.* Dunedin: University of Otago

Darlington (1955). Ida Darlington, *Survey of London: 25, St George's Fields (The Parishes of St. George the Martyr* Southwark and St. Mary Newington). London: London County Council

Darlow (1911). T.H. Darlow and H. F. Moule, *Historical Catalogue of the Printed Editions of Holy Scripture in the Library of the British and Foreign Bible Society.* London: British and Foreign Bible Society

Davids (1882). [Arthur Lumley Davids], Review of 'Mr Davids' Grammar of the Turkish Language', in *The Asiatic Journal and Monthly Miscellany,* 9, 353–56

Davies (1875). C. Maurice Davies, *Unorthodox London: or, Phases of Religious Life in the Metropolis.* Third edition. London: Tinsley Brothers

Davys (1909–10). Owen William Davys, 'The Octogenarian's Recollections of a Member of St. John's College', in the *Eagle,* 31, 181–88

De Bertouch (1904). Baroness de Bertouch, *The Life of Father Ignatius O.S.B. The Monk of Llanthony*. London: Methuen

De Ricci (1969). Seymour de Ricci, *English Book Collectors & Manuscripts (1530–1930) and their Marks of Ownership*. New York: Burt Franklin (Reprint of 1930 ed.)

Dodsworth (2012). Francis Dodsworth and Sophie Watson, 'Into Unorthodox London: The Religious Ethnography of Charles Maurice Davies', in *Victorian Literature and Culture*. 40, 487–508

Drobner (2007). Hubertus R. Drobner, *The Fathers of the Church*. Peabody, MA: Hendrickson Publishers

Drummond (1992). Lewis A. Drummond, *Spurgeon: Prince of Preachers*. Grand Rapids, Michigan: Kregel Publications

Duff (2009). E. Gordon Duff, *Printing in England in the Fifteenth Century*. Revised by Lotta Hellinga. London: The Bibliographical Society

Dunedin Public Library (1924). Dunedin Public Library, New Zealand, *Departmental Reports for the Years 1914–1924*. Dunedin: Whitcombe & Tombs

Edwards (1971). David L. Edwards, *Leaders of the Church of England 1828–1944*. London: Oxford University Press

Ehrman (2013). Bard D. Ehrman, *Forgery and Counterforgery: The Use of Literary Deceit in Early Christian Polemics*. Oxford: Oxford University Press

Eliot (1998). George Eliot, *Middlemarch*. Oxford: Oxford University Press

Elliott (1993). J.K. Elliott, *The Apocryphal New Testament: A Collection of Apocryphal Christian Literature in an English Translation*. Oxford: Oxford University Press

Embry (1931). J. Embry, *The Catholic Movement and the Society of the Holy Cross*. London: The Faith Press

Esplin (1960). David G. Esplin, 'STC (Short Title Catalogue) and Wing STC Books in Dunedin', in *New Zealand Libraries*, 23, nos. 9, 10, and 11, 229–32, 254–63, 292–4

Evans (1828). R.H. Evans, *A Catalogue of the Valuable and Extensive Library of Samuel Parr*. London: Evans

Evelyn (1955). John Evelyn, *Diary*. Edited by Esmond de Beer. Oxford: Clarendon Press

Field (1828). William Field, *Memoirs of the Life, Writings, and Opinions of the Rev. Samuel Parr, LL.D.* London: Henry Colburn

Fischer (1966). Hans Fischer, 'Conrad Gesner (1516–1565) as Bibliographer and Encyclopedist', in *The Library*, 5th Series, XXI, 269–81

Fitzpatrick (1995). Barbara Laning Fitzpatrick, 'Charles Rivington', *Dictionary of Literary Biography*, 154. Detroit: Bruccoli Clark Layman Book Gale Research, 237–47

Flanders (2102). Judith Flanders, *The Victorian City: Everyday Life in Dickens' London*. London: Atlantic Books

Fletcher (1902). William Younger Fletcher, *English Book Collectors*. London: Kegan Paul, Trench, Trübner

Flood (2010). John L. Flood, 'The History of the Book in Germany', in *The Oxford Companion to the Book*. Edited by Michael F. Suarez and H. R. Woudhuysen. 1: Essays A–C. Oxford: Oxford University Press, 223–36

Gardner (1851). Robert Gardner, *History, Gazetteer, and Directory of Cambridgeshire*. Peterborough: Robert Gardner
Gerrard (2003), Christine Gerrard, *Aaron Hill. The Muses Projector 1685–1750*. Oxford: Oxford University Press
Gibbon (1776–1789). Edward Gibbon, *Decline and Fall of the Roman Empire*. London, Strahan & Cadell
Glassie (2012). John Glassie, *Man of Misconceptions: The Life of an Eccentric in an Age of Change*. New York: Penguin Putnam
Godwin (1839). George Godwin, *The Churches of London: A History and Description of the Ecclesiastical Edifices of the Metropolis*. London: C. Tilt
Grafton (1975). Anthony Grafton, 'Joseph Scaliger and Historical Chronologies. The Rise and Fall of a Discipline', in *History and Theory*, 14, 2, 156–85
Grafton (2001). ——, *Bring Out Your Dead: The Past as Revelation*. Cambridge, MA: Harvard University Press
Greenwood (1981). James Greenwood, *The Seven Curses of London*. Edited by Jeffrey Richards. Oxford: Basil Blackwell

Hamilton (1852). William Hamilton, *Discussion on Philosophy and Literature, Education and University Reform*. London: Longman, Brown, Green and Longman
Handbook of Rome (1881). *Handbook of Rome and its Environs*. London: John Murray
Härdelin (1965). Alf Härdelin, *The Tractarian Understanding of the Eucharist*. Stockholm: Almqvist & Wiksell
Hargreaves (1993). Ray Hargreaves, *Selwyn College's First Century: A History*. Dunedin: Centennial Committee, Selwyn College Board of Governors
Harman (1978). Marion Harman, *Incunabula in the University of Illinois Library at Urbana-Champaign*. Robert B. Downs Publication Fund, 5, The University of Illinois Library and Graduate School of Library Science. Urbana, Illinois: University of Illinois Press
Hart (1970). A. Tindal Hart, *The Curate's Lot: The Story of the Unbeneficed English Clergy*. London: John Baker
Hazlitt (1968). W.C. Hazlitt, 'An Alphabetical Roll of Book Collectors from 1316 to 1898', XII, in Bernard Quaritch, *Contributions towards a Dictionary of English Book-collectors*. New York: Burt Franklin (Reprint of 1892–1921 ed.)
Heitland (1921–1922). William E. Heitland, Review of T. G. Bonney's 'Memories', in the *Eagle*, XLII, 284
Hewitt (2013). Martin Hewitt, *The Dawn of the Cheap Press in Victorian Britain: the End of the 'Taxes on Knowledge', 1849–1869*. London: Bloomsbury

Hill (2007). Rosemary Hill, *God's Architect: Pugin and the Building of Romantic Britain*. London: Allen Lane

Hilton (2011). Boyd Hilton, 'The Nineteenth Century', in *St. John's College Cambridge*. Edited by Peter Linehan. Woodbridge, Suffolk: Boydell Press

Historical Register (1917). *Historical Register of the University of Cambridge to the Year 1910*. Edited by J.R. Tanner. Cambridge: Cambridge University Press

History of the County of Surrey (1967). *History of the County of Surrey. IV: Borough of Southwark*. Edited by H.E. Malden. London: The University of London Institute of Historical Research; reprinted by Dawsons of Pall Mall

Hoche (1889). Richard Hoche, 'Reinesius, Thomas', in *Allgemeine Deutsche Biographie* 28, 29–30

Hodgson (1861). J. Hodgson, *Catalogue of the Sale of Library of College of Advocates in Doctors' Commons*. London: Hodgson

Hollingshead (1986). John Hollingshead, *Ragged London in 1861*. London: Dent

Hoppen (2008). K. Theodore Hoppen, *The Mid-Victorian Generation 1846–1886*. Oxford: Clarendon Press

Horace (1942). Horace, *Satires, Epistles and Ars Poetica*. London: Heinemann, 1942

Hort (1896). Arthur Fenton Hort, *Life and Letters of Fenton John Anthony Hort*. 2 vols. London: Macmillan

Houghton (1991). Esther Rhoades Houghton and Josef L. Altholz, 'The "British Critic", 1824–1843', in *Victorian Periodicals Review*, 24, 3, 111–18

Hubay (1970). Ilona Hubay, *Incunabula aus der Staatlichen Bibliothek Neuburg/Donau [und] in der Benediktiner-Abtei Ottobeuren*. Wiesbaden: Harrassowitz, xiv–xvii

Humphry (1864). William Gilson Humphry, *'Our Sufficiency is of God': A Sermon preached in the Chapel Royal, Whitehall on Sunday, December 20th, 1863*. London: W. H. Dalton

Ignatius (1896). Father Ignatius [Joseph Leycester Lyne], 'Autobiography of Reverend Father Ignatius', in *Llanthony Tracts*, 2. Abergavenny: Llanthony Abbey

International Dictionary (2001). *International Dictionary of Library Histories*. Edited by David H. Stam. London: Routledge

Irving (1880). Joseph Irving, *The Annals of Our Time*. London: Macmillan

Irwin (2007). Robert Irwin, *For Lust of Knowing: The Orientalists and their Enemies*. London: Penguin

Jackson (1981). Holbrook Jackson, *The Anatomy of Bibliomania*. New York: Avenel Books

Jamieson (1965). D.G. Jamieson, 'Selwyn College Library', in *New Zealand Libraries*, September, 179–81

Jay (1986). Elisabeth Jay, *Faith and Doubt in Victorian Britain*. London: Macmillan

Jimenes (2009). Rémi Jimenes, 'The French Bibliophile illustrated and the Bachelin-Deflorenne bookstore', in *New Review of Old Books*, 2, 59–64

Julian (1892). John Julian, *Dictionary of Hymnology*. London: John Murray

Kaplan (1966). H.G. Kaplan, *A First Census of Incunabula in Australia and New Zealand*. Sydney: Public Library of New South Wales

Katzenstein (1988). Ranee Katzenstein and Emile Savage-Smith, *The Leiden Aratea: Ancient Constellations in a Medieval Manuscript*. Malibu, California: J. Paul Getty Museum

Keating (2004). Daniel Keating, *The Appropriation of Divine Life in Cyril of Alexandria*. Oxford: Oxford University Press

Kelly (1843). W. Kelly, *The Small Edition of the Post Office London Directory*. London: Frederic Kelly

Kelly & Co (1858). Kelly & Co., *Post Office Directory of Cambridge, Norfolk and Suffolk*. London: Kelly & Co

Kerney (1968). Michael Kerney, 'Colonel Thomas Stanley', in Bernard Quaritch, *Contributions towards a Dictionary of English Book-collectors*. New York: Burt Franklin (Reprint of 1892–1921 ed.)

Kerr (2006). Donald Jackson Kerr, *Amassing Treasures for All Times: Sir George Grey, Colonial Bookman and Collector*. Dunedin: Otago University Press

Kerr (2015). ——, *Hocken. Prince of Collectors*. Dunedin: Otago University Press

Kircher (2004). *Athanasius Kircher: The Last Man Who Knew Everything*. Edited by Paula Findlen. New York: Routledge

Lambert (1806). B. Lambert, *History and Survey of London and its Environs*, III. London: T. Hughes

Larsen (2016). Anne R. Larsen, *Anna Maria van Schurman: 'The Star of Utrecht'*. Abingdon: Routledge

Larsen (2011), Timothy Larsen, *A People of One Book: The Bible and the Victorians*. Oxford: Oxford University Press

Law Society (1871). Law Society of the United Kingdom, *Catalogue of the Mendham Collection being a Selection of Books and Pamphlets from the Library of the Late Rev. Joseph Mendham*. London: Printed for the Incorporated Law Society of the United Kingdom

Law Society (1994). ——, *Catalogue of the Law Society's Mendham Collection, Lent to the University of Kent at Canterbury and Housed in Canterbury Cathedral Library. Compiled & Edited from the Catalogue of Helen Carron and Others*. Edited by Sheila Hingley and David Shaw. London: The Law Society

Lear (1907). Edward Lear, *Letters*. London: T. F. Unwin

Lear (1911). ——, *Later Letters*. London: T. F. Unwin

Leigh, Sotheby (1859). Leigh, Sotheby and John Wilkinson, *Catalogue of the Collection of Greek and Latin Classics Forming the First Portion of the Library of John Mitford*. London: Leigh, Sotheby and John Wilkinson

Lewis (1849). John Delaware Lewis, 'The Fast Cantab', *Sketch of Cantabs*. London: G. Earle

Linn (2009). Richard Linn, 'Christianization, Secularization, and the Transformation of Public Life', in *A Companion to Late Antiquity*. Edited by Philip Rousseau with the assistance of Jutta Raithel. Chichester, West Sussex: Wiley-Blackwell, 497–511

Litwa (2015). M. David Litwa, *Refutation of all Heresies*. Atlanta: SBL Press

Lough (1962). A.G. Lough, *The Influence of John Mason Neale*. London: SPCK

Lowder (1887). C. Lowder, *Twenty-one Years in St. George's Mission*. London: Rivington

McCarthy (1997). D.P. McCarthy, 'The Biblical Chronology of James Ussher', in *Irish Astronomical Journal*, 24, 1, 73–82

McCormick (1974). E.H. McCormick, *Alexander Turnbull: His Life, His Circle, His Collections*. Wellington: Alexander Turnbull Library

McGuckin (1994). John Anthony McGuckin, *Saint Cyril of Alexandria and the Christological Controversy*. Leiden: E. J. Brill

McKechnie (1992). Paul McKechnie, 'Tertullian's De Pallio and life in Roman Carthage', in *Prudentia*, 24, 2, 44–66

McKitterick (2018). David McKitterick, *The Invention of Rare Books. Private Interest and Public Memory, 1600–1840*. Cambridge: Cambridge University Press

Maggs (1964). Maggs, *Early Presses and Monastic Libraries of North-west Europe: A Catalogue of Manuscripts and Printed Books up to A.D. 1520*. 890. London: Maggs

Magnuson (1982). Torgil Magnuson, *Rome in the Age of Bernini*. Stockholm: Almqvist & Wiksell International

Maitland (1756). William Maitland, *History and Survey of London*. London: T. Osborne and J. Shipton

Mallalieu (2002). H.L. Mallalieu, *Dictionary of British Watercolour Artists up to 1920*. 2 vols. Woodbridge, Suffolk: Antique Collectors' Club

Manion (1989). Margaret Manion, Vera Vines, and Christopher de Hamel, *Medieval and Renaissance Manuscripts in New Zealand Collections*. Melbourne: Thames & Hudson

Manning (1867). Henry Edward Manning, *England and Christendom*. London: Longmans, Green

Maslen (1962). Keith Maslen, 'Eighteenth-century Books in New Zealand Libraries', in *New Zealand Libraries*, 25, 102–8

Mayor (1910). Joseph B. Mayor, 'College Reform in the Fifties', in the *Eagle*, 31, 189–94

Measom (1863). George S. Measom, *The Official Illustrated Guide to South-Eastern and North and Mid-Kent Railways*. London: Charles Griffin

Miller (2017). Duane Alexander Miller, 'Anglican Mission in the Middle East up to 1910', in *The Oxford History of Anglicanism, III: Partisan Anglicanism and its Global Expansion 1829–c.1914*. Oxford: Oxford University Press, 276–295

Miller (1961). Edward Miller, *Portrait of a College: A History of the College of Saint John the Evangelist in Cambridge*. Cambridge: Cambridge University Press

Morrell (1969). W. P. Morrell, *University of Otago: A Centennial History.* Dunedin: University of Otago Press

Muensterberger (1994). Werner Muensterberger, *Collecting, An Unruly Passion: Psychological Perspectives.* Princeton, New Jersey: Princeton University Press

Munby (1956). A.N.L. Munby, *The Formation of the Phillipps Library from 1841 to 1872.* Phillipps Studies IV. Cambridge: Cambridge University Press

Naiditch (2011). P.G. Naiditch, *The Library of Richard Porson.* Bloomington, Indiana: Xlibris

Nelson (1989). James G. Nelson, *Elkin Mathews: Publisher to Yeats, Joyce, Pound.* Madison, WI: University of Wisconsin Press

Newman (1845). John Henry Newman, *An Essay on the Development of Christian Doctrine.* London: James Toovey

Nicholls (2003). J. Nicholls and I. Howat, *The Streets Paved with Gold: The Story of the London City Mission.* London: Christian Focus

Nicoll (1959). Allardyce Nicoll, *A History of English Drama 1660-1900.* Second edition. Cambridge: Cambridge University Press

Nihill (1870). Henry D. Nihill, *The Rights of English Churchmen. A Sermon Preached before the Church of England Working Men's Society, at their First Anniversary.* London: Church of England Working Men's Society

Nihill (1887). ——, *The Sisters of St. Mary at the Cross: Sisters of the Poor and their Work.* London: Kegan Paul, Trench & Co

Official Guide (1991). *Official Guide to Bunhill Fields.* London: Corporation of London

Orens (2003). John Richard Orens, *Stewart Headlam's Radical Anglicanism: The Mass, the Masses, and the Music Hall.* Urbana: University of Illinois Press

The Organisation of Knowledge (2005). *The Organisation of Knowledge in Victorian Britain.* Edited by Martin Daunton. Oxford: Oxford University Press

Otten (2018). S. Otten, 'St. Jean-Baptiste-Marie Vianney', in *Catholic Encyclopedia*, 8. New York: Robert Appleton Company

Oxford Illustrated Literary Guide (1981). *Oxford Illustrated Literary Guide to Great Britain and Ireland.* Edited by Dorothy Eagle and Hilary Carnell. Oxford: Oxford University Press

Palmer (1993). Bernard Palmer, *Reverend Rebels: Five Victorian Clerics and their Fight against Authority.* London: Darton, Longman and Todd

Pearson (1994). David Pearson, *Provenance Research in Book History: A Handbook.* London: The British Library

Pearson (2011). ——, *Books as History.* London: The British Library

Pearson (2014). ——, 'A Taste for the Antique: Examples of Antiquarian Imitation in

Bookbindings and Bookplates', in *Transactions of the Cambridge Bibliographical Society*, 15, 3, 103–23

Pearson (2019). ——, *Provenance Research in Book History: A Handbook*. New Castle, Delaware: Oak Knoll Press

Pickering (1967). W.S.F. Pickering, 'The 1851 Religious Census – A Useless Experiment?', in *The British Journal of Sociology*, 18, 382–407

Pickering (1989). ——, *Anglo Catholicism: A Study in Religious Ambiguity*. London: Routledge

Pingree (2003). Isabelle Pingree, 'A Catalogue of the Bindings of the Fifteenth Century Bookbinder called the Rood and Hunt Binder', in *The Library*, 4, 4, 371–401

Pinnock (1855). W.H. Pinnock, *The Laws and Usages of the Church and Clergy: The Unbeneficed Clerk*. Cambridge: J. Hall & Sons

Pointer (1749). John Pointer, *Oxoniensis Academia: or, The Antiquities and Curiosities of the University of Oxford*. London: Printed for S. Birt, and J. Ward

Potts (1855). Robert Potts, *Liber Cantabrigiensis: An Account of the Aids afforded to Poor Students, the Encouragements offered to Diligent Students, and the Rewards conferred on Successful Students, in the University of Cambridge*. I. Cambridge: Printed at the University Press

Potts (1863). ——, *Liber Cantabrigiensis*. II. London: John W. Parker, Son, and Bourn

Proctor (1881). Richard A. Proctor, 'To Our Readers', in *Knowledge*, 3

Proctor (1902). Robert Proctor, 'The French Royal Greek Types and the Eton *Chrysostom*', in *The Library*, 1, 49–74

Quaritch (1856). Bernard Quaritch, *General Catalogue of Books: Forming a Portion of the Stock of Bernard Quaritch, 16, Castle Street, Leicester Square*. London: Bernard Quaritch

Quaritch (1968). ——, *Contributions towards a Dictionary of English Book-collectors*. New York: Burt Franklin (Reprint of 1892–1921 ed.)

Raby (1991). Peter Raby, *Samuel Butler: A Biography*. London: Hogarth Press

Reed (1968). A.H. Reed, *Rare Books and Manuscripts: The Story of the Dunedin Public Library's Alfred and Isabel Reed Collection*. Wellington: Reed

Reed (2017). John Shelton Reed, *Glorious Battle: The Cultural Politics of Victorian Anglo-Catholicism*. Chapel Hill, North Carolina: Bozart Books

Review (1809). Review, the Rev. Josiah Thomas, *Strictures on Subjects Chiefly Relating to the Established Religion and the Clergy* (1807), in *British Critic*, 33, 307–9

'Review of Books' (1830). 'Review of Books: *The Pilgrim's Progress* with a Life of John Bunyan by R. Southey' in the *London Literary Gazette*, 1

Reynolds (1967). J. S. Reynolds, *Canon Christopher of St Aldate's Oxford*. Abingdon: The Abbey Press

Rhodes (1975). Dennis E. Rhodes, 'Lillies and a Library', in *The Book Collector*, 24, 417–20

Richardson (1989). Ruth Richardson, 'George Godwin of *The Builder:* Indefatigable Journalist and Instigator of a Fine Victorian Visual Resource', in *Visual Resources*, 4, 121–40

Rivington (1894). *Publishing House of Rivington.* Edited by Septimus Rivington. London: Rivington, Percival

Roach (1959). John P.C. Roach, 'The University of Cambridge: The Age of Reforms (1800-82)', in *A History of the County of Cambridge and the Isle of Ely: 3, the City and University of Cambridge.* London: Oxford University Press

Roach (1986). ——, *A History of Secondary Education in England 1800–1870.* London: Longman

Roberts (1997). Emma Roberts, *The Liverpool Academy and Other Exhibitions.* Liverpool: Liverpool University Press

Roberts (1895). William Roberts, *The Bookhunter in London.* London: Elliot & Stock

Robinson (1869). Henry Crabb Robinson, *Diary, Reminiscences and Correspondence,* I. London: Macmillan

Roby (1909–1910). Henry John Roby, 'College Reform under the Cambridge University Act of 1856', in the *Eagle*, XXXI, 195–209

Romilly (2000). [Joseph Romilly], *Romilly's Cambridge Diary 1848–1864.* Edited by M.E. Bury and J.D. Pickles. Cambridge: Cambridge Records Society

Rosenblum (1997). Joseph Rosenblum, 'Sir Thomas Phillipps', in *Dictionary of Literary Biography,* 184. Detroit: Bruccoli Clark Layman Book Gale Research, 338–53

Royal Asiatic Society (1824). Royal Asiatic Society, 'Charter of Incorporation', in *Transactions of the Royal Asiatic Society of Great Britain and Ireland,* 1. London: The Society

The Rule of Saint Benedict (1952). *The Rule of Saint Benedict.* Edited by Abbot Justin McCann. London: Burns Oates

The Rule of Saint Benedict (1997). *The Rule of Saint Benedict: Latin & English.* Translated by Luke Dysinger. Santa Anna, California: Source Books

Said (2003). Edward Said, *Orientalism.* London: Penguin

St. John's College (1895). St. John's College, *Lists of Past Occupants of Rooms in St. John's College.* Compiled by G.C. Moore Smith. Cambridge: E. Johnston

St. John's College (1984). ——, *Use and Occupancy of Rooms in St. John's College.* Edited by N. F. M. Henry and A. C. Crook. Cambridge: Printed for the College

Sanday (1897). William Sanday, 'The Life and Letters of F. J. A. Hort', in *American Journal of Theology*, 1, 1, 95–117

Sandys (1908). John Edwin Sandys, *A History of Classical Scholarship,* II. Cambridge: Cambridge University Press

Satterley (2011). Renae Satterley, 'Doctors' Common', in *The Middle Templar*, 51, 46–7

The Scenery of London (1905). *The Scenery of London*. London: A. & C. Black

Scott (1975). Patrick Scott, 'Victorian Religious Periodicals: Fragments that Remain', in *The Materials Sources and Methods of Ecclesiastical History*. Oxford: Basil Blackwell, 325–339

Searby (2004). Peter Searby, *A History of the University of Cambridge. III: 1750–1870*. Cambridge: Cambridge University Press

Selwyn College (1956). Selwyn College, *The Selwyn College List, The Register of Students of Selwyn College, Dunedin, New Zealand from 1892 to 1956*. Dunedin: Selwyn College

Shahan (1907). Thomas Joseph Shahan, 'Augustinus, Antonius', in *Catholic Encyclopedia*, 2. New York: Robert Appleton, 105–6

Shrosbree (1988). Colin Shrosbree, *Public Schools and Private Education: The Clarendon Commission 1861–64 and the Public Schools Acts*. Manchester: Manchester University Press

Shuger (2006). Debora Shuger, *Censorship and Cultural Sensibility: The Regulation of Language in Tudor-Stuart England*. Philadelphia: University of Pennsylvania Press

Simmons (1997). Clare A. Simmons, 'Richard Heber', in *Dictionary of Literary Biography*, 184. Detroit: Bruccoli Clark Layman Book Gale Research, 219–26

Sister Mary Agnes (1890). Sister Mary Agnes [Povey, Jane Mercy], *Nunnery Life in the Church of England, or, Seventeen Years with Father Ignatius*. London: Hodder and Stoughton

Skinner (2004). S. A. Skinner, *Tractarians and the 'Condition of England': The Social and Political Thought of the Oxford Movement*. Oxford: Clarendon Press

Sotheby (1938). Sotheby, *Catalogue of Valuable Printed Books Illuminated and Other Manuscripts: Wednesday, June 29th to Friday, July 1st 1938*. London: Sotheby

Sotheby, Wilkinson (1873). Sotheby, Wilkinson and Hodge, *Catalogue of the Valuable Manuscripts & Printed Books forming the Antiquarian & Miscellaneous Library of the Late Rev. William Henry Black, F.S.A. Retired Assistant Keeper of Public Records*. London: Dryden Press

Sparrow (1956). John Sparrow, 'Some Uncollected Authors IX: Samuel Parr (1747–1825)', in *The Book Collector*, 5, 63–72

Squibb (1977). G. D. Squibb, *Doctors' Commons: A History of the College of Advocates and Doctors of Law*. Oxford: Clarendon Press

Stackhouse (1722). Thomas Stackhouse, *The Miseries and Great Hardships of the Inferior Clergy, in and about London*. London: T. Payne

Staikos (2000). Konstantinos Sp. Staikos, *The Great Libraries. From Antiquity to the Renaissance (3000 B.C. to A.D. 1600)*. New Castle, Delaware: Oak Knoll Press

Starr (2013). Brian Daniel Starr, *Dictionary of Saints*. New York: Xlibris

Stephen (1865). Leslie Stephen, *Sketches from Cambridge*. London: Macmillan

Sterling (2018). Gregory E. Sterling, 'Philo of Alexandria's Life of Moses. An Introduction to the Exposition of the Law', in *The Studia Philonica Annual*, 30, 31–46

Stevens (1930). T.P. Stevens, *Southwark Cathedral 606–1930*. London: Sampson Low & Co

Stewart (1862). C.J. Stewart, *Catalogue of Works in Patristic and Medieval Literature*. London: Charles J. Stewart

Stow (1598). John Stow, *Survey of London*. London: John Windet

Strachan (1995). Michael Strachan, *Esmond de Beer (1895–1990) Scholar and Benefactor: A Personal Memoir*. Norwich: Michael Russell

Stray (1998). Christopher Stray, *Classics Transformed. Schools, Universities, and Society in England, 1830–1960*. Oxford: Clarendon Press

Stray (2001). ——, 'The Shift from Oral to Written Examination: Cambridge and Oxford 1700–1900', in *Assessment in Education: Principles, Policy & Practice*. 8, 33–50

Stray (2007). ——, 'Sir William Smith and his Dictionaries: A Study in Scarlet and Black', in *Bulletin of the Institute of Classical Studies*. Suppl. 101, 35–54

Stray (2008). [Charles Astor Bristed], *An American in Victorian Cambridge. Charles Astor Bristed's 'Five Years in an English University'*. Edited by Christopher Stray. Exeter: University of Exeter Press

Subtelny (2011). M.E. Subtelny, 'Kamal-al-Din Hosayn Wa 'Ez Kāšefi', in *Encyclopædia Iranica*, XV. New York: Encyclopædia Iranica Foundation, 6, 658–61

Taine (1872). Hippolyte Taine, *Notes on England*. London: Strahan

Taylor (1987). Archer Taylor, *Book Catalogues: Their Varieties and Uses*. Second edition, revised by William P. Barlow. New York: Frederic C. Bell

Taylor (1955). David M. Taylor, *The Oldest Manuscripts in New Zealand*. Wellington, New Zealand: Council for Educational Research

Thomas (1975). Alan G. Thomas, *Great Books and Book Collectors*. London: Chancellor Press

Thomas (1887). Joseph Thomas, *The Universal Dictionary of Biography and Mythology*. London: Virtue

Thompson (2008). David M. Thompson, *Cambridge Theology in the Nineteenth Century: Enquiry, Controversy and Truth*. London: Ashgate

Timperley (1839). Charles Henry Timperley, *Dictionary of Printers and Printing, with the Progress of Literature*. London: H. Johnson

Tindall (2006). Gillian Tindall, *The House by the Thames and the People who lived there*. London: Chatto & Windus

Tinniswood (2001). Adrian Tinniswood, *His Invention So Fertile: A Life of Christopher Wren*. London: Jonathan Cape

Traue (1991). J. E. Traue, '"For the Ultimate Good of the Nation": The Contribution of New Zealand's First Book Collectors', in *Committed to Print. Selected Essays in Praise of the Common Culture of the Book*. Wellington: Victoria University Press, 28–42

Tuckwell (1901). William Tuckwell, *Reminiscences of Oxford*. London: Cassell

Turner (1981). Frank M. Turner, *The Greek Heritage in Victorian Britain*. New Haven: Yale University Press

Uglow (2017). Jenny Uglow, *Mr Lear: A Life of Art and Nonsense*. London: Faber and Faber
University of Otago Library (2003). University of Otago Library, *Annual Report*. Dunedin: The Library

Van Hal (2010). Toon Van Hal, 'On the Scythian Theory Reconstructing the Outlines of Johannes Elichmann's 1601/1602–1639 Planned Archaeologia Harmonica', in *Language and History*, 53, 2, 70–80
Vance (1997). Norman Vance, *The Victorians and Ancient Rome*. Oxford: Blackwell
Venn (1913). John Venn, *Early Collegiate Life*. Cambridge: W. Heffer and Sons
Verner (1966). Mathilde Verner, 'Johann Albert Fabricius, Eighteenth-Century Scholar and Bibliographer', in *The Papers of the Bibliographical Society of America*, 60, 3, 281–326
Victorian Faith (1990). *Victorian Faith in Crisis. Essays on Continuity and Change in Nineteenth-Century Religious Belief*. Edited by Richard J. Helmstadter and Bernard Lightman. Stanford, California: Stanford University Press
Vidler (1966). Alec R. Vilder, *F. D. Maurice and Company*. London: SCM Press

Wakefield (1804). Gilbert Wakefield, *Memoirs of the Life of Gilbert Wakefield*, II. London: J. Johnson
Wakefield (1813). ——, *Correspondence of the Late Gilbert Wakefield, B. A., with the Late Right Honourable Charles James Fox*. London: T. Cadell & W. Davies
Walford (1880). Edward Walford, 'Preface', in *Antiquary*, 1, iii–iv
Walker (1864). Charles Walker, *Three Months in an English Monastery*. London: Murray
Walsh (1991). James E. Walsh, *Catalogue of Fifteenth-Century Printed Books in the Harvard University Library*. Binghamton, New York: Centre for Medieval and Early Renaissance Studies, State University of New York at Binghamton
White (1990). James F. White, *Introduction to Christian Worship*. Nashville: Abingdon Press
Willey (1964). Basil Willey, *Nineteenth Century Studies. Coleridge to Matthew Arnold*. London: Chatto & Windus
Williams (2005). D.H. Williams, *Evangelicals and Tradition: The Formative Influence of the Early Church*. Grand Rapids, Michigan: Baker Academic
Williams (1999). S.C. Williams, *Religious Belief and Popular Culture in Southwark c.1880–1939*. Oxford: Oxford University Press
Williams (1965). Thomas Jay Williams, *Priscilla Lydia Sellon: The Restorer after Three Centuries of the Religious Life in the English Church*. London: SPCK

Wilson (2000). A.N. Wilson, *God's Funeral*. London: Abacus

Winstanley (1935). D.A. Winstanley, *Unreformed Cambridge: A Study of Certain Aspects of the University in the Eighteenth Century*. Cambridge: Cambridge University Press

Wisbey (1859). Charles Wisbey, *Valuable Collection of Books, being Duplicate Volumes from Trinity College Library, Cambridge, Friday, November 11, 1859*. Cambridge: W. Metcalfe

Yarnold (2000). Edward Yarnold, *Cyril of Jerusalem*. London: Routledge

'Z, Y.' (1860). 'Y.Z', 'Correspondence', in the *Eagle*, II, IX, 207–11

Zachs (2014). Fruma Zachs and Sharon Halevi, *Gendering Culture in Greater Syria: Intellectuals and Ideology in the Late Ottoman Period*. London: I. B. Tauris

UNPUBLISHED SOURCES

Bridges (1866–1936). Dame Paulina Bridges, 'Refferences (sic) To Fr W. A. Scholts [sic] from the Transcript of the Document: Memoirs of Dame Paulina Bridges OSB'. [Elizabeth Mary Bridges], 25 January 1866 to 24 July 1936.

De Hamel (2009). Christopher de Hamel, 'Fragments in Book Bindings'. Lyell Lecture, Oxford University

Orr-Ewing (2018). Dr the Rev. Francis Orr-Ewing, 'Thomas Joseph Gaster. An Urban Missionary in Historical and Theological Context'. PhD thesis, King's College, London.

OXFORD DICTIONARY OF NATIONAL BIOGRAPHY (ODNB) WEB SEARCHES

Anderson (2004). J.G.C. Anderson and Peter W. Lock. 'Ramsay, Sir William Mitchell (1851–1939), classical scholar and archaeologist.'

Boase (2018). G.C. Boase and Elizabeth Baigent. 'Hill, Pascoe Grenfell (1804–1882), Church of England clergyman and author.'

Bonham (2004). Valerie Bonham, 'Carter, Thomas Thellusson (1808–1901), Church of England clergyman.'

Cooper (2004). Thompson Cooper and Richard J. Schiefen. 'Tierney, Mark Aloysius (1795–1862), historian.'

Courtney (2004). W.P. Courtney and James Edgar Barcus, 'Mitford, John (1781–1859), literary scholar and Church of England clergyman.'

Cowie (2004a). Leonard W. Cowie, 'Beveridge, William (bap. 1637, d. 1708), bishop of St Asaph.'

Cowie (2004b). ——, 'Parr, Samuel (1747–1825), schoolmaster.'

Crolley (2004). Terence Crolley and Judith Blezzard. 'Gauntlett, Henry John (1805–1876), organist, organ designer, and composer.'

De Quehen (2008). Hugh de Quehen, 'Henry Hammond, (1605–1660), Church of England clergyman and theologian.'

Ditchfield (2006). G.M. Ditchfield, 'Mendham, Joseph (1769–1856), Church of England clergyman and religious controversialist.'

Drain (2004). Susan Drain, 'Neale, John Mason (1818–1866), Church of England clergyman and author.'

Ford (2004). Alan Ford, 'Ussher, James (1581–1656), Church of Ireland archbishop of Armagh and scholar.'

Freeman (2004). Arthur Freeman and Janet Ing Freeman. 'Phillipps, James Orchard Halliwell- (1820–1889), antiquary and literary scholar.'

Gerrard (2007). Christine Gerrad, 'Hill, Aaron (1685–1750), writer and entrepreneur.'

Gibson (2004). William Gibson, 'Chishull, Edmund (1671–1733), Church of England clergyman and antiquary.'

Giles (2008). Gordon Giles, 'Julian, John (1839–1913), Church of England clergyman and hymnologist.'

Gilley (2004). Sheridan Gilley, 'Ward, William George (1812–1882), theologian and philosopher.'

Graver (2004). Bruce E. Graver, 'Wakefield, Gilbert (1756–1801), biblical scholar and religious controversialist.'

Hamilton (2006). Alastair Hamilton, 'Gregory, John (1607–1646), orientalist.'

Hamilton (2008). ——, 'Huntington, Robert (bap. 1637, d. 1701), orientalist and bishop of Raphoe.'

Hunt (2004). William Hunt and M. C. Curthoys. 'Jacobson, William (1803–1884), bishop of Chester and theologian.'

Jupp (2004). P. J. Jupp, 'Yonge, Charles Duke (1812–1891), classical scholar and historian.'

Lemmings (2004). David Lemmings, 'Lee, Sir William (1688–1754), judge.'

Louth (2004). Andrew Louth, 'Taylor, Thomas (1758–1835), philosopher and translator.'

McConnell (2014). Anita McConnell, 'Lee [formerly Fiott], John (1783–1866), antiquary and astronomer.'

Matthew (2004). H. C. G. Matthew, 'Jeremie, James Amiraux (1802–1872), dean of Lincoln.'

Milton (2015). Anthony Milton, 'Heylyn, Peter (1599–1662), Church of England clergyman and historian.'

Minton (2008). Gretchen E. Minton, 'Cave, William (1637–1713), Church of England clergyman and patristic scholar.'

Mitchell (2012). Rosemary Mitchell, 'Dolman, Charles (1807–1863), Roman Catholic publisher.'

Newsome (2006). David Newsome, 'Wilberforce, Robert Isaac (1802–1857), Roman Catholic convert.'

Nockles (2004). Peter B. Nockles, 'Palmer, William Patrick (1803–1885), Church of England clergyman and theologian.'

Nockles (2014). ——, 'Rose, Hugh James (1795–1838), Church of England clergyman.'

Nurse (2004). Bernard Nurse, 'Black, William Henry (1808–1872), antiquary.'

Oldroyd (2004). David Oldroyd, 'Bonney, Thomas George (1833–1923), geologist.'

Palmer (2004). Bernard Palmer, 'Palmer, George Josiah (1828–1892), newspaper founder and editor.'

Pawley (2009). Margaret Pawley, 'Lee, Frederick George (1832–1902), writer on theology.'

Rigg (2004). J.M. Rigg and David Maskell. 'Maskell, William (1814–1890), Roman Catholic convert and liturgical scholar.'

Scott (2004). Richard Scott, 'Veitch, James, Lord Elliock (1712–1793), judge.'

Seccombe (2004). Thomas Seccombe and M. C. Curthoys. 'Babington, Churchill (1821–1889), scholar.'

Sharp (2004). Richard Sharp, 'Parker, Samuel (1681–1730), nonjuror and theological writer.'

Shaw (2008). A.G.L. Shaw, 'FitzGerald, Charles (1791–1887), naval officer and colonial governor.'

Taylor (2004). Miles Taylor, 'Urquhart, David (1805–1877), diplomatist and writer.'

Thompson (2015). Michael Welman Thompson, 'Wright, Thomas (1810–1877), historian and antiquary.'

Woodhead (2004). Christine Woodhead, 'Knolles, Richard (late 1540s–1610), historian and translator.'

Woolven (2004). Robin Woolven, 'Walford, Edward (1823–1897), writer and compiler of reference works.'

Wykes (2004). David L. Wykes, 'Henry, Matthew (1662–1714), Presbyterian minister.'

ઢ

OTHER WEB SEARCHES

British History Online http://www.british-history.ac.uk/vch/cambs/vol5/pp251-263 [accessed 8 April 2020], particularly footnote 305 and reference H.O. 129/140/3/6/5

Daneshgar (2017). Majid Daneshgar, 'A "Baptized" Qurʾān? On a Unique Illuminated Manuscript at the University of Otago', in *Mizan*. Boston University & ILEX Foundation http://www.mizanproject.org/a-baptized-qur%CA%BEan/

'Edward Lear Diaries' (1858–1859). 'Edward Lear Diaries, The Private Journals of a Landscape Painter, 22 December 1858, and 25 February 1859'. Transcribed by Marco Graziosi from Houghton Library, Harvard University, MS Eng. 797.3.] *The Lear Diaries* (leardiaries.wordpress.com)

Faulkner (c.1990). Gordon and Barbara Faulkner, 'The Faulkner Family of London and Bristol' Appendix II, Wills: 1 and 6: Mary Ann Faulkner, 2 April 1855, 54; John Dodds, 1819, 56–8, http://www.faulkner-history.co.uk/Faulkner_files/02Wills.pdf

Kirwan (1999). Kevin M. Kirwan, Preface, in Réné-Francois Guettée, *The Papacy*, 1999, http://orthodoxinfo.com/inquirers/Guettee_ThePapacy.pdf

London Institution (2021). en.wikipedia.org/wiki/London_Institution

St. Augustine's Lyre (c.2020). tosingistopraytwice.wordpress.com/

Vanière (2021). fr.wikipedia.org/wiki/Jacques_Vanière

Young (2011). Susan D. Young, Kent OPC Project, http://www.kent-opc.org/Parishes/Thanet-Ramsgate2011.html.

ஓ

SPECIAL COLLECTIONS, UNIVERSITY OF OTAGO WEB LINKS

Exhibitions

Initials. In the Beginning (2007) www.otago.ac.nz/library/exhibitions/initials/index.html

From Pigskin to Paper: The Art and Craft of Bookbinding (2013) www.otago.ac.nz/library/exhibitions/bindings/

Maths, Politics and Concrete: The Legacy of the Classical World (2013) www.otago.ac.nz/library/exhibitions/classical_world/

500 Years On. Martin Luther and the Protestant Reformation (2017) www.otago.ac.nz/library/exhibitions/luther/

A Middle Eastern Odyssey: Constantinople to Palmyra (2018): www.otago.ac.nz/library/exhibitions/middle_east/

General Link: www.otago.ac.nz/library/specialcollections/exhibitions.html

E-Publications

Incunabula. Special Collections (2009): www.otago.ac.nz/library/treasures/incunabula/index.php

Manuscripts in Special Collections, University of Otago (2011): www.otago.ac.nz/library/pdf/Manuscripts_in_Special_Collections.pdf

Special Collections at the University of Otago (2011): www.otago.ac.nz/library/pdf/speccollbrochure.pdf

ஓ

NEWSPAPERS

Birmingham Daily Post
Bury & Norwich Post
Cambridge Chronicle
Cambridge Chronicle and Journal
Cambridge Independent Press
Church News
Cheshire Observer & Chester, Birkenhead and North Wales Times
Daily News
Essex Standard
Evening Star (Dunedin, NZ)
Guardian
Ipswich Journal
Kentish Gazette (Canterbury, UK)
Liverpool Mercury
London Evening Standard
Morning Chronicle
Morning Post
Oswestry Advertiser
Otago Daily Times
Otago Witness
Reynolds Newspaper
South London Chronicle
Standard
Times (London)
Weekly Mail
Western Morning News (Plymouth, Devon, UK)
York Herald

❧

PERIODICALS

Antiquary
Archaeological Journal
Asiatic Journal and Monthly Register for British and Foreign India, China, and Australasia
Athenaeum
British Apollo
British Critic
British Magazine
British Medical Journal

Catholic Magazine
Christian Remembrancer
Church Association Monthly Intelligence
Church Times
Eagle (St John's College, Cambridge)
English Review
European Magazine
Gentleman's Magazine
Graphic
Illustrated London News
Knowledge
Literary Gazette and Journal of the Belles Lettres, Arts, Sciences
London Literary Gazette
London News
Magazine of Science, and School of Arts
Morning Chronicle
Musical Times and Singing Class Circular
North American Review
Portfolio
Punch
Quarterly Review
Royal Female Magazine
Transactions of the Royal Asiatic Society of Great Britain and Ireland
Transactions of the Royal Society of Literature of the United Kingdom
Universal Magazine

INDEX

Abbey, Robert and Susannah, 159
Abergavenny, Wales, 124
Adam, Stephen Condon (contemporary), 37
Adam of St. Victor (poet), 157
Adamnanus, 58
al-'Adim, Kamal al-Din 'Umar ibn Ahmad ibn, 209
Aemilius, Antonius, 67
Aeschylus, 262
Aesop, 51
agriculture, 229, 231
Ahmad, 'Alī ibn, 202
Albanell, Antonio Agustin y, 187
Albricus, 46
Alchorne, Stanesby (book collector), 55
Aldines, 56, 232, 300
Aleman, Mateo, 302
Aleppo, 209, 265
Alexander Turnbull Library, Wellington, 221
Alexis (poet), 46
'Ali, Ikram, 203
'Alī Khān (also known as Asīr), Muzaffar, 203
Allacci, Leone, 59
Allcard vs Skinner (1887), 132
Allen, George, 11
Allen, Hugh, 123
Allen, Sir James, 297
Allen, William H. (bookseller), 200
Altick, Richard, 255
Amberg Franciscan Library, Bavaria, 223, 258
Ammonius, 69
Anacreon, 278
Andrewes, Lancelot, 2
Anglican Church, 1, 2, 12, 19, 42, 50, 71, 75, 107, 112, 115, 120, 129, 145, 170
Anglicus, Bartholomaeus, 224
Anglo-Catholic Movement, 2, 6–7, 107, 113, 116, 120, 131, 145, 146, 169

Anglo-Catholics (Anglo-Catholicism), 6–7, 42, 50, 107, 109, 113, 116, 120, 130, 145, 160, 169, 250, 252, 255, 307, 309
Annan, Noel, 29
Anson, Peter, 113
Anstey, Henry, 121, 123, 127
Apollinaris, Sidonius, 259
Apollinius of Tyna, 180, 278
Apostolic Fathers, 174
Aprosio, Angelico, 231
Apuleius, 268
Arabic books
  – Bible, 110, 209
  – grammars, 207–8
  – fables, 207
  – guidebooks, 208
  – history, 209–10
  – literature, 210–1
  – medicine, 228
  – philosophy, 211
  – poetry, 210
  – science, 212
  – scriptural works, 208–9
Aratus of Soli, 164, 278
Archilochus, 272
Architectural Society (UK), 246–7
Arculf, Bishop, 216
Arderne, Henry (grandfather), 14
Arianism (Arius), 170, 173, 179–80, 254
Aristophanes, 278
Aristotle, 141
Armstrong, John, 252
Arnold, Thomas Kerchever, 276
Arundel marbles, 215, 273
Asäad, Jāny Muhammad, 205
Ashburnham, Bertram, 4th Earl of (book collector), 57
Ashe, Thomas, 45
Ashmole, Elias, 273
Ashmole Library, 235
Ashmolean Museum, Oxford, 273

Asiatic Society of Bengal, 203
Astesanus de Ast, 222, pl.20
Athenaeus, 46
Auckland City Library, Auckland, 221, 309
Augusta of Saxe-Gotha-Altenburg, 244
Augustinian Fathers, Antwerp, 260
Avienus, Rufus Festus, 164

Babington, Churchill, 75, 77, 247
Bach, J. S, 41
Bachelin, Antoine, 249
Badger, George Percy, 163
Badius (Bade), Josse, printer, 64, 176, 224–5
al-Baghdadi, Muwaffaq al-Din 'Abd al-Latif, 209
Bagster, Samuel, publisher, 213
Baily, Walter (contemporary), 38, 40
Baker, Thomas, 265
Baldi, Bernardino, 274
Baldigiani, Antonio (book collector), 266
Balfour, Francis, 203
Ball, T.I., 152
Balme, Edward, Vicar of Finchingfield, Essex, 140
Baluze, Étienne, 48
Bamford, T. W, 18
Barberini, Francesco (library), 231, 235–6, 260
Barker, Edmund Henry, 67, 271
Barker, William Burckhardt, 206
Barnett, Samuel Augustus, 19, 71
Baronio (Baronius), Caesare (Cardinal), 156, 305
Barrow, Isaac, 305
Barstow, Henry Clements (contemporary), 39
Barufaldi, Girolamo (of Ferrara), 155
Bateson, William Henry, 31, 34, 75, 77
Baumgartner, Henry Algernon, 75–6
Bavarian State Library (Bayerische Staatsbibliothek), 52
Beattie, William, 63
Becher, Johann Joachim, 269
Beckford, William (book collector), 56
Belfour, F.C., 204
Bell and Daldy (booksellers; publishers), 55

Bellarmine (Bellarmino), Robert, 3, 49, 187, 286
Beloe, William, 231, 250
Belon, Pierre, 214
Benedictine Orders, 112–3, 115–7, 122–3, 131, 137, 147, 155, 169, 182–3, 258
Benjamin of Tudela (Rabbi), 216
Bennett, William Sterndale, Professor of Music, 24
Benson, Christopher, 59
Bentham, William, 1
Bergler, Stephen (translator), 271
Berlin Royal Library (Berolinensi), 261
Bernard, Edward, 3, 235
Bernegger, Matthias, 67–8
Beroaldus, Philippus, 229
Bertochus, Dionysius, 228
Besant, Walter, 26, 31
Bessarion, Johannes, 300
Bessel, Gottfried (Abbot), 183
Bethell, Christopher, 50
Bethleham (Bedlam) Hospital, Southwark, 9
Betschart, Paul, 182
Beveridge, William, Bishop of St. Asaph, 280–1, 305
Beza, Theodore, 184, 186, 212
Bibles, 56–7, 169–71, 176–7, 183–4, 206, 222, 274, pl. 19
 – Authorised Version (Barker; Baskett), 184
 – Old Testament, 176, 183–6
 – Genesis and Exodus, 186, 188, 200
 – New Testament, 57, 171, 183–7, 212, 241
 – Gospels, 186, 209
 – Geneva Breeches Bible, 184
 – Gutenberg Bible, 236
 – Hebrew Bible, 213, 272
 – Hodgson's Bible, 209
 – Plantin Polyglot Bible, 213
 – Sistine Vulgate, 171
 – Vulgate, 171, 177, 184
 – Wilson's Bible, 16, 51, 184
biblical criticism, 169
bibliography, 231–4

Biblioteca Conte di Aquila, 172
Biblioteca Magliabechiana, Florence, 228
Biblioteca Medicea Laurenziana (Laurentian Library), Florence, 289
Biblioteca Vallicelliana, Rome, 172
Bibliotheca Grenvilliana, 57
Bibliotheca Parriana, 270
Bibliotheca Pinelli, 267
Biblioth[eca] Prevckiana Borussica, 259
Bibliotheca Regia Monacensis (Bayerische Staatsbibliothek, Munich), 258
Bibliothecae Academicae Ingolstadii (University Library, Ingolstadt), 259
Bibliothecae Gorlicensis (Stadtbibliothek, Görlitz, Germany), 258
Bibliothèque du Roi, France, 234
Bickham, George (Junior), 215
Biggs, Louis Coutier, 152
Birrell, T. A, 6
Black, William Henry, 267, 273–5
 – employment, publications, and associations, 273
Blake, William, 103
Blandford, Marquess of (book collector), 55, 57
Bleeck, Arthur Henry, 204
Bliss, William Henry, 165
Blomfield, Charles James, 59–60, 284
Blomfield, Frederic George, 106, 108
Boccaccio, Giovanni, 227, 231
Bochart, Samuel, 212, 264
Bodleian Library, Oxford, 152, 157, 235, 237
 – Ashmole 1285, f. 38, 152
 – Liturgical Misc. 366, f.21, 157
 – MS. Barlow, No.41, 151
Bodley, Thomas, 235
Boeckh, August, 272
Boethius, 182, 301
Bohn, Henry George (bookseller), 54, 216, 280
Bohn, John, 270–1
Bolzani, Pierio Valeriano, 264
Bona, Giovanni (Cardinal), 288–9
Bonaparte, Napoleon, 166, 257, 259
Bonclerici family, 259
Bongars, Jacques, 141

Bonnet, Antoine, 260
Bonney, Thomas George, 24, 32, 34–5, 43, 75, 78
Bonomini, Paolo, 155
Book collecting scene (19th century), 54–7
Book of Common Prayer, 57, 73, 114, 126, 169–170, 184, 186–7
Books of Hours, 57, 63
Boone, Thomas and William (booksellers), 54
Booth, Charles, 104, 143
Borchardt, D. H. (librarian), 304
Borromeo, Saint Charles, 260
Bose, Johann Andreas, 69
Bossus, Matthaeus, 300
Bourdillon, Jacob, 288
Boutflower, Douglas (Bernard), 123
Bowling, Edward Woodley, 45
Boyd, Charlotte, 126–7, 167
Bradley, George Granville, Dean of Westminster, 109
Brahe, Tycho, 306
Brancard, Nicolaus, 69
Brant, Sebastian, 226
Brasch, Charles, 305
Breviaries, 114, 127, 137, 147, 152–5, 170, 182–3, 290, 297–8
Bridge, Stephen, 78
Bridges, Sister (Dame) Paulina, 121, 164–8
Bright, William, 254
Bristed, Charles Astor, 32
British and Foreign Bible Society, 206, 209
British Archaeological Association (BAS), 246, 273
British Library, 149, 154
British Museum, 54, 62, 81, 86, 152–3, 157, 165, 167, 180, 222, 264
 – Harleian 2929 (11th c French Psalter), 152
 – Harleian 2961, f.230 (Leofric Collectar), 152
 – Julius A. vi. f. 36b (11th c. calendar), 152
 – MS. Cotton Claudius E. iv., 110
 – Vespasian D. xi-xii. f. 43b; 153b (Lawrence of
 – Durham mss; Glossed Hymnal), 152
British National Association of Spiritualists, 120

INDEX 339

Brooks, James, 132
Brougham, Henry Peter, first Baron Brougham and Vaux, 244
Brown, James, 268
Brown, John Carter (book collector), 57
Browne, Edward Harold, Professor of Divinity, 24
Brunet, Jacques-Charles (bibliographer), 3, 232–3
Brydges, Samuel Egerton, 67
Buccleuch, Duke of (book collector), 57
Buckingham, Duke of (book collector), 58
Buckler, Benjamin, 278
Budé, Guillaume, 64
The Builder (periodical), 13, 248
Bulkley, Edward (donor), 294, 296
Bullock, William Greenaway (contemporary), 74, 81
Bunhill, and Bunhill Fields, Hoxton, 103–4, 134
Bunsen, Christian, 3
Bunyan, John, 103
Bury, Lancashire, 18
Butler, Samuel, 26, 35
Buxtorf, Johann, 213
Byron, Lord, 3
Byzantine philology, 216

Cailleau, Andrè-Charles (bookseller), 223
Caius, John, 280
Calcagnini, Celio, 266–7
Calder-Marshall, Arthur, 116
Calmet, Augustin, 295
Calvert, Arthur, 75, 77
Camberwell, London, 21, 57, 75–6, 260
Cambridge Antiquarian Society, 77, 247
Cambridge Architectural Society, 41–2
Cambridge Camden Society, 2, 41–2, 131, 147, 154
Cambridge University, 2, 5, 16–7, 27–8, 30, 40, 51, 110, 135, 235, 247, 292
 – Admissions (19th century), 17, 19
 – Overview (19th century), 17, 23, 24
 – Statute Changes, 1849, 1860, 27

 – Reform Act, 1856, 27
 – Status of Dissenters, 27
 – Curriculum, 19, 28, 30
 – Examinations, 23, 28–31
 – Classical Tripos, 29–30
 – Moral Sciences Tripos, 30
 – Natural Sciences Tripos, 30
 – position of Wrangler, 29, 33–4, 40
 – Senior Optimes, 29, 40
 – Junior Optimes, 29, 40
 – private coaches, 33–4, 36
 – sizars, 23–4, 36
 – tuition costs, 36
 – Extracurricular activities, 40–1, 43
 – Bachelor of Divinity, 134–7
 – Doctor of Divinity, 135–6, 139
Cambridge Colleges
 Christ's College, 26
 Gonville and Caius College, 30
 Emmanuel College, 136
 Jesus College, 174
 Peterhouse College, 41
 Queen's College, 104
 St. Catherine's College, 51–2
 St. John's College, 1, 5, 7, 19–21, 23–5, 28–30, 32–8, 41, 43, 72, 74–8, 81, 134, 150, 169, 182, 187, 244, 276, 292
 – Matriculation numbers (1856–60), 24
 – Categories of students, 24
 – Academic dress, 24
 – Examinations, 28–31, 33, 36–40
 – Fees, 24
 – Routines (Chapel and Hall), 32–3
 – Food, 32
 – Rooms, 33
 – Contemporaries, 33, 37–40
 – Old Chapel, pl.2
 Sidney Sussex College, 220
 Trinity College, 20, 29–30, 32, 41, 53, 59, 67, 69, 74, 136, 261
Cambridge University Library, 7, 77, 136, 301
Cambridge University Musical Society, 41, 78
Cambridge University Press, 292
Camm, Reginald, 129

Campanus, Johannes Antonius, 300
Cano, Melchor, 287
Cappel, Leo, 213
Capper, John Longford, 109
Carlyle, Joseph Dacre, 209
Carlyle, Thomas, 43, 109
Carocci, Vincenzo, 262
Carpzov, Friedrich Benedict, 3, 231, 236
Carpzov, Johann Benedict, 271
Carter, Thomas Thellusson, 253
Casaubon, Isaac, 59, 68, 305
Cassianus, Johannes, 226
Castelli, David, 211
Catalán, Juan Francisco Marco y, 48
Catenas, 183
Catius, 277
Catholic Counter-Reformation, 187, 259
Catholic Prayer Book, 139
Catholic revival, 84, 107, 113
Catholic traditions, 42, 51–2, 61, 133
Cato, 229
Cavalieri, Giovanni Michele, 155, 305
Cave, William, 188
Cavendish, William, Sixth Duke of Devonshire (book collector), 55
Caxton, William, 55–6, 227
Cay, Alfred, 84
Celestines of Amiens convent, 302
Cellarius, Christoph (philologist), 271, 275, 277
Celotti (book collector), 56
Celsus, Julius, 69, 176, 280
Census of Religious Worship of 1851, 12
Cerri, Antonio, 66
Chadwick, Owen, 250
Chalmers, Alexander, 278
Chambers, J. D., 152
Chambers, Robert, 138
Champollion, Jean-François, 214
Chappelow, Leonard, 207
Charles II, King of England, 302
Charles II, King of Spain, 164
Charles V (Emperor), 52
Chartist riots (Birmingham), 10

Chaucer, Geoffrey, 57
Chell, George (contemporary), 23, 37
Cheltenham (Grammar), 18
Chevallier, Clement, 138
Chidiac, Fares (Faris El-Shidiac), 109, 208
Chishull, Edmund, 214, 264
Chodzko, Aleksander Borejko, 205
Christian schools, 175–7
Chronicon Paschale (Chronicum Alexandrinum), 175, 183
Church Fathers, 4, 6, 49, 169–70, 172, 174, 177, 183, 187
Church Mission Society, 78
Church News, 109, 252
Church of England, 27, 42, 50, 53, 103, 107, 110–2, 120, 122, 128, 145, 234
Church of Rome, 42–3
Church reunion, 234
Church Times, 109, 132
Church, Richard William, 252
Churches
  Aldborough Hatch, Essex, 84
  All-Hallows-the-Great, London, 70
  All Angels, Shoreditch, 132
  All Saints', Newington, 84
  All Saints', Notting Hill, 81
  Biggleswade Church, Bedfordshire, 104
  Carleton Rode, Norfolk, 84
  Christ Church, Lee, Kent, 74, 81
  Collingham All Saints, Newark, 83
  Great St. Mary's, Cambridge, 135
  Holy Trinity, Brompton, Kensington, 159
  Holy Trinity, Newington, 83–4
  Holy Trinity, Twickenham, 84
  St. Agatha's, Shoreditch, 145
  St. Agnes, Kennington Park, London, 128
  St. Alban's, Cheetwood, Manchester, 130–1
  St. Alban's, Holborn, 146
  St. Bartholomew's, Cripplegate, London, 116, 126, 144
  St. Edmund the Martyr, Lombard Street, City, 1, 107, 117, 119, 142–5
  St. Ethelburga, Bishopsgate, London, 117
  St. George Cathedral, Southwark, 11

St. George's-in-the-East, 84, 113
St. Giles, Camberwell, 76, 78
St. John's, Walworth, 83
St. Jude's, Whitechapel, 71
St. Luke, Chelsea, 159
St. Michael's, Shoreditch, 1, 60, 107, 111, 116, 130–4, 142, 169
– ritualistic ceremonies, 132–3
St. Nicholas, Deptford, Kent, 188
St. Nicholas Acons, 142–4
St. Olave's, Tooley Street, Southwark, 10–2, 14
– Fire (1843) and restoration, 11
– Parish, 11
– Demolished and hospital replacement, 12
St. Paul's, Bunhill Row, Hoxton, 1, 104–8, 112, 117
St. Paul's, Walworth, 83
St. Paul's Cross, Cambridge, 135
St. Peter's, Plymouth, 113
St. Peter's, Walworth, 1, 78–80, 84–5, 111
St. Philip's, Earl's Court, Kensington, 74
St. Saviour, Southwark, 11
St. Stephen's, Norwich, 84
Cicero, 18, 30, 51, 177, 266, 306
Cipelli, Giovanni Battista (Egnazio), 259
City of London College for Ladies, 105
Clark, G. Kitson, 250
Clarke, Samuel, 210
Classical curricula, 17–9
Claudianus, Claudius, 179
Cléry, Jean-Baptiste, 240
Clewer House of Mercy, 253
Clichtoveus, Jodorus, 158
Clive, Edward, 1st Earl of Powis, 55
Clodius, Johann Christian, 213
Clüver, Philipp, 137
Cocceius, Johann Heinrich, 65
Cockayne, Oswald (philologist), 279
Codd, Henry Frederic (contemporary), 37, 39
Coghlan, Peter (publisher), 155
Colbert, Jean-Baptiste (collector), 266, 273
Coleridge, Henry Nelson, 259

Coleridge, Samuel Taylor, 259, 282
College de France, 218
College of Advocates, Doctors' Common, London, 186, 262–6
– history and associates, 262
– *Catalogue of the Books in the Library*, 262–3
Collins, Captain Grenville, 302
Collinson, John, 265
Colomiès, Paul, 69
Colquhoun, J. C. (chair of the Church Association), 145
Colucia, Franciscus, 229
Columella, 229
Community of St. John Baptist, 253
Community of St. Mary at the Cross (Sisters of the Poor), 131–2
Compagnie de la Grand-Navire, Paris, 177
Comte, Auguste, 1
Conder, Josiah, 274
Confraternity of the Blessed Sacrament, 253
Conrad of Brundelsheim, 220
Conrad of Halberstadt, 219–20, 306
Constantine (Emperor), 180
Constantinople (Istanbul), 180
Contarini, Vincenzio, 66
Conybeare, William, 54
Corfu, 160–2, 210
Corporation and Test Acts (1661; 1673), 103
Corser, Thomas (book collector), 57
Coteiba, Ibn (Ibn Qutaybah), 210
Cotham, George Toulson, 83–4
Cotton, George (Bishop), 78
Council of Trent (1545-63), 51
Cowes School, Cowes, 20
Crawford, Earl of (book collector), 57
Creeds, 136–7
Crimean War, 43
Crispus, son of Constantine the Great, 178
Currer, Frances Mary Richardson (book collector), 57–8
Curriculum (Grammar schools), 18
Curzon Park Abbey, Chester, 123

Dalberg-Acton, John Emerich Edward, 1st Baron Acton, 167
Daldianus, Artemidorus, 59
Dale, Anton van, 141, 270
Dale, Arthur Murray, 127–9
Dale, Thomas Pelham, 128
Danesghar, Majid, 308
Daniel, Hermann Adalbert, 150, 152–3
Daniel, Samuel, 256
Daniell, John Frederic, 109
Daniell, William (artist), 245
Dante Alighieri, 56–7, 306
Darwinism, 169
Dasque, Claude, 66
Dathe, Johann August, 212
Davids, Arthur Lumley, 206
Davies, Charles Maurice, 2, 120–1
al-Dawlah, Captin Maqbūl, 203
Dayman, E. A., 152
Dayr al-Suryan (Monastery of the Syrians), Wadi Natrum, Egypt, 167
De Beauvais, Juste, 208
De Beer, Esmond, 8, 295, 305
De Bertouch, Baroness, 119, 124–5
De Billy, Jacques, 181
De Bordone, Karolus de Blanchis (scribe), 298
De Braine, Jean-François Bled, 208
De Brienne, Étienne Charles de Loménie, Archbishop of Sens, 236
De Bure, Guillaume-François, 3, 228, 232
De Busti, Bernardinus, 229, 258
De Carnago, Johannes (scribe), 298
De Casale, Ubertino, 228, 230
De Hamel, Christopher, 7, 227, 298, 306–8
De Larroque, Matthieu, 281
De Leon, Ponce, 181
De Lyra, Nicholas, 227, 308
De Mayno, Jason, 229–30
De Oliveyra, Solomon b. David, 213
De Ratisbona, Augustinus, 224–5
De Ricci, Seymour, 56–7, 61–62, 235
De Rogissart, Alexandre, 139
De Sacy, Silvestre, 210, 217, 264
De Sommal, Henri, 172

De Spina, Alphonsus, Bishop, 225
De Tessé, Charles Louis Froulay, Bishop of Le Mans, 155
De Toledo, Francisco, 186
De Turrecremata, Johannes, 225, 230
De Utino, Leonardus Matthaei, 222, 258
De Voragine, Jacobus, 299
Deflorrene, Madame, 249
Defoe, Daniel, 103, 241
Deighton, Bell & Co, Cambridge, 47
Demosthenes, 18, 30
Denton, William, 116–7
Dering, Sir Edward, 54
Devonshire, 6th Duke of (book collector), 55, 257
Dibdin, Thomas Frognall (book collector), 56–7, 232, 266
Dibdinian tradition, 3
Dickens, Charles, 9, 43, 241, 255
Digby Library, 235
Dindorf, Gottlieb Immanuel, 213
Diocese of Dunedin, New Zealand, 293
Diocletian (Emperor), 178
Diodati, Elia, 67
Dionysius of Halicarnassus, 46, 53
Dionysius the humble, 281
Dixon, William, 20–1, 75–6
Dodds, Elizabeth Arderne (grandmother), 14
Dodds, John (great grandfather), 14
  – Children: John (b.1789); Mary Ann Faulkner (b.1787); Elizabeth Arderne (b. 1792;, Shoults's grandmother), 14
  – Library, 14
Dolman, Charles, 253
Dommer, Gysbertus (editor), 271
D'Orbellis, Nicolas, 228
Douglas, Bishop, 72
Drakenborch, Arnold, 289
Drechsler, Wolfgang, 214
Drobner, Hubertus R., 170
Drury, George, 113–4
Dryden, Henry E. L., 246
Dunedin Public Library, Dunedin, 297
Du Pin, Louis Ellies, 3, 234

Duport, James, 139
Durandus, Guilielmus, 299
Durell, John Vasasor (contemporary), 40, 71
Dyce, Alexander, 63

Eagle (St. John's College), 45, 47, 53, 77, 244, 276
Early Imprint Project (EIP), British Library, 306
Easley, Ann (Sister Winifred), 126–7
Eastern Church, 43, 123
Ecclesiastical Commission, 107–8, 132
Ecclesiastical history, 7, 82, 170, 188, 307, 309
Ecclesiological Society, 41–2
Eck, Johann, 300
Eckhart, Johann Georg van, 261
École Spéciale de langues Orientales Vivantes, 217
Edwards, Francis (bookdealer), 55
Edwards, James (Pall Mall bookseller), 236, 267
Effendi, Mahmoud, 206
Egyptology (Egypt), 208, 214
Einsiedeln Abbey, 182
Elephant and Castle, Southwark, 9
Elichmann, Johan, 211
Elliot, Sir Henry Miers, 204
Elliot Stock (bookdealer), 55
Ellis, F. S (bookdealer), 55
Elzevir (publications), 4, 59, 65, 68, 137, 140–1, 153–4, 179, 184, 186, 207, 213, 277, 283, 285, 289
Emmius, Ubbo, 268
Empiricus, Sextus, 69
Encyclopedia of Islam, 218
English Catholics, 122
English College, Rome, 48
Epictetus, 211, 283
Epistles of St. Paul, 185–6
Erasmus (of Rotterdam), 64, 153, 186, 300
Erpenius, Thomas (van Erpe), 207, 212, pl. 23
Esplin, David G., 301–4
Estienne, Henri, 139, 184, 186
Estienne, Robert, 179, 182

Eton, 16, 18, 25
Eucharist, 49, 51–2, 114–5, 124, 130, 169–70, 174, 288
Euclid, 18, 23, 25, 28–9, 34, 38, 264
Euripides, 278
Eusebius of Caesarea, 179–80, 188, 226
Evans, R.H. of Pall Mall (auctioneers), 55–6, 227, 264, 270
Evelyn, John, 283, 306
Everett, William, 29

Faber, Basil, 269
Fabricius, Johann Albert, 3, 69, 187, 234–5
al-Farghani, Muhammad ibn Kathir (Alfraganus), 212
Farman, Samuel (contemporary), 37
Father Ignatius, 2, 5, 42, 112–3, 120–1, 123, 128, 130–1, 133, 144–5, 154, 166, 169, 172, 182, 239, 253, 270, pl. 7
– early education, 112–3
– positions held (deacon), 113
– Claydon, Ipswich, 114
– Elm Hill Priory, Norwich, 115–6
– Laleham, Staines, 118–9, 121
– 51 Hunter Street, Bloomsbury, Brunswick Square, 118–20
– Feltham Priory, or Feltham Nunnery, 118–9, 121–3, 128–30, 166, 253, pl. 9 and pl. 10
– Capel-y-ffin Abbey, Wales (1869), 112, 114, 122–7, 130, 169, 239, pl. 8
– Library at the Monastery, 128
– rituals and schedules of Order, 114, 118–9, 121, 125–6
– Observances, 118
– Beliefs, 115–7, 122, 128, 130
– travels, 116
– attacks on, 144–5
– death, 129
Faulkner, Mary Ann (great aunt) – book gift (1855), 16
Faulkner, William Elisha, 145
Faulkner, William Woodthorpe, 14, 16
Feder, Ludovic, 64
Fell, Dr John, 176

Fell, Dr Thomas, 220, 294, 296
  gift of books, 296
Ferguson, Richard Saul (contemporary), 40
Ferrari, Giovanni Baptista, 138, 262
Festival days, 48–52, 85, 139
Field, William, 272
Fischer, J. C., 261
Fisher, John, pl. 22
Fitchett, William Alfred Robinson, 297
Fitness of study certificates (universities), 19–20
FitzGerald, Charles, 140
Fléchier, Vossius Espirit, Bishop of Nimes, 261
Fletcher, James (auctioneer), 55
Flitcroft, Henry, 11
Florus, 68
Fogg, Sam (art dealer, London), 298
Folger Shakespeare Library, Washington, 301
Forbes, G. H. (hymnologist), 41
Ford, Henry, 209
Formularium procuratorum (1493), 225
Forster Education Act (1870), 55
Fort William College, Calcutta, 203, 205
Foster, William Shrubsole (contemporary), 40
Foulis publications (Glasgow), 240
France, Francis, 34–6, 75
Francis A. Countway Library of Medicine,
  – Boston, 299–300
  – Lewis Collection, 299
Franciscan Order, 228
François, I, 179
Freeling, Sir Francis (book collector), 55
Freeman-Mitford, John, 1st Baron Redesdale, 63
Freiburg im Breisgau University Library, 260
French Academy of Science, 10
Freytag, Georg Wilhelm Friedrich, 209, 265
Froben, Hieronymus, 213
Froben, Johann, 213
Frontinus, 279
Froude, James, 1
Fruterius, Lucas, 65
Fulgentius, Fabius Planciades, 65

Gaignat, Louis-Jean, 228, 232
Gaisford, Thomas, Dean of Christ Church, 17
Galatino, Pietro Colonna, 52, 258
Galilei, Galileo, 49, 68
Galland, Antoine, 218
Gallican Church, 234
Gallus, Abbot of Aula Regia, Bohemia, near Prague, 220
Gamble, Stephen (related to Peter Martin Shoults), 305
Gardner, John Dunn (book collector), 58
Gaster, Thomas Joseph, 76, 78
Gauntlett, Henry John, 12
Gautier, Léon, 152, 158
Gavanto, Bartolommeo, 154
Gay, John, 160, 240
Gelen, Sigmund, 177
George III (King), 56, 246
Germanicus, Claudius Caesar, 164
Gersdorf, Ephraim Gotthelf, 174
Gesenius, Wilhelm, 213
Gesner, Conrad, 3, 233
Gevaerts, Jean-Gaspard, 260
Gibbon, Edward, 1, 283
Giddy, Albert Edward (Cuthbert), 123
Giffen, Hubert van, 66
Giselinus, Victor, 153
Gladstone, W.E. (book collector), 57, 170
Glassius, Salomon, 213
Glastonbury Abbey, 126
Gnosticism, 175
Godwin, George, 143, 248
Goethe, Johann Wolfgang von, 3
Going, John, 83–4
Golestān (The Rose Garden), 201
Golius, Jacob, 207–8
Gorman case (G. C. Gorham, 1847), 62
Gosford, Earl of (book collector), 57
The Gospels, 38–9, 179, 209, 211, 241
Gospel of James, 211
Gospel of John, 241
Gospel of Thomas, 211
Gothic Revival, 15, 132
Göttweig Abbey, Krems, Austria, 183

INDEX

Graevius, Johann Georg, 271
Graham Commissioners' Enquiry, 135
Graphic (1875), 145, 147
Gratian, 138, 187
Gray, Robert (Bishop of Capetown), 133
Gray, Thomas, 3, 63
Graziani, Giovanni, 263
The Great Fire (1666), 143, 220
Greek Apologists, 174–5
Green, George (contemporary), 37
Greenwood, James, 9
Gregory, John, 240
Grelot, Guillaume-Joseph, 215
Grenville, Richard Plantagenet, 2nd Duke (book collector), 55–6
Grenville, Richard Temple Nugent Brydges Chandos, first Duke of Buckingham and Chandos, (book collector), 55–6
Grenville, Thomas (book collector), 55
Grey, Sir George (book collector), 221, 309
Grimm, Brothers, 7
Grist, William (contemporary), 37, 39
Grodeck, Johann, 181
Gronovius, Johann Friedrich, 289
Grotius, Hugo, 164, 186
Grylls, William, 261
Guettée, René-François (Father Vladimir), 253
Guy, Thomas, 9
Guy's Hospital, Southwark, 9, 291
Gyraldus, 45

Hackney Phalanx, 250
Hagen, Johann van der, 183
Haghia Sophia, 215
Hales, G. C. (*Bibliotheca Graeca*), 234
Halliwell, James Orchard, 245–6
Hamilton, Alexander, 10th Duke, 7th Duke of Brandon (book collector) 56
Hammond, Henry, 186
Handel, George Frideric, 146
Hankinson, Thomas Edwards, 184, 187, 296
Hansom, Joseph Aloysius, 248
Harbin, George (book collector), 56
Härdelin, Alf, 49

Hardwick, Charles, Professor of Divinity, 24
Hare, Sir Ralph (Exhibition), 23
Hargreaves, Ray, 294–5
Harles, G. C., 188
Harley, Edward, 2nd Earl of Oxford (book collector), 153, 275
Harley, Robert, 1st Earl of Oxford (book collector), 153, 275
Harleian Catalogue, 153
Harleian Library, 231, 235
Harman, Marion, 299
Hart, Tindal, 72
Hartmann, Christopher, 182
Harvest Festival (St Edmund's, 1875), 145, pl. 13
Harwood, Edward, 235
Hastings, Warren, 54, 203
Hawkins, B. Waterhouse, 109
Hawtrey, Edward Craven (book collector), 58
Hay, Robert William, 214
Haymo of Halberstadt, Bishop, 225
Hazlitt, W. Carew, 267
Headlam, J. W, 30
Hearne, Thomas (Bodleian Library), 237
Heath, Benjamin, headmaster of Harrow, 216
Heath, William (bookseller), 68
Heber, Richard (book collector), 54–6, 266
Hebrew (psalters, dictionaries, grammars), 56, 213, 272, 274
Hegel, Georg Wilhelm Friedrich, 69
Heineccius, Johann Gottlieb, 269
Heinsius, Daniel, 175, 186
Heinsius, Nicolaas, 179
Heitland, William E, 32–4
Heliodorus, 141
Helmore, Thomas, 114
Henry, Matthew, 186
Her Majesty's Chapel Royal, Whitehall, 73, 81
Herbelot, Barthélemy d', 217–8
Herbert v. Purchas case (1871), 111
Hereford, 124
Heretical works, 173, 177, 181, 228, 230
Hermann, Gottfried, 272
Herodian, 69

Herodotus, 18, 38
Hesiod, (poet), 59
Hesse, Léopold Auguste Constantin, 231, 237
Hessels, Franz, 269
Hesychus of Alexandria, 305
Hexapla, 176
Heylyn, Peter, 48, 251
Heynlin, Johann, 225
Hibbert, George (book collector), 55
Hierocles, Sossianus, Governor of Bythnia, 180
Hiley, Simeon, 31
Hill, Aaron (poet), 243
Hill, John, 64
Hill, Pascoe Grenfell, 117, 140, 142, 144–6
– publications, 142
Hill, Rowland Beevor, 145
Hillyard, Edwin Augustus (Norwich), 124
Hoare, John Newenham, 159
Hoare, Thomas (contemporary), 23, 37–8, 40, 71
Hocken, Thomas Morland (book collector), 294
Hodgson, John (contemporary), 37
Hodgson, Sarah (printer), 209
Hodgson and Co, London (auctioneer), 262
Hogarth, William, 278
Holcot, Robert, 224
Holford, Robert Stayner, 56–7
Hollingshead, John, 9
Holste, Lukas, 236
Holt, Neville (book collector), 58
Holzenberg, Eric, librarian, Grolier Club, New York, 306
Homer, 18, 30, 59, 64, 137, 139
Hooght, Everadus van der, 272
Hooke, Robert, 143
Hooker, Richard, 257, 305
Horace, 18, 276–7
Hort, Arthur Fenton, 136
Hort, Fenton John Anthony, 136, 247
Hosius, Stanislaus, 50–1
Howard, Henry, 6th Duke of Norfolk, 273
Howard, Thomas, 21st Earl of Arundel, 273

Howlett, J. H, 73, 81
Hoxton, London, 57, 103–5
Hudson, John, 53
Hughes, John, 174
Hume, David, 1, 69
Humphry, William Gilson, 73
Huntington, Robert, 59–60
Huth, Henry, 55, 57
Hutchins, Hassill (Jonathan Blackburne sale, 1785), 231
Huygen, Christian, 306
Hyde, Thomas (Bodleian Library), 237
Hymns, hymnology, 12, 41, 70, 103, 145–6, 148–54, 156–8, 169, 183, 278, 290

Ignatius of Antioch, 174
Incunables (incunabula), 3–4, 6–7, 56–7, 221–31, 297–8, 300, 309
– Basel, 225, 258
– Bologna, 298–300
– Brescia, 228, 230
– Cologne, 298–9
– Lyon, 224
– Mantua, 226
– Milan, 228–9, 258, 301
– Parma, 228
– Pavia, 228–9
– Reggio Emilia, 228–9
– Rome, 226, 298–300
– Speyer, 221–2, 258
– Strasbourg, 222–3, 298–9, 301
– Stuttgart, 223
– Venice, 227–8, 298–9
Index Expurgatorius Librorum (Indexes), 173, 234
India, 245
Indian Mutiny, 43
Ionian Academy, Corfu, 161
Iremonger, Frederick, 252
Irenaeus of Lyons, 175
Islam, 210
Islamic beliefs and practices, 211
Islamic numismatics, 216
ISTC, 300

Jackson, George (contemporary), 37
Jackson, Holbrook, 7
Jahan, Shah (Emperor of India), 204
Jamieson, Don. G (librarian), 303–4
Jansson, Jan (publisher; cartographer), 214
Jarrett, Thomas, Professor of Hebrew, 24
Al-Jazūlī, Muhammed ibn Sulaymān, 201
Jelf, William Edward, 241
Jenson, Nicolaus, 227
Jeremie, James Amiraux, Professor of Divinity, 24, 65, 135
Jesus Christ, 116, 180, 185, 188, 201, 211-2
Johnson, Samuel, 270, 307
Jolley, Thomas (book collector), 58
Jones, Sir William, 203, 270
Joyce, Arthur J., 216
Judas Iscariot, 211
Julger, J. F., 261
Julian, John, 148-9, 156, 158, 276
 – *Dictionary of hymnology*, 148–50, 156, 158, 276
 – Wincobank, Sheffield, 149, 156
Justin Martyr, 174-5
Justinianus, Laurentius, 226
Justinus, Marcus Junianus, 271

Kamehameha III (King, Hawaii), 10
Kant, Immanuel, 1
Kāŝefi, Hosayn Wa 'Ez, 205
Kāshānī, Mīrzā Hasan, 209
Kayat, Assaad Yacoob, 208
Keats, John, 9
Keble, John, 2, 42, 49, 110, 152
Keene, Henry George, 2-5
Kempis, Thomas a, 137
Kenney, Arthur H, 10-1, 74
Kent Archaeology Society, 83
Kentish Gazette, 15, 19
Kepler, Johannes, 67
Ker, John Edgar (book collector), 301
Kerr, Donald, 306, 308
Kilan, Wolfgang (engraver, Augsburg), 175
King, Bryan, 84, 113
King, Peter, first Baron King, 281

King's College London, 111
Kingsley, Charles, 43
Kinnamos, Johannes (John Cinnamus), 67
Kircher, Athanasius, 214
 – publications, 214
Kirmani, Mir Hussain Ali Khan, 205
Kirsop, Wallace (bibliographer), 306
Klemp, Jean, 295, 305
Kloss, Georg Franz Burkhard (book collector), 219–20, 299
Knolles, Richard, 217
Knollys, J. W. Erskine, 84
Knox, Ronald, 6
Koberger, Anton (printer), 225
Koellin, Conrad, 300
Korangi (Coringa), 10
Küster, Ludolph, 185

La Vallière, Louis César de la Baume Le Blanc, duc de Vaujours, 223
Labbé, Philippe, 233–4
Lack, Frances (Hargrave Road, Islington), 126–7
Lactantius, 177–8, 298
Laire, François-Xavier (de Brienne Library), 231, 236
Lambeck, Peter, 237
Lambeth Bishops Conference (1888), 292, 294
Lambeth Palace Library, London, 59, 69
Lanceotz, Corneille, 172
Landor, Walter Savage, 270
Lane, Edward William, 217
Langhorne, John, 160
Languages
 – Arabic, 3, 60, 110, 200, 203, 211–3, 264
 – Aramaic, 212
 – Armenian, 183, 279
 – Basque, 241
 – Chaldean, 200
 – Chinese, 241
 – Coptic, 183, 209, 214
 – English, 3, 18, 30, 203, 209
 – French, 139, 152
 – Greek, 3, 17–9, 23, 25, 28, 30, 32–3, 40, 47,

69, 70, 82, 139, 176, 183–5, 211–3, 241
– Hebrew, 3, 60, 82, 200, 203, 213
– Latin, 3, 17–9, 25, 28, 30, 69, 139, 176, 203, 211–3
– Osmanli (Turkish), 206
– Ottoman Turkish, 200–1, 203, 205–6
– Persian, 3, 60, 200–1, 203, 209
– Portuguese, 213
– Sanskrit, 203, 274
– Syriac, 60, 200, 203, 212–3
– Urdu, 203
Latini, Latino, 67, 177, 270, 275
Laud, Archbishop William, 2
Laurentius, Josephus, 67
Lazcano, Francisco Javier, 183
Le Breton, William Corbet, 12
Lear, Edward, 161–3
– guests (along with Ogle), 162–1
Lee, Frederick George, 252–3
Lee, John (John Fiott), 205, 210, 263–6
– life and interests, 263
Hartwell and Colwell Libraries, 264–6
Lee, Samuel, 110, 209, 212
Lee, William, Lord Justice, 265–6
'Leiden Aratea' MS.VLQ 79, 164
Leiden Universiteitsbibliotheek, Leiden, 164
Leigh and S. Sotheby (auctioneers), 69
Lenox, James (book collector), 57
Leo, Friedrich, 158
Leopold, Emperor, 237
Lettou, John (printer), 227
Lettsom, William Nanson, 13
Leusden, Johannes, 213, 272
Lewis, John Delaware, 25
Library catalogues, 235–7, 263
Library profession, 237
Lightfoot, Joseph Barber, Professor of Divinity, 74, 81, 247
Lilly, Joseph (bookseller), 54
Linacre, Thomas, 65
Lindner, Johan Gottlieb, 178
Lipsius, Justus, 273
Little, Edward Delanoy, 45
Littledale, Richard Frederick, 160

Liveing, George Downing, 30
Livingstone, David, 43
Livy, 18, 30, 289, pl. 17
Llanfihangel Crucorney, Monmouthshire, 124
Llanthony, Wales, 112, 116, 122, 124–5, 128, 270
Lloyd, Robert (Charles Honeycombe), 244
Locke, John, 306, 308
Lombard, Peter, 224
Lomeier, Johannes, 237
London Institution, 224
London Metropolitan Archives, London, 74, 82, 84
Longley, Charles Thomas, Archbishop of Canterbury, 115
Lorenzana, Francisco Antonio de (Cardinal), 154
Lough, A.G., 42
Louis XIV, King of France, 164, 273
Louth, Lincolnshire, 18
Lowder, Charles Fuge, 2, 113, 120
Lowth, Robert, 213
Lucan, 140, 269
Lucas, William (contemporary), 37
Lucretius, 30, 109
Ludwig I, King of Bavaria, 258
Lumby, J. Rawson, 136
Lunn, John Robert, Professor of Music, 41, 75, 78
Luqman (Lokman) the sage, 207
Luther, Martin, 188, 269, 299–300, 308
Lutherans, 50
Lutterell, Henry, 63
Lyford, Charles, 131–2
Lyne, Francis, 116, 130
Lyne, Joseph Leycester – see Father Ignatius

Macdonnell, George Alcock, 80
Mackonochie, A. H., 146–7
McEldowney, W. J. (Jock), librarian, 303
McKitterick, David, librarian, 307
McMullin, Brian, bibliographer, 306
McNab, Robert, 8
Madan, Falconer, 157

Magazines and periodicals, 13, 47, 241–55
  (magazines not held), 304
  – 18th century (20), 242–4
    general, 242–3
    historical, 243–4
    female readership, 244
  – 19th century (30), 244–55
    general, 244–5
    antiquarianism, 245–8
    industry, 248
    history, 248
    science, 248–9
    book collecting, 249–50
    religion, 250–4
Maggs Bros (booksellers), 55, 298, 302
Magister, Thomas, 69
Mahdī-'Alī-Khān, Ihān al-Mulk Muhammed, 203
Maire, Johan, 211
Maittaire, Michel, 69–70, 210
Manchester Corn Office, 130
Mandeville, John, 216
Manion, Margaret M., 307
Manners-Sutton, Charles, Archbishop of Canterbury, 78
Manning, Henry Edward, 2, 49, 110
Manuscripts, 6, 60, 110, 200, 220–1, 309
  – Arabic, 165, 200–2
  – English, 220–1
  – Greek, 171
  – Hebrew, 56
  – Latin, 221
  – Ottoman Turkish, 201
  – Persian, 200–2
  – Syriac, 165, 167, 183, 200
  – Turkish, 200–2
Manutius, Paulus, 300
Marcus, Lewis, 104–8, 111, 112, 144
  – publications, 105
Al-Maqrizi (Taki-Eddin-Ahmed Makrizi), 210
Marebon, John, 182
Marena, L, 105
Marks and Co (bookseller), 298

Marlborough Grammar School, 18
Marlow, John, 274, 302
Marrack, John Read (contemporary), 37, 40
Marshalsea Prison, Southwark, 9
Martin, Benjamin, 14
Martin's Bank, Lombard Street, 143
Martyrs, martyology, 156
Maskell, William, 54, 61–62
  – collection overview, 61–62
  – publications, 62
  – sale of library, 62
Maslen, Keith, bibliographer, 304, 306
Mas'ud, Ahmad ibn 'Ali ibn, 208
Mathematics, 28–30, 32–4, 39–40
Matthaeus de Cracovia, 221, 258
Maundrell, Henry, 216
Maurokordatos, Nikolaos, 271
Maximus the Confessor, 183
May, Frederick Schiller, 294
Mayor, John Eyton Bickersteth, 75, 77, 247
Mayor, Joseph Bickersteth, 30, 35, 45, 75, 77
Mazlum, Maksimus ibn Jurjis (Archbishop), 208
Mead, Dr Richard, 278
Mearns, James, Rushden, Buntingford, North Herefordshire, 149
medicine, 228, 231
Medieval manuscripts, 3–4, 7, 56–7, 219–20, 297–8, 302, 306
Mela, Pomponius, 227
Melanchthon, Philip, 299
Melmoth, William, 266
Mendham, Joseph, 54, 60–1
  – collection overview, 60–1
  – publications, 60
  – dispersal of books, 60–1
Meninski, Franciscus (Franciszek) à Mesgnien, 205
Menke, Frideric August, 272
Merriman, Joseph (contemporary), 37, 40, 71
Merula, Georgius, 229
Mesuë, Johannes (Yuhanna Ibn Masawayh), 228, 231
Metropolitan Tabernacle, 9

Meursius, Johannes, 269
Middle Eastern publications, 203–18
  – Arabic, 207–12
  – Hebrew, 213
  – Persian, 203–5
  – Syriac, 212
  – Turkish, 205–6
  – Urdu, 203
Migne, Jacques-Paul, 152, 154
Miles, William (Colonel, translator), 205
Mill, James Stuart, 1
Mill, John, 185
Mill Hall School, London, 142
Miller, Douglas Stewart, Warden of Selwyn, 303
Miller, Edward, 27
Milton, Anthony, 48
Milton, John, 307
Minucius Felix, Marcus, 177–8, 269
Mīranjīr, Shaykh, 202
Mirkhvand (1433-98), 204
Mitchell, Oliver, 84
Mitford, John, 63–4, 271–8
  – life and collection overview, 63
  – publications, 63
  – sales of library, 63
  – books in Shoults, 64–70, 271, 278
Mitford, William, 64
Molyneux, Georgina, 110
Monasticism, 113, 115–6, 123, 167, 171, 182–3, 226
Mone, Franz Joseph, 150, 152–3
Mons Casinus (Monte Cassino), 182
Montagu, Richard, Bishop of Chichester, 148
Montaigne, Michel, 69, 165
Moore, Robert Bendle, 84
More, Thomas, 64
Morelli, Jacob, 236
Moretus, Balthasar, 154
Morhof, Daniel Georg, 3, 66–8
Moroni, Carlo, 236
Morrell, W. P., 292
Moses, 177
Moullin, Daniel Alfred, 83–4
Moultrie, Gerard (South Leigh, Oxford), 124, 145

Mozarabic Breviary and rites, 153–4
Mozley, J. B., 252
Mudie's Library, 55
Muhammad (Prophet), 203, 210
Mulling, William Edward, 45
Muensterberger, Werner, 3
Muncker, Thomas, 46, 51
Münster, Sebastian, 213
Murray II, John, 245
Musée de Picardie (Society of, Amiens), 247
Musée Napoléon (Amiens), 247

Napoleonic Wars, 55, 257
Nares, Robert (Archdeacon), 250
Nassau-Orange Library, Dillenburg, Germany, 261
National Society of Prevention of Cruelty to Children, 291
Neale, Edward Vansittart, 51
Neale, John Mason, 2, 41–2, 114, 126, 131, 147, 152, 154, 158, 252
Nevill, Samuel Tarrett, first Bishop of Dunedin, 5, 7, 292–4, 296–7, 309, pl. 25
  – First books to Selwyn College Library, 292
Newbold, Clare, 84
Newbold, Francis, 84
Newcourt, Richard, 284
  – *Repertorium ecclesiasticum parochiale Londinense*, (1710) – extensive notes by Shoults, 284–5
Newman, John Henry, 2, 42, 49–51, 110, 152, 254
Nicander, 278
Nicean Creed, 179–181, 187
Nicholas of Gorran, 185
Nichols, John, 278
Nicholson, John (librarian), 61
Nicholson, William, Dean of Carlisle, 235
Nihill, Daniel, 60, 284
Nihill, Henry David, 60, 111, 116, 120, 130–4, 284
Nizami (Ganjavi), 205, 264
Nonnus of Panopolis, 186, 259, 278
Noris, Henry, 212

Norris, Henry Handley, 250, 252
North, Brownlow, Bishop of Winchester, 72
North, Frederick, 5th Earl of Guilford, (book collector), 56, 161, 209, 217, 264–5

Oaths of Allegiance and Supremacy, 73, 135, 281
Ockley, Simon, 216
Ogle, Alice (sister-in-law), 160
Ogle, Cecilia Harriette (sister-in-law), 160
Ogle, David Montgomery Richards (brother-in-law), 160
Ogle, Eliza Margaret (mother-in-law; née Maplestone), 160
Ogle, Emily (sister-in-law), 160, 291
Ogle, Isabel (sister-in-law), 160
Ogle, John (brother-in-law), 160
Ogle, John Connell (father-in-law), 160–3, 206, 208, 245
 – residences (London, Corfu, Rome, Trieste, Madras), 161
 – paintings, 160–2
 – death, 161
Ogle, Thomas Edgeworth (brother-in-law), 160
Ogles, Duncan & Cochran (booksellers), 212
Olav (Olaf), King of Norway, 11–2
Oldknow, Joseph, 147
Oldys, William (Harleian Library), 231
Oliver, John, 143
One Thousand and One Nights, 208, 217–8
Order of Servites, Florence (D.S.A. Domus Sanctissimae Annuntiatae), 227–8
Oriental Translation Fund of Great Britain and Ireland, 204–5, 210, 264
Orientalism, 217
Origen of Alexandria, 136, 174, 176, 179, 280, 286
Orme, William, 282
Orsini, Fulvio, 274
Osman, Sayyid Muhammad (Mehmet) ibn Hāf, iz, 201
Ouseley, Sir William, 204
Ovid, 51, 269, 278, 298
Owen, Richard, 43

Oxford Declaration (July 1864), 107
Oxford Movement, 2, 42, 48, 50, 59, 110, 129, 251–2
Oxford University, 2, 16–7, 19, 27, 60–1, 235
 Colleges
 – All Souls College, 237
 – Corpus Christi College, 19, 128
 – Jesus College, 130
 – Merton College, 109
 – Oriel College, 49, 63–4, 68, 266
 – Oxford University Press, 176

Palaeography, 256
Paley, William, 28, 38
Palgrave, Francis, 299
Palgrave, Francis Turner, 299
Palladius, 229
Palmer, Edward Henry, 77
Palmer, Elizabeth Georgina (donor), 293–4
Palmer, George Josiah, 109, 252
Palmer, John Horsley (banker), 293
Palmer, William, 47–8
Papias of Hierapolis, 174
Parker, Samuel, 188
Parkinson, Stephen, 34–5, 38, 134, 136
Parochial Mission Women Fund (1860), 71
Parowns, E. H, 81
Parr, Samuel (book collector), 67, 267, 270–3
 – friends and employment, 270
Pattison, Mark, 252
Pauline works (Epistles; Paraphrases), 185–6
Paulo, Petro, 279
Payne (Thomas P. II) and Foss (Henry), booksellers, 54
Peacock, George, the Dean of Ely, 31, 134
Peale Museum, Philadelphia and Baltimore, 288
Pearson, David, 265, 306
Peck, Pierre, 266
Peckover, Edmund George (contemporary), 74, 81
Peignot, Gabriel, 232–3
Pelham, John Thomas, Bishop of Norwich, 114
Penny Magazine (periodical), 13, 245, 248, 250, 255

The Pentateuch, 177, 188
Peregrinus of Oppeln, 223
Pereira, Benedictus, 186, 262
Perkins, Henry (sale, 1872–73), 57
Perry, Charles, 215
Persian history, 204–5
Persian poets, poems, thinkers, 201–2, 205
Pertz, G.H., 165
Peshitta (in Serto script), 212
Pétau, Denis, 271
Petrarch, 57, 69, 226, 231, 306
Petronius, 239, pl. 21
Pew, James, 76
Phaedrus, 18
Phillipps, Sir Thomas (book collector), 56–7, 246, 257
Phillpotts, Henry, Bishop of Exeter, 61–2, 287–8
Philo of Alexandria (Philo Judaeus), 176–7
Philocrates, 141
Philological Society, 78
Philology, 7, 233, 246–7, 309
Photius, 175
Pickering, William (bookseller), 54
Pindar, 18, 272
Pinelli, Maffeo (book collector), 231, 236, 266–7
Pinnock, W.H., 74, 80–2, 86
Pithou, Pierre, 65
Plantin editions, 59, 65, 153–4, 171–2, 214, 240, 273, 300
Platina, Bartholomaeus, 301
Plautus, 299
Plato, 45
Plutarch, 45, 267
Pococke, Edward, 209–10
Poelmann, Theodore, 153
Poleni, Giovanni, 274
Pollard, A. W, 4, 222, 231, 254
Pollard and Redgrave *STC*, 301
Poole, Alfred, 2
Pope, Alexander, 3
Popes
 – Benedict XVI, 176
 – Clement VIII, 171
 – Clement IX, 236
 – Clement XI, 260
 – Clement XII, 260
 – Clement XIV, 260
 – Gregory, 122
 – John XXI (Petrus Hispanus), 228–9
 – Leo XIII, 165–6
 – Paul V, 50
 – Pius II (Aeneas Sylvius Piccolomini), 224
 – Pius V, 155
 – Pius VII, 260
 – Pius IX, 116, 180
 – Pius X, 167
 – Pius XI, 110
 – Urban VIII (Maffeo Barberini), 156
Porson, Richard, 69, 282
Post-Tractarians, 129
Potter, John, 137
Potts, Robert, 17, 138
Povey, Jane Mercy (Sister Mary Agnes), 119, 127–8
Powell, David Thomas, 16, 58
Pratt, Charles, 184
Preston, Theodore, Professor of Arabic, 24
Previte, William (contemporary), 40, 71
Prewett, F. J., 82
Price, Richard, 59
Prideaux, Humphrey, 215
Priestley, Joseph, 270
Primitive Church, 2, 188, 281–2
Printer device, 176, 223
Printers (incunabula period), 171–231, 257–8, 298–302
 – Amerbach, Johann, 225–6
 – Bertochus, Dionysius, 229
 – Bevilaqua, Simon, 298–9
 – Bononiensis, Peregrinus de Pasqualibus, 228
 – de Benedictus, Franciscus, 300
 – de Bonetis, Andreas, 228
 – de Boninis, Boninus, 298
 – de Boscho, Johannes Andreas, 229
 – de Carcano, Antonius, 229

– de Garaldis, Michael and Bernardinus, 229
– de Mantegatiis, Cassanus, Philippus, 229
– de Montalli, Johannes Antonius, 228
– de Monteferrato, Manfredus de Bonellis, 227
– de Moyllis, Damianus, 228
– de Paltaasichis, Andreas, 298
– de Seligenstadt, Johannes Herbort, 171, 227
– de Vingle, Jean, 224
– Drach, Peter, 222, 257
– Flach, Martin, 299
– Furter, Michael, 225, 258
– Girardengus, Franciscus, 229
– Han, Ulrich (Udalricus Gallus), 171, 226
– Husner, Georg, 223, 299, 301
– Jenson, Nicolaus, 171
– Mentelin, Johann, 222, 302
– Pachel, Leonardus, 229, 258
– Printer of Butigella, 229
– Printer of the 'Erwahlung Maximilians', 178, 223
– Printer of the *Gesta Christi*, 221, 257
– Prüss, Johann, 223
– Richel, Bernard, 225
– Schallus, Johannes, 179, 226
– Silber, Eucharius, 300
– Treschel, Johannes, 172, 224
– Ungarus, Petrus (Pierre Hongre), 224
– Zarotus, Antonius (for Johannes de Legnano), 301
– Zel, Ulrich, 299
Prior, Matthew, 3
Procter, Francis, 51–2, 187
Proctor, Richard A., 249
Proctor, William Addy (contemporary), 40, 71
Protestant College of Malta, 206
Protestant Reformation, 257–8, 260
Provenance, 256
Provenance details, 7, 48, 52, 59–60, 64–5, 67, 69, 109, 137–42, 171, 173, 179, 181, 184, 188, 204–5, 207, 209, 211–2, 214–5, 219–21, 223–6, 229–30, 234, 236–7, 246, 251, 257–75, 299, 300–2

– book labels, 270–1
– bookplates (Ex Libris), 256, 263–6, 268–9
Prudentius, Aurelius, 153
Prynne, George Rundle, 113
pseudo-Albertus Magnus, 299
pseudo-Augustinian texts, 172, 279–280
pseudo-Clementine, 174
pseudo-Lactantius, 178
pseudo-Origen, 176
Psalters, 212
Public Worship Regulation Act (1874-1875), 133
Pugin, Ann, 16
Pugin, Augustus Welby Northmore, 11, 15–6
Punch, 132–3
Purchas, John (Herbert v. Purchas case, 1871), 111
Pusey, Edward Bouverie, 2, 42, 110, 113, 116
Puttick, Thomas (auctioneer), 55
Pythagoras, 211

Quaritch, Bernard (bookseller; publisher), 57–8, 138, 204, 206, 208
Quatremère, Étienne Marc, 210
Queen's University, Belfast, 177
Quintilian, 289
Qur'an (Koran), 200–2, 209, pl. 24

Raleigh, Walter, 240
Ramsey, Sir William Mitchell, 165
Ramsgate, 15
  – Population (1851), 15
  – Development, 15
  – Churches: St. George; St. Lawrence (Laurence); St. Augustine (Catholic), Randolph, Thomas, 15
  – schools, 18
Randolph, Thomas (Corpus Christi College, Oxford), 179
Raphelengius, Franciscus, 207, 213
Rascol, E, (bookseller, 4 Brydes Street, Covent Garden), 250
Rawlinson, Thomas (book collector), 300
al-Razzāq, 'Abd, 202

Record Commission, 159
Redhouse, Sir James William, 206
Redi, Francesco, 288
Reed, A.H., 8
Reeland, Adrian, 211
Regis, Jean-François, 260
Reinesius, Thomas, 69
Reiske, Johann Jakob, 215–6
Religious Tract Society, 250
Renouard, Antoine-Augustin, 232
Reuchlin, Johannes, 52
Revivalism, 41, 42, 84, 107, 112–3, 116–7, 129, 169
Reyner, George Fearns, 31, 35, 75, 77
Rhodiginus, Lodovicus Caelius, 45–6, 51, 276
Richards, Isaac, Bishop of Dunedin, 297
Richardson, George (contemporary), 40, 71
Richardson, James, 106
Richelieu, Armand Jean du Plessis, 208
Rinkart, Martin, 147
Ritualism (ritualistic), 2, 7, 42, 61, 83, 107, 109, 111, 114, 125, 128, 130, 131, 133, 144–6, 153, 169, 241, 252–3, 255, 288
Rivet, André, 285
Rivington, Francis and John, 50, 250–1, 265
Rivington, George Charles, 265
Rivola, Francesco, 279
Roach, John, 18
Robert, Anthony (compiler), 137
Robertson, James Craigie, 111
Robinson, Henry Crabb, 278
Robinson, Thomas, Professor of Arabic, Cambridge, 212
Robson & Clarke (New Bond Street booksellers), 236, 267
Rodd, Thomas (bookseller), 54
Rogers, Samuel, 63
Rogers, Shef, 307
Roman Catholic Church (Roman Catholics), 12, 49, 50, 52, 62, 83, 103, 110, 120, 123, 133, 153, 155, 160, 167, 171–3, 234, 250, 252–3
Romilly, Sir John, 110
Rood and Hunt binders, Oxford, 227, 308, pl. 19
Rose, Hugh James, 251
Rosenmüller, Ernst Friedrich Karl, 208

Ross, Alexander, 138
Rouen Cathedral Library (Bibliotheca Ecclesia, Rothomagensis), 261
Routledge Railway series, 55
Roxburghe Library sale (1812), 55
Royal Archaeological Institute of Great Britain and Ireland (RAI), 240, 245–6
Royal Asiatic Society (RAS), 204, 210
Royal Geographical Society, 79
Royal Institute of British Architects (RIBA), 58
Royal Society of Literature, 246
Rufinus of Aquileia (Tyrannius Rufinus), 174
Rugby Grammar School, 16, 25
Ruinart, Thierry, 182
Ruskin, John (book collector), 57
Rycaut, Sir Paul, 217

Sach, J. E., 82
al-Sādiq, Ja'far, 202
St. Alexander and Theodor Benedictine Abbey (Swabian Escorial), Ottobeuran, Germany, 222, 258
St. André, Nathaniel, 278
St. Bartholomew massacre, Poland, 51
St. Bertin Abbey, Saint-Omer, France, 164
St. George's Fields, London, 9
St. John's College, Auckland, 292
St. Margaret's Sisterhood, East Grinstead, Sussex, 42
St. Martin of Tours, 59
St. Maur (Maurists), 172
St.-Omer, near Lille, France, 164, 240
St. Paul's Cathedral, Dunedin, 305
Saint-Hilaire, Étienne Geoffrey, 8
Saints
– Acacius of Amida, 180
– Albertus Magnus, 57
– Ambrose of Milan, 153, 170–1
– Anselm, 172, 279–80
– Athanasius of Alexandria, 170–1, 226, 254
– Augustine of Hippo, 122, 152, 170–2, 180, 224, 226, 280, 286, 302, 305
– Barnabas, 169

– Basil the Great, 170–1, 173, 280
– Benedict of Nursia, 182
– Bernard, 172, 279–80
– Bonaventura, 223, 302
– Clement of Alexandria, 175
– Clement of Rome, 174
– Cyprian of Carthage, 177–8, 223
– Cyril of Alexandria, 123, 181
– Cyril of Jerusalem, 123, 180–1
– Dunstan, 122
– Epiphanius of Constantia, 181
– Eucherius of Lyon, 181
– Eustathius, 64
– Gregory of Nazianzus, 170–1, 173–4, 183, 280
– Gregory of Nyssa, 49
– Gregory the Great, 170–1
– Hilary of Poitiers, 179–80
– Hippolytus of Rome, 176
– Jerome (Hieronymus) of Stridonium, 170–1, 175, 188, 297–8
– John Chrysostom, Archbishop of Constantinople, 170–1, 173–4
– John of Damascus, 183
– Philip Neri, 50
– Oswald, 122
– Paul, 143, 171, 226
– Peter, 143
– Polycarp of Smyrna, 174
– Prosper, 259
– Thomas Aquinas, 222
– Thomas Cantelupe (Cantilupe), 124
– Wilfrid, 122
Saintsbury, George, 242
Salden, William, 68
Sale, George, 215
Salmon, Thomas, 305
Salvian (Salvianus) of Marseilles, 48, 181
Sammonicus, Serenus, 65
Sardi, Alessandro, 274
Saumaise, Claude, 68, 177, 211
Savary, Claude-Étienne, 208
Savile, Sir Henry, 54, 173
Savile, Sir John, 54

Scaliger, Caesar, 282–3
Scaliger, Joseph Justus, 3, 66, 68, 179–80, 186, 231, 269, 275, 283, 307
– publications, 66, 283
Scarlett, Nathaniel, 185
Scheidius, Everard, 207
Scheidius, Jacobus, 207
Schiller, Friedrich von, 3
Schlegel, August, 3
Schlegel, Friedrich, 3
Sclater (Schlater, Slater), William, 281–2
Scott, A. J, 109
Scott, Charles [Isabel] (contemporary), 40
Scott, William, 252
Scriptores rei rusticae (1496), 229, 231
Searby, Peter, 27
Selden, John, 273–5
Sellon, Priscilla Lydia, 113
Sellwood, Charles (contemporary), 37, 39
Selwyn, William, Professor of Divinity, 24
Selwyn College, Dunedin, 5, 7, 229–30, 292, 294–8, 301–4, 309–10
Sequester, Vibius, 269
Septuaginta, 141, 176, 270, 274
Serarius, Nikolaus, 259
Servius, 45
Severus, Sancus Endelechius, 59
Severus, Sulpicius, 58–9
Seward, H. R, 74
Sfondrati, Celestino, 260–1, 285
Shaftesbury, Lord, 71
Shakespeare, William, 9
Shakespeare Folios, 56, 302
Shaw, Henry (book collector, Auckland), 221
Shea, David, 204
Shelley, Percy Bysshe, 3, 16, 51
Sheppard, Thomas, Southville, Wandsworth, 279
Shepreth, Cambridgeshire, 20
Sheridan, Richard B, 70
Sherratt, John, 220
Shilleto, Richard, 30, 35
Shillingfleet, Henry J. W (Clement), 129
Shīrāzī, Sa'dī, 201

Shoreditch, London, 71
Shoults, Eliza Katherine (wife, née Ogle), 1, 5, 7, 134, 140–1, 142, 158–160, 163, 166, 184, 201, 206, 239, 244, 291–4, 301, 309
 – residences, 160, 291
 – will, 291–2
Shoults, Elizabeth Arderne (mother, née Dodds), 10, 14–7, 19, 21, 39–40, 54, 185, 244
 – book gift to son (1859), 54
Shoults, Maria Susannah (sister), 14, 22, 71, 147, 159, 239, 291
Shoults, Peter Martin (great grandfather), 305
Shoults, William (grandfather), 12
 – Injury, 12
 – Bankruptcy, 12
 – Death (1846), 12
 – Children: Ann, Cecila, Frances, Edward, William, 12–3
Shoults, William (father), 10, 12–7, 21–2, 40, 42, 71, 81, 87, 245, 248
 – Book collection, 13
 – Book gift to son (1870), 13
 – Resident in Cambridge, 21
 – death (1878), 147, 159, 239
 – will, 147, 239
Shoults, William Arderne, pl.1, 14–6, 20–1, 39, 121, 299
 – Birth, 1, 5
 – Baptism (St. Olave's, Tooley Street), 10
 – Book from great-grandfather's library (Dodds), 14
 – Book from Great aunt (Mary Ann Faulkner), 16
 – As 'Scholar', 15
 – First book (1851), 16
 – Certificate of fitness for study, 20
 – Admittance to St. John's College (July 1856), 21, 23
 – Sizar Elected Examination (1856), 23
 – Hare Exhibition, 23
 – St. John's College Prizeman (1857), 38
 – 'Little-Go' Previous Examination (1858), 28, 38–9
 – 'Prizeman' (June 1858), 39
 – Mathematical Tripos (1860), 21, 40
 – Terms kept, 36
 – First appearance in print, 45
 – Nom-de-plume (G. de A. Decurio), 46–7
 – Feast days, 48, 85, 138, 153–4
 – Marks and position in class, 23, 37–40, pl. 3
 – M.A. (April 1863), 71, Voluntary Theological Examination, 31, 72
 – Ordination (Deacon), 72–8
 – Ordination (Priest), 81–3
 – Parish responsibilities, 80, 84–6, 145
 – Character, 108, 124
 – Churches (attached to)
 – St. Peter's Church, Walworth, 1, 74, 76, 78–9, 81, 103, pl.5
 – St. Paul's Church, Bunhill Row, Hoxton, 1, 86, 103, 107, 123, pl.6
 – St. Michael's Church, Shoreditch, 1, 123, 125, 127, 130, 132, 134, 284, pl.11
 – St. Edmund the Martyr, Lombard Street, 1, 143–5, 159, 239, 284, pl.12
 – Harvest Festival, St Edmund's (1875), 145, 147, p.13
 – 'Father Cyril' (Shoults), 123–4, 154
 – Translations and languages, 127, 154, 200
 – Hymn publications, 150–1, 156, pl. 14
 – Bachelor of Divinity (1874), 25, 134–40, 157, 169
 – Doctor of Divinity, 135–6, 299
 – Marriage, 141, 159
 – Final acquisitions, 239–241
 – Presentation copies, 54, 140–2, 159, 164, 201, 213, 240, 270, pl. 15
 – Use by Shoults (marginalia, notes etc), 68, 276–290
 – Collecting interests, 3–4, 170
 – Residence
   8 Weston Street, Southwark, 10
   5 Trafalgar Place, Ramsgate (1847), 15, 19
   33 South Wood, St Lawrence (1851), 15
   Madingley Road, Cambridge (1856-1859), 21, 26, 36, pl. 4
   24 New Olney Street, 78, 82, 86
   St. Michael's Vicarage, Mark Street

(1874), 134
  71 Robert Street, London (1878), 159
  37 Camberwell Grove, Camberwell, 79, 81, 87, 147, 160, 239, 291, pl. 16
– Salary, 2, 57, 134
– travel, 1, 5, 163–8
– Death (of tuberculosis), 1, 20, 291
– Legacy, 7, 309–10
Shoults Collection, Selwyn College, 220–1, 302, pl. 26, pl. 27
– dispersal, 2, 221, 230, 297–302
– arrival in New Zealand, 294
– condition of collection (post-1893 to 1960s), 295, 301
– official transfer to University Library, 303–4
Shoults Collection, Special Collections, University of Otago, 4–5, 7, 13, 39, 47, 51, 57, 61–3, 70, 135, 163, 171, 179, 241, 266, 273, 283, 304–7
– classification, 4–5
– exhibitions, 305–6, 308–9
– use of the collection, 305–7
Shrewsbury Grammar, 25
Shrosbee, Colin, 19
Sike, Henry, 211
Silius, 269
Simes, Nathaniel Phillips (book collector), 170
Simplicius of Cilicia, 211, 283
Simpson, William (auctioneer), 55
Sionita, Gabriel, 214
Sister Mary Agnes - see Povey, Jane Mercy
Sister Gertrude of the Third Order, 120
Sisterhood of Mercy (Church of England), 113
Slade, Sir Adolphus, 216
Slight, John Bullivant (contemporary), 37
Skinner, Hannah (Sister Monica), 132
Skinner, James, 152
Smith, Charles James Eliseo (contemporary), 39, 40, 71
Smith, Emma, 148
Smith, Jason (contemporary), 40
Smith, John, 25
Smith, Romilly, 308

Smith, Samuel, 75–6
Smith, W. H (booksellers), 55
Smith, William, 241
Soane, Sir John, 78
Société Asiatique, 217
Society for Promoting Christian Knowledge (SPCK), 50
Society for the Diffusion of Useful Knowledge (SDUK), 244, 245
Society for the Promotion of Christian Knowledge (SPCK), 250
Society for the Propagation of the Gospel, 209
Society for the Publication of Oriental Texts, 204, 205
Society for the Relief of Distress (1860), 71
Society of Antiquities (London), 247, 273
Society of Jesus (Jesuits and libraries), 257, 260
Society of St. John the Evangelist, 126
Society of the Holy Cross (S. S. C.), 2, 113, 116, 120, 131
Solinus, 68
Sophocles, 30
Sotheby and Wilkinson (auctioneers), 56, 59, 68, 267
Sotheby, Samuel (auctioneer), 55
Sotheby, Samuel Leigh (auctioneer), 55
Sotheby's (auctioneer), 298–9
Sotheby's, Wilkinson, and Hodge (auctioneers), 273
Sotheran and Willis (bookdealers), 55
Southgate, Horatio, 216
Southey, Robert, 103
Southwark, London, 5, 9, 11, 14–5, 21, 71, 148, 179, 246
– Fires (June 1841); (August 1843), 11
– population, 9
Southwark Priory, 152
Speed, John, 302
Spencer, George John, second Earl (book collector), 55–6
Spence, John (Cuthbert), 123
Spencer-Churchill, George, 5th Duke of Marlborough, Marquess of Blandford (book collector), 55
Spirituals in Tuscany (strict Franciscan

order), 228
Sprenger, Aloys, 210
Spurgeon, Charles Haddon, 9, 43, 121
Stahl, Georg Ernst, 270
Stanhope, Philip Dormer, 4th Earl of Chesterfield (book collector), 70
Stanley, Arthur Penrhyn, Dean of Westminster, 109
Stanley, Thomas (Colonel), 227
Stanley, Thomas (translator), 262
Statham, Francis Freeman, 76–80, 82, 84–6, 103, 111
– publications, 79
Statham, Jane Lee (née Kington), 79
Steams, Justin (Princeton), 306
Steinfeld Abbey, Cologne, 259
Stevens, Thomas (Rector, founder of Bradfield College), 179
Stevenson, Joseph, 152, 165
Stewart, Charles J. (bookseller), 55, 58
Stirling, James (contemporary), 40
Stock, Elliot, (bookdealer), 55
Stocqueler, Jaochim Hayward, 216
Struve, Burkhard Gotthelf, 261
Sturtz, Friedrich Wilhelm, 70, 231
Suarès, Joseph Marie, 140, 159
Subtractarians, 129
Sumner, Charles Richard, Bishop of Winchester, 78
Surrey Archaeological Society, 247
Sussex, Prince Augustus Frederick, Duke of (book collector), 55–6, 181, 266, 275, 299
Swainson, Charles Anthony, 109
Sykes, Sir Mark Masterman (book collector), 55
Sylburg, Friedrich, 175
Synkellos, George, 180
Synods: Nicea (325); Alexandria (362); Constantinople (381); Ephesus (431); Chalcedon (451), 50, 180–1, 187

Tacitus, Cornelius, 18, 64
Tait, Archibald Campbell, Bishop of London, 73, 76–77, 81, 83, 105–6, 108, 112, 119, 120–121, 129–32, 144–5

al-Talghamtī, Alī ibn al-Mabrūk, 201
Tankard, Paul, 307
Tapper, Ruard, 259, pl. 18
Tapson, Robert, 78
Tasso, 306
Tatian, 175
Tattam, Henry, 209
Tauchnitz publications, 172, 174, 289
Taylor, David, 7, 296, 304, 307
Taylor, Jeremy, 2, 160
Taylor, Robert West (contemporary), 40, 71
Taylor, Thomas (translator), 267
Taylor, William Bramley (friend of the Shoults family), 291
Tenison, Archbishop, 54
Tennyson, Lord Alfred, 43
Terence, 70
Tertullian, 67, 177–8, 286
Themistius, 271
Theophylact of Ochrida (Archbishop), 171, 226
Thirty-nine Articles of the Anglican faith, 49, 73, 82, 135
Thomas, Josiah, 251
Thomasius, J. M., 152
Thompson, William Hepworth, Professor of Greek, 24
Thomson, William (1st Baron Kelvin), 35
Thorpe, Thomas (bookseller), 54
Thornton, Thomas, 216
Thucydides, 18, 30
Tickell, Richard, 70
Tierney, Mark Aloysius, 179, 215
Tinker, Elizabeth, librarian, 305–6
Tipu, Sultan Fateh Ali Sahab (Tipu, Tiger of Mysore), 205
Tite, Sir William (book collector), 57
Tithes (tithing), 148, 251
Todd, Henry John, 185
Todd case (1873), 129
Tofts, Mary, 278
Toleration Act (1689), 281
Tollius, Cornelius, 67
Townley Gallery Library, 231

Tractarianism - (see Oxford Movement)
Tracts (bound publications), 70, 74, 109, 241, 278
Tracts for the Times (1833-41), 50, 251
Traue, Jim E, librarian, 309
Treaty of Waitangi (New Zealand), 10
Tregelles, Samuel Prideaux, 213
The Trinity (Trinitarianism), 170, 173, 177, 179–81, 200, 224
Trinity College Dublin, 48, 83, 142
Trinity College, Glenalmond, 113
Turkish Company, Smyrna, 215
Turnbull, Alexander Horsburgh (book collector, Wellington), 221
Turner, Dawson (book collector), 58
Turner, Page (book collector), 56
Turton, Thomas, 76
Tutill, C. E., 147

'Udī, Husayn ibn 'Alī al-Mas, 210
Universities (England)
 – entrance (19th century), 19–20
University of California Los Angeles (UCLA), 301
University of Illinois at Urbana-Champaign, 299
 – Denison Collection, 299
University of Otago Library, Dunedin, 295, 301–7, 310
University of Paris Library, 260
University of Toronto Library, Toronto, Canada, 301
Upham, Edward, 216
Urie, Robert, 185
Urquhart, David, 248
Ussher, James, 176, 274
Utterson, Edward Vernon (book collector), 58

Valens (Emperor), 180
Valentinus, 175
Valeriano, Piero, 66–7
Valois, Henry, 179
Valpy, Richard, 18, 55
Vanière, Jacques, 260

Varro, 229
Vatican Archives, 165–7
Vatican City, 165
Vatican Commission on Plainchant, 167
Vatican Library, 165–8, 200, 260, 289
Vegetarian Society, 78
Veitch, James Lord Elliock (Eliock), book collector, 141, 267–70, 275
 – education and travel, 267–8
 – family, 268, 270
 – library, 268, 270
Venn, John, 30, 32, 34, 43
Vianney, Jean-Baptiste-Marie, 110
Victoria (Queen), 205
Vincent, William, 70, 278
Vincentian Canon, 181–182
Vincentius (Vincent) of Lérins, 181, 281, 286
Vines, Vera F., 307
Vinson, Richard Henry, 12
Virgil, 18, 30, 38–39, 45, 51, 65, 266, 269, 274, 278, 300
Vitruvio, 274
Vossius, Gerrit (Gerardus) Janszoon (Vos), 260, 277
Vossius, Isaac, 164
Vulcanius, Bonaventura, 181

Wace, Frederic Charles, 45, 47
Wackernagel, Carl Eduard Philipp, 152–3
Wadham College, Oxford, 109
Wakefield, Gilbert, 277
Walford, Edward, 247
Walker, J. K., 246
Waller, Edmund, 256
Walworth, London, 79, 104, 134, 145, 148
Walsh, Robert, 216
Walsingham, Thomas, 110
Wanley, Humfrey, 154, 235
Waring, Robert, 138
Warren, Richard (father), 138
Warren, Richard (son), 138
Wase, Christopher, 286
Watson, Joshua, 250, 252
Watts, Isaac, 103, 150

Way, Albert, 246
Webb, Samuel B., 76, 84
Welchman, Edward, 49–50
Wesley, John, 150
Westminster Abbey, London, 142
Westrop, Kate, 147
Wettstein, Johan Jakob, 305
Whateley, Elizabeth Lucy Welchman, 35
White, Henry Taylor (brother-in-law by marriage), 291
White, Joseph, Professor of Hebrew, Oxford, 209
Whitehead, Louis Grenville 'Algy', Warden of Selwyn, 297–8
Wicking, William Henry (Placidus), 123
Wilberforce, Robert Isaac, 49
Wilberforce, Samuel, Dean of Westminster, 115
Wilberforce, William, 49
Wilkinson, John (auctioneer), 55
William IV (King), 204
William of Malmesbury, 289
Williams, Henry Griffith, Professor of Arabic, 24
Willibald, 216
Wills, Freeman Crofts, 145
Willson, E. N, 79
Windham, William, 69

Wing, Donald (*STC 1641–1700*), 301
Winstanley, D. A., 135
Wisbey, Charles, 21, 53
Withers, Robert Jewell, 107
Wolcot, John (Peter Pindar), 243
Wolf, Hieronymus, 211
Wolleb, Johannes, 138, 307
Woodroffe, Edward, 143
Wooliscroft, Michael, librarian, 305
Wordsworth, Christopher, 54, 185
Worth, G. Henry, 128–9, 165–7
Wrangham, Digby S., 157
Wren, Sir Christopher, 143
Wright, Thomas, 216–7, 245
Wüstenfeld, Heinrich Ferdinand, 210

Xenophon, 18
Ximenes, Jiménez (Cardinal), 154

Yarranton, Andrew John (contemporary), 23
Yonge, Charles Duke, 177
York (ship), 220–1
Yorktown Church, Surrey, 145
Young, Thomas, 214

'Z, Y', 30
al-Zarniji, Burhan al-Islam, 211
Zosimus, 302

www.ingramcontent.com/pod-product-compliance
Lightning Source LLC
LaVergne TN
LVHW081518060526
838200LV00006B/209